PEERS® FOR YOUNG ADULTS

PEERS® for Young Adults presents the first evidence-based group treatment program for young adults with Autism Spectrum Disorder (ASD), as well as other neurodevelopmental disorders and social challenges. Inside, readers will find a critical step forward in the dissemination of effective behavioral interventions for young adults in the form of 16 engaging group session outlines that are both user-friendly and backed by empirical research. Each session is accompanied by homework assignments and practice suggestions designed to reinforce the group's understanding of the skills learned during each meeting. This practical resource will prove to be an invaluable reference for any clinician or educator working with this population.

Dr. Elizabeth A. Laugeson is a licensed clinical psychologist and an assistant clinical professor in the Department of Psychiatry and Biobehavioral Sciences at the UCLA Semel Institute for Neuroscience and Human Behavior. Dr. Laugeson is the director of The Help Group—UCLA Autism Research Alliance, a collaborative research initiative dedicated to developing and expanding applied clinical research in the treatment of children and adolescents with ASD. She is also the training director for the UCLA Tarjan Center for Excellence in Developmental Disabilities (UCEDD), and the founder and director of the UCLA PEERS® Clinic, an outpatient hospital-based program providing parent-assisted social skills training for individuals with ASD, Attention-Deficit/Hyperactivity Disorder (ADHD), depression, anxiety, and other social impairments across the lifespan.

PEERS® FOR YOUNG ADULTS

Social Skills Training for Adults with Autism Spectrum Disorder and Other Social Challenges

Elizabeth A. Laugeson

Routledge
Taylor & Francis Group

NEW YORK AND LONDON

First published 2017
by Routledge
711 Third Avenue, New York, NY 10017

and by Routledge
2 Park Square, Milton Park, Abingdon, Oxon, OX14 4RN

Routledge is an imprint of the Taylor & Francis Group, an informa business

Library of Congress Cataloging in Publication Data
Names: Laugeson, Elizabeth A., author.
Title: PEERS for young adults : social skills training for adults with autism
spectrum disorder and other social challenges / by Elizabeth A. Laugeson.
Description: New York, NY : Routledge, 2016. | Includes bibliographical
references and index.
Identifiers: LCCN 2016030396| ISBN 9781138238688 (hbk : alk. paper) |
ISBN 9781138238718 (pbk : alk. paper) | ISBN 9781315297057 (ebk)
Subjects: LCSH: Autism spectrum disorders—Patients—Rehabilitation. |
Autism in adolescence—Social aspects. | Developmental disabilities—
Patients—Rehabilitation. | Developmental disabilities—Social aspects.
Classification: LCC RC553.A88 L383 2016 | DDC 616.85/882—dc23
LC record available at https://lccn.loc.gov/2016030396

ISBN: 978-1-138-23868-8 (hbk)
ISBN: 978-1-138-23871-8 (pbk)
ISBN: 978-1-315-29705-7 (ebk)

Typeset in Stone Sans
by Florence Production Ltd, Stoodleigh, Devon, UK

Visit the companion website: www.routledge.com/cw/laugeson

This book is dedicated to my mother,
Janet Tate, who was my first social coach.

CONTENTS

TABLES

PREFACE

This manual is based upon the original work, *Social Skills for Teenagers with Developmental and Autism Spectrum Disorders: The PEERS® Treatment Manual* (Laugeson & Frankel, 2010), which is a parent-assisted social skills program for adolescents with Autism Spectrum Disorder (ASD) and other social challenges. The research upon which the original work with adolescents and the derivative work with young adults were funded through two separate National Research Service Awards through the National Institutes of Health Training Grant NIH T32-MH17140 (Andrew Leuchter, Principal Investigator). The research with young adults was further supported by a grant from the Organization for Autism Research (Alexander Gantman, Principal Investigator).

This manual includes several adaptations and additions to the original *PEERS® Treatment Manual*. In addition to modifying content to be more developmentally appropriate for young adults, the original parent-assisted model has been replaced with a caregiver-assisted model. Under the new manual, social coaching outside of the treatment setting is now conducted by caregivers, who often include parents, adult siblings, other family members, life coaches, job coaches, and peer mentors. Another departure from the original *PEERS® Treatment Manual* for adolescents is that this curriculum includes four sessions on dating etiquette. These sessions were initially created for inclusion in the original *PEERS® Treatment Manual*; however, after a series of focus groups with parents of adolescents with developmental disabilities, including those with ASD, the dating didactics were removed by parent request. The concern cited by parents was that socially immature adolescents were not developmentally prepared to learn about dating etiquette. Arguably, this concern is not generally expressed by caregivers of young adults with ASD and other social challenges. Although very few of the young adults who attend the UCLA PEERS® Clinic (where this program is researched) are actively dating, the majority are curious to know more. Consequently, the inclusion of the dating didactics in this new manual should not be aversive and may be highly motivating for some participants.

The *PEERS® for Young Adults* manual is also different from the original manual in that it includes 16 weeks of lessons, as opposed to the 14 weeks offered in the adolescent parent-assisted program. The supplement of two additional weeks of material includes four new lessons on dating etiquette and the removal of lessons on good sportsmanship and changing a bad reputation. Those professionals seeking strategies for these social challenges should refer to the original PEERS® manuals for adolescents, including the *PEERS® Curriculum for School-Based Professionals* (Laugeson, 2014), the second installment in the PEERS® treatment series.

Just as the didactic content for PEERS® has evolved, so too have the *Role Play Demonstrations*, which highlight the targeted skills. New and updated *Role Play Demonstrations* of appropriate and inappropriate social behavior are offered in this manual to help facilitators provide a means for teaching the skills. New *Role Play Demonstrations* include humorous examples of **bragging**, **policing**, and **getting too personal** during conversations, inappropriate use of **eye contact** and **body boundaries**, and new tactics for **starting conversations**, **getting contact information**, and **handling rumors and gossip**, just to highlight a few. Video demonstrations of the role plays highlighted in this manual are also now available through an online video library, which can be found at www.routledge.com/cw/laugeson. The *FriendMaker* mobile app also includes dozens of *Role Play Video Demonstrations* of targeted skills, as well as bullet-pointed content from the PEERS® intervention. These videos provide facilitators with additional tools for delivering the lessons in fun and engaging ways, as well as providing added support outside of the treatment sessions, including virtual coaching through the *FriendMaker* mobile app.

Another significant addition in the *PEERS® for Young Adults* manual is the use of ***Perspective Taking Questions*** throughout the lessons. The UCLA PEERS® Clinic, where this intervention was originally developed and tested, uses ***Perspective Taking Questions*** as a matter of standard practice in research and clinical groups for teens and adults. These questions follow good and bad *Role Play Demonstrations* of targeted social skills in order to improve social cognition. ***Perspective Taking Questions*** include *"What do you think that was like for that person?"*, *"What do you think they thought of the other person?"*, and *"Do you think they'll want to talk to the other person again?"* Appropriate responses are provided at the end of each series of ***Perspective Taking Questions*** to enhance teaching and promote discussion. These questions have been added to this manual given research findings suggesting improved social cognition following treatment, in addition to overall improvements in social skills and friendships.

While the overarching content of this curriculum is based upon the original *PEERS® Treatment Manual* for adolescents, it is expected that the developmental modifications, supplement of new lessons, and didactic content, as well as the addition of new *Role Play Demonstrations* and ***Perspective Taking Questions***, will provide new users and even seasoned experts of the PEERS® intervention with useful new strategies for teaching social skills. Although the program was originally developed for transitional youth with ASD, PEERS® is also widely used for youth with other social challenges. Given the fact that the intervention teaches ***ecologically valid social skills***—that is, social behavior exhibited by socially successful individuals—PEERS® might be used with any adults interested in learning how to develop close meaningful relationships.

ACKNOWLEDGMENTS

The publication of this manual is a long time in the making and represents over a decade of research and clinical practice. The research and clinical work upon which this manual is based has only been possible through the contributions of a dedicated and talented team of researchers, clinicians, and graduate students at the UCLA PEERS® Clinic. I wish to gratefully acknowledge the hard work and steadfast commitment of these individuals. Most particularly, a special thanks to Mina Park, Shannon Bates, Jennifer Sanderson, Elina Veytsman, Ruth Ellingsen, Enjey Lin, Catherine Mogil, Jessica Hopkins, Courtney Bolton, Vindia Fernandez, Ted Hutman, Kalina Babeva, and Mera West for the exceptional care and compassion you've shown to our families through your clinical work—you are the heart of our program and I am proud to call you friends and colleagues. To our talented research team, I especially want to acknowledge the amazing contributions of Alex Gantman, Yasamine Bolourian, Lara Tucci, Josh Mandelberg, James Yang, Jilly Chang, Ashley Dillon, Aarti Nair, and Allison Vreeland—you are the backbone of our program, the credibility in our work, and I am eternally grateful for your tireless efforts. To our team of *role players*, Elina Veytsman, Jordan Albright, Gabe Aviera, James Yang, and Allison Vreeland, who lent their excellent acting abilities toward the development of our role play videos, I thank you for sharing your creativity and for consistently making us laugh at our cadre of social faux pas. A special thanks to my editorial team, Angela Dahiya, Ana Mendoza, Peggy Hsieh, Leilani Forby, Rhideeta Jalal, Morgan Joliffe, Gozi Egbuong, Mera West, Elina Veytsman, and James Yang, who, in addition to being superb copy-editors, are also brilliant graduate students. To the rest of *Team PEERS®*, I would like to thank all of our students, interns, research assistants, and behavioral coaches who go above and beyond the call of duty—thank you for lightening the load and being the legs on which we stand. We couldn't do this work without you!

I would also like to give special thanks to my friends and colleagues at UCLA and The Help Group, with particular appreciation to Drs. Peter Whybrow, Barbara Firestone, Jim McCracken, Susan Berman, and Philip Levin for their support of my research and this work. To my research mentors, Mary O'Connor, Blair Paley, and Fred Frankel—thank you for helping me find my path, so that I can help others do the same. And to Andy Leuchter, who has been the most generous of mentors—there are no words to adequately express my gratitude for your support throughout the years. I humbly thank you for your guidance and your friendship.

To my research colleagues across the globe, I thank you for being ambassadors for PEERS® and for providing objective and cultural validation through your replications of our program. Most especially, I wish to thank Amy Van Hecke, Heejeong Yoo, Ofer Golan, Ralph Adolphs, Angela Scarpa, Mirella Dapretto, Adam McCrimmon, Kirstin Greaves-Lord, Tomoko Yamada, and Masatsugu Tsujii. Your investigation and support of this research program is what gives it credibility and salience in the real world. We are thrilled to have you in our research family!

It is also important to acknowledge the generosity of donors such as the Friends of the Semel Institute at UCLA, who have helped to support my work for over a decade. In particular, I would like to thank Vicky Goodman and Sally Weil for their unwavering kindness and generosity through their support of our research programs. To Janet Lang, Barry Lang, Vera Guerin, and the Shapell and Guerin Family Foundation, I am truly grateful for your heartfelt support or our research and training—your generosity will have a far greater impact than you will ever know.

To my family and friends, who tolerate the constant travel and patiently support the never-ending writing retreats, this work would not have been possible without your love and support. To my mother, Janet Tate, thank you for setting the example of what a strong woman can be. To my *friends forever*, Jennifer Wilkerson, Carrie Raia, and Dan Oakley, thank you for embodying the *Characteristics of Good Friends* that I write about in this manual—you personify the concepts and I am eternally grateful for your friendship. Most especially, to my husband, Lance Orozco, whose love and encouragement has been unwavering for over 20 years—thank you for believing in this work and in me.

And last, but by no means least, to the incredible families we have had the privilege of working with these many years, thank you for giving meaning to all we do. Through your loving devotion and boundless support for one another, you create hope and inspiration. Your stories touch us, your lives enrich us, and you bring life to these pages.

AUTHOR BIOGRAPHY

Dr. Elizabeth Laugeson is a licensed clinical psychologist and an Assistant Clinical Professor in the Department of Psychiatry and Biobehavioral Sciences at the UCLA Semel Institute for Neuroscience and Human Behavior. Laugeson is the Founder and Director of the UCLA PEERS® Clinic, which is an outpatient hospital-based program providing parent and caregiver assisted social skills training for individuals across the lifespan with Autism Spectrum Disorder (ASD), Attention-Deficit/Hyperactivity Disorder (ADHD), depression, anxiety, and other social impairments. She is also the Training Director for the UCLA Tarjan Center for Excellence in Developmental Disabilities (UCEDD) and Director of The Help Group—UCLA Autism Research Alliance, which is a collaborative research initiative dedicated to developing and expanding applied clinical research in the treatment of children and adolescents with Autism Spectrum Disorder.

Laugeson has been a principal investigator and collaborator on a number of nationally funded studies investigating social skills training for youth with social difficulties from preschool to early adulthood, and is the co-developer of the *Program for the Education and Enrichment of Relational Skills (PEERS®)*, the evidence-based social skills intervention upon which this manual is based. Since 2010, Laugeson has authored three books related to social skills training: *Social Skills for Teenagers with Developmental and Autism Spectrum Disorders: The PEERS® Treatment Manual* (Laugeson & Frankel, 2010), *The Science of Making Friends: Helping Socially Challenged Teens and Young Adults* (Laugeson, 2013), and *The PEERS® Curriculum for School-Based Professionals: Social Skills Training for Adolescents with Autism Spectrum Disorder* (Laugeson, 2014).

She received her doctorate in Clinical Psychology from Pepperdine University in 2004, and completed a predoctoral psychology internship and a postdoctoral research fellowship at UCLA in 2004 and 2007, respectively. Considered one of the world's leading experts in evidence-based social skills training, she was a two-time recipient of the Ruth L. Kirschstein National Research Service Award from the National Institutes of Health in 2004 and 2006, recipient of the Semel Scholar Award for Junior Faculty Career Development in 2008, and received the Distinguished Alumnus Award from Pepperdine University in 2010.

Having trained thousands of mental health professionals, educators, and families in the PEERS® method, Laugeson is dedicated to developing and testing evidence-based treatments to improve social skills across the lifespan, and disseminating these empirically supported programs across the globe. At present, the PEERS® manuals have been translated into over a dozen languages and the program is used in over 25 countries. Laugeson has presented her groundbreaking research at international conferences throughout the world, including the United States, Canada, England, Finland, Holland, Spain, Italy, Portugal, Australia, India, Hong Kong, Iceland, Russia, and Japan. Her work has been featured on national and international media outlets such as *People Magazine*, *USA Today*, the *LA Times*, *New York Times*, *Washington Post*, CBS, ABC, NBC, Fox, NPR, and Channel 4 in the United Kingdom.

In this current work, Laugeson shares her research-supported strategies for teaching social skills to young adults with Autism Spectrum Disorder and other social challenges.

GETTING STARTED

Purpose of the *PEERS® for Young Adults Manual*

The *Program for the Education and Enrichment of Relational Skills (PEERS®)* was originally developed as a parent-assisted intervention focusing on teens in middle school and high school who were having difficulty making and keeping friends. The program has been field-tested extensively with teens and young adults with Autism Spectrum Disorder (ASD), and to a lesser extent with teens diagnosed with Intellectual Disabilities (ID) and Fetal Alcohol Spectrum Disorders (FASD), as well as teens and young adults with Attention-Deficit/Hyperactivity Disorder (ADHD). PEERS® is also used clinically with teens and young adults with depression, anxiety, and other social challenges.

The *PEERS® for Young Adults* curriculum is an adaptation and extension of the original intervention, utilizing caregiver assistance through real-world social coaching. The intervention is intended for higher-functioning adults without significant cognitive impairments, focusing on skills related to making and keeping friends, developing romantic relationships, and managing conflict and rejection. Lessons include starting and maintaining conversations, finding a source of friends, electronic forms of communication, using humor appropriately, entering and exiting conversations, organizing and having successful get-togethers, dating etiquette, managing disagreements, and handling direct and indirect bullying and other forms of rejection. Rules and steps of social behavior are developed from research evidence regarding: (1) the common social errors often committed by those with ASD; (2) the core social skills needed to make and keep friends and develop romantic relationships; and (3) the ecologically valid ways in which socially accepted individuals handle peer conflict and rejection.

The *PEERS® for Young Adults* manual is meant to be used as a complete program in its entirety. Lessons are intended to be delivered in the order they are presented as each skill builds upon the last. The orientation of the manual is cognitive-behavioral in the sense that material is presented as a series of rules or steps to be followed by young adults. *Didactic Lessons* are based upon ecologically valid social skills known to be used by socially successful people. The techniques used, such as *Role Play Demonstrations*, *Behavioral Rehearsal Exercises*, and *Homework Assignments*, have been shown to improve social skills outcomes through research.

The *PEERS® for Young Adults* program has been used in university-based medical settings, university-affiliated clinics, and outpatient mental health programs in North America and abroad. The effectiveness of the treatment was established through our research at the UCLA PEERS® Clinic, where we have conducted multiple research trials and social skills groups with hundreds of young adults with ASD and other social challenges. The efficacy and effectiveness of the program is being further validated through multiple studies conducted inside and outside of the United States by research teams unaffiliated with UCLA.

Delivery methods for instruction have been modified over the past eight years based upon research outcomes and therapist feedback. The current manual and techniques reflect many years of research and clinical practice with adults with social skills challenges. Clinicians need not have much experience running social skills groups in order to use the manual effectively, but they should have background knowledge in working with young adults with ASD or other social challenges and their caregivers.

Inclusion of Social Coaches

A highly unique aspect of *PEERS® for Young Adults* that differs from other social skills groups is the inclusion of caregivers as social coaches. This model involves simultaneously occurring social coaching groups that meet in tandem with young adult groups. Essentially, while young adults are learning about social skills in their own group, caregivers attend a concurrent social coaching group to learn about how to assist young adults in the development and maintenance of relationships. Caregivers typically include parents, but may also include adult siblings, other family members, job coaches, life coaches, friends, partners, and peer mentors. The rationale behind including caregivers as social coaches is that the skills will more easily generalize to other settings and improvements will be more durable over time for the following reasons:

1. *Social coaching in natural social settings.* Greater generalization of skills is expected through social coaching because caregivers will be able to provide social coaching during *coachable moments* in natural social settings. Better durability of treatment outcomes over time is expected because social coaches (when chosen appropriately) will be able to provide social coaching long after the group treatment has ended.

2. *Assistance with weekly socialization assignments.* Generalization of skills will be promoted through the completion of weekly socialization *Homework Assignments.* Caregivers are often integral to ensuring completion of these practice assignments by regularly following up with young adults throughout the week and helping troubleshoot any barriers to homework completion. Durability of treatment outcomes is further enhanced by the inclusion of social coaches in treatment in that caregivers continue to encourage the use of the PEERS® skills even after the program has ended and no formal assignments are given.

3. *Assistance with finding a source of friends.* Inclusion of caregivers is also useful in assisting young adults in finding a source of friends outside of the treatment setting. The purpose of *PEERS® for Young Adults* is not to provide *friendship matching*, where group members become friends with other group members. Instead, we attempt to teach young adults how to more independently find friends in the real world. Caregivers can be very helpful throughout this process by assisting young adults in identifying various social activities in the community where young adults might find accepting groups of peers with common interests. Moreover, caregivers not only assist in helping to enroll young adults in these activities and ensure that they attend these activities regularly, but they also ensure that young adults continue to attend these types of social activities long after the group treatment has ended, thereby further enhancing the durability of treatment gains.

Organization of the Manual

PEERS® for Young Adults is conducted using a structured group format, focusing on teaching young adults the social skills necessary to develop and maintain meaningful relationships with others. An overview of the 16 didactic sessions is presented in Table 1.1.

This manual is intended to serve as a step-by-step outline for each lesson. Through our work with clinicians, we have found that an outline format (rather than a narrative script) facilitates a more spontaneous-sounding presentation of the material and is easier to follow as it allows the group leader to ad lib with material consistent with each lesson. This manual is meant to be used at the time of each group. Memorization of the material in the manual is neither required nor encouraged. Young adults seem comfortable with group leaders having the manual open in front of them as they guide the group through the skills. The rationale for following the manual closely is that the group leader needs to cover all the necessary elements of the skills being taught to maintain treatment fidelity and enhance treatment outcomes.

The current chapter provides an introduction to the curriculum and includes information about the organization of the manual, composition of groups, required personnel, teaching methods, and

Table 1.1 Overview of Manual

Week	Didactic Lesson	Homework Review	Behavioral Rehearsal Activity	Materials Needed	Homework Assignments
1	Trading Information and Starting Conversations	None	*Jeopardy*	Board, markers, *Jeopardy* answer sheets, scissors, pens	1. In-group call or video chat 2. Practice starting a conversation and trading information with social coach
2	Trading Information and Maintaining Conversations	1. In-group call or video chat 2. Practice starting a conversation and trading information with social coach	*Jeopardy*	Board, markers, *Jeopardy* answer sheets, scissors, pens	1. In-group call or video chat 2. Practice starting and maintaining a conversation and trading information with social coach
3	Finding a Source of Friends	1. In-group call or video chat 2. Practice starting and maintaining a conversation and trading information with social coach	*Jeopardy*	Board, markers, *Jeopardy* answer sheets, scissors, pens	1. Find a source of friends 2. In-group call or video chat 3. Practice starting and maintaining a conversation and trading information with social coach 4. Personal item
4	Electronic Communication	1. Find a source of friends 2. In-group call or video chat 3. Practice starting and maintaining a conversation and trading information with social coach 4. Personal item	Trading information about personal items	Board, markers, young adult personal items	1. Find a source of friends 2. Start a conversation and trade information with a peer 3. In-group call or video chat 4. Practice starting and ending a phone call and trading information with social coach 5. Personal item
5	Appropriate Use of Humor	1. Find a source of friends 2. Start a conversation and trade information with a peer 3. In-group call or video chat 4. Practice starting and ending a phone call and trading information with social coach 5. Personal item	Trading information about personal items	Board, markers, young adult personal items	1. Find a source of friends 2. Start a conversation and trade information with a peer 3. Pay attention to humor feedback 4. In-group call or video chat 5. Personal item
6	Entering Group Conversations	1. Find a source of friends 2. Start a conversation and trade information with a peer 3. Pay attention to humor feedback 4. In-group call or video chat 5. Personal item	Entering group conversations	Board, markers, young adult personal items	1. Find a source of friends 2. Enter a group conversation with social coaches 3. Enter a group conversation with peers 4. Pay attention to humor feedback 5. In-group call or video chat 6. Personal item

Table 1.1 Overview of Manual (continued)

Week	Didactic Lesson	Homework Review	Behavioral Rehearsal Activity	Materials Needed	Homework Assignments
7	Exiting Conversations	1. Find a source of friends 2. Enter a group conversation with social coaches 3. Enter a group conversation with peers 4. Pay attention to humor feedback 5. In-group call or video chat 6. Personal item	Entering and exiting conversations	Board, markers, young adult personal items	1. Enter and exit a group conversation with social coaches 2. Enter a group conversation with peers 3. Pay attention to humor feedback
8	Get-Togethers	1. Enter and exit a group conversation with social coaches 2. Enter a group conversation with peers 3. Pay attention to humor feedback	Get-togethers	Board, markers, board games, card games Optional: video games, iPads, laptops	1. Get-together 2. Enter and exit a group conversation with social coaches 3. Enter a group conversation with peers 4. Pay attention to humor feedback
9	Dating Etiquette: Letting Someone Know You Like Them	1. Get-together 2. Enter and exit a group conversation with social coaches 3. Enter a group conversation with peers 4. Pay attention to humor feedback	Get-togethers	Board, markers, board games, card games Optional: video games, iPads, laptops	1. Get-together 2. Practice letting someone know you like them 3. Enter and exit a group conversation with social coaches 4. Enter a group conversation with peers
10	Dating Etiquette: Asking Someone on a Date	1. Get-together 2. Practice letting someone know you like them 3. Enter and exit a group conversation with social coaches 4. Enter a group conversation with peers	Get-togethers	Board, markers, board games, card games Optional: video games, iPads, laptops	1. Get-together 2. Practice letting someone know you like them 3. Enter a group conversation with peers
11	Dating Etiquette: Going on Dates	1. Get-together 2. Practice letting someone know you like them 3. Enter a group conversation with peers	Get-togethers	Board, markers, board games, card games Optional: video games, iPads, laptops	1. Get-together 2. Practice letting someone know you like them, ask them on a date, and/or go on date 3. Enter a group conversation with peers
12	Dating Etiquette: Dating Do's and Don'ts	1. Get-together 2. Practice letting someone know you like them, ask them on a date, and/or go on date 3. Enter a group conversation with peers	Get-togethers	Board, markers, board games, card games Optional: video games, iPads, laptops	1. Get-together 2. Practice letting someone know you like them, ask them on a date, and/or go on date 3. Enter a group conversation with peers

13	Handling Disagreements	1. Get-together 2. Practice letting someone know you like them, ask them on a date, and/or go on date 3. Enter a group conversation with peers	Get-togethers	Board, markers, board games, card games Optional: video games, iPads, laptops	1. Get-together 2. Practice handling a disagreement with social coach 3. Practice handling a disagreement with a friend or partner 4. Practice letting someone know you like them, ask them on a date, and/or go on date
14	Handling Direct Bullying	1. Get-together 2. Practice handling a disagreement with social coach 3. Practice handling a disagreement with a friend or partner 4. Practice letting someone know you like them, ask them on a date, and/or go on date	Get-togethers	Board, markers, board games, card games Optional: video games, iPads, laptops	1. Get-together 2. Practice handling teasing with social coach 3. Practice handling direct bullying with peers 4. Practice handling a disagreement with social coach 5. Practice handling a disagreement with a friend or partner 6. Practice letting someone know you like them, ask them on a date, and/or go on date
15	Handling Indirect Bullying	1. Get-together 2. Practice handling teasing with social coach 3. Practice handling direct bullying with peers 4. Practice handling a disagreement with social coach 5. Practice handling a disagreement with a friend or partner 6. Practice letting someone know you like them, ask them on a date, and/or go on date	Get-togethers	Board, markers, board games, card games Optional: video games, iPads, laptops	1. Get-together 2. Practice spreading the rumor about yourself with social coach 3. Practice handling teasing with social coach 4. Practice handling direct or indirect bullying with peers 5. Practice handling a disagreement with a friend or partner 6. Practice letting someone know you like them, ask them on a date, and/or go on date
16	Moving Forward and Graduation	1. Get-together 2. Practice spreading the rumor about yourself with social coach 3. Practice handling teasing with social coach 4. Practice handling direct or indirect bullying with peers 5. Practice handling a disagreement with a friend or partner 6. Practice letting someone know you like them, ask them on a date, and/or go on date	Graduation party and ceremony	Post-test measures, graduation diplomas, food, beverages, plates, napkins, cups, silverware, decorations, TV, DVD player, movies	None

behavioral management techniques. This chapter also includes information about how to track progress and previous research outcomes. Chapters 2–17 include therapist guides highlighting the 16-week PEERS® curriculum. The material includes information about *Preparing for the Lessons*, how to conduct the *Homework Review*, how to present *Didactic Lessons*, including *Role Play Demonstrations*, procedures for conducting *Behavioral Rehearsal Exercises*, guidelines for conducting *Reunification* between young adults and their social coaches, as well as *Social Coaching Handouts*, which are meant to be photocopied and distributed to young adults and their social coaches each week.

Format of the Chapters

- **Social Coaching Therapist Guide**
  - **Preparing for the Social Coaching Group.** The rationale for each lesson is presented in this section to help the social coaching group leader place appropriate emphasis on the most important material. Possible issues that may arise during the social coaching group are discussed and suggestions for how to overcome these issues are provided.
  - **Homework Review.** Each social coaching group begins with a review of the previous *Homework Assignments*. This section of each chapter provides concrete questions for group leaders to ask social coaches during the *Homework Review*.
  - **Didactic Lesson.** The didactic material for each lesson is presented in this section of each chapter through the presentation of concrete rules and steps of social behavior. Guidelines for the optional use of video *Role Play Demonstrations* to underscore the skills are provided.
  - **Homework Assignments.** In order to generalize the newly learned skills outside of the treatment setting, weekly socialization *Homework Assignments* are given. This section of each chapter provides a comprehensive description of the upcoming *Homework Assignments*, along with recommendations for appropriate **social coaching** and **Perspective Taking Questions** to be asked before and after practicing of the skills.
  - **Social Coaching Tips.** This section of each chapter includes *Social Coaching Tips* that may be used by social coaches when helping to rehearse and reinforce newly learned skills with young adults.
- **Young Adult Therapist Guide**
  - **Preparing for the Young Adult Group.** The rationale for each lesson is presented in this section to help the young adult group leader prepare for the session and understand the rationale for teaching the targeted skill. Possible issues that may arise during the young adult group are discussed in this section and suggestions for how to overcome these issues are provided.
  - **Homework Review.** Each young adult group begins with a review of the previous *Homework Assignments*. This section of each chapter provides concrete questions for group leaders to ask young adults during the *Homework Review*.
  - **Didactic Lesson.** This section of each chapter provides a structured outline of how to present the *Didactic Lesson*. The didactic material is usually presented using a Socratic method and/or through the use of *Role Play Demonstrations*. These methods of instruction keep the young adults engaged and give them a feeling of competence that they (at least collectively) are generating the rules or steps of the lesson themselves.
- **Young Adult Behavioral Rehearsal**
  - The next step for young adults to begin to translate the didactic material into their daily lives is to practice newly learned skills in the group, while receiving performance feedback from the treatment team. This occurs during the *Behavioral Rehearsal* activities. The *Young Adult Behavioral Rehearsal* is not only an opportunity for young adults to practice newly learned skills in a less structured manner, but is also a fun and engaging part of the group. Within the *Young Adult Behavioral Rehearsal* portion of each chapter, the following sections are included:
    - **Materials Needed.** A list of materials needed for the activity is presented in the *Young Adult Behavioral Rehearsal* section. Items should be secured prior to the start of the group.

- ■ **Rules.** Specific instructions on how to facilitate the activity are provided in the *Young Adult Behavioral Rehearsal* section, including how to provide social coaching and performance feedback during the activity.
- ● **Reunification**
  - ○ Each chapter of the *PEERS® for Young Adults* manual includes a section outlining *Reunification* between young adults and social coaches, which occurs at the end of every session. The *Reunification* section of each chapter includes guidelines for how to provide a brief overview of the *Didactic Lesson*, a summary of the upcoming *Homework Assignments*, and suggestions for how to individually check out with group members to negotiate the completion of these *Homework Assignments*.
- ● **Social Coaching Handouts**
  - ○ *Social Coaching Handouts* appear at the end of every chapter. The handouts are suitable for photocopying purposes and should be distributed to social coaches at the beginning of each *Didactic Lesson*, and to young adults at the beginning of the *Homework Assignment* portion of *Reunification*. *Social Coaching Handouts* are provided as a tool to help young adults and social coaches remember the skills being taught and to provide an overview of weekly *Homework Assignments*. *Social Coaching Handouts* should be photocopied and distributed to group members EVERY WEEK and should be hand delivered or emailed to absent group members for the corresponding missed sessions.

Lesson Format

PEERS® for Young Adults is intended to be implemented as a weekly social skills group, taught once per week for 90 minutes. Young adult groups meet concurrently with social coaching groups, but in separate rooms.

Format for the Social Coaching Group

- ● **Homework Review (50 minutes).** Review the *Homework Assignments* from the previous week at the beginning of the group using the guidelines in the *Social Coaching Therapist Guide*.
- ● **Didactic Lesson and *Role Play Demonstrations* (20 minutes).** Present the *Didactic Lesson*, including optional *Video Role Play Demonstrations*, following the guidelines in the *Social Coaching Therapist Guide*. Distribute the *Social Coaching Handouts* to social coaches during the *Didactic Lesson*, which includes a discussion of the upcoming *Homework Assignments*.
  - ○ *Social Coaching Homework Assignment Worksheets* can be found in Appendix I. These worksheets should be photocopied and distributed to the social coaches at the beginning of the *Homework Assignment* portion of the *Didactic Lesson* and should be completed and returned in the next session. The *Social Coaching Homework Assignment Worksheets* are intended to assist social coaches in organizing their responsibilities during the *Homework Assignments* and provide more succinct review of those assignments in the following session. Because some social coaches may forget to bring their completed *Social Coaching Homework Assignment Worksheets* from the previous week, extra copies may be made available during the *Homework Review* each week.
- ● **Reunification with Young Adults (10 minutes).** Social coaches will listen as young adults provide an overview of the *Didactic Lesson* during *Reunification*. A review of the *Homework Assignments* is announced during the *Reunification*, and *Homework Assignments* are individually and privately negotiated with young adults and social coaches before leaving the group.

Format for the Young Adult Group

- ● **Homework Review (30 minutes).** Review the *Homework Assignments* from the previous week at the beginning of the group using the guidelines in the *Young Adult Therapist Guide*.

- **Didactic Lesson and *Role Play Demonstrations* (30 minutes).** Present the *Didactic Lesson*, including *Role Play Demonstrations*, following the guidelines in the *Young Adult Therapist Guide*.
- **Young Adult Behavioral Rehearsal (20 minutes).** Have young adults practice newly learned skills through *Behavioral Rehearsal Exercises* outlined in the *Young Adult Behavioral Rehearsal* section of each chapter.
- **Reunification with Social Coaches (10 minutes).** Have young adults provide an overview of the *Didactic Lesson* in the presence of the social coaches and then review the *Homework Assignments* for the coming week as outlined in the *Reunification* section of each chapter. Distribute *Social Coaching Handouts* to young adults during *Reunification* just prior to assigning homework. *Homework Assignments* are individually and privately negotiated with young adults and social coaches before leaving the group.

Composition of the Group

- **Social Motivation.** One of the most important deciding factors about who should be included in your group relates to social motivation. Only young adults and social coaches expressing an interest in learning about making and keeping friends, developing romantic relationships, and/or learning how to manage conflict and rejection should be included in the group. Including those who do not want to be there is a recipe for disaster and will likely result in attrition and/or a negative contagion. One way to assess for social motivation involves proper screening of group members before inclusion in treatment. Many clinicians conduct phone screening and in-person intake interviews with potential group members prior to intervention. It will be critical to assess willingness and interest in participation for both young adults and caregivers during this screening and intake process. One way to assess for social motivation during screening and intake is to say, *"We have a social skills group called PEERS® for Young Adults that teaches people how to make and keep friends, develop romantic relationships, and handle conflict and rejection in relationships. (Describe the program a bit further.) Does this sound like something you would be interested in participating in?"* Not only will it be imperative that you assess motivation during an intake interview with young adults and social coaches prior to treatment, but you may also want to assess social motivation over the phone before ever scheduling an intake interview. In our experience at the UCLA PEERS® Clinic, only about 25% of requests for treatment come directly from young adults. More often, caregivers are the ones to request services. In order to avoid misunderstandings, you may consider speaking with both young adults and social coaches on the phone to assess social motivation and treatment compliance before scheduling an intake appointment.
- **Group Size.** The recommended PEERS® group size is between seven and 10 young adults, although we have tested the program in groups comprising as many as 12 young adults. Including more than 12 young adults per group could be difficult, but not impossible with some adaptations. For example, time allotted for the *Homework Review* and *Young Adult Behavioral Rehearsal* would have to be adjusted accordingly and a larger treatment team would be required in order to provide performance feedback during *Behavioral Rehearsal Exercises*. Running groups with fewer than six young adults is somewhat risky in that group members may drop out of treatment and absences can occur, significantly decreasing the size of the group.
- **Age Distribution of the Group.** Groups may have a wide range in age, provided there is more than one young adult around the same general age. Most *PEERS® for Young Adults* groups include participants between 18 and 30 years of age, although the program has been used with older adults, as well as adolescents. It is important to note that at the time of writing this manual, the effectiveness of the *PEERS® for Young Adults* program has only been established through research with young adults 18–24 years of age, although research with older adults is currently underway.
- **Gender Distribution of the Group.** Anecdotally, men and women have been easily mixed in *PEERS® for Young Adults* groups without problems. In our experience through the UCLA PEERS® Clinic, men are more likely to present for social skills treatment, so it is likely that groups will be composed of fewer women. It is recommended that groups with only one female member

be avoided when possible, unless the woman agrees prior to treatment. In cases where only one female presents for treatment, be sure to notify the woman beforehand, and consider giving her the option to wait for another group if she is uncomfortable being the only female group member.

- **Including Young Adults without ASD.** It has been repeatedly observed that youth with ASD are often most comfortable and appear to thrive more successfully in social skills groups with other youth with ASD. This may be because all of the atypical behaviors and idiosyncrasies often exhibited by those with ASD are either unnoticed or unremarkable in groups of other youth with ASD. Therefore, homogeneous PEERS® groups for young adults with ASD are quite common and have the capacity to create an accepting and safe environment in which to learn social skills without judgment or discomfort. However, young adults with ADHD, depression, anxiety, and other social behavioral problems who are accepting of the unique challenges of young adults with ASD might also be included in these groups. Although the *PEERS® for Young Adults* curriculum was initially developed for young adults with ASD, we have also seen lasting benefits for young adults not on the autism spectrum. Since PEERS® targets skill development through instruction of ***ecologically valid social skills*** (those behaviors exhibited by socially accepted young adults), the treatment may have widespread applicability regardless of the diagnosis of the person. We suspect that any young adult who does not know the rules for developing and maintaining relationships or managing conflict and rejection could benefit from this intervention.

Required Personnel

When social coaching groups and young adults groups are taught concurrently, two group leaders are needed for *PEERS® for Young Adults*. Group leaders typically include psychologists, psychiatrists, marriage and family therapists, social workers, speech and language pathologists, occupational therapists, recreational therapists, vocational counselors, and other mental health professionals and educators. Whatever the professional background, young adult group leaders should have previous experience working with high-functioning adults with ASD or other social challenges, and social coaching group leaders should have experience working with parents and/or caregivers. Group leaders should also be fully trained on all aspects of the PEERS® curriculum either by reading this manual beforehand or attending a *PEERS® Certified Training Seminar*.

In addition to having two group leaders, it will be essential to have one or two behavioral coaches to assist with the young adult group. Behavioral coaches often include undergraduate students, graduate students, or trainees studying psychology or some related mental health field, as well as other mental health professionals and educators. Some *PEERS® for Young Adults* groups have even included neurotypical peer mentors or siblings as coaches in the young adult groups, although the effectiveness of this approach has yet to be tested. Behavioral coaches should be trained on all aspects of the PEERS® curriculum and have a good understanding of behavior reinforcement and management strategies. Behavioral coaches are often responsible for conducting *Role Play Demonstrations*, providing performance feedback through coaching during *Behavioral Rehearsal Exercises*, and assisting the young adult group leader with reinforcement and behavior management. When possible, it is best to have at least one male and one female behavioral coach in order to demonstrate and practice skills related to dating etiquette in *Sessions 9–12*. In order to avoid heterosexism in the practicing of targeted skills in these sessions, young adults should have the option of choosing a male or female coach to practice the skills related to dating etiquette.

Physical Facilities

The skills taught in *PEERS® for Young Adults* should be presented much like a class, particularly during the *Homework Review* and *Didactic Lesson*. For the young adult group, the room should have a whiteboard and markers with a large conference table and chairs for young adults to sit facing the board. Smart boards may be used, but rules and steps from the lesson should not be created prior to the group as the lesson should appear to be generated organically by the young adults using a Socratic method. Sufficient space should be available in the young adult room (or in additional rooms) to break the group into dyads or smaller groups during *Young Adult Behavioral Rehearsal Exercises*. For the social coaching group, the room should include a large conference table with chairs for the social coaches to sit around facing the group leader. One of the group rooms should be large enough to conduct *Reunification* for all the young adults and social coaches to stand or sit comfortably.

Materials Needed

The following materials are needed for the group:

- **Dry Erase Board and Markers.** A dry erase board and markers used for writing the rules and steps from the *Didactic Lessons* will be essential tools for the young adult group.
- **Phone Roster.** A roster including each young adult's name and phone number is needed for *Sessions 1–6* to practice conversational skills during the *in-group phone call or video chat* assignments. This roster should be distributed to social coaches and young adults in the first week of the group (see Appendix D). You may need to obtain a *release of information* during the intake interview in order to provide this information to group members in *Session 1*.
- **In-Group Call Assignment Log.** This sheet is needed to track the *in-group phone call or video chat* assignments during *Sessions 1–6*, while young adults are practicing conversational skills with one another. Keeping careful track of which young adults are assigned to call one another will enable group leaders to switch the order of *"caller"* and *"receiver"* for these assignments, while ensuring that young adults call different group members throughout this process (see Appendix E).
- **Social Coaching Handouts.** *Social Coaching Handouts* should be photocopied from the manual and distributed every week during the *Didactic Lesson* of the social coaching group and during *Reunification* for young adults. *Social Coaching Handouts* should also be made available for absent group members, to provide an overview of the missed lesson and *Homework Assignments*, and can be shared with other caregivers (e.g., family members, counselors, job coaches, etc.) who are not present at the groups.
- **Homework Compliance Sheets.** These sheets are meant to be photocopied each week and highly recommended to track weekly progress and completion of *Homework Assignments*. The *Homework Compliance Sheets* should be completed by a member of the treatment team in both the young adult and social coaching groups, and might be filed for future reference to track treatment compliance (see Appendix F).
- **Behavioral Rehearsal Materials.** Additional materials needed for the behavioral rehearsal activities are provided in the *Young Adult Behavioral Rehearsal* section of each chapter. For example, indoor games (e.g., video games, card games, board games) are needed for mock get-togethers in *Sessions 8–15*.
- **Graduation Flyers.** In *Sessions 14 and 15*, graduation flyers should be distributed to announce the culmination of the group and the graduation party and ceremony that mark the event (see Appendix G for an example).
- **Certificates of Completion.** These certificates are given at the graduation ceremony on the last day of the group. It is strongly encouraged that certificates be awarded as a way of honoring the accomplishments of the young adults and celebrating their achievements (see Appendix H for an example).
- **Social Coaching Homework Assignment Worksheets.** These worksheets should be photocopied and distributed to the social coaches at the beginning of the *Homework Assignment* portion of the *Didactic Lesson* and should be completed and returned in the next session (see Appendix I).
- **Optional: DVD players, iPads, laptops, gaming consoles.** DVD players, iPads, and laptops are needed when showing *Video Role Play Demonstrations* of targeted skills in the social coaching group or the young adult group. Gaming consoles, iPads, and laptops may also be useful items for the

mock get-togethers, conducted during the *Young Adult Behavioral Rehearsal* portions of *Sessions 8–15*. Portable gaming devices are not recommended.

- **Optional: Outcome Measures.** You are strongly encouraged to track treatment progress using outcome measures collected prior to the start of your group and at the end of the group. The *Test of Young Adult Social Skills Knowledge (TYASSK)* is a criterion-based measure that assesses knowledge of the skills taught in *PEERS®* (see Appendix A). The *Quality of Socialization Questionnaire (QSQ)* provides frequency counts of social engagement through organized get-togethers with peers and dates with romantic partners (see Appendix B). Both tests are recommended as outcome measures to track treatment progress. Additional recommendations for outcome measures are presented in the *Tracking Progress* section of this chapter.

Teaching Methods

- **Didactic Lessons Using Concrete Rules and Steps.** Many young adults with ASD have a penchant for rules and are likely to follow them. This may be due to the fact that the world is generally unpredictable, and rules provide a stable means of understanding social surroundings. Those with ASD are also known for thinking in very concrete and literal ways. Taking into account this preference for rules and the tendency to think in black-and-white terms, PEERS® teaches social skills using concrete rules and steps of social behavior. Sophisticated and sometimes complex social behaviors are deconstructed into smaller rules and steps in order to aid comprehension during *Didactic Lessons*. This method of instruction is not only beneficial for young adults with ASD, but can be a very effective teaching tool for adults with other social challenges.
- **Ecologically Valid Social Skills.** One aspect of PEERS® that is unique from other social skills programs is the use of *ecologically valid social skills*. This essentially involves teaching social behaviors that are naturally used by those who are socially accepted. In other words, you will not be teaching young adults what we *THINK* people should do in social situations, but what actually *WORKS* according to research. What we *think* works isn't always appropriate in reality.
- **Socratic Method.** Another important teaching method utilized in PEERS® includes the use of the Socratic method. This involves asking certain questions or demonstrating certain behaviors through role play exercises that elicit specific responses from group members. This method essentially leads young adults and social coaches to give certain answers, without actually giving them the answers. The power in this approach for young adults is that it gives group members the sense that they or their peers are generating the rules and steps of social behavior. Rather than lecturing, having the group members generate elements of the lessons using a Socratic method ensures that they are more likely to believe what is taught and remember what is learned.
- **Use of Buzzwords.** Another unique aspect of the PEERS® curriculum is the use of *buzzwords*. Terms that are *bold and italicized* in the manual are *buzzwords* and represent important concepts from the curriculum. The buzzwords symbolize complex social behaviors that can be identified in just a few simple words. Using the *buzzwords* as much as possible will help to develop a common language between young adults, social coaches, and the treatment team. When group leaders come across the first instance of buzzwords in the lesson guide, they should emphasize the words when speaking and write them down on the board in the young adult group.
- **Board Writing.** A great deal of didactic material is covered in each lesson of *PEERS® for Young Adults*. Consequently, it is STRONGLY recommended that *buzzwords* related to the rules and steps of social behavior be written on the board during the young adult group. It is NOT recommended that the *Social Coaching Handout* be distributed during the *Young Adult Didactic Lesson* (as is done in the social coaching group) because this would eliminate the impact of using the Socratic method. Young adults should feel as though they and their peers are generating the rules and steps of the lesson in order to enhance memorization and acceptance of the skills. Likewise, PowerPoint slides or pre-made electronic presentations of the skills are also discouraged in the young adult group. The creation of the rules and steps of social behavior should feel more organic during the young adult session; therefore, board writing is strongly encouraged.

- *Role Play Demonstrations.* The modeling of appropriate and inappropriate social behavior is a critical ingredient to understanding social skills. *Role Play Demonstrations* are used throughout the *PEERS® for Young Adults* manual to illustrate specific rules and steps of social etiquette. Examples of *Role Play Demonstrations* are provided in a scripted format in the shaded boxes in the *Young Adult Therapist Guides* to assist group leaders and behavioral coaches in understanding how to demonstrate certain behaviors. These scripts are not intended to be read verbatim, but instead serve as an example of what a *Role Play Demonstration* might look and sound like. *Video Role Play Demonstrations* of many of the targeted skills are also available through other resources, including the *PEERS® Role Play Video Library*, which can be found at www.routledge.com/cw/laugeson and the *FriendMaker* app, which is available in the Apple App Store.

- **Perspective Taking Questions.** In order to promote better social cognition, **Perspective Taking Questions** are provided following *Role Play Demonstrations*. These questions will help facilitate discussion with young adults about appropriate and inappropriate social behavior, while assisting young adults with reading social cues and understanding the perspectives of others. **Perspective Taking Questions** are repetitive in nature and generally include the following three questions: *"What was that like for the other person?"*, *"What did they think of me?"*, and *"Are they going to want to talk to me again?"* Using the same **Perspective Taking Questions** after each *Role Play Demonstration* will help to improve social cognition and ensure that young adults begin to consider these same questions in their own social interactions.

- **Behavioral Rehearsal Exercises.** In order to fully comprehend a particular set of social skills, it is necessary to actually use them through practice and repetition. The use of *Behavioral Rehearsal Exercises* occurs in every session of the young adult group as a separate activity. In some cases, particularly during the dating didactics, the *Behavioral Rehearsal Exercises* may also occur during the *Didactic Lesson. Behavioral Rehearsal Exercises* are a critical ingredient to skill acquisition and should always be paired with social coaching with performance feedback from the treatment team.

- **Coaching with Performance Feedback.** To receive the full benefit of behavioral rehearsal opportunities, it is critical that the treatment team provide performance feedback through coaching. Social coaches are also encouraged to provide coaching in the home and community, as described in the *Social Coaching Handouts*. Coaching is an important component of PEERS® because not all young adults will perfect these skills immediately, and will instead need additional assistance in mastering and generalizing the skills being taught.

- **Homework Assignments.** Each lesson includes *Homework Assignments* to promote the use of skills in more natural settings. Some of the assignments are intended to be completed by young adults and social coaches in order to promote social coaching outside of the group. In other cases, young adults will complete assignments independently, with behind-the-scenes assistance from social coaches. Completion of *Homework Assignments* is critical to generalization of skills to natural social settings and overall success in PEERS®. Our research suggests that those who more frequently completed their *Homework Assignments* have significantly better outcomes following treatment. On the other hand, those who do not complete their *Homework Assignments* exhibit less benefit. Consequently, you should strongly encourage the practicing of newly learned skills outside of the group and hold group members accountable for these assignments through the weekly *Homework Review*.

- **Homework Review.** In order to ensure that group members are using the skills outside of your group, you will conduct the *Homework Review* at the beginning of every young adult and *Social Coaching Session*. The *Homework Review* consists of an examination of completed assignments from the previous week, focused on practicing newly learned skills. A considerable amount of time is spent on the *Homework Review* in each session (i.e., approximately 30 minutes in the young adult group and 50 minutes in the social coaching group), emphasizing the importance of behavioral rehearsal and practice in natural social settings. Social skills are not expected to generalize to other settings without the completion of *Homework Assignments*, so plan to spend a substantial amount of time reviewing homework. The *Homework Review* is also the time in which you will individualize the treatment for each young adult by assessing what's working and what's not working and troubleshooting any issues that may arise.

- **Flexibility with the Manual.** One of the common criticisms of manualized treatments is that they represent *"one size fits all"* approaches. Obviously, very little in life is *"one size fits all,"* and manualized treatments should not be treated in this manner. Instead, the *PEERS® for Young Adults* curriculum is intended to be used flexibly. That means rules and steps of social behavior should be modified accordingly when necessary. A good example of this relates to cultural variation in social skills. The skills taught in PEERS® represent the common social customs utilized in North America and other Western cultures (although the program is used globally). However, even within Western society, there is great cultural variation. Consequently, group leaders should modify the curriculum according to the social customs of the group members. Because not every group member will affiliate with the same culture, the *Homework Review* may afford an excellent opportunity to individualize the treatment for each young adult. The purpose of the *Homework Review* is not only to ensure that skills are being practiced appropriately in natural settings, but to provide an opportunity to troubleshoot and adapt the program for anyone for whom it is not working. Flexibility with the manual (without too much deviation from the core curriculum) is also an essential ingredient to ensuring that all group members will benefit from the treatment.

Behavioral Management Techniques

Although very few group members will be disruptive during the group, you may occasionally require behavioral management techniques to modify periodic disruptions. Three particular types of behaviors that will require attention include: (1) inattention (e.g., trouble focusing or maintaining attention); (2) disruption (e.g., engaging in behaviors that distract or disturb the lesson); and (3) disrespect (e.g., teasing, bullying, rude or inappropriate comments). Suggestions for how to handle these behaviors are listed below.

- **Verbal Praise.** One of the most powerful behavioral management techniques you have with socially motivated young adults and their social coaches is the use of verbal praise. Periodically praising the group or individual group members for behaviors you want to see will probably increase their frequency. For example, saying, *"You all did a great job completing your Homework Assignments,"* or *"I like how you're really taking this seriously and practicing the skills outside of the group"* are nice ways to reinforce and encourage group members to act in desired ways.
- **Using Names to Redirect Attention.** It is fairly common for young adults to appear to drift off during lessons. They will sometimes appear distracted, although it is difficult to know for sure. If you suspect a young adult is having trouble paying attention, rather than interrupting the lesson to bring them back to task, simply use their name as you're presenting the lesson. For example, you might say, *"So David, one of the rules for trading information is . . ."* or *"So the goal of trading information is to find common interests, right David?"* (nodding your head yes to prompt him). Using names to redirect attention is a nice way to bring young adults back to task without causing embarrassment, appearing punitive, or pausing the group.
- **Using Peer Pressure.** Young adults will occasionally make inappropriate comments or behave improperly from time to time. Rather than scold young adults in front of their peers, causing defensiveness or embarrassment, state the behavior you want to see and then apply a little peer pressure to utilize the situation as a coachable moment. You can do this by using the very handy sentence stem, ***"What could be the problem with . . . ?"*** followed by responses from young adults uninvolved with the inappropriate behavior. Never ask the young adult who is engaging in the inappropriate behavior what the problem with their behavior is, as that will not work. Instead, ask the other young adults what could be wrong with a certain behavior, and they will be happy to answer your question. Avoid asking questions such as, *"What was wrong with David's behavior?"* since this is too personal. The question should be vague and general. The vast majority of young adults will not argue with their peers over these points and you can simply move on. Here are some common examples of how it works:
  - When a young adult repeatedly talks out of turn and disrupts the group, you might say, *"We need to raise our hands. What could be the problem with not raising our hands in this group?"*

○ When a young adult inappropriately laughs at someone else's comment, you might say, *"We need to be respectful. What could be the problem with laughing at people?"*

○ When a young adult repeatedly tries to make jokes during the group, you might say, *"We need to be serious. What could be the problem with making jokes in group?"*

○ When a young adult points out another group member's mistake, you might say, *"Let's be careful not to police people. What could be the problem with policing?"*

These comments will help redirect the young adults toward the behavioral expectations you have established, while avoiding being too punitive. By using this method, you are applying peer pressure without directly calling out the misbehaving young adult. Although some young adults (particularly younger group members) may test limits initially, if you address these situations with respect, you will be able to minimize the negative effects.

- **Stating Your Expectations.** One helpful way to redirect inappropriate behavior from the group is to state your expectations. Using the examples above, comments include statements such as *"We need to raise our hands,"* or *"We need to be respectful,"* or *"We need to be serious."* After stating your expectations, you quickly move on as if you fully expect them to comply. If you wait for young adults to agree, you may find yourself in a standoff. Generally, when you state your expectations to a group of socially motivated young adults and you expect them to comply, they usually will. You should also use the pronoun *"we"* rather than *"I"* when stating your expectations. This gives the impression that you are speaking on behalf of the group, which also applies a bit of healthy peer pressure.

- **Offering Timeouts.** If a young adult is particularly disruptive in the group, or appears to be behaviorally or emotionally disregulated, you can offer to let him or her take a timeout. This timeout is not meant to be punitive, as that would not be developmentally appropriate, but rather an opportunity for the young adult to regulate him or herself. For example, offering a timeout could include nonjudgmental questions such as *"David, do you need to take a little time out?"* or *"David, do you need to take a little break?"* It is not uncommon for young adults to agree to these timeouts, particularly when the material presented is emotionally charged for them. When this happens, it is helpful to send a behavioral coach with the young adult to assist in regulating emotions, but be careful not to provide too much reinforcement for these behaviors or you will run the risk of attention-seeking through frequent timeouts. In extreme cases, and when sanctioned by the young adult, you may also opt to get the social coach to assist with de-escalating the situation. Once the young adult returns to group, wipe the slate clean and do not mention the timeout or the inappropriate behavior in the group. You can arrange to have a ***side meeting*** with the young adult and his or her social coach after the group if necessary. Timeouts are rare in most *PEERS® for Young Adults* groups and should be used sparingly.

PEERS® without the Social Coaching Group

Although the inclusion of social coaches as part of treatment is HIGHLY recommended, the reality is that some *PEERS® for Young Adults* programs will not include social coaching groups. We fondly and jokingly call this type of deviation from the original treatment "PEERS® Lite" because these modified versions of PEERS® represent slimmed down versions of the original evidence-based intervention. Lack of inclusion of social coaches occurs for many reasons, including lack of resources and staffing among the treatment team, as well as difficulty in finding appropriate and available social coaches. Because we cannot confidently guarantee the effectiveness of modified versions of our program, we do not advocate the use of "PEERS® Lite" approaches to teaching social skills to young adults with ASD and other social challenges. However, knowing that deviation from the original program is inevitable in certain cases for practical reasons, a few suggestions are provided for how to best involve caregivers in treatment, even when a social coaching group is not possible.

Even when implementation of a social coaching group is not feasible, it is highly recommended that clinicians include caregivers in the program as much as possible. Caregivers might include parents, adult siblings, other family members, job coaches, life coaches, friends, partners, peer mentors, counselors, or any other person involved in the social world of the young adult. The simplest and most straightforward way to include caregivers is by distributing *Social Coaching Handouts* each week. These handouts can be found at the end of each chapter and should be photocopied and sent to caregivers when possible. Many clinicians have opted to scan *Social Coaching Handouts* and send them as electronic documents directly to caregivers over email. Because these handouts are intended to be photocopied and distributed to young adults and their social coaches as part of the program, you will not be breaking copyright restrictions in sharing them with others.

Another method of involving caregivers in treatment when social coaching groups are not an option is to recommend additional resources for caregivers to utilize. *The Science of Making Friends: Helping Socially Challenged Teens and Young Adults* (Laugeson, 2013) is a book for parents and other caregivers to use to help teens and young adults learn to make and keep friends and handle peer conflict and rejection. Most of the skills taught in *PEERS® for Young Adults* (apart from dating etiquette) are summarized in this book through *narrative sections* with *Social Coaching Tips* for parents and caregivers and *chapter summaries* for teens and young adults. A DVD companion is included with *Video Role Play Demonstrations* of targeted skills with **Perspective Taking Questions** to follow. *Chapter exercises* are also provided to help generalize the skills to natural social settings. When social coaching groups are not feasible, you may consider suggesting that relevant caregivers access *The Science of Making Friends* to obtain information about how to provide social coaching to young adults outside of the treatment setting.

Another inexpensive method for including caregivers in treatment when a social coaching group is not possible is to recommend the use of the *FriendMaker* mobile app. *FriendMaker* is a mobile application for smartphones intended to act as a *"virtual social coach"* for teens and young adults. The *FriendMaker* app outlines the concrete rules and steps for making and keeping friends and handling peer conflict and rejection using bullet-pointed material. It can easily and affordably be accessed in the iOS App Store, and is not only a useful tool for providing *virtual coaching* to those struggling socially, but is also a good resource for caregivers seeking more information about the PEERS® program.

Whatever the method of inclusion, involvement of caregivers as social coaches will likely improve the effectiveness and generalizability of your program through the use of social coaching outside of the treatment setting, and therefore is highly encouraged when possible.

Using This Manual with Adults with Intellectual Disabilities

Although the *PEERS® for Young Adults* curriculum is intended for use with individuals without Intellectual Disabilities, given the paucity of evidence-based treatments for adults, we recognize that some of you will be using this curriculum with different populations. For some young adults with Intellectual Disabilities, learning differences, or executive functioning challenges, the number of rules and steps presented in each lesson may be overwhelming. In that case, the following four recommendations are suggested for use with young adults with Intellectual Disabilities or other learning or cognitive challenges.

1. **Slow down the intervention.** The general speed of *PEERS® for Young Adults* is rapid and fast-paced. For young adults with Intellectual Disabilities or other learning or cognitive challenges, feel free to slow down the pace of the program. For example, you might consider *"doubling the dose"* and lengthening the 16-week intervention into a 32-week intervention.
2. **Provide more opportunities for behavioral rehearsal.** In our experience at the UCLA PEERS® Clinic, although some young adults with Intellectual Disabilities (i.e., IQ scores below 70) may not be able to articulate all of the rules and steps of the social skills we are teaching, they are generally able to follow the rules and use the steps. The best way to ensure acquisition of these skills will be through repeated practice attempts. Therefore, providing more behavioral rehearsal opportunities with performance feedback through social coaching inside and outside of the group is strongly recommended.

3. **Simplify the lessons.** Another way in which to adapt the *PEERS® for Young Adults* curriculum for those with Intellectual Disabilities or other learning or cognitive challenges is to simplify the lessons to include abbreviated steps and/or basic rules. Table 1.2 provides an example of abbreviated steps from *Session 1* on *Starting Individual Conversations*. Table 1.3 presents suggestions for how you might abbreviate the lesson for *Session 6* on *Entering Group Conversations*.

4. **Use visual supports.** The use of visual supports is another possible adaptation for individuals with learning difficulties, and may provide an alternative method for comprehension of the material. Future research on PEERS® will more closely examine the benefit of these adapted approaches for youth with Intellectual Disabilities. In the meantime, our clinical observations have revealed treatment benefit using these modified methods of instruction.

Table 1.2 Abbreviated Steps for Starting Individual Conversations

Traditional Steps	Abbreviated Steps
1. Casually Look Over *2. Use a Prop* *3. Find a Common Interest* *4. Mention the Common Interest* *5. Trade Information* *6. Assess Interest* *7. Introduce Yourself*	*1. Find a Common Interest* *2. Mention the Common Interest* *3. Trade Information*

Table 1.3 Abbreviated Steps for Entering Group Conversations

Traditional Steps	Abbreviated Steps
1. Listen to the Conversation *2. Watch from a Distance* *3. Use a Prop* *4. Identify the Topic* *5. Find a Common Interest* *6. Move Closer* *7. Wait for a Pause* *8. Mention the Topic* *9. Assess Interest* *10. Introduce Yourself*	*1. Watch and Listen* *2. Wait for a Pause* *3. Move Closer* *4. Mention the Topic*

Additional Resources for Young Adults and Social Coaches

For young adults and social coaches requiring or requesting additional resources to be used during or after treatment, the following additional resources are recommended. *The Science of Making Friends: Helping Socially Challenged Teens and Young Adults* (Laugeson, 2013) is a book for parents, social coaches, and youth interested in learning how to make and keep friends and handle peer conflict and rejection. This book provides a comprehensive overview of most of the skills taught in *PEERS® for Young Adults* (with the exception of dating etiquette) using narrative sections for parents and social coaches, chapter summaries for teens and young adults, chapter exercises to practice the skills, and a companion DVD including *Video Role Play Demonstrations* with **Perspective Taking Questions**. Additionally, the *FriendMaker* mobile application for smartphones provides *"virtual social coaching"* to young adults and social coaches seeking a quick review of the skills taught in PEERS®. Outlines of the rules and steps of social etiquette related to friendship development and maintenance are provided, including 25 embedded *Video Role Play Demonstrations* of targeted skills with **Perspective Taking Questions** to follow. Many young adults use the *FriendMaker* app in natural social settings as a *virtual coach* when live coaching is not possible or is inappropriate.

Resources for Children and Adolescents

For those working with children or adolescents with ASD and other social challenges, the following evidence-based social skills treatment manuals are recommended.

- *Social Skills for Teenagers with Developmental and Autism Spectrum Disorders: The PEERS® Treatment Manual* (Laugeson & Frankel, 2010).
  This evidence-based manual is suggested for those interested in implementing weekly parent-assisted social skills groups for adolescents in middle and high school. This treatment manual includes 14 weekly 90-minute sessions for parents and adolescents in secondary school settings.
- *The PEERS® Curriculum for School-Based Professionals: Social Skills Training for Adolescents with Autism Spectrum Disorder* (Laugeson, 2014).
  This evidence-based curriculum is recommended for educators and clinicians seeking a daily lesson format for adolescents in middle and high school. The curriculum includes 16 daily 30- to 50-minute lessons for adolescents in secondary school settings. Although there is not a parent group component to this program, comprehensive *Parent Handouts* are included.
- *Children's Friendship Training* (Frankel & Myatt, 2003).
  This treatment manual is recommended for those working with elementary school-aged children. This evidence-based program includes 12 weekly 60-minute sessions for parents and children in primary school settings, focusing on the skills for making and keeping friends.

Tracking Progress

Tracking progress is an essential part of determining whether your program is working. It is how a program maintains quality control. Below is a list of the tests we have used in our published scientific studies with PEERS®. Several standardized assessments of social functioning are included. These measures are widely available and have shown substantial change following the program. They also impose little demands upon young adults and social coaches to complete, and when used as a pre- and post-test assessment of social functioning, these measures provide a good evaluation of treatment outcome.

Test of Young Adult Social Skills Knowledge (Appendix A)

The *TYASSK* is a 30-item criterion-referenced test developed for *PEERS® for Young Adults* to assess young adults' knowledge about the specific social skills taught during the intervention. Items are derived from key elements from each of the 15 *Didactic Lessons*. Young adults are presented with sentence stems and asked to choose the best option from two possible answers. Scores range from 0 to 30, with higher scores reflecting greater knowledge of adult social skills. The *TYASSK* is a modified version of the *Test of Adolescent Social Skills Knowledge* (*TASSK*; Laugeson & Frankel, 2010), which has a coefficient alpha of .56. This moderate level of internal consistency is acceptable, given the large domain of questions on the scale. Previous research using the *TYASSK* to track treatment outcome in *PEERS® for Young Adults* generally yields a six- to eight-point raw score improvement from pre- to post-test among young adults with ASD. The *TYASSK* takes approximately five minutes to complete and can be found in Appendix A.

Quality of Socialization Questionnaire (Appendix B)

The *QSQ* is independently administered to young adults (*Quality of Socialization Questionnaire—Young Adult*; *QSQ-YA*) and social coaches (*Quality of Socialization Questionnaire—Caregiver*; *QSQ-C*) to assess the frequency of get-togethers with peers and romantic dates in the previous month, and the level of conflict during get-togethers with peers. The *Social Initiation Scale* consists of three items, measuring the number of hosted get-togethers and romantic dates in the previous month, and the number of different friends the young adult hosted. The *Social Reciprocity Scale* measures the number of get-togethers and romantic dates the young adult was invited to in the previous month, and the number of different friends that invited the young adult to these get-togethers. The 12 items that make up the *Conflict Scale* ask young adults and caregivers to report the degree of peer conflict in the last get-together (e.g., *"We got upset with each other"*) using a four-point Likert scale ranging from *"not at all true," "just a little true," "pretty much true,"* or *"very much true."* The QSQ was adapted from the *Quality of Play Questionnaire* (QPQ; Frankel & Mintz, 2009), which was developed through factor analysis of 175 boys and girls. Coefficient alpha was .87 for the *Conflict Scale*. This scale also demonstrated convergent validity with the *SSRS Problem Behaviors Scale* (ρ = .35, p < .05) and significantly discriminated community from clinic-referred samples (p < .05). Reported frequency of hosted and invited get-togethers also significantly discriminated community-referred from clinic samples (p's < .005). Spearman correlation between adolescent and parent ratings on the QSQ at baseline for *PEERS® for Adolescents* was .55 for the *Conflict Scale*, .99 for the frequency of hosted get-togethers, and .99 for the frequency of invited get-togethers (deleting reports of "0" get-togethers resulted in correlations of .97 and .94, respectively, all p's < .001). Previous research using the QSQ to track treatment outcome in PEERS® generally reveals two to four additional get-togethers per month from pre- to post-test among youth with ASD. The QSQ takes approximately five minutes to complete and can be found in Appendix B.

Social Responsiveness Scale—Second Edition (SRS-2; Constantino & Gruber, 2012)

The *SRS-2* consists of 65 items assessing the presence and severity of social deficits (i.e., social awareness, social cognition, social communication, social motivation, and restricted interests and repetitive behaviors) associated with Autism Spectrum Disorder (ASD) as they occur in natural social settings. The *SRS-2* can be completed by young adults and social coaches. It was normed on a representative national sample and has good internal consistency (α = .95), inter-rater agreement reliability (r = .61), and convergent validity (Constantino & Gruber, 2012). Previous research using the *SRS-2* to track treatment outcome in PEERS® generally yields a full standard deviation improvement (10 T-score points) from pre- to post-test on parent reports of social functioning among youth with ASD. The *SRS-2* takes approximately 10 minutes to complete.

Social Skills Improvement System (SSIS; Gresham & Elliot, 2008).

The *SSIS* is a standardized, 75-item measure that assesses social skills (communication, cooperation, assertion, responsibility, empathy, engagement, self-control) and problem behaviors (externalizing and internalizing behaviors, bullying, hyperactivity and inattention, Autism Spectrum Disorder-related behaviors). Although developed for youth between 13 and 18 years, the *SSIS* has been used successfully with young adults to track change in social skills following PEERS® (Gantman et al., 2012; Laugeson et al., 2015). Using a four-point rating system, young adults and social coaches rate the frequency and relative importance of various social skills and problem behaviors. Previous research using the *SSIS* to track treatment outcome in PEERS® typically reveals nearly a standard deviation improvement (10 standard score points) from pre- to post-test on parent reports of social functioning among youth with ASD. The *SSIS* takes approximately 10 minutes to complete.

Empathy Quotient (EQ; Baron-Cohen & Wheelwright, 2004)

The *EQ* is a young adult and caregiver-reported measure of empathy. Eighty-one percent of adolescents and adults with ASD score less than 30 on the *EQ*, compared to 12% of neurotypical controls. The *EQ* demonstrates excellent internal consistency (.92) and test-retest reliability (.97). Higher scores represent greater empathic abilities. Previous research using the *EQ* to track treatment outcome in PEERS® typically reveals approximately a seven-point raw score improvement from pre- to post-test on parent reports of social functioning among youth with ASD. The *EQ* takes approximately 10 minutes to complete.

Social and Emotional Loneliness Scale (SELSA; DiTommaso & Spinner, 1993)

The *SELSA* is a 37-item self-report measure of romantic, social, and family loneliness. Validated on neurotypical college students, the internal consistency for the *SELSA* ranges from .89 to .93. Higher scores represent more loneliness. Previous research using the *SELSA* to track treatment outcome in *PEERS® for Young Adults* typically reveals approximately a 12-point raw score improvement from pre- to post-test among young adults with ASD. The *SELSA* takes approximately 10 minutes to complete.

What You Can Expect: The Research Evidence

While social skills training is an important treatment priority for many young adults with ASD and other social challenges, much of the research literature in this area has focused on interventions with children. Very few social skills intervention studies have been devoted to investigating the efficacy and effectiveness of social skills training for young adults. Moreover, few social skills programs focus on the development and maintenance of friendships and romantic relationships. Even among the social skills intervention studies conducted with the ASD population, most have not been formally tested in terms of improving social competence or the development of close friendships, nor have they assessed the benefit of including caregivers in training in order to promote social functioning. The lack of evidence-based social skills instruction to improve social competence and promote the formation of friendships for young adults with ASD and other social challenges is what inspired the development of this manual.

Bridging off of our work conducted at the UCLA PEERS® Clinic with adolescents with ASD, the *PEERS® for Young Adults* manual utilizes a caregiver-assisted model. Like *PEERS® for Adolescents*, which involves a parent-assisted model for social coaching, the current manual utilizes caregivers as social coaches to reinforce skill usage outside of the treatment setting.

The first randomized controlled trial of PEERS® using parent assistance was published in the *Journal of Autism and Developmental Disorders* (Laugeson, Frankel, Mogil, & Dillon, 2009). This study compared 33 teens 13–17 years of age with ASD in two different conditions. Adolescents were randomly assigned to either receive a parent-assisted version of the PEERS® intervention or were placed in a delayed treatment control group. Results revealed that in comparison with the control group, the treatment group significantly improved their knowledge of social skills, increased their frequency of hosted get-togethers, showed changes in their friendship quality, and improved in overall social skills, as reported by parents. Changes in social skills reported by teachers also showed a strong trend toward improvement.

In a second clinical trial using the parent-assisted version of PEERS®, published in the *Journal of Autism and Developmental Disorders*, original findings were replicated for a different group of 28 teens with ASD (Laugeson, Frankel, Gantman, Dillon, & Mogil, 2012). Results revealed improvements in parent-reported overall social skills, specifically in the areas of improved cooperation, assertion, and responsibility for those receiving the PEERS® intervention in comparison to those waiting for treatment. Results further showed a significant decrease in autism symptoms related to social responsiveness in the areas of improved social motivation, social communication, social cognition, and social awareness, as well as a decrease in autistic mannerisms for treatment participants. Increases in teen reports of frequency of hosted get-togethers and improved knowledge of social etiquette were also observed. These treatment gains were generally maintained at the end of a 14-week follow-up assessment period, and in some cases improved even more. Furthermore, the 14-week follow-up assessment revealed significant improvements in overall social functioning, particularly in the area of assertion, according to teacher reports. This latter finding is of particular import as teachers in this study were blind to the conditions under investigation, noticing demonstrable improvements in teens' social functioning, yet unaware these teens had participated in a social skills treatment group.

Using a similar caregiver-assisted model, *PEERS® for Young Adults* includes social coaches, such as parents, adult siblings, peer mentors, job coaches, life coaches, or other family members, to help improve social skills in socially motivated young adults. In the first randomized controlled trial for

PEERS® for Young Adults, published in the *Journal of Autism and Developmental Disorders*, 17 young adults with ASD ranging from 18 to 23 years of age participated in a study with their caregivers testing the effectiveness of the intervention (Gantman, Kapp, Orenski, & Laugeson, 2012). Participants were randomly assigned to a treatment or a delayed treatment control group. Results revealed that the treatment group improved significantly more than the delayed treatment control group at post-test in young adult self-reported social and emotional loneliness and social skills knowledge. Caregiver reports of social functioning also showed significant improvement for the treatment group in social responsiveness in the areas of social communication and decreased autistic mannerisms. Improved social skills in the areas of cooperation, self-control, and assertion, as well as improved empathy and increased frequency of hosted and invited get-togethers, were also reported by caregivers.

In a second randomized controlled trial published in the *Journal of Autism and Developmental Disorders*, 22 young adults with ASD ranging from 18 to 24 years of age participated with their caregivers to test the effectiveness of the *PEERS® for Young Adults* intervention (Laugeson, Gantman, Kapp, Orenski, & Ellingsen, 2015). Participants were randomly assigned to either a treatment group or a delayed treatment control group. Results revealed that, according to caregiver reports, the treatment group improved significantly in overall social skills, particularly in the areas of assertion and cooperation. Significant reductions in ASD symptoms were also reported by caregivers in the treatment group in overall social responsiveness in the areas of improved social motivation and decreased autistic mannerisms. Social skills knowledge and the frequency of social engagement through hosted and invited get-togethers also significantly improved following PEERS®. Furthermore, most treatment gains were maintained at a 16-week follow-up assessment with new improvements observed.

Conclusion. These combined research findings support the effectiveness of parent- and caregiver-assisted PEERS® interventions in improving the social functioning of transitional youth with ASD. Although not extensively tested with youth with other social challenges, *PEERS® for Adolescents* and *PEERS® for Young Adults* are also used clinically for those with ADHD, depression, anxiety, and other developmental disabilities, and are expected to yield similar results.

TRADING INFORMATION AND STARTING CONVERSATIONS

Social Coaching Therapist Guide

Preparing for the Social Coaching Session

The purpose of the first *Social Coaching Session* is to orient caregivers to the structure of the group and solidify the expectations for treatment, while also presenting the first lesson on conversational skills. The development of clear expectations and session structure is critical to maintain the integrity of the program. Without these core components, the sessions may get sidetracked and thereby minimize the effectiveness of the intervention.

At the time of writing this manual, no evidence-based social skills programs for young adults with Autism Spectrum Disorder (ASD) exist, apart from PEERS®, and very few empirically supported programs for adolescents with ASD are available. Consequently, caregivers entering PEERS® are often discouraged through years of efforts at trying to help their young adults use methods that have not worked. They often come with varying degrees of frustration and desperation. On the one hand, they hope you can help them, and on the other hand, they may show high levels of resistance. They sometimes assume that the young adult will not change as a result of treatment, probably because this is what has happened with numerous experiences they have had before. This may manifest as frustration and skepticism in the beginning stages of treatment, and may even impact treatment compliance. In order to overcome this type of treatment resistance, it can be helpful to first provide empathy for these frustrations and then explain how PEERS® is different. Unlike other social skills programs for transitional youth, PEERS® has a strongly established evidence base supporting its effectiveness in improving social skills for adolescents and young adults with ASD. At the time of writing, over a dozen scientific papers have been published in peer-reviewed journals highlighting the efficacy and effectiveness of PEERS® for transitional youth with ASD. One way to combat caregiver skepticism about treatment is to provide a brief overview of the treatment outcome research on PEERS® and emphasize that if they and the young adults follow the program in the ways suggested, they too can expect similar outcomes.

You will find that most social coaches and young adults want and need your help and are highly rewarding to work with. They will be grateful to you for providing the group and eager to do their best to complete *Homework Assignments*. Once they see improvement in the young adults, they will be excited. However, there is a subset of social coaches who may present challenges for the group. Perhaps 90% of all challenging behaviors in the social coaching groups are generated from less than 10% of all caregivers. This section, along with much of the structure of the *Social Coaching Sessions*, is aimed at addressing these challenging behaviors, so that young adults will stand a better chance of benefiting from PEERS® and the help provided to the other social coaches in the group will not be diminished. Closely adhering to the group structure provided is the best overall means of ensuring that participants will benefit from PEERS®.

When you encounter treatment-resistant social coaches, it is important to recognize these symptoms and quickly take appropriate action before difficult and challenging behaviors derail the group. The *Preparing for the Lesson* section in each chapter is designed to help troubleshoot some of the common issues that come up from week to week. However, since it is impossible to anticipate every possible issue that may come up, it is highly recommended that the social coaching group leader have a strong mental health background with comprehensive clinical training and expertise in running groups. In our experience, facilitating the social coaching group is often more clinically challenging than leading the young adult group, and requires strong clinical acumen.

One common and fairly benign occurrence that comes up frequently in the first *Social Coaching Session* involves caregivers jumping ahead and asking specific questions about content that is not ready to be covered yet. For example, questions such as *"How do I teach my son to meet new people?"* or *"How do I help my daughter turn down sexual advances?"* may come up in this first session. Questions that are addressed in later lessons should be saved for future sessions. You might say, *"That's a really important question and we will get to that eventually. We're not there yet, so hold on to that question and we'll get back to it in a future session."* Questions that do not relate to the intervention, such as *"What causes autism?"* or *"Is there a cure for autism?"* should be clearly but gently classified as such. In this case, you might say, *"While that's a good question, I want to be careful to keep us focused on our goal for the group, which is to help our young adults develop and maintain close meaningful relationships. We only have a limited amount of time so we should all be cautious not to get sidetracked and lose the focus of the group."* This redirection turns out to be comforting to social coaches as they know exactly what to expect and can more easily focus upon what PEERS® has to offer. Questions unrelated to the focus of PEERS® can be addressed in individual one-on-one **side meeting**s before or after the group, when appropriate.

Because the structure of the group is new for the social coaches, caregivers may also make off-topic comments and ask off-track questions, such as *"My son has a lot of sensory issues. How can I help him with that?"* or *"How can I get my daughter to go to class?"* To avoid getting sidetracked and ultimately running out of time for the lesson, you can also use the structure of the group to redirect caregivers by saying something such as *"That's a good question, but we have a lot to cover today and unfortunately we do no have time to discuss that right now. If you want to speak after the group, we can do that."* For particularly challenging groups that frequently deviate from the lesson, you might need to write the agenda down on a board to highlight this point. It can also be helpful from the outset to let social coaches know that you may need to interrupt them from time to time by saying something such as *"We have a lot of material to cover each week, so I may have to occasionally interrupt you to keep us focused, but please understand that this is necessary to keep us on track so you can all get the full benefit of the program."* In cases where social coaches are bringing up problems that may be impacting treatment, it is best to meet with them outside of the group, rather than derail the group process, and be prepared to provide additional referrals if necessary.

You will begin the first session by having young adults and social coaches meet in the same room for introductions with the treatment team and other group members. This introduction should only take about five minutes and is meant to "break the ice" and help group members feel more welcome and secure. The *Identifying Strengths* portion of the *Social Coaching Session* involves an exercise in identifying positive characteristics in the young adults. This exercise is intended to help caregivers focus on the positive attributes in their young adults that may be appealing to peers and potential partners. In mental health settings, we often focus on negative attributes, pathologizing certain behaviors and sometimes ignoring special qualities. Because PEERS® is a strength-based approach, it is helpful to begin the first *Social Coaching Session* by focusing on what caregivers like best about their young adults. Most caregivers will have no trouble finding positive attributes in young adults, which you will want to reframe as characteristics important toward the development and mainten-ance of close meaningful relationships. However, some caregivers will find it difficult to identify positive qualities in their young adult. As heartbreaking as that is to imagine, it will be important for you to consider the clinical implications. In some cases, the caregiver may not understand the exercise, which will require you to explain the intent in more detail. In other cases, it may be that the caregiver has a negative way of perceiving their young adult, which will require you to consider how this negative attribution bias may affect the social coaching moving forward. Either way, you should immediately troubleshoot potential clinical issues by redirecting negative caregivers toward the positive as necessary.

The remainder of the session is focused on orienting the social coaches to the structure and expectations of the group and presenting the first lesson and corresponding *Homework Assignments*. Be prepared to distribute photocopies of the *Social Coaching Handout* to all social coaches and young adults at this and all future sessions. These handouts can be found in the manual at the end of every chapter. They are distributed during every social coaching group, and may also be shared with young adults at the end of *Reunification*.

Another common issue that may arise in this session involves social coaches making excuses for why their young adult will have trouble with the first *Homework Assignments*. Some social coaches, known as "helicopter parents" or "hoverers," will try to complete the assignments for the young adults or provide too much prepping. In order to prevent enabling and foster more independence, have these social coaches back off a bit for the first assignments to see how they do before stepping in to help. For example, discourage social coaches from providing scripts or doing in vivo coaching during the *In-Group Phone Call* assignments. Instead, encourage these caregivers to social coach young adults before and after the phone call, rather than during.

Introductions

- At the beginning of the first group, have all young adults and social coaches meet in the same room with the treatment team for introductions.
  - Provide name badges for all participants and treatment team members. These name badges should be worn every week throughout the program.
- Begin by welcoming the group and introducing each member of the treatment team by highlighting their professional background and their role in PEERS®.
- Go around the room and have young adults and social coaches introduce themselves in the following manner:
  - Young adults should say their name, age, and where they work or go to school if relevant.
  - Social coaches should say their name, identify their young adult, and state their relationship with the young adult (e.g., parent, sibling, family member, peer mentor, job coach, life coach, etc.).
  - In groups where people travel long distances, they might also say what city they live in to add more content and context to the introduction.
- Explain that the young adult and social coaching groups will be meeting in separate rooms, but that you will all be reuniting again during the last 10 minutes of each group to talk about what was discussed and how you will practice these skills in the coming week.
- After the introductions, adjourn to separate young adult and social coaching group rooms.

Maintaining Confidentiality

- Review limits of confidentiality (this will vary according to the region within which one practices).
  - Explain, *"If we have information that a young person is being abused or neglected or that there is risk of harm to that person or others, we are required to report this information to the proper authorities."*
- Encourage group members to keep what they hear in the group confidential.
  - Explain, *"We ask that you and the young adults maintain the confidentiality of other group members. That means you should not discuss things brought up here with anyone outside of the group. Although we hope everyone will respect this rule, please remember that we can't control whether group members follow this rule."*

Purpose of PEERS®

- Explain, *"PEERS® is a social skills group to help young adults develop and maintain close meaningful relationships, including friendships and romantic relationships."*
- The following skills will be addressed in PEERS®:
  - Characteristics and types of friendships and romantic relationships.
  - Starting and maintaining conversations.

- ○ Finding an appropriate source of friends.
- ○ Rules about electronic communication.
- ○ Entering and exiting conversations with peers.
- ○ Appropriate use of humor.
- ○ Organizing and having successful get-togethers with friends.
- ○ Dating etiquette, including:
  - ■ Letting someone know you like them.
  - ■ Asking someone on a date.
  - ■ Handling rejection and unwanted sexual advances.
  - ■ General dating do's and don'ts.
- ○ Handling arguments and disagreements.
- ○ Handling teasing and bullying.
- ○ Managing rumors and gossip.
- Explain that social coaches and young adults will meet in separate rooms simultaneously.
  - ○ *Social Coaching Tips* will be given to caregivers to help young adults utilize the skills they learn in PEERS®.
- Explain that the group will be meeting once a week for 90 minutes for 16 weeks.
  - ○ The last week will be a graduation party and ceremony for the young adults, with tips on where to go from here for social coaches.
- Distribute the *Planned Absence Sheet* (see Appendix C).
  - ○ The *Planned Absence Sheet* should include the dates of the groups and corresponding week number, but not the topic of the session as to avoid picking and choosing sessions among group members.
- Remind social coaches that it is extremely important for them to attend all sessions.
- Have social coaches complete and return the *Planned Absence Sheet* if they know they will be missing any sessions.
  - ○ You may consider scheduling off a week if several group members plan to be absent.

Structure of Social Coaching Sessions

Homework Review (50 minutes)

- The session begins with a review of the previous *Homework Assignment*.
- You and your young adult will be given *Homework Assignments* each week to practice the newly learned skills.
- The level of social coaching in homework completion depends on the need and comfort level of the young adult.
  - ○ This will be determined individually and privately through negotiation with the treatment team during *Reunification* at the end of every session.
  - ○ You must at least discuss the homework with your young adult.
- We will only focus on COMPLETED *Homework Assignments*.
  - ○ We will not be spending time talking about why homework did not happen, unless to trouble-shoot how to overcome a problem.
  - ○ The success of the program depends on the completion of the *Homework Assignments*.

Didactic Lesson (20 minutes)

- Each week there will be a new *Didactic Lesson* focusing on relationship skills.
- *Social Coaching Handouts* will be provided each week for you and your young adult.
  - ○ We recommend you save these handouts and place in a binder to be brought to group each week.
  - ○ We suggest you share these handouts with other caregivers.
- Additional treatment options:
  - ○ You may be shown *Role Play Video Demonstrations* of targeted skills from the *PEERS® Role Play Video Library* (www.routledge.com/cw/laugeson) or *FriendMaker* mobile app.

  ○ Social coaches and young adults may want to read corresponding chapters from *The Science of Making Friends* (Laugeson, 2013) throughout the program for additional information.

Homework Assignments (10 minutes)

- Homework is assigned each week for newly and previously learned skills in order to generalize skills outside of the group.
- The *Social Coaching Handout* provides a comprehensive description of the *Homework Assignments* with *Social Coaching Tips*.
- Additional treatment option:
  ○ Young adults may want to use the *FriendMaker* mobile app as an additional "virtual coach" when social coaches are unavailable during homework completion.
- The *Social Coaching Homework Assignment Worksheet* provides space to take notes on weekly homework and should be returned to the group leader each week.

Reunification (10 minutes)

- Social coaches and young adults will reunite at the end of every group to review the lesson, assign the homework, and individually and privately negotiate the *Homework Assignments* for the coming week.

Structure of Young Adult Sessions

Briefly explain that the structure of the young adult session is very similar, although the time allotted to the sections is different and a behavioral rehearsal component is added:

- *Homework Review* (30 minutes).
- *Didactic Lesson* with *Role Play Demonstrations* (30 minutes).
- *Behavioral Rehearsal Exercises* (20 minutes).
  ○ This involves practice of newly learned and/or previously learned skills.
- *Reunification* (10 minutes).

Treatment Expectations

- Distribute the *Social Coaching Handout*.
  ○ Sections in **bold print** in the *Social Coaching Therapist Guide* come directly from the *Social Coaching Handout*.
- Explain that terms that are ***bold and italicized*** are ***buzzwords*** and represent important concepts from the PEERS® curriculum.
  ○ The ***buzzwords*** represent complex social behaviors that can be identified in just a few simple words.
  ○ Try to use the ***buzzwords*** as much as possible to develop a common language between therapists, social coaches, and young adults.

What to Expect from PEERS®

The purpose of PEERS® is to:

- **Help young adults learn how to develop and maintain friendships and romantic relationships, and handle peer conflict and peer rejection.**
- **Teach ecologically valid social skills that are used by socially successful adults.**
- **Help young adults find a source of friends and romantic partners with assistance from social coaches.**
- **Provide young adults with support through social coaching.**
- **Ultimately help young adults foster independence in social relationships.**

PEERS® Methods of Instruction

- Each *Young Adult Session* and *Social Coaching Session* will involve the following methods of instruction:
  - *Didactic Lesson* with concrete rules and steps of social behavior.
  - *Role Play Demonstrations* of targeted skills.
  - *Behavioral Rehearsal Exercises* for young adults to practice newly learned skills.
  - *Homework Assignments* to practice newly learned skills.
  - Review of homework to troubleshoot any problems and individualize treatment.
- The three most important jobs of the social coaches are to:
  - Provide social coaching to young adults outside of PEERS®.
  - Help young adults find an accepting source of friends outside of PEERS® through involvement in meet-up groups, social recreational activities, hobbies, clubs, and/or sports.
  - Support young adults as they arrange get-togethers with friends and dates with potential romantic partners.

What NOT to Expect from PEERS®

- PEERS® is not a support group or a group to help you find out about psychological disorders or developmental issues.
- PEERS® will not solve all of your problems or the challenges you face.
- PEERS® is not a "friendship-matching group."
  - You should not expect to make lasting friendships with other group members.
    - PEERS® teaches young adults how to develop relationships outside of the treatment group through practice with other group members.
  - You will not be allowed to socialize with other group members during the group.
    - You may socialize with group members after the group has ended if you choose and the other member(s) agree.
    - Socializing with other groups members during PEERS® is problematic because:
      - Conflicts may arise and group members do not want to return to the group.
      - Cliques form and other group members feel excluded.
      - Group dynamics change and the group becomes more about hanging out with friends and less about learning how to make and keep friends and other relationships.
- Young adults will not improve unless you:
  - Attend the groups regularly and come on time.
  - Attempt to do each *Homework Assignment*.
  - Use the skills outside of PEERS®.
  - Find an accepting peer group with the help of social coaches.

Identifying Strengths

- Explain, *"PEERS® is a skill-building group, focusing on helping young adults to develop and maintain meaningful relationships. Unlike other programs, it is a strength-based approach. Despite individual challenges, we believe every person has important strengths. It's often these strengths that make us better friends and partners. We often spend a lot of time focusing on our young adults' problems, but instead we're going to begin by focusing on our young adults' strengths."*
- Ask, *"What do you like best about your young adult?"*
- Go around the room and have every social coach identify one of their young adult's strengths.
  - If they focus on something negative, redirect them to finding something positive.
- Repeat what the social coach liked best about their young adult succinctly and reframe how that strength is important to making and keeping friendships and relationships.
- Explain, *"All of the strengths you identified in your young adults will be important characteristics for developing and maintaining close meaningful relationships with people."*

Didactic Lesson: Characteristics of Good Friendships

- Explain, *"Since the purpose of PEERS® is to help young adults learn how to make and keep friends and develop close meaningful relationships, it's important for us all to agree on what makes a good friend. The young adults will be brainstorming the characteristics of good friendships, which are generally described on your Social Coaching Handout."*
- Present the characteristics of good friendships and after each characteristic ask, *"Why would that be a good characteristic to have in a friendship?"*
  - *Sharing of Common Interests*
    - Friends share similar interests, likes, and hobbies.
    - Common interests give you things to talk about and do together.
  - *Kindness and Caring*
    - Good friendships are based on kindness, fondness, warmth, affection, and mutual caring.
    - Kindness includes gestures of friendship that are considerate, generous, and focus on concern for the other person.
    - Caring involves feeling and showing compassion, concern, and empathy.
  - *Support*
    - Support involves providing help and assistance when needed.
    - Support includes giving encouragement and reassurance when times are hard.
  - *Mutual Understanding*
    - Your friend gets you and understands your likes and dislikes.
    - Your friend understands and may even anticipate your thoughts and feelings.
  - *Commitment and Loyalty*
    - Commitment is a promise that you'll be there for each other in tough times.
    - Loyalty includes actions that show your support and allegiance.
  - *Honesty and Trust*
    - Without honesty, there is little trust or security in friendship.
    - Trust is an assurance that your friend will support you and have your back.
  - *Equality*
    - In equal friendships, no one person dominates the other.
    - The needs of both are equally important, and enjoyment is reciprocal and shared.
  - *Ability to Self-Disclose*
    - Self-disclosure is sharing your private thoughts, feelings, and history.
    - Even casual friends may share some thoughts and feelings with one another.
  - *Conflict Resolution*
    - Even close friends argue from time to time, but they can resolve the conflict.
    - Ability to resolve conflict is often determined by caring, commitment, and trust.

Types of Friendships

- Explain, *"There are generally four types of friendships. Sometimes it can be confusing for young adults to know what type of friendship they have. Even when they know about these types, it can still be difficult to determine which type they share with another person. One of the easiest ways to determine what type of friendship we have and also whether this is a good choice in a friend is to consider how many characteristics of a good friendship this relationship has."*

- *Acquaintances*
  - These are people that may know each other by name, but do not know each other well and do not usually associate outside of work or school.
  - Ask, *"Do acquaintances have many of the characteristics of a good friend?"*
    - Answers: No; they don't know each other well enough.

- *Casual Friends*
  - These are people that know each other by name and interact sporadically, but do not spend a lot of time together socially.
  - Ask, *"Do casual friends have many of the characteristics of a good friend?"*
    - Answers: Not many; they don't know each other that well.

- *Regular Friends*
  - These are friends that hang out in the same social circle; they may go to the same parties and get-togethers, and spend time with each other outside of school or work.
  - Ask, *"Do regular friends have many of the characteristics of a good friend?"*
    - Answers: Yes; they have many, but not necessarily all.

- *Best Friends*
  - These are friends that hang out frequently; they are often in the same *clique* and spend much of their free time together.
  - Ask, *"Do best friends have many of the characteristics of a good friend?"*
    - Answers: Yes; they should have most, if not all.

- Explain, *"The characteristics of romantic relationships are very similar to friendships, with one important distinction. Romantic relationships also include mutual physical attraction, which may include passion, love, and deeper emotional and/or physical intimacy. Just like there are different types of friendships, there are different types of romantic relationships. These types will be explored in greater detail when we talk about dating etiquette."*

- Explain, *"When young adults are struggling to determine whether someone is a friend, or they are unsure what type of a friend the person is, it can be helpful to go back to the characteristics of good friendships and do a quick assessment."*

Didactic Lesson: Rules for Trading Information

- Explain, *"Now that we're clear on the different types of friendships, we need to talk about how to strengthen these friendships and get to know people better. The way we do that is by talking and trading information. Trading information is what people naturally do when they're having a good conversation. It involves the sharing or exchanging of thoughts, ideas, and interests. The most important goal of trading information is to find common interests so that you can find out if there are things you might enjoy talking about or doing together."*

- *Ask the other person questions*
  - Say, *"One of the first rules for trading information is to ask the other person questions. You might ask them about their interests, their hobbies, or what they like to do on the weekend."*
  - Ask, *"What are some common questions young adults might ask?"*
    - Answers: Questions about interests; weekend activities; movies; TV shows; video games; sports; books; music; school; or work.
  - Ask, *"Why is it important to ask the other person questions?"*
    - Answers: Because this is how you discover their interests, hobbies, and likes; it helps you discover if you have **common interests**.

- *Answer your own question*
  - Say, *"Another rule for trading information is that we need to answer our own questions and share something related about ourselves. This includes sharing our own interests, likes, or hobbies. Sometimes the person will ask you the same questions back, but if they don't, you can answer your own question."*
  - Ask, *"Why is it important to answer your own question?"*
    - Answer: Because they may not ask you the same question, and in order to trade information, you need to tell them about you too.

- *Find common interests*
  - Say, *"The most important goal of trading information is to find common interests. That's because friendships are based on common interests. These are the things we talk about and these are the things we do together. It can also be helpful to find out what people don't like so we can avoid talking about or doing these things together."*
  - Ask, *"Why is it so important to find common interests?"*
    - Answers: Because they keep the conversation going and they give you things to talk about and things to do together; because *friendships are based on common interests*.

- *Ask follow-up questions*
  - ○ Say, *"One way we can keep the conversation going is by asking follow-up questions. What are follow-up questions?"*
    - ■ Answer: Questions that are on the same topic.
  - ○ Ask, "Why is it important to ask follow-up questions?"
    - ■ Answers: Because that's how we get to know more about the person; if we **topic switch** too much, it's jarring to the other person and can end up sounding like an interview.

- *Share the conversation*
  - ○ Say, *"Another rule for trading information is to share the conversation. That means pausing occasionally and giving the other person a chance to ask questions and make comments."*
  - ○ Ask, *"Why is it important to share the conversation?"*
    - ■ Answers: This is how we **trade information** and have a **two-way conversation**; **sharing the conversation** is how we get to know one another.
  - ○ Explain, "Sharing the conversation means we are having a two-way conversation. When we don't share the conversation we end up having a one-way conversation."

- *Don't be a conversation hog*
  - ○ Explain, *"One of the rules for trading information is don't be a conversation hog. That means we don't want to monologue or lecture to the other person and never give them a chance to speak."*
  - ○ Ask, *"What could be the problem with being a conversation hog?"*
    - ■ Answers: It's boring for the other person; you seem selfish and rude; it's a **one-way conversation**; it's all about you; you never learn about the other person.
  - ○ [Optional: Show the Role Play Video Demonstration of **conversation hogging** from the *PEERS*® *Role Play Video Library* (www.routledge.com/cw/laugeson) or *FriendMaker* mobile app, then ask the **Perspective Taking Questions** that follow the role play.]

- *Don't be an interviewer*
  - ○ Explain, *"One of the rules for trading information is don't be an interviewer. That means don't ask question after question and never share anything about yourself."*
  - ○ Ask, *"What could be the problem with being an interviewer?"*
    - ■ Answers: It's boring and exhausting for the other person; you seem nosy and intrusive; it's a **one-way conversation**; it's all about the other person; they never learn about you.
  - ○ [Optional: Show the Role Play Video Demonstration of **being an interviewer** from the *PEERS*® *Role Play Video Library* (www.routledge.com/cw/laugeson) or *FriendMaker* mobile app, then ask the **Perspective Taking Questions** that follow the role play.]

- *Don't get too personal at first*
  - ○ Say, *"One of the rules for trading information is don't get too personal at first. Why is it important that when we're first getting to know someone we avoid getting too personal?"*
    - ■ Answer: Sharing private thoughts and feelings or asking personal questions might make the other person feel uncomfortable.
  - ○ Ask, *"As you become closer friends, is it okay to get more personal?"*
    - ■ Answer: Yes, if both of you are comfortable with that.
  - ○ [Optional: Show the Role Play Video Demonstration of **getting too personal at first** from the *PEERS*® *Role Play Video Library* (www.routledge.com/cw/laugeson) or *FriendMaker* mobile app, then ask the **Perspective Taking Questions** that follow the role play.]

Didactic Lesson: Steps for Starting Conversations

- Explain, *"Now that we know a little bit about how to trade information, we need to figure out how to start a conversation with someone. Knowing how to strike up a conversation with someone can be difficult. Sometimes people even give the wrong advice about what to do. What are young adults often told to do to meet new people?"*
  - ○ Answer: Go up and say *"hi"* or go up and introduce yourself.

- Explain, *"That's NOT actually how it's done. Imagine what would happen if you went up and randomly said, 'Hi,' or walked over and said, 'Hi, I'm (insert name).' What do you think the other people would think of you?"*
  - ○ Answers: That you're weird; odd; strange.
- Explain, *"Instead of doing something that might seem strange, we're going to talk about the specific steps young adults can follow for starting conversations."*

1. **Casually Look Over**
   - Explain, *"When you're considering starting a conversation with someone, it's helpful to first show interest in the person by casually looking at them for a second or two, but not staring at them."*
   - Ask, *"Why would it be a good idea to casually look over?"*
     - ○ Answer: It shows you are interested in them.

2. **Use a Prop**
   - Explain, *"As you're casually looking over, it's helpful to use a prop like a mobile phone, gaming device, or a book to give the appearance that you're focused on some other activity."*
   - Ask, *"Why would it be a good idea to use a prop?"*
     - ○ Answers: Then you don't look like you're staring at them; you look distracted by something else.

3. **Find a Common Interest**
   - Explain, *"While you're casually and covertly watching the person, you need to find some kind of common interest that you both appear to share."*
   - Ask, *"Why is it important to have a common interest?"*
     - ○ Answers: It gives you something to talk about; it's an excuse for starting a conversation.

4. **Mention the Common Interest**
   - Explain, *"Once you've identified a common interest, you'll want to make a comment, ask a question, or give a compliment about the common interest."*
   - Ask, *"Why is it important to mention the common interest?"*
     - ○ Answer: This is your excuse for talking to them.

5. **Trade Information**
   - Explain, *"Next, you need to trade information about the common interest by asking follow-up questions, answering your own questions, and sharing relevant information about yourself."*
   - Ask, *"Why is it important to trade information?"*
     - ○ Answer: This is how you will get to know each other.

6. **Assess Interest**
   - Say, *"Then you need to assess the interest of the person you're trying to talk to. If they don't seem interested in talking to you, should you move on?"*
     - ○ Answer: Yes.
   - Explain, *"You can tell if someone wants to talk to you by asking yourself the following questions . . ."*
     - ○ **Are they talking to me?**
     - ○ **Are they looking at me?**
     - ○ **Are they facing me (or are they giving me the cold shoulder)?**

7. **Introduce Yourself**
   - Say, *"If they seem interested in talking to you, the final step for starting a conversation is to introduce yourself if you've never met. If they don't seem interested, should you move on without introducing yourself?"*
     - ○ Answer: Yes.

- [Optional: Show BAD and GOOD *Role Play Video Demonstrations* of **starting individual conversations** from the *PEERS®* Role Play Video Library (www.routledge.com/cw/laugeson) or *FriendMaker* mobile app, then ask the **Perspective Taking Questions** that follow the role plays.]

- Say, *"So those are the rules and steps for starting conversations and trading information. Be prepared to provide social coaching as your young adults practice starting conversations and trading information during Homework Assignments this week."*

Homework Assignments

[Distribute the *Social Coaching Homework Assignment Worksheet* (Appendix I) for social coaches to complete and return at the next session.]

1. ***In-group call or video chat.***
   - The young adult group leader will assign the phone calls each week and will read the call assignment aloud during the Reunification.
     - ○ Members of the treatment team will individually and privately negotiate with young adults about where social coaches will be during the call.
   - Arrange a phone call or video chat with another member of the group to trade information.
   - Young adults and social coaches should schedule the day and time of the call with the other group member before leaving the group.
   - Go over the rules for *trading information* before the call.
   - Social coaches should ask young adults the following *social coaching questions* after the call:
     - ○ ***What was the common interest?***
     - ○ ***What could you do with that information if you were going to hang out?***

2. Young adults and social coaches should practice *starting a conversation, trading information,* and *finding common interests.*
   - Go over the rules for *starting a conversation* and *trading information* before practicing.
   - Social coaches should ask young adults the following *social coaching questions* after practicing:
     - ○ ***What was the common interest?***
     - ○ ***What could we do with that information if we were going to hang out?***

Social Coaching Tips

- Explain, *"Giving feedback during social coaching can be difficult. It is easy to sound critical when you want to sound encouraging. Try following these simple steps for giving feedback when social coaching."*

1. *Praise*
   - Begin by offering praise about something the young adult did well.
     - ○ Example: *"Nice job trading information and finding common interests."*

2. *Offer suggestions*
   - This step involves giving **corrective feedback**.
   - Troubleshoot problems by offering suggestions about what to do differently next time.
     - ○ Suggestions can often be given with statements that start with, *"How about if . . ."*
       - ■ Good example: *"How about if next time, you ask your friend what he likes to do, too?"*
     - ○ Suggestions can also be given with statements that start with, *"Let's be careful not to . . ."*
       - ■ Good example: *"Let's be careful not to be a conversation hog next time."*

3. *Use errorless learning*
   - Do not overtly tell young adults they did something wrong.
     - ○ This may discourage them or make them feel embarrassed.
       - ■ Bad example: *"You didn't trade information the right way!"*

4. *Use buzzwords*
   - Explain, *"Always use buzzwords when social coaching as this avoids lecturing. Young adults may check out and stop listening once you start lecturing. Social coaching should be succinct and to the point. Feedback should be positive and encouraging, while simultaneously corrective."*

TRADING INFORMATION AND STARTING CONVERSATIONS

Young Adult Therapist Guide

Preparing for the Young Adult Session

The primary goal of the first lesson is to orient the young adults to the structure of the group and establish group cohesion through a *Didactic Lesson* and *Behavioral Rehearsal Exercise*. It will be very important for you to establish clear expectations in the first lesson and to minimize any misbehavior. Unlike child and adolescent groups, there is rarely misbehavior in young adult groups, particularly if you screened for social motivation. However, if misbehavior does occur, see the *Behavioral Management Techniques* section in Chapter 1 of this manual for assistance.

A controlled and predictable environment is important to ensure that young adults get the maximum benefit from the didactic portion of the lesson. Young adults should generally have to raise their hands in order to speak and should not be allowed to talk over one another or engage in long or overly personal stories. However, flexibility with this rule should be exercised with young adults. Being overly punitive and inflexible about talking out of turn is not developmentally appropriate. If a young adult begins to launch into an unrelated discussion, you should avoid allowing the young adult to get too far off track by redirecting him or her by saying, *"Is this on topic?"* You should also not hesitate to redirect tangential young adults who give overly lengthy responses to questions, as this also takes away from the group. In such cases, it can be helpful to say, *"Okay, we're going to have to move on. We have a lot to cover."* If the young adult persists, you might say, *"If we have time later, we can talk about that."* However, it is not advisable to revisit the topic, as this only reinforces tangential comments.

It is very important for you to establish a fun atmosphere for the group. Creating a fun environment involves getting the young adults actively engaged in the process of generating the rules for the lessons. PEERS® uses a very specific curriculum involving concrete rules and steps for social behavior. The process by which these rules and steps are generated is through a Socratic method of questioning, and through role playing demonstrations. The former involves asking specific questions in such a way that you elicit the response you were seeking. The latter involves specific demonstrations of both appropriate and inappropriate behaviors, in order to generate the rules for some complex social behavior (e.g., demonstrating what it looks like to be a **conversation hog** and then asking, **"What did I do WRONG in that conversation?"**). These methods of instruction are used to keep the young adults' attention during the *Didactic Lessons* and help them to more readily buy into the skills being taught. Young adults are far more likely to believe what you have to teach them if they believe they or their peers are generating the rules. They are also more likely to remember these rules and steps if they or their peers are engaged in the process of creating them.

When presenting the rules and steps for social behavior, avoid asking **open-ended questions** such as, *"Does anyone have any ideas about how to trade information?"* Questions such as this are too broad and often result in inappropriate responses from the young adults who do not know the rules of social etiquette yet. Instead, stick to the questions outlined in the didactic portion of this manual.

In this session, you will be conducting a series of inappropriate and appropriate *Role Play Demonstrations* in conjunction with the *Didactic Lesson*. THE SCRIPTS PROVIDED IN THE MANUAL

ARE NOT MEANT TO BE READ VERBATIM. They simply serve as a guide for what you might say. You should feel free to make up your own inappropriate and appropriate role play scenarios to demonstrate the skills. Inappropriate *Role Play Demonstrations* generally represent common social errors committed by young adults with Autism Spectrum Disorder (ASD) and other social challenges. Appropriate *Role Play Demonstrations* represent ***ecologically valid social skills*** used by socially accepted young adults. The social errors demonstrated in the inappropriate role plays should be quite obvious to the young adults and somewhat over the top (for instructive as well as entertainment value). However, for groups of older adults, you may want to be less dramatic with your demonstrations, as they may think you are talking down to them.

The inappropriate role plays are often very humorous and will help to engage the young adults in the group. Some young adults will use this as an opportunity to make jokes. It is important you remain serious when eliciting feedback from the young adults about what went wrong in the role play, as to avoid losing control of the group. If a young adult provides an inappropriate comment about the role play in an effort to make a joke, rather than engaging in a debate about why this was an inappropriate response, you should **open this comment up to the group** by asking in a general way why the suggestion might be inappropriate. For example, if a young adult made the comment that a particular role play was inappropriate because the coach should have told the group leader to *"mind her own business,"* rather than getting into a debate, it is more advisable to generally say to the group, **"What could be the problem with telling someone to 'mind their own business'?"** Then elicit responses from other group members, not the person who made the inappropriate comment. Using the sentence stem, **"What could be the problem with . . ."** as a means of handling inappropriate behavior from young adults is far more effective in defusing the situation and makes it far less likely that other young adults will follow in this inappropriate behavior. The goal is not to embarrass the young adult, which is why it is important for you to remain serious and respectful, but rather to provide just enough peer pressure to make the behavior less reinforcing. Most young adults will back down from any oppositional behavior if you **open up their comments to the group**. Once this has been done, it is critical to move on to a more appropriate topic immediately.

Inappropriate *Role Play Demonstrations* generally lead to the formation of specific rules and steps of social etiquette. As you are generating these rules and steps, be sure to write them on the board where the young adults can easily view the material. This includes all of the bullet points and **buzzwords** from the lessons, which are easily identified in the manual as they are ***bold and italicized***. Remember that it is important to stress these **buzzwords** and use them frequently since they are the common language used between you, the young adults, and their social coaches. *Buzzwords* are helpful because they allow you to refer to sophisticated social behavior in only a few words, and help you to avoid lecturing during social coaching. Consequently, all **buzzwords** should be listed on the board along with the other rules and steps. Do not write the **buzzwords** or the rules and steps on the board before the group begins (or create PowerPoint slides), as this would defeat the purpose of the Socratic method and having the young adults help generate the rules. The same is true if you are using a smart board. Avoid having any material preprogrammed into screens, as this would give the impression that the young adults are not generating the rules and steps.

Finally, although PEERS® should be treated as a class, it should be fun and lively for the young adults. That does not mean that you should be silly and make a lot of jokes, as this may result in a loss of control and difficulty staying on track. Each group leader will bring his or her own style to the group, so you should feel free to be yourself. Do not try to act cool for the young adults. They will see right through that. Just be yourself, and if there are things they bring up that you do not know, feel free to ask them if it is relevant. They are usually very happy to talk about the latest video games, comic books, and so on, if you are unfamiliar with them. You do not have to know every little detail about their personal interests. There will be plenty of time to learn more as the group progresses.

Introductions

- At the beginning of the first group, have young adults and social coaches all meet in the same room with the treatment team for introductions.

- ○   Provide name badges for all participants and treatment team members. These name badges should be worn every week throughout the program.
- Begin by welcoming the group and introducing each member of the treatment team by highlighting their professional background and their role in PEERS®.
- Go around the room and have young adults and social coaches introduce themselves in the following manner:
  - ○   Young adults should say their name, age, and where they work or go to school if relevant.
  - ○   Social coaches should say their name, identify their young adult, and state their relationship with the young adult (e.g., parent, sibling, family member, peer mentor, job coach, life coach, etc.).
  - ○   In groups where people travel long distances, they might also say what city they live in to add more content and context to the introduction.
- Explain that the young adult and social coaching groups will be meeting in separate rooms, but that you will all be meeting again during the last 10 minutes of each group to talk about what was discussed and how you will practice these skills in the coming week.
- After the introductions, adjourn to separate young adult and social coaching group rooms.

Rules for the Group

Present the following rules and ask, *"Why is this a good rule to have?"* after each rule:

1. Raise your hand.
2. Listen to the others (e.g., no talking when others are speaking, no texting).
3. Follow directions.
4. Be respectful (e.g., no teasing or making fun of others, no swearing, no sleeping).
5. No touching (e.g., no hitting, kicking, pushing, hugging, etc.).
6. Cell phones off.

Overview of PEERS®

Purpose of the Group

- Tell the young adults that the name of the group is PEERS®.
- Ask them, *"What is a peer?"*
  - ○   Answers: Someone else your age; a friend; a classmate; a coworker.
- PEERS® is a social skills group to help young adults develop and maintain close meaningful relationships, including friendships and romantic relationships.
- The group will be meeting once a week for 90 minutes for the next 16 weeks.
- At the end of the 16 weeks, there will be a graduation party and ceremony.

Structure of the Group

Homework Review (30 minutes)
- The session begins with a review of the previous *Homework Assignment*.
- You and your social coach will be given *Homework Assignments* each week.
- These are FUN assignments and will help you practice the newly learned skills.
- The level of social coaching in homework completion depends on the need and comfort level of the young adult.
  - ○   This will be determined individually through negotiation with the treatment team during *Reunification* at the end of every session.
  - ○   You must at least discuss the homework with your social coaches.
    - ■   Have all young adults verbally agree to do this.
- The success of the program depends on the completion of the *Homework Assignments*.

Didactic Lesson (30 minutes)

- Each week there will be a new *Didactic Lesson* focusing on relationship skills.
- *Social Coaching Handouts* will be provided each week for you and your social coach and are distributed to young adults during the *Reunification*.
  - We recommend you save these handouts and place them in a binder.
- Additional treatment option:
  - Young adults and social coaches may want to read corresponding chapters from *The Science of Making Friends* (Laugeson, 2013) throughout the program for additional information.

Behavioral Rehearsal (20 minutes)

- Each week, there will be a *Behavioral Rehearsal Exercise* to practice newly learned skills.
- These activities are less structured than the *Homework Review* and *Didactic Lesson* and provide an opportunity to practice skills while receiving coaching from the treatment team.
- Behavioral rehearsal activities include games such as *Jeopardy*, **trading information** about personal items, and mock get-togethers with other group members.

Reunification (10 minutes)

- Young adults and social coaches will reunite at the end of every group to review the lesson, assign the homework, and individually and privately negotiate the *Homework Assignments* for the coming week.
- Homework is assigned each week for newly and previously learned skills in order to generalize skills outside of the group.
- The *Social Coaching Handout* provides a comprehensive description of the *Didactic Lesson* and the *Homework Assignment* with *Social Coaching Tips*.
- Additional treatment option:
  - Young adults may want to use the *FriendMaker* mobile app as an additional "virtual coach" when social coaches are unavailable during homework completion.

Didactic Lesson: Characteristics of Good Friendships

- Explain, *"The name of this group is PEERS®. Peers are sometimes friends or potential friends. The purpose of this group is for us to learn how to make and keep friends and develop close meaningful relationships. That means it's important for us all to agree on what makes a good friend."*
- Ask the following questions and allow the young adults to briefly discuss:
  - *"What is a friend?"*
  - *"How do you know when you have a friend?"*
  - *"What do friends have in common?"*
  - *"What is a best friend?"*
- Use this as a brainstorming activity in which you write good responses on the board.
- Try to reframe the answers the young adults provide into the **buzzwords** used below to describe the *Characteristics of Good Friendships*:
  - *Sharing of Common Interests*
    - Friends share similar interests, likes, and hobbies.
    - Common interests give you things to talk about and do together.
  - *Kindness and Caring*
    - Good friendships are based on kindness, fondness, warmth, affection, and mutual caring.
    - Kindness includes gestures of friendship that are considerate, generous, and focus on concern for the other person.
    - Caring involves feeling and showing compassion, concern, and empathy.
  - *Support*
    - Support involves providing help and assistance when needed.
    - Support includes giving encouragement and reassurance when times are hard.

- ○ *Mutual Understanding*
  - ■ Your friend gets you and understands your likes and dislikes.
  - ■ Your friend understands and may even anticipate your thoughts and feelings.
- ○ *Commitment and Loyalty*
  - ■ Commitment is a promise that you'll be there for each other in tough times.
  - ■ Loyalty includes actions that show your support and allegiance.
- ○ *Honesty and Trust*
  - ■ Without honesty there is little trust or security in friendship.
  - ■ Trust is an assurance that your friend will support you and have your back.
- ○ *Equality*
  - ■ In equal friendships, no one person dominates the other.
  - ■ The needs of both are equally important, and enjoyment is reciprocal and shared.
- ○ *Ability to Self-Disclose*
  - ■ Self-disclosure is sharing your private thoughts, feelings, and history.
  - ■ Even casual friends may share some thoughts and feelings with one another.
- ○ *Conflict Resolution*
  - ■ Even close friends argue from time to time, but they can resolve the conflict.
  - ■ Ability to resolve conflict is often determined by caring, commitment, and trust.

Types of Friendships

- Explain, *"There are generally four types of friendships. Sometimes it can be confusing to know what type of friendship we have. One of the easiest ways to determine what type of friendship we have, and also whether this is a good choice in a friend, is to consider how many characteristics of a good friendship our relationship has."*

- *Acquaintances*
  - ○ These are people that may know each other by name, but do not know each other well and do not usually associate outside work or school.
  - ○ Ask, *"Do acquaintances have many of the characteristics of a good friend?"*
    - ■ Answers: No; they don't know each other well enough.

- *Casual Friends*
  - ○ These are people that know each other by name and interact sporadically, but do not spend a lot of time together socially.
  - ○ Ask, *"Do casual friends have many of the characteristics of a good friend?"*
    - ■ Answers: Not many; they don't know each other that well.

- *Regular Friends*
  - ○ These are friends that hang out in the same social circle; they may go to the same parties and get-togethers, and spend time with each other outside of school or work.
  - ○ Ask, *"Do regular friends have many of the characteristics of a good friend?"*
    - ■ Answers: Yes; they have many, but not necessarily all.

- *Best Friends*
  - ○ These are friends that hang out frequently; they are often in the same *clique* and spend much of their free time together.
  - ○ Ask, *"Do best friends have many of the characteristics of a good friend?"*
    - ■ Answers: Yes; they should have most, if not all.

- Explain, *"The characteristics of romantic relationships are very similar to friendships, with some important distinctions. Romantic relationships also include mutual physical attraction, which may include passion, love, and deeper emotional and/or physical intimacy. Just like there are different types of friendships, there are different types of romantic relationships. These types will be explored in greater detail when we talk about dating etiquette."*

- Explain, *"If we're ever struggling to determine whether someone is a friend, or if we're unsure what type of a friend the person is, it can be helpful to go back to the characteristics of good friendships and do a quick assessment."*

Didactic Lesson: Trading Information

- Explain, *"Now that we're clear on the different types of friendships, we need to talk about how to strengthen these friendships and get to know people better. The way we do that is by talking and trading information. Trading information is what people naturally do when they're having a good conversation. It involves the sharing or exchanging of thoughts, ideas, and interests. The most important goal of trading information is to find common interests so that you can find out if there are things you might enjoy talking about or doing together."*

- [Present the rules for **trading information**. **Buzzwords** are **bold and italicized** and should be written on the board and emphasized as they represent a common language between therapists, young adults, and social coaches. Do not erase the rules until the end of the lesson. Each role play with a ⊙ symbol includes a corresponding role play video from the *PEERS® Role Play Video Library* (www.routledge.com/cw/laugeson).]

- *Ask the other person questions*
  - Say, *"One of the first rules for trading information is to ask the other person questions. You might ask them about their interests, their hobbies, or what they like to do on the weekend."*
  - Ask, *"What are some common questions young adults might ask?"*
    - Answers: Questions about interests; weekend activities; movies; TV shows; video games; sports; books; music; school; or work.
  - Ask, *"Why is it important to ask the other person questions?"*
    - Answers: Because this is how you discover their interests, hobbies, and likes; it helps you discover if you have **common interests**.

- *Answer your own question*
  - Say, *"Another rule for trading information is that we need to answer our own questions and share something related about ourselves. This includes sharing our own interests, likes, or hobbies. Sometimes the person will ask you the same questions back, but if they don't, you can answer your own question."*
  - Ask, *"Why is it important to answer your own question?"*
    - Answer: Because they may not ask you the same question, and in order to trade information, you need to tell them about you too.

- *Find common interests*
  - Say, *"The most important goal of trading information is to find common interests. That's because friendships are based on common interests. These are the things we talk about and these are the things we do together. It can also be helpful to find out what people don't like so we can avoid talking about or doing these things together."*
  - Ask, *"Why is it so important to find common interests?"*
    - Answers: Because they keep the conversation going and they give you things to talk about and things to do together; because **friendships are based on common interests**.

- *Ask follow-up questions*
  - Say, *"One way we can keep the conversation going is by asking follow-up questions. What are follow-up questions?"*
    - Answer: Questions that are on the same topic.
  - Ask, *"Why is it important to ask follow-up questions?"*
    - Answers: Because that's how we get to know more about the person; if we **topic switch** too much, it's jarring to the other person and can end up sounding like an interview.

> Example of an APPROPRIATE Role Play
> - Group leader: *"Ask me what I like to do on the weekend and then ask me three follow-up questions."*
> - Behavioral coach: *"What do you like to do on the weekend?"*
> - Group leader: *"I like to go hiking."*

- Behavioral coach: *"Where do you go hiking?"*
- Group leader: *"On this trail by my house."*
- Behavioral coach: *"Do you go for long hikes or short hikes."*
- Group leader: *"Usually short hikes."*
- Behavioral coach: *"Who do you usually go with?"*
- Group leader: *"I usually go with friends."*

Behavioral Rehearsal: Ask Follow-Up Questions

- Explain, *"Now we're going to have each of you practice asking follow-up questions. I'm going to give each of you a different starter question and then I want you to ask me three follow-up questions on the same topic while everyone watches."*
- Go around the room and have each young adult come up with THREE *follow-up questions* for the following topics of conversation:
  - *"What kind of TV shows do you like?"*
  - *"What kind of movies do you like?"*
  - *"What kind of music do you like?"*
  - *"What kind of books do you like?"*
  - *"What kind of food do you like?"*
  - *"What sports do you like?"*
  - *"What games do you like?"*
  - *"What videogames do you like?"*
  - *"What do you like to do on the weekends?"*
  - *"What classes are you taking?"*
- End by giving a round of applause to each young adult after their practice.
- [Note: If a young adult has difficulty coming up with *follow-up questions*, privately assign an extra *Homework Assignment* during *Reunification* to practice this during the week with the social coach.]
- **Share the conversation**
  - Say, *"Another rule for trading information is to share the conversation. That means pausing occasionally and giving the other person a chance to ask questions and make comments."*
  - Ask, *"Why is it important to share the conversation?"*
    - Answer: This is how we **trade information** and get to know one another.
  - Explain, *"Sharing the conversation means we are having a two-way conversation. When we don't share the conversation, we end up having a one-way conversation."*
- **Don't be a conversation hog** ▶
  [The group leader and behavioral coach should do an INAPPROPRIATE role play with the group leader being a conversation hog.]
  - Begin by saying, *"Watch this and tell me what I'm doing WRONG."*

Example of an INAPPROPRIATE Role Play

- Group leader: *"Hi, (insert name). What have you been up to?"*
- Behavioral coach: *"Not much. Just going to school and hanging out. What about you?"*
- Group leader: *"Well, I had a really fun weekend. I went to the movies and we saw that new sci-fi movie."*
- Behavioral coach: *"Oh, I heard that was good . . ."*
- Group leader: (Interrupts) *"Yeah, it was. And then we went out to eat at my favorite restaurant and I ate a whole pizza on my own. And then the next day I went to the mall and we went to this really cool gaming store and played video games all day . . ."*
- Behavioral coach: *"Oh, you like video games . . ."*
- Group leader: (Interrupts) *"Yeah, and then we went home and watched some movies and I didn't go to sleep until really late and I'm so tired today. I thought I'd fall asleep . . ."*

> - Behavioral coach: (Looks bored)
> - Group leader: *". . . and tomorrow I have so much work to do, so I'm going to have to stay up really late again . . ."*
> - Behavioral coach: (Looking around, appears bored)

- ○ End by saying, *"Okay, so time out on that. So what did I do WRONG in that conversation?"*
  - ■ Answers: You were not letting the other person talk; you were being rude.
- ○ Ask the following *Perspective Taking Questions*:
  - ■ *"What was that like for (name of coach)?"*
    - □ Answers: Annoying; frustrating; boring.
  - ■ *"What do you think (name of coach) thought of me?"*
    - □ Answers: Selfish; boring; obnoxious; self-centered.
  - ■ *"Is (name of coach) going to want to talk to me again?"*
    - □ Answers: No; too obnoxious; too self-centered.
- ○ Ask the behavioral coach the same *Perspective Taking Questions*:
  - ■ *"What was that like for you?"*
  - ■ *"What did you think of me?"*
  - ■ *"Would you want to talk to me again?"*
- ○ Explain, *"One of the rules for trading information is don't be a conversation hog. That means don't monopolize the conversation or lecture. When you're being a conversation hog you're having a one-way conversation and it's all about you. That's boring for the other person."*

- ● ***Don't be an interviewer*** ⊙
  [The group leader and behavioral coach should do an INAPPROPRIATE role play with the group leader being an interviewer.]
  - ○ Begin by saying, *"Watch this and tell me what I'm doing WRONG."*

> **Example of an INAPPROPRIATE Role Play**
>
> - ■ Group leader: *"Hi, (insert name). How are you doing?"*
> - ■ Behavioral coach: *"Fine. How are you?"*
> - ■ Group leader: *"I'm good. Hey, I was wondering, what kind of movies do you like?"*
> - ■ Behavioral coach: *"Oh, I like action adventure movies and comedies. What about you?"*
> - ■ Group leader: *"Yeah, and what's your favorite movie?"*
> - ■ Behavioral coach: *"I guess my favorite is (insert current movie). What's your favorite?"*
> - ■ Group leader: *"Yeah, that was good. What about TV shows? What kind of TV shows do you watch?"*
> - ■ Behavioral coach: *"I like sitcoms. What about you?"*
> - ■ Group leader: *"Well, what's your favorite TV show?"*
> - ■ Behavioral coach: (Looks annoyed) *"I guess (insert current TV sitcom) is my favorite."*
> - ■ Group leader: *"So what kind of music do you like?"*
> - ■ Behavioral coach: (Looking around, appears bored) *"I guess I like (insert genre of music)."*

- ○ End by saying, *"Okay, timeout on that. So what did I do WRONG in that conversation?"*
  - ■ Answers: You were asking question after question; you never shared anything about yourself.
- ○ Ask the following *Perspective Taking Questions*:
  - ■ *"What was that like for (name of coach)?"*
    - □ Answers: Annoying; exhausting; a lot of work; frustrating; boring.
  - ■ *"What do you think (name of coach) thought of me?"*
    - □ Answers: Like a drill sergeant; interrogator; nosy; annoying; weird.
  - ■ *"Is (name of coach) going to want to talk to me again?"*
    - □ Answers: No; too exhausting; too much work
- ○ Ask the behavioral coach the same *Perspective Taking Questions*:

- *"What was that like for you?"*
- *"What did you think of me?"*
- *"Would you want to talk to me again?"*

○ Explain, *"One of the rules for trading information is don't be an interviewer. That means don't ask question after question without sharing anything about you. That's also a one-way conversation. This time, it's all about them, but it's still boring."*

- **Don't get too personal at first** ▶
  [The group leader and behavioral coach should do an INAPPROPRIATE role play with the group leader getting too personal.]

  ○ Begin by saying, *"Watch this and tell me what I'm doing WRONG."*

Example of an INAPPROPRIATE Role Play

- Group leader: *"Hey, (insert name). What are you doing this weekend?"*
- Behavioral coach: *"I'm going to my mom and stepdad's house."*
- Group leader: *"Your stepdad? Are your parents divorced?"*
- Behavioral coach: (Surprised) *"Yeah."*
- Group leader: *"When did that happen?"*
- Behavioral coach: (Confused) *"When I was 12."*
- Group leader: *"Why?"*
- Behavioral coach: (Uncomfortable) *"I don't know."*
- Group leader: *"Was that hard on you?"*
- Behavioral coach: (Uncomfortable) *"I don't know."*
- Group leader: *"Did they tell you why?"*
- Behavioral coach: *"Can we talk about something else?"*
- Group leader: *"Do you see one of them more than the other? Do they get jealous?"*
- Behavioral coach: (Uncomfortable) *"I don't know."*
- Group leader: *"Do they fight over you? Is it awkward?"*
- Behavioral coach: (Looks uncomfortable) *"Can we talk about something else?"*
- Group leader: *"My parents got divorced when I was younger and they still fight all the time. It's really awkward."*
- Behavioral coach: (Looks uncomfortable)
- Group leader: *"Sometimes they yell and call each other names. It can be really uncomfortable."*
- Behavioral coach: (Looks uncomfortable)

○ End by saying, *"Okay, timeout on that. So what did I do WRONG in that conversation?"*
- Answers: You were asking really personal questions; you shared too much personal information.
○ Ask the following **Perspective Taking Questions**:
- *"What was that like for (name of coach)?"*
  □ Answers: Uncomfortable; awkward; embarrassing; creepy; weird.
- *"What do you think (name of coach) thought of me?"*
  □ Answers: Creepy; stalker; nosy; weird.
- *"Is (name of coach) going to want to talk to me again?"*
  □ Answers: No; too uncomfortable; too creepy.
○ Ask the behavioral coach the same **Perspective Taking Questions**:
- *"What was that like for you?"*
- *"What did you think of me?"*
- *"Would you want to talk to me again?"*
○ Explain, *"One of the rules for trading information is don't get too personal at first. When we ask personal questions or share personal information before we get to know someone, it may make them uncomfortable. As you become closer friends, it may be okay to get more personal, but it's risky at first."*

Role Play: Trading Information ⊙

[The group leader and behavioral coach should do an APPROPRIATE role play of trading information.]

- Begin by saying, *"Now that we know some of the rules for trading information, watch this and tell me what we're doing RIGHT."*

> Example of an APPROPRIATE Role Play
>
> ○ Group leader: *"Hey, (insert name)! How are you doing?"*
> ○ Behavioral coach: *"I'm fine. How are you?"*
> ○ Group leader: *"I'm great. So how was your weekend?"*
> ○ Behavioral coach: *"It was good. I went to the movies with some friends."*
> ○ Group leader: *"That sounds fun. What did you see?"*
> ○ Behavioral coach: *"We saw that new sci-fi movie everyone's been talking about."*
> ○ Group leader: *"How cool! I've been wanting to see that. Was it good?"*
> ○ Behavioral coach: *"Yeah, it was really good. I might see it again. Do you like sci-fi movies?"*
> ○ Group leader: *"Yeah, I love them! I like reading sci-fi books, too."*
> ○ Behavioral coach: *"Me too. I read them all the time."*
> ○ Group leader: *"Same here."*

- Say, *"Timeout on that. Who can tell me what we did RIGHT in that conversation?"*
  - ○ Answers: **Traded information; asked each other questions; answered your own questions; found common interests; asked follow-up questions; shared the conversation; didn't conversation hog; didn't interview; didn't get too personal**.
- Ask the following *Perspective Taking Questions*:
  - ○ *"What was that like for (name of coach)?"*
    - ■ Answers: Nice; pleasant.
  - ○ *"What do you think (name of coach) thought of me?"*
    - ■ Answers: Nice; interesting; pretty cool.
  - ○ *"Is (name of coach) going to want to talk to me again?"*
    - ■ Answer: Yes.
- Ask the behavioral coach the same *Perspective Taking Questions*:
  - ○ *"What was that like for you?"*
  - ○ *"What did you think of me?"*
  - ○ *"Would you want to talk to me again?"*

Didactic Lesson: Starting Conversations

- Explain, *"Now that we know a little bit about how to trade information, we need to figure out how to start a conversation with someone. Knowing how to strike up a conversation with someone can be difficult. Sometimes people even give the wrong advice about what to do. What are young adults often told to do to meet new people?"*
  - ○ Answer: Go up and say *"Hi"* or go up and introduce yourself.
- Explain, *"That's NOT actually how it's done. Imagine what would happen if you went up and randomly said, 'Hi,' or walked over and said, 'Hi, I'm (insert name).' What do you think the other people would think of you?"*
  - ○ Answers: That you're weird; odd; strange.
- Explain, *"Instead of doing something that might seem strange, we're going to talk about the specific steps young adults can follow for starting conversations."*

Bad Role Play: Starting a Conversation ⊙

[The group leader and behavioral coach should do an INAPPROPRIATE role play with the group leader starting a random conversation.]

- Begin by saying, *"We're going to do a role play. Watch this and tell me what I'm doing WRONG in starting this conversation."*

> **Example of an INAPPROPRIATE Role Play**
>
> - Behavioral coach: (Looking at iPhone)
> - Group leader: (Walks up abruptly) *"Hi!"*
> - Behavioral coach: (Confused)
> - Group leader: *"I'm (insert name)."*
> - Behavioral coach: (Confused) *"Umm. Hi."*
> - Group leader: (Overly eager) *"Did you go to the comic book convention last night?"*
> - Behavioral coach: (Confused) *"What?"*
> - Group leader: *"The comic book convention. Were you there?"*
> - Behavioral coach: (Confused) *"The comic book convention?"*
> - Group leader: *"Yeah, did you go last night?"*
> - Behavioral coach: (Confused) *"Umm . . . no."*
> - Group leader: *"Oh, I was there. It was awesome. You should have gone. Do you like comic books?"*
> - Behavioral coach: (Annoyed, looking at iPhone) *"Umm . . . yeah I do."*
> - Group leader: (Interrupts) *"Why didn't you go then? You should have gone. Everyone was there."*
> - Behavioral coach: (Sarcastic, annoyed, looking at iPhone) *"That's great."*
> - Group leader: *"So are you going next week?"*
> - Behavioral coach: (Annoyed) *"What?"*
> - Group leader: *"You should go. It's going to be really good."*
> - Behavioral coach: (Annoyed, looking at iPhone, ignoring) *"Okay."*
> - (Long awkward pause)

- End by saying, *"Timeout on that. So what did I do WRONG in trying to start that conversation?"*
  - Answer: You walked up and talked about something completely random.
- Ask the following *Perspective Taking Questions*:
  - *"What was that like for (name of coach)?"*
    - Answers: Confusing; weird; odd.
  - *"What do you think (name of coach) thought of me?"*
    - Answers: Weird; odd; strange.
  - *"Is (name of coach) going to want to talk to me again?"*
    - Answers: No; too weird.
- Ask the behavioral coach the same *Perspective Taking Questions*:
  - *"What was that like for you?"*
  - *"What did you think of me?"*
  - *"Would you want to talk to me again?"*
- Explain, "Instead of doing something that might seem strange or random, we're going to talk about the specific steps you can follow for starting conversations."

Steps for Starting Conversations

1. *Casually Look Over*
   - Explain, *"When you're considering starting a conversation with someone, it's helpful to first show interest in the person by casually looking at them for a second or two, but not staring at them."*
   - Ask, "Why would it be a good idea to casually look over?"
     - Answer: It shows you are interested in them.

2. *Use a Prop*
   - Explain, *"As you're casually looking over, it's helpful to use a prop like a mobile phone, gaming device, or a book to give the appearance that you're focused on some other activity."*
   - Ask, "Why would it be a good idea to use a prop?"

    ○   Answers: Then you don't look like you're staring at them; you look distracted by something else.

3. ***Find a Common Interest***
   - Explain, *"While you're casually and covertly watching the person, you need to find some kind of common interest that you both appear to share."*
   - Ask, *"Why is it important to have a common interest?"*
     - ○ Answers: It gives you something to talk about; it gives you an excuse for starting a conversation.

4. ***Mention the Common Interest***
   - Explain, *"Once you've identified a common interest, you'll want to make a comment, ask a question, or give a compliment about the common interest."*
   - Ask, *"Why is it important to mention the common interest?"*
     - ○ Answer: This is your excuse for talking to them.

5. ***Trade Information***
   - Explain, *"Next you need to trade information about the common interest by asking follow-up questions, answering your own questions, and sharing relevant information about yourself."*
   - Ask, *"Why is it important to trade information?"*
     - ○ Answer: This is how you will get to know each other.

6. ***Assess Interest***
   - Say, *"Then you need to assess the interest of the person you're trying to talk to. If they don't seem interested in talking to you, you should move on. How can you tell if someone wants to talk to you?"*
     - ○ Answers: Body language; eye contact; verbal clues.
   - Explain, *"You can assess interest by asking yourself the following questions . . ."*
     - ○ ***Are they talking to me?***
     - ○ ***Are they looking at me?***
     - ○ ***Are they facing me (or are they giving me the cold shoulder)?***

7. ***Introduce Yourself***
   - Say, *"If they seem interested in talking to you, the final step for starting a conversation is to introduce yourself if you've never met. How do you introduce yourself?"*
     - ○ Answer: *"By the way, my name is . . ."* or *"We haven't met, but I'm . . ."*
   - Ask, *"If they don't seem interested, should you move on without introducing yourself?"*
     - ○ Answer: Yes.

Good Role Play: Starting a Conversation ▶

[The group leader and behavioral coach should do an APPROPRIATE role play with the group leader following the steps for starting a conversation.]

- Begin by saying, *"We're going to do another role play. Watch this and tell me what I'm doing RIGHT in starting this conversation."*

> Example of an APPROPRIATE Role Play
> - ○ Group leader & behavioral coach: (Standing a few feet away from each other)
> - ○ Behavioral coach: (Looking at iPhone)
> - ○ Group leader: (Holding iPhone, looks over at coach) *"Hey, is that the new iPhone?"*
> - ○ Behavioral coach: (Looks over and smiles) *"Yeah, it is."*
> - ○ Group leader: (Smiles) *"Oh, that's cool. I've been wanting to get one."*
> - ○ Behavioral coach: *"You should. It's great."*
> - ○ Group leader: *"I know. I have the old one. Is the new one better?"*
> - ○ Behavioral coach: *"Oh yeah, it's awesome. It's lightweight too."*

- o Group leader: *"Yeah, I definitely need to get one. I thought they were sold out."*
- o Behavioral coach: *"They might be. I ordered mine early."*
- o Group leader: *"That was smart."*
- o Behavioral coach: (Smiles casually)
- o Group leader: *"I'm (insert name) by the way."*
- o Behavioral coach: *"Oh, hi. I'm (insert name)."*
- o Group leader & behavioral coach: (Smile, don't shake hands)

- End by saying, *"Timeout on that. So what did I do RIGHT in starting that conversation?"*
  - o Answers: ***Casually looked over; used a prop; found a common interest; mentioned the common interest; traded information; assessed interest; introduced yourself.***
- Ask, *"Did it seem like (insert name) wanted to talk to me?"*
  - o Answer: Yes.
- Ask, *"How could you tell?"*
  - o Answers: ***Talked to you; looked at you; faced you.***
- Ask the following *Perspective Taking Questions*:
  - o *"What was that like for (name of coach)?"*
    - ■ Answers: Nice; normal; pleasant.
  - o *"What do you think (name of coach) thought of me?"*
    - ■ Answers: Friendly; cool; interesting.
  - o *"Is (name of coach) going to want to talk to me again?"*
    - ■ Answers: Yes; probably.
- Ask the behavioral coach the same *Perspective Taking Questions*:
  - o *"What was that like for you?"*
  - o *"What did you think of me?"*
  - o *"Would you want to talk to me again?"*
- Explain, *"So those are the rules and steps for starting conversations and trading information. It's important that we use those steps when meeting new people and we trade information when we're talking to anyone."*

TRADING INFORMATION AND STARTING CONVERSATIONS

Young Adult Behavioral Rehearsal

Jeopardy

Materials Needed

- Whiteboard and markers
- *Jeopardy Answer Sheets* for each young adult
- Pens
- Scissors

Rules

- Young adults will compete against themselves in this game of *trading information*.
- Like the North American TV game show *Jeopardy*, young adults will be given answers and asked to respond in the form of a question.
  - Example:
    - Group leader: *"The answer is Jimmy's favorite sport."*
    - Young adult: *"What is football?"*
  - The young adult does not have to answer in the form of a question (most do not).
  - If this group is being conducted in a country where *Jeopardy* is unknown, feel free to change the name and alter the rules accordingly.
- To promote interest and cooperation, points will be given for correct responses.
- The purpose of *Jeopardy* is not to practice *trading information* perfectly, since the young adults will sound like they are *interviewing* when asking the questions.
- The true purpose of *Jeopardy* is to improve:
  - *Topic initiation*
    - Talking about a variety of topics, rather than only restricted interests.
  - *Listening skills*
    - Listening and remembering what people share about themselves.

How to Play

- Pass out *Jeopardy Answer Sheets* (found at the end of this section).
- Have young adults fill in responses and return to the group leader.
- Write the *Jeopardy Topics* on the board where young adults can see them.
  - *Favorite music*
  - *Favorite weekend activity*
  - *Favorite sport*
  - *Favorite game*
  - *Favorite movie*
  - *Favorite television show*

- ○ *Favorite book*
- ○ *Eye color* [Note: This is NOT to be asked, but noticed by using good eye contact. If conducting this group in a place where most people share the same eye color, feel free to replace this category.]
- Have young adults practice *trading information* about the *Jeopardy Topics* in small groups for two or three minutes each.
  - ○ Change the groups a few times (depending on the time).
  - ○ Prompt young adults to ask relevant questions about the *Jeopardy Topics* when necessary.
- While young adults are *trading information*:
  - ○ Cut the *Jeopardy Answer Sheets* into individual boxes along the lines provided.
  - ○ Separate the *Jeopardy Answer Sheets* according to category and mix the order of the answer sheets.
- Once the young adults have finished *trading information*, reconvene as a group and begin the *Jeopardy Challenge*.
  - ○ Begin by having the young adult who appears to have participated the most that week choose the first category.
  - ○ Notify the group that if they raise their hand before the question has been asked, they are disqualified from answering.
  - ○ The person who raises their hand first gets to take the first guess.
  - ○ If they provide the wrong answer, the person who raised their hand second has a chance to answer, and so on.
  - ○ The young adults get only one guess per question.
  - ○ Do not give clues.
- You may need to enforce a time limit if young adults take a long time to answer.
- Do not correct the young adults if they answer the questions in the incorrect format (i.e., instead of saying *"What is football?"* they say *"Football"*).
  - ○ All that matters is that they remembered the information they obtained through *trading information*.
- The person who answers the question correctly gets a point and gets to choose the next category.
- If no one answers correctly, the person about whom the last question relates gets to pick the next category.
- Encourage the young adults to clap and cheer for each other during the game.
- Give points for correct responses and keep track of the points on the board.
- At the end of the game, the person with the most points is the *Jeopardy Challenge Winner*.
- SAVE YOUNG ADULT *JEOPARDY ANSWER SHEETS* FOR NEXT WEEK.

Jeopardy Answer Sheets

Music to Your Ears	**TGIF**
The answer is: _____'s favorite band. (Name) The question is: What is _____ (favorite band)	The answer is: _____'s favorite weekend activity. (Name) The question is: What is _____ (favorite weekend activity)
Sports and Leisure	**Game Time**
The answer is: _____'s favorite sport. (Name) The question is: What is _____ (favorite sport)	The answer is: _____'s favorite game. (Name) The question is: What is _____ (favorite game)
Movies, Movies, Movies	**TV Time**
The answer is: _____'s favorite movie. (Name) The question is: What is _____ (favorite movie)	The answer is: _____'s favorite TV show. (Name) The question is: What is _____ (favorite TV show)
Bestseller List	**The "Eyes" Have It**
The answer is: _____'s favorite book. (Name) The question is: What is _____ (favorite book)	The answer is: The color of _____'s eyes. (Name) The question is: What is _____ (your eye color)

TRADING INFORMATION AND STARTING CONVERSATIONS

Reunification

- Announce that young adults should join their social coaches.
  - Have young adults stand or sit next to their social coaches.
  - Be sure to have silence and the full attention of the group before starting with *Reunification*.
  - Have young adults generate the content from the lesson while social coaches listen.
- Say, *"Today we talked about the characteristics of good friendships, types of friendships, and how to trade information and start conversations. Who can tell us some of the rules for trading information?"*
- Have young adults generate the rules for **trading information**:
  - *Ask the other person questions*
  - *Answer your own questions*
  - *Find common interests*
  - *Ask follow-up questions*
  - *Share the conversation (two-way conversation)*
  - *Don't be a conversation hog (one-way conversation)*
  - *Don't be an interviewer (one-way conversation)*
  - *Don't get too personal at first*
- Say, *"We also talked about the steps for starting conversations. Who can tell us the steps for starting conversations?"*
  1. *Casually Look Over*
  2. *Use a Prop*
  3. *Find a Common Interest*
  4. *Mention the Common Interest*
  5. *Trade Information*
  6. *Assess Interest*
     - *Are they talking to me?*
     - *Are they looking at me?*
     - *Are they facing me (or are they giving me the cold shoulder)?*
  7. *Introduce Yourself (if they seem interested)*
- Say, *"This group did a great job of practicing trading information today. Let's give them a round of applause."*
- Say, *"The group also played a game called Jeopardy where they practiced trading information. Tonight's Jeopardy Challenge Winner was (insert name). Let's give (insert name) a round of applause."*

Homework Assignments

Distribute the *Social Coaching Handout* to young adults and announce the following *Homework Assignments*:

1. ***In-group call or video chat.***
   - Arrange a phone call or video chat with another group member to trade information.
   - Young adults and social coaches should schedule the day and time of the call with the other group member before leaving the group.
   - Go over the rules for ***trading information*** before the call.
   - Social coaches should ask young adults the following ***social coaching questions*** after the call:
     - ***What was the common interest?***
     - ***What could you do with that information if you were going to hang out?***

2. Young adults and social coaches should practice ***starting a conversation, trading information,*** and ***finding common interests.***
   - Go over the rules for ***starting a conversation*** and ***trading information*** before practicing.
   - Social coaches should ask young adults the following ***social coaching questions*** after practicing:
     - ***What was the common interest?***
     - ***What could we do with that information if we were going to hang out?***

- Read off the in-group call assignment (Appendix E) and remind social coaches to make a note of who is calling whom.
- Go over the Phone Roster with young adults and social coaches (Appendix D) and tell them they will use the Phone Roster to note the day and time of the scheduled call each week.
- Young adults and social coaches should let all relevant people know if they wish to be called at a different number or if there are any errors on the current Phone Roster.
  - In the event that there are changes, a new Phone Roster should be distributed the next week.

Individual Check-Out

Once the calls have been scheduled, individually and privately negotiate with each young adult and social coach:

1. Where the social coach will be during the ***in-group call or video chat.***

2. When young adults and social coaches will practice ***starting a conversation, trading information,*** and ***finding common interests.***

TRADING INFORMATION AND STARTING CONVERSATIONS

Social Coaching Handout

What to Expect from PEERS®

The purpose of PEERS® is to:

- Help young adults learn how to develop and maintain friendships and romantic relationships, and handle peer conflict and peer rejection.
- Teach ecologically valid social skills that are used by socially successful adults.
- Help young adults find a source of friends and romantic partners with assistance from social coaches.
- Provide young adults with support through social coaching.
- Ultimately help young adults foster independence in social relationships.

PEERS® Methods of Instruction

- Each *Young Adult Session* and *Social Coaching Session* will involve the following methods of instruction:
  - *Didactic Lessons* with concrete rules and steps of social behavior.
  - *Role Play Demonstrations* of targeted skills.
  - *Behavioral Rehearsal Exercises* for young adults to practice newly learned skills.
  - *Homework Assignments* to practice newly learned skills.
  - Review of homework to troubleshoot any problems and individualize treatment.
- The three most important jobs of the social coaches are to:
  - Provide social coaching to young adults outside of PEERS®.
  - Help young adults find an accepting source of friends outside of PEERS® through involvement in meet-up groups, social recreational activities, hobbies, clubs, and/or sports.
  - Support young adults as they arrange get-togethers with friends and dates with potential romantic partners.

What NOT to Expect from PEERS®

- PEERS® is not a support group or a group to help you find out about psychological disorders or developmental issues.
- PEERS® will not solve all of your problems or the challenges you face.
- PEERS® is not a "friendship-matching group."
  - You should not expect to make lasting friendships with other group members.
  - You will not be allowed to socialize with other group members during the group.
  - You may socialize with group members after the group has ended if you choose and the other member(s) agree.
- Young adults will not improve unless you:
  - Attend the groups regularly and come on time.
  - Attempt to do each *Homework Assignment*.

○ Use the skills outside of PEERS®.
○ Find an accepting peer group with the help of social coaches.

Characteristics of Good Friendships

- *Sharing of Common Interests*
- *Kindness and Caring*
- *Support*
- *Mutual Understanding*
- *Commitment and Loyalty*
- *Honesty and Trust*
- *Equality*
- *Ability to Self-Disclose*
- *Conflict Resolution*

Types of Friendships

- *Acquaintances*
- *Casual Friends*
- *Regular Friends*
- *Best Friends*

Rules for Trading Information*

- *Ask the other person questions*
- *Answer your own question*
- *Find common interests*
- *Ask follow-up questions*
- *Share the conversation (two-way conversation)*
- *Don't be a conversation hog (one-way conversation)**
- *Don't be an interviewer (one-way conversation)**
- *Don't get too personal at first**

Steps for Starting Conversations*

1. *Casually Look Over*
2. *Use a Prop*
3. *Find a Common Interest*
4. *Mention the Common Interest*
5. *Trade Information*
6. *Assess Interest*
   ○ *Are they talking to me?*
   ○ *Are they looking at me?*
   ○ *Are they facing me (or are they giving me the cold shoulder)?*
7. *Introduce Yourself*

Homework Assignments

1. *In-group call or video chat.*
   - Arrange a phone call or video call with another group member to trade information.
   - Young adults and social coaches should schedule the day and time of the call with the other group member before leaving the group.
   - Go over the rules for *trading information* before the call.
   - Social coaches should ask young adults the following *social coaching questions* after the call:
     ○ *What was the common interest?*
     ○ *What could you do with that information if you were going to hang out?*

2. Young adults and social coaches should practice *starting a conversation, trading information,* and *finding common interests.*
    - Go over the rules for *starting a conversation* and *trading information* before practicing.
    - Social coaches should ask young adults the following *social coaching questions* after practicing:
        ○ *What was the common interest?*
        ○ *What could we do with that information if we were going to hang out?*

* See *The Science of Making Friends* DVD (Laugeson, 2013) or the *FriendMaker* mobile app for a *Video Role Play Demonstration* of the corresponding rule.

TRADING INFORMATION AND MAINTAINING CONVERSATIONS

Social Coaching Therapist Guide

Preparing for the Social Coaching Session

The skills taught in PEERS® are meant to be presented in a stepwise fashion where one skill builds upon another in an organized and preconceived manner. The lessons are not intended to be modular where one picks and chooses the order or inclusion. Since each skill naturally flows into the next, the group is not appropriate for rolling admission. In other words, group members should not be joining the group partway through. If this were to happen, latecomers would be lost and unable to follow session content, **buzzwords** would be unfamiliar, and *Homework Assignments* would be confusing. Consequently, it is strongly recommended that all group members enroll starting in Session 1. With a few minor exceptions, one or two group members might be allowed to start in week 2. Newcomers should be given *Social Coaching Handouts* from the previous week, but providing separate individual sessions is discouraged as it might reinforce future absences by giving too much extra attention to those who were not present. Instead, content from the handout in conjunction with the repetition of instruction that often accompanies the *Homework Review* should be sufficient to get new group members up to speed.

The most important *Homework Assignment* from the previous week is the **in-group call or video chat**, so make sure to save time for that during the *Homework Review*. Begin by asking who completed the call or attempted to complete the call. Avoid going around the room (e.g., from left to right), as this will waste valuable time on excuse making from those who did not complete the assignment. If there is time, you can attempt to **troubleshoot** with those who did not complete the assignment by saying, *"For those that were unable to do this assignment, let's figure out how to get it done this week."* Listening to the reasons why they could not complete the assignments is only productive if the debriefing is short and ends with a solution to the barrier. Long accounts of how busy the social coach was or how over-scheduled the young adult is are not very productive. In response to such excuses, focus may be placed on how necessary homework completion is for good treatment outcome. Coming to group each week but failing to do assignments will not generalize the skills to other settings and may end up being a waste of time, sadly. It is helpful for the group leader to set up these realistic expectations and parameters from the beginning.

Another issue that might come up at this point is the social coach not being present for the **in-group call or video chat**. One possible reason for this may be that the young adult was uncomfortable with the social coach being present. This should have been negotiated at *Reunification* in the previous week and the young adult should have agreed to at least share the details of the call with the social coach. In this case, homework negotiation may need to be revisited during *Reunification* and the young adult may need to be reminded that he or she needs to discuss the call with the social coach at the very least. Another reason might be that the time of the call was inconvenient for the social coach to be present. This type of reason is more common among social coaches who do not reside with their young adult. Although more than 90% of social coaches we have worked with through the UCLA PEERS® Clinic consist of parents, other social coaches have included job coaches, life coaches, peer mentors, adult siblings, and other family members. These individuals are not always easily accessible to the young adult, nor do they have frequent or even daily contact with the young adult. While greater involvement and access to social coaches is preferable, when contact is limited it will be important to schedule *Homework Assignments* carefully. For example, the day and time of the **in-group call or video chat** should be scheduled during *Reunification* before group members leave. It is not only important that both young adults be available for these calls, but social coaches must also be present. Take this as an opportunity to highlight the importance of having social coaches present during these calls and ensure that all parties are present for the call in the coming week. Remind social coaches that they should be coaching before and after the call, and when they are not present their young adults miss valuable coaching opportunities.

A related issue that may come up during the *Homework Review* is that the call did not take place when it was supposed to. Even though the call should have been scheduled during *Reunification* in the previous week, plans can change and life gets in the way. The result is often that the call takes place at an unscheduled and spontaneous time. One issue with unexpected calls is that the social coach on the receiving end may not be present, and therefore misses the opportunity to coach before and after the call. The other issue is the young adult on the receiving end may have been anxiously awaiting a call that never took place, thereby further increasing anxiety. In either case, this is not fair to those on the receiving end. Take the opportunity to point out these possibilities during instances when the call did not take place at the scheduled time, and encourage social coaches to reschedule the call if plans change.

Another issue that may come up is that some social coaches will attempt to be "script writers" in which the whole phone call is written out in advance using a script. In PEERS®, we are not very fond of scripts. The problem with scripts is that the other person doesn't know their lines and you are lost before you ever get started. The other issue with scripts is that if they include a series of questions, they may end up sounding like an interview. Instead, **trading information** should involve the natural flow of **asking questions, answering your own questions, asking follow-up questions**, and generally **sharing the conversation**. Several more rules apply and will be discussed in greater detail in this session. In the meantime, for social coaches attempting to provide scripts for young adults, praise their intent, but redirect them to help their young adult have more spontaneous conversations following the rules of **trading information**. If the concern is that the young adult will run out of things to talk about, use this as an opportunity to explain the purpose of *Jeopardy*, the game we play in the young adult session in which common conversational topics are discussed, providing "schematic scripts" for future use. Schematic scripts are essentially ideas of common topics for conversations (e.g., movies, games, TV shows, sports, music, books, weekend activities, school, work, etc.). Social coaches might consider sticking to schematic scripts, such as those used in *Jeopardy*, to promote better topic initiation and avoid sounding preprogrammed. In fact, during the first *Homework Review*, many social coaches will report that their young adults were **trading information** about topics they don't normally talk about. In most of these cases, the young adults were talking about topics covered during *Jeopardy* in the previous week. Although these conversations are often a huge improvement over former repetitive conversations about restricted interests, they can still sound a bit stiff and stilted—even a bit like an interview. Take this as an opportunity to reassure social coaches that we are just getting started and that new didactic content for **maintaining conversations** will be covered in the current lesson, which should further enhance conversational skills and **trading information**.

Homework Review

[Go over the following *Homework Assignments* and **troubleshoot** any potential problems. Start with completed homework first. If you have time, you can inquire as to why others were unable to complete the assignment and try to **troubleshoot** how they might get it done for the coming week. When reviewing homework, be sure to relabel descriptions using the **buzzwords** (identified by **bold and italicized** print). Spend the majority of the *Homework Review* on the **in-group call or video chat**, as this is the most important assignment.]

1. *In-group call or video chat.*
   - Say, *"One of your assignments this week was for your young adult to have a phone call or video chat with someone in the group in order to practice trading information. Whose young adult did the in-group call or video chat?"*
   - Ask the following questions:
     ○ *"Who did your young adult talk to and who called whom?"*
     ○ *"What social coaching did you do before the call?"*
     ○ *"Where were you during the call?"*
     ○ *"Did they trade information and find a common interest?"*
     ○ *"What social coaching did you do after the call?"*
       ▪ Appropriate *social coaching questions*:
         □ **What was your common interest?**
         □ **What could you do with that information if you were going to hang out?**
   - Have the other social coach who participated in the call or video chat give their account immediately after, but not at the same time.

2. Young adults and social coaches should have practiced **starting a conversation**, **trading information**, and **finding common interests**.
   - Say, *"Another assignment this week was to practice starting a conversation, trading information, and finding common interests with your young adult. Who completed or attempted to complete this assignment?"*
   - Focus on completed or attempted assignments by asking the following questions:
     ○ *"Did your young adult practice starting a conversation with you?"*
     ○ *"Did you go over the rules and steps before practicing?"*
       ▪ *Steps for Starting a Conversation*:
         1. **Casually Look Over**
         2. **Use a Prop**
         3. **Find a Common Interest**
         4. **Mention the Common Interest**
         5. **Trade Information**
         6. **Assess Interest**
            □ **Are they talking to me?**
            □ **Are they looking at me?**
            □ **Are they facing me (or are they giving me the cold shoulder)?**
         7. **Introduce Yourself**
     ○ *"Did your young adult practice trading information?"*
     ○ *"Did you ask the social coaching questions after practicing?"*
       ▪ Appropriate *social coaching questions*:
         □ **What was the common interest?**
         □ **What could we do with that information if we were going to hang out?**

- [Collect the *Social Coaching Homework Assignment Worksheets*. If social coaches forgot to bring the worksheets, have them complete a new form to hold them accountable for the assignments.]

Didactic Lesson: Conversational Topics

- Distribute the *Social Coaching Handout*.
  ○ Sections in **bold print** in the *Social Coaching Therapist Guide* come directly from the *Social Coaching Handout*.
  ○ Remind social coaches that terms that are in ***bold and italicized*** print are **buzzwords** and represent important concepts from the PEERS® curriculum that should be used as much as possible when social coaching.
- Explain, *"Today, we're going to continue our discussion about trading information and having good conversations. In particular, we're going to talk about how to maintain conversations with others. Before*

Table 3.1 Common Conversational Topics Among Young Adults

School or work gossip	Video games/computer games	Classes/major
Problems with friends	Computers/technology	Exams/papers/schoolwork
Problems with family	Comic books/anime/manga	Professors/supervisors
Boyfriends/girlfriends	Movies	College and job applications
Dating	TV shows	Sports
Parties/get-togethers	YouTube videos/viral videos	Cars/motorcycles/bikes
Weekend activities	Internet websites	Celebrities
Meet-up groups	Music/concerts	Fashion/clothes
Social clubs/activities	Books	Shopping
Hobbies/interests	News/media/politics	Makeup/hair

we get into the rules of trading information and maintaining conversations, it might be helpful to review common topics young adults talk about."
- Ask, *"What are common topics of conversation for young adults?"*
- Point out that the table in the *Social Coaching Handout* lists common topics of conversation for young adults.
  - Mention a few of the topics listed in the table if they did not come up.

Didactic Lesson: Trading Information and Maintaining Conversations

Explain, *"So now that we have some ideas about WHAT our young adults may talk about, we need to figure out HOW to help them talk to peers and have good conversations. They can do this by trading information and maintaining conversations."*

- *Trade information*
  - Explain, *"Last week, we talked about some of the rules for trading information and starting conversations. Who can remember some of the rules for trading information?"*
    - Answers:
      - *Ask the other person questions*
      - *Answer your own questions*
      - *Find common interests*
      - *Ask follow-up questions*
      - *Share the conversation*
      - *Don't be a conversation hog*
      - *Don't be an interviewer*
      - *Don't get too personal at first*
  - Say, *"The rules for maintaining a conversation also include these same rules for trading information. Now we'll be talking about additional rules for trading information."*

- *Don't be repetitive*
  - Say, *"Another rule for trading information and maintaining conversations is don't be repetitive. That means we don't talk about the same thing over and over."*
  - Ask, *"What could be the problem with being repetitive?"*
    - Answers: It's boring for the other person, even if the topic is a **common interest**; people prefer to talk about a variety of topics, not just one.

- *Listen to your friend*
  - Say, *"Another rule for trading information and maintaining conversations is that we need to listen to our friends. What could be the problem with not listening in conversations?"*
    - Answers: Your friend will think you don't care about what they have to say; when you listen, it shows that you're interested in your friend.

- *Ask open-ended questions*
  - ○ Explain, *"Another rule for trading information and maintaining conversations is to ask open-ended questions. Open-ended questions are those where the answers are longer and can lead to more conversation. Closed-ended questions are those that only require a short response, like yes or no answers."*
  - ○ Say, *"This doesn't mean you can't ask closed-ended questions, but what could be the problem with asking too many closed-ended questions?"*
    - ■ Answer: You'll sound like *an interviewer*.

- *Don't brag*
  - ○ Say, *"Another rule for trading information and maintaining conversations is don't brag. That means we shouldn't brag about our possessions or talk about how much money we have or how smart we are. What could be the problem with bragging?"*
    - ■ Answers: *Bragging* can seem condescending; you will appear egotistical; people may think you're shallow and superficial.
  - ○ [Optional: Show the *Role Play Video Demonstration* of **bragging** from the *PEERS® Role Play Video Library* (www.routledge.com/cw/laugeson).]

- *Don't be argumentative*
  - ○ Say, *"Another rule for trading information and maintaining conversations is don't be argumentative. That means don't argue over every little thing or frequently disagree with other people's opinions. What could be the problem with being argumentative?"*
    - ■ Answers: Other people don't like to be argued with; just because you don't agree with someone doesn't mean you have to point that out; you could seem rude; you could seem aggressive.
  - ○ [Optional: Show the *Role Play Video Demonstration* of **being argumentative** from the *PEERS® Role Play Video Library* (www.routledge.com/cw/laugeson).]

- *Don't police*
  - ○ Say, *"Another rule for trading information and maintaining conversations is don't police others. That means we shouldn't criticize or point out other people's mistakes. What could be the problem with policing?"*
    - ■ Answers: *Policing* others is annoying and embarrassing to the other person; it will make you look like a know-it-all.
  - ○ [Optional: Show the *Role Play Video Demonstration* of **policing** from the *PEERS® Role Play Video Library* (www.routledge.com/cw/laugeson) or *FriendMaker* mobile app, then ask the **Perspective Taking Questions** that follow the role play.]

- *Don't tease*
  - ○ Explain, *"Another rule for trading information and maintaining conversations is don't tease others. Teasing or bantering is risky behavior if you're trying to make and keep friends. Bantering is the equivalent of teasing among friends. It's usually meant playfully, but it's still risky. What could be the risk with bantering?"*
    - ■ Answer: It can escalate and feelings can get hurt.
  - ○ [Optional: Show the *Role Play Video Demonstration* of **teasing** from the *PEERS® Role Play Video Library* (www.routledge.com/cw/laugeson) or *FriendMaker* mobile app, then ask the **Perspective Taking Questions** that follow the role play.]

- *Use good volume control*
  - ○ Say, *"Another rule for trading information and maintaining conversations is to use good volume control. That means we don't want to speak too loudly or the person may get annoyed or bothered. What could be the problem with speaking too loudly?"*
    - ■ Answers: It can be seen as obnoxious or annoying; we might embarrass the person if others are around.
  - ○ Say, *"We also don't want to speak too quietly or the person may not be able to hear us. What could be the problem with speaking too quietly?"*

- Answers: The other person may think we're shy or depressed; it's too much work for them; they may not want to talk to us because it's hard to understand.
    - ○ Explain, *"Good volume control depends on where you are, so you will need to be prepared to provide social coaching in the moment as needed."*
- ○ [Optional: Show the TWO *Role Play Video Demonstration*s of **using good volume control** from the *PEERS*® *Role Play Video Library* (www.routledge.com/cw/laugeson) or *FriendMaker* mobile app, then ask the **Perspective Taking Questions** that follow the role plays.]

- *Use good body boundaries*
    - ○ Say, *"Another rule for trading information and maintaining conversations is to use good body boundaries. What could be the problem with standing too close?"*
        - Answers: It's very uncomfortable; it could come off as creepy.
    - ○ Ask, *"What could be the problem with standing too far away?"*
        - Answers: Seems odd or strange; could be embarrassing for the other person if there are people around.
    - ○ Explain, *"The general rule is to stand about an arm's length away, but don't go up and measure first!"*
    - ○ [Optional: Show the TWO *Role Play Video Demonstration*s of **using good body boundaries** from the *PEERS*® *Role Play Video Library* (www.routledge.com/cw/laugeson) or *FriendMaker* mobile app, then ask the **Perspective Taking Questions** that follow the role plays.]

- *Use good eye contact*
    - ○ Say, *"Another rule for trading information and maintaining conversations is to make good eye contact. What could be the problem with not looking at the other person?"*
        - Answers: You seem disinterested; it could seem odd or weird; it's confusing for the other person.
    - ○ Ask, *"What could be the problem with staring at the other person?"*
        - Answers: It's uncomfortable; it can feel predatory; they might think you're creepy.
    - ○ Explain, *"Good eye contact involves looking at the other person, but also occasionally looking away."*
    - ○ [Optional: Show the TWO *Role Play Video Demonstration*s of **using good eye contact** from the *PEERS*® *Role Play Video Library* (www.routledge.com/cw/laugeson) or *FriendMaker* mobile app, then ask the **Perspective Taking Questions** that follow the role plays.]
    - ○ [Optional: Show the *Role Play Video Demonstration* of **trading information** from the *PEERS*® *Role Play Video Library* (www.routledge.com/cw/laugeson) or *FriendMaker* mobile app, then ask the **Perspective Taking Questions** that follow the role play.]

- Say, *"So those are the rules for trading information and maintaining conversations. Be prepared to provide social coaching as your young adults practice trading information and maintaining conversations during Homework Assignments this week."*

Homework Assignments

[Distribute the *Social Coaching Homework Assignment Worksheet* (Appendix I) for social coaches to complete and return at the next session.]

1. *In-group call or video chat.*
    - The young adult group leader will assign the phone calls each week and will read the call assignment aloud during the *Reunification*.
        - ○ Members of the treatment team will individually and privately negotiate with young adults about where social coaches will be during the call.
    - **Arrange a phone call or video chat with another group member to trade information.**
    - **Young adults and social coaches should schedule the day and time of the call with the other group member before leaving the group.**

- Go over the rules for *trading information* before the call.
- Social coaches should ask young adults the following *social coaching questions* after the call:
  - *What was the common interest?*
  - *What could you do with that information if you were going to hang out?*

2. Young adults and social coaches should practice *starting and maintaining a conversation, trading information,* and *finding common interests.*
   - Go over the rules for *starting and maintaining a conversation* and *trading information* before practicing.
   - Social coaches should ask young adults the following *social coaching questions* after practicing:
     - *What was the common interest?*
     - *What could we do with that information if we were going to hang out?*

Social Coaching Tips

- Explain, *"Remember that it's important for you to provide social coaching around these Homework Assignments and whenever your young adult is practicing these skills. Follow these simple steps for giving feedback when social coaching."*

1. *Praise*
   - Begin by offering praise about something the young adult did well.
     - Example: *"Nice job trading information and finding common interests."*

2. *Offer suggestions*
   - Troubleshoot problems by offering *corrective feedback* through suggestions about what to do differently next time.
     - Example: *"How about if next time, you ask more follow-up questions?"*
     - Example: *"Let's be careful with our volume control next time."*

3. *Use errorless learning*
   - Explain, *"Do not overtly tell young adults they did something wrong as this may discourage them or make them feel embarrassed."*
     - Bad example: *"You didn't trade information the right way!"*

4. *Use buzzwords*
   - Explain, *"Always use buzzwords when social coaching as this avoids lecturing. Young adults may check out and stop listening if you sound like you're lecturing."*
   - Explain, *"It will also be critical for you to start using Perspective Taking Questions from this point forward in ALL of your social coaching."*
     - *Perspective Taking Questions for Social Coaching:*
       - *What was that like for that person?*
       - *What do they think of you?*
       - *Are they going to want to talk to you again?*

- Explain, *"These three Perspective Taking Questions are presented after every Role Play Demonstration in the young adult group. They help young adults improve their social cognition and their ability to take on the perspectives of others. Be sure to use these three questions when assessing social situations from this point forward."*
- Explain, *"If you are reading* The Science of Making Friends *or using the FriendMaker app, you will notice that these three Perspective Taking Questions follow every Role Play Demonstration, so feel free to use them as a tool in your own social coaching."*

TRADING INFORMATION AND MAINTAINING CONVERSATIONS

Young Adult Therapist Guide

Preparing for the Young Adult Session

The focus of the *Didactic Lesson* this week is to continue the discussion about the rules for conversational skills, including **trading information** and **maintaining conversations**. It will be critical to engage the young adults in this lesson and win over any young adults that may be ambivalent about the group at this point. This session also involves a number of *Role Play Demonstrations*, which will afford a nice opportunity to engage and entertain the young adults. Perhaps the best method of engaging the young adults is to have them generate the rules for the lesson. The use of a Socratic method of instruction in combination with *Role Play Demonstrations* of inappropriate conversations is a fun and engaging way for the young adults to learn. This method of showing bad examples (i.e., what not to do) has been found to be highly effective in encouraging young adults to generate rules of social etiquette, thereby making them more likely to believe what you are teaching them. Inappropriate role plays should always be introduced by saying, *"Watch this and tell me what I'm doing WRONG."* At the end of the role play, ask the question, *"So what did I do WRONG in that conversation?"* The demonstrations should be overdramatized and obvious to the young adults, which they will find amusing and easy to decode. Of course, following the presentation of the full *Didactic Lesson* should be the demonstration of an appropriate role play of good methods of conversation. Appropriate role plays of good social behavior are also critical to success in the program, in that they will demonstrate the *ecologically valid social skills* that the young adults should actually be following. The appropriate role plays are often demonstrated at the end of the *Didactic Lesson*, preceded by the statement, *"Watch this and tell me what I'm doing RIGHT."* and followed by the question, *"So what did I do RIGHT in that conversation?"*

All *Role Play Demonstrations*, whether inappropriate or appropriate, should be followed with **Perspective Taking Questions**. These questions are intended to improve social cognition and assist young adults in reading social cues while understanding the perspectives of others. The **Perspective Taking Questions** are almost always the same and include: (1) *"What do you think that was like for that person?"*; (2) *"What do you think that person thought of me?"*; and (3) *"Do you think that person will want to talk to me again?"* The questions remain the same because when asked repetitively throughout the program, young adults are more likely to begin to ask themselves the same questions when they are interacting with others.

Some of the rules for **trading information** and **maintaining conversations** do not involve *Role Play Demonstrations*. In these cases, it is helpful to begin by presenting the rule and immediately asking, *"Why is it important to . . . (state the rule)?"* or *"What could be the problem with . . . (state the rule)?"* These methods of rule generating are effective in that young adults are being asked to generate rationales for the rules, thereby making it more likely that they will believe and remember what they are being taught. Young adults are more likely to believe what you have to teach them if they and their peers imagine that they are generating the ideas themselves.

Finally, because people have different types of learning styles, it will be helpful to present the material in each lesson in multiple formats. This should not only include verbal instruction and behavioral demonstration, but also writing the bullet points and **buzzwords** (identified by **bold and italicized** print) on the board. These bullet points and **buzzwords** should be visually accessible to the young adults during *Behavioral Rehearsal Exercises* and should not be erased until the end of the group.

Homework Review

[Go over the following *Homework Assignments* and **troubleshoot** any potential problems. Start with completed homework first. If you have time, you can inquire as to why others were unable to complete the assignment and try to **troubleshoot** how they might get it done for the coming week. When reviewing homework, be sure to relabel descriptions using the **buzzwords** (identified by **bold and italicized** print). Spend the majority of the *Homework Review* on the **in-group call or video chat**, as this is the most important assignment.]

1. *In-group call or video chat.*
   - Say, *"One of your assignments this week was to have a phone call or video chat with someone in the group in order to practice trading information. Raise your hand if you did the in-group call or video chat."*
   - Ask the following questions:
     - *"Who did you talk to and who called whom?"*
     - *"Did you trade information and did you find a common interest?"*
     - *"What could you do with that information if you were going to hang out?"*
   - Have the other person who participated in the call or video chat give their account immediately after, but not at the same time.

2. Young adults and social coaches should have practiced **starting a conversation, trading information**, and **finding common interests**.
   - Say, *"Another assignment this week was to practice starting a conversation, trading information, and finding common interests with a social coach. Raise your hand if you traded information with your social coach this week."*
   - Ask the following questions:
     - *"Did you practice starting a conversation and which steps did you follow?"*
       - *Steps for Starting Conversation*
         1. *Casually Look Over*
         2. *Use a Prop*
         3. *Find a Common Interest*
         4. *Mention the Common Interest*
         5. *Trade Information*
         6. *Assess Interest*
            - *Are they talking to me?*
            - *Are they looking at me?*
            - *Are they facing me (or are they giving me the cold shoulder)?*
         7. *Introduce Yourself*
     - *"Did you trade information and did you find common interests?"*
     - *"What could you do with that information if you were going to hang out with your social coach?"*

Didactic Lesson: Conversational Topics

- Explain, *"Today, we're going to continue our discussion about trading information and having good conversations. In particular, we're going to talk about how to maintain conversations with others. Before we get into the rules of trading information and maintaining conversations, it might be helpful to brainstorm what kinds of things to talk about."*
- Ask the question, *"What do young adults talk about?"*
- Have the group brainstorm common topics of conversation for young adults.
- Mention the following topics if the group does not think of them on their own.

Table 3.1 Common Conversational Topics Among Young Adults

School or work gossip	Video games/computer games	Classes/major
Problems with friends	Computers/technology	Exams/papers/schoolwork
Problems with family	Comic books/anime/manga	Professors/supervisors
Boyfriends/girlfriends	Movies	College and job applications
Dating	TV shows	Sports
Parties/get-togethers	YouTube videos/viral videos	Cars/motorcycles/bikes
Weekend activities	Internet websites	Celebrities
Meet-up groups	Music/concerts	Fashion/clothes
Social clubs/activities	Books	Shopping
Hobbies/interests	News/media/politics	Makeup/hair

Didactic Lesson: Trading Information and Maintaining Conversations

Explain, *"So now that we have some ideas about WHAT to talk about, we need to figure out HOW to talk to our friends and have good conversations. We can do this by trading information and maintaining conversations."*

[Present the rules for **trading information** and **maintaining conversations** by writing the following bullet points and **buzzwords** (identified by **bold and italicized** print) on the board. Do not erase the rules until the end of the lesson. Each role play with a ⊙ symbol includes a corresponding role play video from the *PEERS® Role Play Video Library* (www.routledge.com/cw/laugeson).]

- *Trade information*
  - ○ Explain, *"Last week, we talked about some of the rules for trading information and starting conversations. Who can remember some of the rules for trading information?"*
    - ■ Answers:
      - □ *Ask the other person questions*
      - □ *Answer your own questions*
      - □ *Find common interests*
      - □ *Ask follow-up questions*
      - □ *Share the conversation*
      - □ *Don't be a conversation hog*
      - □ *Don't be an interviewer*
      - □ *Don't get too personal at first*
  - ○ Say, *"The rules for maintaining a conversation also include the same rules for trading information. Now we'll be talking about additional rules for trading information."*
- *Don't be repetitive*
  - ○ Explain, *"Another rule for trading information and maintaining conversations is don't be repetitive. That means we don't talk about the same thing over and over."*
  - ○ Ask, *"Just because you find a common interest with someone, does that mean that's the only thing you should talk about?"*
    - ■ Answer: No, you should talk about a variety of things.
  - ○ Ask, *"What could be the problem with being repetitive?"*
    - ■ Answers: It's boring for the other person; even if the topic is a **common interest**, you need to find different topics to talk about now and then to keep it interesting.
- *Listen to your friend*
  - ○ Explain, *"Another rule for trading information and maintaining conversations is that we need to listen to our friends."*
  - ○ Ask, *"If you ask your friend a question, do you think you should listen to the answer?"*
    - ■ Answer: Yes.
  - ○ Ask, *"What could be the problem with not listening to the answer?"*

- Answers: Your friend will think you don't care about what they have to say; when you listen, it shows that you're interested in your friend.
- *Ask open-ended questions*
  - Explain, *"One of the rules for trading information and maintaining conversations is to ask open-ended questions. Open-ended questions are those where the answers are longer and can lead to more conversation. Closed-ended questions are those that only require a short response, like yes or no answers."*
  - Say, *"This doesn't mean you can't ask closed-ended questions, but what could be the problem with asking too many closed-ended questions?"*
    - Answer: You'll sound like **an interviewer**.
  - Explain, *"For example, if the closed-ended question were, 'What's your favorite movie?' an open-ended question might be, 'What kind of movies do you like?' The open-ended question could lead to a longer answer and more conversation."*

Behavioral Rehearsal: Ask Open-Ended Questions

- Explain, *"Now we're going to have each of you practice asking open-ended questions. I'm going to give each of you an example of a closed-ended question and then I want you to give me an example of an open-ended question on the same topic while everyone watches."*
- Go around the room and have each young adult generate an **open-ended question** from the stem of a **closed-ended question** for the following topics of conversation:
  - *"What is your favorite TV show?"*
  - *"What is your favorite movie?"*
  - *"What is your favorite band?"*
  - *"What is your favorite song?"*
  - *"What is your favorite book?"*
  - *"What is your favorite food?"*
  - *"What is your favorite sport?"*
  - *"What is your favorite game?"*
  - *"What is your favorite video game?"*
  - *"What is your favorite thing to do on the weekend?"*
- End by giving a round of applause to each young adult after their practice.
- [Note: If a young adult has difficulty coming up with **open-ended questions**, privately assign an extra *Homework Assignment* during *Reunification* to practice this during the week with the social coach.]
- *Don't brag* ⊚
  [The group leader and behavioral coach should do an INAPPROPRIATE role play with the group leader bragging]
  - Begin by saying, "Watch this and tell me what I'm doing WRONG."

Example of an INAPPROPRIATE Role Play

- Group leader: *"Hey, (insert name). Check out my new phone!"*
- Behavioral coach: *"That's cool. It's new?"*
- Group leader: *"Yeah, I just got it. It's the most expensive phone they had in the store! Almost no one has it . . . they probably can't afford it!"*
- Behavioral coach: (Surprised) *"I guess."*
- Group leader: *"Well, you know my family has a lot of money so I can pretty much buy whatever I like."*
- Behavioral coach: (Annoyed, looking around) *"Oh, good for you."*
- Group leader: *"It's pretty complicated to use, too, but I'm really smart so it's not a problem for me."*
- Behavioral coach: (Bored, looking around, planning an escape) *"Okay."*
- (Long awkward pause)

- ○ End by saying, *"Okay, timeout on that. So what did I do WRONG in that conversation?"*
  - ■ Answer: You were bragging.
- ○ Ask the following *Perspective Taking Questions*:
  - ■ *"What was that like for (name of coach)?"*
    - □ Answers: Annoying; irritating; boring.
  - ■ *"What do you think (name of coach) thought of me?"*
    - □ Answers: Arrogant; condescending; superficial; shallow.
  - ■ *"Is (name of coach) going to want to talk to me again?"*
    - □ Answers: No; too annoying; too vain.
- ○ Ask the behavioral coach the same *Perspective Taking Questions*:
  - ■ *"What was that like for you?"*
  - ■ *"What did you think of me?"*
  - ■ *"Would you want to talk to me again?"*
- ○ Say, *"One of the rules for trading information and maintaining conversations is don't brag. What could be the problem with bragging?"*
  - ■ Answers: When you brag, it can also seem condescending and egotistical; people will think you're shallow and superficial.

- ● *Don't be argumentative* ▶
  [The group leader and behavioral coach should do an INAPPROPRIATE role play with the group leader being argumentative.]
  - ○ Begin by saying, *"Watch this and tell me what I'm doing WRONG."*

Example of an INAPPROPRIATE Role Play

- ■ Group leader: *"Hey, (insert name). How's it going?"*
- ■ Behavioral coach: *"Pretty good."*
- ■ Group leader: *"What are you doing this weekend?"*
- ■ Behavioral coach: *"I'm just going to hang out and watch some movies."*
- ■ Group leader: *"Cool. What are you going to watch?"*
- ■ Behavioral coach: *"I'm going to do a Star Wars marathon. Starting with The Phantom Menace . . . it's the best!"*
- ■ Group leader: (Astonished, upset) *"Actually, it's NOT the best. Everyone knows that Attack of the Clones is the BEST Star Wars movie."*
- ■ Behavioral coach: (Surprised) *"Oh. Well I kind of like Episode One better."*
- ■ Group leader: (Astonished, enraged) *"How could you think Episode One is better than Episode Two?!"*
- ■ Behavioral coach: (Confused, annoyed) *"I don't know. I just do."*
- ■ Group leader: (Astonished, enraged) *"That's just clearly WRONG! When Obi-Wan Kenobi uncovers the sinister plot that leads to war . . ."*
- ■ Behavioral coach: (Annoyed) *"Uh-huh."*
- ■ Group leader: (Insistent) *". . . or when Anakin Skywalker has to choose between his Jedi duties or his forbidden love . . ."*
- ■ Behavioral coach: (Annoyed, bored, looking around) *"Okay."*
- ■ Group leader: (Astonished, enraged) *". . . I mean how could you beat that?! It has something for everyone!"*
- ■ Behavioral coach: (Annoyed) *"Sure. Whatever."*
- ■ Group leader: (Condescending) *"I'm just saying . . . clearly Attack of the Clones is the better movie."*
- ■ (Long awkward pause)

- ○ End by saying, *"Okay, timeout on that. So what did I do WRONG in that conversation?"*
  - ■ Answer: You were being argumentative.
- ○ Ask the following *Perspective Taking Questions*:

- ■ *"What was that like for (name of coach)?"*
  - □ Answers: Annoying; obnoxious.
- ■ *"What do you think (name of coach) thought of me?"*
  - □ Answers: Rude; arrogant; argumentative; condescending.
- ■ *"Is (name of coach) going to want to talk to me again?"*
  - □ Answers: No; too rude.
- ○ Ask the behavioral coach the same *Perspective Taking Questions*:
  - ■ *"What was that like for you?"*
  - ■ *"What did you think of me?"*
  - ■ *"Would you want to talk to me again?"*
- ○ Say, *"One of the rules for trading information and maintaining conversations is don't be argumentative. That means don't argue over every little thing or disagree with other people's opinions. What could be the problem with being argumentative?"*
  - ■ Answers: It's annoying, obnoxious; rude
- ○ Explain, *"Other people don't like to be argued with; just because you don't agree with someone doesn't mean you have to point that out; you could seem rude; you could seem aggressive."*

- ● ***Don't police*** ⊙
  [The group leader and behavioral coach should do an INAPPROPRIATE role play with the group leader policing.]
  - ○ Begin by saying, *"Watch this and tell me what I'm doing WRONG."*

> Example of an INAPPROPRIATE Role Play
>
> - ■ Group leader: *"Hey, (insert name). How's it going?"*
> - ■ Behavioral coach: *"I'm doing good."*
> - ■ Group leader: *"Actually, it's 'You're doing well.' 'Well' is an adverb and 'good' is an adjective, and in this situation you actually want to use the adverb 'well.'"*
> - ■ Behavioral coach: (Annoyed) *"Okay, sorry. I'm doing well."*
> - ■ Group leader: *"Well, you know it's for your benefit."*
> - ■ Behavioral coach: (Annoyed) *"Yeah, right."*
> - ■ Group leader: *"So, what did you do this weekend?"*
> - ■ Behavioral coach: (Looking around, planning an escape) *"I don't know."*
> - ■ (Long awkward pause)

- ○ End by saying, *"Okay, timeout on that. So what did I do WRONG in that conversation?"*
  - ■ Answers: You were correcting the person's grammar; you were being bossy; you were being a know-it-all.
- ○ Ask the following *Perspective Taking Questions*:
  - ■ *"What was that like for (name of coach)?"*
    - □ Answers: Annoying; obnoxious; embarrassing.
  - ■ *"What do you think (name of coach) thought of me?"*
    - □ Answers: Rude; arrogant; know-it-all; bossy; controlling.
  - ■ *"Is (name of coach) going to want to talk to me again?"*
    - □ Answers: No; too annoying; too rude.
- ○ Ask the behavioral coach the same *Perspective Taking Questions*:
  - ■ *"What was that like for you?"*
  - ■ *"What did you think of me?"*
  - ■ *"Would you want to talk to me again?"*
- ○ Say, *"One of the rules for trading information and maintaining conversations is don't police others. That means don't criticize or point out other people's mistakes. What could be the problem with policing?"*
  - ■ Answers: *Policing* others is annoying; it will make you look bossy and controlling; you will seem like a know-it-all; it embarrasses other people and they won't want to be around you.

- *Don't tease* ⊙

  [The group leader and behavioral coach should do an INAPPROPRIATE role play with the group leader teasing.]

  ○ Begin by saying, *"Watch this and tell me what I'm doing WRONG."*

  > Example of an INAPPROPRIATE Role Play
  >
  > ■ Group leader: *"Hey, (insert name). What did you do this weekend?"*
  > ■ Behavioral coach: *"I actually hung out with my parents."*
  > ■ Group leader: (Teasing) *"You hung out with your parents?! Who hangs out with their parents on the weekend?!"*
  > ■ Behavioral coach: (Uncomfortable) *"I don't know."*
  > ■ Group leader: (Teasing) *"What are you a momma's boy or something? Does your mom lay out your clothes on your bed too?"*
  > ■ Behavioral coach: (Uncomfortable) *"No."*
  > ■ Group leader: (Teasing) *"Does she know where you are right now? Maybe you should text her. She might be worried."*
  > ■ Behavioral coach: (Embarrassed, looking away)
  > ■ Group leader: (Teasing) *"Make sure she knows where you are. She's your mommy."*
  > ■ Behavioral coach: (Looking around for an escape)

  ○ End by saying, *"Okay, timeout on that. So what did I do WRONG in that conversation?"*
    ■ Answers: You were teasing the other person; you were being mean.
  ○ Ask the following *Perspective Taking Questions*:
    ■ *"What was that like for (name of coach)?"*
      □ Answers: Irritating; annoying; hurtful; embarrassing.
    ■ *"What do you think (name of coach) thought of me?"*
      □ Answers: Mean; unfriendly; unkind; rude; annoying.
    ■ *"Is (name of coach) going to want to talk to me again?"*
      □ Answers: No; too mean
  ○ Ask the behavioral coach the same *Perspective Taking Questions*:
    ■ *"What was that like for you?"*
    ■ *"What did you think of me?"*
    ■ *"Would you want to talk to me again?"*
  ○ Say, *"One of the rules for trading information and maintaining conversations is don't tease others. Teasing or bantering is risky behavior if you're trying to make and keep friends. Bantering is the equivalent of teasing among friends. It's usually meant playfully, but it's still risky. What could be the risk with bantering?"*
    ■ Answers: It can escalate and feelings can get hurt; this is especially true when you're FIRST getting to know someone and they don't know your sense of humor yet.

- *Use good volume control* ⊙

  [The group leader and behavioral coach should do an INAPPROPRIATE role play with the group leader speaking too loudly.]

  ○ Begin by saying, *"Watch this and tell me what I'm doing WRONG."*

  > Example of an INAPPROPRIATE Role Play
  >
  > ■ Group leader: (Speaking very loudly) *"Hi, (insert name). How's it going?"*
  > ■ Behavioral coach: (Startled, covers ears, moves back) *"Oh, it's going well."*
  > ■ Group leader: (Speaking very loudly) *"What have you been up to?"*
  > ■ Behavioral coach: (Embarrassed, moving further away) *"Oh, not much."*
  > ■ Group leader: (Speaking very loudly) *"So what did you do over the weekend?"*
  > ■ Behavioral coach: (Looking around, trying to escape) *"I don't know."*
  > ■ (Long awkward pause)

- ○ End by saying, *"Okay, timeout on that. So what did I do WRONG in that conversation?"*
  - ■ Answer: You were speaking too loudly.
- ○ Ask the following *Perspective Taking Questions*:
  - ■ *"What was that like for (name of coach)?"*
    - □ Answers: Irritating; annoying; embarrassing.
  - ■ *"What do you think (name of coach) thought of me?"*
    - □ Answers: Weird; obnoxious; annoying.
  - ■ *"Is (name of coach) going to want to talk to me again?"*
    - □ Answers: Probably not; too weird.
- ○ Ask the behavioral coach the same *Perspective Taking Questions*:
  - ■ *"What was that like for you?"*
  - ■ *"What did you think of me?"*
  - ■ *"Would you want to talk to me again?"*
- ○ Say, *"One of the rules for trading information and maintaining conversations is to use good volume control. What could be the problem with speaking too loudly?"*
  - ■ Answers: The person may get annoyed or bothered by you; it can also be embarrassing when someone is speaking too loudly in public.

[The group leader and behavioral coach should do an INAPPROPRIATE role play with the group leader speaking too quietly.]
- ○ Begin by saying, *"Watch this and tell me what I'm doing WRONG."*

Example of an INAPPROPRIATE Role Play

- ■ Group leader: (Whispering) *"Hi, (insert name). How's it going?"*
- ■ Behavioral coach: (Straining to hear) *"What?"*
- ■ Group leader: (Whispering) *"How's it going?"*
- ■ Behavioral coach: (Looking confused) *"Oh, fine thanks."*
- ■ Group leader: (Whispering) *"So what have you been up to?"*
- ■ Behavioral coach: (Straining to hear, moving closer) *"What?"*
- ■ Group leader: (Whispering) *"What have you been up to?"*
- ■ Behavioral coach: (Looking around, appears bored) *"What have I been up to? Oh, not much."*
- ■ (Long awkward pause)

- ○ End by saying, *"Okay, timeout on that. So what did I do WRONG in that conversation?"*
  - ■ Answer: You were speaking too quietly.
- ○ Ask the following *Perspective Taking Questions*:
  - ■ *"What was that like for (name of coach)?"*
    - □ Answers: Confusing; annoying; exhausting; a lot of work.
  - ■ *"What do you think (name of coach) thought of me?"*
    - □ Answers: Weird; maybe a little shy; maybe depressed.
  - ■ *"Is (name of coach) going to want to talk to me again?"*
    - □ Answers: Probably not; too much work.
- ○ Ask the behavioral coach the same *Perspective Taking Questions*:
  - ■ *"What was that like for you?"*
  - ■ *"What did you think of me?"*
  - ■ *"Would you want to talk to me again?"*
- ○ Say, *"Remember, one of the rules for trading information and maintaining conversations is to use good volume control. What could be the problem with speaking too quietly?"*
  - ■ Answers: The person may not hear you; it's a lot of effort to understand you; they may avoid speaking to you in the future because it's too much work.

- • *Use good body boundaries* ⊙
  [The group leader and behavioral coach should do an INAPPROPRIATE role play with the group leader standing too close.]
  - ○ Begin by saying, *"Watch this and tell me what I'm doing WRONG."*

Example of an INAPPROPRIATE Role Play

- Group leader: (Standing too close) *"Hi, (insert name). How are you doing?"*
- Behavioral coach: (Startled, moves back) *"Oh gosh . . . I'm fine."*
- Group leader: (Moves forward) *"What have you been up to?"*
- Behavioral coach: (Looking annoyed, moving further back) *"Uhh . . . not much."*
- Group leader: (Moves forward again) *"So how's work going?"*
- Behavioral coach: (Looking around, trying to escape) *"Umm . . . I don't know."*

○ End by saying, *"Okay, timeout on that. So what did I do WRONG in that conversation?"*
   - Answer: You were standing too close.
○ Ask the following *Perspective Taking Questions*:
   - *"What was that like for (name of coach)?"*
     □ Answers: Uncomfortable; irritating; annoying; embarrassing.
   - *"What do you think (name of coach) thought of me?"*
     □ Answers: Weird; creepy; stalker.
   - *"Is (name of coach) going to want to talk to me again?"*
     □ Answers: Definitely not; too creepy.
○ Ask the behavioral coach the same *Perspective Taking Questions*:
   - *"What was that like for you?"*
   - *"What did you think of me?"*
   - *"Would you want to talk to me again?"*
○ Say, *"One of the rules for trading information and maintaining conversations is to have good body boundaries. What could be the problem with standing too close?"*
   - Answers: Standing too close may make them feel uncomfortable; they may avoid you and not want to talk to you again.

[The group leader and behavioral coach should do an INAPPROPRIATE role play with the group leader standing too far away.]
○ Begin by saying, "Watch this and tell me what I'm doing WRONG."

Example of an INAPPROPRIATE Role Play

- Group leader: (Standing across the room) *"Hi, (insert name). How are you doing?"*
- Behavioral coach: (Straining to hear and looking confused) *"Oh, hi."*
- Group leader: (Still standing across the room) *"How are you doing?"*
- Behavioral coach: (Looking confused, embarrassed) *"Fine."*
- Group leader: (Still standing across the room) *"So what have you been up to?"*
- Behavioral coach: (Looking confused, looking around the room, trying to escape) *"Not much."*
- (Long awkward pause)

○ End by saying, *"Okay, timeout on that. So what did I do WRONG in that conversation?"*
   - Answer: You were standing too far away.
○ Ask the following *Perspective Taking Questions*:
   - *"What was that like for (name of coach)?"*
     □ Answers: Confusing; strange; embarrassing.
   - *"What do you think (name of coach) thought of me?"*
     □ Answers: Weird; odd; strange; oblivious.
   - *"Is (name of coach) going to want to talk to me again?"*
     □ Answers: Probably not; too embarrassing.
○ Ask the behavioral coach the same *Perspective Taking Questions*:

- ■ *"What was that like for you?"*
- ■ *"What did you think of me?"*
- ■ *"Would you want to talk to me again?"*
- ○ Say, *"Remember, one of the rules for trading information and maintaining conversations is to have good body boundaries. What could be the problem with standing too far away?"*
  - ■ Answers: It's awkward and strange; they may feel like your conversation is too public; it could be embarrassing for the other person if people are listening.
- ○ Explain, *"The general rule is to stand about an arm's length away (demonstrate an arm's length away), but don't go up and measure first!"*
  - ■ [Note: If young adults are having trouble gauging **an arm's length away**, they can practice by measuring with their social coaches.]

- • **Use good eye contact** ▷
  [The group leader and behavioral coach should do an INAPPROPRIATE role play with the group leader making too little eye contact.]
  - ○ Begin by saying, *"Watch this and tell me what I'm doing WRONG."*

  > **Example of an INAPPROPRIATE Role Play**
  >
  > - ■ Group leader: (Looking away) *"Hi, (insert name)."*
  > - ■ Behavioral coach: (Making eye contact) *"Hey, (insert name)!"*
  > - ■ Group leader: (Looking away) *"How's it going?"*
  > - ■ Behavioral coach: (Confused) *"I'm good. How are you?"*
  > - ■ Group leader: (Looking away) *"I'm fine. What did you do this weekend?"*
  > - ■ Behavioral coach: (Trying to make eye contact) *"I went hiking."*
  > - ■ Group leader: (Looking around) *"Oh, that's cool, I like to hike."*
  > - ■ Behavioral coach: (Trying to make eye contact) *"Yeah, I like hiking too."*
  > - ■ Group leader: (Looking around) *"Who did you go with?"*
  > - ■ Behavioral coach: (Confused) *"I went with my sister."*
  > - ■ Group leader: (Looking away) *"Oh, that's cool."*
  > - ■ (Long awkward pause)

  - ○ End by saying, *"Okay, timeout on that. So what did I do WRONG in that conversation?"*
    - ■ Answer: You were not making eye contact.
  - ○ Ask the following ***Perspective Taking Questions***:
    - ■ *"What was that like for (name of coach)?"*
      - □ Answers: Confusing; awkward; weird.
    - ■ *"What do you think (name of coach) thought of me?"*
      - □ Answers: Disinterested; weird; strange; spacey.
    - ■ *"Is (name of coach) going to want to talk to me again?"*
      - □ Answers: Probably not; too weird; didn't seem interested.
  - ○ Ask the behavioral coach the same ***Perspective Taking Questions***:
    - ■ *"What was that like for you?"*
    - ■ *"What did you think of me?"*
    - ■ *"Would you want to talk to me again?"*
  - ○ Say, *"One of the rules for trading information and maintaining conversations is to make good eye contact. What could be the problem with not looking at the other person when you're talking?"*
    - ■ Answers: It seems strange and confusing; if you don't look at them, they will think you're not interested.

  [The group leader and behavioral coach should do an INAPPROPRIATE role play with the group leader making too much eye contact.]
  - ○ Begin by saying, *"Watch this and tell me what I'm doing WRONG."*

> Example of an INAPPROPRIATE Role Play
>
> - Group leader: (Staring) *"Hey, (insert name), how's it going?"*
> - Behavioral coach: *"I'm good, how are you doing?"*
> - Group leader: (Staring) *"I'm fine. What did you do this weekend?"*
> - Behavioral coach: (Uncomfortable, looking away) *"I went hiking."*
> - Group leader: (Still staring) *"That's cool! Who'd you go with?"*
> - Behavioral coach: (Looking away) *"My sister."*
> - Group leader: (Still staring) *"Nice, I like to go hiking too."*
> - Behavioral coach: (Uncomfortable, looking away) *"Yeah?"*
> - Group leader: (Still staring) *"There's this trail I like to go to by my house."*
> - Behavioral coach: (Uncomfortable, looking away) *"Great."*
> - (Long awkward pause)

- End by saying, *"Okay, timeout on that. So what did I do WRONG in that conversation?"*
  - Answers: You were making too much eye contact; you were staring at the person.
- Ask the following *Perspective Taking Questions*:
  - *"What was that like for (name of coach)?"*
    - Answers: Uncomfortable; awkward; creepy; weird.
  - *"What do you think (name of coach) thought of me?"*
    - Answers: Stalker; predator; creepy; weird.
  - *"Is (name of coach) going to want to talk to me again?"*
    - Answers: No; too creepy; too awkward.
- Ask the behavioral coach the same *Perspective Taking Questions*:
  - *"What was that like for you?"*
  - *"What did you think of me?"*
  - *"Would you want to talk to me again?"*
- Say, *"Remember, one of the rules for trading information and maintaining conversations is to make good eye contact. What could be the problem with staring at the other person and never looking away?"*
  - Answers: You may make the other person uncomfortable; it may seem predatory and creepy.
- Explain, *"It's important to make eye contact to show interest, but we don't want to stare at the other person. Instead, we should look away once in awhile so we don't make people uncomfortable."*

Role Play: Trading Information and Maintaining Conversations ⊙

[The group leader and a coach should demonstrate an APPROPRIATE role play using all of the rules for *trading information* and *maintaining conversations*.]

- Begin by saying, *"Now that we know the rules for trading information and maintaining conversations, watch this and tell us what we're doing RIGHT."*

> Example of an APPROPRIATE Role Play
>
> - Group leader: (Standing about an arm's length away, maintaining good eye contact, using appropriate volume) *"Hi, (insert name). How's it going?"*
> - Behavioral coach: *"Oh, it's going well. How are you?"*
> - Group leader: *"I'm fine. So what have you been up to lately?"*
> - Behavioral coach: *"Oh, not much. Just working and studying a lot, but I'm going to the movies this weekend."*
> - Group leader: *"Oh, yeah. So what are you going to see?"*
> - Behavioral coach: *"I think I'm going to see that new sci-fi movie. What are you doing this weekend?"*
> - Group leader: *"I was thinking about going to the movies, too, but I already saw that one."*

- Behavioral coach: *"Oh, yeah. Was it good?"*
- Group leader: *"Yeah, it was really good. Do you like sci-fi?"*
- Behavioral coach: *"Yeah. They're my favorite! What about you?"*
- Group leader: *"I love sci-fi movies, too!"*
- Behavioral coach: *"Cool. What's your favorite movie?"*

- End by saying, *"Okay, timeout on that. So what did we do RIGHT in that conversation?"*
    - Answers: *Asked open-ended questions; not repetitive; listened; didn't brag; didn't police; didn't tease; used good volume control; used good body boundaries; used good eye contact.*
- Ask, *"Did it seem like we wanted to talk to each other?"*
    - Answer: Yes.
- Ask, *"How could you tell?"*
    - Answers: *Talking to each other; looking at each other; facing each other.*
- Ask the following *Perspective Taking Questions*:
    - *"What was that like for (name of coach)?"*
        - Answers: Nice; pleasant.
    - *"What do you think (name of coach) thought of me?"*
        - Answers: Nice; interesting; pretty cool.
    - *"Is (name of coach) going to want to talk to me again?"*
        - Answer: Yes.
- Ask the behavioral coach the same *Perspective Taking Questions*:
    - *"What was that like for you?"*
    - *"What did you think of me?"*
    - *"Would you want to talk to me again?"*
- Say, *"So those are the rules for trading information and maintaining conversations. You will be practicing trading information and maintaining conversations during your Homework Assignments this week."*

TRADING INFORMATION AND MAINTAINING CONVERSATIONS

Young Adult Behavioral Rehearsal

Jeopardy

Materials Needed

- Whiteboard and markers
- *Jeopardy Answer Sheets* for each young adult
- Pens
- Scissors

Rules

- Young adults will compete against themselves in this game of **trading information**.
- Like the North American TV game show *Jeopardy*, young adults will be given answers and asked to respond in the form of a question.
  - Example:
    - Group leader: *"The answer is Jimmy's favorite sport."*
    - Young adult: *"What is football?"*
  - The young adult does not have to answer in the form of a question (most do not).
  - If this group is being conducted in a country where *Jeopardy* is unknown, feel free to change the name and alter the rules accordingly.
- To promote interest and cooperation, points will be given for correct responses.
- The purpose of *Jeopardy* is not to practice **trading information** perfectly, since the young adults will sound like they are **interviewing** when asking the questions.
- The true purpose of *Jeopardy* is to improve:
  - *Topic initiation*
    - Talking about a variety of topics, rather than only restricted interests.
  - *Listening skills*
    - Listening and remembering what people share about themselves.

How to Play

- You should have saved completed *Jeopardy Answer Sheets* from the previous session.
  - If you forgot to save the answer sheets, you can have young adults complete the answer sheets found at the end of this section.
- Write the *Jeopardy Topics* on the board where young adults can see them.
  - *Favorite music*
  - *Favorite weekend activity*
  - *Favorite sport*
  - *Favorite game*
  - *Favorite movie*

- o *Favorite television show*
- o *Favorite book*
- o *Eye color* [Note: This is NOT to be asked, but noticed by using good eye contact. If conducting this group in a place where most people share the same eye color, feel free to replace this category.]
- Have young adults practice *trading information* about the *Jeopardy Topics* in small groups for two or three minutes each.
  - o Change the groups a few times (depending on the time).
  - o Prompt young adults to ask relevant questions about the *Jeopardy Topics* when necessary.
- Once the young adults have finished *trading information*, reconvene as a group and begin the *Jeopardy Challenge*.
  - o Begin by having the young adult who appears to have participated the most that week choose the first category.
  - o Notify the group that if they raise their hand before the question has been asked, they are disqualified from answering.
  - o The person who raises their hand first gets to take the first guess.
  - o If they provide the wrong answer, the person who raised their hand second has a chance to answer, and so on.
  - o The young adults get only one guess per question.
  - o Do not give clues.
- You may need to enforce a time limit if young adults take a long time to answer.
- Do not correct the young adults if they answer the questions in the incorrect format (i.e., instead of saying *"What is football?"* they say *"Football"*).
  - o All that matters is that they remembered the information they obtained through *trading information*.
- The person who answers the question correctly gets a point and gets to choose the next category.
- If no one answers correctly, the person about whom the last question relates, gets to pick the next category.
- Encourage the young adults to clap and cheer for each other during the game.
- Give points for correct responses and keep track of the points on the board.
- At the end of the game, the person with the most points is the *Jeopardy Challenge Winner*.
- SAVE YOUNG ADULT *JEOPARDY ANSWER SHEETS* FOR NEXT WEEK.

Jeopardy Answer Sheets

Music to Your Ears	**TGIF**
The answer is:	The answer is:
_____'s favorite band. (Name)	_____'s favorite weekend activity. (Name)
The question is:	The question is:
What is _____ (favorite band)	What is _____ (favorite weekend activity)
Sports and Leisure	**Game Time**
The answer is:	The answer is:
_____'s favorite sport. (Name)	_____'s favorite game. (Name)
The question is:	The question is:
What is _____ (favorite sport)	What is _____ (favorite game)
Movies, Movies, Movies	**TV Time**
The answer is:	The answer is:
_____'s favorite movie. (Name)	_____'s favorite TV show. (Name)
The question is:	The question is:
What is _____ (favorite movie)	What is _____ (favorite TV show)
Bestseller List	**The "Eyes" Have It**
The answer is:	The answer is:
_____'s favorite book. (Name)	The color of _____'s eyes. (Name)
The question is:	The question is:
What is _____ (favorite book)	What is _____ (your eye color)

TRADING INFORMATION AND MAINTAINING CONVERSATIONS

Reunification

- Announce that young adults should join their social coaches.
  - ○ Have young adults stand or sit next to their social coaches.
  - ○ Be sure to have silence and the full attention of the group before starting with *Reunification*.
  - ○ Have young adults generate the content from the lesson while social coaches listen.
- Say, *"Today, we talked about how to trade information and maintain conversations. Who can tell us some of the new rules for trading information and maintaining conversations?"*
- Have young adults generate the new rules for **trading information** and **maintaining conversations**:
  - ○ **Don't be repetitive**
  - ○ **Listen to your friend**
  - ○ **Ask open-ended questions**
  - ○ **Don't brag**
  - ○ **Don't be argumentative**
  - ○ **Don't police**
  - ○ **Don't tease**
  - ○ **Use good volume control**
  - ○ **Use good body boundaries**
  - ○ **Use good eye contact**
- Say, *"This group did a great job of practicing trading information and maintaining conversations today. Let's give them a round of applause."*
- Say, *"The group also played Jeopardy again where they practiced trading information. Tonight's Jeopardy Challenge Winner was (insert name). Let's give (insert name) a round of applause."*

Homework Assignments

Distribute the *Social Coaching Handout* to young adults and announce the following *Homework Assignments*:

1. ***In-group call or video chat.***
   - Arrange a phone call or video chat with another group member to trade information.
   - Young adults and social coaches should schedule the day and time of the call with the other group member before leaving the group.
   - Go over the rules for **trading information** before the call.
   - Social coaches should ask young adults the following **social coaching questions** after the call:
     - ○ **What was the common interest?**
     - ○ **What could you do with that information if you were going to hang out?**

2. Young adults and social coaches should practice **starting and maintaining a conversation, trading information**, and **finding common interests**.

- Go over the rules for ***starting and maintaining a conversation*** and ***trading information*** before practicing.
- Social coaches should ask young adults the following ***social coaching questions*** after practicing:
  - ***What was the common interest?***
  - ***What could you do with that information if you were going to hang out?***
- Read off the in-group call assignment (Appendix E) and remind social coaches to make a note of who is calling whom.
- Encourage the young adults and social coaches to use the Phone Roster (Appendix D) to note the day and time of the scheduled call each week.
  - Pass out a new Phone Roster if there were changes from the previous week.
- Young adults and social coaches should let all relevant people know if they wish to be called at a different number or if there are any errors on the current Phone Roster.
  - In the event that there are more changes, a new Phone Roster should be distributed the next week.

Individual Check-Out

Once the calls have been scheduled, individually and privately negotiate with each young adult and social coach:

1. Where the social coach will be during the ***in-group call or video chat***.

2. When young adults and social coaches will practice ***starting and maintaining a conversation***, ***trading information***, and ***finding common interests***.

TRADING INFORMATION AND MAINTAINING CONVERSATIONS

Social Coaching Handout

Conversational Topics

Table 3.1 Common Conversational Topics Among Young Adults

School or work gossip	Video games/computer games	Classes/major
Problems with friends	Computers/technology	Exams/papers/schoolwork
Problems with family	Comic books/anime/manga	Professors/supervisors
Boyfriends/girlfriends	Movies	College and job applications
Dating	TV shows	Sports
Parties/get-togethers	YouTube videos/viral videos	Cars/motorcycles/bikes
Weekend activities	Internet websites	Celebrities
Meet-up groups	Music/concerts	Fashion/clothes
Social clubs/activities	Books	Shopping
Hobbies/interests	News/media/politics	Makeup/hair

Trading Information and Maintaining Conversations*

- *Don't be repetitive*
- *Listen to your friend*
- *Ask open-ended questions*
- *Don't brag*
- *Don't be argumentative*
- *Don't police**
- *Don't tease**
- *Use good volume control**
- *Use good body boundaries**
- *Use good eye contact**

Perspective Taking Questions for Social Coaching

- *What was that like for that person?*
- *What do they think of you?*
- *Are they going to want to talk to you again?*

Homework Assignments

1. *In-group call or video chat.*
   - Arrange a phone call or video chat with another group member to **trade information**.
   - Young adults and social coaches should schedule the day and time of the call with the other group member before leaving the group.
   - Go over the rules for **trading information** before the call.
   - Social coaches should ask young adults the following *social coaching questions* after the call:
     - *What was the common interest?*
     - *What could you do with that information if you were going to hang out?*

2. Young adults and social coaches should practice **starting and maintaining a conversation, trading information**, and **finding common interests**.
   - Go over the rules for **starting and maintaining a conversation** and **trading information** before practicing.
   - Social coaches should ask young adults the following *social coaching questions* after practicing:
     - *What was the common interest?*
     - *What could we do with that information if we were going to hang out?*

* See *The Science of Making Friends* DVD (Laugeson, 2013) or *FriendMaker* mobile app for a video Role Play Demonstration of the corresponding rule.

FINDING A SOURCE OF FRIENDS

Social Coaching Therapist Guide

Preparing for the Social Coaching Session

The structure of the *Social Coaching Session* helps keep caregivers on track, which is absolutely necessary to keep the session productive. The sequence of *Homework Review, Didactic Lesson, Homework Assignments,* and *Reunification* is pretty straightforward, and social coaches will catch onto the routine quickly. For social coaches who missed the previous session, it is important to avoid giving "extra time" during the group, as this is unfair to those who attend regularly. The same is true for group members who arrive late. This special treatment gives the message that it is not important to attend regularly and on time, and may reinforce absences and tardiness. Similarly, if a different caregiver "filled in" during the previous session, do not count on them conveying enough of the session content to be sufficient to complete the assignments. Instead, give the handout of the missed session to the returning social coach and use the *Homework Review* with other caregivers as a way of informing them of what they missed. Sending *Social Coaching Handouts* in the previous week to absent group members via email is another option, but be sure to always have extra handouts from previous sessions on hand in case group members are absent.

The main focus of this lesson is on helping young adults *find a source of friends*. This may not be an issue for some young adults that already have *social activities* from which they can draw accepting friends. For those young adults that do not currently have a *source of friends*, this may be one of the more challenging aspects of the program. Most young adults will require additional support from social coaches in identifying *social activities* where they might meet accepting peers with *common interests*. It will be important for you to stress that this social coaching role is one of the most important jobs the caregivers have in PEERS®.

Some social coaches whose young adults are isolated with no current *source of friends* may exhibit some resistance around this session. For example, some social coaches may suggest *social activities* that fall short and do not include accepting peers. Other social coaches may suggest *social activities* the young adult has been attending without benefit of generating closer friendships. For instance, a young adult may enjoy attending a religious youth group, but would not consider asking any of the members to hang out outside of this group. Just because a young adult enjoys a particular activity does not mean it fits the parameters of a *good source of friends*. Now may be a good time to find NEW *social activities* since the young adult will be more socially motivated. Social coaches should judge whether an activity is socially productive or not, and if not, discuss this with young adults and encourage them to find better alternatives. Good parameters of a social activity include those that: (1) are based on the young adult's interests; (2) meet weekly or at least every other week; (3) include accepting peers similar in age; (4) include unstructured time to interact with others; and (5) start within the next couple of weeks.

Although social coaches are expected to *scout out social activities* by doing some background investigating of possible options, it will be critical to involve the young adult in the process of joining an appropriate activity where he or she has access to a *good potential source of friends* with *common interests*. It should be less a question of *DO* they want to join a *social activity*, and instead *WHICH* one. Some young adults may be reluctant to do this, but if the young adult is socially motivated, then, with a little help from you and the social coaches, it will probably go more smoothly. If the young adult is already enrolled in an appropriate *social activity* with good friend options, they do not need to look for new activities.

Homework Review

[Go over the following *Homework Assignments* and **troubleshoot** any potential problems. Start with completed homework first. If you have time, you can inquire as to why others were unable to complete the assignment and try to **troubleshoot** how they might get it done for the coming week. When reviewing homework, be sure to relabel descriptions using the **buzzwords** (identified by **bold and italicized** print). Spend the majority of the *Homework Review* on the **in-group call or video chat**, as this is the most important assignment.]

1. ***In-group call or video chat***
   - Say, *"One of the assignments this week was for your young adult to have a phone call or video chat with someone in the group in order to practice trading information. Whose young adult did the in-group call or video chat?"*
   - Ask the following questions:
     - *"Who did your young adult talk to and who called whom?"*
     - *"What social coaching did you do before the call?"*
     - *"Where were you during the call?"*
     - *"Did they trade information and find a common interest?"*
     - *"What social coaching did you do after the call?"*
       - Appropriate ***social coaching questions***:
         - ***What was your common interest?***
         - ***What could you do with that information if you were going to hang out?***
   - Have the other social coach who participated in the call or video chat give their account immediately after, but not at the same time.

2. Young adults and social coaches should have practiced ***starting and maintaining a conversation, trading information***, and ***finding common interests***.
   - Say, *"Another assignment this week was to practice starting and maintaining a conversation, trading information, and finding common interests with your young adult. Who completed or attempted to complete this assignment?"*
   - Focus on completed or attempted assignments and ask the following questions:
     - *"Did your young adult practice starting and maintaining a conversation with you?"*
     - *"Did you go over the rules and steps before practicing?"*
       - ***Steps for Starting a Conversation:***
         1. ***Casually Look Over***
         2. ***Use a Prop***
         3. ***Find a Common Interest***
         4. ***Mention the Common Interest***
         5. ***Trade Information***
         6. ***Assess Interest***
            - ***Are they talking to me?***
            - ***Are they looking at me?***
            - ***Are they facing me (or are they giving me the cold shoulder)?***
         7. ***Introduce Yourself***
     - *"Did your young adult practice trading information?"*
     - *"Did you ask the social coaching questions after practicing?"*
       - Appropriate ***social coaching questions***:
         - ***What was the common interest?***
         - ***What could we do with that information if we were going to hang out?***
   - [Collect the *Social Coaching Homework Assignment Worksheets*. If social coaches forgot to bring the worksheets, have them complete a new form to hold them accountable for the assignments.]

Didactic Lesson: Finding a Source of Friends

- Distribute the *Social Coaching Handout*.
  - Sections in **bold print** in the *Social Coaching Therapist Guide* come directly from the *Social Coaching Handout*.
  - Remind social coaches that terms that are in ***bold and italicized*** print are ***buzzwords*** and represent important concepts from the PEERS® curriculum that should be used as much as possible when social coaching.
- Explain, *"Today, we're talking about finding a source of friends. PEERS® is a program that helps young adults learn to make and keep friends and develop close meaningful relationships, but it is not a friendship-matching group. That means we need to teach young adults how to find a source of friends outside of this group. You will be a HUGE part of that process as social coaches. To begin this process, we need to understand that friendship is a choice."*
- Ask, *"Do we get to be friends with everyone?"*
  - Answer: No.
- Ask, *"Does everyone get to be friends with us?"*
  - Answer: No.
- Explain, *"That's because having a friend is a CHOICE and it's important that we CHOOSE our friends wisely. Now that we understand that friendship is a CHOICE, and there are good choices and bad choices, we need to talk about WHERE young adults might find some of these good choices for friends."*

Social Groups

- Explain, *"In most places, there are different groups of people that hang out, and they share some common interest. We call them 'social groups' and they usually have names, like gamers or techies. What are some other social groups common to young adults?"*
- Have social coaches brainstorm the different ***social groups***.
  - See Table 4.1 for an overview of commonly identified ***social groups***.
  - Some coaches will be unfamiliar with the ***social groups*** listed in Table 4.1, so be prepared to explain unfamiliar groups.
  - [Note: ***Social groups*** will be different according to culture. Do not rely on Table 4.1 as a comprehensive list. Instead, have social coaches generate the list of ***social groups***, as they change with time and culture.]

Table 4.1 Different Social Groups Identified by Young Adults

Jocks/athletes	Computer geeks/techies	Gamers/video game geeks
Sports teams	Science geeks/IT	Nerds
Sports fans	Robotics club	Brains
Cheerleaders/pep squad	Sci-fi geeks	Hip hop
Popular	Trekkies	Metalheads
Greeks/fraternities/sororities	Comic book geeks/anime geeks	Skaters
Student government	Cosplayers	Surfers
Drama/theater arts	LARPers	Hipsters
Choir/chorus/Glee club	Math geeks/mathletes	Hippies/granolas
Musicians	Newsies	Debate club/debate team
Artists	Movie buffs/movie geeks	Political groups
Ravers/partiers	Band geeks	Military groups
Preppies	Bronies/Pegasisters	Ethnic groups/cultural groups
Bookworms	Chess club/chess team	Religious groups
History buffs	Goths	LGBTQ
Animal lovers/pet lovers	Emos	Majors (source of college study)
Equestrians	Scenesters	Departments (work settings)
Motorheads/gearheads	Bikers	Industries (work settings)

Finding Social Activities

- Explain, *"One of the MOST IMPORTANT jobs you each have as a social coach is to help your young adult find a source of friends. One of the best ways of doing that is by helping young adults enroll in social activities based on their interests. This will give them access to people from some of these social groups. When chosen wisely, the social activities they join should include people with common interests. We know that friendships are based on common interests, so it's important for us to help find social activities where they might meet people that have the same interests."*

- Present each of the interests listed in Table 4.2 and ask the question, *"So if our young adult likes (insert interest), where can he or she meet other people that like (insert interest)?"*

Table 4.2 Possible Social Activities

Interests	Related Social Activities
Computers/ technology	Take computer classes; attend events through computer/IT department; join a technology related meet-up group; join a technology club; join a computer meet-up group; join a computer club
Video games	Go to adult video arcades with friends; go to gaming conventions; visit gaming stores; join a gaming meet-up group; join a gaming club
Science	Go to science museum events; take science classes; join a science-related meet-up group; join a science club; join a robotics club
Comic books/anime	Attend comic book conventions (i.e., Comic Con); go to comic book/anime stores; take comic book/anime drawing classes; join a comic book/anime meet-up group; join a comic book/anime club
Chess	Visit gaming stores where they play chess; attend chess tournaments; join a chess meet-up group; join a chess club
Cosplay (costume play)	Attend comic book conventions (i.e., Comic Con); take sewing classes to make costumes; join a cosplay meet-up group; join a cosplay club
LARPing (live action role playing)	Attend comic book conventions (i.e., Comic Con); take sewing classes to make costumes; attend LARPing events; join a LARPing meet-up group; join a LARPing club
Movies	Join an audiovisual club; join a movie-related meet-up group; join a movie club
Sports	Try out for a sports team; play sports at community recreation centers or parks; join a sports league; go to sporting events; attend sports camps (e.g., spring training); join a sports-related meet-up group; join a sports club
Cars	Go to car shows; visit car museums; take auto shop courses; join a car-related meet-up group; join a car club
Music	Go to concerts; join the college band; take music classes; join a music-related meet-up group; join a music club

Finding People with Common Interests

- Say, *"In some cases, it may be difficult to find social activities based on your young adult's interests. When that happens it can be helpful to identify individual people with common interests. Let's talk about other ways we can identify and find potential friends outside of social activities. How can you tell which social group someone belongs to and what their interests are?"*

Clues About Social Groups and Common Interests

- Appearance, clothing, hair
- Their interests, what they talk about
- What they do during free time
- Who they hang out with
- Where they hang out
- Social activities they belong to

- Ask, *"If your young adult is a techie and wants to meet other people who like computers and technology, how will he or she find them if there's not a computer club or tech club to join?"*
  - Answers: Techies may hang out in the computer labs on campus; take computer classes; work in IT departments or technology related industries; study information technology in college; carry around laptops and other types of technology; talk about computers with their friends; and wear T-shirts with computer or technology logos.
- Ask, *"If your young adult is a gamer and wants to meet other people who like video games, how will he or she find them if there's not a gaming club to join?"*
  - Answers: Gamers may carry around portable gaming devices; play video games during breaks and before and after class or work; they talk about video games with their friends; and often wear T-shirts with gaming logos.
- Ask, *"If your young adult is a comic book geek or an anime geek and wants to meet other people who like comics or anime, how will he or she find them if there's not a comic book or anime club to join?"*
  - Answers: Comic book geeks and anime geeks often carry around magazines of their favorite comics; they may draw characters on their possessions; take art classes to improve their drawing; talk about comic books or anime with their friends; talk about attending comic book conventions; and wear T-shirts with comic book or anime characters.
- Ask, *"If your young adult is a science geek and wants to meet other people who like science, how will he or she find them if there's not a science club to join?"*
  - Answers: Science geeks may hang out in science labs on campus; take science classes; work in science-related industries; carry around science books or sci-fi books; talk about science with their friends; and wear T-shirts with science or sci-fi-related logos.
- Explain, *"So there are lots of ways to identify people with common interests, even if we don't have access to social activities."*

Assessing Peer Acceptance or Rejection

- Explain, *"As your young adults begin to identify which social groups they might fit in with, it will be important to think about how you can tell if they're accepted or not accepted by people from those groups. How can you tell if someone wants to be friends? Some people think it's just a feeling you get. It's true that there are feelings, but there are also concrete behaviors that tell us if we're accepted or not accepted."*
- Ask the following questions and use Table 4.3 to guide the discussion.
  - *"How can you tell if you're ACCEPTED by someone?"*
  - *"How can you tell if you're NOT ACCEPTED by someone?"*

Table 4.3 Signs of Acceptance and Lack of Acceptance from Social Groups

Signs You Are Accepted	Signs You Are Not Accepted
They seek you out to do things individually or in the group	They do not seek you out to do things
They talk to you and respond to your attempts to talk	They ignore you and/or do not respond to your attempts
They give you their contact information	They do not give you their contact information
They ask for your contact information	They do not ask for your contact information
They text message, instant message, email, or call you just to talk	They do not text message, instant message, email, or call you
They respond to your text messages, instant messages, emails, or phone calls	They do not accept or return your calls or messages
They invite you to do things	They do not invite you to do things
They accept your invitations to do things	They do not accept your invitations or put off your invitations to do things
They add you to their social networking pages	They ignore your friend requests on social networking sites
They say nice things to you and give you compliments	They laugh at you or make fun of you

- Explain, *"We know that it feels bad when people don't want to be friends with our young adults, but we need to be prepared to provide social coaching when that happens. If someone doesn't want to be friends, it is helpful to remind them of the following statement and then redirect them to people who do want to be friends."*
  - ○ **Friendship is a choice. We don't get to be friends with everyone and everyone doesn't get to be friends with us.**
- Explain, *"This week, with a LOT of help from you, young adults are going to begin to identify social activities where they can find potential sources of friends."*

Homework Assignments

[Distribute the *Social Coaching Homework Assignment Worksheet* (Appendix I) for social coaches to complete and return at the next session.]

1. Find a *source of friends*.
   - Young adults and social coaches should DISCUSS and DECIDE on *social activities* based on the young adult's interests.
   - BEGIN TO ENROLL in these activities immediately.
     - ○ Criteria for a good *social activity*:
       - ▪ Is based on the young adult's interests.
       - ▪ Meets weekly or at least every other week.
       - ▪ Includes accepting peers similar in age.
       - ▪ Includes unstructured time to interact with others.
       - ▪ Activity starts within the next couple of weeks.

2. *In-group call or video chat*.
   - Arrange a phone call or video chat with another group member to trade information.
   - Young adults and social coaches should schedule the day and time of the call with the other group member before leaving the group.
   - Go over the rules for *trading information* before the call.
   - Social coaches should ask young adults the following *social coaching questions* after the call:
     - ○ *What was the common interest?*
     - ○ *What could you do with that information if you were going to hang out?*

3. Young adults and social coaches should practice *starting and maintaining a conversation, trading information*, and *finding common interests*.
   - Go over the rules for *starting and maintaining a conversation* and *trading information* before practicing.
   - Social coaches should ask young adults the following *social coaching questions* after practicing:
     - ○ *What was the common interest?*
     - ○ *What could we do with that information if we were going to hang out?*

4. Bring a *personal item* to *trade information*.
   - Bring a *personal item* to *trade information* with other group members next week (e.g., music, game, book, pictures).

Social Coaching Tips

1. *Scout out* possible *social activities* for your young adult.
   - Identify your young adult's interests and hobbies.
     - ○ If you don't know their interests, consider the **common interests** they have identified through *trading information*.
   - Start to investigate options for him or her.
   - Do your own independent investigating first.

2. Bring your ideas back to your young adult for feedback.
   - Your young adult ultimately gets to choose the *social activities*, so don't try to force ideas on him or her.

3. Begin to collaborate with your young adult on ideas and start to investigate together.
   - Example: Go online to find meet-up groups for adults (e.g., www.meetup.com).

4. Help your young adult start to enroll in these *social activities*.
   - Example: Sending an email request to the meetup.com organizer.

5. Help *troubleshoot* the logistics.
   - Identify how your young adult will get to and from these *social activities*.
   - Identify any costs or materials needed for these *social activities*.

6. Remind your young adult when these *social activities* take place.
   - Be prepared to drive your young adult to and from these *social activities* if needed and developmentally appropriate.

FINDING A SOURCE OF FRIENDS

Young Adult Therapist Guide

Preparing for the Young Adult Session

Young adults find themselves embedded in a multilevel system of peer affiliations. At the most intimate level of peer affiliation is the *clique*. This typically includes a few close friends, often identified as best friends. The next level of peer affiliation is the *social group*. This may include dozens of peers, all sharing some *common interest*. These *social groups* are often identified with a name or label, such as the gamers or the techies, which defines their *common interest*. Research shows that many people belong to more than one *social group*, floating naturally between different friendship networks, and often finding their best friends from among these *social groups*. The last level of peer affiliation is the *larger peer group*. This group typically includes young adults around the same age, made up of individuals from different *cliques* or *social groups*, but who do not necessarily share *common interests* or socialize with one another. For most young adults, the *larger peer group* may include the entire student body of their college or university, or all of the coworkers in their place of work.

Although several levels of peer affiliation are present across the lifespan, the *social group*, which includes dozens of peers with *common interests*, is particularly relevant during adolescence and early adulthood. It is this level of peer affiliation that typically defines the social world of transitional youth, often determining their reputation and defining who they will become friends with. Yet, for many young adults with Autism Spectrum Disorder (ASD) and other social challenges, affiliation with a *social group* is not necessarily something they have given much thought. The problem with this oversight is that not identifying with a particular *social group*, or at least individuals with whom they share *common interests*, makes it difficult to find a *source of friends*. The purpose of this lesson is to help overcome this lapse.

Problems with group identification are often a characteristic of many individuals referred for social skills training. Typically, those struggling with social skills fall into two main categories: *socially neglected* or *peer rejected*. *Socially neglected* young adults are those that often fail to identify a *social group* and are socially isolated. They are typically seen as shy, timid, or withdrawn, and they rarely seek out others—sometimes expecting others to come to them. They do not seek out their peers and are consequently neglected and alone. *Socially neglected* young adults often end up either completely withdrawn from peer social networks (i.e., the *loners*) or on the periphery of one or more peer groups (i.e., the *floaters*). In addition to developmental disorders such as Autism Spectrum Disorder (ASD), they sometimes have diagnoses of anxiety and/or depression. On the other hand, *peer-rejected* young adults are those that have often repeatedly attempted to make friends with peers from inappropriate or unaccepting *social groups*. Unlike the *socially neglected* young adults, *peer rejected* youth are actively seeking out their peers, but they are actively getting rejected. They often make social errors such as *policing*, *conversation hogging*, or barging into conversations. They may be teased or made fun of by their classmates or work colleagues, and in some cases they may even be bullied and have bad reputations with these peers, making it difficult for them to make and keep friends. In addition to developmental disorders such as ASD, peer rejected young adults sometimes are diagnosed with impulse control disorders such as ADHD. Although *socially neglected* and *peer rejected* young adults look rather different in presentation, they are both struggling to find a source of friends, albeit for different reasons. It will be important for you to identify which category of peer acceptance young adults fit into. Although the skills you will be teaching will be the same *ecologically valid skills* used by socially accepted young adults, the challenges these two groups will face in finding an accepting social group will be somewhat different. *Socially neglected* young adults may have a reputation as being shy or slow to warm up. Since being shy is not generally viewed as a negative personality trait, these young adults may be able to make friends from preexisting sources of known people. However, some *peer rejected* young adults may come to your group with such a negative reputation that choosing a *social group* from within their school or workplace may not be a viable option. In these cases, it will be essential for social coaches to help find a source of friends outside of the school or work setting while their reputation dies down. [Note: For a review of the steps for changing a bad reputation, see *Social Skills for Teenagers with Developmental and Autism Spectrum Disorders: The PEERS® Treatment Manual* (Laugeson & Frankel, 2010), *The Science of Making Friends: Helping Socially Challenged Teens and Young Adults* (Laugeson, 2013), or *The PEERS® Curriculum for School-Based Professionals: Social Skills Training for Adolescents with Autism Spectrum Disorder* (Laugeson, 2014).]

By helping young adults understand the function of *social groups*, you will assist them in identifying appropriate *sources of friends*. Young adults will be looking to you as an expert in these matters, as most will have heard of these *social groups* but will not have given much thought to the function of them (e.g., *"If I like video games, I should try to make friends with other gamers"*). Thus, it is important for you to have a good understanding of these *social groups* prior to the *Didactic Lesson*.

Some young adults will incorrectly state that they would fit in with *social groups* that may not be accepting. One of the most important parts of the lesson is for you to gently dissuade young adults from attempting to fit in with inappropriate *social groups*, while identifying more appropriate options based on the young adult's interests. You will do this by asking, *"Have you ever tried to hang out with that group?"* If they say yes, you will ask, *"Did it seem like they accepted you?"* If they say yes, you will ask, *"How could you tell?"* Lesson content has young adults identify behavioral signs of acceptance or rejection. If this discussion leads to the realization or admission of previous rejection, you will need to follow up by assisting the young adult with finding a more appropriate *social group*. While these realizations can be painful, you will want to help normalize the experience by frequently using the buzz phrase, *"Friendship is a choice. We don't get to be friends with everyone, and everyone doesn't get to be friends with us."*

For young adults who are not working or attending school, the concept of *social groups* is less relevant. However, this lesson will still be quite helpful in identifying sources of new friends through enrollment in social activities. The support of social coaches in identifying social activities will be essential to success in finding young adults new potential friends with *common interests*. If organized social activities are rare or limited in your community, simply identifying a few young adults with *common interests* will be sufficient to get started.

Challenge young adults that choose an antisocial group (e.g., gangs, taggers) by *opening it up to the group* and asking, *"What could be the problem with choosing to hang out with (insert name of social group)?"* Do not allow young adults to choose "floaters" (i.e., young adults that float from one group to another) or "loners," as neither is a true *social group*. Make sure to write down the *social groups* and social activities the young adults chose for future reference.

Homework Review

[Go over the following *Homework Assignments* and *troubleshoot* any potential problems. Start with completed homework first. If you have time, you can inquire as to why others were unable to complete the assignment and try to *troubleshoot* how they might get it done for the coming week. When reviewing homework, be sure to relabel descriptions using the *buzzwords* (identified by **bold and italicized** print). Spend the majority of the *Homework Review* on the **in-group call or video chat**, as this is the most important assignment.]

1. ***In-group call or video chat***
   - Say, *"One of your assignments this week was to have a phone call or video chat with someone in the group in order to practice trading information. Raise your hand if you did the in-group call or video chat."*
   - Ask the following questions:
     ○ *"Who did you talk to and who called whom?"*
     ○ *"Did you trade information and did you find a common interest?"*
     ○ *"What could you do with that information if you were going to hang out?"*
   - Have the other person who participated in the call or video chat give their account immediately after, but not at the same time.

2. Young adults and social coaches should have practiced ***starting and maintaining a conversation, trading information***, and ***finding common interests***.
   - Say, *"Another assignment you had this week was to practice starting and maintaining a conversation, trading information, and finding common interests with a social coach. Raise your hand if you traded information with your social coach this week."*
   - Ask the following questions:
     ○ *"Did you practice starting a conversation and which steps did you follow?"*
       ▪ ***Steps for Starting Conversation***
         1. ***Casually Look Over***
         2. ***Use a Prop***
         3. ***Find a Common Interest***
         4. ***Mention the Common Interest***
         5. ***Trade Information***
         6. ***Assess Interest***
            □ ***Are they talking to me?***
            □ ***Are they looking at me?***
            □ ***Are they facing me (or are they giving me the cold shoulder)?***
         7. ***Introduce Yourself***
     ○ *"Did you trade information and did you find common interests?"*
     ○ *"What could you do with that information if you were going to hang out with your social coach?"*

Didactic Lesson: Finding a Source of Friends

- Explain, *"Today, we're talking about finding a source of friends. PEERS® is a program that helps young adults learn to make and keep friends and develop close meaningful relationships, but it is not a friendship-matching group. That means that you're not here to make lasting friendships with other people in the group. If that happens, that's great. Meanwhile, we need to teach you how to find a source of friends outside of this group. To begin, we need to understand that friendship is a choice."*
- Ask, *"Do we get to be friends with everyone?"*
  ○ Answer: No.
- Ask, *"Does everyone get to be friends with us?"*
  ○ Answer: No.
- Explain, *"That's because having a friend is a CHOICE and it's important that we CHOOSE our friends wisely. There are good choices and bad choices for choosing potential friends."*
- Present each of the GOOD suggestions below for choosing friends by saying, *"Do you want to choose someone who . . ."* (while nodding your head yes). Follow each point by saying, *"Why is it important to choose someone who . . . ?"*

- o *". . . is nice and friendly to you?"*
- o *". . . is interested in you?"*
- o *". . . likes the same things as you?"*
- o *". . . is a similar age as you?"*
- Present each of the BAD suggestions below for choosing friends by saying, *"Do you want to choose someone who . . . ?"* (while shaking your head no). Follow each point by saying, *"What could be the problem with choosing someone who . . . ?"*
  - o *". . . is mean to you or makes fun of you?"*
  - o *". . . ignores you?"*
  - o *". . . takes advantage of you or uses you?"*
  - o *". . . could get you into trouble?"*

Social Groups

- Explain, *"Now that we understand that friendship is a CHOICE, and there are good choices and bad choices, we need to talk about WHERE you might find some of these good choices for friends. In most places, there are different groups of people that hang out, and they share some common interest. We call them 'social groups' and they usually have names, like gamers or techies. What are some other social groups?"*
- Have young adults brainstorm the different *social groups*.
  - o See Table 4.1 for an overview of commonly identified *social groups*.
  - o [Note: *Social groups* will be different according to culture. Do not rely on Table 4.1 as a comprehensive list. Instead, have young adults generate the list of *social groups*, as they change with time and culture.]
- Write the names of the *social groups* on the board and do not erase until the end of the lesson.

Table 4.1 Different Social Groups Identified by Young Adults

Jocks/athletes	Computer geeks/techies	Gamers/video game geeks
Sports teams	Science geeks/IT	Nerds
Sports fans	Robotics club	Brains
Cheerleaders/pep squad	Sci-fi geeks	Hip hop
Popular	Trekkies	Metalheads
Greeks/fraternities/sororities	Comic book geeks/anime geeks	Skaters
Student government	Cosplayers	Surfers
Drama/theater arts	LARPers	Hipsters
Choir/chorus/Glee club	Math geeks/mathletes	Hippies/granolas
Musicians	Newsies	Debate club/debate team
Artists	Movie buffs/movie geeks	Political groups
Ravers/partiers	Band geeks	Military groups
Preppies	Bronies/Pegasisters	Ethnic groups/cultural groups
Bookworms	Chess club/chess team	Religious groups
History buffs	Goths	LGBTQ
Animal lovers/pet lovers	Emos	Majors (source of college study)
Equestrians	Scenesters	Departments (work settings)
Motorheads/gearheads	Bikers	Industries (work settings)

- [Note: When the young adults begin to identify the different types of geeks, it will be important to present the following information and make a good pitch for being a geek. If you normalize and even promote the affiliation of being a geek, many of the young adults will identify themselves with one or more of these groups.]
- Say, *"There are lots of different kinds of geeks, and it's actually kind of cool to be a geek. That's because a 'geek' is someone that's really interested in something and really good at it. You can't just be interested in something to be a geek; you have to know about it too. For example, I might be really interested in computers, but if I don't know much about computers, do I get to be a computer geek?"*

- ○ Answer: No, absolutely not.
- Say, *"So computer geeks are really interested in computers and really good at using them. Does that mean they're proud to call themselves computer geeks?"*
  - ○ Answer: Yes, absolutely.
- Ask, *"What are some other kinds of geeks?"*
  - ○ Answers: Video game geeks or gamers; comic book geeks; anime geeks; science geeks; sci-fi geeks; math geeks; band geeks; movie geeks.
- Ask the following question about some of the different types of geeks listed below: *"What do the . . . geeks have in common?"* Follow each point by asking, *"And are they proud to call themselves . . . geeks?"*
  - ○ Computer geeks or techies
  - ○ Video game geeks or gamers
  - ○ Comic book geeks
  - ○ Science geeks

Finding Social Activities

- Explain, *"Something important to remember about these social groups is that they all share something in common with one another. A lot of these social groups hang out and even meet each other through social activities, sports, or clubs. So if our goal is to make and keep friends, and we know that friendships are based on common interests, then it's important for us to find social activities where we might meet people that have the same interests as us."*
- Present each of the interests listed in Table 4.2 and ask the question, *"So if we like (insert interest), where can we meet other people that like (insert interest)?"*

Table 4.2 Possible Social Activities

Interests	Related Social Activities
Computers/technology	Take computer classes; attend events through computer/IT department; join a technology related meet-up group; join a technology club; join a computer meet-up group; join a computer club
Video games	Go to adult video arcades with friends; go to gaming conventions; visit gaming stores; join a gaming meet-up group; join a gaming club
Science	Go to science museum events; take science classes; join a science-related meet-up group; join a science club; join a robotics club
Comic books/anime	Attend comic book conventions (i.e., ComicCon); go to comic book/anime stores; take comic book/anime drawing classes; join a comic book/anime meet-up group; join a comic book/anime club
Chess	Visit gaming stores where they play chess; attend chess tournaments; join a chess meet-up group; join a chess club
Cosplay (costume play)	Attend comic book conventions (i.e., ComicCon); take sewing classes to make costumes; join a cosplay meet-up group; join a cosplay club
LARPing (live action role playing)	Attend comic book conventions (i.e., ComicCon); take sewing classes to make costumes; attend LARPing events; join a LARPing meet-up group; join a LARPing club
Movies	Join an audiovisual club; join a movie-related meet-up group; join a movie club
Sports	Try out for a sports team; play sports at community recreation centers or parks; join a sports league; go to sporting events; attend sports camps (e.g., spring training); join a sports-related meet-up group; join a sports club
Cars	Go to car shows; visit car museums; take auto shop courses; join a car-related meet-up group; join a car club
Music	Go to concerts; join the college band; take music classes; join a music-related meet-up group; join a music club

Finding People with Common Interests

- Ask, *"So now that we've identified all of these different social groups and talked about some of the places we might find young adults who have common interests, let's talk about other ways we can identify and find these people outside of social activities. How can you tell which social group someone belongs to?"*
  - ○ Answers:
    - Appearance, clothing, hair.
    - Their interests, what they talk about.
    - What they do during free time.
    - Who they hang out with.
    - Where they hang out.
    - Social activities they belong to.
- Ask, *"If I'm a techie and I want to meet other people who like computers and technology, how will I find them if there's not a computer club or tech club to join?"*
  - ○ Answers: Techies may hang out in the computer labs on campus; take computer classes; work in IT departments or technology related industries; study information technology in college; carry around laptops and other types of technology; talk about computers with their friends; and wear T-shirts with computer or technology logos.
- Ask, *"If I'm a gamer and I want to meet other people who like video games, how will I find them if there's not a gaming club to join?"*
  - ○ Answers: Gamers may carry around portable gaming devices; play video games during breaks and before and after class or work; they talk about video games with their friends; and often wear T-shirts with gaming logos.
- Ask, *"If I'm a comic book geek or an anime geek and I want to meet other people who like comics or anime, how will I find them if there's not a comic book or anime club to join?"*
  - ○ Answers: Comic book geeks and anime geeks often carry around magazines of their favorite comics; they may draw characters on their possessions; take art classes to improve their drawing; talk about comic books or anime with their friends; talk about attending comic book conventions; and wear T-shirts with comic book or anime characters.
- Ask, *"If I'm a science geek and I want to meet other people who like science, how will I find them if there's not a science club to join?"*
  - ○ Answers: Science geeks may hang out in science labs on campus; take science classes; work in science-related industries; carry around science books or sci-fi books; talk about science with their friends; and wear T-shirts with science or sci-fi-related logos.
- Explain, *"So there are lots of ways to identify people with common interests even if we don't have access to social activities."*

Assessing Peer Acceptance or Rejection

- Explain, *"Now that we've talked about WHO we might become friends with and WHERE we might find them, we need to talk about how we can tell if we're accepted by people from these social groups. Remember that friendship is a choice. We don't get to be friends with everyone and everyone doesn't get to be friends with us. There are good choices and bad choices. Sometimes people try to be friends with people that don't want to be friends with them. That would be a bad choice."*
- Explain, *"So how can you tell if someone wants to be friends with you? Some people think it's just a feeling you get. It's true that there are feelings, but there are also concrete behaviors that tell us if we're accepted or not accepted."*
- Ask the following questions and use Table 4.3 to guide the discussion.
  - ○ Ask, *"How can you tell if you're ACCEPTED by someone?"*
  - ○ Ask, *"How can you tell if you're NOT ACCEPTED by someone?"*

Table 4.3 Signs of Acceptance and Lack of Acceptance from Social Groups

Signs You Are Accepted	Signs You Are Not Accepted
They seek you out to do things individually or in the group	They do not seek you out to do things
They talk to you and respond to your attempts to talk	They ignore you and/or do not respond to your attempts to talk
They give you their contact information	They do not give you their contact information
They ask for your contact information	They do not ask for your contact information
They text message, instant message, email, or call you just to talk	They do not text message, instant message, email, or call you
They respond to your text messages, instant messages, emails, or phone calls	They do not accept or return your calls or messages
They invite you to do things	They do not invite you to do things
They accept your invitations to do things	They do not accept your invitations or put off your invitations to do things
They add you to their social networking pages	They ignore your friend requests on social networking sites
They say nice things to you and give you compliments	They laugh at you or make fun of you

- Explain, *"We know that it feels bad when people don't want to be our friend, but we have to remember that friendship is a choice. We don't get to be friends with everyone and everyone doesn't get to be friends with us. If someone doesn't want to be our friend, we need to move on and find other people that do."*

Identifying a Source of Friends

- Explain, *"We've spent a lot of time the last two weeks trading information about the things you like to do. Now we need to think about which social groups we might fit in with based on our interests. We're going to go around the room and I want everyone to think of two or three groups that you might fit in with based on your interests. Then I want you to think of a few social activities or clubs where you might find other people who like these same things."* (See Table 4.2 for assistance.)
- Ask each young adult the following questions:
  - *"So which groups do you think you might fit in with based on your interests?"*
    - Quickly name the appropriate groups mentioned.
    - Actively ignore inappropriate groups mentioned.
  - *"Have you ever tried to hang out with people from that group before?"*
  - *"Did it seem like they accepted you?"*
    - If they say yes, ask, *"How could you tell?"*
  - *"Where can you find other young adults who are (insert social group)?"*
- After each young adult answers the questions, summarize which groups are appropriate and have a behavioral coach make a note of these groups on the *Homework Compliance Sheet* (Appendix F) to read aloud at *Reunification* with social coaches.
- Explain, *"This week, with the help of social coaches, we're going to begin to identify social activities where we can find these potential sources of friends."*

FINDING A SOURCE OF FRIENDS

Young Adult Behavioral Rehearsal

Jeopardy

Materials Needed

- Whiteboard and markers
- *Jeopardy Answer Sheets* for each young adult
- Pens
- Scissors

Rules

- Young adults will compete against themselves in this game of *trading information*.
- Like the North American TV game show *Jeopardy*, young adults will be given answers and asked to respond in the form of a question.
  - Example:
    - Group leader: *"The answer is Jimmy's favorite sport."*
    - Young adult: *"What is football?"*
  - The young adult does not have to answer in the form of a question (most do not).
  - If this group is being conducted in a country where *Jeopardy* is unknown, feel free to change the name and alter the rules accordingly.
- To promote interest and cooperation, points will be given for correct responses.
- The purpose of *Jeopardy* is not to practice *trading information* perfectly, since the young adults will sound like they are *interviewing* when asking the questions.
- The true purpose of *Jeopardy* is to improve:
  - *Topic initiation*
    - Talking about a variety of topics, rather than only restricted interests.
  - *Listening skills*
    - Listening and remembering what people share about themselves.

How to Play

- You should have saved completed *Jeopardy Answer Sheets* from the previous session.
  - If you forgot to save the answer sheets, you can have young adults complete the answer sheets found at the end of this section.
- Write the *Jeopardy Topics* on the board where young adults can see them.
  - *Favorite music*
  - *Favorite weekend activity*
  - *Favorite sport*
  - *Favorite game*
  - *Favorite movie*

- ○ *Favorite television show*
- ○ *Favorite book*
- ○ *Eye color* [Note: This is NOT to be asked, but noticed by using good eye contact. If conducting this group in a place where most people share the same eye color, feel free to replace this category.]
- Have young adults practice *trading information* about the *Jeopardy Topics* in small groups for two or three minutes each.
  - ○ Change the groups a few times (depending on the time).
  - ○ Prompt young adults to ask relevant questions about the *Jeopardy Topics* when necessary.
- Once the young adults have finished *trading information*, reconvene as a group and begin the *Jeopardy Challenge*.
  - ○ Begin by having the young adult who appears to have participated the most that week chose the first category.
  - ○ Notify the group that if they raise their hand before the question has been asked, they are disqualified from answering.
  - ○ The person who raises their hand first gets to take the first guess.
  - ○ If they provide the wrong answer, the person who raised their hand second has a chance to answer, and so on.
  - ○ The young adults get only one guess per question.
  - ○ Do not give clues.
- You may need to enforce a time limit if young adults take a long time to answer.
- Do not correct the young adults if they answer the questions in the incorrect format (i.e., instead of saying *"What is football?"* they say *"Football"*).
  - ○ All that matters is that they remembered the information they obtained through *trading information*.
- The person who answers the question correctly gets a point and gets to choose the next category.
- If no one answers correctly, the person about whom the last question relates gets to pick the next category.
- Encourage the young adults to clap and cheer for each other during the game.
- Give points for correct responses and keep track of the points on the board.
- At the end of the game, the person with the most points is the *Jeopardy Challenge Winner*.

Jeopardy Answer Sheets

Music to Your Ears The answer is: _____'s favorite band. (Name) The question is: What is _____ (favorite band)	**TGIF** The answer is: _____'s favorite weekend activity. (Name) The question is: What is _____ (favorite weekend activity)
Sports and Leisure The answer is: _____'s favorite sport. (Name) The question is: What is _____ (favorite sport)	**Game Time** The answer is: _____'s favorite game. (Name) The question is: What is _____ (favorite game)
Movies, Movies, Movies The answer is: _____'s favorite movie. (Name) The question is: What is _____ (favorite movie)	**TV Time** The answer is: _____'s favorite TV show. (Name) The question is: What is _____ (favorite TV show)
Bestseller List The answer is: _____'s favorite book. (Name) The question is: What is _____ (favorite book)	**The "Eyes" Have It** The answer is: The color of _____'s eyes. (Name) The question is: What is _____ (your eye color)

FINDING A SOURCE OF FRIENDS

Reunification

- Announce that young adults should join their social coaches.
  - ○ Have young adults stand or sit next to their social coaches.
  - ○ Be sure to have silence and the full attention of the group before starting with *Reunification*.
  - ○ Have young adults generate the content from the lesson while social coaches listen.
- Say, *"Today, we talked about finding a source of friends. In most places, there are groups of people that hang out based on some common interest. We call them social groups. Our young adults brainstormed the different types of social groups, where you might find individuals from these groups, and which groups they might fit in with based on their interests. We're going to read off the social groups identified by each young adult, so social coaches please make a note of this."*
  - ○ Have a behavioral coach read off the **social groups** identified by each young adult and then confirm these choices with the young adult.
  - ○ Have social coaches make a note of these social groups.
  - ○ Avoid having young adults identify their possible **source of friends** as they may not remember or may identify inappropriate groups.
- Say, *"This group did a great job of identifying potential sources of friends. Let's give them a round of applause."*
- Say, *"The group also played Jeopardy again where they practiced trading information. Tonight's Jeopardy Challenge Winner was (insert name). Let's give (insert name) a round of applause."*

Homework Assignments

Distribute the *Social Coaching Handout* to young adults and announce the following *Homework Assignments*:

1. Find a **source of friends**.
   - Young adults and social coaches should DISCUSS and DECIDE on **social activities** based on the young adult's interests.
   - BEGIN TO ENROLL in these activities immediately.
     - ○ Criteria for a good **social activity**:
       - ■ Is based on the young adult's interests.
       - ■ Meets weekly or at least every other week.
       - ■ Includes accepting peers similar in age.
       - ■ Includes unstructured time to interact with others.
       - ■ Activity starts within the next couple of weeks.

2. **In-group call or video chat.**
   - Arrange a phone call or video chat with another group member to trade information
   - Young adults and social coaches should schedule the day and time of the call with the other group member before leaving the group.
   - Go over the rules for **trading information** before the call.

- Social coaches should ask young adults the following *social coaching questions* after the call:
  - *What was the common interest?*
  - *What could you do with that information if you were going to hang out?*

3. Young adults and social coaches should practice *starting and maintaining a conversation, trading information*, and *finding common interests*.
   - Go over the rules for *starting and maintaining a conversation* and *trading information* before practicing.
   - Social coaches should ask young adults the following *social coaching questions* after practicing:
     - *What was the common interest?*
     - *What could we do with that information if we were going to hang out?*

4. Bring a *personal item* to *trade information*.
   - Bring a *personal item* to *trade information* with other group members next week (e.g., music, game, book, pictures).

- Read off the in-group call assignment (Appendix E) and remind social coaches to make a note of who is calling whom.
- Encourage the young adults and social coaches to use the Phone Roster (Appendix D) to note the day and time of the scheduled call each week.
  - Pass out a new Phone Roster if there were changes from the previous week.
- Young adults and social coaches should let all relevant people know if they wish to be called at a different number or if there are any errors on the current Phone Roster.
  - In the event that there are more changes, a new Phone Roster should be distributed the next week.

Individual Check-Out

Once the calls have been scheduled, individually and privately negotiate with each young adult and social coach:

1. What type of *social activity* they are interested in joining.
   - If they are already in a *social activity*, confirm that the activity:
     - Is based on the young adult's interests.
     - Meets weekly or at least every other week.
     - Includes accepting peers similar in age.
     - Includes unstructured time to interact with others.
     - Starts within the next couple of weeks.

2. Where the social coach will be during the *in-group call or video chat*.

3. When young adults and social coaches will practice *starting and maintaining a conversation, trading information*, and *finding common interests*.

4. What *personal item* they plan to bring next week.

FINDING A SOURCE OF FRIENDS

Social Coaching Handout

Social Groups

Table 4.1 Different Social Groups Identified by Young Adults

Jocks/athletes	Computer geeks/techies	Gamers/video game geeks
Sports teams	Science geeks/IT	Nerds
Sports fans	Robotics club	Brains
Cheerleaders/pep squad	Sci-fi geeks	Hip hop
Popular	Trekkies	Metalheads
Greeks/fraternities/sororities	Comic book geeks/anime geeks	Skaters
Student government	Cosplayers	Surfers
Drama/theater arts	LARPers	Hipsters
Choir/chorus/Glee club	Math geeks/mathletes	Hippies/granolas
Musicians	Newsies	Debate club/debate team
Artists	Movie buffs/movie geeks	Political groups
Ravers/partiers	Band geeks	Military groups
Preppies	Bronies/Pegasisters	Ethnic groups/cultural groups
Bookworms	Chess club/chess team	Religious groups
History buffs	Goths	LGBT
Animal lovers/pet lovers	Emos	Majors (source of college study)
Equestrians	Scenesters	Departments (work settings)
Motorheads/gearheads	Bikers	Industries (work settings)

Finding Social Activities

Table 4.2 Possible Social Activities

Interests	Related Social Activities
Computers/technology	Take computer classes; attend events through computer/IT department; join a technology related meet-up group; join a technology club; join a computer meet-up group; join a computer club
Video games	Go to adult video arcades with friends; go to gaming conventions; visit gaming stores; join a gaming meet-up group; join a gaming club
Science	Go to science museum events; take science classes; join a science-related meet-up group; join a science club; join a robotics club
Comic books/anime	Attend comic book conventions (i.e., ComicCon); go to comic book/anime stores; take comic book/anime drawing classes; join a comic book/anime meet-up group; join a comic book/anime club

Chess	Visit gaming stores where they play chess; attend chess tournaments; join a chess meet-up group; join a chess club
Cosplay (costume play)	Attend comic book conventions (i.e., ComicCon); take sewing classes to make costumes; join a cosplay meet-up group; join a cosplay club
LARPing (live action role playing)	Attend comic book conventions (i.e., ComicCon); take sewing classes to make costumes; attend LARPing events; join a LARPing meet-up group; join a LARPing club
Movies	Join an audiovisual club; join a movie-related meet-up group; join a movie club
Sports	Try out for a sports team; play sports at community recreation centers or parks; join a sports league; go to sporting events; attend sports camps (e.g., spring training); join a sports-related meet-up group; join a sports club
Cars	Go to car shows; visit car museums; take auto shop courses; join a car-related meet-up group; join a car club
Music	Go to concerts; join the college band; take music classes; join a music-related meet-up group; join a music club

Finding People with Common Interests

Clues About Social Groups and Common Interests

- Appearance, clothing, hair.
- Their interests, what they talk about.
- What they do during free time.
- Who they hang out with.
- Where they hang out.
- Social activities they belong to.

Assessing Peer Acceptance or Rejection

Table 4.3 Signs of Acceptance and Lack of Acceptance from Social Groups

Signs You Are Accepted	Signs You Are Not Accepted
They seek you out to do things individually or in the group	They do not seek you out to do things
They talk to you and respond to your attempts to talk	They ignore you and/or do not respond to your attempts to talk
They give you their contact information	They do not give you their contact information
They ask for your contact information	They do not ask for your contact information
They text message, instant message, email, or call you just to talk	They do not text message, instant message, email, or call you
They respond to your text messages, instant messages, emails, or phone calls	They do not accept or return your calls or messages
They invite you to do things	They do not invite you to do things
They accept your invitations to do things	They do not accept your invitations or put off your invitations to do things
They add you to their social networking pages	They ignore your friend requests on social networking sites
They say nice things to you and give you compliments	They laugh at you or make fun of you

Important Reminder

Friendship is a choice. We don't get to be friends with everyone and everyone doesn't get to be friends with us.

Homework Assignments

1. Find a *source of friends*.
   - Young adults and social coaches should DISCUSS and DECIDE on *social activities* based on the young adult's interests.
   - BEGIN TO ENROLL in these activities immediately.
     - Criteria for a good *social activity*:
       - Is based on the young adult's interests.
       - Meets weekly or at least every other week.
       - Includes accepting peers similar in age.
       - Includes unstructured time to interact with others.
       - Activity starts within the next couple of weeks.

2. *In-group call or video chat.*
   - Arrange a phone call or video chat with another group member to trade information.
   - Young adults and social coaches should schedule the day and time of the call with the other group member before leaving the group.
   - Go over the rules for *trading information* before the call.
   - Social coaches should ask young adults the following *social coaching questions* after the call:
     - *What was the common interest?*
     - *What could you do with that information if you were going to hang out?*

3. Young adults and social coaches should practice *starting and maintaining a conversation, trading information*, and *finding common interests*.
   - Go over the rules for *starting and maintaining a conversation* and *trading information* before practicing.
   - Social coaches should ask young adults the following *social coaching questions* after practicing:
     - *What was the common interest?*
     - *What could we do with that information if we were going to hang out?*

4. Bring a *personal item* to trade information.
   - Bring a *personal item* to *trade information* with other group members next week (e.g., music, game, book, pictures).

SESSION 4

ELECTRONIC COMMUNICATION

Social Coaching Therapist Guide

Preparing for the Social Coaching Session

The focus of the *Homework Review* in this session should be on identifying **sources of friends** and **social activities**. This may not be an issue for some young adults that already have **social activities** with accepting peers; for others, this assignment may be a struggle. Plan to spend considerable time during the *Homework Review* on helping social coaches identify appropriate **social activities** for their young adults. Avoid passing out lists of possible **social activities** as these lists tend to be outdated before you know it and may not be appropriate for each young adult. More importantly, by giving social coaches a list of possible **social activities**, you fail to teach them and their young adults how to do this independently. Ultimately, your goal is to help group members become as self-sufficient as possible, so they can support one another once the group has come to an end. Handing them a list of possible **sources of friends** is contrary to that goal. Having said that, if you see a young adult struggling to find a **source of friends**, and you or other group members have some good ideas, feel free to share them as appropriate. The latter form of help, which includes offering additional suggestions, is quite different than providing lists of **social activities**, which might give the impression that you are responsible for finding the **source of friends**.

Challenging issues that might come up in the group may include inappropriate behaviors from group members. While the majority of social coaches will be focused and eager to learn, occasionally you may have a social coach who consistently ignores the group discussion, perhaps conversing with other social coaches, texting or listening to voicemail, or even talking on his or her phone. A good rule of thumb is to intervene when the behavior is distracting to the group. One of your jobs as the group leader is to protect your group. Distracting (and even disrespectful) behavior from one group member is unfair to the entire group, so you will need to intervene. One approach to distracting side conversations is to try pausing for a few seconds, looking at the social coaches conversing to see if they will stop. Usually, this nonverbal prompt is enough to redirect their attention. Another approach might be to pause the discussion by saying, *"I'm sorry. I'm having trouble hearing."* Once you have the attention of the whole group, you can politely apologize to whoever was speaking and say, *"I'm sorry. You were saying . . ."* For particularly resistant group members who are unresponsive to these approaches, you might also be more direct by saying, *"Can we have everyone's attention please?"* Then wait for silence before continuing with the session. In extreme cases, you may need to speak to the social coach outside of the group. This is highly unusual and should be handled with delicacy. A private conversation is critical, as you would not want to embarrass the social coach. You might begin by being slightly apologetic (e.g., *"I'm sorry to have to bring this up . . ."*). Then you can briefly mention whatever the distracting behavior is (e.g., *"I noticed the last couple of weeks you've been checking your voicemail and returning text messages throughout the group."*). Then you might point out how this behavior is affecting the group (e.g., *"I'm not sure if you're aware of this, but it's a bit distracting to the group."*). Explain that it's your job to make sure everyone can get the full benefit of the program (e.g., *"I want to make sure everyone can benefit from the information we're covering."*). Then find a solution (e.g., *"I'm wondering what I can do to get your attention back on the group so you and everyone else can benefit from the lessons.").* This conversation may provide new insights into issues of treatment resistance. Often when social coaches behave in this distracting way, they are belittling the importance of the group. You will want to find out why and identify ways to overcome this treatment barrier. Strategies for overcoming treatment resistance will be discussed throughout the manual in the *Preparing for the Lesson* sections.

Homework Review

[Go over the following *Homework Assignments* and **troubleshoot** any potential problems. Start with completed homework first. If you have time, you can inquire as to why others were unable to complete the assignment and try to **troubleshoot** how they might get it done for the coming week. When reviewing homework, be sure to relabel descriptions using the **buzzwords** (identified by **bold and italicized** print). Spend the majority of the *Homework Review* on the **finding a source of friends** assignment, as this is the most important assignment.]

1. Bring a **personal item** to **trade information**.
   - Say, *"One of the assignments this week was to bring a personal item to trade information with other group members. Very quickly, let's hear what young adults brought to trade information about."*
     ○ If items are inappropriate, **troubleshoot** what they might bring next week.

2. Find a **source of friends**.
   - Say, *"Your main assignment this week was to help find a potential source of friends for your young adults and help them begin to enroll in social activities. Who was able to identify a source of friends with your young adult?"*
   - Identify if the **sources of friends** are appropriate and meet the following criteria:
     ○ Are based on the young adult's interests.
     ○ Meet weekly or at least every other week.
     ○ Include accepting peers similar in age.
     ○ Include unstructured time to interact with others.
     ○ Activity starts within the next couple of weeks.

3. **In-group call or video chat.**
   - Say, *"Another assignment this week was for your young adult to have a phone call or video chat with someone in the group in order to practice trading information. Whose young adult did the in-group call or video chat?"*
   - Ask the following questions:
     ○ *"Who did your young adult talk to and who called whom?"*
     ○ *"What social coaching did you do before the call?"*
     ○ *"Where were you during the call?"*
     ○ *"Did they trade information and find a common interest?"*
     ○ *"What social coaching did you do after the call?"*
       ■ Appropriate **social coaching questions**:
         □ **What was your common interest?**
         □ **What could you do with that information if you were going to hang out?**
   - Have the other social coach who participated in the call or video chat give their account immediately after, but not at the same time.

4. Young adults and social coaches should have practiced **starting and maintaining a conversation, trading information**, and **finding common interests**.
   - Say, *"Another assignment this week was to practice starting and maintaining a conversation, trading information, and finding common interests with your young adult. Who completed or attempted to complete this assignment?"*
   - Focus on completed or attempted assignments and ask the following questions:
     ○ *"Did your young adult practice starting and maintaining a conversation with you?"*
     ○ *"Did you go over the rules and steps before practicing?"*

■ *Steps for Starting a Conversation*:
1. **Casually Look Over**
2. **Use a Prop**
3. **Find a Common Interest**
4. **Mention the Common Interest**
5. **Trade Information**
6. **Assess Interest**
    □ *Are they talking to me?*
    □ *Are they looking at me?*
    □ *Are they facing me (or are they giving me the cold shoulder)?*
7. **Introduce Yourself**
○ *"Did your young adult practice trading information?"*
○ *"Did you ask the social coaching questions after practicing?"*
   ■ Appropriate *social coaching questions*:
      □ **What was the common interest?**
      □ **What could we do with that information if we were going to hang out?**

● [Collect the *Social Coaching Homework Assignment Worksheets*. If social coaches forgot to bring the worksheets, have them complete a new form to hold them accountable for the assignments.]

Didactic Lesson: Electronic Communication

● Distribute the *Social Coaching Handout*.
   ○ Sections in **bold print** in the *Social Coaching Therapist Guide* come directly from the *Social Coaching Handout*.
   ○ Remind social coaches that terms that are in **bold and italicized** print are **buzzwords** and represent important concepts from the PEERS® curriculum that should be used as much as possible when social coaching.
● Explain, *"Today, we're going to be talking about electronic communication. This includes things like making phone calls, texting, instant messaging, social networking, emails, video chat, and using the Internet. Electronic communication is a very popular way for young adults to talk to one another, so we need to know what the rules are."*

Exchanging Contact Information

● Explain, *"One of the most popular ways for young adults to communicate is through the phone, especially through texting. In order to text or use any form of electronic communication, we need to exchange contact information. That means exchanging phone numbers and screen names. There are very specific steps for exchanging contact information."*

Steps for Exchanging Contact Information

1. **Trade information multiple times**
   ● Example: *"I remember you saying that you like sci-fi movies."*

2. **Find a common interest**
   ● Example: *"I like sci-fi movies, too. Have you seen that new one that came out last weekend?"*

3. **Use the common interest as a cover story for contact**
   ● Example: *"Maybe we should go see it together."*

4. **Assess their interest**
   ● Signs of interest: They agree; they seem eager; if they're busy, they try to find another time that works.
      ○ If interested, you can proceed to the next step.
   ● Signs of disinterest: They don't agree; they're hesitant; they make excuses; they say they're busy and don't try to find a time that works.

      ○   If NOT interested, shift the subject back to the common interest.
         ■ Example: *"Well anyway, you should definitely check it out."*

5. ***Suggest exchanging contact information***
   - Example: *"We should exchange numbers."*

- [Optional: Show BAD and GOOD *Role Play Video Demonstrations* of **exchanging contact information** from the *PEERS® Role Play Video Library* (www.routledge.com/cw/laugeson).]

Phone Calls

Explain, *"We know most young adults use the phone for text messaging, and not so much for talking, but sometimes they still have to make a call. Because they don't use the phone as much in that way, it can be difficult to know how to begin and end phone calls. There are very specific steps for starting and ending phone calls."*

Steps for Starting Phone Calls

1. ***Ask for the person***
   - Example: *"Hi. May I please speak to Jennifer?"*
   - Exception: You don't need to **ask for the person** if it's a private cell phone and you are certain it's the person you're calling.

2. ***Say who you are***
   - Example: *"Hi, Jennifer. This is Carrie."*
   - Exception: You don't need to **say who you are** if they say hello by using your name because of caller ID.

3. ***Ask how they are***
   - Example: *"How's it going?"*

4. ***Ask if they can talk***
   - Example: *"Can you talk right now?"*

5. ***Give a cover story for why you are calling***
   - Example: *"I was just calling to see how you're doing."*
   - ***Cover stories*** are reasons you do things (in this case, the reason you are calling).
   - Have the social coaches come up with different examples of ***cover stories*** (see Table 5.1).

- [Optional: Show BAD and GOOD *Role Play Video Demonstrations* of **beginning phone calls** from the *PEERS® Role Play Video Library* (www.routledge.com/cw/laugeson).]

Steps for Ending Phone Calls

1. ***Wait for a bit of a pause***
   - This is a transitional moment, so try not to interrupt.

2. ***Give a cover story for why you have to go***
   - Example: *"Well, I better get back to work."*
   - ***Cover stories*** are reasons you do things (in this case, the reason you have to get off the phone).
   - Have the social coaches come up with different examples of ***cover stories*** (see Table 5.1).

3. ***Tell the person it was nice talking***
   - Example: *"It was nice talking to you."*

4. ***Tell the person you will talk to them later***
   - Example: *"I'll talk to you later."*

5. ***Say goodbye***
   - Example: *"Bye."*

- [Optional: Show BAD and GOOD *Role Play Video Demonstrations* of **ending phone calls** from the *PEERS® Role Play Video Library* (www.routledge.com/cw/laugeson).]

Table 5.1 Cover Story Examples

Reasons You Are Calling	Reasons You Have to Hang Up
"Just calling to see how you're doing." *"Just calling to hear what's up with you."* *"I'm calling with a work/school question."* *"I haven't talked to you in a while."* *"I was wondering what you've been up to."*	*"I have to get going."* *"I better let you go."* *"I need to finish studying."* *"It's time for dinner."* *"I have to get back to work."*

Voicemail

Explain, *"Sometimes our young adults call someone on the phone and they get their voicemail. Many young adults feel uncomfortable leaving voicemail, but it doesn't have to be uncomfortable if they know the steps to follow."*

Steps for Leaving Voicemail

1. **Say who you are**
   - Example: *"Hi, this is Carrie."*

2. **Say who you are calling for**
   - Example: *"I'm calling for Jennifer."*
   - Exception: You don't need to **say who you are calling for** if it's a private line (e.g., private cell phone, private work extension).

3. **Say when you are calling**
   - Example: *"It's about 6 o'clock on Thursday night."*

4. **Give a cover story for calling**
   - Example: *"I was just calling to see what you've been up to."*

5. **Leave your phone number**
   - Example: *"Give me a call at 310-555-1212."*
   - Exception: You don't need to leave your phone number if you talk regularly, but don't assume they have you in their contacts or their caller ID.

6. **Say goodbye**
   - Example: *"Talk to you soon. Bye."*

- [Optional: Show BAD and GOOD *Role Play Video Demonstrations* of **leaving voicemail** from the *PEERS® Role Play Video Library* (www.routledge.com/cw/laugeson).]

General Rules for Using Electronic Communication

Explain, "Now that we have some rules and steps for exchanging contact information and making phone calls, it's also important for us to understand the rules for things like texting, instant messaging, emailing, and using social networking sites."

- **Identify yourself when contacting new people**
  - Ask, *"When we're texting, instant messaging, or emailing new people, why would it be important to identify who we are?"*
    - Answer: So they won't ask, *"Who is this?"*
  - Say, *"You NEVER want to start a conversation with 'Who is this?'! Instead, you should identify yourself. How do we do that?"*
    - Answer: *"This is (your name)."*
  - Ask, *"Do we have to identify ourselves with people we normally text, IM, or email?"*
    - Answer: No.

- *Use cover stories for contacting people you don't know well*
  - ○ Explain, *"Just like with phone calls, we need to use cover stories when we're texting, instant messaging, emailing, or video chatting with people we don't know well."*
  - ○ Ask, *"What could be the problem with not using cover stories with people we don't know well?"*
    - ■ Answers: They will wonder why you are contacting them; they may even ask, *"What do you want?"*
  - ○ Say, *"We NEVER want to start a conversation with 'What do you want?'! But do we always need to use cover stories for text messaging, instant messaging, emailing, or video chatting our close friends?"*
    - ■ Answer: No, but it doesn't hurt to use cover stories even with close friends.

- *Don't call or text before or after double digits*
  - ○ Explain, *"Another important rule for electronic communication is don't call or text before or after double digits. That means don't call, video chat, or text someone before 10 a.m. or after 10 p.m."*
  - ○ Ask, *"What could be the problem with calling or texting before or after double digits?"*
    - ■ Answers: You might wake them up; it may be too early or too late.

- *Don't get too personal*
  - ○ Explain, *"Another important rule for using electronic communication is don't get too personal. This is true even if you know the person well."*
  - ○ Ask, *"What could be the problem with getting too personal over texting, instant messaging, email, voicemail, video chat, or social media?"*
    - ■ Answers: **Anyone can see, read, or hear what you sent**; you may embarrass the other person by getting too personal; you may embarrass yourself if other people see, read, or hear what you sent.
  - ○ Explain, *"Since you can't control who sees, reads, or hears what you send, a good rule is to only send what you are comfortable having anyone see, read, or hear. Save the personal stuff for when you're actually in person."*

- *Use the two-message rule*
  - ○ Explain, *"Sometimes when we contact people electronically, we don't get a hold of them. About how many messages can we leave in a row without hearing back before we stop trying?"*
    - ■ Answer: Two or less.
  - ○ Explain, *"The answer is TWO times. It's called the two-message rule and it means that we shouldn't leave more than two messages in a row without hearing back. We can leave one, but we can't leave more than two."*
  - ○ Ask, *"What could be the problem with leaving more than two messages in a row?"*
    - ■ Answers: The other person may be busy; they may not want to talk to you; you may seem creepy; they might think you're a stalker.
  - ○ Ask, *"What if we don't leave a voicemail message? Is it okay to call and hang up more than two times in a row?"*
    - ■ Answers: No, they will see that you called; missed calls count in the **two-message rule**.
  - ○ Ask, *"Does the two-message rule mean that we can leave TWO voicemails, TWO text messages, TWO instant messages, and TWO emails in a row without hearing back?"*
    - ■ Answer: No, the **two-message rule** crosses all forms of electronic communication.
  - ○ Explain, *"There's one exception to the two-message rule. That's if we're trying to 'friend' someone on Facebook or some other social networking site. When we try to 'friend' someone, they have the option to 'accept' or 'ignore' our request."*
  - ○ Ask, *"If someone ignores your 'friend' request, what should you do?"*
    - ■ Answers: **Move on** and find someone else to "friend" that knows you and seems interested in you; do not try to "friend" the same person twice.
  - ○ Ask, *"What could be the problem with sending more than one 'friend' request?"*
    - ■ Answer: They might think you are desperate, creepy, or a stalker.

- *Avoid cold-calling*
  - ○ Say, *"Another rule for using electronic communication is that we need to avoid cold-calling."*
  - ○ Ask, *"Does anyone know what cold-calling is?"*

- ■ Answers: Cold-calling is contacting someone who has not given you their phone number or screen name; it is what telemarketers do.
  - ○ Explain the following:
    - ■ Giving out a phone number, IM, email address, or screen name is giving someone permission to contact you.
    - ■ Just because you may have access to someone's contact information in a school directory or online directory does not give you permission to contact that person.
  - ○ Ask, *"What could be the problem with cold calling someone without their permission?"*
    - ■ Answers: They might think you are strange, weird, creepy or a stalker; they may ask, *"How did you get my phone number?"*
  - ○ Explain, *"You NEVER want to start a conversation with 'How did you get my number?'!"*
  - ○ Ask, *"What if you're Facebook friends with someone and they have their contact information on their profile page . . . does that give you permission to contact them?"*
    - ■ Answers: Not at all; that is still cold-calling and they may think you are creepy and weird.
  - ○ Explain, *"Instead of cold-calling, we should use the steps for exchanging contact information."*

Staying Safe Online

- ● Explain, *"We all know that the Internet is a very popular way for young adults to socialize, and many of your young adults are probably online and even use social networking sites like Facebook. But just like with any kind of communication, there are rules about how to be safe when you're online."*
- ● Explain, *"The main rule about being safe is that young adults should be cautious when using the Internet to make NEW friends online."*
- ● Ask, *"What could be the problem with making NEW friends online?"*
  - ○ Answers: It could be dangerous; you do not know who they are; the person could have bad intentions.
- ● Say, *"The area where this gets confusing for our young adults is when it comes to online friends. What's the difference between 'online friends' and 'real-life friends'?"*
  - ○ Answers: **Online friends** are people you may play games with online, but you do not know in real life; **real-life friends** are people you know in person.
- ● Ask, *"What could be the problem with turning 'online friends' into 'real-life friends'?"*
  - ○ Answers: You do not know who that person is; they could be dangerous; they could have bad intentions.
- ● Ask, *"There is an exception to this rule. It relates to meet-up groups and online dating. Do a lot of adults join meet-up groups and do online dating?"*
  - ○ Answer: Yes.
- ● Say, *"But even with meet-up groups, you have to apply to join them. That helps to protect people so not just anyone can show up to the group. What are some other ways young adults can be safe when attending meet-up groups?"*

  - ○ **Safety tips for attending meet-up groups:**
    - ■ **Only meet in public places where there are lots of people around.**
    - ■ **Do not go anywhere alone with group members.**
    - ■ **Do not accept rides from group members.**
    - ■ **Find your own transportation to and from the meet-up group.**
    - ■ **Let your friends and family know where you're going, with whom, and when.**
    - ■ **Check in with family and friends before and after the meet-up group.**
    - ■ **Attend meet-up groups with other friends when possible.**

- ● Explain, *"The same strategies apply to online dating. There are lots of ways that we can stay safe when meeting people online. When we get to the dating lessons, we will talk about some other ways to stay safe when online dating."*
  - ○ [Note: If any social coaches express concern about their young adult online dating, you may want to have a **side meeting** to go over *Safety Tips for Online Dating* from Session 11.]

- Ask, *"Meanwhile, is it okay for young adults to use the Internet to develop stronger friendships with people they already know, or reconnect with friends they haven't talked to in a while?"*
  - Answer: Yes, absolutely.
- Explain, *"The bottom line is that the Internet is very useful for developing closer friendships with PREEXISTING friends, but young adults should be cautious when using it to make NEW friends."*

  - Suggestions for young adults to stay safe online:
    - Try to avoid giving your personal information to strangers online.
    - Avoid meeting strangers from the Internet unless it's through meet-up groups or online dating websites (and then take precautions).
    - Be cautious about accepting invitations to be "friends" with strangers on Facebook or other social networking sites.

- Explain, *"In fact, 'friending' a person you don't actually know is technically against Facebook's terms and conditions."*

    - Do not send friend requests to strangers.
    - Do not post your contact information on your profile pages.
    - Use privacy settings on Facebook and other social networking sites so your account is not open for anyone to view.

- Explain, *"Those are some of the rules for using electronic communication. We're going have young adults practice using electronic communication this week with social coaches and when trading information during in-group calls or video chats."*

Homework Assignments

[Distribute the *Social Coaching Homework Assignment Worksheet* (Appendix I) for social coaches to complete and return at the next session.]

1. **Find a *source of friends*.**
- Young adults and social coaches should DISCUSS and DECIDE on *social activities* based on the young adult's interests.
- BEGIN TO ENROLL in these activities immediately.
  - Criteria for a good *social activity*:
    - Is based on the young adult's interests.
    - Meets weekly or at least every other week.
    - Includes accepting peers similar in age.
    - Includes unstructured time to interact with others.
    - Activity starts within the next couple of weeks.

2. ***Start a conversation*** and ***trade information*** with a peer (could be from the *source of friends*).
   - Social coaches should go over the rules and steps for *starting and maintaining a conversation* and *trading information* before the practice.
   - Social coaches should ask young adults the following *social coaching questions* after the practice:
     - *Did you start a conversation and with whom?*
     - *Did it seem like they wanted to talk to you and how could you tell?*
     - *Did you trade information and what were your common interests?*
     - *What could you do with that information if you were going to hang out?*
     - *Does this seem like someone you might want to hang out with?*

3. ***In-group call or video chat.***
   - Arrange a phone call or video chat with another group member to trade information.
   - Young adults and social coaches should schedule the day and time of the call with the other group member before leaving the group.

- Go over the rules for *starting and ending phone calls* and *trading information* before the call.
- Social coaches should ask young adults the following *social coaching questions* after the call:
  - *Which steps did you follow for starting the call?*
    - Steps are slightly modified if doing a video chat (i.e., you don't **ask for the person** or *say who you are*).
  - *What was the common interest?*
  - *What could you do with that information if you were going to hang out?*
  - *Which steps did you follow to end the call?*

4. Young adults and social coaches should practice *starting and ending a phone call* while *trading information* and *finding common interests*.
   - Go over the rules for *starting and ending phone calls* and *trading information* before practicing.
   - Social coaches should ask young adults the following *social coaching questions* after practicing:
     - *Which steps did you follow for starting the call?*
     - *What was the common interest?*
     - *What could we do with that information if we were going to hang out?*
     - *Which steps did you follow to end the call?*

5. Bring a *personal item* to *trade information*.
   - Bring a *personal item* to *trade information* with other group members next week (e.g., music, game, book, pictures).

Social Coaching Tips

Additional Strategies to Keep Young Adults Safe on Social Networking Sites

- Social coaches might assist young adults in adjusting privacy settings on their social networking sites so their account is not open for anyone to view.
- Follow or become "friends" with your young adult on their social networking sites.
  - Monitor what they're posting.
  - Make sure their contact information is not on their profile page.
  - Monitor who they're "friends" with or who is following them.
    - If they are "friends" with someone unfamiliar to you, find out how they know them.
    - Discourage attempts to accept strangers' friend requests.
    - Discourage attempts to friend request strangers.
  - If you don't know how to set up your own social networking page:
    - Have your young adult teach you.
    - Have another caregiver monitor for you (e.g., an adult sibling).

ELECTRONIC COMMUNICATION

Young Adult Therapist Guide

Preparing for the Young Adult Session

It seems that with every succeeding generation, young adults learn to use more sophisticated forms of electronic communication. In fact, electronic communication is an integral part of young adult culture, particularly text messaging, instant messaging (IM), and social networking sites. The popularity of online games, MMOs (massively multiplayer online games), and video-sharing websites is also dramatically increasing among young adults. The focus of this lesson will be on how to effectively navigate these forms of electronic communication.

The purpose of this lesson is to help young adults learn the appropriate uses of electronic forms of communication with peers. For some young adults, the portion of the *Didactic Lesson* on using the telephone will already be included in their repertoire. For others, using the telephone, apart from texting or video chatting, will be less familiar. Some young adults will even claim that no one makes phone calls anymore. While it's true that fewer and fewer young adults use the phone just to talk, it is still difficult to get through life and navigate social relationships without knowing how to make a phone call once in a while. The challenge with this part of the lesson may be to keep young adults' interest until you move onto more sophisticated forms of electronic communication. The *Role Play Demonstrations* will be helpful in this respect. It can also be helpful to point out to the young adults that although some of them may already know these skills, it is very easy to forget one or two of the steps. You might even have them think of a time when someone forgot one of the steps and how it affected their conversation. For example, you might say, *"I know it seems obvious that you should identify yourself when calling someone on the phone, but how many of you have had people call that didn't identify themselves and you had no idea who you were talking to? It seems obvious and yet people often forget!"*

During the online safety portion of the *Didactic Lesson*, it is common for one or two young adults to challenge the point that we should be cautious about turning **online friends** into **real-life friends**. With the rising popularity of social networking sites, young adults often use the Internet to communicate with strangers as well as friends. While the latter is perfectly appropriate, the former has the capacity to be dangerous if certain precautions are not taken. As described in previous lessons, the best way to handle objections from young adults is to open it up to the group by asking, **"What could be the problem with . . . ?"** In this case, you can ask the group, *"What could be the problem with turning online friends into real-life friends?"* The other young adults will quickly offer that it can be unsafe and may even launch into news stories about online relationships that turned dangerous. This discussion should be bridged with caution, particularly as the concept relates to meet-up groups and online dating. Meet-up groups are social networking groups for adults that share some **common interest**. At the time of writing this manual, websites such as www.meetup.com have become quite popular across the globe, and may provide a good **source of friends** with **common interests** for young adults. In order to join these groups, you have to contact the group organizer and apply. This protects the group and the person applying, as not just anyone can show up to the meet-up group. Online dating has also become a very popular method for meeting potential romantic partners. However, since meet-up groups and online dating could involve certain risks, precautions should be taken (e.g., meeting in public, notifying family and friends where you are going, checking in with family and friends before and after the date, etc.). Many of these precautions will be described in detail during the current lesson. However, for young adults currently online dating, be prepared for additional questions to arise during this session. Although we will discuss additional strategies for being safe when online dating during the dating lessons, you may want to review the section on *Safety Tips for Online Dating* in Session 11 should questions arise. Once you have made the point about being cautious when turning **online friends** into **real-life friends**, remind young adults that the Internet can also be very helpful in strengthening current friendships and developing friendships with preexisting acquaintances.

Homework Review

[Go over the following *Homework Assignments* and **troubleshoot** any potential problems. Start with completed homework first. If you have time, you can inquire as to why others were unable to complete the assignment and try to **troubleshoot** how they might get it done for the coming week. When reviewing homework, be sure to relabel descriptions using the **buzzwords** (identified by **bold and italicized** print). Spend the majority of the *Homework Review* on the **finding a source of friends** assignment, as this is the most important assignment.]

1. Bring a **personal item** to **trade information**.
   - Say, *"One of the assignments this week was to bring a personal item to trade information with other group members. Very quickly, let's hear what you brought to trade information."*
     - Have young adults place these items somewhere off to the side of the room to avoid distractions.
     - If items are inappropriate, **troubleshoot** what they might bring next week.

2. Find a **source of friends**.
   - Say, *"Your main assignment this week was to find a potential source of friends with the help of your social coaches and begin to enroll in social activities. Who was able to identify a source of friends?"*
   - Identify if the **sources of friends** are appropriate and meet the following criteria:
     - Are based on the young adult's interests.
     - Meet weekly or at least every other week.
     - Include accepting peers similar in age.
     - Include unstructured time to interact with others.
     - Activity starts within the next couple of weeks.

3. **In-group call or video chat**.
   - Say, *"Another assignment you had this week was to have a phone call or video chat with someone in the group in order to practice trading information. Raise your hand if you did the in-group call or video chat."*
   - Ask the following questions:
     - *"Who did you talk to and who called whom?"*
     - *"Did you trade information and did you find a common interest?"*
     - *"What could you do with that information if you were going to hang out?"*
   - Have the other person who participated in the call or video chat give their account immediately after, but not at the same time.

4. Young adults and social coaches should have practiced **starting and maintaining a conversation**, **trading information**, and **finding common interests**.
   - Say, *"Another assignment this week was to practice starting and maintaining a conversation, trading information, and finding common interests with a social coach. Raise your hand if you traded information with your social coach this week."*
   - Ask the following questions:

○ *"Did you practice starting a conversation and which steps did you follow?"*
  ▪ **Steps for Starting Conversation**
    1. **Casually Look Over**
    2. **Use a Prop**
    3. **Find a Common Interest**
    4. **Mention the Common Interest**
    5. **Trade Information**
    6. **Assess Interest**
       ▫ **Are they talking to me?**
       ▫ **Are they looking at me?**
       ▫ **Are they facing me (or are they giving me the cold shoulder)?**
    7. **Introduce Yourself (if they seem interested)**
○ *"Did you trade information and did you find common interests?"*
○ *"What could you do with that information if you were going to hang out with your social coach?"*

Didactic Lesson: Electronic Communication

- Explain, *"Today, we're going to be talking about electronic communication. This includes things like making phone calls, texting, instant messaging, social networking, emails, video chat, and using the Internet. Electronic communication is a very popular way for young adults to talk to one another, so we need to know what the rules are."*

- [Present the rules and steps for electronic communication by writing the following bullet points and buzzwords (identified by bold and italicized print) on the board. Do not erase the rules until the end of the lesson. Each role play with a sc symbol includes a corresponding role play video from the PEERS® Role Play Video Library (www.routledge.com/cw/laugeson).]

Exchanging Contact Information ⊙

- Say, *"One of the most popular ways for young adults to communicate is through the phone, especially through texting. In order to text or use any form of electronic communication, we need to exchange contact information. That means exchanging phone numbers and screen names. There are very specific steps for exchanging contact information."*

Bad Role Play: Exchanging Contact Information ⊙

[The group leader and behavioral coach should do an INAPPROPRIATE role play of exchanging contact information.]

- Begin by saying, *"Watch this and tell me what I'm doing WRONG."*

Example of an INAPPROPRIATE Role Play

○ Behavioral coach: (Looking at cell phone)
○ Group leader: (Abruptly walks up) *"Hey. Can I get your number?"*
○ Behavioral coach: (Startled, confused) *"What?"*
○ Group leader: (Overly eager) *"Can I get your number?"*
○ Behavioral coach: (Startled, confused, uncomfortable) *"Umm, I don't think so."*
○ Group leader: (Moving closer, overly eager) *"Oh, come on. Let me get your number."*
○ Behavioral coach: (Moving away, looking away, annoyed) *"No, I don't think so."*
○ Group leader: *"Why not?"*
○ Behavioral coach: (Looking away, trying to find an escape)

- End by saying, *"Timeout on that. So what did I do WRONG in trying to exchange contact information?"*
  ○ Answer: You just walked up and randomly asked for their number and wouldn't take no for an answer.

- Ask the following *Perspective Taking Questions*:
  - ○ *"What was that like for (name of behavioral coach)?"*
    - ▪ Answers: Strange; confusing; weird; uncomfortable.
  - ○ *"What do you think (name of behavioral coach) thought of me?"*
    - ▪ Answers: Weird; odd; creepy; stalker.
  - ○ *"Is (name of behavioral coach) going to want to talk to me again?"*
    - ▪ Answers: No; too creepy.
- Ask the behavioral coach the same *Perspective Taking Questions*:
  - ○ *"What was that like for you?"*
  - ○ *"What did you think of me?"*
  - ○ *"Would you want to talk to me again?"*

Steps for Exchanging Contact Information

1. *Trade information multiple times*
   - Example: *"I remember you saying that you like sci-fi movies."*

2. *Find a common interest*
   - Example: *"I like sci-fi movies, too. Have you seen that new one that came out last weekend?"*

3. *Use the common interest as a cover story for contact*
   - Example: *"Maybe we should go see it together."*

4. *Assess their interest*
   - Signs of interest: They agree; they seem eager; if they're busy, they try to find another time that works.
     - ○ If interested, you can proceed to the next step.
   - Signs of disinterest: They don't agree; they're hesitant; they make excuses; they say they're busy and don't try to find a time that works.
     - ○ If NOT interested, shift the *subject* back to the *common interest*.
       - ▪ Example: *"Well anyway, you should definitely check it out."*

5. *Suggest exchanging contact information*
   - Example: *"We should exchange numbers."*
     - ○ Explain the following about *exchanging contact information*:
       - ▪ Sometimes the person hands you their phone.
         - □ They do that so you can program your number in their phone.
       - ▪ Sometimes the person dials your number and lets it ring.
         - □ Don't answer the call! Just let it ring and then hang up.
         - □ They do that so you both have your numbers in your phone history. You are meant to program their name in later.

Good Role Play: Exchanging Contact Information ⊙

[The group leader and behavioral coach should do an APPROPRIATE role play of exchanging contact information.]

- Begin by saying, *"Watch this and tell me what I'm doing RIGHT."*

Example of an APPROPRIATE Role Play

- ○ Behavioral coach: (Looking at cell phone)
- ○ Group leader: (Walks over) *"Hi, (insert name)."*
- ○ Behavioral coach: (Looks up) *"Hi, (insert name)."*
- ○ Group leader: *"Did you have a good weekend?"*

> ○ Behavioral coach: (Friendly) *"Yeah, I did. I went to the movies."*
> ○ Group leader: (Interested, curious) *"Oh yeah? Did you see that new sci-fi movie? I remember you saying you like sci-fi."*
> ○ Behavioral coach: (Disappointed) *"I didn't, but I really want to see it."*
> ○ Group leader: (Casual) *"Yeah, me too. (pause) Maybe we should see it together."*
> ○ Behavioral coach: (Eager) *"That would be cool!"*
> ○ Group leader: (Eager) *"Great. So I guess I should get your number."*
> ○ Behavioral coach: (Friendly, eager, takes out phone) *"Sure."*
> ○ Group leader: (Takes out phone) *"Okay, what is it?"*
> ○ Behavioral coach: *"310-555-1212."*
> ○ Group leader: (Types in phone and lets it ring)
> ○ Behavioral coach: (Hangs up call without answering) *"Cool. Now I have yours too."*
> ○ Group leader: (Friendly) *"Great. So I'll text you later to make plans."*
> ○ Behavioral coach: (Friendly) *"Sounds good!"*

- End by saying, *"Timeout on that. So what did I do RIGHT in exchanging contact information?"*
  - Answers: You **traded information multiple times**; **found a common interest**; **used the common interest as a cover story for contact**; **assessed interest**; and **suggested exchanging contact information**.
- Ask the following **Perspective Taking Questions**:
  - *"What was that like for (name of behavioral coach)?"*
    - Answers: Fine; comfortable; pleasant.
  - *"What do you think (name of behavioral coach) thought of me?"*
    - Answers: Normal; cool; friendly.
  - *"Is (name of behavioral coach) going to want to talk to me again?"*
    - Answer: Yes.
- Ask the behavioral coach the same **Perspective Taking Questions**:
  - *"What was that like for you?"*
  - *"What did you think of me?"*
  - *"Would you want to talk to me again?"*

Behavioral Rehearsal: Exchanging Contact Information

- Explain, *"Now we're going to go around the room and have each of you practice exchanging contact information. We're going to figure out what you like to do on the weekends and then imagine I like to do the same thing. Then you will practice suggesting exchanging contact information with me while everyone watches."*
- Go around the room and have each young adult practice **exchanging contact information** with the group leader in the following way:
  - Ask, *"What do you like to do on the weekend?"*
  - Say, *"Now imagine that I like to do that too, and we've traded information about that multiple times. Now follow the steps for exchanging contact information with me."*
- End by giving a round of applause to each young adult after their practice.
- [Note: If a young adult has difficulty **exchanging contact information**, privately assign an extra *Homework Assignment* during *Reunification* to practice this during the week with the social coach.]

Phone Calls

- Say, *"We know most young adults use the phone for text messaging, and not so much for talking, but sometimes you just have to make a call. Because we don't use the phone as much in that way, it can be difficult to know how to begin and end phone calls. There are very specific steps for starting and ending phone calls."*

Bad Role Play: Starting Phone Calls ⊙

[The group leader and behavioral coach should do an INAPPROPRIATE role play of starting a phone call.]

- Begin by saying, *"Watch this and tell me what I'm doing WRONG."*

> **Example of an INAPPROPRIATE Role Play**
>
> ○ Group leader: (Hold a cell phone to your ear) *"Ring, ring."*
> ○ Behavioral coach: (Pick up a cell phone) *"Hello?"*
> ○ Group leader: *"Hey. What are you doing?"*
> ○ Behavioral coach: (Confused, looking at phone) *"Umm, watching TV."*
> ○ Group leader: *"Oh, what are you watching?"*
> ○ Behavioral coach: (Confused, looking at phone again) *"I'm watching the game."*
> ○ Group leader: *"Oh yeah? What game?"*
> ○ Behavioral coach: (Confused, annoyed) *"Umm, (mention two popular sports teams)."*
> ○ Group leader: *"So which team are you rooting for?"*
> ○ Behavioral coach: (Confused, annoyed, looking at phone again) *"Umm . . . I don't know."*

- End by saying, *"Timeout on that. So what did I do WRONG in starting that phone call?"*
  - ○ Answers: You did not ask for the person; didn't give your name; didn't ask how the person was doing; didn't ask if the person could talk; didn't give a reason for calling.
- Ask the following **Perspective Taking Questions**:
  - ○ *"What was that like for (name of behavioral coach)?"*
    - ▪ Answers: Strange; confusing; weird
  - ○ *"What do you think (name of behavioral coach) thought of me?"*
    - ▪ Answers: Weird; odd; creepy; stalker.
  - ○ *"Is (name of behavioral coach) going to want to talk to me again?"*
    - ▪ Answers: Probably not; too weird.
- Ask the behavioral coach the same **Perspective Taking Questions**:
  - ○ *"What was that like for you?"*
  - ○ *"What did you think of me?"*
  - ○ *"Would you want to talk to me again?"*

Steps for Starting Phone Calls

1. **Ask for the person**
   - Example: *"Hi. May I please speak to Jennifer?"*
     - ○ Exception: You don't need to **ask for the person** if it's a private cell phone and you are certain it's the person you're calling.

2. **Say who you are**
   - Example: *"Hi, Jennifer. This is Carrie."*
     - ○ Exception: You don't need to **say who you are** if they say hello by using your name because of caller ID.

3. **Ask how they are**
   - Example: *"How's it going?"*

4. **Ask if they can talk**
   - Example: *"Can you talk right now?"*

5. **Give a cover story for why you are calling**
   - Example: *"I was just calling to see how you're doing."*
   - **Cover stories** are reasons you do things (in this case, the reason you are calling).
   - Have the young adults come up with different examples of **cover stories** (see Table 5.1).

Table 5.1 Cover Story Examples

Reasons You Are Calling	Reasons You Have to Hang Up
"Just calling to see how you're doing." *"Just calling to hear what's up with you."* *"I'm calling with a work/school question."* *"I haven't talked to you in a while."* *"I was wondering what you've been up to."*	*"I have to get going."* *"I better let you go."* *"I need to finish studying."* *"It's time for dinner."* *"I have to get back to work."*

Good Role Play: Starting Phone Calls ⊙

[The group leader and behavioral coach should do an APPROPRIATE role play of starting a phone call.]

- Begin by saying, *"Watch this and tell me what I'm doing RIGHT."*

> Example of an APPROPRIATE Role Play
>
> ○ Group leader: (Hold a cell phone to your ear) *"Ring, ring."*
> ○ Behavioral coach: (Pick up a cell phone) *"Hello?"*
> ○ Group leader: *"Hi. Can I speak to (insert name)?"*
> ○ Behavioral coach: *"This is (insert name)."*
> ○ Group leader: *"Hi. This is (insert name)."*
> ○ Behavioral coach: *"Oh, hey! How's it going?"*
> ○ Group leader: *"Pretty well. How are you?"*
> ○ Behavioral coach: *"I'm good."*
> ○ Group leader: *"So can you talk right now?"*
> ○ Behavioral coach: *"Sure."*
> ○ Group leader: *"So I was just calling to see how you've been doing."*
> ○ Behavioral coach: *"Oh, I'm good. Just watching the game."*
> ○ Group leader: *"Oh yeah? Which game?"*
> ○ Behavioral coach: *"(Mention two popular sports teams.)"*
> ○ Group leader: (Playfully) *"So who are you rooting for?"*
> ○ Behavioral coach: (Excited) *"Definitely (mention one of the teams)!"*

- End by saying, *"Timeout on that. So what did I do RIGHT in starting that phone call?"*
  - ○ **Answers: Asked for the person; said who you were; asked how they were doing; asked if they could talk; gave a cover story for calling.**
- Ask the following *Perspective Taking Questions*:
  - ○ *"What was that like for (name of behavioral coach)?"*
  - ○ Answers: Fine; comfortable; pleasant.
  - ○ *"What do you think (name of behavioral coach) thought of me?"*
    - ■ Answers: Normal; cool; friendly.
  - ○ *"Is (name of behavioral coach) going to want to talk to me again?"*
    - ■ Answer: Probably yes.
- Ask the behavioral coach the same *Perspective Taking Questions*:
  - ○ *"What was that like for you?"*
  - ○ *"What did you think of me?"*
  - ○ *"Would you want to talk to me again?"*

Bad Role Play: Ending Phone Calls ⊙

[The group leader and behavioral coach should do an INAPPROPRIATE role play of ending a phone call.]

- Begin by saying, *"So we're going to pick up where we left off in MIDDLE of the phone call. Watch this and tell me what I'm doing WRONG."*

> **Example of an INAPPROPRIATE Role Play**
>
> ○ Group leader & behavioral coach: (Pick-up where you left off with cell phones to ears)
> ○ Group leader: *"So which game are you watching?"*
> ○ Behavioral coach: *"(Mention two popular sports teams.)"*
> ○ Group leader: (Playfully) *"So who are you rooting for?"*
> ○ Behavioral coach: (Excited) *"Definitely (mention one of the teams)!"*
> ○ Group leader: (Disappointed, confused, awkward) *"Oh."*
> ○ Behavioral coach: (Confused, curious) *"Do you like (mention the team)?"*
> ○ Group leader: (Awkward, uncomfortable) *"No, not really."*
> ○ Behavioral coach: (Uncomfortable) *"Oh. (long pause) Okay."*
> ○ Group leader: (Looks panicked, not sure what to do, hangs up phone)
> ○ Behavioral coach: (Looks confused, stunned)

- End by saying, *"Timeout on that. So what did I do WRONG in ending that phone call?"*
  - Answers: You did not wait for a pause; give a reason for getting off the phone; say it was nice talking to the person; say you would talk to the person later; or say goodbye.
- Ask the following *Perspective Taking Questions*:
  - *"What was that like for (name of behavioral coach)?"*
    - Answers: Strange; confusing; weird.
  - *"What do you think (name of behavioral coach) thought of me?"*
    - Answers: Weird; odd; strange.
  - *"Is (name of behavioral coach) going to want to talk to me again?"*
    - Answers: Probably not; too weird.
- Ask the behavioral coach the same *Perspective Taking Questions*:
  - *"What was that like for you?"*
  - *"What did you think of me?"*
  - *"Would you want to talk to me again?"*

Steps for Ending Phone Calls

1. **Wait for a bit of a pause**
   - This is a transitional moment, so try not to interrupt.
2. **Give a cover story for why you have to go**
   - Example: *"Well, I better get back to work."*
   - *Cover stories* are reasons you do things (in this case, the reason you have to get off the phone).
   - Have the young adults come up with different examples of *cover stories* (see Table 5.1).
3. **Tell the person it was nice talking**
   - Example: *"It was nice talking to you."*
4. **Tell the person you will talk to them later**
   - Example: *"I'll talk to you later."*
5. **Say goodbye**
   - Example: *"Bye."*

Good Role Play: Ending Phone Calls ⊙

[The group leader and behavioral coach should do an APPROPRIATE role play of ending a phone call.]

- Begin by saying, *"So we're going to pick up where we left off in the MIDDLE of the phone call. Watch this and tell me what I'm doing RIGHT."*

Example of an APPROPRIATE Role Play

- Group leader & behavioral coach: (Pick up where you left off with cell phones to ears)
- Group leader: *"So which game are you watching?"*
- Behavioral coach: *"(Mention two popular sports teams.)"*
- Group leader: (Playfully) *"So who are you rooting for?"*
- Behavioral coach: (Excited) *"Definitely (mention one of the teams)!"*
- Group leader: (Surprised) *"Oh."*
- Behavioral coach: (Curious) *"Do you like (mention the team)?"*
- Group leader: (Casual) *"Not really. But that's cool that you like them."*
- Behavioral coach: (Curious) *"So what teams do you like?"*
- Group leader: (Eager) *"I like (mention a different sports team)."*
- Behavioral coach: (Excited) *"Oh yeah? Me too!"*
- Behavioral coach: (Excited) *"That's cool!"*
- Group leader: (Brief pause) *"Well, it looks like my manager is calling. I guess my break is over, so I better get going."*
- Behavioral coach: (Friendly) *"Okay."*
- Group leader: *"It was good talking to you."*
- Behavioral coach: *"You too. Thanks for calling."*
- Group leader: *"I'll talk to you later."*
- Behavioral coach: *"Sounds good."*
- Group leader: *"Okay, bye!"*
- Behavioral coach: *"Bye!"*
- Group leader & behavioral coach: (Hang up phones)

- End by saying, *"Timeout on that. So what did I do RIGHT in ending that phone call?"*
  - ***Answers: You waited for a pause; gave a cover story for why you had to go; told them it was nice talking; told them you would talk later; and said goodbye.***
- Ask the following ***Perspective Taking Questions***:
  - *"What was that like for (name of behavioral coach)?"*
    - Answers: Fine; normal.
  - *"What do you think (name of behavioral coach) thought of me?"*
    - Answers: Friendly; pleasant; normal.
  - *"Is (name of behavioral coach) going to want to talk to me again?"*
    - Answer: Probably yes.
- Ask the behavioral coach the same ***Perspective Taking Questions***:
  - *"What was that like for you?"*
  - *"What did you think of me?"*
  - *"Would you want to talk to me again?"*

Behavioral Rehearsal: Starting and Ending Phone Calls

- Explain, *"Now we're going to have each of you practice starting and ending phone calls with each other. Each of you will practice being a caller where you start the call and a receiver where you end the call."*
- Take a few moments (approximately five minutes) to do individual behavioral rehearsals of ***starting and ending phone calls***.
  - Break up young adults into dyads to practice simultaneously.
    - If there is an uneven number of young adults, you can have one young adult practice with a behavioral coach or create one triad.
  - Assign a caller and a receiver:
    - The caller will start the call.
    - The receiver will end the call.
  - Then switch the caller and the receiver so that everyone has a chance to practice both parts of the call.

- [Note: If a young adult has difficulty **starting and ending phone calls**, privately assign an extra *Homework Assignment* during *Reunification* to practice this during the week with the social coach.]

Voicemail

- Explain, *"Sometimes we call someone on the phone and we get their voicemail. Lots of people feel uncomfortable leaving voicemail, but it doesn't have to be uncomfortable if we know the steps to follow."*

Bad Role Play: Leaving Voicemail ⊙

[The group leader and behavioral coach should do an INAPPROPRIATE role play of leaving a voicemail message.]

- Begin by saying, *"Watch this and tell me what I'm doing WRONG."*

> Example of an INAPPROPRIATE Role Play
>
> ○ Group leader: (Hold a cell phone to your ear) *"Ring, ring."*
> ○ Behavioral coach: (Voicemail message) *"Hi. We can't get to the phone right now. Please leave a message. Beep."*
> ○ Group leader: *"Are you watching the game? I just turned it on. Did you see that last play? Hmm. (pause) Hello? Why aren't you there? I thought you'd be home."* (Hang up cell phone)

- End by saying, *"Timeout on that. So what did I do WRONG in leaving that voicemail message?"*
  - Answers: You didn't say your name; didn't say who you were calling for; didn't say when you were calling; didn't give a **cover story** for calling; didn't leave a phone number; didn't say goodbye.
- Ask the following **Perspective Taking Questions**:
  - *"What is (name of behavioral coach) going to think of that message?"*
    - Answers: Strange; weird.
  - *"What do you think (name of behavioral coach) is going to think of me?"*
    - Answers: Weird; odd; strange.
  - *"Is (name of behavioral coach) going to want to talk to me after that?"*
    - Answers: Probably not; won't know who to call anyway.
- Ask the behavioral coach the same **Perspective Taking Questions**:
  - *"What would you think of that message?"*
  - *"What would you think of me?"*
  - *"Would you want to talk to me after that?"*

Steps for Leaving Voicemail

1. *Say who you are*
   - Example: *"Hi, this is Carrie."*

2. *Say who you are calling for*
   - Example: *"I'm calling for Jennifer."*
   - Exception: You don't need to **say who you are calling for** if it's a private line (e.g., private cell phone, private work extension).

3. *Say when you are calling*
   - Example: *"It's about 6 o'clock on Thursday night."*

4. *Give a cover story for calling*
   - Example: *"I was just calling to see what you've been up to."*

5. ***Leave your phone number***
   - Example: *"Give me a call at 310-555-1212."*
   - Exception: You don't need to leave your phone number if you talk regularly, but don't assume they have you in their contacts or their caller ID.

6. ***Say goodbye***
   - Example: *"Talk to you soon. Bye."*

Good Role Play: Leaving Voicemail ⊙

[The group leader and behavioral coach should do an APPROPRIATE role play of leaving a voicemail message.]

- Begin by saying, *"Watch this and tell me what I'm doing RIGHT."*

> **Example of an APPROPRIATE Role Play**
>
> ○ Group leader: (Hold a cell phone to your ear) *"Ring, ring."*
> ○ Behavioral coach: (Voicemail message) *"Hi. We can't get to the phone right now. Please leave a message. Beep."*
> ○ Group leader: *"Hi, this is (insert name). I'm calling for (insert name). It's about 6 o'clock on Thursday evening. I was just calling to see what you've been up to. Give me a call at 310-555-1212. Talk to you soon. Bye."*

- End by saying, *"Timeout on that. So what did I do RIGHT in leaving that voicemail message?"*
  - ***Answers: Said who you were; said who you were calling for; said when you called; gave a cover story for calling; left your phone number; said goodbye.***
- Ask the following ***Perspective Taking Questions***:
  - *"What is (name of behavioral coach) going to think of that message?"*
    - Answers: Fine; normal.
  - *"What do you think (name of behavioral coach) is going to think of me?"*
    - Answers: Friendly; normal.
  - *"Is (name of behavioral coach) going to want to talk to me after that?"*
    - Answer: Probably yes.
- Ask the behavioral coach the same ***Perspective Taking Questions***:
  - *"What would you think of that message?"*
  - *"What would you think of me?"*
  - *"Would you want to talk to me after that?"*

Behavioral Rehearsal: Leaving Voicemail

- Explain, *"Now we're going to have each of you practice leaving voicemail with each other. Each of you will practice being a caller where you leave a voicemail and a receiver where you pretend to be the outgoing message."*
- Take a few moments (approximately five minutes) to do individual behavioral rehearsals of ***leaving voicemail***.
  - Break up young adults into dyads to practice simultaneously.
    - If there is an uneven number of young adults, you can have one young adult practice with a behavioral coach or create one triad.
  - Assign a caller and a receiver:
    - The caller will leave the voicemail.
    - The receiver will pretend to be the outgoing message.
  - Then switch the caller and the receiver so that everyone has a chance to practice leaving a voicemail.

- [Note: If a young adult has difficulty **leaving voicemail**, privately assign an extra *Homework Assignment* during *Reunification* to practice this during the week with the social coach.]

General Rules for Using Electronic Communication

Explain, *"Now that we have some rules and steps for exchanging contact information and making phone calls, it's also important for us to understand the rules for things like texting, instant messaging, emailing, and using social networking sites."*

- *Identify yourself when contacting new people*
  - Ask, *"When we're texting, instant messaging, or emailing new people, why would it be important to identify who we are?"*
    - Answer: So they won't ask, *"Who is this?"*
  - Say, *"You NEVER want to start a conversation with 'Who is this?'! Instead, you should identify yourself. How do we do that?"*
    - Answer: *"This is (your name)."*
  - Ask, *"Do we have to identify ourselves with people we normally text, IM, or email?"*
    - Answer: No.

- *Use cover stories for contacting people you don't know well*
  - Explain, *"Just like with phone calls, we need to use cover stories when we're texting, instant messaging, emailing, or video chatting people we don't know well."*
  - Ask, *"What could be the problem with not using cover stories with people we don't know well?"*
    - Answers: They will wonder why you are contacting them; they may even ask, *"What do you want?"*
  - Say, *"We NEVER want to start a conversation with 'What do you want?'! But do we always need to use cover stories for text messaging, instant messaging, emailing, or video chatting our close friends?"*
    - Answer: No, but it doesn't hurt to use *cover stories* even with close friends.
  - Have young adults generate some examples of *cover stories*.
  - Examples:
    - *"Wondering what you've been up to."*
    - *"Just checking to see what you're doing this weekend."*
    - *"Wanted to know if you're going to the game."*

- *Don't call or text before or after double digits*
  - Explain, *"Another important rule for electronic communication is don't call or text before or after double digits. That means don't call, video chat, or text someone before 10 a.m. or after 10 p.m."*
  - Ask, *"What could be the problem with calling or texting before or after double digits?"*
    - Answers: You might wake them up; it may be too early or too late.

- *Don't get too personal*
  - Explain, *"Another important rule for using electronic communication is don't get too personal. This is true even if you know the person well."*
  - Ask, *"What could be the problem with getting too personal over texting, instant messaging, email, voicemail, video chat, or Facebook?"*
    - Answers: **Anyone can see, read, or hear what you sent**; you may embarrass the other person by getting too personal; you may embarrass yourself if other people see, read, or hear what you sent.
  - Explain, *"Since you can't control who sees, reads, or hears what you send, a good rule is to only send what you are comfortable having anyone see, read, or hear. Save the personal stuff for when you're actually in person."*

- *Use the two-message rule*
  - Explain, *"Sometimes when we contact people electronically, we don't get a hold of them."*

○ Ask, *"About how many VOICEMAIL MESSAGES can we leave in a row without hearing back before we stop calling?"*
   ▪ Go around the room and have everyone cast a vote.
○ Explain, *"The answer is TWO times. It's called the two-message rule and it means that we shouldn't leave more than two messages in a row without hearing back. We can leave one, but we can't leave more than two."*
○ Ask, *"What could be the problem with leaving more than two messages in a row?"*
   ▪ Answers: The other person may be busy; they may not want to talk to you; you may seem creepy; they might think you're a stalker.
○ Ask, *"What if we don't leave a voicemail message? Is it okay to call and hang up more than two times in a row?"*
   ▪ Answers: No, they will see that you called; missed calls count in the **two-message rule**.
○ Ask, *"About how many TEXT MESSAGES can we send in a row without hearing back before we stop texting?"*
   ▪ Go around the room and have everyone cast a vote.
○ Explain, *"The answer is TWO times. It's called the two-message rule!"*
○ Ask, *"What could be the problem with sending more than two text messages in a row?"*
   ▪ Answers: The other person may be busy; they may not want to talk to you; you may seem creepy; they might think you're a stalker.
○ Ask, *"About how many INSTANT MESSAGES can we send in a row without hearing back before we stop IMing?"*
   ▪ Go around the room and have everyone cast a vote.
○ Explain, *"The answer is TWO times. It's called the two-message rule!"*
○ Ask, *"What could be the problem with sending more than two instant messages in a row?"*
   ▪ Answers: The other person may be busy; they may not want to talk to you; you may seem creepy; they might think you're a stalker.
○ Ask, *"About how many EMAILS can we send in a row without hearing back before we stop emailing?"*
   ▪ Go around the room and have everyone cast a vote.
○ Explain, *"The answer is TWO times. It's called the two-message rule!"*
○ Ask, *"What could be the problem with sending more than two emails in a row?"*
   ▪ Answers: The other person may be busy; they may not want to talk to you; you may seem creepy; they might think you're a stalker.
○ Ask, *"Does the two-message rule mean that we can leave TWO voicemail, TWO text messages, TWO instant messages, and TWO emails in a row without hearing back?"*
   ▪ Answer: No, the **two-message rule** crosses all forms of electronic communication.
○ Explain, *"There's one exception to the two-message rule. That's if we're trying to 'friend' someone on Facebook or some other social networking site. When we try to 'friend' someone, they have the option to 'accept' or 'ignore' our request."*
○ Ask, *"If someone ignores your 'friend' request, what should you do?"*
   ▪ Answers: **Move on** and find someone else to "friend" that knows you and seems interested in you; do not try to "friend" the same person twice.
○ Ask, *"What could be the problem with sending more than one 'friend' request?"*
   ▪ Answer: They might think you are desperate, creepy, or a stalker.

● *Avoid cold-calling*
   ○ Say, *"Another rule for using electronic communication is that we need to avoid cold-calling."*
   ○ Ask, *"Does anyone know what cold-calling is?"*
      ▪ Answers: Cold-calling is contacting someone who has not given you their phone number or screen name; it is what telemarketers do.
   ○ Explain the following:
      ▪ Giving out a phone number, IM, email address, or screen name is giving someone permission to contact you.
      ▪ Just because you may have access to someone's contact information in a school directory or online directory does not give you permission to contact that person.

- ○ Ask, *"What could be the problem with cold-calling someone without their permission?"*
  - Answers: They might think you are strange, weird, creepy or a stalker; they may ask, *"How did you get my phone number?"*
- ○ Explain, *"You NEVER want to start a conversation with 'How did you get my number?'!"*
- ○ Ask, *"What if you're Facebook friends with someone and they have their contact information on their profile page . . . does that give you permission to contact them?"*
  - Answers: Not at all; that is still **cold-calling** and they may think you are creepy and weird.
- ○ Explain, *"Instead of cold calling, we should use the steps for exchanging contact information."*

Staying Safe Online

- Explain, *"We all know that the Internet is a very popular way for young adults to socialize, and many of you are probably online and even use social networking sites like Facebook. But just like with any kind of communication, there are rules about how to be safe when you're online."*
- Explain, *"The main rule about being safe is that young adults should be cautious when using the Internet to make NEW friends online."*
- Ask, *"What could be the problem with making NEW friends online?"*
  - ○ Answers: It could be dangerous; you do not know who they are; the person could be out to harm you.
- Ask, *"What's the difference between 'online friends' and 'real-life friends'?"*
  - ○ Answers: **Online friends** are people you may play games with online, but you do not know in real life; **real-life friends** are people you know in person.
- Ask, *"What could be the problem with turning 'online friends' into 'real-life friends'?"*
  - ○ Answers: You do not know who that person is; they could be dangerous; they could be out to harm you.
- Ask, *"There is an exception to this rule. It relates to meet-up groups and online dating. Do a lot of adults join meet-up groups and do online dating?"*
  - ○ Answer: Yes.
- Say, *"But even with meet-up groups, you have to apply to join them. That helps to protect people so not just anyone can show up to the group. What are some other ways we can stay safe when attending meet-up groups?"*
  - ○ Go over safety tips for attending meet-up groups:
    - Only meet in public places where there are lots of people around.
    - Do not go anywhere alone with group members.
    - Do not accept rides from group members.
    - Find your own transportation to and from the meet-up group.
    - Let your friends and family know where you're going, with whom, and when.
    - Check in with family and friends before and after the meet-up group.
    - Attend meet-up groups with other friends when possible.
- Explain, *"The same strategies apply to online dating. There are lots of ways that we can stay safe when meeting people online. When we get to the dating lessons, we will talk about some other ways to stay safe when online dating."*
  - ○ [Note: For anyone who is currently online dating, you may want to have a **side meeting** to go over *Safety Tips for Online Dating* from Session 11.]
- Ask, *"Meanwhile, is it okay to use the Internet to develop stronger friendships with people we already know, or reconnect with friends we haven't talked to in a while?"*
  - ○ Answer: Yes, absolutely.
- Explain, *"The bottom line is that the Internet is very useful for developing closer friendships with PREEXISTING friends, but we should be cautious when using it to make NEW friends."*
  - ○ **Suggestions for young adults to stay safe online:**
    - Try to avoid giving your personal information to strangers online.
    - Avoid meeting strangers from the Internet unless it's through meet-up groups or online dating websites (and then take precautions).

- Be cautious about accepting invitations to be "friends" with strangers on Facebook or other social networking sites.
- Do not send friend requests to strangers.
- Do not post your contact information on your profile pages.
- Use privacy settings on Facebook and other social networking sites so your account is not open for anyone to view.

● Explain, *"Those are some of the rules for using electronic communication. We're going to continue to have you practice using electronic communication with your social coaches this week and by trading information during your in-group calls or video chats."*

ELECTRONIC COMMUNICATION

Young Adult Behavioral Rehearsal

Trading Information About Personal Items

Materials Needed

- Young adults bring *personal items* to *trade information* with other group members.
- If young adults forget to bring *personal items*:
  - Cell phones with music and/or pictures may be used.
  - T-shirts with logos of favorite pastimes are relevant.
  - Young adults can simply talk about their interests without *personal items*.

Behavioral Rehearsal

- Break up young adults into dyads.
- Have young adults practice *trading information* and having *two-way conversations* about their *personal items*.
- Encourage young adults to identify *common interests* through *trading information*.
- Prompt young adults to ask questions when appropriate.
- Rotate young adults approximately every five minutes.
  - It may be necessary to create a triad if there is an uneven numbers of young adults.
- If there is time, debrief during the final five minutes of the group.
  - Have young adults recall what they learned about their peers through *trading information*.
  - Have young adults identify *common interests*.
    - Follow up by asking, *"What could you do with that information if you were going to hang out?"*

ELECTRONIC COMMUNICATION

Reunification

- Announce that young adults should join their social coaches.
  - Have young adults stand or sit next to their social coaches.
  - Be sure to have silence and the full attention of the group before starting with *Reunification*.
  - Have young adults generate the content from the lesson while social coaches listen.
- Say, *"Today, we talked about rules for using electronic communication. What are some of the general rules for electronic communication?"*
  - *Use the steps for exchanging contact information.*
  - *Follow the steps for starting and ending phone calls.*
  - *Follow the steps for leaving voicemail.*
  - *Identify yourself when contacting new people.*
  - *Use cover stories for contacting people you don't know well.*
  - *Don't call or text before or after double digits.*
  - *Don't get too personal.*
  - *Use the two-message rule.*
  - *Avoid cold-calling.*
  - *Be cautious about turning online friends into real-life friends.*
- Say, *"This group did a great job of practicing using electronic communication. Let's give them a round of applause."*

Homework Assignments

Distribute the *Social Coaching Handout* to young adults and announce the following *Homework Assignments*:

1. Find a *source of friends*.
   - Young adults and social coaches should DISCUSS and DECIDE on *social activities* based on the young adult's interests.
   - BEGIN TO ENROLL in these activities immediately, if you haven't already.
     - Criteria for a good *social activity*:
       - Is based on the young adult's interests.
       - Meets weekly or at least every other week.
       - Includes accepting peers similar in age.
       - Includes unstructured time to interact with others.
       - Activity starts within the next couple of weeks.

2. *Start a conversation* and *trade information* with a peer (could be from the *source of friends*).
   - Social coaches should go over the rules and steps for *starting and maintaining a conversation* and *trading information* before the practice.
   - Social coaches should ask young adults the following *social coaching questions* after the practice:

      ○ *Did you start a conversation and with whom?*
      ○ *Did it seem like they wanted to talk to you and how could you tell?*
      ○ *Did you trade information and what were your common interests?*
      ○ *What could you do with that information if you were going to hang out?*
      ○ *Does this seem like someone you might want to hang out with?*

3. *In-group call or video chat*.
- Arrange a phone call or video chat with another group member to trade information.
- Young adults and social coaches should schedule the day and time of the call with the other group member before leaving the group.
- Go over the rules for *starting and ending phone calls* and *trading information* before the call.
- Social coaches should ask young adults the following *social coaching questions* after the call:
  - *Which steps did you follow for starting the call?*
  - *What was the common interest?*
  - *What could you do with that information if you were going to hang out?*
  - *Which steps did you follow to end the call?*

4. Young adults and social coaches should practice *starting and ending a phone call* while *trading information* and *finding common interests*.
- Go over the rules for *starting and ending phone calls* and *trading information* before practicing.
- Social coaches should ask young adults the following *social coaching questions* after practicing:
  - *Which steps did you follow for starting the call?*
  - *What was the common interest?*
  - *What could we do with that information if we were going to hang out?*
  - *Which steps did you follow to end the call?*

5. Bring a *personal item* to *trade information*.
- Bring a *personal item* to *trade information* with other group members next week (e.g., music, game, book, pictures).

- Read off the in-group call assignment (Appendix E) and remind social coaches to make a note of who is calling whom.
- Encourage the young adults and social coaches to use the Phone Roster (Appendix D) to note the day and time of the scheduled call each week.

Individual Check-Out

Once the calls have been scheduled, individually and privately negotiate with each young adult and social behavioral coach:

1. What type of *social activity* they are interested in joining, if they haven't already.
- If they are already in a *social activity*, confirm that the activity:
  - Is based on the young adult's interests.
  - Meets weekly or at least every other week.
  - Includes accepting peers similar in age.
  - Includes unstructured time to interact with others.
  - Starts within the next couple of weeks.

2. Where the social coach will be during the *in-group call or video chat*.

3. When young adults and social coaches will *practice starting and ending a phone call* while *trading information* and *finding common interests*.

4. What *personal item* they plan to bring next week.

SESSION 4

ELECTRONIC COMMUNICATION

Social Coaching Handout

Steps for Exchanging Contact Information

1. *Trade information multiple times*
2. *Find a common interest*
3. *Use the common interest as a cover story for contact*
4. *Assess their interest*
5. *Suggest exchanging contact information*

Steps for Starting and Ending Phone Calls

Table 5.2 Steps for Starting and Ending Phone Calls

Starting Phone Calls	Ending Phone Calls
1. Ask for the person	1. Wait for a bit of a pause
2. Say who you are	2. Give a cover story for why you have to go
3. Ask how they are	3. Tell the person it was nice talking
4. Ask if they can talk	4. Tell the person you will talk to them later
5. Give a cover story for why you are calling	5. Say goodbye

Cover Story Examples

Table 5.1 Cover Story Examples

Reasons You Are Calling	Reasons You Have to Hang Up
"Just calling to see how you're doing."	"I have to get going."
"Just calling to hear what's up with you."	"I better let you go."
"I'm calling with a work/school question."	"I need to finish studying."
"I haven't talked to you in a while."	"It's time for dinner."
"I was wondering what you've been up to."	"I have to get back to work."

Steps for Leaving Voicemail

1. *Say who you are*
2. *Say who you are calling for*
3. *Say when you are calling*
4. *Give a cover story for calling*
5. *Leave your phone number*
6. *Say goodbye*

General Rules for Using Electronic Communication

- *Identify yourself when contacting new people*
- *Use cover stories for contacting people you don't know well*
- *Don't call or text before or after double digits*
- *Don't get too personal (anyone can see, read, or hear what you sent)*
- *Use the two-message rule*
- *Avoid cold-calling*

Safety Tips for Attending Meet-Up Groups

- Only meet in public places where there are lots of people around.
- Do not go anywhere alone with group members.
- Do not accept rides from group members.
- Find your own transportation to and from the meet-up group.
- Let your friends and family know where you're going, with whom, and when.
- Check in with family and friends before and after the meet-up group.
- Attend meet-up groups with other friends when possible.

Suggestions for Young Adults to Stay Safe Online

- Try to avoid giving your personal information to strangers online.
- Avoid meeting strangers from the Internet unless it's through meet-up groups or online dating websites (and then take precautions).
- Be cautious about accepting invitations to be "friends" with strangers on Facebook or other social networking sites.
- Do not send friend requests to strangers.
- Do not post your contact information on your profile pages.
- Use privacy settings on Facebook and other social networking sites so your account is not open for anyone to view.

Homework Assignments

1. Find a *source of friends*.
   - Young adults and social coaches should DISCUSS and DECIDE on *social activities* based on the young adult's interests.
   - BEGIN TO ENROLL in these activities immediately, if you haven't already.
     - Criteria for a good *social activity*:
       - Is based on the young adult's interests.
       - Meets weekly or at least every other week.
       - Includes accepting peers similar in age.
       - Includes unstructured time to interact with others.
       - Activity starts within the next couple of weeks.

2. *Start a conversation* and *trade information* with a peer (could be from the *source of friends*).
   - Social coaches should go over the rules and steps for *starting and maintaining a conversation* and *trading information* before the practice.
   - Social coaches should ask young adults the following *social coaching questions* after the practice:
     - *Did you start a conversation and with whom?*
     - *Did it seem like they wanted to talk to you and how could you tell?*
     - *Did you trade information and what were your common interests?*
     - *What could you do with that information if you were going to hang out?*
     - *Does this seem like someone you might want to hang out with?*

3. *In-group call or video chat.*
   - Arrange a phone call or video chat with another group member to trade information.
   - Young adults and social coaches should schedule the day and time of the call with the other group member before leaving the group.
   - Go over the rules for *starting and ending phone calls* and *trading information* before the call.
   - Social coaches should ask young adults the following *social coaching questions* after the call:
     - *Which steps did you follow for starting the call?*
     - *What was the common interest?*
     - *What could you do with that information if you were going to hang out?*
     - *Which steps did you follow to end the call?*

4. Young adults and social coaches should practice *starting and ending a phone call* while *trading information* and *finding common interests*.
   - Go over the rules for *starting and ending phone calls* and *trading information* before practicing.
   - Social coaches should ask young adults the following *social coaching questions* after practicing:
     - *Which steps did you follow for starting the call?*
     - *What was the common interest?*
     - *What could we do with that information if we were going to hang out?*
     - *Which steps did you follow to end the call?*

5. Bring a *personal item* to *trade information*.
   - Bring a *personal item* to *trade information* with other group members next week (e.g., music, game, book, pictures).

SESSION 5

APPROPRIATE USE OF HUMOR

Social Coaching Therapist Guide

Preparing for the Social Coaching Session

The focus of this lesson is on *appropriate use of humor*. While this lesson will not be critical to all of the young adults you will be working with, there is a certain subset that require instruction in this area. These are the young adults that are constantly cracking jokes and trying to be funny. Unfortunately, for many of them, no one else is laughing—or if others are laughing, they may be *laughing AT them* rather than *laughing WITH them*. Perhaps due to deficits in social cognition and perspective taking, many young adults with social challenges are unaware of their *humor feedback* and may be pushing people away in their quest to be funny. They often do this because they know how captivating and alluring humor can be. The reality is that when used appropriately, humor is intoxicating and magnetic. People often want to be around other people that are funny and make them laugh. However, when used inappropriately, *humor is one of the fastest ways to push people away*.

One of the challenges for this session is helping social coaches to understand that when their young adult tells a joke that is not funny, they actually do them a disservice by laughing. Caregivers commonly laugh at jokes they know aren't funny, or that they have heard a dozen times. They often do this because they care for their young adults and don't want to hurt their feelings. Perhaps they also find them charming and endearing when they tell jokes others might not appreciate. In this session, it will be important for you to encourage social coaches to start giving honest and constructive feedback about humor. If they fail to do this and the young adult persists in using humor inappropriately, success in the program is jeopardized. One of the ways we have found helpful for explaining this concept to young adults and their social coaches is by saying, *"You could master ALL of the skills in PEERS, but if you keep trying to tell jokes when no one else is laughing, it's going to be very hard to make and keep friends."* We typically follow this up by explaining, *"Humor is one of the fastest ways to push people away. If your goal is to make and keep friends, then telling inappropriate jokes is risky."* It can also be helpful to point out that if the young adult is attempting to socially engage others with his or her humor, *"We have a much less risky way of connecting with others: TRADING INFORMATION!"* Ultimately, young adults get to decide what to do with this information. Although they may initially be reluctant to let go of ineffective joke telling, the more they *pay attention to their humor feedback*, the less likely they will be to use humor inappropriately.

Young adults will be provided with behavioral signs of *humor feedback* during the lesson. For example, two of the signs that alert you to someone *laughing at you* are when they roll their eyes or make sarcastic comments. For some individuals with Autism Spectrum Disorder (ASD), interpreting sarcasm will be difficult and may not be a reliable sign of feedback. In these cases, it is best to rely upon other behavioral signs of *humor feedback* (i.e., eye rolling, making a face, pointing at you, etc.).

Once social coaches are open to providing *humor feedback* to young adults, you need to provide them with some strategies for how to do that. As in every session, *Social Coaching Tips* are provided at the end of the *Homework Assignment* section of the manual. These tips are not included in the

Social Coaching Handout because those handouts are also distributed to young adults at *Reunification*, and could be misconstrued by young adults as slightly condescending. Consequently, we recommend that social coaches take notes about *Social Coaching Tips* when appropriate. This may be a lesson where coaches whose young adults are struggling with **appropriate use of humor** may wish to take such notes, as there are several tips presented.

The first *Social Coaching Tip* is that caregivers should begin to have an open dialogue with young adults about **appropriate uses of humor**. They might do this by first getting permission from young adults to start pointing out instances of **inappropriate uses of humor**. If the young adult agrees, it is recommended that they jointly come up with some sort of sign to be used when others are around to help young adults **pay attention to their humor feedback**. For example, if the young adult was using humor inappropriately in some public place, where social coaching is restricted, the social coach might use some predetermined benign phrase or question (e.g., *"What time are we going to . . . ?"*) to alert the young adult to pay attention to **humor feedback**. Alternatively, a discrete verbal prompt that others cannot hear (e.g., whispering *"humor check"*) can also be helpful. A discrete hand gesture (e.g., moving hair out of face, rubbing hands together) might also help young adults to **pay attention to humor feedback** during coachable moments in public.

Whether or not young adults agree to be discretely coached in public settings, social coaches should be strongly urged to privately debrief about instances of **inappropriate uses of humor**. The simplest way to do this is by first mentioning the incident, and then following up with the social coaching questions, **"What was your humor feedback"** and **"How could you tell?"** This might lead to more in-depth discussions about whether it is better to be a **joke teller** or **joke lover**, and whether we should persist in telling jokes when our **humor feedback** is not good.

Homework Review

[Go over the following *Homework Assignments* and **troubleshoot** any potential problems. Start with completed homework first. If you have time, you can inquire as to why others were unable to complete the assignment and try to **troubleshoot** how they might get it done for the coming week. When reviewing homework, be sure to relabel descriptions using the **buzzwords** (identified by **bold and *italicized*** print). Spend the majority of the *Homework Review* on the **finding a source of friends** assignment, as this is the most important assignment.]

1. Bring a **personal item** to **trade information**.
   - Say, *"One of the assignments this week was to bring a personal item to trade information with other group members. Very quickly, let's hear what young adults brought to trade information about."*
     ○ If items are inappropriate, **troubleshoot** what they might bring next week.

2. Find a **source of friends**.
   - Say, *"Your main assignment this week was to help find a potential source of friends for your young adults and help them begin to enroll in social activities, if you haven't already. Who was able to identify a source of friends with your young adult?"*
   - Identify if the **sources of friends** are appropriate and meet the following criteria:
     ○ Are based on the young adult's interests.
     ○ Meet weekly or at least every other week.
     ○ Include accepting peers similar in age.
     ○ Include unstructured time to interact with others.
     ○ Activity starts within the next couple of weeks.

3. **Start a conversation** and **trade information** with a peer.
   - Say, *"Another assignment this week was for young adults to practice starting a conversation and trading information with a peer. This could have happened within the context of social activities. Who completed or attempted to complete this assignment?"*
   - Ask the following questions:
     ○ *"Where and with which peer did your young adult start a conversation?"*
     ○ *"Did you go over the rules and steps before the practice?"*

- **Steps for Starting a Conversation**:
  1. **Casually Look Over**
  2. **Use a Prop**
  3. **Find a Common Interest**
  4. **Mention the Common Interest**
  5. **Trade Information**
  6. **Assess Interest**
     - **Are they talking to me?**
     - **Are they looking at me?**
     - **Are they facing me (or are they giving me the cold shoulder)?**
  7. **Introduce Yourself**
- Ask, *"What social coaching did you do after the practice?"*
  - Appropriate *social coaching questions*:
    - **Did you start a conversation and with whom?**
    - **Did it seem like they wanted to talk to you and how could you tell?**
    - **Did you trade information and what were your common interests?**
    - **What could you do with that information if you were going to hang out?**
    - **Does this seem like someone you might want to hang out with?**

4. **In-group call or video chat**.
   - Say, *"Another assignment this week was for your young adult to have a phone call or video chat with someone in the group in order to practice starting and ending phone calls and trading information. Whose young adult did the in-group call or video chat?"*
   - Ask the following questions:
     - *"Who did your young adult talk to and who called whom?"*
     - *"What social coaching did you do before the call?"*
     - *"Where were you during the call?"*
     - *"How did the call start?"*
     - *"Did they trade information and find a common interest?"*
     - *"How did the call end?"*
     - *"What social coaching did you do after the call?"*
       - Appropriate *social coaching questions*:
         - **What was your common interest?**
         - **What could you do with that information if you were going to hang out?**
   - Have the other social coach who participated in the call or video chat give their account immediately after, but not at the same time.

Table 6.1 Steps for Starting and Ending Phone Calls

Starting Phone Calls	*Ending Phone Calls*
1. Ask for the person	1. Wait for a bit of a pause
2. Say who you are	2. Give a cover story for why you have to go
3. Ask how they are	3. Tell the person it was nice talking
4. Ask if they can talk	4. Tell the person you will talk to them later
5. Give a cover story for why you are calling	5. Say goodbye

5. Young adults and social coaches should practice **starting and ending a phone call, trading information**, and **finding common interests**.
   - Say, *"Another assignment this week was to practice starting and ending a phone call, trading information, and finding common interests with your young adult. Who completed or attempted to complete this assignment?"*
   - Focus on completed or attempted assignments and ask the following questions:
     - *"Did your young adult practice starting and ending a phone call with you?"*

- ○ *"Did you go over the rules and steps before practicing?"*
- ○ *"How did the call start?"*
- ○ *"Did your young adult practice trading information?"*
- ○ *"How did the call end?"*
- ○ *"Did you ask the social coaching questions after practicing?"*
  - ■ Appropriate *social coaching questions*:
    - □ **What was the common interest?**
    - □ **What could we do with that information if we were going to hang out?**

- [Collect the *Social Coaching Homework Assignment Worksheets*. If social coaches forgot to bring the worksheets, have them complete a new form to hold them accountable for the assignments.]

Didactic Lesson: Appropriate Use of Humor

- Distribute the *Social Coaching Handout*.
  - ○ Sections in **bold print** in the *Social Coaching Therapist Guide* come directly from the *Social Coaching Handout*.
  - ○ Remind social coaches that terms that are in **bold and italicized** print are **buzzwords** and represent important concepts from the PEERS® curriculum that should be used as much as possible when social coaching.
- Explain, *"Today, we're going to be talking about appropriate use of humor. Humor is one way that people communicate and connect with each other. When used appropriately, humor can be very magnetic. The problem is that when humor is used inappropriately, it's one of the FASTEST ways to push people away. Unfortunately, some of our young adults don't use humor appropriately, so we need to help them understand the rules about using humor and how to pay attention to their humor feedback when they tell jokes."*
- *Be a little more serious when you're FIRST getting to know someone.*
  - ○ Say, *"The first rule for appropriate use of humor is to be a little more serious when you're FIRST getting to know someone. What could be the problem with acting silly and trying to be funny when you're FIRST getting to know someone?"*
    - ■ Answers: They may not understand your sense of humor; they may think you're making fun of them; they may think you're weird.
  - ○ Ask, *"Have you ever met someone for the first time and you think they just told a joke, but you're not sure, and you don't know if you're supposed to laugh? What's that like for you?"*
    - ■ Answers: Awkward; uncomfortable; confusing.
  - ○ Say, *"It's a lot less risky if we're a little more serious at first. After you've gotten to know them better, then is it okay to be less serious?"*
    - ■ Answer: Yes, if your *humor feedback* is good.
- *Don't repeat jokes with people who've heard them.*
  - ○ Say, *"Another rule for appropriate use of humor is don't repeat jokes with people who've already heard them. What could be the problem with repeating jokes to people that have already heard them?"*
    - ■ Answers: A joke usually isn't funny if you've already heard it; it may look like you've got no material.
  - ○ Explain, *"Sometimes we laugh when our young adult tells a joke, even if we don't think it's funny or we've heard it a dozen times. We're going to discourage you from laughing at jokes you don't find funny or that you've heard before, and instead use this as an opportunity to provide humor feedback. Later in the session, we'll talk about how you can do that."*
- *Avoid insult jokes.*
  - ○ Say, *"Another rule for appropriate use of humor is to avoid insult jokes. These are jokes that make fun of people. Insult jokes often include making fun of someone's ethnicity, religion, gender, sexual orientation, or appearance. What could be the problem with telling insult jokes?"*
    - ■ Answers: You might insult them; you might hurt their feelings; they might not want to be friends with you; you could get a bad reputation for being mean.
  - ○ Explain, *"We know insult jokes are common, but if your goal is to make and keep friends, telling insult jokes is risky."*

- *Avoid dirty jokes.*
  - Say, *"Another important rule about humor is to avoid telling dirty jokes. Dirty jokes are usually about sex or body parts. What could be the problem with telling dirty jokes?"*
    - Answers: Dirty jokes may make people uncomfortable; they could give you a bad reputation.
  - Ask, *"What could the other person think of you if you tell a dirty joke?"*
    - Answer: That you're weird or perverted.
  - Explain, *"We know dirty jokes may be common among certain people, but if your goal is to make and keep friends, telling dirty jokes is risky."*

- *Avoid inside jokes with people who won't get them.*
  - Explain, *"Another rule for appropriate use of humor is to avoid inside jokes with people who won't get them. Inside jokes are shared jokes that only a few people understand. They're usually specific to some context and are only shared by certain people."*
  - Say, *"There's nothing wrong with inside jokes, but what could be the problem with telling inside jokes with people who won't get them?"*
    - Answers: The people not in on the joke won't get it; they might feel left out; you might hurt their feelings.
  - Ask, *"What should we do if we accidentally tell an inside joke in front of someone who doesn't get it?"*
    - Answer: Apologize and explain the joke.
  - Ask, *"But is a joke ever funny if you have to explain it?"*
    - Answer: No, hardly ever.

- *Don't tell jokes to people in authority.*
  - Say, *"Another rule for appropriate use of humor is to avoid telling jokes to people in authority. Who are some people in authority?"*
    - Answers: Professors; deans; supervisors; bosses; law enforcement officers.
  - Ask, *"What could be the problem with telling jokes to people in authority?"*
    - Answers: You could seem disrespectful, rude, or bad-mannered because there is a power differential; you could get in trouble.
  - Explain, *"We know some people tell jokes to people in authority without problems, but remember that it's still risky."*

- *Don't laugh for no reason.*
  - Say, *"Another rule for appropriate use of humor is don't laugh for no reason. For example, you might have a funny thought and you laugh out loud, but no one knows why you're laughing. What could be the problem with laughing for no reason?"*
    - Answers: People may think you're laughing at them; they might think you're strange or weird; people might even think you're psychotic and having hallucinations.
  - Ask, *"What should we do if we accidentally laugh out loud for no reason?"*
    - Answer: Say, *"I'm sorry, I just had a funny thought."*

- *Humor should be age-appropriate.*
  - Explain, *"It's also important that humor be age-appropriate. That means when young adults are telling jokes to peers, they shouldn't be telling knock-knock jokes or really immature jokes that a 5-year-old might tell."*
  - Ask, *"What could be the problem with telling jokes that aren't age-appropriate?"*
    - Answers: People won't think your jokes are funny; you might seem immature or weird.
  - Ask, *"What if you're telling a joke to a 5-year-old. Then is it okay to tell immature jokes?"*
    - Answer: Yes, because that joke is ***age-appropriate*** for a 5-year-old.

- *Humor should be context-appropriate.*
  - Say, *"It's also important that humor be context-appropriate. That means the joke needs to make sense in the context you're in. For example, if you told a joke about robotics engineering to a group of people who didn't know anything about robotics, would they think it was funny?"*
    - Answer: No, they probably wouldn't get it.
  - Ask, *"But if you told the same joke in your robotics club, would they think it was funny?"*

- ■ Answer: Maybe, if it was a good joke.
  - ○ Ask, *"What could be the problem with telling jokes that aren't context-appropriate?"*
    - ■ Answers: People won't think your jokes are funny if they don't get them or they're out of context; they might think you're weird or odd.

- **Think about whether it's the right time to tell jokes.**
  - ○ Explain, *"It's also important to think about whether it's the RIGHT time or the WRONG time to tell jokes."*
  - ○ Ask, *"When would be the RIGHT time to tell jokes?"*
    - ■ Answers: Parties; get-togethers; free time; lunch breaks; when other people are telling jokes.
  - ○ Ask, *"When would be the WRONG time to tell jokes?"*
    - ■ Answers: During a lecture; when the professor is talking; during exams; when you're supposed to be working; when people are sad because this could seem insensitive.

- **Give a courtesy laugh if someone tells a joke.**
  - ○ Explain, *"Sometimes people tell us jokes and we may not think they're funny. If we don't laugh or we say, 'That's not funny', we might make them feel bad. If our goal is to make and keep friends, what should we do if someone tells a joke that we don't think is funny?"*
    - ■ Answers: **Give a courtesy laugh**; politely smile; say, *"That's funny."*
  - ○ [Optional: Show BAD and GOOD *Role Play Video Demonstrations* of **giving a courtesy laugh** from the *PEERS® Role Play Video Library* (www.routledge.com/cw/laugeson).]

- **Pay attention to your humor feedback.**
  - ○ Explain, *"One of the most important rules for using humor appropriately is that if you're going to tell a joke, you need to pay attention to your humor feedback. Humor feedback is the reaction people give you after you've told a joke."*
  - ○ Ask, *"What could be the problem with not paying attention to your humor feedback?"*
    - ■ Answers: People may not think the joke was funny and you may end up pushing people away; they may think you're weird or strange and may not want to be your friend.
  - ○ Explain, *"When you're paying attention to your humor feedback, there are four types of reactions you should look for ..."*
    - ■ **Don't laugh at all**
    - ■ **Giving a courtesy laugh**
    - ■ **Laughing at you**
    - ■ **Laughing with you**
  - ○ Ask, *"What does it mean if they DON'T LAUGH at all?"*
    - ■ Answers: They don't think what you said was funny; this is **BAD humor feedback**.
  - ○ Ask, *"What does it mean if they give you a COURTESY LAUGH?"*
    - ■ Answers: They're laughing to be polite, but don't think what you said was funny; this is **BAD humor feedback**.
  - ○ Ask, *"What does it mean when they LAUGH AT YOU and what does that look like?"*
    - ■ Answers: See Table 6.2; this is **BAD humor feedback**.
  - ○ Ask, *"What does it mean when they LAUGH WITH YOU and what does that look like?"*
    - ■ Answers: See Table 6.2; this is the only **GOOD humor feedback**.
  - ○ Explain, *"The biggest mistake people make when paying attention to their humor feedback is they don't LOOK at the other person, and they only listen."*
  - ○ Ask the following question using the sentence stem *"Can you HEAR people ..."*
    - ■ *"... roll their eyes?"*
    - ■ *"... make a face?"*
    - ■ *"... point at you?"*
    - ■ *"... smile at you?"*
    - ■ *"... nod their head?"*
  - ○ Explain, *"In order to pay attention to our humor feedback, we need to LOOK and LISTEN. That means you must WATCH the other person for their reaction. Simply listening to whether they laugh, will not give you enough feedback."*

○ [Optional: Show the *laughing at* and *laughing with* Role Play Video Demonstrations of *humor feedback* from the *PEERS® Role Play Video Library* (www.routledge.com/cw/laugeson).]

Table 6.2 Humor Feedback Signs

Laughing AT You	Laughing WITH You
Laugh and roll their eyes	Laugh and smile
Look at someone else and then laugh	Compliment your joke or sense of humor
Laugh before the joke is over	Laugh and nod their head yes
Long pause before they laugh	They say, *"That's a good one"* and smile
Laugh and make a face	They say, *"You're funny"* and smile
Laugh and point at you	Ask you to tell another joke
Laugh and shake their head no to someone else	Say, *"I'll have to remember that one."*
Make sarcastic comments (this may be difficult to interpret)	They start telling jokes

Identifying Joke Tellers

Explain, *"Everyone has a different relationship with humor. Some people like to tell jokes, many people like to hear jokes, and some people don't like jokes at all. There are basically three types of people when it comes to humor."*

- **Joke Tellers**
  ○ Explain, *"Joke tellers are people who like to tell jokes CONSTANTLY. They consider themselves jokesters or class clowns, but the reality is that it's difficult to be funny ALL the time. Unfortunately, sometimes people aren't laughing WITH them; they're laughing AT them. Very few people are good joke tellers ALL the time."*

- **Joke Lovers**
  ○ Explain, *"Joke lovers (or joke fans) are people who enjoy humor, sometimes tell jokes or make funny comments, but aren't trying to be funny ALL the time. Joke lovers like to laugh and occasionally tell jokes or joke around, but their identity isn't wrapped up in being a jokester or a class clown. Most people are joke lovers."*

- **Joke Haters**
  ○ Explain, *"Joke haters (or joke refusers) are people who don't enjoy humor. They don't like telling jokes or hearing jokes. Humor may make them uncomfortable or feel confused."*
  ○ Ask, *"While it's perfectly fine not to like jokes, if you're more of a joke hater, is it your business to tell people not to tell jokes?"*
    ■ Answer: No, that would be **policing**.
  ○ Explain, *"So if your young adult is not comfortable with humor, then remind them that friendship is a choice, and being friends with joke tellers may not be a good choice for them, but it's not their business to be policing people about their humor."*
- Explain *"Tonight, your young adults will be identifying whether they think they're more of a joke teller, joke lover, or joke hater. We will go over their responses at Reunification. Hopefully there won't be any surprises. One of your jobs moving forward will be to help them pay attention to their humor feedback. We'll give you some tips on how to do that once we've talked about the Homework Assignments."*
- Explain, *"For some of our young adults, the realization that they're not getting good humor feedback may come as a shock and a blow. Consider that they're most likely telling jokes because they want to engage others and connect with them. That's a good thing. But now we have a far more effective and less risky way of doing that: TRADING INFORMATION!"*

Homework Assignments

[Distribute the *Social Coaching Homework Assignment Worksheet* (Appendix I) for social coaches to complete and return at the next session.]

1. Find a *source of friends*.
   - Young adults and social coaches should DISCUSS and DECIDE on *social activities* based on the young adult's interests.

   - BEGIN TO ENROLL in these activities immediately, if you haven't already.
     - Criteria for a good *social activity*:
       - Is based on the young adult's interests.
       - Meets weekly or at least every other week.
       - Includes accepting peers similar in age.
       - Includes unstructured time to interact with others.
       - Activity starts within the next couple of weeks.

2. *Start a conversation* and *trade information* with a peer (could be from the *source of friends*).
   - Social coaches should go over the rules and steps for *starting and maintaining a conversation* and *trading information* before the practice.
   - Social coaches should ask young adults the following *social coaching questions* after the practice:
     - *Did you start a conversation and with whom?*
     - *Did it seem like they wanted to talk to you and how could you tell?*
     - *Did you trade information and what were your common interests?*
     - *What could you do with that information if you were going to hang out?*
     - *Does this seem like someone you might want to hang out with?*

3. *Pay attention to humor feedback.*
   - If young adults happen to tell jokes (this is NOT the assignment), *pay attention to humor feedback.*
   - Social coaches should PRIVATELY ask the following *social coaching questions* after attempts at humor by young adults:
     - *What was your humor feedback?*
     - *How could you tell?*

4. *In-group call or video chat.*
   - Arrange a phone call or video chat with another group member to trade information.
   - Young adults and social coaches should schedule the day and time of the call with the other group member before leaving the group.
   - Go over the rules for *starting and ending phone calls* and *trading information* before the call.
   - Social coaches should ask young adults the following *social coaching questions* after the call:
     - *Which steps did you follow for starting the call?*
       - Steps are slightly modified if doing a video chat (i.e., you don't *ask for the person* or *say who you are*).
     - *What was the common interest?*
     - *What could you do with that information if you were going to hang out?*
     - *Which steps did you follow to end the call?*

5. Bring a *personal item* to *trade information*.
   - Bring a *personal item* to *trade information* with other group members next week (e.g., music, game, book, pictures).

Social Coaching Tips

- Begin to have an open dialogue with young adults about *appropriate uses of humor*.
  - Get permission to start pointing out instances of *inappropriate uses of humor*.
- Come up with a sign you can use when others are around to help young adults *pay attention to humor feedback*:

- ○ Benign phrase or question (e.g., *"What time are we going to . . . ?"*).
- ○ Discrete verbal prompt that others cannot hear (e.g., whispering *"humor check"*).
- ○ Discrete hand gesture (e.g., moving hair out of face, rubbing hands together).
- Discuss instances of *humor feedback* privately by asking:
  - ○ *What was your humor feedback?*
    - ■ *Not laughing at all*
    - ■ *Giving a courtesy laugh*
    - ■ *Laughing AT them*
    - ■ *Laughing WITH them*
  - ○ *How could you tell?*
- Avoid laughing at jokes that aren't funny.
  - ○ You will be doing your young adult a disservice if you laugh at jokes that others might find odd or annoying.
  - ○ Instead ask, *"What was your humor feedback?"* in the manner described above.
- For young adults committed to being *joke tellers* when it's not working for them:
  - ○ Normalize the experience of wanting to tell jokes, but remind them:
    - ■ *"If your goal is to make and keep friends, this is really risky!"*
    - ■ *"We have a less risky way of connecting with others: TRADING INFORMATION!"*

APPROPRIATE USE OF HUMOR

Young Adult Therapist Guide

Preparing for the Young Adult Session

While most of us recognize that a good sense of humor can be socially magnetic and charming, *inappropriate use of humor is one of the fastest ways to push people away*. One inappropriate joke or off-color remark from an acquaintance and most people are done with that person. Unfortunately, humor is perhaps one of the more outstanding and obvious social deficits for many people with Autism Spectrum Disorder (ASD). Young adults with ASD often have substantial deficits in understanding punch lines to jokes, particularly when sarcasm is involved. Moreover, due to difficulty with social cognition and perspective taking, it is often difficult for people with ASD to understand and interpret *humor feedback* and read the social cues about responses to joke telling. Even with these deficits, many young adults with ASD like to tell jokes—although they don't always get a laugh—or perhaps, sadly, people are *laughing AT them* rather than *laughing WITH them*.

While some young adults with ASD will relish in telling jokes, others are so confused by humor that they get upset, even angry, when people tell jokes. We call these young adults *joke haters*. While they make up only a minority of young adults with ASD, *joke haters* must come to understand that it is not their job to *police* others and insist that they not tell jokes. Instead, it will be important to remember that *friendship is a choice*. They don't have to be friends with *joke tellers*, and *joke tellers* don't have to be friends with them.

For some young adults in your group, learning to use humor appropriately will be of paramount importance to developing relationships, particularly for those who engage in silly or immature humor, or joke telling that no one else seems to understand. Many *peer-rejected* young adults are oblivious to the negative *humor feedback* they receive. This causes them to be further rejected and may even result in a bad reputation among peers. Young adults who regularly engage in *inappropriate use of humor* are often seen as strange or weird by their peers, which may ultimately lead to teasing and bullying, if not simply *peer rejection* and social exclusion. Therefore, paying attention to one's *humor feedback* and learning to use humor appropriately will be critical for a select group of rejected young adults that consider themselves *joke tellers*. For some young adults, failing to develop this one core skill may be the difference between success and failure in PEERS®. In other words, even if a young adult was able to successfully master all of the other skills outlined in the PEERS® curriculum, if they continue to persist with *inappropriate use of humor*, it is likely that they will continue to experience rejection from peers.

One issue that may come up in this lesson relates to the misunderstanding about the role of *joke lovers* and *joke tellers*. To clarify, *joke lovers* enjoy jokes. In fact, most *joke lovers* also tell jokes or joke around from time to time. But unlike *joke tellers*, who consider themselves jokesters, class clowns, and full-time comedians, *joke lovers* are not trying to be funny ALL of the time. It will be important for you to explain the difference and stress that very few people can be successful *joke tellers* all of the time. Since *humor is one of the fastest ways to push people away*, if our goal is to make and keep friends, we should be careful with our humor and always *pay attention to our humor feedback*. If young adults are not comfortable with the words "*lover*" or "*hater*," you can also use the terms *joke fans* or *joke refusers*.

Another issue that may come up in this lesson will be young adults who challenge the rules by claiming that most jokes are *insult jokes*, or that *dirty jokes* are very common among boys and men. You should respond to these comments by acknowledging that these statements are true. Insult jokes are very common, and in certain circles dirty jokes are too. The point that you will need to stress is that this behavior is very *risky* if you are trying to make and keep friends. You can present this idea by saying, *"Remember that humor is one of the fastest ways to push people away. If your goal is to make and keep friends, then telling these types of jokes is risky."* Like everything you teach in PEERS®, you are simply providing information about *ecologically valid skills* related to making and keeping friends. You are sharing what we know works through research. It is up to the young adults to decide whether they will use that information.

Perhaps the greatest challenge in this lesson will involve addressing mistaken beliefs about successful joke telling. Approximately 25% of young adults presenting for social skills treatment at the UCLA PEERS® Clinic report being *joke tellers*. The likelihood that all are successful *joke tellers* is slim given the fact that humor is a social magnet when used appropriately. By virtue of their attendance in your group, and the fact that they are struggling socially, it is unlikely that they are wildly successful *joke tellers*. Instead, it is more common that young adults think they are successful *joke tellers*, but have rarely paid attention to whether others are *laughing WITH them*. As they learn to *pay attention to their humor feedback*, many of these young adults start to notice that others are either not laughing, or they may be *laughing AT them* or giving a *courtesy laugh*. This can be a shocking blow to some young adults. Be prepared to empathize and normalize this experience by explaining that very few people are successful *joke tellers* all the time. Most people are *joke lovers (or joke fans)*, meaning they enjoy humor and even joke around, but they're not trying to be funny all the time. This is also a good opportunity to remind young adults that they have a good replacement behavior for humor. *Trading information* is a highly effective and far less risky method for connecting with other people. You will want to encourage young adults to do more *trading information* and less joke telling if their goal is to make and keep friends.

From this point on in the program, it will be important for you to discreetly point out any violations of the rules of *appropriate use of humor* in the group. *Joke tellers* often like to tell jokes during the group, even though this is not the right time to tell jokes. Take this as an opportunity for a coachable moment. For example, if a young adult makes an inappropriate joke during the group and no one laughs, or worse, the group *laughs AT him or her*, you might gently ask, *"What was your humor feedback?"* Most young adults will be able to admit that their feedback was not good. This will give you the opportunity to remind the young adult, *"Humor is one of the fastest ways to push people away, so if our goal is to make and keep friends, we need to be careful with our humor."* If the feedback was good (i.e., the group was *laughing WITH him or her*), you can still use this as a coachable moment to ask, *"Is this the right time to be telling jokes?"* Most young adults will be able to admit that it is not, and you can follow up with a statement such as, *"We need to be serious."*

Homework Review

[Go over the following *Homework Assignments* and *troubleshoot* any potential problems. Start with completed homework first. If you have time, you can inquire as to why others were unable to complete the assignment and try to *troubleshoot* how they might get it done for the coming week. When reviewing homework, be sure to relabel descriptions using the *buzzwords* (identified by *bold and italicized* print). Spend the majority of the *Homework Review* on the *finding a source of friends* assignment, as this is the most important assignment.]

1. Bring a *personal item* to *trade information*.
    - Say, *"One of the assignments this week was to bring a personal item to trade information with other group members. Very quickly, let's hear what you brought to trade information."*
        ○ Have young adults place these items somewhere off to the side of the room to avoid distractions.
        ○ If items are inappropriate, *troubleshoot* what they might bring next week.

2. Find a *source of friends*.
   - Say, *"Your main assignment this week was to find a potential source of friends with the help of your social coaches and begin to enroll in social activities, if you haven't already. Who was able to identify a source of friends?"*
   - Identify if the *sources of friends* are appropriate and meet the following criteria:
     - Are based on the young adult's interests.
     - Meet weekly or at least every other week.
     - Include accepting peers similar in age.
     - Include unstructured time to interact with others.
     - Activity starts within the next couple of weeks.

3. *Start a conversation* and *trade information* with a peer.
   - Say, *"Another assignment this week was to practice starting a conversation and trading information with a peer. This could have happened within the context of your social activities. Raise your hand if you did this assignment."*
   - Ask the following questions:
     - *"Where and with whom did you start a conversation?"*
     - *"How did you start the conversation?"*
       - **Steps for Starting a Conversation**:
         1. **Casually Look Over**
         2. **Use a Prop**
         3. **Find a Common Interest**
         4. **Mention the Common Interest**
         5. **Trade Information**
         6. **Assess Interest**
            - **Are they talking to me?**
            - **Are they looking at me?**
            - **Are they facing me (or are they giving me the cold shoulder)?**
         7. **Introduce Yourself**
     - *"Did it seem like they wanted to talk to you and how could you tell?"*
     - *"Did you trade information and what were your common interests?"*
     - *"What could you do with that information if you were going to hang out?"*
     - *"Does this seem like someone you might want to hang out with?"*

4. *In-group call or video chat*.
   - Say, *"Another assignment you had this week was to have a phone call or video chat with someone in the group in order to practice starting and ending phone calls and trading information. Raise your hand if you did the in-group call or video chat."*
   - Ask the following questions:
     - *"Who did you talk to and who called whom?"*
     - *"How did the call start?"* (only ask the caller)
     - *"Did you trade information and did you find a common interest?"*
     - *"What could you do with that information if you were going to hang out?"*
     - *"How did the call end?"* (only ask the person that ended the call)
   - Have the other person who participated in the call or video chat give their account immediately after, but not at the same time.

Table 6.1 Steps for Starting and Ending Phone Calls

Starting Phone Calls	Ending Phone Calls
1. Ask for the person	1. Wait for a bit of a pause
2. Say who you are	2. Give a cover story for why you have to go
3. Ask how they are	3. Tell the person it was nice talking
4. Ask if they can talk	4. Tell the person you will talk to them later
5. Give a cover story for why you are calling	5. Say goodbye

5. Young adults and social coaches should have practiced *starting and ending a phone call*, *trading information*, and *finding common interests*.
   - Say, *"Another assignment this week was to practice starting and ending a phone call, trading information, and finding common interests with a social coach. Raise your hand if you traded information with your social coach this week."*
   - Ask the following questions:
     - *"How did the call start?"*
     - *"Did you trade information and did you find common interests?"*
     - *"What could you do with that information if you were going to hang out with your social coach?"*
     - *"How did the call end?"*

Didactic Lesson: Appropriate Use of Humor

- Explain, *"Today, we're going to be talking about appropriate use of humor. Humor is one way that people communicate and connect with each other. When used appropriately, humor can be very magnetic. The problem is that when humor is used inappropriately, it's one of the FASTEST ways to push people away. So it's important that we understand the rules about using humor appropriately when trying to make and keep friends and develop close meaningful relationships."*
- [Present the rules for *appropriate use of humor* by writing the following bullet points and *buzzwords* (identified by *bold and italicized* print) on the board. Do not erase the rules until the end of the lesson. Each role play with a ⊙ symbol includes a corresponding role play video from the *PEERS® Role Play Video Library* (www.routledge.com/cw/laugeson).]

- *Be a little more serious when you're FIRST getting to know someone*
  - Explain, *"The first rule for appropriate use of humor is to be a little more serious when you're FIRST getting to know someone."*
  - Ask, *"What could be the problem with acting silly and trying to be funny when you're FIRST getting to know someone?"*
    - Answers: They may not understand your sense of humor; they may think you're making fun of them; they may think you're weird.
  - Ask, *"Have you ever met someone for the first time and you think they just told a joke, but you're not sure, and you don't know if you're supposed to laugh? What's that like for you?"*
    - Answers: Awkward; uncomfortable; confusing.
  - Explain, *"We know people sometimes try to be funny when they're first getting to know someone, but if your goal is to make and keep friends, this is really risky!"*
  - Ask, *"After you've gotten to know them better, then is it okay to be less serious?"*
    - Answer: Yes, if your *humor feedback* is good.

- *Don't repeat jokes with people who've heard them*
  - Explain, *"Another rule for appropriate use of humor is don't repeat jokes with people who've already heard them."*
  - Ask, *"What could be the problem with repeating jokes to people that have already heard them?"*
    - Answers: A joke usually isn't funny if you've already heard it; it looks like you've got no material.
  - Ask, *"What if I tell my friend Shannon a joke one day and she laughs. Then the next day our friend Lara is there with me and Shannon. Lara hasn't heard the joke, but Shannon has. Is it okay to repeat the joke?"*
    - Answer: No, never tell the same joke more than once in front of the same person (unless it's an *inside joke*).
  - Ask, *"What if Shannon asks me to tell Lara the joke. Then is it okay to repeat the joke?"*
    - Answer: Yes, but only when the person who has heard the joke asks you to repeat it.
  - Ask, *"What if I tell a joke to Shannon one day, and the next day Lara is there, but Shannon isn't. Can I tell Lara the joke if Shannon isn't there?"*
    - Answer: Yes, because Lara hasn't heard the joke and Shannon isn't there.

- Explain, *"We know people sometimes repeat jokes with people who've already heard them, but if your goal is to make and keep friends, this is really risky!"*

- **Avoid insult jokes**
  - Explain, *"Another rule for appropriate use of humor is to avoid insult jokes. These are jokes that make fun of people. Insult jokes often include making fun of someone's ethnicity, religion, gender, sexual orientation, or appearance."*
  - Ask, *"What could be the problem with telling insult jokes?"*
    - Answers: You might insult them; you might hurt their feelings; they might not want to be friends with you; you could get a bad reputation for being mean.
  - Ask, *"For example, what could be the problem with telling a racist joke?"*
    - Answers: The other person might think you're a racist; you could insult or offend them; they might not want to be friends with you; you could get a bad reputation for being a racist.
  - Ask, *"What if the person isn't of that race. Then is it okay to tell the joke?"*
    - Answers: No, absolutely not; many people find these jokes offensive, even if they're not from the targeted group.
  - Ask, *"What if your friends are telling racist jokes. Then is it okay to tell racist jokes?"*
    - Answers: No, absolutely not; even if the people you're telling the joke to are not offended, someone overhearing the joke may be upset; you could get a bad reputation for being a racist.
  - Explain, *"We know insult jokes are common, but if your goal is to make and keep friends, this is really risky!"*

- **Avoid dirty jokes**
  - Explain, *"Another important rule about humor is to avoid telling dirty jokes. Dirty jokes are usually about sex or body parts."*
  - Ask, *"What could be the problem with telling dirty jokes?"*
    - Answers: Dirty jokes may make people uncomfortable; could give you a bad reputation.
  - Ask, *"What could the other person think of you if you tell a dirty joke?"*
    - Answer: That you're weird or perverted.
  - Ask, *"What if your friends are telling dirty jokes. Then is it okay to tell them?"*
    - Answers: No, you could still get a bad reputation if someone overhears; people might think you're weird or perverted.
  - Explain, *"We know dirty jokes are fairly common, but if your goal is to make and keep friends, this is really risky!"*

- **Avoid inside jokes with people who won't get them**
  - Explain, *"Another rule for appropriate use of humor is to avoid inside jokes with people who won't get them. Inside jokes are shared jokes that only a few people understand. They're usually specific to some context and are only shared by certain people."*
  - Say, *"There's nothing wrong with inside jokes, but what could be the problem with telling inside jokes with people who won't get them?"*
    - Answers: The people not in on the joke won't get it; they might feel left out; you might hurt their feelings.
  - Ask, *"What if I have an inside joke with my friends Shannon and Lara. One day the three of us are with our friend Ruth and I want to tell the joke. Shannon and Lara are in on the joke, but Ruth isn't. Is it okay for me to tell the inside joke?"*
    - Answer: No, because Ruth won't get the joke and she might feel left out.
  - Ask, *"What should I do if I accidentally tell the inside joke in front of Ruth who doesn't get it?"*
    - Answer: Apologize and explain the joke to Ruth.
  - Ask, *"But is a joke ever funny if you have to explain it?"*
    - Answer: No, hardly ever.
  - Explain, *"We know people sometimes tell inside jokes with people who don't get them, but if your goal is to make and keep friends, this is really risky!"*

- *Don't tell jokes to people in authority*
  - ○ Say, *"Another rule for appropriate use of humor is to avoid telling jokes to people in authority. Who are some people in authority?"*
    - Answers: Professors; deans; supervisors; bosses; law enforcement officers.
  - ○ Ask, *"What could be the problem with telling jokes to people in authority?"*
    - Answers: You could seem disrespectful, rude, or bad-mannered; you could get in trouble.
  - ○ Ask, *"What if your professor or supervisor is telling jokes. Is it okay for you to tell jokes then?"*
    - Answers: No, it is still risky; you could still get in trouble; you could still seem disrespectful; you could get a bad reputation with that person.
  - ○ Explain, *"We know people sometimes tell jokes to people in authority, but it's really risky!"*

- *Don't laugh for no reason*
  - ○ Explain, *"Another rule for appropriate use of humor is don't laugh for no reason. For example, you might have a funny thought and you laugh out loud, but no one knows why you're laughing."*
  - ○ Ask, *"What could be the problem with laughing for no reason?"*
    - Answers: People may think you're laughing at them; they might think you're strange or weird; people might even think you're psychotic and having hallucinations.
  - ○ Ask, *"What should we do if we accidentally laugh out loud for no reason?"*
    - Answer: Say, *"I'm sorry, I just had a funny thought."*
  - ○ Explain, *"We know people sometimes laugh to themselves, but if your goal is to make and keep friends, this is really risky!"*

- *Humor should be age-appropriate*
  - ○ Explain, *"It's also important that humor be age-appropriate. That means when young adults are telling jokes to peers, they shouldn't be telling knock-knock jokes or really immature jokes that a 5-year-old might tell."*
  - ○ Ask, *"What could be the problem with telling jokes that aren't age-appropriate?"*
    - Answers: People won't think your jokes are funny; you might seem immature or weird.
  - ○ Ask, *"What if you're telling a joke to a 5-year-old. Then is it okay to tell immature jokes?"*
    - Answer: Yes, because that joke is **age-appropriate** for a 5-year-old.
  - ○ Explain, *"We know people sometimes tell jokes that aren't age-appropriate, but if your goal is to make and keep friends, this is really risky!"*

- *Humor should be context-appropriate*
  - ○ Say, *"It's also important that humor be context-appropriate. That means the joke needs to make sense in the context you're in. For example, if you told a joke about robotics engineering to a group of people who didn't know anything about robotics, would they think it was funny?"*
    - Answer: No, they probably wouldn't get it.
  - ○ Ask, *"But if you told the same joke in your robotics club, would they think it was funny?"*
    - Answer: Maybe, if it was a good joke.
  - ○ Ask, *"What could be the problem with telling jokes that aren't context-appropriate?"*
    - Answers: People won't think your jokes are funny if they don't get them or they're out of context; they might think you're weird or odd.
  - ○ Explain, *"We know people sometimes tell jokes that are out of context, but if your goal is to make and keep friends, this is really risky!"*

- *Think about whether it's the right time to tell jokes*
  - ○ Explain, *"It's also important to think about whether it's the RIGHT time or the WRONG time to tell jokes."*
  - ○ Ask, *"When would be the RIGHT time to tell jokes?"*
    - Answers: Parties; get-togethers; dates; free time; lunch breaks; when other people are telling jokes.
  - ○ Ask, *"When would be the WRONG time to tell jokes?"*
    - Answers: During a lecture; when the professor is talking; during exams; when you're supposed to be working; when people are sad.
  - ○ Say, *"Some people think it's a good time to tell jokes when someone is sad, like they might cheer the person up. What could be the problem with telling jokes when someone is sad?"*

- ■ Answers: It makes you look insensitive; you might seem like you don't care; it might look like you have no empathy.
  - ○ Explain, *"We know people sometimes tell jokes when other people are sad, but if your goal is to make and keep friends, this is really risky!"*
- ● *Give a courtesy laugh if someone tells a joke*
  - ○ Explain, *"Sometimes people tell us jokes and we may not think they're funny. If we don't laugh or say, 'That's not funny', we might make them feel bad. If our goal is to make and keep friends, what should we do if someone tells a joke that we don't think is funny?"*
    - ■ Answers: *Give a courtesy laugh*; politely smile; say, *"That's funny."*

Bad Role Play: Giving a Courtesy Laugh ⊙

[Two behavioral coaches should do an INAPPROPRIATE role play of *giving a courtesy laugh*. If you do not have two behavioral coaches, the group leader can be a substitute for one of the coaches.]

- ● Begin by saying, *"We're going to do a role play. Watch this and tell me what (name of behavioral coach 2) is doing WRONG in giving a courtesy laugh."*

Example of an INAPPROPRIATE Role Play

- ○ Behavioral coach 2: *"Hi, (insert name). How are you?"*
- ○ Behavioral coach 1: *"I'm pretty good. How are you?"*
- ○ Behavioral coach 2: *"I'm fine. So what did you do over the break?"*
- ○ Behavioral coach 1: *"I got together with some friends and went skiing."*
- ○ Behavioral coach 2: *"Oh cool. Are you a pretty good skier?"*
- ○ Behavioral coach 1: *"I guess so, but funny story . . . so this last trip we were skiing black diamonds and I made it almost all the way down the mountain with no problems and then totally wiped out in front of the 'DANGER' sign!"*
- ○ Behavioral coach 2: (Over-the-top laughing) *"That's hysterical! You're so funny! That's the funniest thing I've ever heard!"*
- ○ Behavioral coach 1: (Uncomfortable, awkward)

- ○ End by saying, *"Timeout on that. So what did (name of behavioral coach 2) do WRONG in giving that courtesy laugh?"*
  - ■ Answers: Was over the top; seemed insincere; seemed desperate; looked like he/she was trying too hard.
- ○ Ask the following *Perspective Taking Questions*:
  - ■ *"What was that like for (name of coach 1)?"*
    - □ Answers: Uncomfortable; awkward.
  - ■ *"What do you think (name of coach 1) thought of (name of coach 2)?"*
    - □ Answers: Overly enthusiastic; trying too hard; desperate.
  - ■ *"Is (name of coach 1) going to want to talk to (name of coach 2) again?"*
    - □ Answer: Probably not.
- ○ Ask behavioral coach 1 the same *Perspective Taking Questions*:
  - ■ *"What was that like for you?"*
  - ■ *"What did you think of (name of coach 2)?"*
  - ■ *"Are you going to want to talk to (name of coach 2) again?"*

Good Role Play: Giving a Courtesy Laugh ⊙

[Two behavioral coaches should do an APPROPRIATE role play demonstrating *giving a courtesy laugh*. If you do not have two behavioral coaches, the group leader can be a substitute for one of the coaches.]

- ● Begin by saying, *"We're going to do another role play. Watch this and tell me what (name of behavioral coach 2) is doing RIGHT in giving a courtesy laugh."*

Example of an APPROPRIATE Role Play
- Behavioral coach 2: *"Hi, (insert name). How are you?"*
- Behavioral coach 1: *"I'm pretty good. How are you?"*
- Behavioral coach 2: *"I'm fine. So what did you do over the break?"*
- Behavioral coach 1: *"I got together with some friends and went skiing."*
- Behavioral coach 2: *"Oh cool. Are you a pretty good skier?"*
- Behavioral coach 1: *"I guess so, but funny story . . . so this last trip we were skiing black diamonds and I made it almost all the way down the mountain with no problems and then totally wiped out in front of the 'DANGER' sign!"*
- Behavioral coach 2: (Courtesy laugh) *"That's pretty funny."*
- Behavioral coach 1: (Smiling, comfortable) *"Yeah, it was classic."*

- End by saying, *"Timeout on that. So what did (name of behavioral coach 2) do RIGHT in giving a courtesy laugh?"*
  - Answers: Not over the top; seemed normal; seemed like he/she thought it was funny.
- Ask the following *Perspective Taking Questions*:
  - *"What was that like for (name of coach 1)?"*
    - Answers: Nice; flattering; comfortable.
  - *"What do you think (name of coach 1) thought of (name of coach 2)?"*
    - Answers: Nice; friendly.
  - *"Is (name of coach 1) going to want to talk to (name of coach 2) again?"*
    - Answer: Yes.
- Ask behavioral coach 1 the same *Perspective Taking Questions*:
  - *"What was that like for you?"*
  - *"What did you think of (name of coach 2)?"*
  - *"Are you going to want to talk to (name of coach 2) again?"*

Behavioral Rehearsal: Giving a Courtesy Laugh

- Explain, *"Now we're going to have each of you practice giving a courtesy laugh to one of our behavioral coaches."*
- Go around the room and have each young adult practice *giving a courtesy laugh* to one of the behavioral coaches while everyone else is watching.
- Have the behavioral coach tell the same story to each young adult and have them practice *giving a courtesy laugh* at the end:
  - Say, *"So I went skiing with some friends last week and funny story . . . we were skiing black diamonds and I made it almost all the way down the mountain with no problems and then totally wiped out in front of the 'DANGER' sign!"*
- Provide *social coaching* as needed and *troubleshoot* any problems that may arise.
- End by giving a round of applause to each young adult after their practice.

- *Pay attention to your humor feedback*
  - Explain, *"One of the most important rules for using humor appropriately is that if you're going to tell a joke, you need to pay attention to your humor feedback. Humor feedback is the reaction people give you after you've told a joke."*
  - Ask, *"What could be the problem with not paying attention to your humor feedback?"*
    - Answers: People may not think the joke was funny and you may end up pushing people away; they may think you're weird or strange and may not want to be your friend.
  - Explain, *"When you're paying attention to your humor feedback, there are four types of reactions you should look for . . ."*
    - *Don't laugh at all*
    - *Giving a courtesy laugh*

- ■ *Laughing at you*
- ■ *Laughing with you*
- ○ Ask, *"What does it mean if they DON'T LAUGH at all?"*
  - ■ Answers: They don't think what you said was funny; this is **BAD humor feedback**.
- ○ Ask, *"What does it mean if they give you a COURTESY LAUGH?"*
  - ■ Answers: They're laughing to be polite, but don't think what you said was funny; this is **BAD humor feedback**.
- ○ Ask, *"What does it mean when they LAUGH AT YOU and what does that look like?"*
  - ■ Answers: See Table 6.2; this is **BAD humor feedback**.
- ○ Ask, *"What does it mean when they LAUGH WITH YOU and what does that look like?"*
  - ■ Answers: See Table 6.2; this is the only **GOOD humor feedback**.
- ○ Explain, *"The biggest mistake people make when paying attention to their humor feedback is they don't LOOK at the other person, and they only listen."*
- ○ Ask the following question using the sentence stem *"Can you HEAR people . . ."*
  - ■ *". . . roll their eyes?"*
  - ■ *". . . make a face?"*
  - ■ *". . . point at you?"*
  - ■ *". . . smile at you?"*
  - ■ *". . . shake their head?"*
- ○ Explain, *"In order to pay attention to humor our feedback, we need to LOOK and LISTEN. That means you must WATCH the other person for their reaction. Simply listening to whether they laugh will not give you enough feedback."*

Table 6.2 Humor Feedback Signs

Laughing AT You	Laughing WITH You
Laugh and roll their eyes	Laugh and smile
Look at someone else and then laugh	Compliment your joke or sense of humor
Laugh before the joke is over	Laugh and nod their head yes
Long pause before they laugh	They say, *"That's a good one"* and smile
Laugh and make a face	They say, *"You're funny"* and smile
Laugh and point at you	Ask you to tell another joke
Laugh and shake their head no to someone else	Say, *"I'll have to remember that one."*
Make sarcastic comments (this may be difficult to	They start telling jokes

Role Play: Paying Attention to Humor Feedback ▶

- Explain, *"Now we're going to practice paying attention to humor feedback. Remember that the best way to pay attention to humor feedback is to LOOK with your eyes and LISTEN with your ears. That means we need to WATCH the other person's reaction. Listening for whether they laughed is not enough, since they could be rolling their eyes or making a face."*
- Explain, *"(Name of behavioral coach) and I are going to practice first. (Name of behavioral coach) is going to tell the same joke twice. This joke is not meant to be funny. In fact, it's a good example of humor that is not age-appropriate for adults. The reason we're using it is because it's simple and most people have heard the joke before. The first time he/she tells the joke, his/her eyes will be closed. The second time he/she tells the joke, his/her eyes will be opened and looking at me. Both times, he/she has to guess if I was laughing AT him/her or laughing WITH him/her. Then we'll check to see which was easier: eyes opened or eyes closed."*

[The group leader and behavioral coach should do a role play of paying attention to humor feedback.]

Example of NOT LOOKING During Humor Feedback

- ○ Behavioral coach: (Turned around with eyes closed, cannot see group leader) *"Why did the chicken cross the road?"*
- ○ Group leader: (Curious, smiling) *"I don't know."*
- ○ Behavioral coach: (Still turned around with eyes closed) *"To get to the other side."*
- ○ Group leader: (Laughs WITH the coach, smiling, nodding head yes)
- ○ Group leader: (Brief pause) *"So timeout on that. Go ahead and turn around. So do you think I was laughing AT you or laughing WITH you?"*
- ○ Behavioral coach: (Uncertain, confused) *"I'm not sure. Were you laughing AT me?"*
- ○ Group leader: (Turn to young adults) *"What do you think group . . . was I laughing AT him/her or laughing WITH him/her?"*
- ○ Young adults: (Answer: You were laughing WITH him/her.)
- ○ Group leader: *"How could you tell?"*
- ○ Young adults: (Answers: You were smiling and nodding your head yes; did not roll your eyes or make a face.)
- ○ Group leader: (Turn to coach) *"I was actually laughing WITH you. It's hard to tell when you're not looking at the person!"*

Example of LOOKING during humor feedback

- ○ Group leader: (Still facing coach) *"Now try paying attention to your humor feedback with your eyes opened and looking at me."*
- ○ Behavioral coach: (Looking at the group leader) *"Why did the chicken cross the road?"*
- ○ Group leader: (Neutral) *"I don't know."*
- ○ Behavioral coach: (Still looking at the group leader) *"To get to the other side."*
- ○ Group leader: (Laughs AT the coach, rolling eyes, making a face, pointing at the coach)
- ○ Group leader: (Brief pause) *"So timeout on that. So do you think I was laughing AT you or laughing WITH you?"*
- ○ Behavioral coach: (Certain, confident) *"You were laughing AT me."*
- ○ Group leader: (Turn to young adults) *"What do you think group . . . was I laughing AT him/her or laughing WITH him/her?"*
- ○ Young adults: (Answer: You were laughing AT him/her.)
- ○ Group leader: *"How could you tell?"*
- ○ Young adults: (Answers: You were rolling your eyes; making a face; pointing at the coach.)
- ○ Group leader: (Turn to coach) *"That's right! I was laughing AT you. So which was easier . . . eyes opened or eyes closed?"*
- ○ Behavioral coach: (Certain, confident) *"Definitely eyes opened."*

Behavioral Rehearsal: Paying Attention to Humor Feedback ⊙

- Explain, *"Now we're going to have each of you practice paying attention to your humor feedback. We're going to go around the room and each of you is going to say the same joke twice. The first time you tell the joke, you will be facing away from me with your eyes closed. The second time you tell the joke, you will be facing me with your eyes opened. In both cases, you have to guess if I'm laughing AT you or laughing WITH you. We're all going to be telling the same joke. It's not about the joke; it's about paying attention to your humor feedback."*
- Young adults will be telling the SAME JOKE to the group leader while the rest of the group watches.
  - ○ Young adult: *"Why did the chicken cross the road?"*
  - ○ Group leader: *"I don't know."*
  - ○ Young adult: *"To get to the other side."*
  - ○ Group leader: (**Laughs AT** or **laughs WITH**)

- Be sure that each young adult uses the same joke or the group may get out of control and the lesson will become a competition about who has the funniest joke.
- The group leader should randomly alternate between demonstrating *laughing AT* (e.g., laughing, rolling eyes, making a face, pointing, shaking head no) and *laughing WITH* (e.g., laughing, smiling, nodding head yes).
- On the FIRST OCCASION, the young adults should have their EYES CLOSED and be turned away when telling the joke and *paying attention to their humor feedback.*
  - When the joke is finished and the group leader has given a reaction, have the young adult interpret the *humor feedback*.
    - Say, *"Okay, now open your eyes. So do you think that was laughing AT you or laughing WITH you?"*
  - Allow the young adult to take a guess and then have the rest of the young adults (who had their eyes opened) interpret the *humor feedback.*
  - The group leader will tell them if they were correct or incorrect.
- On the SECOND OCCASION, the young adults should have their EYES OPEN looking at the group leader when telling the joke and *paying attention to their humor feedback.*
  - When the joke is finished and the group leader has given a reaction, have the young adult interpret the *humor feedback*.
    - Say, *"So do you think that was laughing AT you or laughing WITH you?"*
  - Allow the young adult to take a guess and then have the rest of the young adults also interpret the *humor feedback.*
  - The group leader will tell them if they were correct or incorrect.
- Ask the practicing young adult, *"Which was easier . . . eyes opened or eyes closed?"*
  - Answer: Eyes opened.
  - If the young adult responds that it was easier with eyes closed, open it up to the group by asking, *"What do we think everyone. Is it generally easier to pay attention to humor feedback with eyes opened or eyes closed?"*
    - Answer: Eyes opened.
- After all adults have practiced paying attention to their *humor feedback*:
  - Say, *"The purpose of this exercise is to demonstrate how important it is to WATCH the other person for their reaction when we tell a joke. When you don't WATCH the other person's reaction, you may miss out on the humor feedback."*
- [Optional: Instead of doing live demonstrations of *laughing AT* and *laughing WITH*, you may show *Role Play Video Demonstrations* of *humor feedback* from the *PEERS® Role Play Video Library* (www.routledge.com/cw/laugeson). Have young adults individually guess if the person was *laughing at* or *laughing with*, while alternating between closing their eyes and opening their eyes. There are 20 *humor feedback* video demonstrations, which should be shown randomly during the behavioral rehearsal.]

Identifying Joke Tellers

- Explain, *"Everyone has a different relationship with humor. Some people like to tell jokes, many people like to hear jokes, and some people don't like jokes at all. There are basically three types of people when it comes to humor."*

- ***Joke Tellers***
  - Explain, *"Joke tellers are people who like to tell jokes CONSTANTLY. They consider themselves jokesters or class clowns, but the reality is that it's difficult to be funny ALL the time. Unfortunately, sometimes people aren't laughing WITH them; they're laughing AT them. Very few people are good joke tellers ALL the time."*
- ***Joke Lovers***
  - Explain, *"Joke lovers (or joke fans) are people who enjoy humor, sometimes tell jokes or make funny comments, but aren't trying to be funny ALL the time. Joke lovers like to laugh and occasionally tell*

jokes or joke around, but their identity isn't wrapped up in being a jokester or a class clown. Most people are joke lovers."

- **Joke Haters**
  - ○ Explain, *"Joke haters (or joke refusers) are people who don't enjoy humor. They don't like telling jokes or hearing jokes. Humor may make them uncomfortable or feel confused."*
  - ○ Ask, *"While it's perfectly fine not to like jokes, if you're more of a joke hater, is it your business to tell people not to tell jokes?"*
    - ■ Answer: No, that would be *policing*.
  - ○ Explain, *"So if we're not comfortable with humor, then we should remember that friendship is a choice, and being friends with joke tellers may not be a good choice for us, but it's not our business to be policing people about their humor."*
- Go around the room and have each young adult identify if they think they are more of a *joke teller*, *joke lover*, or *joke hater*.
  - ○ Have a behavioral coach take notes about this on the *Homework Compliance Sheet* in case anyone doesn't remember when we announce this at *Reunification*.
  - ○ Remind any young adult claiming to be a *joke teller* that it is very difficult to be a successful *joke teller* all the time and you expect them to **pay VERY close attention to their humor feedback**.
  - ○ Praise those who claim to be *joke lovers*. Normalize this by saying most people are *joke lovers* but they still tell jokes or joke around sometimes.
    - ■ It can be helpful if the group leader and behavioral coaches also self-identify as *joke lovers*.
  - ○ Normalize anyone who claims to be a *joke hater* by saying, *"Friendship is a CHOICE and you don't have to be friends with people who are joke tellers if you don't like that or it makes you uncomfortable."*
    - ■ It can also be helpful to remind *joke haters* that even if someone's humor makes us uncomfortable, it's not our job to *police* them and tell them not to tell jokes. We don't have to be friends with people if we don't like their humor.

- Explain, *"So those are some of the rules for appropriate use of humor. Remember that when humor is used inappropriately, it's one of the fastest ways to push people away, so we need to pay attention to our humor feedback if we're going to tell jokes. If we're not getting good humor feedback, then we need to stop telling jokes."*
- Say, *"Remember, if we're trying to socially engage and connect with others, we have a much better way that's far less risky. How do we connect with others and get to know them?"*
  - ○ Answer: **TRADING INFORMATION!!!**

APPROPRIATE USE OF HUMOR

Young Adult Behavioral Rehearsal

Trading Information About Personal Items

Materials Needed

- Young adults bring *personal items* to *trade information* with other group members.
- If young adults forget to bring *personal items*:
  - Cell phones with music and/or pictures may be used.
  - T-shirts with logos of favorite pastimes are relevant.
  - Young adults can simply talk about their interests without *personal items*.

Behavioral Rehearsal

- Break up young adults into dyads.
- Have young adults practice *trading information* and *having two-way conversations* about their *personal items*.
- Encourage young adults to identify *common interests* through *trading information*.
- Prompt young adults to ask questions when appropriate.
- Rotate young adults approximately every five minutes.
  - It may be necessary to create a triad if there is an uneven numbers of young adults.
- If there is time, debrief during the final five minutes of the group.
  - Have young adults recall what they learned about their peers through *trading information*.
  - Have young adults identify *common interests*.
    - Follow up by asking, *"What could you do with that information if you were going to hang out?"*

APPROPRIATE USE OF HUMOR

Reunification

- Announce that young adults should join their social coaches.
  - ○ Have young adults stand or sit next to their social coaches.
  - ○ Be sure to have silence and the full attention of the group before starting with *Reunification*.
  - ○ Have young adults generate the content from the lesson while social coaches listen.
- Say, *"Today, we talked about the rules for appropriate use of humor. What are some of the rules for appropriate use of humor?"*
  - ○ **Be a little more serious when you're FIRST getting to know someone.**
  - ○ **Don't repeat jokes with people who've heard them.**
  - ○ **Avoid insult jokes.**
  - ○ **Avoid dirty jokes.**
  - ○ **Avoid inside jokes with people who won't get them.**
  - ○ **Don't tell jokes to people in authority.**
  - ○ **Don't laugh for no reason.**
  - ○ **Humor should be age-appropriate.**
  - ○ **Humor should be context-appropriate.**
  - ○ **Think about whether it's the right time to tell jokes.**
  - ○ **Give a courtesy laugh if someone tells a joke.**
  - ○ **Pay attention to your humor feedback.**
- Say, *"One of the things we talked about today was if we're more of a joke teller, joke lover (or joke fan), or joke hater (or joke refuser). Who can tell us the difference between the three?"*
  - ○ Quickly have a young adult identify the differences.
- Say, *"So let's go around the room and quickly have young adults identify whether they think they're more of a joke teller, joke lover, or joke hater. Social coaches should make a note of this. Hopefully there are no surprises."*
  - ○ Go around the room and have each young adult identify if they think they're more of a *joke teller*, *joke lover*, or *joke hater*.
    - ■ The behavioral coach should have taken notes about this on the *Homework Compliance Sheet* in case a young adult doesn't remember.
  - ○ Point out that it is VERY difficult to be a successful *joke teller* all the time, so those who identified themselves as *joke tellers* need to pay special **attention to their humor feedback**.
- Say, *"This group did a great job of paying attention to their humor feedback. Let's give them a round of applause."*

Homework Assignments

Distribute the *Social Coaching Handout* to young adults and announce the following *Homework Assignments*:

1. Find a *source of friends*.
   - Young adults and social coaches should DISCUSS and DECIDE on *social activities* based on the young adult's interests.
   - BEGIN TO ENROLL in these activities immediately, if you haven't already.
     - Criteria for a good *social activity*:
       - Is based on the young adult's interests.
       - Meets weekly or at least every other week.
       - Includes accepting peers similar in age.
       - Includes unstructured time to interact with others.
       - Activity starts within the next couple of weeks.

2. *Start a conversation* and *trade information* with a peer (could be from the *source of friends*).
   - Social coaches should go over the rules and steps for *starting and maintaining a conversation* and *trading information* before the practice.
   - Social coaches should ask young adults the following *social coaching questions* after the practice:
     - *Did you start a conversation and with whom?*
     - *Did it seem like they wanted to talk to you and how could you tell?*
     - *Did you trade information and what were your common interests?*
     - *What could you do with that information if you were going to hang out?*
     - *Does this seem like someone you might want to hang out with?*

3. Pay attention to *humor feedback*.
   - If young adults happen to tell jokes (this is NOT the assignment), *pay attention to humor feedback*.
   - Social coaches should PRIVATELY ask the following *social coaching questions* after attempts at humor by young adults:
     - *What was your humor feedback?*
     - *How could you tell?*

4. *In-group call or video chat*.
   - Arrange a phone call or video chat with another group member to trade information.
   - Young adults and social coaches should schedule the day and time of the call with the other group member before leaving the group.
   - Go over the rules for *starting and ending phone calls* and *trading information* before the call.
   - Social coaches should ask young adults the following *social coaching questions* after the call:
     - *Which steps did you follow for starting the call?*
     - *What was the common interest?*
     - *What could you do with that information if you were going to hang out?*
     - *Which steps did you follow to end the call?*

5. Bring a *personal item* to *trade information*.
   - Bring a *personal item* to *trade information* with other group members next week (e.g., music, game, book, pictures).

- Read off the in-group call assignment (Appendix E) and remind social coaches to make a note of who is calling whom.
- Encourage the young adults and social coaches to use the Phone Roster (Appendix D) to note the day and time of the scheduled call each week.

Individual Check-Out

Once the calls have been scheduled, individually and privately negotiate with each young adult and social coach:

1. What type of *social activity* they are interested in joining, if they haven't already.
   - If they are already in a *social activity*, confirm that the activity:
     - Is based on the young adult's interests.
     - Meets weekly or at least every other week.
     - Includes accepting peers similar in age.
     - Includes unstructured time to interact with others.
     - Starts within the next couple of weeks.

2. Who they plan to *trade information* with at this *social activity*.

3. Where the social coach will be during the *in-group call or video chat*.

4. When young adults and social coaches will practice *starting and ending a phone call* while *trading information* and *finding common interests*.

5. What *personal item* they plan to bring next week.

APPROPRIATE USE OF HUMOR

Social Coaching Handout

Rule About Appropriate Use of Humor

- *Be a little more serious when you're FIRST getting to know someone.*
- *Don't repeat jokes with people who've heard them.*
- *Avoid insult jokes.*
- *Avoid dirty jokes.*
- *Avoid inside jokes with people who won't get them.*
- *Don't tell jokes to people in authority.*
- *Don't laugh for no reason.*
- *Humor should be age-appropriate.*
- *Humor should be context-appropriate.*
- *Think about whether it's the right time to tell jokes.*
- *Give a courtesy laugh if someone tells a joke.*
- *Pay attention to your humor feedback.*
  - *Don't laugh at all.*
  - *Giving a courtesy laugh.*
  - *Laughing at you.*
  - *Laughing with you.*

Table 6.2 Humor Feedback Signs

Laughing AT You	Laughing WITH You
Laugh and roll their eyes	Laugh and smile
Look at someone else and then laugh	Compliment your joke or sense of humor
Laugh before the joke is over	Laugh and nod their head yes
Long pause before they laugh	They say, *"That's a good one"* and smile
Laugh and make a face	They say, *"You're funny"* and smile
Laugh and point at you	Ask you to tell another joke
Laugh and shake their head no to someone else	Say, *"I'll have to remember that one."*
Make sarcastic comments (this may be difficult to interpret)	They start telling jokes

Homework Assignments

1. Find a *source of friends*.
   - Young adults and social coaches should DISCUSS and DECIDE on *social activities* based on the young adult's interests.
   - BEGIN TO ENROLL in these activities immediately, if you haven't already.
     - Criteria for a good *social activity*:
       - Is based on the young adult's interests.

- Meets weekly or at least every other week.
- Includes accepting peers similar in age.
- Includes unstructured time to interact with others.
- Activity starts within the next couple of weeks.

2. *Start a conversation* and *trade information* with a peer (could be from the *source of friends*).
   - Social coaches should go over the rules and steps for *starting and maintaining a conversation* and *trading information* before the practice.
   - Social coaches should ask young adults the following *social coaching questions* after the practice:
     - *Did you start a conversation and with whom?*
     - *Did it seem like they wanted to talk to you and how could you tell?*
     - *Did you trade information and what were your common interests?*
     - *What could you do with that information if you were going to hang out?*
     - *Does this seem like someone you might want to hang out with?*

3. *Pay attention to humor feedback.*
   - If young adults happen to tell jokes (this is NOT the assignment), *pay attention to humor feedback*.
   - Social coaches should PRIVATELY ask the following *social coaching questions* after attempts at humor by young adults:
     - *What was your humor feedback?*
     - *How could you tell?*

4. *In-group call or video chat.*
   - Arrange a phone call or video chat with another group member to trade information.
   - Young adults and social coaches should schedule the day and time of the call with the other group member before leaving the group.
   - Go over the rules for *starting and ending phone calls* and *trading information* before the call.
   - Social coaches should ask young adults the following *social coaching questions* after the call:
     - *Which steps did you follow for starting the call?*
     - *What was the common interest?*
     - *What could you do with that information if you were going to hang out?*
     - *Which steps did you follow to end the call?*

5. Bring a *personal item* to *trade information*.
   - Bring a *personal item* to *trade information* with other group members next week (e.g., music, game, book, pictures).

SESSION 6

ENTERING GROUP CONVERSATIONS

Social Coaching Therapist Guide

Preparing for the Social Coaching Session

The focus for this session is teaching young adults to appropriately enter group conversations with accepting peers. Socially challenged young adults often have difficulty with this higher level social skill, typically making one of two mistakes. Those young adults experiencing **peer rejection** will often barge into conversations and be **off topic**, resulting in further rejection. **Socially neglected** young adults may not attempt to enter at all. Instead, they may be hoping the group will speak to them, which they often do not. In either case, these attempts to make and keep friends are usually unsuccessful.

The advice often given to young adults is also fraught with mistakes. When attempting to meet a new group of people, most adults will say they have been given the advice to *"go up and say hi"* or *"go up and introduce yourself."* As with the previous examples, these tactics are not **ecologically valid**. Imagine if you were to go up and say *"hi"* or introduce yourself to a group of strangers. What might they think? At the very least, they might think that's a bit odd or random. At worst, they might think you're weird or creepy. Other advice young adults are given is to *"just be yourself"* or *"go up and talk to them."* It's difficult to know what these suggestions mean or what they would look like, but again this could seem strange or random if there is no context for what you choose to talk about. The bottom line is that young adults are often given the wrong advice from well-meaning caregivers about how to behave in social situations. This lesson will focus on correcting some of that bad advice and instead providing **ecologically valid strategies** for **entering group conversations**.

For any social coaches feeling skeptical about the program, this session is often pivotal in getting them on board. What person has not had to navigate their way around a social gathering, mixing and mingling? Even for the most socially savvy person, this can be a bit daunting and anxiety-provoking at moments. Fortunately, because this lesson highlights a sophisticated social skill that most of us need to use from time to time, any unconvinced social coaches tend to become convinced. They will often make statements such as, *"I could use this!"* or *"I wish I knew this when I was younger."*

Although most social coaches who have been on the fence about the program will reach a turning point in this session, there may still be one or two that are a bit treatment-resistant. One common type of treatment resistance is the frequent latecomer. These are the social coaches that frequently arrive late with their young adult, often missing 30 minutes or more of the session. Because the *Homework Review* in the *Social Coaching Session* includes approximately 50 minutes of *Homework Review*, they will sometimes mistakenly think they didn't miss anything (apart from other social coaches reporting on their assignments). This is actually untrue. By consistently arriving 30 minutes or more late, the social coach not only missed valuable *Social Coaching Tips* offered during the review of others' assignments, but the young adult will have missed the entire *Homework Review* in the young adult group. This means the repetition of instruction that is fundamental to the *Homework Review* (i.e., relabeling homework attempts using the **buzzwords**) and **troubleshooting** issues that arise during the *Homework Review* is completely lost for the young adult.

When social coaches arrive late to the group, it will be important not to allow their tardiness to disrupt the group by backtracking and trying to fill in the gaps of what they have missed. Likewise, avoid reviewing *Homework Assignments* that have already been discussed, as this will only serve to reinforce tardiness. If social coaches arrive in the middle of the *Didactic Lesson*, you can pass them a *Social Coaching Handout* without directly addressing their tardiness. Do not encourage excuses for lateness, as it takes valuable time away from the session. Chronic lateness should be addressed with the social coach outside of the session, having the caregiver wait after session and speaking to them away from their young adult. If the young adult is the cause of the tardiness, then a conversation with him or her is recommended as well. You can remind them of the portions of the sessions they have missed and how it will decrease the benefits their young adult might reap from the program. You might also mention that arriving late can be disruptive to the group and is unfair to other group members who have arrived on time.

Homework Review

[Go over the following *Homework Assignments* and **troubleshoot** any potential problems. Start with completed homework first. If you have time, you can inquire as to why others were unable to complete the assignment and try to **troubleshoot** how they might get it done for the coming week. When reviewing homework, be sure to relabel descriptions using the **buzzwords** (identified by **bold and italicized** print). Spend the majority of the *Homework Review* on **finding a source of friends** (if they haven't already reported on this) and **starting a conversation** and **trading information** with a peer, as these were the most important assignments.]

1. Bring a **personal item** to **trade information**.
   - Say, *"One of the assignments this week was to bring a personal item to trade information with other group members. Very quickly, let's hear what young adults brought to trade information about."*
     - If items are inappropriate, **troubleshoot** what they might bring next week.

2. Find a **source of friends**.
   - Say, *"Your main assignment this week was to help find a potential source of friends for your young adults and help them begin to enroll in social activities, if you haven't already. Who was able to identify a source of friends with your young adult?"*
   - Identify if the **sources of friends** are appropriate and meet the following criteria:
     - Are based on the young adult's interests.
     - Meet weekly or at least every other week.
     - Include accepting peers similar in age.
     - Include unstructured time to interact with others.
     - Activity starts within the next couple of weeks.

3. **Start a conversation** and **trade information** with a peer.
   - Say, *"Another assignment this week was for young adults to practice starting a conversation and trading information with a peer. This could have happened within the context of social activities. Who completed or attempted to complete this assignment?"*
   - Ask the following questions:
     - *"Where and with which peer did your young adult start a conversation?"*
     - *"Did you go over the rules and steps before the practice?"*
       - **Steps for Starting a Conversation**:
         1. **Casually Look Over**
         2. **Use a Prop**
         3. **Find a Common Interest**
         4. **Mention the Common Interest**
         5. **Trade Information**
         6. **Assess Interest**
            - **Are they talking to me?**
            - **Are they looking at me?**
            - **Are they facing me (or are they giving me the cold shoulder)?**
         7. **Introduce Yourself**

- ○ *"What social coaching did you do after the practice?"*
  - ■ Appropriate *social coaching questions*:
    - ❑ **Did you start a conversation and with whom?**
    - ❑ **Did it seem like they wanted to talk to you and how could you tell?**
    - ❑ **Did you trade information and what were your common interests?**
    - ❑ **What could you do with that information if you were going to hang out?**
    - ❑ **Does this seem like someone you might want to hang out with?**

4. *Pay attention to humor feedback.*
   - Say, *"Last week, we talked about appropriate use of humor. One of your assignments this week was for young adults to pay attention to their humor feedback if they happened to tell a joke. The assignment was NOT to tell a joke. Who completed this assignment or attempted to complete this assignment?"*
   - Ask the following questions:
     - ○ *"Did your young adult attempt to tell jokes and did he/she pay attention to the humor feedback?"*
     - ○ *"What did you do to provide social coaching around humor feedback?"*
       - ■ Appropriate *social coaching questions*:
         - ❑ **What was your humor feedback?**
         - ❑ **How could you tell?**

5. *In-group call or video chat.*
   - Say, *"Another assignment this week was for your young adult to have a phone call or video chat with someone in the group in order to practice starting and ending phone calls and trading information. Whose young adult did the in-group call or video chat?"*
   - Ask the following questions:
     - ○ *"Who did your young adult talk to and who called whom?"*
     - ○ *"What social coaching did you do before the call?"*
     - ○ *"Where were you during the call?"*
     - ○ *"How did the call start?"*
     - ○ *"Did they trade information and find a common interest?"*
     - ○ *"How did the call end?"*
     - ○ *"What social coaching did you do after the call?"*
       - ■ Appropriate *social coaching questions*:
         - ❑ **What was your common interest?**
         - ❑ **What could you do with that information if you were going to hang out?**
   - Have the other social coach who participated in the call or video chat give their account immediately after, but not at the same time.

Table 7.1 Steps for Starting and Ending Phone Calls

Starting Phone Calls	*Ending Phone Calls*
1. Ask for the person	*1. Wait for a bit of a pause*
2. Say who you are	*2. Give a cover story for why you have to go*
3. Ask how they are	*3. Tell the person it was nice talking*
4. Ask if they can talk	*4. Tell the person you will talk to them later*
5. Give a cover story for why you are calling	*5. Say goodbye*

- [Collect the *Social Coaching Homework Assignment Worksheets*. If social coaches forgot to bring the worksheets, have them complete a new form to hold them accountable for the assignments.]

Didactic Lesson: Entering Group Conversations

- Distribute the *Social Coaching Handout*.
  - ○ Sections in **bold print** in the *Social Coaching Therapist Guide* come directly from the *Social Coaching Handout*.

- ○ Remind social coaches that terms that are in ***bold and italicized*** print are ***buzzwords*** and represent important concepts from the PEERS® curriculum that should be used as much as possible when social coaching.
- Say, *"One way for young adults to make new friends is by talking to the people they're trying to get to know better. Young adults are often given advice about how to do this. Unfortunately, the advice they get is often wrong. What are most young adults told to do to meet new groups of people?"*
  - ○ Answers: Just be yourself; go up and talk to them; go up and introduce yourself; go up and say *"hi."*
- Say, *"Imagine what that would look like. What will people think of me if I go up and say 'hi' and introduce myself for no reason?"*
  - ○ Answers: They'll think that's odd and random; they'll think you're weird.
- Explain, *"Instead, we need to follow very specific steps for entering group conversations. These are not the steps we follow for joining conversations with people we already know well. With good friends we can just walk up and say hello. These are the steps we use for entering group conversations with people we either don't know or only know slightly."*

1. *Listen to the Conversation*
- Explain, *"Before you try to enter a group conversation between people you either don't know or only know slightly, you first need to discreetly listen to the conversation."*
- Ask, *"Why is it important to listen to the conversation?"*
  - ○ Answer: You need to know what the topic is before you try to enter.

2. *Watch from a Distance*
- Say, *"While you're listening, you should also be inconspicuously watching from a distance. Why would it be important to watch from a distance?"*
  - ○ Answer: It shows you're interested in the group.
- Ask, *"But do we want to stare at the group?"*
  - ○ Answer: No, absolutely not.
- Ask, *"What could be the problem with staring at the group?"*
  - ○ Answers: It will look like you're eavesdropping (which you are); they may think you're weird or creepy; they may think you're a stalker.

3. *Use a Prop*
- Explain, *"While you're listening and watching the conversation, it's helpful to use a prop like a mobile phone, a gaming device, or a book to make it look like you're focused on something else."*
- Ask, *"Why would it be a good idea to use a prop?"*
  - ○ Answers: It makes it seem like you're occupied with something else; doesn't look like you're eavesdropping (even though you are).

4. *Identify the Topic*
- Say, *"The most important goal of listening to the conversation will be to identify the topic being discussed. Why is it important to identify the topic?"*
  - ○ Answer: Because you need to be able to talk about that topic if you're going to enter the conversation.

5. *Find a Common Interest*
- Say, *"Before you attempt to enter a conversation, you need to make sure you share a common interest in the topic. Why is it important to find a common interest?"*
  - ○ Answer: Your ***common interest*** will be your excuse for entering.
- Ask, *"What could be the problem with trying to enter a conversation where you don't know anything about the topic?"*
  - ○ Answers: You will slow that conversation down; it will be boring for the group; it will be boring for you.

6. *Move Closer*
- Say, *"Once you've found a common interest and decided to enter the conversation, you should move a bit closer to the group. Usually about an arm or two lengths away is good. Why is it important to move closer?"*

○ Answers: It shows interest; it alerts the group you are entering; standing far away and trying to talk to the group would seem weird.

7. *Wait for a Pause*
   - Say, *"The next step is to wait for a brief pause in the conversation just before entering. Why is it important to wait for a pause in the conversation?"*
     ○ Answer: If you don't wait for a brief pause, you may be interrupting the conversation.
   - Explain, *"Some young adults will wait for the PERFECT PAUSE, particularly those who are a little more socially anxious. There's never a perfect pause, so we just tell them to try not to interrupt too much. The best time to enter is when one person stops talking and another is just beginning to talk."*

8. *Mention the Topic*
   - Say, *"You should enter the conversation by making a comment, asking a question, or giving a compliment about the topic. Why is it important to mention the topic?"*
     ○ Answer: This is your reason for entering the conversation.

9. *Assess Interest*
   - Explain, *"You also need to make sure the group wants to talk to you. What are the three behavioral signs we identified that tell us when someone wants to talk to us?"*
     ○ Answers: They're talking to you, looking at you, and facing you.
   - Explain, *"So after you've attempted to enter a conversation, you need to assess interest by asking yourself the following questions . . ."*
     ○ *Are they talking to me?*
       ▪ Explain, *"That means they're answering your questions, asking you questions, making comments, and not giving short responses or making rude comments."*
     ○ *Are they looking at me?*
       ▪ Explain, *"That means they're looking at you with interest, maybe even smiling, and not rolling their eyes or making a face."*
     ○ *Are they facing me (did they open the circle or close the circle)?*
       ▪ Explain, *"When people talk in groups, they talk in circles. When they want to talk to you, they open the circle. When they don't want to talk to you, they close the circle or give you the cold shoulder."*

10. *Introduce Yourself*
    - Explain, *"If you've been accepted, the final step for entering a group conversation is to introduce yourself to anyone you don't know. This step is optional and you only do this after you've been talking for several minutes and you're sure you've been accepted into the conversation."*
    - Ask, *"How do we introduce ourselves?"*
      ○ Answers: *"By the way, I'm (your name)"* or *"We haven't met. I'm (your name)."*
    - Explain, *"Of course, if they don't seem interested in talking to us, we should move on. Next week, we'll be giving young adults more concrete strategies for exiting conversations."*

- [Optional: Show BAD and GOOD *Role Play Video Demonstrations* of **entering group conversations** from the *PEERS® Role Play Video Library* (www.routledge.com/cw/laugeson) or *FriendMaker* mobile app, then ask the **Perspective Taking Questions** that follow the role plays.]

Homework Assignments

[Distribute the *Social Coaching Homework Assignment Worksheet* (Appendix I) for social coaches to complete and return at the next session.]

1. Find a *source of friends*.
   - **Young adults and social coaches should DISCUSS and DECIDE on *social activities* based on the young adult's interests.**
   - **BEGIN TO ENROLL in these activities immediately, if you haven't already.**
     ○ **Criteria for a good *social activity*:**
       ▪ **Is based on the young adult's interests.**

- Meets weekly or at least every other week.
- Includes accepting peers similar in age.
- Includes unstructured time to interact with others.
- Activity starts within the next couple of weeks.

2. *Enter a group conversation* with social coaches.
   - Young adults should practice *entering group conversations* with their social coach and another person (who will be ACCEPTING them into the conversation).
   - Social coaches should go over the rules and steps for *entering group conversations* before the practice.
   - Social coaches should ask young adults the following *social coaching questions* after the practice:
     - *Did it seem like we wanted to talk to you?*
     - *How could you tell?*
     - *What were our common interests?*
     - *What could we do with that information if we were going to hang out?*

3. *Enter a group conversation* with peers (could be from the *source of friends*).
   - Social coaches should go over the rules and steps for *entering group conversations* before the practice.
   - Social coaches should ask young adults the following *social coaching questions* after the practice:
     - *Where did you enter a conversation and with whom?*
     - *Which steps did you follow?*
     - *Did it seem like they wanted to talk to you and how could you tell?*
     - *Did you trade information and what were your common interests?*
     - *What could you do with that information if you were going to hang out?*
     - *Do these seem like people you might want to hang out with?*

4. *Pay attention to humor feedback.*
   - If young adults happen to tell jokes (this is NOT the assignment), *pay attention to humor feedback.*
   - Social coaches should PRIVATELY ask the following *social coaching questions* after attempts at humor by young adults:
     - *What was your humor feedback?*
     - *How could you tell?*

5. *In-group call or video chat.*
   - Arrange a phone call or video chat with another group member to trade information.
   - Note: This is the LAST in-group call or video chat.
   - Young adults and social coaches should schedule the day and time of the call with the other group member before leaving the group.
   - Go over the rules for *starting and ending phone calls* and *trading information* before the call.
   - Social coaches should ask young adults the following *social coaching questions* after the call:
     - *Which steps did you follow for starting the call?*
       - Steps are slightly modified if doing a video chat (i.e., you don't **ask for the person** or **say who you are**).
     - *What was the common interest?*
     - *What could you do with that information if you were going to hang out?*
     - *Which steps did you follow to end the call?*

6. Bring a *personal item* to *trade information.*
   - Bring a *personal item* to *trade information* with other group members next week (e.g., music, game, book, pictures).

Social Coaching Tips

- One of the assignments is for young adults to practice *entering group conversations* with their social coach and another person.
  - It is best if the other person is aware of the practice so that you can provide social coaching in the moment as needed.
    - Spouses, adult siblings, and other family members are often good options.
- The best time to set-up this extra practice is right before the young adult plans to *enter group conversations* with peers.
  - For example, before the young adult attends his or her *social activity*, you might go over the rules and steps for *entering group conversations* and then have him or her practice with you so that it's fresh in his/her mind when attempted with peers.
- Plan to provide coaching around the common mistakes that are made during these practice attempts.
  - Those with impulse control issues (e.g., ADHD) tend to barge into conversations without *watching* and *listening* or *waiting for a pause*.
    - *Social coaching questions* to ask in these situations:
      - *What are we supposed to be waiting for?*
      - *What are we doing while we're waiting for a pause?*
  - Those with internalizing issues (e.g., anxiety, depression) tend to wait for the *perfect pause*.
    - *Social coaching questions* to ask in these situations:
      - *Do you know the topic?*
        - [Note: If they don't know the topic, praise them for not joining and change the topic to something they know.]
      - *What are we waiting for?*
      - *Is there ever a perfect pause?*
- Make sure you ACCEPT your young adult into these conversations.
  - If they do something inappropriate, call a *"timeout"* and provide social coaching.
  - They will learn the steps for *exiting conversations* when they are NOT accepted next week.
- Encourage young adults to use the *FriendMaker* mobile app as a "virtual coach" to assist with real-life situations when they are *entering group conversations*.
  - Their phone can be *used as a prop* as they review the steps for *entering group conversations* in their *FriendMaker* app.

ENTERING GROUP CONVERSATIONS

Young Adult Therapist Guide

Preparing for the Young Adult Session

Knowing how to enter conversations with others is a critical ingredient for making and keeping friends and developing relationships. This is the process by which we meet people. If you were to ask young adults what advice they are often given to meet new people, they will probably tell you that they are told to *"go up and introduce yourself"* or *"go up and say hi."* Sadly, these are not *ecologically valid social skills* used by socially successful young adults. In fact, those strategies are likely to result in some form of rejection. Research suggests that successful entries into conversations begin with low-risk tactics such as waiting and listening. Unsuccessful entry attempts might include disrupting an ongoing conversation by asking for information or disagreeing.

Young adults will be taught the basic steps of *peer entry* (i.e., how to *enter group conversations* with peers). When teaching *peer entry*, it is helpful to break down these complex social behaviors into discrete steps. Young adults with Autism Spectrum Disorder (ASD) often think in concrete and literal ways. Breaking down complex social skills into easily digestible parts through the presentation of steps of behavior will make the skills far more understandable. The breaking down of these steps into concrete parts is equally helpful to young adults with other social challenges as it helps them to more easily conceptualize exactly what they will need to do.

A critical aspect of success with *peer entry* skills will be identifying the appropriate *social group* or members of a *social group* with which to *enter conversations*. This point cannot be understated. If young adults choose to *enter group conversations* with peers who are likely to reject them, perhaps because of poor choices in *social groups* or *social activities*, this may only make them feel defeated and increase social anxiety and avoidant behavior. At *Reunification*, you will need to be very specific with young adults in having them identify which *social group* they plan to enter conversation with and where. If there are serious questions about whether the young adult will be accepted by this group, it may be advisable to have the young adult choose a different *social group* for the time being that is less likely to reject them.

One of the more common difficulties with this lesson for socially anxious young adults is trouble initiating all of the steps for *entering a group conversation* during the in-group *Behavioral Rehearsal Exercise*. One way to overcome this anxiety is to walk through the steps with the young adult, side by side, essentially *entering the group conversation* together. This may ease some nervousness so that the young adult may be able to independently *enter group conversations* during future rehearsals. For young adults that are particularly socially anxious and reluctant to complete this rehearsal or assignment, it may be helpful to have them practice just the first few steps of *entering group conversations*, which involve *listening, watching, identifying the topic*, and *finding common interests*, while establishing proximity and interest in the group. In subsequent sessions, the young adult may be encouraged to add additional steps as he or she feels more comfortable.

Another common issue that comes up in the behavioral rehearsal for *entering group conversations* is that young adults will often *wait for the perfect pause*. Perhaps it is due to their tendency to follow rules and be exacting in their utilization of rules that compels them to wait for the *perfect pause* during *peer entry*. You will notice this immediately when you observe a young adult *listening* and *watching from a distance* with no effort to move toward the group. You can coach the young adult in the moment by asking questions such as, *"Do you know what they're talking about?"*, *"Do you know anything about that topic?"*, *"What are you waiting for?"*, *"Is there ever a PERFECT pause?"*, and *"There's never a PERFECT pause, so go ahead and enter, just try not to interrupt too much."* You might even point out moments when it would be appropriate to enter, such as when the conversation is going from one person to the next.

Another issue that may come up during the behavioral rehearsal is that young adults choose not to **enter group conversations** because they don't know about the topic that is being discussed. Since this is a very appropriate response, you will want to praise them for having good judgment. Then, in order to facilitate practice, you should ask the other group members to change the topic so the young adult can appropriately enter. This will be artificial, but the young adults won't mind since this is just for practice. Be sure that the new topic is something that the young adult attempting to enter knows something about.

Homework Review

[Go over the following *Homework Assignments* and **troubleshoot** any potential problems. Start with completed homework first. If you have time, you can inquire as to why others were unable to complete the assignment and try to **troubleshoot** how they might get it done for the coming week. When reviewing homework, be sure to relabel descriptions using the **buzzwords** (identified by **bold and italicized** print). Spend the majority of the *Homework Review* on **finding a source of friends** (if they haven't already reported on this) and **starting a conversation** and **trading information** with a peer, as these were the most important assignments.]

1. Bring a **personal item** to **trade information**.
    - Say, *"One of the assignments this week was to bring a personal item to trade information with other group members. Very quickly, let's hear what you brought to trade information."*
        ○ Have young adults place these items somewhere off to the side of the room to avoid distractions.
        ○ If items are inappropriate, **troubleshoot** what they might bring next week.

2. Find a **source of friends**.
    - Say, *"Your main assignment this week was to find a potential source of friends with the help of your social coaches and begin to enroll in social activities, if you haven't already. Who was able to identify a source of friends?"*
    - Identify if the **sources of friends** are appropriate and meet the following criteria:
        ○ Are based on the young adult's interests.
        ○ Meet weekly or at least every other week.
        ○ Include accepting peers similar in age.
        ○ Include unstructured time to interact with others.
        ○ Activity starts within the next couple of weeks.

3. **Start a conversation** and **trade information** with a peer.
    - Say, *"Another assignment this week was to practice starting a conversation and trading information with a peer. This could have happened within the context of your social activities. Raise your hand if you did this assignment."*
    - Ask the following questions:
        ○ *"Where and with whom did you start a conversation?"*
        ○ *"How did you start the conversation?"*
            ■ *Steps for Starting a Conversation*:
                1. *Casually Look Over*
                2. *Use a Prop*
                3. *Find a Common Interest*
                4. *Mention the Common Interest*

5. ***Trade Information***
6. ***Assess Interest***
   - ☐ ***Are they talking to me?***
   - ☐ ***Are they looking at me?***
   - ☐ ***Are they facing me (or are they giving me the cold shoulder)?***
7. ***Introduce Yourself***
- ○ *"Did it seem like they wanted to talk to you and how could you tell?"*
- ○ *"Did you trade information and what were your common interests?"*
- ○ *"What could you do with that information if you were going to hang out?"*
- ○ *"Does this seem like someone you might want to hang out with?"*

4. ***Pay attention to humor feedback.***
   - Say, *"Last week, we talked about appropriate use of humor. One of your assignments this week was to pay attention to your humor feedback if you happened to tell a joke. The assignment was NOT to tell a joke. If you happened to tell a joke this week, raise your hand if you paid attention to your humor feedback."*
   - Ask the following questions:
     - ○ *"I don't want to know what joke you told, I just want to know what your humor feedback was. Were they laughing AT you, laughing WITH you, giving a courtesy laugh, or NOT laughing at all?"*
     - ○ *"How could you tell?"*
     - ○ *"So are you done paying attention to your humor feedback?"*
       - ▪ Answer: No.
     - ○ *"When will you pay attention to your humor feedback?"*
       - ▪ Answer: Every time they tell a joke.
     - ○ *"How will you pay attention to your humor feedback?"*
       - ▪ Answer: By LOOKING and LISTENING.

5. ***In-group call or video chat.***
   - Say, *"Another assignment you had this week was to have a phone call or video chat with someone in the group in order to practice starting and ending phone calls and trading information. Raise your hand if you did the in-group call or video chat."*
   - Ask the following questions:
     - ○ *"Who did you talk to and who called whom?"*
     - ○ *"How did the call start?"* (only ask the caller)
     - ○ *"Did you trade information and did you find a common interest?"*
     - ○ *"What could you do with that information if you were going to hang out?"*
     - ○ *"How did the call end?"* (only ask the person that ended the call)
   - Have the other person who participated in the call or video chat give their account immediately after, but not at the same time.

Table 7.1 Steps for Starting and Ending Phone Calls

Starting Phone Calls	*Ending Phone Calls*
1. Ask for the person	*1. Wait for a bit of a pause*
2. Say who you are	*2. Give a cover story for why you have to go*
3. Ask how they are	*3. Tell the person it was nice talking*
4. Ask if they can talk	*4. Tell the person you will talk to them later*
5. Give a cover story for why you are calling	*5. Say goodbye*

Didactic Lesson: Entering Group Conversations

- Say, *"One way to make new friends is by talking to the people we're trying to get to know better. Young adults are often given advice about how to do this. Unfortunately, the advice you get is often wrong. What are most young adults told to do to meet new groups of people?"*

- ○ Answers: *"Just be yourself;" "go up and talk to them;" "go up and introduce yourself;" "go up and say hi."*
- Say, *"The truth is this isn't very good advice. What will people think of me if I go up and say 'hi' and introduce myself for no reason?"*
  - ○ Answers: They'll think that's odd and random; they'll think you're weird.
- Explain, *"Instead, we need to follow very specific steps for entering group conversations. These are not the steps we follow for joining conversations with people we already know well. With good friends, we can just walk up and say hello. These are the steps we use for entering group conversations with people we either don't know or only know slightly."*

[The group leader should do an INAPPROPRIATE role play demonstrating barging into a conversation between two behavioral coaches. If you do not have a second behavioral coach, you can show the BAD Role Play Video Demonstration of **entering group conversations** from the *PEERS® Role Play Video Library* (www.routledge.com/cw/laugeson) or *FriendMaker* mobile app, then ask the **Perspective Taking Questions** that follow the role play.]

Bad Role Play: Entering a Group Conversation ▶

- Begin by saying, *"We're going to do a role play where I'll try to enter a group conversation with people I don't know well. Watch this and tell me what I'm doing WRONG."*

> Example of an INAPPROPRIATE Role Play
>
> - ○ Group leader: (Standing several feet from the two behavioral coaches)
> - ○ Behavioral coach 1: *"Hi, (insert name). How was your weekend?"*
> - ○ Behavioral coach 2: *"It was good. How was yours?"*
> - ○ Behavioral coach 1: *"It was pretty good. What did you do?"*
> - ○ Behavioral coach 2: *"I just hung out and watched some movies."*
> - ○ Behavioral coach 1: *"Oh yeah? What movies did you watch?"*
> - ○ Behavioral coach 2: *"I watched a couple of sci-fi movies."*
> - ○ Behavioral coach 1: *"Really? I love sci-fi movies. Which ones did you . . ."*
> - ○ Group leader: (Walks over abruptly, interrupts) *"Are you guys going to the big gaming convention?"*
> - ○ Behavioral coach 1: (Startled, confused) *"Umm . . . no."* (Turning away from the group leader) *"So anyway, you were saying that you watched some sci-fi movies . . ."*
> - ○ Group leader: (Interrupts) *"I'm going to this really cool gaming convention next week. Have you guys ever been to one?"*
> - ○ Behavioral coach 2: (Looking annoyed, rolling eyes) *"Umm . . . no."* (Turning away from the group leader) *"So, anyway. Yeah, I just hung out and watched some movies. Have you ever seen . . ."*
> - ○ Group leader: (Interrupts) *"You guys should really go to this gaming convention. It's really cool! They have all the latest video games and there's lots of free stuff . . ."*
> - ○ Behavioral coaches 1 & 2: (Looking annoyed, ignoring comments, rolling eyes)

- End by saying, *"Timeout on that. So what did I do WRONG in trying to enter that conversation?"*
  - ○ Answer: You barged in and were **off topic**.
- Ask, *"Did it seem like they wanted to talk to me?"*
  - ○ Answer: No.
- Ask, *"How could you tell?"*
  - ○ Answers: They weren't **talking to you**; weren't **looking at you**; weren't **facing you**.
- Ask the following **Perspective Taking Questions**:
  - ○ *"What was that like for (names of coaches)?"*
    - ■ Answers: Irritating; annoying; frustrating.
  - ○ *"What do you think (names of coaches) thought of me?"*

- ■ Answers: Rude; obnoxious; annoying; weird.
  - ○ *"Are (names of coaches) going to want to talk to me again?"*
    - ■ Answers: No; too annoying.
- Ask the behavioral coaches the same *Perspective Taking Questions*:
  - ○ *"What was that like for you?"*
  - ○ *"What did you think of me?"*
  - ○ *"Would you want to talk to me again?"*

Steps for Entering a Group Conversation

[Present the rules and steps for *entering group conversations* by writing the following bullet points and *buzzwords* (identified by *bold and italicized* print) on the board. Do not erase the rules and steps until the end of the lesson.]

1. *Listen to the Conversation*
   - Explain, *"Before you try to enter a group conversation between people you either don't know or only know slightly, you first need to discreetly listen to the conversation."*
   - Ask, *"Why is it important to listen to the conversation?"*
     - ○ Answer: You need to know what the topic is before you try to enter.

2. *Watch from a Distance*
   - Explain, *"While you're listening, you should also be inconspicuously watching from a distance. This means you should occasionally look over toward the group for a second or two at a time, without staring at them."*
   - Ask, *"Why would it be important to watch from a distance?"*
     - ○ Answer: It shows you're interested in the group.
   - Ask, *"But do we want to stare at the group?"*
     - ○ Answer: No, absolutely not.
   - Ask, *"What could be the problem with staring at the group?"*
     - ○ Answers: It will look like you're eavesdropping (which you are); they may think you're weird or creepy; they may think you're a stalker.

3. *Use a Prop*
   - Explain, *"While you're listening and watching the conversation, it's helpful to use a prop like a mobile phone, a gaming device, or a book to make it look like you're focused on something else."*
   - Ask, *"Why would it be a good idea to use a prop?"*
     - ○ Answers: It makes it seem like you're occupied with something else; doesn't look like you're eavesdropping (even though you are).

4. *Identify the Topic*
   - Explain, *"The most important goal of listening to the conversation will be to identify the topic being discussed."*
   - Ask, *"Why is it important to identify the topic?"*
     - ○ Answer: Because you need to be able to talk about that topic if you're going to enter the conversation.

5. *Find a Common Interest*
   - Say, *"Before you attempt to enter a conversation, you need to make sure you share a common interest in the topic. Why is it important to find a common interest?"*
     - ○ Answer: Your *common interest* will be your excuse for entering.
   - Ask, *"If you don't have a common interest and you don't know anything about the topic, should you try to enter that conversation?"*
     - ○ Answer: No.
   - Ask, *"What could be the problem with trying to enter a conversation where you don't know anything about the topic?"*
     - ○ Answers: You will slow that conversation down; it will be boring for the group; it will be boring for you.

6. *Move Closer*
   - Explain, *"Once you've found a common interest and decided to enter the conversation, you should move a bit closer to the group. Usually about an arm or two lengths away is good."*
   - Ask, *"Why is it important to move closer?"*
     - Answers: It shows interest; alerts the group you are about to enter; to stand far away and try to talk to the group would seem weird.

7. *Wait for a Pause*
   - Say, *"The next step is to wait for a brief pause in the conversation just before entering. Why is it important to wait for a pause in the conversation?"*
     - Answer: If you don't wait for a brief pause, you may be interrupting the conversation.
   - Ask, *"Is there ever a PERFECT PAUSE?"*
     - Answer: No.
   - Explain, *"There's never a perfect pause, so just try not to interrupt too much. The best time to enter is when one person stops talking and another is just beginning to talk."*

8. *Mention the Topic*
   - Explain, *"You should enter the conversation by making a comment or asking a question about the topic."*
   - Ask, *"Why is it important to mention the topic?"*
     - Answer: This is your reason for entering the conversation.

9. *Assess Interest*
   - Explain, *"You also need to make sure the group wants to talk to you. What are the three behavioral signs we identified that tell us when someone wants to talk to us?"*
     - Answers: They're **talking to you**, **looking at you**, and **facing you**.
   - Explain, *"So after you've attempted to enter a conversation, you need to assess interest by asking yourself the following questions . . ."*
     - *Are they talking to me?*
       - Explain, *"That means they're answering your questions, asking you questions, making comments, and not giving short responses or making rude comments."*
     - *Are they looking at me?*
       - Explain, *"That means they're looking at you with interest, maybe even smiling, and not rolling their eyes or making a face."*
     - *Are they facing me (did they open the circle or close the circle)?*
       - Explain, *"When people talk in groups, they talk in circles. When they want to talk to you, they open the circle. When they don't want to talk to you, they close the circle or give you the cold shoulder."*

10. *Introduce Yourself*
    - Explain, *"If you've been accepted, the final step for entering a group conversation is to introduce yourself to anyone you don't know. This step is optional and you only do this after you've been talking for several minutes and you're sure you've been accepted into the conversation."*
    - Ask, *"How do we introduce ourselves?"*
      - Answers: *"By the way, I'm (your name)"* or *"We haven't met. I'm (your name)."*
    - Ask, *"If they don't seem interested in talking to us, should we introduce ourselves?"*
      - Answer: No, we should **move on**.

Good Role Play: Entering a Group Conversation ⊙

[The group leader should do an APPROPRIATE role play demonstrating *entering a group conversation* between two behavioral coaches. If you do not have a second behavioral coach, you can show the GOOD Role Play Video Demonstration of *entering group conversations* from the *PEERS® Role Play Video Library* (www.routledge.com/cw/laugeson) or *FriendMaker* mobile app, then ask the **Perspective Taking Questions** that follow the role play.]

- Begin by saying, *"We're going to do another role play. Watch this and tell me what I'm doing RIGHT in entering this conversation."*

Example of an APPROPRIATE Role Play
- ○ Group leader: (Standing several feet from the two behavioral coaches, looking at a cell phone)
- ○ Behavioral coach 1: "Hi, (insert name). How was your weekend?"
- ○ Behavioral coach 2: "It was good. How was yours?"
- ○ Behavioral coach 1: "It was pretty good. What did you do?"
- ○ Behavioral coach 2: "Oh, I just hung out and watched some movies."
- ○ Group leader: (Looks over at coaches, shows interest, then looks away)
- ○ Behavioral coach 1: "Oh yeah? What movies did you watch?"
- ○ Behavioral coach 2: "I watched a couple of sci-fi movies."
- ○ Group leader: (Looks over at coaches, shows interest, then looks away)
- ○ Behavioral coach 1: "How fun. I love sci-fi!"
- ○ Behavioral coach 2: "Really? That's cool."
- ○ Behavioral coach 1: "So which ones did you watch?"
- ○ Behavioral coach 2: "I did a little Star Wars marathon."
- ○ Group leader: (Looks over at coaches, shows interest, then looks away)
- ○ Behavioral coach 1: "That's awesome. Those are classic."
- ○ Behavioral coach 2: "I know right? Phantom Menace is my favorite. How about you?"
- ○ Behavioral coach 1: "Definitely Episode 1! Hard to beat that one."
- ○ Group leader: (Looks over at coaches, starts walking over, makes eye contact)
- ○ Behavioral coaches 1 & 2: (Look at the group leader)
- ○ Group leader: (Waits for a brief pause) "So you guys are into Star Wars?"
- ○ Behavioral coaches 1 & 2: (Look at the group leader) "Yeah. Are you?"
- ○ Group leader: "Oh definitely. Actually, I'm not sure if you heard, but they're showing Episodes 1–3 next week at this old theater downtown."
- ○ Behavioral coach 2: (Opens the circle) "No way!"
- ○ Behavioral coach 1: (Opens the circle) "Really? I hadn't heard about that."
- ○ Behavioral coach 2: "That's so cool."
- ○ Group leader: "I know. I've never seen them on the big screen."
- ○ Behavioral coach 1: "Me neither. I'm going to have to check that out."
- ○ Group leader: "You should." (Brief pause) "I'm (insert name) by the way."
- ○ Behavioral coach 2: (Smiles) "Oh cool. I'm (insert name)."
- ○ Behavioral coach 1: (Smiles) "Hi, I'm (insert name)."

- End by saying, "Timeout on that. So what did I do RIGHT in entering that conversation?"
  - ○ Answers: *Listened and watched; used a prop; identified the topic; found a common interest; moved closer; waited for a pause; mentioned the topic; assessed interest; introduced yourself.*
- Ask, "Did it seem like they wanted to talk to me?"
  - ○ Answer: Yes.
- Ask, "How could you tell?"
  - ○ Answers: *They were talking to you, looking at you, and facing you (they opened the circle).*
- Ask the following *Perspective Taking Questions*:
  - ○ "What was that like for (names of coaches)?"
    - Answers: Nice; pleasant.
  - ○ "What do you think (names of coaches) thought of me?"
    - Answers: Nice; interesting; pretty cool.
  - ○ "Are (names of coaches) going to want to talk to me again?"
    - Answer: Yes, probably.
- Ask the behavioral coaches the same *Perspective Taking Questions*:
  - ○ "What was that like for you?"
  - ○ "What did you think of me?"
  - ○ "Would you want to talk to me again?"
- Explain, "So those are the steps for entering a group conversation with people we either don't know or only know slightly. You're going to be practicing this as you trade information about your personal items, and you will continue to practice during your Homework Assignments this week."

ENTERING GROUP CONVERSATIONS

Young Adult Behavioral Rehearsal

Entering Group Conversations

Materials Needed

- Young adults bring *personal items* to *trade information* about.
- If young adults forget to bring *personal items*:
    - Cell phones with music and/or pictures may be used.
    - T-shirts with logos of favorite pastimes are relevant.
    - Young adults can simply talk about their interests without *personal items*.

Behavioral Rehearsal

- Break up young adults into small groups (no less than three young adults per group).
- Have young adults practice *trading information* about their *personal items* while taking turns *entering a group conversation*.
- For young adults practicing *trading information* about *personal items*:
    - Encourage young adults to identify *common interests* through *trading information*.
    - Inform the young adults that they should accept the entering person into these conversations.
- For young adults practicing *entering a group conversation*:
    - Separate the young adult from the group and have him or her identify the *steps for entering group conversations* before practicing (they may need to look at the board at first).
    - You may need to provide Socratic prompting to the young adult for identifying the specific steps by using some of the following *social coaching questions*:
        - *"What do you want to do with your ears?"*
        - *"What are you listening for?"*
        - *"What do you want to do with your eyes?"*
        - *"Should you be staring at them?"*
        - *"What could you use while you're listening?"*
        - *"Do you want to join from across the room?"*
        - *"Should you barge right in or wait for something?"*
        - *"Is there ever a PERFECT PAUSE?"*
        - *"When you join, what should you be talking about?"*
    - Then have the young adult practice using these steps by *entering the group conversation* with their peers in which the others will be *trading information* about their *personal items*.
    - You may need to provide Socratic prompting to the young adult if they have trouble following the steps by using some of the following *social coaching questions*:
        - *"Do you know what they're talking about?"*
        - *"Do you know anything about that topic?"*
            - [Note: If they don't know the topic, praise them for not joining and have the young adults change the topic to something they know.]

- *"Do you want to use anything while you're listening?"*
- *"What are you waiting for before you enter?"*
- *"Is there ever a PERFECT PAUSE?"*
- *"Do you want to move closer before you enter?"*
- *"When you enter, do you want to be on topic?"*

- In the event that a young adult incorrectly **enters the group conversation**, call a *"timeout"* and use this as a coachable moment to offer praise and then gently point out the error, while providing feedback on how to more appropriately attempt to enter.
  - Have the young adult try again until he or she is successful at following the steps.
- Once the young adult has successfully entered, call a *"timeout"* and have the other young adults applaud.
- Have each young adult practice **entering a group conversation** at least once.

ENTERING GROUP CONVERSATIONS

Reunification

- Announce that young adults should join their social coaches.
  - ○ Have young adults stand or sit next to their social coaches.
  - ○ Be sure to have silence and the full attention of the group before starting with *Reunification*.
  - ○ Have young adults generate the content from the lesson while social coaches listen.
- Say, *"Today we talked about the rules and steps for entering group conversations. What are the steps for entering group conversations?"*
  1. *Listen to the Conversation*
  2. *Watch from a Distance*
  3. *Use a Prop*
  4. *Identify the Topic*
  5. *Find a Common Interest*
  6. *Move Closer*
  7. *Wait for a Pause*
  8. *Mention the Topic*
  9. *Assess Interest*
     - *Are they talking to me?*
     - *Are they looking at me?*
     - *Are they facing me (did they open the circle or close the circle)?*
  10. *Introduce Yourself*
- Say, *"The young adults practiced entering group conversation while people were trading information about their personal items and the group did a great job. Let's give them a round of applause."*

Homework Assignments

Distribute the *Social Coaching Handout* to young adults and announce the following *Homework Assignments*:

1. Find a *source of friends*.
   - Young adults and social coaches should DISCUSS and DECIDE on *social activities* based on the young adult's interests.
   - BEGIN TO ENROLL in these activities immediately, if you haven't already.
     - ○ Criteria for a good *social activity*:
       - Is based on the young adult's interests.
       - Meets weekly or at least every other week.
       - Includes accepting peers similar in age.
       - Includes unstructured time to interact with others.
       - Activity starts within the next couple of weeks.

2. *Enter a group conversation* with social coaches.
   - Young adults should practice *entering group conversations* with their social coach and another person (who will be ACCEPTING them into the conversation).

- Social coaches should go over the rules and steps for *entering group conversations* before the practice.
- Social coaches should ask young adults the following *social coaching questions* after the practice:
  - *Did it seem like we wanted to talk to you?*
  - *How could you tell?*
  - *What were our common interests?*
  - *What could we do with that information if we were going to hang out?*

3. *Enter a group conversation* with peers (could be from the *source of friends*).
    - Social coaches should go over the rules and steps for *entering group conversations* before the practice.
    - Social coaches should ask young adults the following *social coaching questions* after the practice:
      - *Where did you enter a conversation and with whom?*
      - *Which steps did you follow?*
      - *Did it seem like they wanted to talk to you and how could you tell?*
      - *Did you trade information and what were your common interests?*
      - *What could you do with that information if you were going to hang out?*
      - *Do these seem like people you might want to hang out with?*

4. *Pay attention to humor feedback.*
    - If young adults happen to tell jokes (this is NOT the assignment), *pay attention to humor feedback*.
    - Social coaches should PRIVATELY ask the following *social coaching questions* after attempts at humor by young adults:
      - *What was your humor feedback?*
      - *How could you tell?*

5. *In-group call or video chat.*
    - Arrange a phone call or video chat with another group member to trade information.
    - Note: This is the LAST in-group call or video chat.
    - Young adults and social coaches should schedule the day and time of the call with the other group member before leaving the group.
    - Go over the rules for *starting and ending phone calls* and *trading information* before the call.
    - Social coaches should ask young adults the following *social coaching questions* after the call:
      - *Which steps did you follow for starting the call?*
      - *What was the common interest?*
      - *What could you do with that information if you were going to hang out?*
      - *Which steps did you follow to end the call?*

6. Bring a *personal item* to *trade information*.
    - Bring a *personal item* to *trade information* with other group members next week (e.g., music, game, book, pictures).

- Read off the in-group call assignment (Appendix E) and remind social coaches to make a note of who is calling whom.
- Encourage the young adults and social coaches to use the Phone Roster (Appendix D) to note the day and time of the scheduled call each week.

Individual Check-Out

Once the calls have been scheduled, individually and privately negotiate with each young adult and social coach:

1. What type of *social activity* they are interested in joining, if they haven't already.
   - If they are already in a *social activity*, confirm that the activity:
     - Is based on the young adult's interests.
     - Meets weekly or at least every other week.
     - Includes accepting peers similar in age.
     - Includes unstructured time to interact with others.
     - Starts within the next couple of weeks.

2. When they plan to *enter a group conversation* with social coaches.
   - Which other person they would be comfortable practicing with.

3. Where, when, and with whom they plan to *enter a group conversation* with peers.
   - Whether this is an accepting *social group* and how they can tell.

4. Where the social coach will be during the *in-group call or video chat*.

5. What *personal item* they plan to bring next week.

ENTERING GROUP CONVERSATIONS

Social Coaching Handout

Steps for Entering Group Conversations*

1. *Listen to the Conversation*
2. *Watch from a Distance*
3. *Use a Prop*
4. *Identify the Topic*
5. *Find a Common Interest*
6. *Move Closer*
7. *Wait for a Pause*
8. *Mention the Topic*
9. *Assess Interest*
   - *Are they talking to me?*
   - *Are they looking at me?*
   - *Are they facing me (did they open the circle or close the circle)?*
10. *Introduce Yourself*

Homework Assignments

1. Find a *source of friends*.
   - Young adults and social coaches should DISCUSS and DECIDE on *social activities* based on the young adult's interests.
   - BEGIN TO ENROLL in these activities immediately, if you haven't already.
     - Criteria for a good *social activity*:
       - Is based on the young adult's interests.
       - Meets weekly or at least every other week.
       - Includes accepting peers similar in age.
       - Includes unstructured time to interact with others.
       - Activity starts within the next couple of weeks.

2. *Enter a group conversation* with social coaches.
   - Young adults should practice *entering group conversations* with their social coach and another person (who will be ACCEPTING them into the conversation).
   - Social coaches should go over the rules and steps for *entering group conversations* before the practice.
   - Social coaches should ask young adults the following *social coaching questions* after the practice:
     - *Did it seem like we wanted to talk to you?*
     - *How could you tell?*
     - *What were our common interests?*
     - *What could we do with that information if we were going to hang out?*

3. *Enter a group conversation* with peers (could be from the *source of friends*).
   - Social coaches should go over the rules and steps for *entering group conversations* before the practice.
   - Social coaches should ask young adults the following *social coaching questions* after the practice:
     - *Where did you enter a conversation and with whom?*
     - *Which steps did you follow?*
     - *Did it seem like they wanted to talk to you and how could you tell?*
     - *Did you trade information and what were your common interests?*
     - *What could you do with that information if you were going to hang out?*
     - *Do these seem like people you might want to hang out with?*

4. *Pay attention to humor feedback*.
   - If young adults happen to tell jokes (this is NOT the assignment), *pay attention to humor feedback*.
   - Social coaches should PRIVATELY ask the following *social coaching questions* after attempts at humor by young adults:
     - *What was your humor feedback?*
     - *How could you tell?*

5. *In-group call or video chat*.
   - Arrange a phone call or video chat with another group member to trade information.
   - Young adults and social coaches should schedule the day and time of the call with the other group member before leaving the group.
   - Go over the rules for *starting and ending phone calls* and *trading information* before the call.
   - Social coaches should ask young adults the following *social coaching questions* after the call:
     - *Which steps did you follow for starting the call?*
     - *What was the common interest?*
     - *What could you do with that information if you were going to hang out?*
     - *Which steps did you follow to end the call?*

6. Bring a *personal item* to *trade information*.
   - Bring a *personal item* to *trade information* with other group members next week (e.g., music, game, book, pictures).

* See *The Science of Making Friends* DVD (Laugeson, 2013) or *FriendMaker* mobile app for a video Role Play Demonstration of the corresponding rule.

SESSION 7

EXITING CONVERSATIONS

Social Coaching Therapist Guide

Preparing for the Social Coaching Session

At this point in the group, there have been six weeks of *Homework Assignments*. You will quickly notice that patterns develop among group members with regard to homework completion. Most social coaches will take their responsibility of helping their young adult complete his or her assignments very seriously. They will attend sessions regularly, come on time, and spend considerable effort providing good social coaching outside of the group. However, a minority of social coaches may demonstrate less commitment to the process. They may minimize the importance of the group by regularly stating that they or their young adult was too busy to complete the assignments. They may indicate that their young adult refused to do the assignments. They may also say that their young adult does not need to practice certain skills because he or she *"already knows how to do that."* There are many causes for this type of treatment resistance, which is one of the reasons we highly recommend that the social coaching group leader have extensive clinical training and experience running groups. Whatever the cause may be, it is important for the group leader not to give this resistance too much time during the group, as this will take away from other group members. However, if a pattern of treatment resistance is observed, often exhibited through lack of homework compliance, the group leader should address this with the social coach and young adult in an individual *side meeting* outside of the group. Considering that you are now nearly halfway through the program, all treatment refractory issues should be dealt with by now (if not much sooner).

Individual *side meeting*s with social coaches and young adults may be a regular occurrence in your program. They are often necessary to deal with crises that may come up, questions families may have that do not relate to the group but may impact treatment, and also to manage treatment resistance and lack of homework completion. It is recommended that *side meeting*s are brief and take place immediately before or after the group. The content and structure of these meetings will vary, but for conversations regarding lack of homework compliance, the following tactic is recommended.

1. You might begin by asking if you can speak to the young adult and social coach briefly after the group. If either person seems anxious, you will want to reassure them that they are not in trouble, you just want to discuss something with them.
2. Begin the meeting by mentioning that you have noticed they haven't been doing their *Homework Assignments*. You might refer to your *Homework Compliance Sheets* before this meeting to have a more concrete understanding of their homework completion history.
3. It is then helpful to ask them if they are also aware of this pattern and identify if there are certain issues that are getting in the way of completing assignments.
4. You will then want to *troubleshoot* these treatment barriers and try to find ways to help young adults and social coaches to get the assignments done.
5. This is also a good opportunity to point out the importance of doing *Homework Assignments* by making a statement such as, *"You could come every week and learn all the skills in PEERS®, but if you're not doing your assignments and practicing outside of the group, don't expect to get the full benefit of the program."* You might also point out, *"If your goal is to make and keep friends and develop*

relationships, you MUST do your assignments." Our research indicates that homework completion is highly predictive of success in PEERS®. Those who do their assignments tend to be successful in the program. Those who do not do their assignments tend to have less success. It is your responsibility as a group leader to make certain group members understand this concept.

6. In concluding the **side meeting**, you might have young adults and social coaches reaffirm their commitment to the program and in completing their assignments, much like they did during the intake interview.

The focus of the *Didactic Lesson* in this session is on **exiting conversations**. No formal assignment to practice **exiting conversations** with peers is given (unless it happens naturally). Consequently, young adults should be practicing **exiting conversations** with their social coach and some other person they feel comfortable with (e.g., a parent, sibling, family member, friend). The *Social Coaching Tips* section of the *Social Coaching Therapist Guide* provides suggestions for how to do this. Be sure to emphasize to social coaches that this may be one of the few opportunities for their young adults to practice these important skills, so be sure to do the assignment.

Although the practice assignments with social coaches in this session and in previous sessions should be the easiest assignments to organize, since both have made a commitment to the group, they are oddly the assignments that group members forget the most. In anticipation of this, you might make a statement when assigning this homework by saying, *"One of your assignments this week is for young adults to practice entering and exiting a conversation with you and another person. Although this should be one of the easier assignments to complete, many people forget to do this homework. So don't forget."* Making a brief statement such as this may help to clarify expectations and increase homework compliance in the group.

Homework Review

[Go over the following *Homework Assignments* and **troubleshoot** any potential problems. Start with completed homework first. If you have time, you can inquire as to why others were unable to complete the assignment and try to **troubleshoot** how they might get it done for the coming week. When reviewing homework, be sure to relabel descriptions using the **buzzwords** (identified by **bold and italicized** print). Spend the majority of the *Homework Review* on **entering a group conversation** with social coaches and **entering a group conversation** with peers, as these were the most important assignments. There are six assignments in this *Homework Review*, so manage your time carefully.]

1. Bring a **personal item** to **trade information**.
   - Say, *"One of the assignments this week was to bring a personal item to trade information with other group members. Very quickly, let's hear what young adults brought to trade information about."*
     ○ If items are inappropriate, **troubleshoot** what they might bring next week.

2. **Enter a group conversation** with social coaches.
   - Say, *"One of the main assignments this week was for young adults to practice entering a group conversation with you and another person. Who completed this assignment or attempted to complete it?"*
   - Ask the following questions:
     ○ *"Who did you and your young adult practice with?"*
     ○ *"What social coaching did you do before the practice?"*
     ○ *"Which steps did your young adult follow?"*
       1. **Listen to the Conversation**
       2. **Watch from a Distance**
       3. **Use a Prop**
       4. **Identify the Topic**
       5. **Find a Common Interest**
       6. **Move Closer**
       7. **Wait for a Pause**
       8. **Mention the Topic**
       9. **Assess Interest**
       10. **Introduce Yourself**

　　　○　*"What social coaching did you do after the practice?"*
　　　　　■　Appropriate *social coaching questions*:
　　　　　　□　**Did it seem like we wanted to talk to you?**
　　　　　　□　**How could you tell?**
　　　　　　□　**What were our common interests?**
　　　　　　□　**What could we do with that information if we were going to hang out?**

3. **Enter a group conversation** with peers (could be from the **source of friends**).
   - Say, *"Another one of the main assignments this week was for young adults to practice entering group conversations with peers. Who completed this assignment or attempted to complete it?"*
   - Ask the following questions:
     ○　*"Where and with whom did your young adult practice?"*
     ○　*"What social coaching did you do before the practice?"*
     ○　*"Which steps did your young adult follow?"*
     ○　*"What social coaching did you do after the practice?"*
     　　■　Appropriate *social coaching questions*:
     　　　□　**Where did you enter a conversation and with whom?**
     　　　□　**Which steps did you follow?**
     　　　□　**Did it seem like they wanted to talk to you and how could you tell?**
     　　　□　**Did you trade information and what were your common interests?**
     　　　□　**What could you do with that information if you were going to hang out?**
     　　　□　**Do these seem like people you might want to hang out with?**

4. Find a **source of friends**.
   - Say, *"Another assignment this week was to help find a potential source of friends for your young adults and help them begin to enroll in social activities, if you haven't already. Who was able to identify a source of friends with your young adult?"*
   - Identify if the **sources of friends** are appropriate and meet the following criteria:
     ○　Are based on the young adult's interests.
     ○　Meet weekly or at least every other week.
     ○　Include accepting peers similar in age.
     ○　Include unstructured time to interact with others.
     ○　Activity starts within the next couple of weeks.

5. **Pay attention to humor feedback**.
   - Say, *"Another assignment this week was for young adults to pay attention to their humor feedback if they happened to tell a joke. The assignment was NOT to tell a joke. Who completed this assignment or attempted to complete this assignment?"*
   - Ask the following questions:
     ○　*"Did your young adult attempt to tell jokes and did he/she pay attention to the humor feedback?"*
     ○　*"What did you do to provide social coaching around humor feedback?"*
     　　■　Appropriate *social coaching questions*:
     　　　□　**What was your humor feedback?**
     　　　□　**How could you tell?**

6. **In-group call or video chat**.
   - Say, *"Another assignment this week was for your young adult to have a phone call or video chat with someone in the group in order to practice starting and ending phone calls and trading information. Whose young adult did the in-group call or video chat?"*
   - Ask the following questions:
     ○　*"Who did your young adult talk to and who called whom?"*
     ○　*"What social coaching did you do before the call?"*
     ○　*"Where were you during the call?"*
     ○　*"Did they trade information and find a common interest?"*
     ○　*"What social coaching did you do after the call?"*
     　　■　Appropriate *social coaching questions*:

> □ *What was your common interest?*
> □ *What could you do with that information if you were going to hang out?*
- Have the other social coach who participated in the call or video chat give their account immediately after, but not at the same time.

- [Collect the *Social Coaching Homework Assignment Worksheets.* If social coaches forgot to bring the worksheets, have them complete a new form to hold them accountable for the assignments.]

Didactic Lesson: Exiting Conversations

- Distribute the *Social Coaching Handout.*
  - Sections in **bold print** in the *Social Coaching Therapist Guide* come directly from the *Social Coaching Handout.*
  - Remind social coaches that terms that are in **bold and italicized** print are **buzzwords** and represent important concepts from the PEERS® curriculum that should be used as much as possible when social coaching.
- Explain, *"Last week, we talked about the steps for entering group conversations. This week, we're going to talk about exiting conversations. Research suggests that 50% of peer entry attempts are unsuccessful. That means half the time we try to enter group conversations, we're not going to be accepted, and it's not a big deal. It happens to everyone."*

Reasons for Not Being Accepted in Conversations

- Explain, *"There are many reasons for not being accepted in conversations. Even though we won't be included half of the time, it's important to think about why we might not be accepted and what we can do differently next time."*
- Using the Socratic method, have social coaches come up with reasons for being turned down and what could be done differently next time (see Table 8.1 for examples).
  - Ask the question, *"What are some reasons we might not be accepted?"*
  - Follow up each answer with, *"What could we do differently next time?"*

Table 8.1 Reasons for Not Being Accepted in Conversations

Reasons for Not Being Accepted	What to Do Differently Next Time
They want to talk privately	Try again later and listen before you join
They are rude or mean	Try a different group
You broke one of the rules for entering	Try again later, following the steps
You got too personal	Try a different group, don't get too personal
They are in a clique and don't want to make new friends	Try a different group
They are talking about something you do not know about	Try a different group that is talking about something you know
You have a bad reputation with them	Try a different group that does not know or care about your reputation
They did not understand that you were trying to join	Try again later, following the steps

Exiting Conversations

- Explain, *"There are basically three scenarios where we will have to exit conversations: when we're never accepted; when we're initially accepted and then excluded; and when we're fully accepted but we have to leave. Just like with entering group conversations, there are very specific steps to follow for exiting conversations."*

Steps for Exiting When Never Accepted

- Explain, *"These are the steps for exiting when NEVER accepted. That means they never talked to us or let us into their conversation."*

1. *Keep Your Cool*
   - Say, *"The first step for exiting a conversation when never accepted is to keep your cool. This means don't get upset or try to force them to talk to you. What could be the problem with getting upset and losing your cool?"*
     - ○ Answers: They're going to think you're weird; they will be less likely to want to talk to you in the future; they may tell others about your reaction, which could give you a bad reputation.

2. *Look Away*
   - Say, *"The next step for exiting a conversation when never accepted is to look away. What does it tell the group when you start to look away?"*
     - ○ Answers: Your attention is now somewhere else; you're not interested in what they're talking about anymore.

3. *Turn Away*
   - Say, *"After we've kept our cool and looked away, the next step for exiting the conversation is to turn away. What does it tell the group when you turn away?"*
     - ○ Answers: That you're about to walk away; that you've lost interest in what they're saying; that you're preparing to leave.

4. *Walk Away*
   - Say, *"The last step for exiting a conversation when never accepted is to walk away. This doesn't mean storming off or walking away quickly. Instead, you will want to SLOWLY and calmly walk away. What could be the problem with walking away quickly?"*
     - ○ Answers: Walking away quickly will draw attention to you; instead, you want to walk away so casually they don't even notice you've left.

- [Optional: Show the *Role Play Video Demonstrations* of **exiting when never accepted** from the *PEERS®
Role Play Video Library* (www.routledge.com/cw/laugeson) or *FriendMaker* mobile app, then ask the **Perspective Taking Questions** that follow the role plays.]

Steps for Exiting When Initially Accepted and Then Excluded

- Explain, *"In some cases, we may initially be accepted into a conversation, they might speak to us for a couple of exchanges, but then something happens and we get excluded. These are the steps for exiting when initially accepted and then excluded."*

1. *Keep Your Cool*
   - Say, *"The first step for exiting a conversation when initially accepted and then excluded is to keep your cool. Just like before, you need to stay calm and not get upset. What could be the problem with getting upset?"*
     - ○ Answers: They may think you're weird; they will be less likely to want to talk to you in the future; they may tell others about your reaction, which could give you a bad reputation.

2. *Look Away*
   - Say, *"The next step is to slowly look away, as if you're distracted by something. What does it tell the group when you start to look away?"*
     - ○ Answers: Your attention is now somewhere else; you're not interested in what they're talking about anymore.

3. *Wait for a BRIEF Pause*
   - Say, *"The next step is to wait for a brief pause in the conversation before you say something. Why would you need to wait for a brief pause before saying something?"*
     - ○ Answer: They might be annoyed if you interrupted them.

4. *Give a BRIEF Cover Story for Leaving*
   - Explain, *"The next step is to give a brief cover story for leaving the conversation. Remember, cover stories are reasons you have to do something. Some examples are . . ."*
     - ○ *"Well, gotta go."*

- ○ *"I'd better go."*
- ○ *"Take care."*
- ○ *"See you later."*
- Say, *"In this case, cover stories need to be VERY BRIEF. The reality is they're done talking to you, so they're not really that concerned with where you're going. Why do we need to give a cover story or some kind of acknowledgment before leaving?"*
  - ○ Answer: Even though they're done talking to you, if you don't give some acknowledgment that you're leaving it will seem weird.

5. ***Walk Away***
- Say, *"The last step for exiting a conversation when initially accepted and then excluded is to walk away. Should we wait for them to make some kind of reply to our cover story before we walk away?"*
  - ○ Answers: No; after you've **given a brief cover story**, don't wait for the group to respond; just casually and calmly walk away.

- [Optional: Show the Role Play Video Demonstration of **exiting when initially accepted and then excluded** from the *PEERS® Role Play Video Library* (www.routledge.com/cw/laugeson) or *FriendMaker* mobile app, then ask the **Perspective Taking Questions** that follow the role play.]

Steps for Exiting When Fully Accepted

- Say, *"Sometimes we have to exit conversations even when we've been fully accepted. Just like when we're not accepted, there are specific steps we need to follow."*

1. ***Wait for a Pause***
- Say, *"The first step for exiting a conversation when fully accepted is to wait for a brief pause in the conversation before saying anything about leaving. Why is it important to wait for a brief pause in the conversation before saying anything?"*
  - ○ Answer: It would be rude to interrupt someone unless it was urgent.

2. ***Give a SPECIFIC Cover Story for Leaving***
- Explain, *"The next step is to give a SPECIFIC cover story for why you're leaving. In this case, because you've been fully accepted, your cover story will be specific and a little longer."*
- Ask, *"If you just said, 'Gotta go,' what do you think your friends are going to think?"*
  - ○ Answers: Your friends may think you don't want to talk to them; they may wonder where you're going; they may even ask, "Where are you going?"
- Explain, *"Instead, be more specific by saying something like, 'Well I better get to class,' or 'I have to head home now,' or 'My break is over.' In this case, you need to give some SPECIFIC reason for why you have to leave so your friends won't be confused or offended."*

3. ***Say You'll See Them Later***
- Say, *"If you're planning on seeing your friends again, the next step usually involves saying something like, 'Talk to you later' or 'See you later.' Why would it be a good idea to say, 'Talk to you later' or 'See you later'?"*
  - ○ Answer: It lets your friends know that you want to hang out again and that you're just leaving because you have to go, not because you want to go.

4. ***Say Goodbye***
- Say, *"As you're leaving, the next step is to say goodbye. Some people will also wave, give a hug or kiss, or give a fist bump or a pound. Why is it important to say goodbye before you leave?"*
  - ○ Answer: It's polite and doesn't feel as abrupt as simply walking away without saying goodbye.

5. ***Walk Away***
- Explain, *"The last step for exiting a conversation when fully accepted is to walk away. In this case, if you've followed all the steps, walking away won't seem rude or abrupt to your friends."*

- [Optional: Show the *Role Play Video Demonstrations* of **exiting when fully accepted** from the *PEERS® Role Play Video Library* (www.routledge.com/cw/laugeson) or *FriendMaker* mobile app, then ask the **Perspective Taking Questions** that follow the role plays.]

Homework Assignments

[Distribute the *Social Coaching Homework Assignment Worksheet* (Appendix I) for social coaches to complete and return at the next session.]

1. *Enter and exit group conversations* with social coaches.
   - Young adults should practice *entering and exiting group conversations* with their social coach and another person.
     - Practice exiting when NEVER ACCEPTED.
     - Practice exiting when INITIALLY ACCEPTED AND THEN EXCLUDED.
     - Practice exiting when FULLY ACCEPTED.
   - Social coaches should go over the rules and steps for *entering and exiting group conversations* before the practice.
   - Social coaches should ask young adults the following *social coaching questions* after each practice:
     - *Did it seem like we wanted to talk to you?*
     - *How could you tell?*

2. *Enter a group conversation* with peers (could be from the *source of friends*).
   - Social coaches should go over the rules and steps for *entering and exiting group conversations* before the practice.
   - The assignment is NOT to *exit the conversation* unless they naturally need to.
   - Social coaches should ask young adults the following *social coaching questions* after the practice:
     - *Where did you enter a conversation and with whom?*
     - *Which steps did you follow?*
     - *Did it seem like they wanted to talk to you and how could you tell?*
     - *Did you have to exit the conversation and which steps did you follow?*

3. *Pay attention to humor feedback*.
   - If young adults happen to tell jokes (this is NOT the assignment), *pay attention to humor feedback*.
   - Social coaches should PRIVATELY ask the following *social coaching questions* after attempts at humor by young adults:
     - *What was your humor feedback?*
     - *How could you tell?*

Social Coaching Tips

- One of the assignments is for young adults to practice *entering and exiting group conversations* with their social coach and another person.
  - It is best if the other person is aware of the practice so that you can provide social coaching in the moment as needed.
    - Spouses, adult siblings, and other family members are often good options.
- The best time to set-up this extra practice is right before the young adult plans to *enter group conversations* with peers.
  - For example, before the young adult attends his or her *social activity*, you might go over the rules and steps for *entering and exiting group conversations* and then have him or her practice with you so that it's fresh in mind when attempted with peers.
- Notify your young adult that you are going to be practicing EACH of the following types of *exiting conversations*:
  - Exiting when NEVER ACCEPTED.
  - Exiting when INITIALLY ACCEPTED AND THEN EXCLUDED.
  - Exiting when FULLY ACCEPTED.
- If you think your young adult can remember the steps for each type of exiting, DON'T tell them which one you are practicing beforehand and let them pick up on the behavioral cues.
- If you DO NOT think your young adult will remember the steps for each type of exiting, tell them which one you are practicing beforehand and review the steps.

EXITING CONVERSATIONS

Young Adult Therapist Guide

Preparing for the Young Adult Session

The purpose of this lesson is to help young adults recover from unsuccessful attempts at *entering group conversations*. Some young adults with social challenges are puzzled when they try to enter conversations and their entry attempts do not go as planned. Although this could happen to anyone, for a socially awkward young adult, this can add to their confusion when peers do not respond as expected.

One of the common social errors committed by socially challenged young adults is they may fail to notice when they are not being accepted into conversations. They may persist in forcing conversations, often resulting in frustration and annoyance from their conversational partners, and possibly even resulting in a bad reputation among the larger peer group when this pattern persists. While the previous lesson provides a review of the important social cues to which young adults should attend in order to determine if they are accepted into a conversation (i.e., *are they talking to me* [verbal cues], *are they looking at me* [eye contact], *are they facing me* [body language]), the current lesson provides several role play examples to practice *assessing interest*. The *Role Play Demonstrations*, along with the *Perspective Taking Questions* in this lesson, will be helpful in improving social awareness and understanding of social cognition during *peer entry*. Conducting inappropriate *Role Play Demonstrations* of *peer entry* attempts, followed by questions such as, *"Did it seem like they wanted to talk to me?"*, *"How could you tell?"*, *"What do you think that was like for them?"*, *"What do you think they thought of me?"*, and *"Are they going to want to talk to me again?"* will assist young adults in better understanding the social cues related to acceptance and rejection in conversational entry.

One reason for *peer entry* attempts to be turned down is that the young adult may have a bad reputation among his or her peers. In the event that the young adult has a bad reputation, it will be important to identify other *sources of friends* through involvement in *social activities* in which the young adult is unknown. Whatever the cause of *peer rejection* during *peer entry*, young adults will need to be reassured that this is common and that they do not need to take it too personally. It can be very helpful to normalize this experience by telling the young adults that even you (and perhaps their social coaches) get turned down when trying to *enter group conversations* from time to time. If these confessions are successful in normalizing the experience for the young adults, they will be more willing to attempt to *enter group conversations* in the future.

Although the bulk of this lesson focuses on how to *exit conversations* when either *never accepted*, or when *initially accepted and then excluded*, the lesson also provides strategies for how to *exit when fully accepted*. In this case, the common social error made by young adults with social challenges is to simply walk away when done speaking, with no acknowledgment of their departure or where they are going. Since this behavior is hardly likely to lead to social success, the portion of the lesson on *exiting when fully accepted* will be quite useful.

As explained in *Session 1 Preparing for the Lesson*, although this manual provides scripts of role plays demonstrating inappropriate and appropriate social behavior, ROLE PLAY SCRIPTS ARE NOT INTENDED TO BE READ VERBATIM. They are simply intended to provide a guide for how you might conduct role plays. Hopefully, you have taken this advice to heart and have not been reading the script aloud to your group. In this case, you have been creating your own dialogue and hopefully having fun with the process. One thing to keep in mind with the *Role Play Demonstrations* this week is that when demonstrating INAPPROPRIATE behavior, make sure that everything you are demonstrating is WRONG. In other words, if you are *exiting the conversation* inappropriately, you should also be *entering the group conversation* inappropriately. Likewise, when demonstrating APPROPRIATE behavior, make sure that everything you are demonstrating is RIGHT. In other words, if you are *exiting the conversation* appropriately, you should also be *entering the group conversation* appropriately. To do one aspect of a role play appropriately and the other inappropriately would be confusing for your group.

Homework Review

[Go over the following *Homework Assignments* and **troubleshoot** any potential problems. Start with completed homework first. If you have time, you can inquire as to why others were unable to complete the assignment and try to **troubleshoot** how they might get it done for the coming week. When reviewing homework, be sure to relabel descriptions using the **buzzwords** (identified by **bold and italicized** print). Spend the majority of the *Homework Review* on *entering a group conversation* with social coaches and *entering a group conversation* with peers, as these were the most important assignments. There are six assignments in this *Homework Review*, so manage your time carefully.]

1. Bring a *personal item* to *trade information*.
   - Say, *"One of the assignments this week was to bring a personal item to trade information with other group members. Very quickly, let's hear what you brought to trade information."*
     - Have young adults place these items somewhere off to the side of the room to avoid distractions.
     - If items are inappropriate, *troubleshoot* what they might bring next week.

2. *Enter a group conversation* with social coaches.
   - Say, *"One of the main assignments this week was to practice entering a group conversation with your social coach and another person. Raise your hand if you did this assignment."*
   - Ask the following questions:
     - *"Who did you and your social coach practice with?"*
     - *"Which steps did you follow?"*
       1. **Listen to the Conversation**
       2. **Watch from a Distance**
       3. **Use a Prop**
       4. **Identify the Topic**
       5. **Find a Common Interest**
       6. **Move Closer**
       7. **Wait for a Pause**
       8. **Mention the Topic**
       9. **Assess Interest**
       10. **Introduce Yourself**

3. *Enter a group conversation* with peers (could be from the *source of friends*).
   - Say, *"Another one of the main assignments this week was to practice entering group conversations with peers. Raise your hand if you did this assignment."*
   - Ask the following questions:
     - *"Where and with whom did you practice?"*
     - *"Which steps did you follow?"*
     - *"Did it seem like they wanted to talk to you?"*
     - *"How could you tell?"*
       - *Talking to you?*
       - *Looking at you?*
       - *Facing you (they opened the circle?)*

○ *"What were your common interests and what could you do with that information if you were going to hang out?"*

○ *"Do these seem like people you might want to hang out with?"*

4. Find a *source of friends*.

- Say, *"Another assignment this week was to find a potential source of friends with the help of your social coaches and begin to enroll in social activities, if you haven't already. Who was able to identify a source of friends?"*

- Identify if the *sources of friends* are appropriate and meet the following criteria:
  ○ Are based on the young adult's interests.
  ○ Meet weekly or at least every other week.
  ○ Include accepting peers similar in age.
  ○ Include unstructured time to interact with others.
  ○ Activity starts within the next couple of weeks.

5. *Pay attention to humor feedback.*

- Say, *"Another assignment this week was to pay attention to your humor feedback if you happened to tell a joke. The assignment was NOT to tell a joke. If you happened to tell a joke this week, raise your hand if you paid attention to your humor feedback."*

- Ask the following questions:
  ○ *"I don't want to know what joke you told, I just want to know what your humor feedback was. Were they laughing AT you, laughing WITH you, giving a courtesy laugh, or NOT laughing at all?"*
  ○ *"How could you tell?"*
  ○ *"So are you done paying attention to your humor feedback?"*
     ▪ Answer: No.
  ○ *"When will you pay attention to your humor feedback?"*
     ▪ Answer: Every time they tell a joke.
  ○ *"How will you pay attention to your humor feedback?"*
     ▪ Answer: By LOOKING and LISTENING.

6. *In-group call or video chat.*

- Say, *"Another assignment you had this week was to have a phone call or video chat with someone in the group in order to practice starting and ending phone calls and trading information. Raise your hand if you did the in-group call or video chat."*

- Ask the following questions:
  ○ *"Who did you talk to and who called whom?"*
  ○ *"Did you trade information and did you find a common interest?"*
  ○ *"What could you do with that information if you were going to hang out?"*

- Have the other person who participated in the call or video chat give their account immediately after, but not at the same time.

Didactic Lesson: Exiting Conversations

- Explain, *"Last week, we talked about the steps for entering group conversations. This week, we're going to talk about exiting conversations. Sometimes, even when we follow all of the steps for entering conversations, some people will still not want to talk to us. It happens to everyone and it's not a big deal."*

- Ask, *"For example, if someone tried to join 10 different conversations, on average how many times out of ten do you think they will get turned down?"*
  ○ Go around the room and have everyone take a guess.

- Say, *"The answer is 5 OUT OF 10 TIMES! That means half the time we try to enter group conversations, we're not going to be accepted, and it's not a big deal. It happens to everyone."*

- Ask, *"Do you think we should give up trying?"*
  ○ Answer: No, don't let this stop you from trying in the future.

Reasons for Not Being Accepted in Conversations

- Explain, *"There are many reasons for not being accepted in conversations. Even though we won't be invited to join half of the time, it's important to think about why we might not be accepted and what we can do differently next time."*
- Using the Socratic method, have young adults come up with reasons for being turned down and what they can do differently next time (see Table 8.1 for examples).
  - Ask the question, *"What are some reasons we might not be accepted?"*
  - Follow up each answer with, *"What could we do differently next time?"*

Table 8.1 Reasons for Not Being Accepted in Conversations

Reasons for Not Being Accepted	What to Do Differently Next Time
They want to talk privately	Try again later and listen before you join
They are rude or mean	Try a different group
You broke one of the rules for entering	Try again later, following the steps
You got too personal	Try a different group, don't get too personal
They are in a clique and don't want to make new friends	Try a different group
They are talking about something you do not know about	Try a different group that is talking about something you know
You have a bad reputation with them	Try a different group that does not know or care about your reputation
They did not understand that you were trying to join	Try again later, following the steps

Exiting Conversations

- Explain, *"Since we know that it's common for people to not let us join their conversations, and that it's not a big deal, we need to know what to do in these situations. Just like with entering group conversations, there are very specific steps we need to follow for exiting conversations."*

Bad Role Play: Exiting When Never Accepted ▶

[The group leader should do an INAPPROPRIATE role play of *entering and exiting a conversation* between two behavioral coaches when NEVER ACCEPTED.]

- Begin by saying, *"We're going to do a role play where I'll try to enter a group conversation, but I'm not going to be accepted. Watch this and tell me what I'm doing WRONG."*

Example of an INAPPROPRIATE Role Play

- Group leader: (Standing several feet away)
- Behavioral coach 1: *"Hi, (insert name). How've you been doing?"*
- Behavioral coach 2: *"I've been pretty good. How about you?"*
- Behavioral coach 1: *"I'm good. Hey, didn't you tell me you like comic books? Did you go to that big comic book convention last weekend?"*
- Behavioral coach 2: *"Yeah, I went on Saturday! It was great! Did you . . ."*
- Group leader: (Walks over abruptly, interrupts) *"Hey, guys. What are you talking about?"*
- Behavioral coach 2: (Startled, confused) *"What?"*
- Behavioral coach 1: (Annoyed) *"We were just talking. So anyway, you went to . . ."*
- Behavioral coaches 1 & 2: (Turning away from the group leader, closing the circle)
- Group leader: (Interrupts) *"What are you guys doing this weekend?"*
- Behavioral coach 1: (Annoyed, ignoring, rolling eyes) *"So you went to ComicCon? How was it?"*

> ○ Behavioral coach 2: (Ignoring) *"It was great! Why didn't you go?"*
> ○ Behavioral coach 1: (Ignoring) *"I had other plans, but I was thinking about going to the next one . . ."*
> ○ Group leader: (Interrupts) *"Hey, have you guys seen that new sci-fi movie?"*
> ○ Behavioral coaches 1 & 2: (Annoyed, rolling eyes, ignoring)
> ○ Behavioral coach 2: *"Well, if you do go, let me know because I want to go again . . ."*
> ○ Group leader: (Interrupts) *"Have you seen it? I'm supposed to see it this weekend. Do you know if it's any good?"*
> ○ Behavioral coaches 1 & 2: (Looking annoyed, ignoring comments)
> ○ Behavioral coach 2: (Under breath, rolling eyes): *"How annoying?"*
> ○ Behavioral coach 1: (Making a face, rolling eyes) *"I know, right?"*
> ○ Group leader: (Angry) *"What's your problem? I was just trying to talk to you. You don't have to be so rude!"* (Storms off)
> ○ Behavioral coaches 1 & 2: (Look at each other and laugh)

- End by saying, *"Timeout on that. So what did I do WRONG in trying to join that conversation?"*
  ○ Answer: You barged in and were off topic.
- Ask, *"Did it seem like they wanted to talk to me?"*
  ○ Answer: No.
- Ask, *"How could you tell?"*
  ○ Answers: **Didn't talk to you**; **didn't look at you** (except to roll their eyes and make faces); **didn't face you; closed the circle**.
- Ask, *"What should I have done when I realized they didn't want to talk to me?"*
  ○ Answers: You shouldn't have tried to force them to talk; you shouldn't have gotten upset; you should have **moved on**.
- Ask the following *Perspective Taking Questions*:
  ○ *"What was that like for (names of coaches)?"*
    ▪ Answers: Irritating; annoying; frustrating.
  ○ *"What do you think (names of coaches) thought of me?"*
    ▪ Answers: Rude; obnoxious; annoying; weird.
  ○ *"Are (names of coaches) going to want to talk to me again?"*
    ▪ Answers: No; too annoying.
- Ask the behavioral coaches the same *Perspective Taking Questions*:
  ○ *"What was that like for you?"*
  ○ *"What did you think of me?"*
  ○ *"Would you want to talk to me again?"*

Steps for Exiting When Never Accepted

- Say, *"Instead of getting upset and not taking no for an answer, we need to know how to exit conversations appropriately. In this case, I was NEVER ACCEPTED into that conversation. So these are the steps I should have followed . . ."*
- [Present the rules and steps for *exiting conversations* by writing the following bullet points and **buzzwords** (identified by **bold and italicized** print) on the board. Be sure to label which type of exiting the steps refer to for each of the three scenarios (i.e., *never accepted, initially accepted and then excluded*, and *fully accepted*). Do not erase the rules and steps until the end of the lesson.]

1. *Keep your cool*
   - Explain, *"The first step for exiting a conversation when we've never been accepted is to keep your cool. This means don't get upset or try to force them to talk to you."*
   - Ask, *"What could be the problem with getting upset and losing your cool?"*
     ○ Answers: They're going to think you're weird; they will be less likely to want to talk to you in the future; they may tell others about your reaction, which could give you a bad reputation.

2. **Look away**
   - Explain, *"The next step for exiting a conversation when we've never been accepted is to look away. This means you shouldn't stare. Instead, you should casually stop eye contact and look in a different direction."*
   - Ask, *"What does it tell the group when you start to look away?"*
     - Answers: Your attention is now somewhere else; you're not interested in what they're talking about anymore.
   - Explain, *"We want to be careful not to draw too much attention to ourselves when we look away. That means choosing something to look at that doesn't involve looking over your shoulder or turning your whole head and body around."*
   - Ask, *"What could be the problem with turning your whole head and body around to look away?"* (demonstrate turning in the opposite direction)
     - Answers: This would look strange and would draw attention to your behavior; the group might think the behavior was weird; they might laugh or make fun of you.
   - Explain, *"So just try looking to one side or the other. You could even pull out your cell phone or some other prop as a way of looking away, but only if it's easy to reach."*

3. **Turn away**
   - Explain, *"After we've kept our cool and looked away, the next step for exiting the conversation is to turn away. This means that you casually and slowly turn your body away from the group."*
   - Ask, *"What does it tell the group when you turn away?"*
     - Answers: That you're about to walk away; that you've lost interest in what they're saying; that you're preparing to leave.
   - Say, *"It's also important to turn your body away in the direction that you're already looking. What could be the problem with turning your body in a different direction from where you were looking?"* (demonstrate looking in one direction and turning your body in another)
     - Answers: This would also look strange; this would draw attention to your behavior; the group would think this was odd behavior; they would probably think you're odd.

4. **Walk away**
   - Explain, *"The last step for exiting a conversation when you're never accepted is to walk away. This doesn't mean storming off or walking away quickly. Instead, you will want to SLOWLY and calmly walk away."*
   - Ask, *"What could be the problem with walking away quickly?"*
     - Answers: Walking away quickly will draw attention to you; instead, you want to walk away so casually they don't even notice you've left.
   - Say, *"It's also important that we walk away in the direction that we're looking and facing. What could be the problem with walking in a different direction from where you were looking and facing?"* (demonstrate looking in one direction, turning in another direction, and walking in a separate direction)
     - Answers: This would look very odd; this would draw attention to you; this strange behavior could give you a bad reputation.

Good Role Play: Exiting When Never Accepted ⊙

[The group leader should do an APPROPRIATE role play demonstrating *entering and exiting a conversation* between two behavioral coaches when NEVER ACCEPTED.]

- Begin by saying, *"We're going to do another role play. Watch this and tell me what I'm doing RIGHT in entering and exiting this conversation."*

> Example of an APPROPRIATE Role Play
> - Group leader: (Standing several feet away, looking at a cell phone)
> - Behavioral coach 1: *"Hi, (insert name). How've you been doing?"*
> - Behavioral coach 2: *"I've been pretty good. How about you?"*

> ○ Behavioral coach 1: *"I'm good. Hey, didn't you tell me you like comic books? Did you go to that big comic book convention last weekend?"*
> ○ Group leader: (Looks over briefly, smiles slightly)
> ○ Behavioral coach 2: *"Yeah, I went on Saturday! It was great! Did you go?"*
> ○ Behavioral coach 1: *"I had other plans, but I was thinking about going to the next one."*
> ○ Group leader: (Looks over again)
> ○ Behavioral coach 2: *"Well, if you do go, let me know because I want to go again."*
> ○ Behavioral coach 1: *"Definitely. I'll let you know. That would be fun!"*
> ○ Group leader: (Moves closer, waits for a pause, looks at behavioral coach 2): *"So you went to ComicCon?"*
> ○ Behavioral coaches 1 & 2: (Ignoring, close the circle)
> ○ Behavioral coach 1: *"So did you meet all the famous authors?"*
> ○ Group leader: (Casually looks away)
> ○ Behavioral coach 2: *"Yeah, I did! It was so crazy."*
> ○ Group leader: (Casually turns away)
> ○ Behavioral coach 1: *"Was everyone dressed up?"*
> ○ Group leader: (Slowly walks away in the direction looking and facing)
> ○ Behavioral coach 2: *"So many people were dressed up! It was so much fun!"*
> ○ Behavioral coaches 1 & 2: (Don't appear to notice that the group leader has left)

- End by saying, *"Timeout on that. So what did I do RIGHT in entering that conversation?"*
  - ○ Answers: **Listened and watched**; **used a prop**; **identified the topic**; **found a common interest**; **moved closer**; **waited for a pause**; **mentioned the topic**.
- Ask, *"Did it seem like they wanted to talk to me?"*
  - ○ Answer: No.
- Ask, *"How could you tell?"*
  - ○ Answers: **Didn't talk to you**; **didn't look at you**; **didn't face you (closed the circle)**.
- Ask, *"What did I do RIGHT in exiting that conversation?"*
  - ○ Answers: **Kept your cool**; **looked away**; **turned away**; **walked away**.
- Ask the following *Perspective Taking Questions*:
  - ○ *"What was that like for (names of coaches)?"*
    - ■ Answers: Fine; normal.
  - ○ *"What do you think (names of coaches) thought of me?"*
    - ■ Answers: Not much; didn't notice you.
  - ○ *"Are (names of coaches) going to want to talk to me again?"*
    - ■ Answer: Not sure; maybe.
- Ask the behavioral coaches the same *Perspective Taking Questions*:
  - ○ *"What was that like for you?"*
  - ○ *"What did you think of me?"*
  - ○ *"Would you want to talk to me again?"*

Steps for Exiting When Initially Accepted and Then Excluded

- Explain, *"In some cases, we may initially be accepted into a conversation, but then something happens and we get excluded. For example, you might enter a conversation and initially the group speaks to you, but then you notice that they close the circle, ignore your comments, and no longer talk to you or look at you. In this case, leaving without saying something would seem awkward, so we have different steps for exiting these kinds of conversations."*

1. **Keep Your Cool**
   - Explain, *"The first step for exiting a conversation when initially accepted and then excluded is to keep your cool. Just like before, you need to stay calm and not get upset."*

- Ask, *"What could be the problem with getting upset?"*
  - ○ Answers: They may think you're weird; they will be less likely to want to talk to you in the future; they may tell others about your reaction, which could give you a bad reputation.

2. *Look Away*
   - Explain, *"The next step is to slowly look away, as if you're distracted by something. Just like before, you could look to one side or the other, or look at a personal item like a mobile phone."*
   - Ask, *"What does it tell the group when you start to look away?"*
     - ○ Answers: Your attention is now somewhere else; you're not interested in what they're talking about anymore.

3. *Wait for a BRIEF Pause*
   - Explain, *"The next step is to wait for a BRIEF pause in the conversation before you say something. Just like with entering a conversation, there's never a perfect pause, just try not to interrupt too much."*
   - Ask, *"Why would you need to wait for a BRIEF pause before saying something?"*
     - ○ Answer: They might be annoyed if you interrupted them.
   - Ask, *"Remember, this is a BRIEF pause. We don't want to stick around for too long where we're not wanted."*

4. *Give a BRIEF Cover Story for Leaving*
   - Explain, *"The next step is to give a brief cover story for leaving the conversation. Remember, cover stories are reasons you have to do something. Some examples are . . ."*
     - ○ *"Well, gotta go."*
     - ○ *"I'd better go."*
     - ○ *"Take care."*
     - ○ *"See you later."*
   - Explain, *"In this case, cover stories need to be VERY BRIEF. The reality is they're done talking to you, so they're not really that concerned with where you're going."*
   - Ask, *"Why do we need to give a cover story or some kind of acknowledgment before leaving?"*
     - ○ Answer: Even though they're done talking to you, if you don't give some acknowledgment that you're leaving it will seem weird.

5. *Walk Away*
   - Explain, *"The last step for exiting a conversation when initially accepted and then excluded is to walk away."*
   - Ask, *"Should we wait for them to give some kind of reply to our cover story before we walk away?"*
     - ○ Answers: No; after you've **given a brief cover story**, don't wait for the group to respond; just casually and calmly walk away; they might say *"bye"* but don't wait for them to say anything.

Good Role Play: Exiting When Initially Accepted and Then Excluded ⊙

[The group leader should do an APPROPRIATE role play demonstrating *entering and exiting a group conversation* between two behavioral coaches when INITIALLY ACCEPTED AND THEN EXCLUDED. If you do not have a second behavioral coach, you can show the *Role Play Video Demonstration* of *exiting when initially accepted and then excluded* from the PEERS® Role Play Video Library (www.routledge.com/cw/laugeson) or *FriendMaker* mobile app, then ask the *Perspective Taking Questions* that follow the role play.]

- Begin by saying, *"We're going to do another role play. Watch this and tell me what I'm doing RIGHT in entering and exiting this conversation."*

> **Example of an APPROPRIATE Role Play**
>
> ○ Group leader: (Standing several feet away, looking at a cell phone)
> ○ Behavioral coach 1: *"Hi, (insert name). How've you been doing?"*

> ○ Behavioral coach 2: *"I've been pretty good. How about you?"*
> ○ Behavioral coach 1: *"I'm good. Hey, didn't you tell me you like comic books? Did you go to that big comic book convention last weekend?"*
> ○ Group leader: (Looks over briefly, smiles slightly)
> ○ Behavioral coach 2: *"Yeah, I went on Saturday! It was great! Did you go?"*
> ○ Behavioral coach 1: *"I had other plans, but I was thinking about going to the next one."*
> ○ Group leader: (Looks over again)
> ○ Behavioral coach 2: *"Well, if you do go, let me know because I want to go again."*
> ○ Behavioral coach 1: *"Definitely. I'll let you know. That would be fun!"*
> ○ Group leader: (Moves closer, waits for a pause, looks at behavioral coach 2): *"So you went to ComicCon?"*
> ○ Behavioral coach 2: (Looks over, turns toward group leader) *"Yeah."*
> ○ Group leader: *"I love comic books. I really wanted to go."*
> ○ Behavioral coach 2: *"Oh, you should have. It was cool."*
> ○ Group leader: *"So where was it?"*
> ○ Behavioral coach 2: *"It was downtown."* (Looks away, turns away, starts to close the circle)
> ○ Behavioral coach 1: (Turned away from group leader) *"So anyway, when is the next one?"*
> ○ Group leader: (Begins to look away)
> ○ Behavioral coach 2: *"I'm not sure, but I think it's next month."*
> ○ Behavioral coach 1: *"We should figure out when it is and get tickets."*
> ○ Group leader: (Waits for a brief pause) *"Well, see you later."* (Starts to walk away)
> ○ Behavioral coaches 1 & 2: (Casually look over) *"Yeah. See ya."*

- End by saying, *"Timeout on that. So what did I do RIGHT in entering that conversation?"*
  - Answers: **Listened and watched**; **used a prop**; **identified the topic**; **found a common interest**; **moved closer**; **waited for a pause**; **mentioned the topic**.
- Ask, *"Did it seem like they wanted to talk to me?"*
  - Answer: At first, but then they pushed you out of the conversation.
- Ask, *"How could you tell?"*
  - Answers: They stopped **talking to you**; stopped **looking at you**; **closed the circle**.
- Ask, *"What did I do RIGHT in exiting that conversation?"*
  - Answers: **Kept your cool**; **looked away**; **waited for a pause**; **gave a brief cover story**; **walked away**.
- Ask the following **Perspective Taking Questions**:
  - *"What was that like for (names of coaches)?"*
    - Answers: Fine; normal.
  - *"What do you think (names of coaches) thought of me?"*
    - Answers: Not much; normal.
  - *"Are (names of coaches) going to want to talk to me again?"*
    - Answer: Maybe.
- Ask the behavioral coaches the same **Perspective Taking Questions**:
  - *"What was that like for you?"*
  - *"What did you think of me?"*
  - *"Would you want to talk to me again?"*

Exiting When Fully Accepted

- Say, *"Sometimes we have to exit conversations even when we've been fully accepted. Just like when we're not accepted, there are specific steps we need to follow."*

Bad Role Play: Exiting When Fully Accepted ⏵

[The group leader should do an INAPPROPRIATE role play of **exiting a conversation** with two behavioral coaches when FULLY ACCEPTED.]

- Begin by saying, *"Watch this role play and tell me what I'm doing WRONG in exiting this conversation."*

> Example of an INAPPROPRIATE Role Play
>
> ○ Behavioral coaches 1 & 2 and group leader: (Standing around and talking)
> ○ Group leader: *"So what did you guys do this weekend?"*
> ○ Behavioral coach 1: *"I actually went and saw that new sci-fi movie. I forget what it's called."*
> ○ Behavioral coach 2: *"That fantasy sci-fi one that's in the theaters right now and just came out on Friday?"*
> ○ Behavioral coach 1: *"Yeah. That's the one."*
> ○ Behavioral coach 2: *"Oh, I want to see that."*
> ○ Group leader: *"I know the one you're talking about."*
> ○ Behavioral coach 1: *"Did you see that one?"*
> ○ Group leader: *"Yeah, I saw it last weekend too."*
> ○ Behavioral coach 2: *"Oh, really. How was it?"*
> ○ Behavioral coach 1: *"It was good. I liked it."* (Turns to group leader) *"Did you like it?"*
> ○ Group leader: *"Yeah, I thought it was really good actually."*
> ○ Behavioral coach 2: *"I'm going to try to see it this weekend I think."*
> ○ Behavioral coach 1: *"You really should. It's cool."*
> ○ Group leader: *"It's really good. You should see it."*
> ○ Behavioral coach 2: *"Awesome. I definitely will."*
> ○ Behavioral coaches 1 & 2 and group leader: (Long pause)
> ○ Group leader: (Looks awkward, abruptly walks away)
> ○ Behavioral coaches 1 & 2: (Shocked, confused, look at each other)
> ○ Behavioral coach 2: (Confused) *"What was that all about?"*
> ○ Behavioral coach 1: (Confused) *"I have no idea."*
> ○ Behavioral coaches 1 & 2: (Shake heads in disbelief)

- End by saying, *"Timeout on that. So what did I do WRONG in exiting that conversation?"*
  - ○ Answer: You barged off for no reason.
- Ask the following *Perspective Taking Questions*:
  - ○ *"What was that like for (names of coaches)?"*
    - ▪ Answers: Confusing; surprising; shocking.
  - ○ *"What do you think (names of coaches) thought of me?"*
    - ▪ Answers: Rude; weird; odd.
  - ○ *"Are (names of coaches) going to want to talk to me again?"*
    - ▪ Answer: Not sure; maybe too weird.
- Ask the behavioral coaches the same *Perspective Taking Questions*:
  - ○ *"What was that like for you?"*
  - ○ *"What did you think of me?"*
  - ○ *"Would you want to talk to me again?"*

Steps for Exiting When Fully Accepted

- Explain, *"Instead of just walking away or barging off when we have to leave, we should follow the steps for exiting conversations when we've been fully accepted."*

1. **Wait for a Pause**
   - Explain, *"The first step for exiting a conversation when fully accepted is to wait for a pause in the conversation before saying anything about leaving."*
   - Ask, *"Why is it important to wait for a pause in the conversation before saying anything?"*
     - ○ Answer: It would be rude to interrupt someone unless it was urgent.

2. **Give a SPECIFIC Cover Story for Leaving**
   - Explain, *"The next step is to give a SPECIFIC cover story for why you're leaving. In this case, because you've been fully accepted, your cover story will be SPECIFIC and a little longer."*

- Ask, *"If you just said, 'Gotta go,' what do you think your friends are going to think?"*
  - Answers: Your friends may think you don't want to talk to them; they may wonder where you're going; they may even ask, *"Where are you going?"*
- Explain, *"Instead, be more specific by saying something like, 'Well, I better get to class,' or 'I have to head home now,' or 'My break is over.' In this case, you need to give some SPECIFIC reason for why you have to leave so your friends won't be confused or offended."*

3. **Say You'll See Them Later**
   - Explain, *"If you're planning on seeing your friends again, the next step usually involves saying something like, 'Talk to you later' or 'See you later.'"*
   - Ask, *"Why would it be a good idea to say, 'Talk to you later' or 'See you later'?"*
     - Answer: It lets your friends know that you want to hang out again and that you're just leaving because you have to go, not because you want to go.

4. **Say Goodbye**
   - Explain, *"As you're leaving, the next step is to say goodbye. Some people will also wave, give a hug or kiss, or give a fist bump or a pound."*
   - Ask, *"Why is it important to say goodbye before you leave?"*
     - Answer: It's polite and doesn't feel as abrupt as simply walking away without saying goodbye.

5. **Walk Away**
   - Explain, *"The last step for exiting a conversation when fully accepted is to walk away. In this case, if you've followed all the steps, walking away won't seem rude or abrupt to your friends."*

Good Role Play: Exiting When Fully Accepted ▶

[The group leader should do an APPROPRIATE role play of *exiting a conversation* with two behavioral coaches when FULLY ACCEPTED.]

- Begin by saying, *"Watch this role play and tell me what I'm doing RIGHT in exiting this conversation."*

Example of an APPROPRIATE Role Play
- Behavioral coaches 1 & 2 and group leader: (Standing around and talking)
- Group leader: *"So what did you guys do this weekend?"*
- Behavioral coach 1: *"I actually went and saw that new sci-fi movie. I forget what it's called."*
- Behavioral coach 2: *"That fantasy sci-fi one that's in the theaters right now and just came out on Friday?"*
- Behavioral coach 1: *"Yeah. That's the one."*
- Behavioral coach 2: *"Oh, I want to see that."*
- Group leader: *"I know the one you're talking about."*
- Behavioral coach 1: *"Did you see that one?"*
- Group leader: *"Yeah, I saw it last weekend too."*
- Behavioral coach 2: *"Oh, really. How was it?"*
- Behavioral coach 1: *"It was good. I liked it."* (Turns to group leader) *"Did you like it?"*
- Group leader: *"Yeah, I thought it was really good actually."*
- Behavioral coach 2: *"I'm going to try to see it this weekend I think."*
- Behavioral coach 1: *"You really should. It's cool."*
- Group leader: *"It's really good. You should see it."*
- Behavioral coach 2: *"Awesome. I definitely will."*
- Group leader: (Looks away, waits for a pause) *"Hey guys, my break is over, so I've got to get going."*
- Behavioral coach 2: *"Okay."*

- Behavioral coach 1: *"Alright."*
- Group leader: *"See you later. Bye"* (Waves, smiles, casually walks away)
- Behavioral coach 2: (Waves, smiles) *"Bye, see you."*
- Behavioral coach 1: (Waves, smiles) *"Bye."*

- End by saying, *"Timeout on that. So what did I do RIGHT in exiting that conversation?"*
  - Answers: **Waited for a pause**; **gave a specific cover story**; **said see you later**; **said goodbye**; **walked away**.
- Ask the following **Perspective Taking Questions**:
  - *"What was that like for (names of coaches)?"*
    - Answers: Fine; pleasant; normal; interesting.
  - *"What do you think (names of coaches) thought of me?"*
    - Answers: Friendly; interesting; cool.
  - *"Are (names of coaches) going to want to talk to me again?"*
    - Answers: Yes; definitely.
- Ask the behavioral coaches the same **Perspective Taking Questions**:
  - *"What was that like for you?"*
  - *"What did you think of me?"*
  - *"Would you want to talk to me again?"*

- Explain, *"So those are the steps for exiting conversations. You're going to be practicing this as you trade information about your personal items, and you will continue to practice during your Homework Assignments this week."*

EXITING CONVERSATIONS

Young Adult Behavioral Rehearsal

Entering and Exiting Conversations

Materials Needed

- Young adults bring **personal items** to **trade information** about.
- If young adults forget to bring **personal items**:
    - Cell phones with music and/or pictures may be used.
    - T-shirts with logos of favorite pastimes are relevant.
    - Young adults can simply talk about their interests without **personal items**.

Behavioral Rehearsal

- Break up young adults into small groups (no less than three young adults per group).
- Have young adults practice **trading information** about their **personal items** while taking turns **entering and exiting a group conversation**.
- For young adults practicing **trading information** about **personal items**:
    - Encourage young adults to identify **common interests** through **trading information**.
    - Inform the young adults that they should ACCEPT the entering person into these conversations.
    - DO NOT simulate peer rejection in the behavioral rehearsals.
- For young adults practicing **entering and exiting a group conversation**:
    - Separate the young adult from the group and have him or her identify the **steps for entering and exiting conversations** before practicing (they may need to look at the board at first).
    - There are three possible scenarios for **exiting conversations**. If you don't have time to practice all three (you probably will not), practice the most difficult of the three: **Exiting when NEVER accepted**.
        - Giving a **cover story** is generally not that difficult, but **keeping your cool, looking away, turning away**, and **walking away** when never accepted can be slightly more difficult.
    - You may need to provide Socratic prompting to the young adult for identifying the specific steps to **enter a group conversation** by using some of the following **social coaching questions**:
        - *"What do you want to do with your ears?"*
        - *"What are you listening for?"*
        - *"What do you want to do with your eyes?"*
        - *"Should you be staring at them?"*
        - *"What could you use while you're listening?"*
        - *"Do you want to join from across the room?"*
        - *"Should you barge right in or wait for something?"*
        - *"Is there ever a PERFECT PAUSE?"*
        - *"When you join, what should you be talking about?"*

- ○ Then have the young adult practice using these steps by *entering the group conversation* with their peers in which the others will be *trading information* about their *personal items*.
- ○ You may need to provide Socratic prompting to the young adult if they have trouble following the steps by using some of the following *social coaching questions*:
  - ▪ *"Do you know what they're talking about?"*
  - ▪ *"Do you know anything about that topic?"*
    - □ [Note: If they don't know the topic, praise them for not joining and have the other young adults change the topic to something they know.]
  - ▪ *"Do you want to use anything while you're listening?"*
  - ▪ *"What are you waiting for before you enter?"*
  - ▪ *"Is there ever a PERFECT PAUSE?"*
  - ▪ *"Do you want to move closer before you enter?"*
  - ▪ *"When you enter, do you want to be on topic?"*

- In the event that a young adult incorrectly *enters the group conversation*, call a *"timeout"* and use this as a coachable moment to gently point out the error, while providing feedback on how to more appropriately attempt to enter.
  - ○ Have the young adult try again until he or she is successful at following the steps.
- Once the young adult has successfully entered and been accepted, say the following:
  - ○ *"Timeout. Great job following the steps for entering a group conversation. Now pretend they NEVER accepted you into the conversation. What are the steps for exiting a conversation when we've NEVER been accepted?"*
  - ○ You may need to provide Socratic prompting to the young adult for identifying the specific steps to *exit a conversation when NEVER accepted* by using some of the following *social coaching questions*:
    - ▪ *"Do you want to get upset?"*
    - ▪ *"Should you keep looking at them?"*
    - ▪ *"Where should you be facing?"*
    - ▪ *"Are you going to stick around?"*
- In the event that a young adult incorrectly *exits the conversation*, call a *"timeout"* and use this as a coachable moment to gently point out the error, while providing feedback on how to more appropriately exit.
  - ○ Have the young adult try again until he or she is successful at following the steps.
  - ○ If the young adult looks rigid with his or her motor movements when following the steps for exiting (almost as if moving like a robot), you might say, *"That looks a little stiff. How about just walking away really slowly?"* and that should loosen up the movements.
- Once the young adult has successfully exited, call a *"timeout"* and have the other young adults applaud.
- Have each young adult practice *entering and exiting a conversation* at least once.

EXITING CONVERSATIONS

Reunification

- Announce that young adults should join their social coaches.
    - Have young adults stand or sit next to their social coaches.
    - Be sure to have silence and the full attention of the group before starting with *Reunification*.
    - Have young adults generate the content from the lesson while social coaches listen.
- Say, *"Today, we talked about the rules and steps for exiting conversations. What are the steps for exiting conversations when we're . . ."* (see Table 8.2 for steps for exiting conversations).
    - *". . . NEVER ACCEPTED?"*
    - *". . . INITIALLY ACCEPTED AND THEN EXCLUDED?"*
    - *". . . FULLY ACCEPTED?"*

Table 8.2 Steps for Exiting Conversations

NEVER ACCEPTED	INITIALLY ACCEPTED, THEN EXCLUDED	FULLY ACCEPTED
1. Keep your cool 2. Look away 3. Turn away 4. Walk away	1. Keep your cool 2. Look away 3. Wait for a BRIEF pause 4. Give a BRIEF cover story for leaving 5. Walk away	1. Wait for a pause 2. Give a SPECIFIC cover story for leaving 3. Say you'll see them later 4. Say goodbye 5. Walk away

- Say, *"The young adults practiced entering and exiting group conversations while people were trading information about their personal items and the group did a great job. Let's give them a round of applause."*

Homework Assignments

Distribute the *Social Coaching Handout* to young adults and announce the following *Homework Assignments*:

1. ***Enter and exit group conversations*** with social coaches.
    - Young adults should practice ***entering and exiting group conversations*** with their social coach and another person.
        - Practice exiting when NEVER ACCEPTED.
        - Practice exiting when INITIALLY ACCEPTED AND THEN EXCLUDED.
        - Practice exiting when FULLY ACCEPTED.
    - Social coaches should go over the rules and steps for ***entering and exiting group conversations*** before the practice.
    - Social coaches should ask young adults the following ***social coaching questions*** after each practice:
        - ***Did it seem like we wanted to talk to you?***
        - ***How could you tell?***

2. *Enter a group conversation* with peers (could be from the *source of friends*).
   - Social coaches should go over the rules and steps for *entering and exiting group conversations* before the practice.
   - The assignment is NOT to *exit the conversation* unless they naturally need to.
   - Social coaches should ask young adults the following *social coaching questions* after the practice:
     - *Where did you enter a conversation and with whom?*
     - *Which steps did you follow?*
     - *Did it seem like they wanted to talk to you and how could you tell?*
     - *Did you have to exit the conversation and which steps did you follow?*

3. *Pay attention to humor feedback.*
   - If young adults happen to tell jokes (this is NOT the assignment), *pay attention to humor feedback.*
   - Social coaches should PRIVATELY ask the following *social coaching questions* after attempts at humor by young adults:
     - *What was your humor feedback?*
     - *How could you tell?*

Individual Check-Out

Individually and privately negotiate with each young adult and social coach:

1. When they plan to *enter and exit a group conversation* with social coaches.
   - Which other person they would be comfortable practicing with.

2. Where, when, and with whom they plan to *enter a group conversation* with peers.
   - Whether this is an accepting *social group* and how they can tell.

SESSION 7

EXITING CONVERSATIONS

Social Coaching Handout

Reasons for Not Being Accepted in Conversations

Table 8.1 Reasons for Not Being Accepted in Conversations

Reasons for Not Being Accepted	What to Do Differently Next Time
They want to talk privately	Try again later and listen before you join
They are rude or mean	Try a different group
You broke one of the rules for entering	Try again later, following the steps
You got too personal	Try a different group, don't get too personal
They are in a clique and don't want to make new friends	Try a different group
They are talking about something you do not know about	Try a different group that is talking about something you know
You have a bad reputation with them	Try a different group that does not know or care about your reputation
They did not understand that you were trying to join	Try again later, following the steps

Steps for Exiting Conversations*

Table 8.2 Steps for Exiting Conversations

NEVER ACCEPTED	INITIALLY ACCEPTED, THEN EXCLUDED	FULLY ACCEPTED
1. Keep your cool 2. Look away 3. Turn away 4. Walk away	1. Keep your cool 2. Look away 3. Wait for a BRIEF pause 4. Give a BRIEF cover story for leaving 5. Walk away	1. Wait for a pause 2. Give a SPECIFIC cover story for leaving 3. Say you'll see them later 4. Say goodbye 5. Walk away

Homework Assignments

1. ***Enter and exit group conversations*** with social coaches.
   * Young adults should practice ***entering and exiting group conversations*** with their social coach and another person.
     ○ Practice exiting when NEVER ACCEPTED.
     ○ Practice exiting when INITIALLY ACCEPTED AND THEN EXCLUDED.
     ○ Practice exiting when FULLY ACCEPTED.

- Social coaches should go over the rules and steps for *entering and exiting group conversations* before the practice.
- Social coaches should ask young adults the following *social coaching questions* after each practice:
    - *Did it seem like we wanted to talk to you?*
    - *How could you tell?*

2. *Enter a group conversation* with peers (could be from the *source of friends*).
   - Social coaches should go over the rules and steps for *entering and exiting group conversations* before the practice.
   - The assignment is NOT to *exit the conversation* unless they naturally need to.
   - Social coaches should ask young adults the following *social coaching questions* after the practice:
       - *Where did you enter a conversation and with whom?*
       - *Which steps did you follow?*
       - *Did it seem like they wanted to talk to you and how could you tell?*
       - *Did you have to exit the conversation and which steps did you follow?*

3. *Pay attention to humor feedback.*
   - If young adults happen to tell jokes (this is NOT the assignment), *pay attention to humor feedback*.
   - Social coaches should PRIVATELY ask the following *social coaching questions* after attempts at humor by young adults:
       - *What was your humor feedback?*
       - *How could you tell?*

* See *The Science of Making Friends* DVD (Laugeson, 2013) or *FriendMaker* mobile app for a video Role Play Demonstration of the corresponding rule.

GET-TOGETHERS

Social Coaching Therapist Guide

Preparing for the Social Coaching Session

The focus of this lesson is on helping young adults learn to organize and have successful *get-togethers* with friends. For some young adults that have failed to identify a *source of friends*, the biggest challenge in this lesson is finding someone with whom they can have a *get-together*. When this happens, it will be important for the group leader to help social coaches assess acceptance from peers and other possible causes in order to identify the source of the problem. The most common reasons for lack of *source of friends* include:

1. *No access to accepting peers with common interests.* This is perhaps the simplest and most common explanation when young adults are unable to identify someone with whom to have a *get-together*. In this case, the number-one priority of the social coach moving forward should be to help *find a source of friends*. This will need to be an extra weekly assignment until the *source of friends* is found. Redirecting young adults and social coaches to www.meetup.com and other social groups for young adults may be advisable.

2. *Peer rejection resulting from inappropriate choices in friends.* Another explanation for lack of options for get-togethers may be related to inappropriate choices of friends by the young adult. Some young adults wish to be friends with people who are not interested in return. The result is that they are *peer rejected*. If the social coach is unsure whether the young adult is being rejected, have him or her revisit the *Signs of Acceptance and Lack of Acceptance from Social Groups* in Table 4.3 to do a quick assessment. If the social coach suspects that the young adult is being rejected, it will be helpful to go over these signs with the young adult and remind him or her that *"Friend-ship is a choice. We don't get to be friends with everyone and not everyone gets to be friends with us. We want to make good choices and this may not be a good choice. Let's identify someone who is a good choice."* Then help the young adult to identify more accepting *sources of friends* moving forward.

3. *Bad reputation among peers.* Another reason young adults may be having difficulty *finding a source of friends* is that they have a bad reputation among the larger peer group. This is related to *peer rejection*, but on a larger scale. People get bad reputations for a variety of reasons. Simply doing something other people don't like, such as *being a conversation hog, policing, bragging,* or *being argumentative* can give you a bad reputation. Although issues with bad reputations are more common with adolescents, young adults may also occasionally struggle with bad reputations, and may consequently need to take steps toward changing their reputation if they are unable to escape their current peer group. Although not covered in the current manual, for more information about ecologically valid steps for changing bad reputations, see *The Science of Making Friends: Helping Socially Challenged Teens and Young Adults* (Laugeson, 2013). For more formal group-based lessons on changing a bad reputation, see *Social Skills for Teenagers with Developmental and Autism Spectrum Disorders: The PEERS® Treatment Manual* (Laugeson & Frankel, 2010) or *The PEERS®*

Curriculum for School-Based Professionals: Social Skills Training for Adolescents with Autism Spectrum Disorder (Laugeson, 2014).

4. ***The young adult is not using the skills with his or her peers.*** Another common reason young adults are unable to identify someone with whom to have a ***get-together*** is that they are not using the skills with their peers. Although a less common reason, young adults who are particularly anxious, or those who may be treatment-resistant, may be failing to use the skills taught in PEERS® in other settings. This is often apparent by lack of homework completion. In this event, it will be important to have an individual ***side meeting*** with the young adult and social coach and remind them, *"If your goal is to make and keep friends, you need to practice these skills and do your Homework Assignments."* For a review of how to manage these types of individual ***side meeting***s, see the *Preparing for the Lesson* section in the *Social Coaching Therapist Guide* for Session 7.

In the meantime, for young adults struggling to find a source of friends, another alternative is to give the option of choosing former close friends or relatives around the same age as the young adult. In some cultures, friendships rarely exist outside of the family, so be flexible in allowing peer choices to come from within the family when appropriate.

Homework Review

[Go over the following *Homework Assignments* and ***troubleshoot*** any potential problems. Start with completed homework first. If you have time, you can inquire as to why others were unable to complete the assignment and try to ***troubleshoot*** how they might get it done for the coming week. When reviewing homework, be sure to relabel descriptions using the ***buzzwords*** (identified by ***bold and italicized*** print). Spend the majority of the *Homework Review* on ***entering and exiting group conversations*** with social coaches and ***entering a group conversation*** with peers, as these were the most important assignments.]

1. ***Enter and exit group conversations*** with social coaches.
   - Say, *"One of the main assignments this week was for young adults to practice entering and exiting group conversations with you and another person. Who completed this assignment or attempted to complete it?"*
     - Ask the following questions:
     - *"Who did you and your young adult practice with?"*
     - *"What social coaching did you do before the practice?"*
     - *"Which steps did your young adult follow to enter the group conversation?"*
       1. ***Listen to the Conversation***
       2. ***Watch from a Distance***
       3. ***Use a Prop***
       4. ***Identify the Topic***
       5. ***Find a Common Interest***
       6. ***Move Closer***
       7. ***Wait for a Pause***
       8. ***Mention the Topic***
       9. ***Assess Interest***
       10. ***Introduce Yourself***
     - *"Which steps did your young adult follow to exit the conversations?"*
     - *"What social coaching did you do after the practice?"*
       - Appropriate ***social coaching questions***:
         - ***Did it seem like we wanted to talk to you?***
         - ***How could you tell?***

2. ***Enter a group conversation*** with peers (could be from the ***source of friends***).
   - Say, *"Another one of the main assignments this week was for young adults to practice entering group conversations with peers. Who completed this assignment or attempted to complete it?"*

Table 9.1 Steps for Exiting Conversations

NEVER ACCEPTED	INITIALLY ACCEPTED, THEN EXCLUDED	FULLY ACCEPTED
1. Keep your cool *2. Look away* *3. Turn away* *4. Walk away*	*1. Keep your cool* *2. Look away* *3. Wait for a BRIEF pause* *4. Give a BRIEF cover story for leaving* *5. Walk away*	*1. Wait for a pause* *2. Give a SPECIFIC cover story for leaving* *3. Say you'll see them later* *4. Say goodbye* *5. Walk away*

- Ask the following questions:
  - ○ *"Where and with whom did your young adult practice?"*
  - ○ *"What social coaching did you do before the practice?"*
  - ○ *"Which steps did your young adult follow?"*
  - ○ *"What social coaching did you do after the practice?"*
    - ■ Appropriate *social coaching questions*:
      - □ *Where did you enter a conversation and with whom?*
      - □ *Which steps did you follow?*
      - □ *Did it seem like they wanted to talk to you and how could you tell?*
      - □ *Did you have to exit the conversation and which steps did you follow?*

3. *Pay attention to humor feedback.*
   - Say, *"Another assignment this week was for young adults to pay attention to their humor feedback if they happened to tell a joke. The assignment was NOT to tell a joke. Who completed this assignment or attempted to complete this assignment?"*
   - Ask the following questions:
     - ○ *"Did your young adult attempt to tell jokes and did he/she pay attention to the humor feedback?"*
     - ○ *"What did you do to provide social coaching around humor feedback?"*
       - ■ Appropriate *social coaching questions*:
         - □ *What was your humor feedback?*
         - □ *How could you tell?*

- [Collect the *Social Coaching Homework Assignment Worksheets*. If social coaches forgot to bring the worksheets, have them complete a new form to hold them accountable for the assignments.]

Didactic Lesson: Get-Togethers

- Distribute the *Social Coaching Handout*.
  - ○ Sections in **bold print** in the *Social Coaching Therapist Guide* come directly from the *Social Coaching Handout*.
  - ○ Remind social coaches that terms that are in ***bold and italicized*** print are ***buzzwords*** and represent important concepts from the PEERS® curriculum that should be used as much as possible when social coaching.
- Explain, *"Today, we're going to be talking about how to have successful get-togethers with friends. A good way for young adults to start close friendships is by planning get-togethers. These could be at home or in the community. In order to make sure they're successful, we need to be familiar with the rules and steps for having get-togethers. We organize these rules and steps into five phases: planning, preparing, beginning, during, and ending get-togethers."*

Planning Get-Togethers

- ***Make plans using the five W's***
  - ○ Explain, *"The first part of having a successful get-together involves planning the get-together. This means you need to decide beforehand, with your friend, what you're going to do and who is going to be there. We call these the five W's."*

- ***WHO is going to be there***
  - Say, *"One part of planning involves deciding WHO is going to be there. Why is it important that everyone invited to a get-together know in advance WHO is going to be there?"*
    - Answers: Because you don't want your friends to be surprised if there are other people at the ***get-together***; certain people may not get along and wouldn't want to be around each other.

- ***WHAT you're going to do***
  - Say, *"Another part of planning the get-together involves figuring out WHAT you're going to do beforehand. Why is it important to figure out WHAT you're going to do?"*
    - Answers: Because ***get-togethers*** are easier and more fun if you plan activities; you don't want your friends to get bored if there is nothing to do.
  - Ask, *"What should your activities be based on?"*
    - Answer: Your ***common interests***.
  - Ask, *"We've provided you with a list of some activities that young adults have identified for get-togethers"* (see Table 9.2).

Table 9.2 Common Activity-Based Get-Togethers Identified by Young Adults

Public Activities	Indoor Activities	Amusement Parks
Movie theaters	Video games	Gaming centers
Malls	Computer games	Adult video arcades
Sporting events	Surf the Internet	Laser tag
Bars/night clubs/dance clubs	YouTube videos	Paintball/airsoft
Comic book conventions	Social networking sites	Adult amusement parks
Comic book stores	Listen to music	Miniature golf parks
Gaming conventions	Watching sporting events	Water parks
Gaming stores	Watch awards shows	Go-karting
Science museums	Watch movies	Batting cages
Warhammer	Watch TV shows	Golf ranges/driving ranges
Concerts	Card games	Speedways
Festivals	Board games	Car shows/auto shows
LARPing events	Trivia games	Safari parks/animal parks
Bowling	Darts	Zoos
Pet stores/pet adoptions	Air hockey	Aquariums
Dog parks	Table shuffleboard	State and county fairs
Parks	Crafting	Renaissance fairs
Beach/lake/river	Sewing	Science expos
Mealtime Activities	**Pair Sports**	**Group Sports**
Restaurants	Bike riding/mountain biking	Basketball
Food courts	Hiking/walking/trekking	Football
Food carts/food trucks	Rock climbing	Baseball
Dinner parties	Tennis/raquetball/squash	Soccer
Drinks parties	Skiing/snowboarding	Hockey
Ice cream shops	Sailing/boating/kayaking	Volleyball
Frozen yogurt shops	Surfing/windsurfing/kiteboarding	Badminton
Order pizza	Swimming/snorkeling/diving	Water polo
Food delivery	Golf	Bocce ball
Order takeout/takeaway	Skateboarding	Lacrosse
Barbecue	Pool/billiards/snooker	Rugby
Sushi	Ping-Pong	Cricket
Cook a meal	Shooting baskets	Martial arts groups
Picnic	Frisbee/freestyle/playing catch	Aerobics classes
Baking	Roller skating/rollerblading	Dance classes
Cooking classes	Ice skating	Competitive dance
Food festivals	Fishing/hunting	Rafting
Farmers' market	Weightlifting/working out	Rowing

- *WHERE you're going to get together*
  - Say, *"It's also important to figure out in advance WHERE the get-together is going to take place. Why is it important to figure out WHERE the get-together is going to be?"*
    - Answer: Because the *get-together* may never happen if no one knows where to go.

- *WHEN you're going to get together*
  - Say, *"We also need to figure out in advance WHEN the get-together is going to take place. Why is it important to figure out WHEN the get-together is going to happen?"*
    - Answer: Because if you do not decide in advance when you're going to *get together*, your schedules may become full and the *get-together* might never take place.

- *HOW the get-together is going to happen*
  - Say, *"The fifth W stands for HOW. Depending on what we're doing, we may also need to figure out HOW the get-together is going to happen, like who is going to drive or if we need to get tickets. Some young adults may need more assistance with this part of the planning than others, particularly when it comes to transportation and paying for things."*

Preparing for Get-Togethers

- *Make a follow-up call to finalize plans*
  - Say, *"Even though we've planned the get-together using the five W's, we still need to finalize the plans right before the get-together. When do we do that and how?"*
    - Answer: Usually a text or phone call a day or two before is appropriate.
  - Explain, *"Depending on the activity, you'll want to help young adults follow-up with their friend to make sure plans haven't changed. You may need to help them with the wording and choosing the best time to finalize the plans."*

- *Make sure your space is cleaned up*
  - Explain, *"Another important part of preparing for a get-together is to make sure your personal space is cleaned up. That means if the get-together is in their home, they need to make sure any common areas are picked up. If they're driving, they need to make sure their car isn't messy."*
  - Ask, *"What could be the problem with having a messy home or car?"*
    - Answers: If your home or car is a mess, your friends may think you are a slob; cleaning up before having company over is a sign of respect for your guests; not cleaning up is seen as rude and disrespectful.

- *Have refreshments ready to share*
  - Say, *"When we have get-togethers in our home, we also need to have some refreshments ready to share. Why is it important to have food and beverages ready to share when we have friends over?"*
    - Answers: They might be hungry or thirsty; it would seem rude not to offer them something to eat or drink; they may think you're inconsiderate.
  - Explain, *"If your young adult is going to have people over to his or her home, you may need to help decide what's appropriate."*

- *Put away personal items you don't want others to share, see, or touch*
  - Say, *"Another important part of preparing for a get-together involves putting away any personal items you don't want to share or let other people see or touch. Why would it be important to put away these items beforehand?"*
    - Answers: Because you don't want to be rude and tell your friends they can't see or touch your things; it's easier to put personal items away in advance so your friends don't even know they exist (this includes food you're unwilling to share).
  - Explain, *"Some young adults have prized items that they don't want anyone to touch. Be sure to help them put away these items and anything else they don't want others to share, see, or touch if they're having friends over to their home."*

- *Have other activities ready*
  - Say, *"Even though you should have decided beforehand what you're going to do, if your friend is coming over to your home, you'll need to have some other activities ready. Why would it be important to have other things to do?"*

- ▪ Answers: Because people get bored easily and plans change; you need to have other options ready; having a variety of activities ready to use will be helpful.
  - ○ Ask, *"What should these other activities be based on?"*
    - ▪ Answer: Your ***common interests***.

Beginning Get-Togethers

- Explain, *"Now that we know the rules for planning and preparing for get-togethers, we need to talk about the steps for beginning get-togethers, particularly if they're in your young adult's home."*

1. *Greet your guest*
   - Say, *"When having a get-together in your home, the first step when your guests arrive is to greet them at the door. How do we greet our guests?"*
     - ○ Answers: Say hello and ask them how they're doing; some people will hug or give a casual acknowledgment like a head nod, a pound, or fist bump.

2. *Invite them in*
   - Say, *"The next step is we need to invite them in. This involves saying something like, 'Come in' and moving out of the doorway so they can come inside. What happens if we forget to invite them in?"*
     - ○ Answers: They end up standing at the door waiting to come in; this can feel awkward for your friend.
   - Explain, *"Inviting your friend in may also include taking coats, jackets, or umbrellas."*

3. *Introduce them to anyone they don't know*
   - Say, *"Once we've invited our guest in, we need to introduce them to anyone they don't know. Why is it important to introduce them to anyone they don't know?"*
     - ○ Answers: If they don't know everyone, they might feel awkward and left out; they'll feel more comfortable and welcome if they know everyone.

4. *Show them around*
   - Say, *"If this is the first time your friends have been to your home, you probably want to show them around a little. Why is it important to show your friends around?"*
     - ○ Answers: It's your job to make your guests feel welcome; they should know where the bathroom is located and be familiar with the surroundings in order to feel welcome.

5. *Offer them refreshments*
   - Say, *"As your friend is getting settled, or maybe as you're walking by the kitchen, you might want to offer them something to eat or drink. Why is it important to offer your guests refreshments?"*
     - ○ Answers: They may be hungry or thirsty; it's polite to offer guests in your home food and beverages.

6. *Ask them what they want to do*
   - Say, *"Even though you should have planned with them what you're going to do, you should still ask your guest what they want to do when they're settled. Why is it a good idea to ask them what they want to do?"*
     - ○ Answers: It's your job as the host to make sure your guest has a good time; they might want to do something different in the end.
   - Explain, *"You'll at least want to check in to make sure your friend still wants to do what you planned. If not, then ask them what they want to do and be prepared to go with the flow."*

- [Optional: Show BAD and GOOD *Role Play Video Demonstrations* of **beginning a get-together** from the *PEERS® Role Play Video Library* (www.routledge.com/cw/laugeson).]

Rules for During Get-Togethers

- Explain, *"So now that we know how to begin the get-together, we need to know what to do during the get-together. There are some important rules for making sure your young adult's get-together is a success."*

- *Get-togethers should be activity-based*
  - Explain, *"The first thing we should do when planning a get-together is to figure out what we're going to do beforehand. What could be the problem with just deciding to hang out, but not making any real plans for what to do?"*
    - Answers: It could end up being boring; you may never figure out what to do.
  - Say, *"In order to avoid boring get-togethers, it's best if we have activity-based get-togethers. What should the activities be based on?"*
    - Answer: ***Common interests.***

- *The guests get to pick the activities at your home*
  - Say, *"Another important rule for having a get-together in your home is that the guests get to pick the activities. Why is it important to let the guests pick the activities?"*
    - Answer: Because it's the host's job to make sure the guests have a good time.
  - Ask, *"Should we still have some idea of what we're going to do beforehand and even have some activities ready to go if plans change?"*
    - Answer: Yes, but we need to be flexible.
  - Say, *"Not everyone knows the rule that the guests pick the activities. So what do you do if you're at a friend's house and they want to choose all the activities?"*
    - Answers: ***Don't police your friend; go with the flow in the moment, and remember that friendship is a choice;*** if your friend never wants to do what you want to do, you don't have to hang out with him or her anymore.

- *Go with the flow*
  - Say, *"Another important rule for having a successful get-together is that we need to go with the flow. That means sometimes we need to be flexible and go with whatever is happening that we didn't expect. For example, do plans sometimes change during get-togethers?"*
    - Answer: Yes.
  - Ask, *"What should we do if plans change?"*
    - Answer: Go with the flow.
  - Explain, *"If it really bothers your young adult that their friend keeps changing plans, you can tell them to just go with the flow in the moment, and remember that friendship is a choice. They don't have to hang out with that friend again if it really bothers them."*

- *Don't invite other people into your get-together unexpectedly*
  - Explain, *"Another rule for having successful get-togethers is don't invite other people into your get-together unexpectedly. What could be the problem with inviting another friend into your get-together unexpectedly?"*
    - Answers: Your friend might think you're rude; it's disloyal to your friend; they might feel disappointed or like they're not good enough if you invite others; your friends might not get along.
  - Explain, *"In general, when young adults are planning the get-together, have them think of the five W's as their social contract. If plans change, everyone needs to okay the changes."*

- *Don't ignore your friends*
  - Say, *"Another important rule for having get-togethers is don't ignore your friends. Is it okay to ignore one friend to talk to another friend during a get-together?"*
    - Answers: No; it's your job to make sure all your friends are having fun; your friends should feel like they have your attention.
  - Ask, *"Should we be texting or video chatting with other people during our get-togethers, and what could be the problem with that?"*
    - Answers: It's rude to text or video chat with other people during a get-together; it's disloyal to your friend; your friend might feel left out or ignored; it might not be fun for your friend.

- *Don't tease your friends*
  - Say, *"Another rule for having successful get-togethers is don't tease your friends. What could be the problem with teasing your friends?"*

- ■ Answers: This might hurt their feelings; the teasing could escalate and you could end up in a fight or an argument; they might not want to hang out with you anymore.
  - ○ Ask, *"Do friends sometimes tease each other?"*
    - ■ Answer: Yes, particularly men.
  - ○ Explain, *"We call teasing among friends 'banter.' Banter is a type of teasing, but it's meant to be playful and friendly. Even though banter is really common among friends, what could be the problem with teasing or bantering?"*
    - ■ Answers: Feelings could get hurt; it can escalate into a fight or argument; ***it's risky if your goal is to make and keep friends***.

- ● *Stick up for your friends*
  - ○ Say, *"What if you're hosting a group get-together and one of your friends is teasing another friend. What should you do?"*
    - ■ Answer: You should stick up for your friend and try to keep the peace.
  - ○ Explain, *"If you're the host of the get-together, your friend who's being teased may be looking for you to help them. If you don't stick up for your friend, you may seem disloyal and they may not want to hang out with you again."*

- ● *Don't argue with your friends*
  - ○ Say, *"Another important rule for having successful get-togethers is don't argue with your friends. What could be the problem with arguing with friends during a get-together?"*
    - ■ Answers: It could escalate and people could get angry; feelings could get hurt; your friend may not want to hang out with you again.
  - ○ Explain, *"In a few weeks, we'll be giving young adults strategies for resolving conflicts and handling arguments and disagreements. In the meantime, you can suggest that they go with the flow and avoid arguing with friends during get-togethers."*

- ● *Don't police your friends*
  - ○ Explain, *"Just like when we're trading information, another important rule for having successful get-togethers is don't police your friends. What could be the problem with policing your friends?"*
    - ■ Answers: It's rude; it's annoying; your friends might think you're bossy and controlling; it could be embarrassing for the other person.

- ● *Be a good sport*
  - ○ Say, *"A lot of people like to play games and sports during get-togethers, so another rule for having a successful get-together is that we need to be a good sport. Why is it important to be a good sport?"*
    - ■ Answers: Because your friend will be less likely to want to hang out with you if you're a ***poor sport***; if you're a ***good sport***, they're more likely to have fun and want to hang out again.
  - ○ Ask, *"How can we be a good sport?"*
    - ■ Answers: Praise your friend; don't be competitive; ***don't police*** them or act bossy; don't be a sore loser; don't be a bad winner; share and take turns; play by the rules; don't cheat.

- ● *Suggest a change if you get bored*
  - ○ Say, *"People sometimes get bored during get-togethers, but what could be the problem with saying 'I'm bored' or walking away from your friends during a get-together?"*
    - ■ Answers: You would seem rude; it sounds like you're saying they're boring; they might not want to hang out with you again.
  - ○ Explain, *"Instead of saying you're bored or walking away, you should suggest a change. We can do that by saying, 'How about when we're done with this, we do something else.'"*
  - ○ Ask, *"What should you do if your friend doesn't want to do what you suggest for a change?"*
    - ■ Answers: ***Go with the flow in the moment***, let them pick the activity, and ***remember that friendship is a choice***; if your friend never wants to do what you suggest, you don't have to hang out with him or her.

- ● *Trade information at least 50% of the time*
  - ○ Say, *"Another important rule for having a successful get-together is that you should be talking and trading information at least 50% of the time. Why is it important to trade information at least half of the time?"*

- ■ Answers: Because this is how you get to know one another and **find common interests**; if you don't talk and **trade information**, you won't get to know one another and become closer friends.

- *Keep it short and sweet to start*
  - ○ Say, *"Finally, when we're having get-togethers with friends we don't know that well, it's better to keep it short and sweet. What does it mean to keep it short and sweet?"*
    - □ Answers: Keep the get-together short at first; don't have long get-togethers right away.
  - ○ Explain, *"It's better to keep it short and sweet at first to make sure things go well. As young adults get to know friends better, then they can hang out for longer periods of time. You can help decide what's an appropriate length."*

Ending Get-Togethers

- Explain, *"Now that we know the rules for what to do during a get-together, we need to talk about how to end a get-together."*

1. *Wait for a pause in activities*
   - Say, *"The first step in ending a get-together is to wait for a pause in the activities. That means don't interrupt what you're doing unless you have to. What could be the problem with interrupting an activity to leave or end a get-together?"*
     - ○ Answers: It may seem abrupt; your friends may think you don't want to hang out with them anymore.

2. *Give a cover story for ending the get-together*
   - Say, *"The next step is to give a cover story for leaving or ending the get-together. Remember, cover stories are reasons we do things. What are some examples of reasons you might have to leave or end a get-together?"*
     - ○ Examples:
       - ■ *"I have to go soon."*
       - ■ *"I have to study now."*
       - ■ *"It's getting late and I have an early class."*
       - ■ *"It's late and I have work in the morning."*
   - Ask, *"What could be the problem with not giving a cover story for leaving or ending a get-together?"*
     - ○ Answer: Your friends may think you don't want to hang out with them anymore.

3. *Start walking your friend to the door*
   - Say, *"If the get-together is in your home, the next step is to stand up and start walking your friend to the door. Why is it important to walk your friend to the door?"*
     - ○ Answers: Because it's rude to make them find their way out; if you don't stand up and start walking them to the door, they may not leave; they are waiting for your cue about what to do next.

4. *Thank your friend for getting together*
   - Say, *"The next step for ending a get-together is to thank your friend for getting together. Why is it important to thank your friend?"*
     - ○ Answers: Because it makes them feel nice; it shows that you appreciate them.

5. *Tell your friend you had a good time*
   - Say, *"If you had a good time, you should tell your friend as you're saying goodbye or walking them out. Why is it important to tell your friend you had a good time?"*
     - ○ Answers: It shows them that you enjoy being around them; it makes them feel good.

6. *Say goodbye and you'll see them later*
   - Say, *"Finally, as you're saying goodbye or walking your friend out, it's important to say goodbye. You might even say 'I'll see you later' or 'I'll talk to you soon' as you're saying goodbye. This is also a nice time to try to make future plans to get-together if you like. Why is it important to say goodbye and that you'll see them later?"*
     - ○ Answer: It shows that you enjoyed their company and want to see them again.

- [Optional: Show BAD and GOOD *Role Play Video Demonstrations* of **ending a get-together** from the *PEERS® Role Play Video Library* (www.routledge.com/cw/laugeson).]

Homework Assignments

[Distribute the *Social Coaching Homework Assignment Worksheet* (Appendix I) for social coaches to complete and return at the next session.]

1. Have a *get-together* with a friend.
   - Social coaches should help young adults plan the get-together using the *five W's*:
     - *WHO* they plan to get together with.
     - *WHAT* they plan to do.
     - *WHEN* it will happen.
     - *WHERE* they will meet.
     - *HOW* they will make it happen.
   - Social coaches should go over the rules and steps for *get-togethers* with young adults beforehand.
   - Social coaches should ask young adults the following *social coaching questions* after the *get-together*:
     - *What did you decide to do and who picked the activities?*
     - *Did you trade information and for what percentage of the time?*
     - *What were your common interests and what could you do with that information if you were going to hang out again?*
     - *Did you and your friend have a good time?*
     - *Is this someone you might want to hang out with again?*

2. *Enter and exit group conversations* with social coaches.
   - Young adults should practice *entering and exiting group conversations* with their social coach and another person.
     - Practice exiting when NEVER ACCEPTED.
     - Practice exiting when INITIALLY ACCEPTED AND THEN EXCLUDED.
     - Practice exiting when FULLY ACCEPTED.
   - Social coaches should go over the rules and steps for *entering and exiting group conversations* before the practice.
   - Social coaches should ask young adults the following *social coaching questions* after each practice:
     - *Did it seem like we wanted to talk to you?*
     - *How could you tell?*

3. *Enter a group conversation* with peers (could be from the *source of friends*).
   - Social coaches should go over the rules and steps for *entering and exiting group conversations* before the practice.
   - The assignment is NOT to *exit the conversation* unless they naturally need to.
   - Social coaches should ask young adults the following *social coaching questions* after the practice:
     - *Where did you enter a conversation and with whom?*
     - *Which steps did you follow?*
     - *Did it seem like they wanted to talk to you and how could you tell?*
     - *Did you have to exit the conversation and which steps did you follow?*

4. *Pay attention to humor feedback.*
   - If young adults happen to tell jokes (this is NOT the assignment), *pay attention to humor feedback.*
   - Social coaches should PRIVATELY ask the following *social coaching questions* after attempts at humor by young adults:
     - *What was your humor feedback?*
     - *How could you tell?*

Social Coaching Tips

- Be sure to help young adults plan the *get-together* using the *five W's*.
  - The most common reason *get-togethers* fall through during this assignment is because young adults forget to figure out **WHEN** and **WHERE** and *finalize the plans*.
- If the *get-together* is going to be in the young adult's home, help them:
  - *Make sure their space is cleaned up.*
  - *Have refreshments ready to share.*
  - *Put away personal items they don't want others to share, see, or touch.*
  - *Have other activities ready.*
- If the *get-together* is in your own home (most likely for parents), if it's developmentally appropriate:
  - Allow your young adult's friends to hang out at your home with some privacy.
  - Check on conversations by offering snacks periodically.
    - You might make several trips with food and beverages at various times in order to monitor the *get-together* (e.g., bring the beverages out first, wait for awhile, then bring some snacks out, wait for awhile, then check on refills, wait for awhile, etc.).
    - Unobtrusively observe when bringing in snacks, but do not intrude on conversations unless it is to offer snacks.
  - If something is going wrong, use a *cover story* to pull your young adult out (e.g., *Can you help me with the snacks in the kitchen?"*).
  - Avoid lecturing and keep it BRIEF and positive.
  - Provide *social coaching* using your *Social Coaching Tips* from week 1:
    1. *Begin with praise* (e.g., *"Nice job trading information and finding common interests"*).
    2. *Offer suggestions* (e.g., *"Let's be careful not to be a conversation hog"*).
    3. *Use buzzwords* (e.g., *"How about asking follow-up questions"*).

GET-TOGETHERS

Young Adult Therapist Guide

Preparing for the Young Adult Session

The focus of this lesson is on teaching young adults how to organize and have successful *get-togethers* with potential friends. Socially accepted young adults have frequent *get-togethers* with friends, both in their homes and in the community. They turn school and work acquaintances into close friends by spending time with them outside of these settings. Therefore, learning the skills necessary to be successful at having *get-togethers* is particularly important in helping young adults make and keep friends and develop relationships. Research indicates that the best way to form close friendships is through organizing and frequently having social contact outside of formal settings such as work and school. Since most young adults with Autism Spectrum Disorder (ASD) and other social challenges tend to have fewer social interactions with peers outside of these settings, learning how to organize and have successful *get-togethers* will be a pivotal skill toward the development of closer relationships.

One of the recommendations from this lesson is that *get-togethers should be activity-based*. In other words, *get-togethers* should be organized around some predetermined activity in which all of the attendees share a *common interest*. Having *activity-based get-togethers* lessens the pressure of maintaining conversation throughout the time spent together. Common activities identified by young adults attending PEERS® groups around the globe are highlighted in Table 9.2. The activities chosen by young adults will be different according to culture and *common interests*, so do not consider this list exhaustive. Have young adults come up with their own ideas.

The most common challenge about this lesson is the lack of choices for potential guests for *get-togethers*. The *"gold standard"* is someone with whom the young adult wishes to know better and who appears to be interested in becoming closer friends. Options chosen from accepting individuals from *social groups* and *social activities* are usually helpful in this regard. In the absence of having someone to fill the *gold standard*, a former close friend or a family member around the same age would be acceptable options until someone more appropriate can be identified. The most important part of this assignment is that a *get-together* actually takes place so that the young adult can practice the skills just learned. If such practice does not occur soon after learning, the skills are unlikely to be used at a later time.

For young adults struggling to find someone to have a *get-together* with, identifying an accepting *source of friends* may need to take priority over all other assignments moving forward. Although no longer a formal assignment, any young adult who does not have a potential *source of friends* by this point in the program should be given this extra assignment until he or she is successful at identifying one or two potential friends with *common interests*. Inability to find a *source of friends* could be the difference between success or failure in the program. Suggestions for how to overcome this treatment barrier are discussed in greater detail in the *Preparing for the Social Coaching Session* section of the *Social Coaching Therapist Guide* in this chapter.

Finally, the current lesson includes a rule that *during get-togethers* when games and sports are involved, young adults should be *good sports*. The issue of poor sportsmanship, like that of bad reputations, is more common among adolescents, and is therefore not discussed in detail in the current manual. However, for more information about ecologically valid strategies for good sportsmanship, see *The Science of Making Friends: Helping Socially Challenged Teens and Young Adults* (Laugeson, 2013). For more formal group-based lessons on good sportsmanship, see *Social Skills for Teenagers with Developmental and Autism Spectrum Disorders: The PEERS® Treatment Manual* (Laugeson & Frankel, 2010) or *The PEERS® Curriculum for School-Based Professionals: Social Skills Training for Adolescents with Autism Spectrum Disorder* (Laugeson, 2014).

Homework Review

[Go over the following *Homework Assignments* and **troubleshoot** any potential problems. Start with completed homework first. If you have time, you can inquire as to why others were unable to complete the assignment and try to **troubleshoot** how they might get it done for the coming week. When reviewing homework, be sure to relabel descriptions using the **buzzwords** (identified by **bold and italicized** print). Spend the majority of the *Homework Review* on **entering and exiting group conversations** with social coaches and **entering a group conversation** with peers, as these were the most important assignments.]

1. *Enter and exit group conversations* with social coaches.
   - Say, *"One of the main assignments this week was to practice entering and exiting group conversations with your social coach and another person. Raise your hand if you did this assignment."*
   - Ask the following questions:
     ○ *"Who did you and your social coach practice with and which steps did you follow?"*
       1. *Listen to the Conversation*
       2. *Watch from a Distance*
       3. *Use a Prop*
       4. *Identify the Topic*
       5. *Find a Common Interest*
       6. *Move Closer*
       7. *Wait for a Pause*
       8. *Mention the Topic*
       9. *Assess Interest*
       10. *Introduce Yourself*
     ○ *"Did it seem like they wanted to talk to you and how could you tell?"*
     ○ *"Did you exit the conversation and which steps did you follow?"*

Table 9.1 Steps for Exiting Conversations

NEVER ACCEPTED	INITIALLY ACCEPTED, THEN EXCLUDED	FULLY ACCEPTED
1. Keep your cool	1. Keep your cool	1. Wait for a pause
2. Look away	2. Look away	2. Give a SPECIFIC cover story for leaving
3. Turn away	3. Wait for a BRIEF pause	3. Say you'll see them later
4. Walk away	4. Give a BRIEF cover story for leaving	4. Say goodbye
	5. Walk away	5. Walk away

2. *Enter a group conversation* with peers (could be from the **source of friends**).
   - Say, *"Another one of the main assignments this week was to practice entering group conversations with peers. Raise your hand if you did this assignment."*
   - Ask the following questions:
     ○ *"Where and with whom did you practice?"*
     ○ *"Which steps did you follow?"*
     ○ *"Did it seem like they wanted to talk to you?"*
     ○ *"How could you tell?"*
       ▪ *Talking to you?*

- ■ *Looking at you?*
- ■ *Facing you (they opened the circle)?*
  - ○ *"Did you have to exit the conversation and which steps did you follow?"*

3. *Pay attention to humor feedback.*
   - Say, *"Another assignment this week was to pay attention to your humor feedback if you happened to tell a joke. The assignment was NOT to tell a joke. If you happened to tell a joke this week, raise your hand if you paid attention to your humor feedback."*
   - Ask the following questions:
     - ○ *"I don't want to know what joke you told, I just want to know what your humor feedback was. Were they laughing AT you, laughing WITH you, giving a courtesy laugh, or NOT laughing at all?"*
     - ○ *"How could you tell?"*
     - ○ *"So are you done paying attention to your humor feedback?"*
       - ■ Answer: No.
     - ○ *"When will you pay attention to your humor feedback?"*
       - ■ Answer: Every time they tell a joke.
     - ○ *"How will you pay attention to your humor feedback?"*
       - ■ Answer: By LOOKING and LISTENING.

Didactic Lesson: Get-Togethers

- Explain, *"Today, we're going to be talking about how to have successful get-togethers with friends. Having get-togethers is a nice way to hang out with friends and get to know each other better. This is how close friendships develop. Sadly, if we're not having get-togethers with our friends outside of work or school, we're probably not close friends. A good way to start a close friendship is to plan a get-together. This could be in your home or in the community. If you're planning the get-together in your home, that means you're the host and you'll have a few extra jobs. Whether meeting in your home or somewhere else, in order to make sure that it's successful, we need to be familiar with the rules and steps for having get-togethers."*
- [Present the rules and steps for *get-togethers* by writing the following bullet points and *buzzwords* (identified by *bold and italicized* print) on the board. Do not erase the rules and steps until the end of the lesson. Each role play with a ⊙ symbol includes a corresponding role play video from the *PEERS® Role Play Video Library* (www.routledge.com/cw/laugeson).]

Planning Get-Togethers

- *Make plans using the five W's*
  - ○ Explain, *"The first part of having a successful get-together involves planning the get-together. This means you will need to decide beforehand, with your friend, what you're going to do and who is going to be there. We call these the five W's."*

- *WHO is going to be there*
  - ○ Say, *"One part of planning involves deciding WHO is going to be there. Why is it important that everyone invited to a get-together know in advance WHO is going to be there?"*
    - ■ Answers: Because you don't want your friends to be surprised if there are other people at the *get-together*; certain people may not get along and wouldn't want to be around each other.

- *WHAT you're going to do*
  - ○ Say, *"Another part of planning the get-together involves figuring out WHAT you're going to do beforehand. Why is it important to figure out WHAT you're going to do?"*
    - ■ Answers: Because *get-togethers* are easier and more fun if you plan activities; you don't want your friends to get bored if there is nothing to do.
  - ○ Ask, *"What should your activities be based on?"*
    - ■ Answer: Your *common interests*.
  - ○ Ask, *"What are some activities that young adults enjoy doing during get-togethers?"*
    - ■ Have young adults brainstorm ideas (see Table 9.2 for suggestions).

Table 9.2 Common Activity-Based Get-Togethers Identified by Young Adults

Public Activities	Indoor Activities	Amusement Parks
Movie theaters	Video games	Gaming centers
Malls	Computer games	Adult video arcades
Sporting events	Surf the Internet	Laser tag
Bars/night clubs/dance clubs	YouTube videos	Paintball/airsoft
Comic book conventions	Social networking sites	Adult amusement parks
Comic book stores	Listen to music	Miniature golf parks
Gaming conventions	Watching sporting events	Water parks
Gaming stores	Watch awards shows	Go-karting
Science museums	Watch movies	Batting cages
Warhammer	Watch TV shows	Golf ranges/driving ranges
Concerts	Card games	Speedways
Festivals	Board games	Car shows/auto shows
LARPing events	Trivia games	Safari parks/animal parks
Bowling	Darts	Zoos
Pet stores/pet adoptions	Air hockey	Aquariums
Dog parks	Table shuffleboard	State and county fairs
Parks	Crafting	Renaissance fairs
Beach/lake/river	Sewing	Science expos
Mealtime Activities	**Pair Sports**	**Group Sports**
Restaurants	Bike riding/mountain biking	Basketball
Food courts	Hiking/walking/trekking	Football
Food carts/food trucks	Rock climbing	Baseball
Dinner parties	Tennis/raquetball/squash	Soccer
Drinks parties	Skiing/snowboarding	Hockey
Ice cream shops	Sailing/boating/kayaking	Volleyball
Frozen yogurt shops	Surfing/windsurfing/kiteboarding	Badminton
Order pizza	Swimming/snorkeling/diving	Water polo
Food delivery	Golf	Bocce ball
Order takeout/takeaway	Skateboarding	Lacrosse
Barbecue	Pool/billiards/snooker	Rugby
Sushi	Ping-Pong	Cricket
Cook a meal	Shooting baskets	Martial arts groups
Picnic	Frisbee/freestyle/playing catch	Aerobics classes
Baking	Roller skating/rollerblading	Dance classes
Cooking classes	Ice skating	Competitive dance
Food festivals	Fishing/hunting	Rafting
Farmers' market	Weightlifting/working out	Rowing

- *WHERE you're going to get-together*
  - Say, *"It's also important to figure out in advance WHERE the get-together is going to take place. Why is it important to figure out WHERE the get-together is going to be?"*
    - Answer: Because the *get-together* may never happen if no one knows where to go.

- *WHEN you're going to get-together*
  - Say, *"We also need to figure out in advance WHEN the get-together is going to take place. Why is it important to figure out WHEN the get-together is going to happen?"*
    - Answer: Because if you do not decide in advance when you're going to meet, your schedules may become full and the *get-together* might never take place.

- *HOW the get-together is going to happen*
  - Say, *"The fifth W stands for HOW. Depending on what we're doing, we may also need to figure out HOW the get-together is going to happen, like who is going to drive or if we need to get tickets. Why is it important to figure out HOW the get-together is going to happen?"*
    - Answer: If you don't work out the details in advance, the *get-together* may never happen.

Preparing for Get-Togethers

- *Make a follow-up call to finalize plans*
  - ○ Say, *"Even though we've planned the get-together using the five W's, do we still need to finalize the plans right before the get-together?"*
    - ■ Answer: Yes.
  - ○ Ask, *"When do we do that and how?"*
    - ■ Answer: Usually a text or phone call a day or two before is appropriate.
  - ○ Explain, *"Depending on the activity, you'll want to follow up with your friend a day or two beforehand to make sure plans haven't changed. Social coaches can help with the wording and choosing the best time to finalize the plans."*

- *Make sure your space is cleaned up*
  - ○ Explain, *"Another important part of preparing for a get-together is to make sure your personal space is cleaned up. That means if the get-together is in your home, make sure any common areas your friends might see are picked up. If you're driving, make sure your car isn't messy."*
  - ○ Ask, *"What could be the problem with having a messy home or car?"*
    - ■ Answers: If your home or car is a mess, your friends may think you are a slob; cleaning up before having company over is a sign of respect for your guests; not cleaning up is seen as rude and disrespectful.

- *Have refreshments ready to share*
  - ○ Explain, *"When we have get-togethers in our home, we also need to have refreshments ready to share. That means we need to be prepared to feed people and have beverages."*
  - ○ Ask, *"Why is it important to have refreshments ready to share when we have friends over?"*
    - ■ Answers: They might be hungry or thirsty; it would seem rude not to offer them something to eat or drink; they may think you're inconsiderate.
  - ○ Explain, *"It's always a good idea to have snacks and refreshments available if you're going to have people over to your home. Your coaches can help decide what's appropriate."*

- *Put away personal items you don't want others to share, see, or touch*
  - ○ Say, *"Another important part of preparing for a get-together involves putting away any personal items you don't want to share or let other people see or touch. Why would it be important to put away these things beforehand?"*
    - ■ Answers: Because you don't want to be rude and tell your friends they can't see or touch your things; it's easier to put personal items away in advance so your friends don't even know they're there (this includes food you're unwilling to share).

- *Have other activities ready*
  - ○ Say, *"Even though you should have decided beforehand what you're going to do, if your friend is coming over to your home, you'll need to have some other activities ready. Why would it be important to have other things to do?"*
    - ■ Answers: Because people get bored easily and plans change; you need to have other options ready; having a variety of activities ready will be helpful.
  - ○ Ask, *"What should these other activities be based on?"*
    - ■ Answer: Your *common interests*.

Beginning Get-Togethers

- Explain, *"Now that we know the rules for planning and preparing for get-togethers, we need to talk about the steps for beginning get-togethers at your home."*

Bad Role Play: Beginning a Get-Together ⊙

[The group leader and one behavioral coach should do an INAPPROPRIATE role play of *beginning a get-together*.]

- Begin by saying, *"We're going to do a role play. Watch this and tell me what I'm doing WRONG in beginning this get-together."*

Example of an INAPPROPRIATE Role Play
- (Begin by having the behavioral coach step outside)
- Behavioral coach: (Knocks on door)
- Group leader: (Opens door, stands there, doesn't say anything)
- Group leader & behavioral coach: (Long pause)
- Behavioral coach: (Confused) *"Umm . . . hi, (insert name)."*
- Group leader: (Looking awkward, confused, stunned) *"Hi."*
- Group leader & behavioral coach: (Long pause)
- Behavioral coach: (Confused, unsure what to do) *"How's it going?"*
- Group leader: (Looking awkward, confused) *"Pretty good."*
- Group leader & behavioral coach: (Long pause)
- Behavioral coach: (Confused, awkward) *"Can I come in?"*
- Group leader: (Surprised) *"Oh . . . sure."* (Doesn't move out of the doorway)
- Behavioral coach: (Uncomfortable, awkward) *"Thanks."* (Awkwardly moves around the group leader to get inside)
- Group leader: (Standing in the doorway, holding the door open)
- Group leader & behavioral coach: (Long awkward pause)

- End by saying, *"Timeout on that. So what did I do WRONG in beginning that get-together?"*
  - Answers: Awkwardly stood on the doorstep; never invited friend in.
- Ask the following *Perspective Taking Questions*:
  - *"What was that like for (name of coach)?"*
    - Answers: Uncomfortable; awkward; confusing.
  - *"What do you think (name of coach) thought of me?"*
    - Answers: Odd; strange; weird; unfriendly.
  - *"Is (name of coach) going to want to hang out with me again?"*
    - Answers: Not sure; not a good start.
- Ask the behavioral coach the same *Perspective Taking Questions*:
  - *"What was that like for you?"*
  - *"What did you think of me?"*
  - *"Would you want to hang out with me again?"*

Steps for Beginning Get-Togethers

- Explain, *"Instead of having an awkward start, we need to begin get-togethers in our home following the appropriate steps."*

1. *Greet your guest*
   - Say, *"When having a get-together in your home, the first step when your guests arrive is to greet them at the door. How do we greet our guests?"*
     - Answers: Say hello and ask them how they're doing; some people will hug or give a casual acknowledgment like a head nod, a pound, or fist bump.

2. *Invite them in*
   - Say, *"The next step is we need to invite them in. This involves saying something like, 'Come in' and moving out of the doorway so they can come inside. What happens if we forget to invite them in?"*
     - Answers: They end up standing at the door waiting to come in; this can feel awkward for your friend.
   - Explain, *"Inviting your friend in may also include taking coats, jackets, or umbrellas."*

3. *Introduce them to anyone they don't know*
   - Say, *"Once we've invited our guest in, we need to introduce them to anyone they don't know. Why is it important to introduce them to anyone they don't know?"*
     - Answers: If they don't know everyone, they might feel awkward and left out; they'll feel more comfortable and welcome if they know everyone.

4. *Show them around*
   - Say, *"If this is the first time your friends have been to your home, you probably want to show them around a little. Why is it important to show your friends around?"*
     - Answers: It's your job to make your guests feel welcome; they should know where the bathroom is located and be familiar with the surroundings in order to feel welcome.

5. *Offer them refreshments*
   - Say, *"As your friend is getting settled, or maybe as you're walking by the kitchen, you might want to offer them something. What should you offer them?"*
     - Answers: Something to eat or drink; refreshments.
   - Ask, *"Why is it important to offer your guests refreshments?"*
     - Answers: They may be hungry or thirsty; it's polite to offer guests in your home food and beverages.

6. *Ask them what they want to do*
   - Say, *"Even though you should have planned with them what you're going to do, should you still ask your guest what they want to do when they're settled?"*
     - Answer: Yes.
   - Ask, *"Why is it a good idea to ask them what they want to do?"*
     - Answers: It's your job as the host to make sure your guest has a good time; they might want to do something different in the end.
   - Explain, *"You'll at least want to check in to make sure your friend still wants to do what you planned. If not, then ask them what they want to do and be prepared to go with the flow."*

Good Role Play: Beginning a Get-Together ⏵

[The group leader and two behavioral coaches should do an APPROPRIATE role play of *beginning a get-together*. One coach will be the arriving guest and the other coach will be the guest that has already arrived. If you do not have two behavioral coaches, you can have one of the young adults be the guest that has already arrived.]

- Begin by saying, *"We're going to do a role play. Watch this and tell me what I'm doing RIGHT in beginning this get-together."*

Example of an APPROPRIATE Role Play
- (Begin by having the behavioral coach 1 step outside)
- Behavioral coach 1: (Knocks on door)
- Group leader: (Opens door) *"Hi, (insert name)! How are you?"*
- Behavioral coach 1: *"Hi! I'm fine. How are you?"*
- Group leader: *"Fine, thanks. Come on in."* (Moves aside so the behavioral coach can enter)
- Behavioral coach 1: (Enters) *"Thanks."*
- Group leader: *"I don't think you've met my other friend before. This is (insert name). This is (insert name)."*
- Behavioral coach 1: *"Nice to meet you."*
- Behavioral coach 2: *"You too."*
- Group leader: *"So I know you've never been here before, so let me just show you around real quick. (Give an imaginary tour) This is the living room where we're going to be hanging out. The bathroom is just around the corner, and the kitchen is through there."*
- Behavioral coach: *"Cool. Thanks."*
- Group leader: *"Can I get you something to eat or drink?"*
- Behavioral coach: *"I'm okay. Thanks anyway."*
- Group leader: (Looking at behavioral coaches) *"So do you guys still want to watch the game?"*
- Behavioral coaches 1 & 2: *"Sure!"*

- End by saying, *"Timeout on that. So what did I do RIGHT in beginning that get-together?"*
  - Answers: **Greeted your guest; invited your guest in; introduced your guests; showed your guest around; offered refreshments; asked your guests what they wanted to do.**
- Ask the following *Perspective Taking Questions*:
  - *"What was that like for (names of coaches)?"*
    - Answers: Fine; normal.
  - *"What do you think (names of coaches) thought of me?"*
    - Answers: Friendly; normal, a good host.
  - *"Are (names of coaches) going to want to hang out with me again?"*
    - Answers: Probably; so far so good.
- Ask the behavioral coaches the same *Perspective Taking Questions*:
  - *"What was that like for you?"*
  - *"What did you think of me?"*
  - *"Would you want to hang out with me again?"*

Rules for During Get-Togethers

- Explain, *"So now that we know how to begin the get-together, we need to know what to do during the get-together. There are some important rules for making sure your get-together is a success."*

- *Get-togethers should be activity-based*
  - Explain, *"The first thing we should do when planning a get-together is to figure out what we're going to do beforehand. What could be the problem with just deciding to hang out, but not making any real plans for what to do?"*
    - Answers: It could end up being boring; you may never figure out what to do.
  - Ask, *"Have you ever had the experience where you're hanging out with a friend and you ask them, 'What do you want to do?' and they say, 'I don't know. What do you want to do?' and it keeps going back and forth? What's that like for you and your friend?"*
    - Answers: Boring; frustrating.
  - Say, *"In order to avoid boring get-togethers, it's best if we have activity-based get-togethers. What should the activities be based on?"*
    - Answer: **Common interests**.

- *The guests get to pick the activities at your home*
  - Say, *"Another important rule for having a get-together in your home is that the guests get to pick the activities. Why is it important to let the guests pick the activities?"*
    - Answer: Because it's the host's job to make sure the guests have a good time.
  - Ask, *"Should we still have some idea of what we're going to do beforehand and even have some activities ready to go if plans change?"*
    - Answer: Yes, but we need to be flexible.
  - Say, *"There's one exception to this rule. What should you do if your guest wants to do something that makes you uncomfortable?"*
    - Answers: Don't go along with it; suggest doing something different; consider whether this is a good choice for a friend.
  - Say, *"Not everyone knows the rule that the guests pick the activities. So what do you do if you're at a friend's house and they want to choose all the activities?"*
    - Answers: **Don't police your friend; go with the flow in the moment, and remember that friendship is a choice**; if your friend never wants to do what you want to do, you don't have to hang out with him or her anymore.

- *Go with the flow*
  - Say, *"Another important rule for having a successful get-together is that we need to go with the flow. That means sometimes we need to be flexible and go with whatever is happening that we didn't expect. For example, do plans sometimes change during get-togethers?"*
    - Answer: Yes.

- ○ Ask, *"What should we do if plans change?"*
  - ■ Answer: *Go with the flow.*
- ○ Ask, *"Do people sometimes change their minds and want to do different things?"*
  - ■ Answer: Yes.
- ○ Ask, *"What should we do?"*
  - ■ Answer: *Go with the flow.*
- ○ Explain, *"We need to expect that plans will change and people will change their minds about what they want to do during a get-together. If it really bothers you that your friend keeps changing plans, just go with the flow in the moment, and remember that friendship is a choice. You don't have to hang out with that friend again if it really bothers you."*

- *Don't invite other people into your get-together unexpectedly*
  - ○ Ask, *"What if someone you like unexpectedly calls or texts during your get-together and wants to hang out. Should you invite them over?"*
    - ■ Answers: No, you should wait to call or text them back; don't invite them over.
  - ○ Ask, *"What could be the problem with inviting your other friend into your get-together unexpectedly?"*
    - ■ Answers: Your guest might think you're rude; it's disloyal to your guest; they might feel disappointed and like they're not good enough if you invite others; your friends might not get along.
  - ○ Ask, *"Should you ask your guest if someone else can come over unexpectedly?"*
    - ■ Answer: No, because they may feel obligated to say yes even though they may not want to.
  - ○ Ask, *"What if your friend wants to invite other people into your get-together?"*
    - ■ Answer: *Go with the flow in the moment and remember that friendship is a choice*; if it bothers you that your friend always wants to invite other people into your *get-togethers*, you don't have to hang out with them.
  - ○ Explain, *"In general, when you're planning your get-together, think of the five W's as your social contract. If plans change, everyone needs to okay the changes."*

- *Don't ignore your friends*
  - ○ Say, *"Another important rule for having get-togethers is don't ignore your friends. Is it okay to ignore one friend to talk to another friend during a get-together?"*
    - ■ Answers: No; it's your job to make sure all your friends are having fun; your friends should feel like they have your attention.
  - ○ Ask, *"Should we be texting or video chatting with other people during our get-togethers?"*
    - ■ Answer: No.
  - ○ Ask, *"What could be the problem with texting, video chatting, or talking to other people during your get-together?"*
    - ■ Answers: It's rude; it's disloyal to your friend; your friend might feel left out or ignored; it might not be fun for your friend.
  - ○ Ask, *"What should we do if it's our friend's idea to text or video chat with someone else during our get-together?"*
    - ■ Answer: *Go with the flow in the moment and remember that friendship is a choice*; if it bothers you that your friend always wants to text other people during your *get-togethers*, you don't have to hang out with them.

- *Don't tease your friends*
  - ○ Say, *"Another rule for having successful get-togethers is don't tease your friends. What could be the problem with teasing your friends?"*
    - ■ Answers: This might hurt their feelings; the teasing could escalate and you could end up in a fight or an argument; they might not want to hang out with you anymore.
  - ○ Ask, *"Do friends sometimes tease each other?"*
    - ■ Answer: Yes, particularly men.
  - ○ Explain, *"We call teasing among friends 'banter.' Banter is a type of teasing, but it's meant to be playful and friendly. Even though banter is really common among friends, what could be the problem with bantering?"*

- Answers: It could still hurt their feelings; the banter could escalate and you could end up in a fight or an argument; they might not want to hang out with you anymore.
  - Explain, *"We know teasing and bantering is really common, but if your goal is to make and keep friends, this is really risky."*

- *Stick up for your friends*
  - Say, *"What if you're hosting a group get-together and one of your friends is teasing another friend. What should you do?"*
    - Answer: You should **stick up for your friends** and try to keep the peace (this is especially true if you're the host because your job is to make sure everyone is having a nice time).
  - Explain, *"If you're the host of the get-together, your friend who's being teased may be looking for you to help them. If you don't stick up for your friend, you may seem disloyal and they may not want to hang out with you again."*

- *Don't argue with your friends*
  - Say, *"Another important rule for having successful get-togethers is don't argue with your friends. What could be the problem with arguing with friends during a get-together?"*
    - Answers: It could escalate and people could get angry; feelings could get hurt; your friend may not want to hang out with you again.
  - Explain, *"In a few weeks, we'll be giving you strategies for resolving conflicts and handling arguments and disagreements. In the meantime, try to go with the flow and avoid arguing with friends during get-togethers."*

- *Don't police your friends*
  - Explain, *"Just like when we're trading information, another important rule for having successful get-togethers is don't police your friends. What does it mean to police people?"*
    - Answer: It's when you point out people's mistakes or correct them in some way.
  - Ask, *"What could be the problem with policing your friends?"*
    - Answers: It's rude; it's annoying; your friends might think you're bossy and controlling; it could be embarrassing for the other person.

- *Be a good sport*
  - Say, *"A lot of people like to play games and sports during get-togethers, so another rule for having a successful get-together is that we need to be a good sport. Why is it important to be a good sport?"*
    - Answers: Because your friend will be less likely to want to hang out with you if you're a poor sport; if you're a good sport, they're more likely to have fun and want to hang out again.
  - Ask, *"How can we be a good sport?"*
    - Answers: Praise your friend; don't be competitive; ***don't police*** them or act bossy; don't be a sore loser; don't be a bad winner; share and take turns; play by the rules; don't cheat.
  - Say, *"There are lots of ways to be a good sport. But just because you're a good sport doesn't mean your friends will be good sports. For example, what if your friend is really competitive and doesn't always play by the rules. Should you freak out and tell them they're cheating?"*
    - Answer: No, that just makes you look bad.
  - Explain, *"Instead of freaking out or accusing them of cheating, you might start by casually or playfully mentioning the rules once or twice. If your friend keeps cheating after this, what should you do?"*
    - Answers: **You should go with the flow in the moment, and remember that friendship is a choice**; if it really bothers you that your friend is always cheating, you don't have to hang out anymore.
  - Explain, *"It's always safer to go with the flow in the moment and remember that friendship is a choice. If we still want to be friends, we can also suggest a change in activities and avoid playing games and sports."*

- *Suggest a change if you get bored*
  - Ask, *"Do people sometimes get bored during get-togethers?"*
    - Answer: Yes.
  - Ask, *"What could be the problem with saying 'I'm bored' or walking away from your friends during a get-together?"*

- Answers: You would seem rude; it sounds like you're saying they're boring; they might not want to hang out with you again.
  - ○ Say, *"Instead of saying you're bored or walking away, you should suggest a change. How do you suggest a change?"*
    - Answer: You can say, *"How about when we're done with this, we do something else?"*
  - ○ Ask, *"What should you do if your friend doesn't want to do what you suggest for a change?"*
    - Answers: **Go with the flow in the moment**, let them pick the activity, and **remember that friendship is a choice**; if your friend never wants to do what you suggest, you don't have to hang out with him or her.

- *Trade information at least 50% of the time*
  - ○ Say, *"Another important rule for having a get-together is that you should be talking and trading information at least 50% of the time. Why is it important to trade information at least half of the time?"*
    - Answers: Because this is how you get to know one another and **find common interests**; if you don't talk and **trade information**, you won't get to know one another and become closer friends.

- *Keep it short and sweet to start*
  - ○ Say, *"Finally, when we're having get-togethers with friends we don't know that well, it's better to keep it short and sweet. What does it mean to keep it short and sweet?"*
    - Answers: Keep the get-together short at first; don't have long get-togethers right away.
  - ○ Ask, *"What could be the problem with having long get-togethers too soon?"*
    - Answers: You could get bored with each other; it might be too much too soon.
  - ○ Explain, *"It's better to keep it short and sweet at first to make sure things go well. As you get to know each other better, then you can hang out for longer periods of time. Your coaches can help decide what's an appropriate length."*

Ending Get-Togethers

- Explain, *"Now that we know the rules for what to do during a get-together, we need to talk about how to end a get-together."*

Bad Role Play: Ending a Get-Together ▶

[The group leader and two behavioral coaches should do an INAPPROPRIATE role play of the group leader **ending a get-together**. If you do not have two behavioral coaches, you can demonstrate with just one behavioral coach.]

- Begin by saying, *"We're going to do another role play. Watch this and tell me what I'm doing WRONG in ending this get-together."*

Example of an INAPPROPRIATE Role Play
- ○ Group leader & behavioral coaches: (Sitting down)
- ○ Behavioral coach 1: *"That was a good game!"*
- ○ Behavioral coach 2: *"I know . . . a total upset!"*
- ○ Group leader: (Distracted, looking around, bored)
- ○ Behavioral coach 1: (A little pause) *"Well, this was fun."* (Looking at group leader, unsure what to do)
- ○ Group leader: (Oblivious, looking around, bored)
- ○ Behavioral coach 2: (A little pause) *"Yeah, it was fun."* (Looking at group leader, unsure what to do)
- ○ Group leader: (Stands up, walks away and leaves)
- ○ Behavioral coach 1: (Startled, confused) *"What was that?"*
- ○ Behavioral coach 2: (Confused) *"I have no idea."*
- ○ Behavioral coach 1: (Confused) *"What should we do?"*
- ○ Behavioral coach 2: (Confused, annoyed) *"I guess we should leave."*
- ○ Behavioral coaches 1 & 2: (Stand up, start walking to the door)

- End by saying, *"Timeout on that. So what did I do WRONG in ending that get-together?"*
  - Answers: You just walked away without saying anything; you made your friends find their way out.
- Ask the following *Perspective Taking Questions*:
  - *"What was that like for (names of coaches)?"*
    - Answers: Confusing; annoying; hurtful.
  - *"What do you think (names of coaches) thought of me?"*
    - Answers: Rude; weird; inconsiderate; bad host.
  - *"Are (names of coaches) going to want to hang out with me again?"*
    - Answer: No, probably not.
- Ask the behavioral coaches the same *Perspective Taking Questions*:
  - *"What was that like for you?"*
  - *"What did you think of me?"*
  - *"Would you want to hang out with me again?"*

Steps for Ending Get-Togethers

- Explain, *"Instead of having an awkward ending, we need to end get-togethers following the appropriate steps."*

1. **Wait for a pause in activities**
   - Say, *"The first step in ending a get-together is to wait for a pause in the activities. That means don't interrupt what you're doing unless you have to. What could be the problem with interrupting an activity to leave or end a get-together?"*
     - Answers: It may seem abrupt; your friends may think you don't want to hang out with them anymore.

2. **Give a cover story for ending the get-together**
   - Say, *"The next step is to give a cover story for leaving or ending the get-together. Remember, cover stories are reasons we do things. What are some examples of reasons you might have to leave or end a get-together?"*
     - Examples:
       - *"I have to go soon."*
       - *"I have to study now."*
       - *"It's getting late and I have an early class."*
       - *"It's late and I have work in the morning."*
   - Ask, *"What could be the problem with not giving a cover story for leaving or ending a get-together?"*
     - Answer: Your friends may think you don't want to hang out with them anymore.

3. **Start walking your friend to the door**
   - Say, *"If the get-together is in your home, the next step is to stand up and start walking your friend to the door. Why is it important to walk your friend to the door?"*
     - Answers: Because it's rude to make them find their way out; if you don't stand up and start walking them to the door, they may not leave; they are waiting for your cue about what to do next.

4. **Thank your friend for getting together**
   - Say, *"The next step for ending a get-together is to thank your friend for getting together. Why is it important to thank your friend?"*
     - Answers: Because it makes them feel nice; it shows that you appreciate them.

5. **Tell your friend you had a good time**
   - Say, *"If you had a good time, you should tell your friend as you're saying goodbye or walking them out. Why is it important to tell your friend you had a good time?"*
     - Answers: It shows them that you enjoy being around them; it makes them feel good.

6. *Say goodbye and you'll see them later*
   - Explain, *"Finally, as you're saying goodbye or walking your friend out, it's important to say goodbye. You might even say, 'I'll see you later' or 'I'll talk to you soon' as you're saying goodbye. This is also a nice time to try to make future plans to get-together if you like."*
   - Ask, *"Why is it important to say goodbye and that you'll see them later?"*
     - Answer: It shows that you enjoyed their company and want to see them again.

Good Role Play: Ending a Get-Together ▶

[The group leader and two behavioral coaches should do an APPROPRIATE role play of the group leader *ending a get-together*. If you do not have two behavioral coaches, you can demonstrate with just one behavioral coach.]

- Begin by saying, *"We're going to do another role play. Watch this and tell me what I'm doing RIGHT in ending this get-together."*

Example of an APPROPRIATE Role Play

- Group leader & behavioral coaches: (Sitting down)
- Group leader: *"That was a great game!"*
- Behavioral coach 1: *"I know. It was!"*
- Behavioral coach 2: *"A total upset!"*
- Group leader: (Little pause) *"Well, it's getting kind of late and I know we all have work in the morning."*
- Behavioral coach 1: *"Yeah, we do."*
- Behavioral coach 2: *"I didn't realize how late it was."*
- Group leader: (Stands up and starts walking to the door) *"Thanks for coming over!"*
- Behavioral coach 1: (Follows group leader to the door) *"Thanks for having us over!"*
- Behavioral coach 2: (Follows group leader to the door) *"Yeah, thanks."*
- Group leader: *"It was really fun!"*
- Behavioral coach 1: *"I had a good time."*
- Behavioral coach 2: *"It was cool."*
- Group leader: *"We should hang out again soon."*
- Behavioral coach 1: *"That would be cool."*
- Behavioral coach 2: *"Yeah, that would be fun."*
- Group leader: (Opens the door) *"So I'll talk to you guys later."*
- Behavioral coach 1: *"Okay. Sounds good."* (Walks through the door)
- Behavioral coach 2: *"See ya."* (Walks through the door)
- Group leader: *"Take care. Bye!"* (Waves)
- Behavioral coaches 1 & 2: (Wave) *"Bye!"*

- End by saying, *"Timeout on that. So what did I do RIGHT in ending that get-together?"*
  - Answers: ***Waited for a pause in the activity; gave a cover story; started walking your friends to the door; thanked your friends for coming over; said you had a good time; said you would see your friends later; said goodbye.***
- Ask the following *Perspective Taking Questions*:
  - *"What was that like for (names of coaches)?"*
    - Answers: Fine; normal.
  - *"What do you think (names of coaches) thought of me?"*
    - Answers: Friendly; normal; a good host.
  - *"Are (names of coaches) going to want to hang out with me again?"*
    - Answer: Yes, probably.
- Ask the behavioral coaches the same *Perspective Taking Questions*:
  - *"What was that like for you?"*
  - *"What did you think of me?"*
  - *"Would you want to hang out with me again?"*

GET-TOGETHERS

Young Adult Behavioral Rehearsal

Get-Togethers

Materials Needed

- Indoor games (e.g., video games, card games, board games).
  - If you are going to provide video games as an option, make sure there are enough gaming consoles that each group can play simultaneously together.
  - Do not use small, portable gaming devices as people have to wait to take turns and that can get boring.
  - Several decks of playing cards will be sufficient if you do not have these other resources.
- Optional: iPads or laptops for watching YouTube videos, surfing the Internet, or playing computer games.
  - If you are going to provide iPads or laptops as an option, make sure there are enough that each group can use them simultaneously together.
- [Note: Most PEERS® programs DO NOT have access to gaming consoles, iPads, or laptops. These are luxury items. Just providing a few decks of cards to keep the get-together *activity-based* will be fine.]

Behavioral Rehearsal

- Notify young adults they will be practicing *beginning and ending get-togethers*.
- Break up young adults into small groups (no less than three young adults per group).
- Have EACH young adult practice *beginning a get-together* following the steps.
  - Assign "hosts" and "guests."
    - One young adult will be the *host*.
    - One young adult will be the *arriving guest*.
    - The other young adult(s) will be the *guests that have already arrived*.
  - Begin by having the *host* verbally go over the steps for *beginning a get-together* (they may need to look at the board at first).
  - You may need to provide Socratic prompting to young adults for identifying the specific steps for *beginning a get-together* by using some of the following *social coaching questions*:
    - *"What should you do when your guest knocks on the door?"*
    - *"What should you do when they're standing on the doorstep?"*
    - *"What should you do if they've never met your other friends?"*
    - *"What should you do if they've never been to your home?"*
    - *"Do you want to offer them something?"*
    - *"How will you decide what to do?"*
  - The *arriving guest* should step outside and knock on the door.
  - The *guest(s) that have already arrived* should be seated somewhere nearby.

- ○ Have the *host* follow the steps for *beginning the get-together*.
- ○ You may need to provide Socratic prompting to young adults if they have trouble following the steps by using some of the following *social coaching questions*:
  - ■ *"What should you do when your friend knocks on the door?"*
  - ■ *"Do you think your friend might want to come in?"*
  - ■ *"Have all of your friends met?"*
  - ■ *"Has your friend been to your home?"*
  - ■ *"Do you want to offer your friends something?"*
  - ■ *"How will you and your friends decide what to do?"*
- ○ Once the young adult has practiced, call a *"timeout"* and have the other young adults applaud.
- ○ EACH young adult should practice *beginning a get-together* as a *host*, an *arriving guest*, and a *guest that has already arrived*.
- Have young adults practice following the rules for how to behave **during the get-together** while **trading information, finding common interests**, and playing with games and items provided by the treatment team (e.g., video games, card games, board games, iPads, laptops, etc.).
- Have EACH young adult practice **ending a get-together** following the steps.
  - ○ Assign *hosts* and *guests*.
    - ■ One young adult will be the *host*.
    - ■ The other young adults will be the *guest(s)*.
  - ○ Have the *host* verbally go over the steps for **ending a get-together** (they may need to look at the board at first).
  - ○ You may need to provide Socratic prompting to young adults for identifying the specific steps to **ending a get-together** by using some of the following *social coaching questions*:
    - ■ *"Should you interrupt your friends to end the get-together?"*
    - ■ *"Should you just tell them to leave?"*
    - ■ *"How are they going to find their way out?"*
    - ■ *"Should you thank them for anything?"*
    - ■ *"What should you say if you had a nice time?"*
    - ■ *"What should you say if you're going to see them again?"*
    - ■ *"What's the last thing you should say as they're leaving?"*
  - ○ The *hosts* and *guests* should be seated before they begin the practice so that the *host* has to **stand up and start walking the guests to the door**.
  - ○ Have the *host* follow the steps for **ending the get-together**.
  - ○ You may need to provide Socratic prompting to young adults if they have trouble following the steps by using some of the following *social coaching questions*:
    - ■ *"Do you just tell your friends to leave, or do you need a reason?"*
    - ■ *"How will your friends find their way out?"*
    - ■ *"Do you want to thank them for anything?"*
    - ■ *"What could you say if you had a nice time?"*
    - ■ *"What could you say if you're going to see them again?"*
    - ■ *"What's the last thing you should say as they're leaving?"*
  - ○ *Guests* should actually leave and then come back at the end of the role play.
  - ○ Once the young adult has practiced, call a *"timeout"* and have the other young adults applaud.
  - ○ EACH young adult should practice **ending a get-together** as a *host* and a *guest*.

GET-TOGETHERS

Reunification

- Announce that young adults should join their social coaches.
  - Have young adults stand or sit next to their social coaches.
  - Be sure to have silence and the full attention of the group before starting with *Reunification*.
  - Have young adults generate the content from the lesson while social coaches listen.
- Say, *"Today, we talked about the rules and steps for having successful get-togethers. We talked about planning and preparing for get-togethers, and how to begin and end get-togethers. We also talked about what to do during get-togethers. What were some of the rules for DURING a get-together?"*
  - *Get-togethers should be activity-based*
  - *The guests get to pick the activities at your home*
  - *Go with the flow*
  - *Don't invite other people into your get-together unexpectedly*
  - *Don't ignore your friends*
  - *Don't tease your friends*
  - *Stick up for your friends*
  - *Don't argue with your friends*
  - *Don't police your friends*
  - *Be a good sport*
  - *Suggest a change if you get bored*
  - *Trade information at least 50% of the time*
  - *Keep it short and sweet to start*
- Say, *"The young adults practiced beginning and ending get-togethers while having group get-togethers and the group did a great job. Let's give them a round of applause."*

Homework Assignments

Distribute the *Social Coaching Handout* to young adults and announce the following *Homework Assignments*:

1. Have a *get-together* with a friend.
   - Social coaches should help young adults plan the get-together using the *five W's*:
     - *WHO* they plan to get together with.
     - *WHAT* they plan to do.
     - *WHEN* it will happen.
     - *WHERE* they will meet.
     - *HOW* they will make it happen.
   - Social coaches should go over the rules and steps for *get-togethers* with young adults beforehand.
   - Social coaches should ask young adults the following *social coaching questions* after the *get-together*:

    ○   *What did you decide to do and who picked the activities?*
    ○   *Did you trade information and for what percentage of the time?*
    ○   *What were your common interests and what could you do with that information if you were going to hang out again?*
    ○   *Did you and your friend have a good time?*
    ○   *Is this someone you might want to hang out with again?*

2. *Enter and exit group conversations* with social coaches.
   - Young adults should practice *entering and exiting group conversations* with their social coach and another person.
     ○ Practice exiting when NEVER ACCEPTED.
     ○ Practice exiting when INITIALLY ACCEPTED AND THEN EXCLUDED.
     ○ Practice exiting when FULLY ACCEPTED.
   - Social coaches should go over the rules and steps for *entering and exiting group conversations* before the practice.
   - Social coaches should ask young adults the following *social coaching questions* after each practice:
     ○ *Did it seem like we wanted to talk to you?*
     ○ *How could you tell?*

3. *Enter a group conversation* with peers (could be from the *source of friends*).
   - Social coaches should go over the rules and steps for *entering and exiting group conversations* before the practice.
   - The assignment is NOT to *exit the conversation* unless they naturally need to.
   - Social coaches should ask young adults the following *social coaching questions* after the practice:
     ○ *Where did you enter a conversation and with whom?*
     ○ *Which steps did you follow?*
     ○ *Did it seem like they wanted to talk to you and how could you tell?*
     ○ *Did you have to exit the conversation and which steps did you follow?*

4. *Pay attention to humor feedback.*
   - If young adults happen to tell jokes (this is NOT the assignment), *pay attention to humor feedback*.
   - Social coaches should PRIVATELY ask the following *social coaching questions* after attempts at humor by young adults:
     ○ *What was your humor feedback?*
     ○ *How could you tell?*

Individual Check-Out

Individually and privately negotiate with each young adult and social coach:

1. *WHO* they plan to have a *get-together* with in the coming week.
   - *WHAT* they plan to suggest to their friends.
   - *WHEN* and *WHERE* they will suggest to their friends.
   - *HOW* they will make it happen (e.g., tickets, transportation, etc.).

2. When they plan to *enter and exit a group conversation* with social coaches.
   - Which other person they would be comfortable practicing with.

3. Where, when, and with whom they plan to enter a group conversation with peers.
   - Whether this is an accepting *social group* and how they can tell.

SESSION 8

GET-TOGETHERS

Social Coaching Handout

Planning Get-Togethers

- *Make plans using the five W's*
  - *WHO is going to be there*
  - *WHAT you're going to do*
  - *WHERE you're going to get together*
  - *WHEN you're going to get together*
  - *HOW the get-together is going to happen*

Common Activities for Get-Togethers

Table 9.2 Common Activity-Based Get-Togethers Identified by Young Adults

Public Activities	Indoor Activities	Amusement Parks
Movie theaters	Video games	Gaming centers
Malls	Computer games	Adult video arcades
Sporting events	Surf the Internet	Laser tag
Bars/night clubs/dance clubs	YouTube videos	Paintball/airsoft
Comic book conventions	Social networking sites	Adult amusement parks
Comic book stores	Listen to music	Miniature golf parks
Gaming conventions	Watching sporting events	Water parks
Gaming stores	Watch awards shows	Go-karting
Science museums	Watch movies	Batting cages
Warhammer	Watch TV shows	Golf ranges/driving ranges
Concerts	Card games	Speedways
Festivals	Board games	Car shows/auto shows
LARPing events	Trivia games	Safari parks/animal parks
Bowling	Darts	Zoos
Pet stores/pet adoptions	Air hockey	Aquariums
Dog parks	Table shuffleboard	State and county fairs
Parks	Crafting	Renaissance fairs
Beach/lake/river	Sewing	Science expos

Mealtime Activities	Pair Sports	Group Sports
Restaurants	Bike riding/mountain biking	Basketball
Food courts	Hiking/walking/trekking	Football
Food carts/food trucks	Rock climbing	Baseball
Dinner parties	Tennis/raquetball/squash	Soccer
Drinks parties	Skiing/snowboarding	Hockey
Ice cream shops	Sailing/boating/kayaking	Volleyball
Frozen yogurt shops	Surfing/windsurfing/kiteboarding	Badminton
Order pizza	Swimming/snorkeling/diving	Water polo
Food delivery	Golf	Bocce ball
Order takeout/takeaway	Skateboarding	Lacrosse
Barbecue	Pool/billiards/snooker	Rugby
Sushi	Ping-Pong	Cricket
Cook a meal	Shooting baskets	Martial arts groups
Picnic	Frisbee/freestyle/playing catch	Aerobics classes
Baking	Roller skating/rollerblading	Dance classes
Cooking classes	Ice skating	Competitive dance
Food festivals	Fishing/hunting	Rafting
Farmers' market	Weightlifting/working out	Rowing

Preparing for Get-Togethers

- *Make a follow-up call to finalize plans*
- *Make sure your space is cleaned up*
- *Have refreshments ready to share*
- *Put away personal items you don't want others to share, see, or touch*
- *Have other activities ready*

Steps for Beginning and Ending Get-Togethers

Table 9.3 Steps for Beginning and Ending Get-Togethers in Your Home

Beginning the Get-Together	*Ending the Get-Together*
1. Greet your guest	*1. Wait for a pause in activities*
2. Invite them in	*2. Give a cover story for ending the get-together*
3. Introduce them to anyone they don't know	*3. Start walking your friend to the door*
4. Show them around	*4. Thank your friend for getting together*
5. Offer them refreshments	*5. Tell your friend you had a good time*
6. Ask them what they want to do	*6. Say goodbye and you'll see them later*

Rules for During Get-Togethers

- *Get-togethers should be activity-based*
- *The guests get to pick the activities at your home*
- *Go with the flow*
- *Don't invite other people into your get-together unexpectedly*
- *Don't ignore your friends*
- *Don't tease your friends*
- *Stick up for your friends*
- *Don't argue with your friends*
- *Don't police your friends*
- *Be a good sport*
- *Suggest a change if you get bored*

- *Trade information at least 50% of the time*
- *Keep it short and sweet to start*

Homework Assignments

1. Have a *get-together* with a friend.
   - Social coaches should help young adults plan the get-together using the *five W's*:
     - WHO they plan to get together with.
     - WHAT they plan to do.
     - WHEN it will happen.
     - WHERE they will meet.
     - HOW they will make it happen.
   - Social coaches should go over the rules and steps for *get-togethers* with young adults beforehand.
   - Social coaches should ask young adults the following *social coaching questions* after the *get-together*:
     - *What did you decide to do and who picked the activities?*
     - *Did you trade information and for what percentage of the time?*
     - *What were your common interests and what could you do with that information if you were going to hang out again?*
     - *Did you and your friend have a good time?*
     - *Is this someone you might want to hang out with again?*

2. *Enter and exit group conversations* with social coaches.
   - Young adults should practice *entering and exiting group conversations* with their social coach and another person.
     - Practice exiting when NEVER ACCEPTED.
     - Practice exiting when INITIALLY ACCEPTED AND THEN EXCLUDED.
     - Practice exiting when FULLY ACCEPTED.
   - Social coaches should go over the rules and steps for *entering and exiting group conversations* before the practice.
   - Social coaches should ask young adults the following *social coaching questions* after each practice:
     - *Did it seem like we wanted to talk to you?*
     - *How could you tell?*

3. *Enter a group conversation* with peers (could be from the *source of friends*).
   - Social coaches should go over the rules and steps for *entering and exiting group conversations* before the practice.
   - The assignment is NOT to *exit the conversation* unless they naturally need to.
   - Social coaches should ask young adults the following *social coaching questions* after the practice:
     - *Where did you enter a conversation and with whom?*
     - *Which steps did you follow?*
     - *Did it seem like they wanted to talk to you and how could you tell?*
     - *Did you have to exit the conversation?*
     - *If you had to exit, which steps did you follow?*

4. *Pay attention to humor feedback.*
   - If young adults happen to tell jokes (this is NOT the assignment), *pay attention to humor feedback*.
   - Social coaches should PRIVATELY ask the following *social coaching questions* after attempts at humor by young adults:
     - *What was your humor feedback?*
     - *How could you tell?*

DATING ETIQUETTE: LETTING SOMEONE KNOW YOU LIKE THEM

Social Coaching Therapist Guide

Preparing for the Social Coaching Session

The focus of this session and the next three subsequent sessions will be on appropriate dating etiquette. In particular, the current lesson highlights how to *let someone know you like them*. This is a highly useful skill for those with Autism Spectrum Disorder (ASD) and other social challenges, who often struggle in this area. Research suggests that the majority of adults with ASD are without a romantic partner, even though most express interest in forming romantic relationships. For many, it is not a question of wanting to date, but rather not knowing *how* to date. Consequently, mistakes are often made in the process of trying to secure a romantic partner.

One of the more serious issues that can arise in the pursuit of romantic relationships for those with ASD involves stalking behavior. Research suggests there is a high rate of stalking behavior among adults with ASD, sometimes even resulting in trouble with law enforcement. To be fair, this behavior most likely represents a naiveté about appropriate dating etiquette, rather than the antagonistic intent generally associated with stalking behavior. Technically speaking, stalking behavior includes unwanted or obsessive attention by an individual toward another person, typically involving harassment and intimidation. Although the naive romantic acts of a person with ASD might include unwanted and obsessive attention toward another person, these acts are rarely intended to provoke fear or intimidation. Individuals with ASD are known to have restricted, repetitive, and obsessive interests, which in this case could be a person. Furthermore, because individuals with ASD typically have poor social cognition, difficulty reading social cues, and understanding the perspectives of others, they may fail to recognize when their affections are not being returned, or even when they have crossed the line and frightened someone. They may not understand, for example, that just because you can Google someone and get their address, you do not have permission to go to their house and knock on the door. Acts such as these could be misconstrued as stalking behavior and result in trouble with the law. Thus, teaching appropriate strategies for *letting someone know you like them* is a good first step in teaching dating etiquette to those with ASD and other social challenges.

As with every lesson, *ecologically valid social skills* are provided in this session. However, one *ecologically valid strategy* for *letting someone know you like them* is conspicuously absent. That strategy involves social touch. One common method that typically developing people in Western cultures may use to show romantic interest involves social touch. A light touch of the arm or hand when talking can sometimes signify romantic interest and flirting. Although this strategy is quite common in certain cultures, we do not teach this tactic in PEERS®, as we find it is quite risky for those with ASD, who often have difficulty interpreting and using social touch. Keep this in mind as you teach the lesson. Although young adults rarely know about this strategy, some social coaches may offer social touch as another method for *letting someone know you like them*. While a light touch on the arm or the hand might be appropriate in some cases, being overly touchy (e.g., being clingy or draping yourself on another person) could give the impression of wanting to get more physical than you actually do. To avoid this risk and confusion, we do not teach the tactic of social touch, and for those who have a tendency to be overly tactile with others, we actually recommend limiting physical touch at first. You may also consider having certain young adults limit their physical contact at first, if this is a concern.

Homework Review

[Go over the following *Homework Assignments* and **troubleshoot** any potential problems. Start with completed homework first. If you have time, you can inquire as to why others were unable to complete the assignment and try to **troubleshoot** how they might get it done for the coming week. When reviewing homework, be sure to relabel descriptions using the **buzzwords** (identified by **bold and italicized** print). Spend the majority of the *Homework Review* on **get-togethers** as this was the most important assignment.]

1. Have a **get-together** with a friend.
    - Say, *"One of the main assignments this week was for young adults to have a get-together with a friend. Who completed this assignment or attempted to complete it?"*
    - Ask the following questions:
        ○ *"Did you help your young adult plan the get-together using the five W's?"*
        ○ *"What social coaching did you do before the get-together?"*
        ○ *"What did your young adult decide to do and with whom?"*
        ○ *"How did the get-together begin?"*
        ○ *"Who picked the activities?"*
        ○ *"Did they trade information and what percentage of the time?"*
        ○ *"How did the get-together end?"*
        ○ *"What social coaching did you do after the get-together?"*
            ■ Appropriate *social coaching questions*:
                □ **What did you decide to do and who picked the activities?**
                □ **Did you trade information and for what percentage of the time?**
                □ **What were your common interests and what could you do with that information if you were going to hang out again?**
                □ **Did you and your friend have a good time?**
                □ **Is this someone you might want to hang out with again?**
        ○ *"Does this seem like a good choice for a friend and someone your young adult will want to hang out with again?"*

Table 10.1 Steps for Beginning and Ending Get-Togethers in Your Home

Beginning the Get-Together	Ending the Get-Together
1. Greet your guest	1. Wait for a pause in activities
2. Invite them in	2. Give a cover story for ending the get-together
3. Introduce them to anyone they don't know	3. Start walking your friend to the door
4. Give them a tour	4. Thank your friend for getting together
5. Offer them refreshments	5. Tell your friend you had a good time
6. Ask them what they want to do	6. Say goodbye and you'll see them later

2. **Enter and exit group conversations** with social coaches.
    - Say, *"Another assignment this week was for young adults to practice entering and exiting group conversations with you and another person. Who completed this assignment or attempted to complete it?"*
    - Ask the following questions:
        ○ *"Who did you and your young adult practice with?"*
        ○ *"What social coaching did you do before the practice?"*
        ○ *"Which steps did your young adult follow to enter the group conversation?"*
            1. **Listen to the Conversation**
            2. **Watch from a Distance**
            3. **Use a Prop**

4. *Identify the Topic*
5. *Find a Common Interest*
6. *Move Closer*
7. *Wait for a Pause*
8. *Mention the Topic*
9. *Assess Interest*
10. *Introduce Yourself*
   ○ *"Which steps did your young adult follow to exit the conversations?"*
   ○ *"What social coaching did you do after the practice?"*
      ■ Appropriate *social coaching questions*:
         □ *Did it seem like we wanted to talk to you?*
         □ *How could you tell?*

Table 10.2 Steps for Exiting Conversations

NEVER ACCEPTED	INITIALLY ACCEPTED, THEN EXCLUDED	FULLY ACCEPTED
1. Keep your cool 2. Look away 3. Turn away 4. Walk away	1. Keep your cool 2. Look away 3. Wait for a BRIEF pause 4. Give a BRIEF cover story for leaving 5. Walk away	1. Wait for a pause 2. Give a SPECIFIC cover story for leaving 3. Say you'll see them later 4. Say goodbye 5. Walk away

3. **Enter a group conversation** with peers (could be from the **source of friends**).
   • Say, *"Another assignment this week was for young adults to practice entering group conversations with peers. Who completed this assignment or attempted to complete it?"*
   • Ask the following questions:
      ○ *"Where and with whom did your young adult practice?"*
      ○ *"What social coaching did you do before the practice?"*
      ○ *"Which steps did your young adult follow?"*
      ○ *"What social coaching did you do after the practice?"*
         ■ Appropriate *social coaching questions*:
            □ *Where did you enter a conversation and with whom?*
            □ *Which steps did you follow?*
            □ *Did it seem like they wanted to talk to you and how could you tell?*
            □ *Did you have to exit the conversation and which steps did you follow?*

4. **Pay attention to humor feedback**.
   • Say, *"Another assignment this week was for young adults to pay attention to their humor feedback if they happened to tell a joke. The assignment was NOT to tell a joke. Who completed this assignment or attempted to complete this assignment?"*
   • Ask the following questions:
      ○ *"Did your young adult attempt to tell jokes and did he/she pay attention to the humor feedback?"*
      ○ *"What did you do to provide social coaching around humor feedback?"*
         ■ Appropriate *social coaching questions*:
            □ *What was your humor feedback?*
            □ *How could you tell?*

   • [Collect the *Social Coaching Homework Assignment Worksheets*. If social coaches forgot to bring the worksheets, have them complete a new form to hold them accountable for the assignments.]

Didactic Lesson: Dating Etiquette: Letting Someone Know You Like Them

• Distribute the *Social Coaching Handout*.
   ○ Sections in **bold print** in the *Social Coaching Therapist Guide* come directly from the *Social Coaching Handout*.

- ○ Remind social coaches that terms that are in **bold and italicized** print are **buzzwords** and represent important concepts from the PEERS® curriculum that should be used as much as possible when social coaching.
- Explain, *"Today, we're going to be talking about dating etiquette. By now, your young adults have learned some of the basic elements for making and keeping friends. These social skills are also used in dating. That's because you need to know how to be a friend in order to be more than a friend. The goal of the next several sessions is to provide young adults with some basic tools for dating that go beyond friendship skills. To start, we're going to talk about finding and choosing appropriate people to date and how to let someone know you like them."*

Choosing Appropriate People to Date

- *Dating is a choice*
  - ○ Explain, *"Just like friendship is a choice, dating is a choice, too."*
  - ○ Ask, *"Do we get to date everyone?"*
    - ■ Answer: No.
  - ○ Ask, *"Does everyone get to date us?"*
    - ■ Answer: No.
  - ○ Explain, *"That's because dating is a CHOICE and it's important that we CHOOSE the people we date wisely. There are GOOD choices and BAD choices for choosing potential dates. As social coaches, it will be important for you to help young adults identify GOOD choices and BAD choices."*
- Present each of the *GOOD choices* for dates mentioned below by saying, *"Should your young adults choose someone who . . . ?"* Follow each point by saying, *"Why is it important to choose someone who . . . ?"*
  - ○ *". . . they actually like?"*
  - ○ *". . . seems interested in them?"*
  - ○ *". . . has common interests with them?"*
  - ○ *". . . is around the same age as them?"*
  - ○ *". . . is likely to say 'yes'?"*
- Present each of the *BAD choices* for dates mentioned below by saying, *"Should your young adults choose someone who . . . ?"* Follow each point by saying, *"What could be the problem with choosing someone who . . . ?*
  - ○ *". . . doesn't seem interested in them?"*
  - ○ *". . . doesn't know them?"*
  - ○ *". . . is mean to them or makes fun of them?"*
  - ○ *". . . ignores them?"*
  - ○ *". . . takes advantage of them or uses them?"*
  - ○ *". . . has rejected them before?"*
  - ○ *". . . has a boyfriend or a girlfriend?"*
- Summarize the following:
  - ○ *Dating is a choice*
    - ■ **We don't get to date everyone and everyone doesn't get to date us.**
    - ■ There are *GOOD choices* and there are *BAD choices* when it comes to dating.

Dating Sources

- Explain, *"Now that we understand that dating is a CHOICE, we need to talk about WHERE young adults might find some of these good choices for potential dates."*
- Ask, *"Where do people find potential partners to date?"*
  - ○ See Table 10.3 for an overview of commonly identified *dating sources*.
  - ○ If appropriate, have social coaches brainstorm different Internet dating websites.
    - ■ Some social coaches will be unfamiliar with dating websites, so be prepared to explain any unfamiliar *dating sources*.

- ■ Explain that there are *GOOD choices* for dating websites (e.g., Match, eHarmony), and there are *BAD choices* (e.g., Craigslist).
- ○ [Note: *Dating sources* will be different according to culture. Do not rely on Table 10.3 as a comprehensive or exhaustive list. Instead, have social coaches generate the list of *dating sources*, as they change with time and culture.]

Table 10.3 Dating Sources Identified by Young Adults

Mutual friends	Internet dating sites
Friends of family members	School, college
Parties, get-togethers, social gatherings	Adult classes
Social activities	Workplace
Sporting events	Neighborhood
Dog parks, local parks	Sports clubs, private gyms, recreational centers
Recreational activities (e.g., sports leagues and clubs)	Church, synagogue, mosque, temple, religious gatherings
Meet up groups	
Community gatherings (e.g., concerts, fairs, farmers' market)	Public places (e.g., coffee houses, bars, clubs, bookstores)

Letting Someone Know You Like Them

Explain, *"Now that we know WHO might be a good choice to date and WHERE we might find them, we need to talk about HOW to let someone know you like them."*

- ● *Talk to mutual friends*
  - ○ Say, *"One of the ways to let someone know you like them is by talking to mutual friends. What can we say or ask our mutual friend to let them know we like someone?"* (Identify the following strategies.)
    - ■ *Tell your friend that you like the person.*
      - □ Example: *"You know (insert name)? I like him/her."*
      - □ Example: *"You know (insert name)? He/she is really cute."*
    - ■ *Ask your friend if the person is dating anyone.*
      - □ Example: *"Do you know if (insert name) is going out with anyone?"*
      - □ Example: *"Do you know if (insert name) has a boyfriend/girlfriend?"*
    - ■ *Ask your friend if they think the person would go out with you.*
      - □ Example: *"Do you think (insert name) would go out with me?"*
      - □ Example: *"Do you think (insert name) is interested in me?"*

  - ○ Explain, *"If your mutual friend offers to find out if the person is interested in going out with you, agree but tell them not to say you asked. They may still tell them you asked, but at least they won't say, '(Insert name) wanted me to ask you . . .'"*
  - ○ [Optional: Show *Role Play Video Demonstration* of *talking to mutual friends* from the *PEERS® Role Play Video Library* (www.routledge.com/cw/laugeson).]

- ● *Flirt with your eyes*
  - ○ Explain, *"Another way to let someone know you like them is by flirting with your eyes. This involves following very specific steps in a sequence."*
    1. *Make eye contact*
       - ■ Say, *"The first step for flirting with your eyes is to make eye contact. That does not mean staring at the person. What could be the problem with staring at the person?"*
         - □ Answers: They might think you're a creepy stalker; it seems predatory to stare at someone.
       - ■ Say, *"Instead, you want to casually make eye contact. Once you've made eye contact, then what should you do?"*
         - □ Answer: Smile.

2. *Give a slight smile*
   - Say, *"The next step is to give a slight smile. This is not a big, huge, teeth-baring smile. What could be the problem with giving a big, huge, toothy smile?"*
     - Answers: It may be too much; it might seem overenthusiastic; you might seem like a creepy stalker.
   - Explain, *"Instead, give a slight smile with no teeth."*
3. *Look away*
   - Explain, *"Once you've made eye contact and given a slight smile, the next step in flirting with your eyes is to look away. When you look away, it lets the other person know that you're safe and that you're not a creepy stalker."*
   - Ask, *"Just because we've made eye contact, smiled, and looked away does not mean we're flirting. What's the next step for flirting with your eyes?"*
     - Answer: You need to repeat the whole process again.
4. *Repeat several times*
   - Explain, *"The final step for flirting with your eyes is that you need to repeat the whole cycle again multiple times. The act of looking, smiling, looking away, and repeating is the act of flirting with your eyes. Simply making eye contact once or twice and smiling is NOT flirting."*
- ○ [Optional: Show BAD and GOOD *Role Play Video Demonstrations* of **flirting with your eyes** from the *PEERS® Role Play Video Library* (www.routledge.com/cw/laugeson).]

- **Ask them if they're dating anyone**
  - ○ Explain, *"Another way to let someone know you like them is by asking them if they're dating anyone. This also involves following very specific steps in a sequence."*
  1. *Trade information and find common interests*
     - Say, *"The first step for asking someone if they're dating anyone is to trade information and find common interests."*
       - **Example: *"I heard you went skiing last week. I love skiing."***
  2. *Ask about social activities related to the common interest*
     - Say, *"The next step is to ask about social activities related to the common interest. This gives you a clue about who they spend time with and gives you a context for the next step when you ask about dating, which is also social in nature."*
       - **Example: *"Who did you go skiing with . . . ?"***
  3. *Casually work dating into the conversation*
     - Say, *"The next step for asking someone if they're dating anyone is to casually work dating into the conversation. This gives them the opportunity to mention if they're seeing anyone, and it gives you the opportunity to ask if they're seeing anyone."*
       - **Example: *". . . did you go with your boyfriend/girlfriend?"***
     - Ask, *"How will their response let you know if they're romantically interested in you?"*
       - *GOOD sign*: They say they're not dating anyone while smiling and flirting.
       - *BAD sign*: They say they're dating someone or appear uncomfortable after you ask the question.
  4. *Give a cover story for asking*
     - Say, *"The next step for asking someone if they're dating anyone is to use a cover story for asking. This makes it less awkward for both of you and it gives you a reason for asking."*
       - **Example: *"It just seems like all my friends go skiing with their boyfriends/ girlfriends."***
  5. *Shift the conversation back to the common interest*
     - Explain, *"The last step for asking someone if they're dating anyone is to shift the conversation back to the common interest. This makes it less awkward for both of you. If they want to know about your dating status they can ask."*
       - **Example: *"So are you a pretty good skier?"***
  - ○ [Optional: Show BAD and GOOD *Role Play Video Demonstrations* of **asking them if they're dating anyone** from the *PEERS® Role Play Video Library* (www.routledge.com/cw/laugeson).]

- *Give compliments*
  - ○ Explain, *"Another way to let someone know you like them is by giving compliments. This is the equivalent of verbal flirting. Just like with any of our skills, there are GOOD ways and BAD ways of giving compliments."*
  - ○ *Give SPECIFIC compliments when you DON'T know the person well.*
    - ▪ Say, *"When we're giving compliments to people we DON'T know well, it's better to be SPECIFIC in our compliments, rather than GENERAL. What are some examples of SPECIFIC compliments?"*
      - ◻ **Examples of *SPECIFIC* compliments**:
        - – *"You have a nice smile."*
        - – *"That was a funny joke."*
        - – *"That was interesting."*
  - ○ *Give SPECIFIC or GENERAL compliments when you know the person well.*
    - ▪ Say, *"When we're giving compliments to people we actually know well, we can give SPECIFIC or GENERAL compliments. What are some examples of GENERAL compliments?"*
      - ◻ **Examples of *GENERAL* compliments**:
        - – *"You're so beautiful/handsome."*
        - – *"You're so funny."*
        - – *"You're so smart."*
    - ▪ Ask, *"What could be the problem with giving GENERAL compliments to someone you don't know well?"*
      - ◻ Answers: It could seem insincere; it might seem like you're just trying to flatter them; it might not sound genuine; you don't know them well enough to say those things yet.
  - ○ *Avoid too many physical compliments.*
    - ▪ Say, *"It's also important that when giving compliments, we avoid giving too many physical compliments. What could be the problem with giving too many physical compliments?"*
      - ◻ Answers: It could seem like you're only interested in their looks; it may seem like you only like them for their appearance.
  - ○ *Physical compliments should be from the neck up.*
    - ▪ Say, *"If we're going to give physical compliments, they should only be from the neck up. What could be the problem with giving compliments below the neck?"*
      - ◻ Answers: There are very few physical compliments below the neck that are appropriate; you could seem like you're only interested in their body; they might think you only want something physical with them; you could seem creepy; you could make them uncomfortable.
  - ○ [Optional: Show BAD and GOOD *Role Play Video Demonstrations* of *giving compliments* from the *PEERS® Role Play Video Library* (www.routledge.com/cw/laugeson).]
- *Show interest in them*
  - ○ Explain, *"Another way to let someone know you like them is by showing interest in them. How do we show interest in someone?"*
  - ○ *Trade information*
    - ▪ Explain, *"One of the best ways to show interest in someone is by talking to them and trading information. That means all the skills we learned for starting and maintaining conversations and for entering group conversations apply to dating."*
  - ○ *Find common interests*
    - ▪ Say, *"Just like friendships, romantic relationships are often based on common interests, as well as mutual attraction. Why is it important to find common interests?"*
      - ◻ Answer: It gives you something to talk about and something to do together.
    - ▪ Ask, *"Could you date someone that you have very little in common with?"*
      - ◻ Answer: Yes, but it might be a bit boring.
- *Laugh at their jokes*
  - ○ Say, *"Another way to show interest in someone is to laugh at their jokes. Even if you don't think their jokes are funny, should you still laugh?"*
    - ▪ Answer: Yes.

    ○ Ask, *"What do we call that when we laugh just to be polite?"*
      ■ Answer: A *courtesy laugh*.
    ○ Ask, *"Why would it be important to give a courtesy laugh if we're trying to show interest in someone and let them know we like them?"*
      ■ Answers: It makes them feel comfortable; you seem friendly and approachable; not laughing might make them feel uncomfortable and awkward.
- Explain, *"Those are some of the ways young adults can let people know they like them. For those young adults that are interested in someone romantically, we're going to have them practice using some of these strategies this week."*

Homework Assignments

[Distribute the *Social Coaching Homework Assignment Worksheet* (Appendix I) for social coaches to complete and return at the next session.]

1. Have a *get-together* with a friend.
    - Social coaches should help young adults plan the get-together using the *five W's*:
        ○ WHO they plan to get together with.
        ○ WHAT they plan to do.
        ○ WHEN it will happen.
        ○ WHERE they will meet.
        ○ HOW they will make it happen.
    - Social coaches should go over the rules and steps for *get-togethers* with young adults beforehand.
    - Social coaches should ask young adults the following *social coaching questions* after the *get-together*:
        ○ *What did you decide to do and who picked the activities?*
        ○ *Did you trade information and for what percentage of the time?*
        ○ *What were your common interests and what could you do with that information if you were going to hang out again?*
        ○ *Did you and your friend have a good time?*
        ○ *Is this someone you might want to hang out with again?*

2. Practice *letting someone know you like them.*
    - If young adults are interested in someone romantically, use the strategies for *letting someone know you like them.*
        ○ DO NOT practice unless you are romantically interested in the person.
    - Young adults should practice *letting someone know you like them* with social coaches, if comfortable.
    - Social coaches should go over the rules and steps for *letting someone know you like them* before the practice.
    - Social coaches should ask young adults the following *social coaching questions* after each practice:
        ○ *Who did you practice with?*
        ○ *What did you do to let them know you like them?*
        ○ *How did they respond?*
        ○ *Does this seem like a good choice and is this someone you might want to go on a date with?*

3. *Enter and exit group conversations* with social coaches.
    - Young adults should practice *entering and exiting group conversations* with their social coach and another person.
        ○ Practice exiting when NEVER ACCEPTED.
        ○ Practice exiting when INITIALLY ACCEPTED AND THEN EXCLUDED.
        ○ Practice exiting when FULLY ACCEPTED.

- Social coaches should go over the rules and steps for *entering and exiting group conversations* before the practice.
- Social coaches should ask young adults the following *social coaching questions* after each practice:
  - *Did it seem like we wanted to talk to you?*
  - *How could you tell?*

4. *Enter a group conversation* with peers (could be from the *source of friends*).
   - Social coaches should go over the rules and steps for *entering and exiting group conversations* before the practice.
   - The assignment is NOT to *exit the conversation* unless they naturally need to.
   - Social coaches should ask young adults the following *social coaching questions* after the practice:
     - *Where did you enter a conversation and with whom?*
     - *Which steps did you follow?*
     - *Did it seem like they wanted to talk to you and how could you tell?*
     - *Did you have to exit the conversation and which steps did you follow?*

Social Coaching Tips

For young adults interested in dating and forming romantic relationships, the following *Social Coaching Tips* are suggested:

- Social coaches should begin to have a dialogue with young adults about who they are romantically interested in.
  - Begin to assess if these are *GOOD choices* or *BAD choices*.
  - For those pursuing potential partners who do not appear interested, remind young adults, *"Dating is a choice. We don't get to date everyone, and everyone doesn't get to date us."*
- Encourage young adults who seem to be making *GOOD choices* to start *letting the person know they like them*.
  - Choose one person at a time (i.e., avoid having the young adult practice with multiple people as this could result in hurt feelings or even a bad reputation).
  - Begin by having them choose who they are most interested in and reassess the relationship and their interest periodically.
- Have young adults begin slowly by *talking to mutual friends, flirting with their eyes, giving compliments, showing interest* by *trading information* and *finding common interests*, and *laughing at jokes*.
- Remind young adults that they should also use the skills for making and keeping friends with people they want to date.
  - It may be helpful to explain, *"We need to know how to be a friend in order to be more than a friend."*
- Discourage young adults from asking people out on dates, as we have not covered that skill yet.

DATING ETIQUETTE: LETTING SOMEONE KNOW YOU LIKE THEM

Young Adult Therapist Guide

Preparing for the Young Adult Session

Although many of the young adults in your group will be very interested in the sessions on dating etiquette, it is unlikely that many of them will actually be dating. Among young adults aged 18–30 who have presented for social skills treatment at the UCLA PEERS® Clinic, approximately only 10% were actively dating. The same may be true for your group. Regardless, the majority of these young adults will express interest in dating and will be eager to learn the general rules about dating etiquette.

Since the skills related to dating behavior are complex and multifaceted, you will only be scratching the surface in the four sessions devoted to the topic. However, most of the skills related to friendships that have been covered up until this point are still applicable to dating. For example, just as with friendships, we need to know how to carry on conversations, enter and exit conversations, use electronic communication, and use humor appropriately in order to date. One helpful way to highlight this to young adults is by explaining, *"We need to know how to be a friend in order to be more than a friend."*

This first lesson on dating etiquette involves strategies for choosing appropriate people to date, identifying *dating sources* (i.e., where to meet people to date), and how to *let someone know you like them*. During the *Didactic Lesson*, there will be several role play examples and *Behavioral Rehearsal Exercises*. The more traditional method for conducting role plays in this session is to provide demonstrations between male and female behavioral coaches. You will have to use your clinical judgment whether this method is best for your group. Alternatively, you could provide a combination of mixed-gender and same-gender *Role Play Demonstrations*. Whatever you choose to do, in order to avoid being heterosexist, it is critical that you provide young adults with opportunities to practice with male and female behavioral coaches during the *Behavioral Rehearsal Exercises*. Young adults do not need to identify their sexual orientation during these practice attempts. Instead, you will simply ask them, *"Who would you feel more comfortable practicing with (insert name of female coach) or (insert name of male coach)?"* Providing opportunities to practice newly learned dating skills with either male or female coaches will not only avoid heterosexist teaching, but will also allow those young adults who may be too nervous to practice with a particular gendered coach the option of practicing with someone less intimidating.

One critical mistake occasionally made by beginning group leaders involves having young adult group members practice the strategies related to dating etiquette with one another. This has the potential to be a huge mistake, possibly causing great discomfort to group members. Unlike other lessons, *Behavioral Rehearsal Exercises* focused on dating etiquette should only be practiced with the group leader and/or behavioral coaches during the sessions. Allowing group members to practice with each other could create a serious boundary violation among group members, and has the potential to lead to confusion and/or discomfort. It is best to stick to the treatment guidelines as outlined in the manual to avoid any unnecessary awkwardness or distress. *Behavioral Rehearsal Exercises* related to dating, therefore, take place during the *Didactic Lesson* for all four sessions on dating etiquette.

Additional *Behavioral Rehearsal Exercises* with group members take place following the lesson and focus on having successful get-togethers with friends.

Homework Review

[Go over the following *Homework Assignments* and **troubleshoot** any potential problems. Start with completed homework first. If you have time, you can inquire as to why others were unable to complete the assignment and try to **troubleshoot** how they might get it done for the coming week. When reviewing homework, be sure to relabel descriptions using the **buzzwords** (identified by **bold and italicized** print). Spend the majority of the *Homework Review* on *get-togethers* as this was the most important assignment.]

1. Have a ***get-together*** with a friend.
   - Say, *"One of the main assignments this week was for you to have a get-together with a friend. Raise your hand if you had a get-together with a friend this week."*
   - Ask the following questions:
     - *"Who did you have a get-together with and what did you decide to do?"*
     - *"Did you plan the get-together using the five W's?"*
     - *"How did the get-together begin?"*
     - *"Who picked the activities?"*
     - *"Did you trade information and for what percentage of the time?"*
     - *"How did the get-together end?"*
     - *"Did you and your friend have a good time?"*
     - *"Is this someone you might want to hang out with again?"*

Table 10.1 Steps for Beginning and Ending Get-Togethers in Your Home

Beginning the Get-Together	*Ending the Get-Together*
1. Greet your guest	*1. Wait for a pause in activities*
2. Invite them in	*2. Give a cover story for ending the get-together*
3. Introduce them to anyone they don't know	*3. Start walking your friend to the door*
4. Give them a tour	*4. Thank your friend for getting together*
5. Offer them refreshments	*5. Tell your friend you had a good time*
6. Ask them what they want to do	*6. Say goodbye and you'll see them later*

2. ***Enter and exit group conversations*** with social coaches.
   - Say, *"Another assignment this week was to practice entering and exiting group conversations with your social coach and another person. Raise your hand if you did this assignment."*
   - Ask the following questions:
     - *"Who did you and your social coach practice with and which steps did you follow?"*
       1. **Listen to the Conversation**
       2. **Watch from a Distance**
       3. **Use a Prop**
       4. **Identify the Topic**
       5. **Find a Common Interest**
       6. **Move Closer**
       7. **Wait for a Pause**
       8. **Mention the Topic**
       9. **Assess Interest**
       10. **Introduce Yourself**
     - *"Did it seem like they wanted to talk to you and how could you tell?"*
     - *"Did you exit the conversation and which steps did you follow?"*

Table 10.2 Steps for Exiting Conversations

NEVER ACCEPTED	INITIALLY ACCEPTED, THEN EXCLUDED	FULLY ACCEPTED
1. Keep your cool 2. Look away 3. Turn away 4. Walk away	1. Keep your cool 2. Look away 3. Wait for a BRIEF pause 4. Give a BRIEF cover story for leaving 5. Walk away	1. Wait for a pause 2. Give a SPECIFIC cover story for leaving 3. Say you'll see them later 4. Say goodbye 5. Walk away

3. **Enter a group conversation** with peers (could be from the **source of friends**).
   - Say, *"Another assignment this week was to practice entering group conversations with peers. Raise your hand if you did this assignment."*
   - Ask the following questions:
     - *"Where and with whom did you practice?"*
     - *"Which steps did you follow?"*
     - *"Did it seem like they wanted to talk to you?"*
     - *"How could you tell?"*
       - **Talking to you?**
       - **Looking at you?**
       - **Facing you (they opened the circle)?**
     - *"Did you have to exit the conversation and which steps did you follow?"*

4. **Pay attention to humor feedback**.
   - Say, *"Another assignment this week was to pay attention to your humor feedback if you happened to tell a joke. The assignment was NOT to tell a joke. If you happened to tell a joke this week, raise your hand if you paid attention to your humor feedback."*
   - Ask the following questions:
     - *"I don't want to know what joke you told, I just want to know what your humor feedback was. Were they laughing AT you, laughing WITH you, giving a courtesy laugh, or NOT laughing at all?"*
     - *"How could you tell?"*
     - *"So are you done paying attention to your humor feedback?"*
       - Answer: No.
     - *"When will you pay attention to your humor feedback?"*
       - Answer: Every time they tell a joke.
     - *"How will you pay attention to your humor feedback?"*
       - Answer: By LOOKING and LISTENING.

Didactic Lesson: Dating Etiquette: Letting Someone Know You Like Them

- Explain, *"Today, we're going to be talking about dating etiquette. By now, you've all learned some of the basic elements for making and keeping friends. These social skills are also used in dating. That's because you need to know how to be a friend in order to be more than a friend. The goal of the next several sessions is to provide you with some basic tools for dating that go beyond friendship skills. To start, we're going to talk about finding and choosing appropriate people to date and how to let someone know you like them."*
- [Present the rules and steps for **letting someone know you like them** by writing the following bullet points and **buzzwords** (identified by **bold and italicized** print) on the board. Do not erase the rules and steps until the end of the lesson. Each role play with a ⏵ symbol includes a corresponding role play video from the *PEERS® Role Play Video Library* (www.routledge.com/cw/laugeson).]

Choosing Appropriate People to Date

- **Dating is a choice**
  - Explain, *"Just like friendship is a choice, dating is a choice, too."*

- ○ Ask, *"Do we get to date everyone?"*
  - ▪ Answer: No.
- ○ Ask, *"Does everyone get to date us?"*
  - ▪ Answer: No.
- ○ Explain, *"That's because dating is a CHOICE and it's important that we CHOOSE the people we date wisely. There are good choices and bad choices for choosing potential dates."*
- Present each of the **GOOD choices** for dates mentioned below by saying, *"Do you want to choose someone who . . . ?"* (while nodding your head yes). Follow each point by saying, *"Why is it important to choose someone who . . . ?*
  - ○ *". . . you actually like?"*
  - ○ *". . . seems interested in you?"*
  - ○ *". . . has common interests with you?"*
  - ○ *". . . is around the same age as you?"*
  - ○ *". . . is likely to say 'yes'?"*
- Present each of the **BAD choices** for dates mentioned below by saying, *"Do you want to choose someone who . . . ?"* (while shaking your head no). Follow each point by saying, *"What could be the problem with choosing someone who . . . ?"*
  - ○ *". . . doesn't seem interested in you?"*
  - ○ *". . . doesn't know you?"*
  - ○ *". . . is mean to you or makes fun of you?"*
  - ○ *". . . ignores you?"*
  - ○ *". . . takes advantage of you or uses you?"*
  - ○ *". . . has rejected you before?"*
  - ○ *". . . has a boyfriend or a girlfriend?"*
- Explain, *"Remember that just like friendship, dating and being in romantic relationships is a CHOICE. Other people don't have to date you just because you like them, just like you don't have to date someone just because they ask you out or they like you."*

Dating Sources

- Explain, *"Now that we understand that dating is a CHOICE, and there are good choices and bad choices, we need to talk about WHERE you might find some of these good choices for potential dates."*
- Ask, *"Where do people find potential partners to date?"*
  - ○ See Table 10.3 for an overview of commonly identified **dating sources**.
  - ○ If appropriate, have young adults brainstorm different Internet dating websites.
    - ▪ Some young adults will be unfamiliar with dating websites, so be prepared to explain any unfamiliar **dating sources**.
    - ▪ Explain that there are **GOOD choices** for dating websites (e.g., Match, eHarmony), and there are **BAD choices** (e.g., Craigslist).
  - ○ [Note: **Dating sources** will be different according to culture. Do not rely on Table 10.3 as a comprehensive or exhaustive list. Instead, have young adults generate the list of **dating sources**, as they change with time and culture.]

Table 10.3 Dating Sources Identified by Young Adults

Mutual friends	Internet dating sites
Friends of family members	School, college
Parties, get-togethers, social gatherings	Adult classes
Social activities	Workplace
Sporting events	Neighborhood
Dog parks, local parks	Sports clubs, private gyms, recreational centers
Recreational activities (e.g., sports leagues and clubs)	Church, synagogue, mosque, temple, religious gatherings
Meet up groups	
Community gatherings (e.g., concerts, fairs, farmers' market)	Public places (e.g., coffee houses, bars, clubs, bookstores)

Letting Someone Know You Like Them

- Explain, *"Now that we know WHO might be a good choice to date and WHERE we might find them, we need to talk about HOW to let someone know you like them."*

- ***Talk to mutual friends***
  - Say, *"One of the ways to let someone know you like them is by talking to mutual friends. What is a mutual friend?"*
    - Answer: A friend you have in common.
  - Ask, *"What can we say or ask our mutual friend to let them know we like someone?"* (Identify the following strategies.)
    - ***Tell your friend that you like the person.***
      - Example: *"You know (insert name)? I like him/her."*
      - Example: *"You know (insert name)? He/she is really cute."*
    - ***Ask your friend if the person is dating anyone.***
      - Example: *"Do you know if (insert name) is going out with anyone?"*
      - Example: *"Do you know if (insert name) has a boyfriend/girlfriend?"*
    - ***Ask your friend if they think the person would go out with you.***
      - Example: *"Do you think (insert name) would go out with me?"*
      - Example: *"Do you think (insert name) is interested in me?"*
  - Explain, *"If your mutual friend offers to find out if the person is interested in going out with you, agree but tell them not to say you asked. They may still tell them you asked, but at least they won't say, '(Insert name) wanted me to ask you . . .'"*

Good Role Play: Talking to a Mutual Friend ⊙

[The group leader and a behavioral coach should do an APPROPRIATE role play demonstrating **talking to a mutual friend**.]

- Begin by saying, *"We're going to do a role play. Watch this and tell me what I'm doing RIGHT in talking to a mutual friend."*

> Example of an APPROPRIATE Role Play
>
> - Group leader: *"Hi, (insert name). How's it going?"*
> - Behavioral coach: *"Pretty well. How are you?"*
> - Group leader: *"I'm good. (pause) Hey, aren't you friends with (insert name)?"*
> - Behavioral coach: *"Yeah, we've been friends for years."*
> - Group leader: *"I met him/her the other day. He/she is really cute. I liked him/her."*
> - Behavioral coach: *"Yeah, he/she is pretty cool."*
> - Group leader: *"Do you know if he/she is going out with anyone?"*
> - Behavioral coach: *"No, he/she isn't dating anyone right now."*
> - Group leader: *"Really? Do you think he/she might want to go out with me?"*
> - Behavioral coach: *"I don't know. Do you want me to find out?"*
> - Group leader: *"That would be cool, but don't tell him/her I asked you to find out."*
> - Behavioral coach: *"Okay, no problem."*

- End by saying, *"Timeout on that. So what did I do RIGHT in talking to a mutual friend?"*
  - Answers: ***Told your friend you liked the person; asked your friend if the person was dating anyone; asked your friend if the person might go out with you.***
- Ask the following *Perspective Taking Questions*:
  - *"What was that like for (name of coach)?"*
    - Answers: Fine, normal.

- ○ *"What do you think (name of coach) thought of me?"*
  - ■ Answer: You liked (insert name).
- ○ *"Is (name of coach) going to tell our mutual friend I'm interested in him/her?"*
  - ■ Answer: Yes, probably.
- Ask the behavioral coach the same *Perspective Taking Questions*:
  - ○ *"What was that like for you?"*
  - ○ *"What did you think of me?"*
  - ○ *"Are you going to tell our mutual friend I'm interested in him/her?"*

Behavioral Rehearsal: Talking to a Mutual Friend

- Explain, *"Now we're going to have each of you practice talking to a mutual friend to let someone know you like them. I will pretend to be your mutual friend."*
- Go around the room and have each young adult practice **letting someone know they like them** by **talking to a mutual friend** with the group leader.
- Have each young adult practice using the following strategies in one conversational sequence with the group leader while everyone else is watching:
  - ○ **Tell your friend that you like the person.**
  - ○ **Ask your friend if the person is dating anyone.**
  - ○ **Ask your friend if they think the person would go out with you.**
- Provide *social coaching* as needed and *troubleshoot* any problems that may arise.
- End by giving a round of applause to each young adult after their practice.
- Explain, *"So one way to let someone know you like them is to talk to mutual friends if you have them. If you don't have mutual friends, there are other ways to let someone know you like them."*

- **Flirt with your eyes**
  - ○ Explain, *"Another way to let someone know you like them is by flirting with your eyes. Just like with all the skills we teach, there are GOOD ways and BAD ways of doing this."*

Bad Role Play: Flirting With Your Eyes ⊙

[Two behavioral coaches should do an INAPPROPRIATE role play of **flirting with your eyes**. If you do not have two behavioral coaches, the group leader can be a substitute for one of the coaches.]

- Begin by saying, *"We're going to do a role play. Watch this and tell me what (name of behavioral coach 2) is doing WRONG in flirting with his/her eyes."*

Example of an INAPPROPRIATE Role Play

- ○ Behavioral coaches 1 & 2: (Looking at cell phones, standing a short distance away)
- ○ Behavioral coach 2: (Looks at behavioral coach 1 and begins to stare)
- ○ Behavioral coach 1: (Looks over and notices behavioral coach 2 staring, appears surprised and uncomfortable)
- ○ Behavioral coach 2: (Gives a HUGE teeth-baring smile, continues to stare)
- ○ Behavioral coach 1: (Looks away, turns away, looks very uncomfortable)
- ○ Behavioral coach 2: (Continues to stare, giving a HUGE teeth-baring smile)
- ○ Behavioral coach 1: (Looks back again, appears frightened and uncomfortable)
- ○ Behavioral coach 2: (Continues to stare, does a full body scan looking behavioral coach 1 up and down, giving a HUGE teeth-baring smile)
- ○ Behavioral coach 1: (Looks away, turns away, appears very uncomfortable)
- ○ Behavioral coach 2: (Continues to stare, nodding head "yes," giving a HUGE teeth-baring smile)
- ○ Behavioral coach 1: (Continues to look away, turned away, appears very uncomfortable)

- End by saying, *"Timeout on that. So what did (name of coach 2) do WRONG in flirting with his/her eyes?"*
  - Answers: Stared at the person; gave a huge toothy smile; did a full body scan; never looked away.
- Ask the following *Perspective Taking Questions*:
  - *"What was that like for (name of coach 1)?"*
    - Answers: Uncomfortable; creepy; scary.
  - *"What do you think (name of coach 1) thought of (name of coach 2)?"*
    - Answers: Creepy; stalker; predatory; weird.
  - *"Is (name of coach 1) going to want to talk to (name of coach 2)?"*
    - Answer: No, absolutely not.
- Ask behavioral coach 1 the same *Perspective Taking Questions*:
  - *"What was that like for you?"*
  - *"What did you think of (name of coach 2)?"*
  - *"Are you going to want to talk to (name of coach 2)?"*

Steps for Flirting with Your Eyes

1. **Make eye contact**
   - Say, *"One way to let someone know you like them is to flirt with your eyes. The first step for flirting with your eyes is to make eye contact. Does that mean we should stare at the person?"*
     - Answer: No.
   - Ask, *"What could be the problem with staring at the person?"*
     - Answers: They might think you're a creepy stalker; it seems predatory to stare at someone.
   - Say, *"Instead, you want to casually make eye contact. Once you've made eye contact, then what should you do?"*
     - Answer: Smile at them.

2. **Give a slight smile**
   - Say, *"The next step involves smiling at them. Should we give a big, huge, teeth-baring smile?!"*
     - Answer: No.
   - Ask, *"What could be the problem with giving a big, huge, toothy smile?"*
     - Answers: It may be too much; it might seem overzealous; you might seem like a creepy stalker.
   - Ask, *"Is it okay to give a slight smile with no teeth?"*
     - Answer: Yes.
   - Ask, *"What should we do next? Should we keep smiling and staring?"*
     - Answers: No; you should **look away**.

3. **Look away**
   - Explain, *"Once you've made eye contact and given a slight smile, the next step in flirting with your eyes is to look away. When you look away, it lets the other person know that you're safe and that you're not a creepy stalker."*
   - Ask, *"Just because we've made eye contact, smiled, and looked away does not mean we're flirting. What's the next step for flirting with your eyes?"*
     - Answer: You need to repeat the whole process again.

4. **Repeat several times**
   - Explain, *"The final step for flirting with your eyes is that you need to repeat the whole cycle again multiple times. The act of looking, smiling, looking away, and repeating is the act of flirting with your eyes. Simply making eye contact once or twice and smiling is NOT flirting."*

Good Role Play: Flirting With Your Eyes ⊙

[Two behavioral coaches should do an APPROPRIATE role play demonstrating ***flirting with your eyes***. If you do not have two behavioral coaches, the group leader can be a substitute for one of the coaches.]

- Begin by saying, *"We're going to do another role play. Watch this and tell me what (name of behavioral coach 2) is doing RIGHT in flirting with his/her eyes."*

Example of an APPROPRIATE Role Play

- Behavioral coaches 1 & 2: (Looking at cell phones, standing a short distance away)
- Behavioral coach 2: (Casually looks at behavioral coach 1)
- Behavioral coach 1: (Looks over and notices behavioral coach 2)
- Behavioral coach 2: (Gives a slight smile with no teeth)
- Behavioral coach 1: (Gives a slight smile, looks a little embarrassed)
- Behavioral coach 2: (Looks away, looks back at phone)
- Behavioral coach 1: (Looks away, looks back at phone)
- Behavioral coach 2: (Looks back at behavioral coach 1)
- Behavioral coach 1: (Looks back at behavioral coach 2)
- Behavioral coach 2: (Gives a slight smile)
- Behavioral coach 1: (Gives a slight smile)
- Behavioral coach 2: (Looks away, looks back at phone)
- Behavioral coach 1: (Looks away, looks back at phone)
- Behavioral coach 2: (Looks back at behavioral coach 1)
- Behavioral coach 1: (Looks back at behavioral coach 2)
- Behavioral coach 2: (Gives a slight smile)
- Behavioral coach 1: (Gives a slight smile)
- Behavioral coach 2: (Looks away, looks back at phone)
- Behavioral coach 1: (Looks away, looks back at phone)
- Behavioral coach 2: (Looks back at behavioral coach 1)
- Behavioral coach 1: (Looks back at behavioral coach 2)
- Behavioral coach 2: (Gives a slight smile)
- Behavioral coach 1: (Gives a slight smile)

- End by saying, *"Timeout on that. So what did (name of behavioral coach 2) do RIGHT in flirting with his/her eyes?"*
  - Answers: **Made eye contact; gave a slight smile; looked away; and repeated multiple times.**
- Ask the following *Perspective Taking Questions*:
  - *"What was that like for (name of coach 1)?"*
    - Answers: Nice; flattering; exciting.
  - *"What do you think (name of coach 1) thought of (name of coach 2)?"*
    - Answers: Nice; approachable; cute.
  - *"Is (name of coach 1) going to want to talk to (name of coach 2)?"*
    - Answer: Yes, probably.
- Ask behavioral coach 1 the same *Perspective Taking Questions*:
  - *"What was that like for you?"*
  - *"What did you think of (name of coach 2)?"*
  - *"Are you going to want to talk to (name of coach 2)?"*

Behavioral Rehearsal: Flirting with Your Eyes

- Explain, *"Now we're going to have each of you practice flirting with your eyes with one of our behavioral coaches."*
- Go around the room and have each young adult practice **letting someone know they like them** by **flirting with their eyes** with one of the behavioral coaches.
  - Be sure to have at least one male and one female behavioral coach for young adults to practice with.
  - If you only have one behavioral coach, the group leader can substitute for a missing coach of the same gender.

- ○ Ask, *"Who would you feel more comfortable practicing with, (insert name of female coach) or (insert name of male coach)?"*
- Have each young adult practice flirting with their eyes with one of the behavioral coaches using the following steps while everyone else is watching:
  1. *Make eye contact*
  2. *Give a slight smile*
  3. *Look away*
  4. *Repeat several times*
- Provide **social coaching** as needed and **troubleshoot** any problems that may arise.
- End by giving a round of applause to each young adult after their practice.
- Explain, *"So one way to let someone know you like them is to flirt with your eyes, but remember there are GOOD ways and BAD ways of doing this. There are also other ways to let someone know you like them."*

- **Ask them if they're dating anyone**
  - ○ Explain, *"Another way to let someone know you like them is by asking them if they're dating anyone. There are GOOD ways and BAD ways of doing this."*

Bad Role Play: Ask Them If They're Dating Anyone ⊙

[Two behavioral coaches should do an INAPPROPRIATE role play of **asking them if they're dating anyone**. If you do not have two behavioral coaches, the group leader can be a substitute for one of the coaches.]

- Begin by saying, *"We're going to do a role play. Watch this and tell me what (name of behavioral coach 2) is doing WRONG in asking them if they're dating anyone."*

Example of an INAPPROPRIATE Role Play

- ○ Behavioral coach 1: (Looking at cell phone)
- ○ Behavioral coach 2: (Abruptly walks over) *"Are you dating anyone?"*
- ○ Behavioral coach 1: (Shocked, confused) *"I'm sorry, what?"*
- ○ Behavioral coach 2: (Overly enthusiastic) *"Are you dating anyone?"*
- ○ Behavioral coach 1: (Uncomfortable, awkward) *"Umm . . . I don't know."*
- ○ Behavioral coach 2: (Persistent) *"I just wanted to know. Are you going out with anyone?"*
- ○ Behavioral coach 1: (Uncomfortable, awkward) *"Yeah. I think I have a boyfriend/girlfriend."* (Looks away)

- End by saying, *"Timeout on that. So what did (name of behavioral coach 2) do WRONG in asking them if they're dating anyone?"*
  - ○ Answers: Randomly walked up and asked; no context for asking; kept asking despite the discomfort.
- Ask the following *Perspective Taking Questions*:
  - ○ *"What was that like for (name of coach 1)?"*
    - ▪ Answers: Uncomfortable; creepy; scary.
  - ○ *"What do you think (name of coach 1) thought of (name of coach 2)?"*
    - ▪ Answers: Creepy; stalker; predatory; weird.
  - ○ *"Is (name of coach 1) going to want to talk to (name of coach 2) again?"*
    - ▪ Answer: No, absolutely not.
- Ask behavioral coach 1 the same *Perspective Taking Questions*:
  - ○ *"What was that like for you?"*
  - ○ *"What did you think of (name of coach 2)?"*
  - ○ *"Are you going to want to talk to (name of coach 2) again?"*

Steps for Asking Them If They're Dating Anyone

1. ***Trade information and find common interests***
   - Say, *"The first step for asking someone if they're dating anyone is to trade information. What are we trying to find when we trade information?"*
     - Answer: **Common interests**.

2. ***Ask about social activities related to the common interest***
   - Say, *"The next step is to ask about social activities related to the common interest. Why is it a good idea to ask about social activities?"*
     - Answers: It gives you a clue about who they spend time with; it gives you a context for the next step when you ask about dating, which is also social in nature.

3. ***Casually work dating into the conversation***
   - Say, *"The next step for asking someone if they're dating anyone is to casually work dating into the conversation. Why is it a good idea to work dating into the conversation?"*
     - Answers: It gives them the opportunity to mention if they're seeing anyone; it gives you the opportunity to ask if they're seeing anyone.
   - Ask, *"How will their response let you know if they're romantically interested in you?"*
     - **GOOD sign**: They say they're not dating anyone while smiling and flirting.
     - **BAD sign**: They say they're dating someone or appear uncomfortable after you ask the question.
   - Ask, *"If they're dating someone or seem uncomfortable when you ask the question, should you flirt with them and let them know you like them?"*
     - Answers: It's not a good idea to pursue someone if they don't seem romantically interested in you or if they're dating someone.

4. ***Give a cover story for asking***
   - Say, *"The next step for asking someone if they're dating anyone is to use a cover story for asking. Why is it a good idea to have a cover story for asking about dating?"*
     - Answers: It makes it less awkward for both of you; it gives you a reason for asking.

5. ***Shift the conversation back to the common interest***
   - Explain, *"The last step for asking someone if they're dating anyone is to shift the conversation back to the common interest. Why is it a good idea to shift the conversation away from dating and back to the common interest?"*
     - Answers: It makes it less awkward for both of you; if they want to know about your dating status, they can ask.

Good Role Play: Ask Them If They're Dating Anyone ⊙

[Two behavioral coaches should do an APPROPRIATE role play demonstrating **asking them if they're dating anyone**. If you do not have two behavioral coaches, the group leader can be a substitute for one of the coaches.]

- Begin by saying, *"We're going to do a role play. Watch this and tell me what (name of behavioral coach 2) is doing RIGHT in asking them if they're dating anyone."*

Example of an APPROPRIATE Role Play

- Behavioral coach 2: *"Hi, (insert name). How are you?"*
- Behavioral coach 1: *"I'm pretty good. How are you?"*
- Behavioral coach 2: *"I'm fine. So what did you do over the break?"*
- Behavioral coach 1: *"I actually went skiing for the week."*
- Behavioral coach 2: *"Oh that's so cool! I love skiing."*

- ○ Behavioral coach 1: *"Yeah, me too. It was really fun!"*
- ○ Behavioral coach 2: (Casual, friendly) *"I bet it was! Do you go skiing a lot?"*
- ○ Behavioral coach 1: (Friendly) *"As often as I can."*
- ○ Behavioral coach 2: (Casual) *"So who did you go with . . . did you go with your boyfriend/girlfriend?"*
- ○ Behavioral coach 1: (Smiling, casual) *"No, it was just me and my friends."*
- ○ Behavioral coach 2: (Casual) *"Oh, it just seems like all my friends go skiing with their boyfriends/girlfriends."*
- ○ Behavioral coach 1: (Smiling, flirty) *"No, I usually just go with friends. We're all single."*
- ○ Behavioral coach 2: (Friendly, flirty) *"Well that sounds cool. So are you a pretty good skier?"*

- End by saying, *"Timeout on that. So what did (name of behavioral coach 2) do RIGHT in asking them if they're dating anyone?"*
  - ○ Answers: **Traded information and found a common interest; asked about social activities related to the common interest; casually worked dating into the conversation; gave a cover story for asking; shifted the conversation back to the common interest.**
- Ask the following **Perspective Taking Questions**:
  - ○ *"What was that like for (name of coach 1)?"*
    - ■ Answers: Comfortable; nice; flattering.
  - ○ *"What do you think (name of coach 1) thought of (name of coach 2)?"*
    - ■ Answers: Nice; friendly; cute.
  - ○ *"Is (name of coach 1) going to want to talk to (name of coach 2) again?"*
    - ■ Answer: Yes.
- Ask behavioral coach 1 the same **Perspective Taking Questions**:
  - ○ *"What was that like for you?"*
  - ○ *"What did you think of (name of coach 2)?"*
  - ○ *"Are you going to want to talk to (name of coach 2) again?"*

Behavioral Rehearsal: Ask Them If They're Dating Anyone

- Explain, *"Now we're going to have each of you practice asking one of our behavioral coaches if they're dating anyone."*
- Go around the room and have each young adult practice **letting someone know they like them** by **asking them if they're dating anyone** with one of the behavioral coaches.
  - ○ Be sure to have at least one male and one female behavioral coach for young adults to practice with.
  - ○ If you only have one behavioral coach, the group leader can substitute for a missing coach of the same gender.
  - ○ Ask, *"Who would you feel more comfortable practicing with, (insert name of female coach) or (insert name of male coach)?"*
- Ask the young adult what they like to do and tell them to imagine the coach shares that **common interest** and use that topic for **asking them if they're dating anyone**.
- Have each young adult practice asking one of the behavioral coaches if they're dating anyone using following the steps while everyone else is watching:
  1. **Trade information and find common interests**
  2. **Ask about social activities related to the common interest**
  3. **Casually work dating into the conversation**
  4. **Give a cover story for asking**
  5. **Shift the conversation back to the common interest**
- Encourage young adults to look at the board as they're following the steps.
  - ○ You may need to point to specific steps as they're practicing.
  - ○ Try not to stop the behavioral rehearsal while they're practicing.

- Provide *social coaching* as needed and *troubleshoot* any problems that may arise.
- End by giving a round of applause to each young adult after their practice.
- Explain, *"So one way to let someone know you like them is by asking them if they're dating anyone, but remember there are GOOD ways and BAD ways of doing this. There are also other ways to let someone know you like them."*

- *Give compliments*
  ○ Explain, *"Another way to let someone know you like them is by giving compliments. This is the equivalent of verbal flirting. Just like with any of our skills, there are GOOD ways and BAD ways of giving compliments."*
  ○ *Give SPECIFIC compliments when you DON'T know the person well.*
    ■ Say, *"When we're giving compliments to people we DON'T know well, it's better to be SPECIFIC in our compliments, rather than GENERAL. What are some examples of SPECIFIC compliments?"*
      □ Examples of *SPECIFIC compliments*:
        – *"You have a nice smile."*
        – *"That was a funny joke."*
        – *"That was interesting."*
  ○ *Give SPECIFIC or GENERAL compliments when you know the person well.*
    ■ Say, *"When we're giving compliments to people we actually know well, we can give SPECIFIC or GENERAL compliments. What are some examples of GENERAL compliments?"*
      □ Examples of *GENERAL compliments*:
        – *"You're so beautiful/handsome."*
        – *"You're so funny."*
        – *"You're so smart."*
    ■ Ask, *"What could be the problem with giving GENERAL compliments to someone you don't know well?"*
      □ Answers: It could seem insincere; it might seem like you're just trying to flatter them; it might not sound genuine; you don't know them well enough to say those things yet.
  ○ *Avoid too many physical compliments.*
    ■ Say, *"It's also important that when giving compliments, we avoid giving too many physical compliments. What are physical compliments?"*
      □ Answer: They are compliments about someone's appearance.
    ■ Ask, *"What could be the problem with giving too many physical compliments?"*
      □ Answers: It could seem like you're only interested in their looks; it may seem like you only like them for their appearance.
  ○ *Physical compliments should be from the neck up.*
    ■ Say, *"If we're going to give physical compliments, they should only be from the neck up. What could be the problem with giving compliments below the neck?"*
      □ Answers: There are very few physical compliments below the neck that are appropriate; you could seem like you're only interested in their body; they might think you only want something physical with them; you could seem creepy; you could make them uncomfortable.

Bad Role Play: Giving Compliments ⊙

[Two behavioral coaches should do an INAPPROPRIATE role play of giving a *GENERAL compliment*. If you do not have two behavioral coaches, the group leader can be a substitute for one of the coaches.]

- Begin by saying, *"We're going to do a role play. Watch this and tell me what (name of behavioral coach 2) is doing WRONG in giving a compliment."*

Example of an INAPPROPRIATE Role Play

○   Behavioral coach 2: *"Hi, (insert name). How are you?"*
○   Behavioral coach 1: *"I'm pretty good. How are you?"*
○   Behavioral coach 2: *"I'm fine. So what did you do over the break?"*
○   Behavioral coach 1: *"I got together with some friends and went skiing."*
○   Behavioral coach 2: *"Oh cool. Do you ski a lot?"*
○   Behavioral coach 1: *"When I can."*
○   Behavioral coach 2: (Over the top with enthusiasm) *"You're so athletic!"*
○   Behavioral coach 1: (Uncomfortable, awkward) *"I don't know about that."*

- End by saying, *"Timeout on that. So what did (name of behavioral coach 2) do WRONG in giving a compliment?"*
  ○   Answers: Compliment was too general; they may not know each other well enough to say that; seemed insincere; looked like he/she was trying too hard.
- Ask the following *Perspective Taking Questions*:
  ○   *"What was that like for (name of coach 1)?"*
    ▪   Answers: Uncomfortable; awkward.
  ○   *"What do you think (name of coach 1) thought of (name of coach 2)?"*
    ▪   Answers: Overly enthusiastic; trying too hard; desperate.
  ○   *"Is (name of coach 1) going to want to talk to (name of coach 2) again?"*
    ▪   Answer: Probably not.
- Ask behavioral coach 1 the same *Perspective Taking Questions*:
  ○   *"What was that like for you?"*
  ○   *"What did you think of (name of coach 2)?"*
  ○   *"Are you going to want to talk to (name of coach 2) again?"*

Good Role Play: Giving Compliments ▶

[Two behavioral coaches should do an APPROPRIATE role play of giving a **SPECIFIC compliment**. If you do not have two behavioral coaches, the group leader can be a substitute for one of the coaches.]

- Begin by saying, *"We're going to do a role play. Watch this and tell me what (name of behavioral coach 2) is doing RIGHT in giving a compliment."*

Example of an APPROPRIATE Role Play

○   Behavioral coach 2: *"Hi, (insert name). How are you?"*
○   Behavioral coach 1: *"I'm pretty good. How are you?"*
○   Behavioral coach 2: *"I'm fine. So what did you do over the break?"*
○   Behavioral coach 1: *"I got together with some friends and went skiing."*
○   Behavioral coach 2: *"Oh cool. Do you ski a lot?"*
○   Behavioral coach 1: *"When I can."*
○   Behavioral coach 2: (Casual, flirty, smiling) *"You must be a pretty good skier then."*
○   Behavioral coach 1: (Smiling, flattered) *"I'm okay."*

- End by saying, *"Timeout on that. So what did (name of coach 2) do RIGHT in giving a compliment?"*
  ○   Answers: Gave a **SPECIFIC compliment**; wasn't over the top; wasn't trying too hard.
- Ask the following *Perspective Taking Questions*:
  ○   *"What was that like for (name of coach 1)?"*
    ▪   Answers: Nice; flattering.
  ○   *"What do you think (name of coach 1) thought of (name of coach 2)?"*
    ▪   Answers: Nice; friendly; cute.

- ○ *"Is (name of coach 1) going to want to talk to (name of coach 2) again?"*
  - ■ Answer: Yes.
- Ask behavioral coach 1 the same *Perspective Taking Questions*:
  - ○ *"What was that like for you?"*
  - ○ *"What did you think of (name of coach 2)?"*
  - ○ *"Are you going to want to talk to (name of coach 2) again?"*

Behavioral Rehearsal: Giving SPECIFIC Compliments

- Explain, *"Now we're going to have each of you practice giving a specific compliment to one of our behavioral coaches."*
- Go around the room and have each young adult practice **letting someone know they like them** by **giving a SPECIFIC compliment** to one of the behavioral coaches while everyone else is watching.
  - ○ Be sure to have at least one male and one female behavioral coach for young adults to practice with.
  - ○ If you only have one behavioral coach, the group leader can substitute for a missing coach of the same gender.
  - ○ Ask, *"Who would you feel more comfortable practicing with (insert name of female coach) or (insert name of male coach)?"*
- Provide **social coaching** as needed and **troubleshoot** any problems that may arise.
- End by giving a round of applause to each young adult after their practice.
- Explain, *"So one way to let someone know you like them is to give compliments, but remember there are GOOD ways and BAD ways of doing this. There are also a couple of other ways to let someone know you like them."*

- **Show interest in them**
  - ○ Explain, *"Another way to let someone know you like them is by showing interest in them. How do we show interest in someone?"*
  - ○ **Trade information**
    - ■ Explain, *"One of the best ways to show interest in someone is by talking to them and trading information. That means all the skills we learned for starting and maintaining conversations and for entering group conversations apply to dating."*
    - ■ Ask, *"What is your goal when trading information?"*
      - □ Answer: **Find common interests**.
  - ○ **Find common interests**
    - ■ Explain, *"Just like friendships, romantic relationships are often based on common interests, as well as mutual attraction."*
    - ■ Ask, *"Why is it important to find common interests?"*
      - □ Answer: It gives you something to talk about and something to do together.
    - ■ Ask, *"Could you date someone that you have very little in common with?"*
      - □ Answer: Yes, but it might be a bit boring.

- **Laugh at their jokes**
  - ○ Say, *"Another way to show interest in someone is to laugh at their jokes. Even if you don't think their jokes are funny, should you still laugh?"*
    - ■ Answer: Yes.
  - ○ Ask, *"What do we call that when we laugh just to be polite?"*
    - ■ Answer: *A courtesy laugh*.
  - ○ Ask, *"Why would it be important to give a courtesy laugh if we're trying to show interest in someone and let them know we like them?"*
    - ■ Answers: It makes them feel comfortable; you seem friendly and approachable; not laughing might make them feel uncomfortable and awkward.

DATING ETIQUETTE: LETTING SOMEONE KNOW YOU LIKE THEM

Young Adult Behavioral Rehearsal

Get-Togethers

Materials Needed

- Indoor games (e.g., video games, card games, board games).
    - If you are going to provide video games as an option, make sure there are enough gaming consoles that each group can play simultaneously together.
    - Do not use small, portable gaming devices as people have to wait to take turns and that can get boring.
    - Several decks of playing cards will be sufficient if you do not have these other resources.
- Optional: iPads or laptops for watching YouTube videos, surfing the Internet, or playing computer games.
    - If you are going to provide iPads or laptops as an option, make sure there are enough that each group can use them simultaneously together.
- [Note: Most PEERS® programs DO NOT have access to gaming consoles, iPads, or laptops. These are luxury items. Just providing a few decks of cards to keep the get-together *activity-based* will be fine.]

Behavioral Rehearsal

- Notify young adults they will be practicing *beginning and ending get-togethers*.
- Break up young adults into small groups (no less than three young adults per group).
- Have EACH young adult practice *beginning a get-together* following the steps.
    - Assign *hosts* and *guests*.
        - One young adult will be the *host*.
        - One young adult will be the *arriving guest*.
        - The other young adult(s) will be the *guest(s) that have already arrived*.
    - Begin by having the *host* verbally go over the steps for *beginning a get-together*.
    - You may need to provide Socratic prompting to young adults for identifying the specific steps for *beginning a get-together* by using some of the following *social coaching questions*:
        - *"What should you do when your guest knocks on the door?"*
        - *"What should you do when they're standing on the doorstep?"*
        - *"What should you do if they've never met your other friends?"*
        - *"What should you do if they've never been to your home?"*
        - *"Do you want to offer them something?"*
        - *"How will you decide what to do?"*
    - The *arriving guest* should step outside and knock on the door.
    - The *guest(s) that have already arrived* should be seated somewhere nearby.
    - Have the *host* follow the steps for *beginning the get-together*.

- ○ You may need to provide Socratic prompting to young adults if they have trouble following the steps by using some of the following *social coaching questions*:
  - ▪ *"What should you do when your friend knocks on the door?"*
  - ▪ *"Do you think your friend might want to come in?"*
  - ▪ *"Have all of your friends met?"*
  - ▪ *"Has your friend been to your home?"*
  - ▪ *"Do you want to offer your friends something?"*
  - ▪ *"How will you and your friends decide what to do?"*
- ○ Once the young adult has practiced, call a *"timeout"* and have the other young adults applaud.
- ○ EACH young adult should practice *beginning a get-together* as a *host*, an *arriving guest*, and a *guest that has already arrived*.
- • Have young adults practice following the rules for how to behave *during the get-together* while *trading information*, *finding common interests*, and playing with games and items provided by the treatment team (e.g., video games, card games, board games, iPads, laptops, etc.).
- • Have EACH young adult practice *ending a get-together* following the steps.
  - ○ Assign *hosts* and *guests*.
    - ▪ One young adult will be the *host*.
    - ▪ The other young adults will be the *guests*.
  - ○ Have the *host* verbally go over the steps for *ending a get-together*.
  - ○ You may need to provide Socratic prompting to young adults for identifying the specific steps to *ending a get-together* by using some of the following *social coaching questions*:
    - ▪ *"Should you interrupt your friends to end the get-together?"*
    - ▪ *"Should you just tell them to leave?"*
    - ▪ *"How are they going to find their way out?"*
    - ▪ *"Should you thank them for anything?"*
    - ▪ *"What should you say if you had a nice time?"*
    - ▪ *"What should you say if you're going to see them again?"*
    - ▪ *"What's the last thing you should say as they're leaving?"*
  - ○ The *hosts* and *guests* should be seated before they begin the practice so that the *host* has to *stand up and start walking the guests to the door*.
  - ○ Have the *host* follow the steps for *ending the get-together*.
  - ○ You may need to provide Socratic prompting to young adults if they have trouble following the steps by using some of the following *social coaching questions*:
    - ▪ *"Do you just tell your friends to leave, or do you need a reason?"*
    - ▪ *"How will your friends find their way out?"*
    - ▪ *"Do you want to thank them for anything?"*
    - ▪ *"What could you say if you had a nice time?"*
    - ▪ *"What could you say if you're going to see them again?"*
    - ▪ *"What's the last thing you should say as they're leaving?"*
  - ○ *Guests* should actually leave and then come back at the end of the role play.
  - ○ Once the young adult has practiced, call a *"timeout"* and have the other young adults applaud.
  - ○ EACH young adult should practice *ending a get-together* as a *host* and a *guest*.

DATING ETIQUETTE: LETTING SOMEONE KNOW YOU LIKE THEM

Reunification

- Announce that young adults should join their social coaches.
  - ○ Have young adults stand or sit next to their social coaches.
  - ○ Be sure to have silence and the full attention of the group before starting with *Reunification*.
  - ○ Have young adults generate the content from the lesson while social coaches listen.
- Say, *"Today, we talked about dating etiquette and how to let someone know you like them. What are some of the ways we can let someone know we like them?"*
  - ○ *Talk to mutual friends*
    - ■ *Tell your friend that you like the person.*
    - ■ *Ask your friend if the person is dating anyone.*
    - ■ *Ask your friend if they think the person would go out with you.*
  - ○ *Flirt with your eyes*
    1. *Make eye contact*
    2. *Give a slight smile*
    3. *Look away*
    4. *Repeat several times*
  - ○ *Ask them if they're dating anyone*
    1. *Trade information and find common interests*
    2. *Ask about social activities related to the common interest*
    3. *Casually work dating into the conversation*
    4. *Give a cover story for asking*
    5. *Shift the conversation back to the common interest*
  - ○ *Give compliments*
    - ■ *Give SPECIFC compliments when you DON'T know the person well.*
    - ■ *Give SPECIFIC or GENERAL compliments when you know the person well.*
    - ■ *Avoid too many physical compliments.*
    - ■ *Physical compliments should be from the neck up.*
  - ○ *Show interest in them*
    - ■ *Trade information*
    - ■ *Find common interests*
  - ○ *Laugh at their jokes*
- Say, *"Remember, dating is a choice. We don't get to date everyone and everyone doesn't get to date us. There are GOOD choices and there are BAD choices when it comes to dating. Once we've confirmed that someone is a good choice, we need to let them know we like them. Today, the young adults practiced flirting and letting someone know they like them and the group did a great job. Let's give them a round of applause."*

Homework Assignments

Distribute the *Social Coaching Handout* to young adults and announce the following *Homework Assignments*:

1. Have a *get-together* with a friend.
    - Social coaches should help young adults plan the get-together using the *five W's*:
        - *WHO* they plan to get together with.
        - *WHAT* they plan to do.
        - *WHEN* it will happen.
        - *WHERE* they will meet.
        - *HOW* they will make it happen.
    - Social coaches should go over the rules and steps for *get-togethers* with young adults beforehand.
    - Social coaches should ask young adults the following *social coaching questions* after the *get-together*:
        - *What did you decide to do and who picked the activities?*
        - *Did you trade information and for what percentage of the time?*
        - *What were your common interests and what could you do with that information if you were going to hang out again?*
        - *Did you and your friend have a good time?*
        - *Is this someone you might want to hang out with again?*

2. Practice *letting someone know you like them*.
    - If young adults are interested in someone romantically, use the strategies for *letting someone know you like them*.
        - DO NOT practice unless you are romantically interested in the person.
    - Young adults should practice *letting someone know you like them* with social coaches, if comfortable.
    - Social coaches should go over the rules and steps for *letting someone know you like them* before the practice.
    - Social coaches should ask young adults the following *social coaching questions* after each practice:
        - *Who did you practice with?*
        - *What did you do to let them know you like them?*
        - *How did they respond?*
        - *Does this seem like a good choice and is this someone you might want to go on a date with?*

3. *Enter and exit group conversations* with social coaches.
    - Young adults should practice *entering and exiting group conversations* with their social coach and another person.
        - Practice exiting when NEVER ACCEPTED.
        - Practice exiting when INITIALLY ACCEPTED AND THEN EXCLUDED.
        - Practice exiting when FULLY ACCEPTED.
    - Social coaches should go over the rules and steps for *entering and exiting group conversations* before the practice.
    - Social coaches should ask young adults the following *social coaching questions* after each practice:
        - *Did it seem like we wanted to talk to you?*
        - *How could you tell?*

4. *Enter a group conversation* with peers (could be from the *source of friends*).
    - Social coaches should go over the rules and steps for *entering and exiting group conversations* before the practice.

- The assignment is NOT to *exit the conversation* unless they naturally need to.
- Social coaches should ask young adults the following *social coaching questions* after the practice:
  - *Where did you enter a conversation and with who?*
  - *Which steps did you follow?*
  - *Did it seem like they wanted to talk to you and how could you tell?*
  - *Did you have to exit the conversation and which steps did you follow?*

Individual Check-Out

Individually and privately negotiate with each young adult and social coach:

1. *WHO* they plan to have a *get-together* with in the coming week.
   - *WHAT* they plan to suggest to their friends.
   - *WHEN* and *WHERE* they will suggest to their friends.
   - *HOW* they will make it happen (e.g., tickets, transportation, etc.).

2. How they will practice *letting someone know they like them* and with whom.

3. When they plan to *enter and exit a group conversation* with social coaches.
   - Which other person they would be comfortable practicing with.

4. Where, when, and with whom they plan to *enter a group conversation* with peers.
   - Whether this is an accepting *social group* and how they can tell.

DATING ETIQUETTE: LETTING SOMEONE KNOW YOU LIKE THEM

Social Coaching Handout

Choosing Appropriate People to Date

- *Dating is a choice*
    - ○ *We don't get to date everyone and everyone doesn't get to date us.*
    - ○ There are *GOOD choices* and there are *BAD choices* when it comes to dating.

Dating Sources

Table 10.3 Dating Sources Identified by Young Adults

Mutual friends	Internet dating sites
Friends of family members	School, college
Parties, get-togethers, social gatherings	Adult classes
Social activities	Workplace
Sporting events	Neighborhood
Dog parks, local parks	Sports clubs, private gyms, recreational centers
Recreational activities (e.g., sports leagues and clubs)	Church, synagogue, mosque, temple, religious gatherings
Meet up groups	
Community gatherings (e.g., concerts, fairs, farmers' market)	Public places (e.g., coffee houses, bars, clubs, bookstores)

Letting Someone Know You Like Them

- *Talk to mutual friends*
    - ○ *Tell your friend that you like the person.*
        - ▪ Example: *"You know (insert name)? I like him/her."*
        - ▪ Example: *"You know (insert name)? He/she is really cute."*
    - ○ *Ask your friend if the person is dating anyone.*
        - ▪ Example: *"Do you know if (insert name) is going out with anyone?"*
        - ▪ Example: *"Do you know if (insert name) has a boyfriend/girlfriend?"*
    - ○ *Ask your friend if they think the person would go out with you.*
        - ▪ Example: *"Do you think (insert name) would go out with me?"*
        - ▪ Example: *"Do you think (insert name) is interested in me?"*
- *Flirt with your eyes*
    1. *Make eye contact*
    2. *Give a slight smile*
    3. *Look away*
    4. *Repeat several times*

- *Ask them if they're dating anyone*
  1. *Trade information and find common interests*
     - Example: *"I heard you went skiing last week. I love skiing."*
  2. *Ask about social activities related to the common interest*
     - Example: *"Who did you go skiing with . . . ?"*
  3. *Casually work dating into the conversation*
     - Example: *". . . did you go with your boyfriend/girlfriend?"*
     - *GOOD sign*: They say they're not dating anyone while smiling and flirting.
     - *BAD sign*: They say they're dating someone or appear uncomfortable after you ask the question.
  4. *Give a cover story for asking*
     - Example: *"It just seems like all my friends go skiing with their boyfriend/girlfriend."*
  5. *Shift the conversation back to the common interest*
     - Example: *"So are you a pretty good skier?"*

- *Give compliments*
  - *Give SPECIFIC compliments when you DON'T know the person well.*
    - Examples of *SPECIFIC* compliments:
      - *"You have a nice smile."*
      - *"That was a funny joke."*
      - *"That was interesting."*
  - *Give SPECIFIC or GENERAL compliments when you know the person well.*
    - Examples of *GENERAL* compliments:
      - *"You're beautiful/handsome."*
      - *"You're so funny."*
      - *"You're so smart."*
  - *Avoid too many physical compliments.*
  - *Physical compliments should be from the neck up.*

- *Show interest in them*
  - *Trade information*
  - *Find common interests*

- *Laugh at their jokes*
  - *Give a courtesy laugh*

Homework Assignments

1. Have a *get-together* with a friend.
   - Social coaches should help young adults plan the get-together using the *five W's*:
     - *WHO* they plan to get together with.
     - *WHAT* they plan to do.
     - *WHEN* it will happen.
     - *WHERE* they will meet.
     - *HOW* they will make it happen.
   - Social coaches should go over the rules and steps for *get-togethers* with young adults beforehand.
   - Social coaches should ask young adults the following *social coaching questions* after the *get-together*:
     - *What did you decide to do and who picked the activities?*
     - *Did you trade information and for what percentage of the time?*
     - *What were your common interests and what could you do with that information if you were going to hang out again?*
     - *Did you and your friend have a good time?*
     - *Is this someone you might want to hang out with again?*

2. Practice *letting someone know you like them*.
   - If young adults are interested in someone romantically, use the strategies for *letting someone know you like them*.
     - DO NOT practice unless you are romantically interested in the person.
   - Young adults should practice *letting someone know you like them* with social coaches, if comfortable.
   - Social coaches should go over the rules and steps for *letting someone know you like them* before the practice.
   - Social coaches should ask young adults the following *social coaching questions* after each practice:
     - *Who did you practice with?*
     - *What did you do to let them know you like them?*
     - *How did they respond?*
     - *Does this seem like a good choice and is this someone you might want to go on a date with?*

3. *Enter and exit group conversations* with social coaches.
   - Young adults should practice *entering and exiting group conversations* with their social coach and another person.
     - Practice exiting when NEVER ACCEPTED.
     - Practice exiting when INITIALLY ACCEPTED AND THEN EXCLUDED.
     - Practice exiting when FULLY ACCEPTED.
   - Social coaches should go over the rules and steps for *entering and exiting group conversations* before the practice.
   - Social coaches should ask young adults the following *social coaching questions* after each practice:
     - *Did it seem like we wanted to talk to you?*
     - *How could you tell?*

4. *Enter a group conversation* with peers (could be from the *source of friends*).
   - Social coaches should go over the rules and steps for *entering and exiting group conversations* before the practice.
   - The assignment is NOT to *exit the conversation* unless they naturally need to.
   - Social coaches should ask young adults the following *social coaching questions* after the practice:
     - *Where did you enter a conversation and with whom?*
     - *Which steps did you follow?*
     - *Did it seem like they wanted to talk to you and how could you tell?*
     - *Did you have to exit the conversation?*
     - *If you had to exit, which steps did you follow?*

DATING ETIQUETTE: ASKING SOMEONE ON A DATE

Social Coaching Therapist Guide

Preparing for the Social Coaching Session

The focus of this session is on teaching young adults how to ask potential partners out on romantic dates. The role of the social coaches in this regard will be very much behind the scenes. Because it would not be developmentally appropriate for social coaches to be present when young adults ask others on dates (unless done over online dating), much of the social coaching will occur during the preparation for dates.

Social coaches should be encouraged to help young adults make sure they have done a number of things before ever asking someone on a date. For example, *talking to mutual friends, flirting with their eyes, giving SPECIFIC or GENERAL compliments, asking the person if they're dating anyone,* and *showing interest* by *trading information, finding common interests,* and *laughing at jokes* are all ways social coaches can encourage young adults to *let someone know they like them.* Moreover, social coaches can provide much needed assistance in assessing responses to these overtures. The role social coaches play in helping young adults assess feedback when it comes to *letting someone know they like them* and *asking someone on a date* cannot be underestimated. Inappropriate choices for dates can often be avoided by heeding the warning signs when these factors have been considered. Since young adults often have difficulty interpreting these warning signs, social coaches can provide a much-needed gatekeeping role.

Additionally, in this lesson, young adults will be instructed to find out if their romantic interest has a girlfriend or a boyfriend, and to *consider their dating activity options* before they ever ask them out. The latter part in particular is another critical role social coaches will play in helping young adults to prepare for dates. *Considering their dating activity options* generally encompasses the *five W's,* which include figuring out *WHO* will be there, *WHAT* you plan to do, *WHEN* it will happen, *WHERE* you will meet, and *HOW* you will make it happen. Young adults with social challenges often require assistance with such pragmatic planning. Consequently, social coaches can provide much-needed behind-the-scene assistance during this preparation phase.

Finally, social coaches will also be an integral part of normalizing experiences of rejection that might occur through the process of asking others out on dates. Although young adults will be discouraged from *asking someone on a date* until after they have learned how to behave on a date in the next session, social coaches will begin to receive guidance in how to normalize experiences of rejection in the current session. Social coaches and young adults will be reminded that, like friendship; *Dating is a choice. We don't get to date everyone and everyone doesn't get to date us.* Unfortunately, rejection is just part and parcel of the dating process for everyone. However, if we help young adults follow the general rules for dating etiquette outlined in these sessions, and encourage them to make *GOOD choices,* while avoiding *BAD choices,* we may be able to minimize recurrent experiences of rejection.

Homework Review

[Go over the following *Homework Assignments* and **troubleshoot** any potential problems. Start with completed homework first. If you have time, you can inquire as to why others were unable to complete the assignment and try to **troubleshoot** how they might get it done for the coming week. When reviewing homework, be sure to relabel descriptions using the **buzzwords** (identified by **bold and italicized** print). Spend the majority of the *Homework Review* on **get-togethers** as this was the most important assignment.]

1. Have a **get-together** with a friend.
   - Say, *"One of the main assignments this week was for young adults to have a get-together with a friend. Who completed this assignment or attempted to complete it?"*
   - Ask the following questions:
     - *"Did you help your young adult plan the get-together using the five W's?"*
     - *"What social coaching did you do before the get-together?"*
     - *"What did your young adult decide to do and with whom?"*
     - *"How did the get-together begin?"*
     - *"Who picked the activities?"*
     - *"Did they trade information and what percentage of the time?"*
     - *"How did the get-together end?"*
     - *"What social coaching did you do after the get-together?"*
       - Appropriate **social coaching questions**:
         - **What did you decide to do and who picked the activities?**
         - **Did you trade information and for what percentage of the time?**
         - **What were your common interests and what could you do with that information if you were going to hang out again?**
         - **Did you and your friend have a good time?**
         - **Is this someone you might want to hang out with again?**
     - *"Does this seem like a good choice for a friend and someone your young adult will want to hang out with again?"*

Table 11.1 Steps for Beginning and Ending Get-Togethers in Your Home

Beginning the Get-Together	Ending the Get-Together
1. Greet your guest	1. Wait for a pause in activities
2. Invite them in	2. Give a cover story for ending the get-together
3. Introduce them to anyone they don't know	3. Start walking your friend to the door
4. Give them a tour	4. Thank your friend for getting together
5. Offer them refreshments	5. Tell your friend you had a good time
6. Ask them what they want to do	6. Say goodbye and you'll see them later

2. Practice **letting someone know you like them**.
   - Say, *"Another assignment this week was for young adults to practice letting someone know they like them. The assignment was NOT to practice unless they are romantically interested in the person. Young adults could also have practiced with social coaches, if they were comfortable. Who completed this assignment or attempted to complete it?"*
   - Ask the following questions:
     - *"What social coaching did you do before the practice?"*
     - *"Who did your young adult practice with?"*
     - *"What did they do to let them know they liked them?"*
     - *"How did the person respond?"*
     - *"What social coaching did you do after the practice?"*

- ■ Appropriate *social coaching questions*:
  - □ *Who did you practice with?*
  - □ *What did you do to let them know you like them?*
  - □ *How did they respond?*
  - □ *Is this someone you might want to go on a date with?*
  - ○ "Does this seem like a good choice and is this someone they might want to go on a date with?"

3. ***Enter and exit group conversations*** with social coaches.
   - • Say, *"Another assignment this week was for young adults to practice entering and exiting group conversations with you and another person. Who completed this assignment or attempted to complete it?"*
   - • Ask the following questions:
     - ○ *"Who did you and your young adult practice with?"*
     - ○ *"What social coaching did you do before the practice?"*
     - ○ *"Which steps did your young adult follow to enter the group conversation?"*
       1. **Listen to the Conversation**
       2. **Watch from a Distance**
       3. **Use a Prop**
       4. **Identify the Topic**
       5. **Find a Common Interest**
       6. **Move Closer**
       7. **Wait for a Pause**
       8. **Mention the Topic**
       9. **Assess Interest**
       10. **Introduce Yourself**
     - ○ *"Which steps did your young adult follow to exit the conversations?"*
     - ○ *"What social coaching did you do after the practice?"*
       - ■ Appropriate *social coaching questions*:
         - □ *Did it seem like we wanted to talk to you?*
         - □ *How could you tell?*

Table 11.2 Steps for Exiting Conversations

NEVER ACCEPTED	INITIALLY ACCEPTED, THEN EXCLUDED	FULLY ACCEPTED
1. Keep your cool 2. Look away 3. Turn away 4. Walk away	1. Keep your cool 2. Look away 3. Wait for a BRIEF pause 4. Give a BRIEF cover story for leaving 5. Walk away	1. Wait for a pause 2. Give a SPECIFIC cover story for leaving 3. Say you'll see them later 4. Say goodbye 5. Walk away

4. ***Enter a group conversation*** with peers (could be from the ***source of friends***).
   - • Say, *"Another assignment this week was for young adults to practice entering group conversations with peers. Who completed this assignment or attempted to complete it?"*
   - • Ask the following questions:
     - ○ *"Where and with whom did your young adult practice?"*
     - ○ *"What social coaching did you do before the practice?"*
     - ○ *"Which steps did your young adult follow?"*
     - ○ *"What social coaching did you do after the practice?"*
       - ■ Appropriate *social coaching questions*:
         - □ *Where did you enter a conversation and with whom?*
         - □ *Which steps did you follow?*
         - □ *Did it seem like they wanted to talk to you and how could you tell?*
         - □ *Did you have to exit the conversation and which steps did you follow?*

- [Collect the *Social Coaching Homework Assignment Worksheets*. If social coaches forgot to bring the worksheets, have them complete a new form to hold them accountable for the assignments.]

Didactic Lesson: Dating Etiquette: Asking Someone on a Date

- Distribute the *Social Coaching Handout*.
  - ○ Sections in **bold print** in the *Social Coaching Therapist Guide* come directly from the *Social Coaching Handout*.
  - ○ Remind social coaches that terms that are in ***bold and italicized*** print are ***buzzwords*** and represent important concepts from the PEERS® curriculum that should be used as much as possible when social coaching.
- Explain, *"Today, we're going to continue talking about dating etiquette. Last week, we talked about who to date, where to find people to date, and how to let someone know you like them. This week, we're going to talk about how to ask someone on a date."*

Before Asking Someone on a Date

- Explain, *"Before we ever ask someone on a date, we should have done a number of things to let the person know we like them."*

- ***Talk to mutual friends, if you have them.***
- ***Flirt with your eyes.***
- ***Give SPECIFIC or GENERAL compliments, depending on how well you know them.***
- ***Ask them if they're dating anyone.***
- ***Show interest in them by trading information and finding common interests.***
- ***Laugh at their jokes when appropriate.***

- Explain, *"There are a few more things we need to do before we ever ask someone on a date."*
- ***Assess their romantic interest in you***
  - ○ Say, *"We also need to assess their romantic interest in us. How can you tell if someone is interested in you romantically?"*
    - ■ Answers: Mutual friends tell you they like you; they flirt back; they appear to enjoy your compliments; they show interest in you by trading information; they ask about your dating status.

- ***Find out if they have a girlfriend or boyfriend***
  - ○ Say, *"We also need to find out if they have a girlfriend or a boyfriend before we ask them on a date. How do we find out if they're dating someone?"*
    - ■ Answers: You could ask a mutual friend; check out their relationship status on their social networking profile page (e.g., Facebook); you could ask them directly.

- ***Consider your dating activity options using the five W's***
  - ○ Say, *"Before we ever ask someone on a date, we should also consider our dating activity options. This involves the five W's."*
    - ■ ***WHO* will be there.**
    - ■ ***WHAT* you plan to do.**
    - ■ ***WHEN* it will happen.**
    - ■ ***WHERE* you will meet.**
    - ■ ***HOW* you will make it happen.**

Asking Someone on a Date

- Explain, *"Once we've let the person know we like them, assessed their romantic interest, found out if they have a girlfriend or boyfriend, and considered our dating activity options, the next step is to ask the person out on a date. There are very specific steps to follow when asking someone on a date."*

1. *Wait for an appropriate time to ask*
   - Say, *"The first step for asking someone on a date is to wait for the appropriate time to ask. When are some appropriate times?"*
     - Answers: When no one else is around; when they're not in the middle of doing something; when you're both free to talk; when you're in person; when they're in a good mood.

2. *Trade information*
   - Say, *"The next step for asking someone out is to trade information. Why is it important to trade information before you ask someone out?"*
     - Answer: You don't want to randomly ask them on a date out of the blue.
   - Ask, *"Should you have traded information multiple times before?"*
     - Answer: It is less risky to ask someone out that you know and have talked to several times.

3. *Mention your common interest*
   - Say, *"The next step is to mention your common interest. What common interest should you be mentioning?"*
     - Answer: The **common interest** you plan to suggest for your date.

4. *Ask what they're doing at a certain time*
   - Explain, *"After you've traded information for a bit and mentioned the common interest you plan to suggest for your date, the next step is to ask what they're doing at a certain time."*
   - Ask, *"How do you ask what they're doing at a certain time?"*
     - Example: *"What are you doing this weekend?"*
     - Example: *"What are you doing Friday night?"*
   - Explain, *"By asking what they're doing at a certain time, you protect yourself from possible rejection because you haven't actually asked them out yet."*

5. *Assess their interest*
   - Explain, *"After you've asked them what they're doing at a certain time, you need to assess their interest. What are some good signs and bad signs that they're interested in going out with you?"*
     - **GOOD signs**: They say they're available and are smiling; they seem friendly and enthusiastic; they say they're busy, but seem disappointed.
     - **BAD signs**: They say they're busy and seem uncomfortable; they mention a boyfriend or a girlfriend; they say they're available, but seem uncomfortable; they change the subject.

6. *Use your common interest as a cover story for going out*
   - Explain, *"If they seem interested, the next step for asking someone on a date is to use your common interest as a cover story for going out."*
   - Ask, *"What if your common interest is sci-fi movies, what could be a cover story for asking them on a date?"*
     - Answers: Going to the theater to see the latest sci-fi movie; watching sci-fi movies at one of your homes.

7. *Exchange contact information*
   - Say, *"If they say yes, the next step is to exchange contact information if you don't already have it. How do we exchange contact information?"*
     - Example: *"I should get your number."*
     - Example: *"We should exchange numbers."*

8. *Tell them when you'll follow-up*
   - Explain, *"The last step for asking someone on a date is to tell them when you'll follow up with them."*
   - Ask, *"When is it appropriate to call or text after getting someone's number or asking them on a date?"*
     - Answer: Within one or two days of getting their number or planning the date.

- [Optional: Show BAD and GOOD *Role Play Video Demonstrations* of **asking someone on a date** from the *PEERS® Role Play Video Library* (www.routledge.com/cw/laugeson).]

- Explain, *"After you've asked them out and they've accepted, you still need to do a few more things."*
- *Follow up using the two-day rule*
  - Explain, *"If you're interested in the person, follow up using the two-day rule. That means you should call or text one or two days after getting their number or asking them out. If you call the same day, they might get scared. If you call after three days, they might lose interest or think you're playing games."*
- *Use the five W's to plan the date*
  - Explain, *"When you ask them on the date, you should have a general sense of what you're going to do and when, but use the five W's to solidify the plans when you follow up."*
- *Confirm the plans right before the date*
  - Say, *"You also need to confirm the plans right before the date. Usually a day or two before the date is appropriate, depending on when you asked them out. Social coaches can help young adults decide when the right time to confirm the plans is."*

Accepting Rejection

- Explain, *"Even when we follow all the steps for asking someone on a date, we sometimes get rejected. When this happens, it's important to remember that dating is a choice. We don't get to date everyone, and everyone doesn't get to date us. There are some very specific steps we should follow if we get rejected when we ask someone out."*

1. *Keep your cool*
   - Say, *"The first step for accepting rejection when you ask someone on a date is to keep your cool. Why is it important to keep your cool?"*
     - Answers: If you don't **keep your cool**, you will make them uncomfortable; you will look desperate or foolish if you lose your cool; you could get a bad reputation; other people might not want to date you.

2. *Make a casual statement of acceptance*
   - Say, *"The next step is to make a casual statement of acceptance. What casual statements could you make to show that you accept the rejection?"*
     - Example: *"Okay. No big deal."*
     - Example: *"That's cool. Just thought I'd ask."*
     - Example: *"That's fine. No worries."*

3. *Shift the subject back to the common interest*
   - Say, *"The next step for accepting rejection is to shift the subject back to the common interest. Why is it a good idea to shift the subject back to what you were talking about before?"*
     - Answers: Because it's awkward to focus on the rejection; it's better to shift away from the offer of a date and talk about your **common interest** again.

4. *Use a cover story before exiting*
   - Say, *"At some point, the conversation will come to an end. It's best to have a cover story for leaving. Why is it important to have a cover story for leaving?"*
     - Answer: So it doesn't seem like you're running away because you're embarrassed or upset.

- Explain, *"While you're following the steps for accepting rejection, you need to do a few more things."*
- *Keep it friendly*
  - Say, *"It's important to keep it friendly when you've been rejected. Why it is important to keep it friendly?"*
    - Answer: Because it's awkward for both of you if it doesn't feel friendly.
- *Don't pressure them to go out with you*
  - Say, *"When someone turns you down for a date, it's important not to pressure them to go out with you. That means don't force the issue and keep asking them out. What could be the problem with pressuring them to go out with you or asking again?"*

- ■ Answers: It makes them uncomfortable; you seem desperate; they might think you're a creepy stalker; you could get a bad reputation and others may not want to go out with you.
  - ○ Ask, *"What if the reason they give could change at some point? For example, what if they say they don't want to date right now. What could you say?"*
    - ■ Example: *"Let me know if you change your mind."*
    - ■ Example: *"If something changes, let me know."*

- • *Don't ask for an explanation*
  - ○ Say, *"Even though we may be curious about why they said 'no,' we don't get to ask for an explanation. What could be the problem with asking for an explanation when someone turns you down?"*
    - ■ Answers: It makes you look desperate; it could make them uncomfortable; it's awkward.

- • [Optional: Show BAD and GOOD *Role Play Video Demonstrations* of **accepting rejection** from the *PEERS®* *Role Play Video Library* (www.routledge.com/cw/laugeson).]

Turning Someone Down

- • Explain, *"Sometimes people we're not interested in may ask us out on dates. When this happens, it's important to remember that dating is a choice. We don't get to date everyone, and everyone doesn't get to date us. That means we don't have to say yes just because someone asks us out. There are some very specific steps we should follow if we need to turn someone down when they ask us out."*

1. *Keep your cool*
   - • Say, *"The first step for turning someone down that asks you on a date is to keep your cool. Why is it important to keep your cool?"*
     - ○ Answers: Because if you lose your cool you might embarrass the other person; you might make them feel bad; you could seem mean or rude; you could get a bad reputation.

2. *Politely turn them down*
   - • Say, *"The next step is to politely turn them down. How do we politely turn someone down?"*
     - ○ Example: *"I don't think so."*
     - ○ Example: *"No thank you."*
     - ○ Example: *"I don't think I can."*

3. *Give a cover story for turning them down*
   - • Explain, *"People often want to know why they're being turned down, so it's nice to give a cover story or a reason for turning them down. Try not to be too honest if it will hurt their feelings."*
   - • Ask, *"What are some cover stories for turning someone down?"*
     - ○ Example: *"I just think of you as a friend."*
     - ○ Example: *"I'm sort of interested in someone else."*
     - ○ Example: *"I'm dating someone right now."* (Don't say this if it's not true.)

4. *Thank them for asking you out*
   - • Explain, *"It's generally considered a compliment when someone wants to date you, even if you're not interested in them. That means it's nice to thank them for the offer. How might you thank them for asking you out?"*
     - ○ Example: *"Thanks for asking though."*
     - ○ Example: *"Thanks anyway, I'm flattered."*
     - ○ Example: *"That's nice of you to ask."*

5. *Shift the subject back to the common interest*
   - • Say, *"The next step for turning someone down is to shift the subject back to the common interest. Why is it a good idea to shift the subject back to what you were talking about before?"*
     - ○ Answers: Because it's awkward to focus on the rejection; it's better to shift away from the offer and talk about your **common interest** again.

6. *Use a cover story before exiting*
   - Say, *"At some point, the conversation will come to an end. It's best to have a cover story for leaving. Why is it important to have a cover story for leaving?"*
     - Answer: So it doesn't seem like you're running away because you're embarrassed or uncomfortable.

- Explain, *"While you're following the steps for turning someone down, you need to do a few more things."*
- *Keep it friendly*
  - Say, *"It's important to keep it friendly when you're turning someone down. Why it is important to keep it friendly?"*
    - Answer: Because it's awkward for both of you if it doesn't feel friendly.

- *Don't say yes just because you don't know how to say no*
  - Say, *"Sometimes it can feel awkward to turn someone down, but what could be the problem with saying 'yes' because you don't know how to say 'no'?"*
    - Answers: It's not fair to go out if you don't like them; it will just prolong the inevitable; you shouldn't go out with someone you're not interested in.

- *Don't say yes because you feel sorry for them*
  - Say, *"Sometimes people feel guilty for turning someone down, but what could be the problem with saying 'yes' because you feel sorry for them?"*
    - Answers: It's not fair to them; it will just prolong the inevitable; you shouldn't go out with someone unless you're interested in them.

- *Don't laugh at them or make fun of them*
  - Say, *"Some people laugh and make fun of the people that ask them out. What could be the problem with laughing and making fun of someone who's asked you on a date?"*
    - Answers: It's mean; it's rude; you seem cruel; you could get a bad reputation; other people may not want to ask you out.

- *Don't tell others they asked you out*
  - Say, *"Although it could be tempting to tell people when someone has asked you out, what could be the problem with telling others that you've turned someone down?"*
    - Answers: People may gossip; it could be embarrassing for the other person; it makes you look bad; you might get a bad reputation; others might be afraid to ask you out in the future.
- [Optional: Show BAD and GOOD *Role Play Video Demonstrations* of **turning someone down** from the *PEERS® Role Play Video Library* (www.routledge.com/cw/laugeson).]

- Explain, *"Those are some of the ways young adults can ask someone on a date and also accept rejection and turn people down. Young adults are practicing this in the group today."*

Homework Assignments

[Distribute the *Social Coaching Homework Assignment Worksheet* (Appendix I) for social coaches to complete and return at the next session.]

1. Have a *get-together* with a friend.
   - **Social coaches should help young adults plan the get-together using the *five W's*:**
     - *WHO* **they plan to get together with.**
     - *WHAT* **they plan to do.**
     - *WHEN* **it will happen.**
     - *WHERE* **they will meet.**
     - *HOW* **they will make it happen.**
   - **Social coaches should go over the rules and steps for *get-togethers* with young adults beforehand.**

- Social coaches should ask young adults the following *social coaching questions* after the *get-together*:
  - *What did you decide to do and who picked the activities?*
  - *Did you trade information and for what percentage of the time?*
  - *What were your common interests and what could you do with that information if you were going to hang out again?*
  - *Did you and your friend have a good time?*
  - *Is this someone you might want to hang out with again?*

2. Practice *letting someone know you like them*.
   - If young adults are interested in someone romantically, use the strategies for *letting someone know you like them*.
     - DO NOT practice unless you are romantically interested in the person.
     - DO NOT ask the person on a date, as we have not covered the rules for having successful dates yet.
   - Young adults should practice *letting someone know you like them* and *asking someone on a date* with social coaches, if comfortable.
   - Social coaches should go over the rules and steps for *letting someone know you like them* and *asking someone on a date* before the practice.
   - Social coaches should ask young adults the following *social coaching questions* after each practice:
     - *Who did you practice with?*
     - *What did you do to let them know you like them?*
     - *How did they respond?*
     - *Does this seem like a good choice and is this someone you might want to go on a date with?*

3. *Enter a group conversation* with peers (could be from the *source of friends*).
   - Social coaches should go over the rules and steps for *entering and exiting group conversations* before the practice.
   - The assignment is NOT to *exit the conversation* unless they naturally need to.
   - Social coaches should ask young adults the following *social coaching questions* after the practice:
     - *Where did you enter a conversation and with whom?*
     - *Which steps did you follow?*
     - *Did it seem like they wanted to talk to you and how could you tell?*
     - *Did you have to exit the conversation and which steps did you follow?*

Social Coaching Tips

For young adults interested in dating and forming romantic relationships, the following *Social Coaching Tips* are suggested:

- Encourage young adults to continue to practice **letting someone know they like them**, if appropriate.
- Discourage young adults from **asking someone out on a date**, as we have not covered the skills related to having successful dates yet.
  - If they insist on planning a date now, make sure they schedule it for some time after the next lesson on dating etiquette.
- Young adults can practice **asking someone on a date** with their social coach, if they feel comfortable.
  - Review the steps before the practice.
  - Allow them to follow the steps for **asking someone on a date** by using the *Social Coaching Handout* during the practice if necessary.
  - Review which steps were followed after the practice.

DATING ETIQUETTE: ASKING SOMEONE ON A DATE

Young Adult Therapist Guide

Preparing for the Young Adult Session

The common social error made by young adults with Autism Spectrum Disorder (ASD) and other social challenges when **asking someone on a date** is to either randomly ask, *"Do you want to go on a date?"* with no buildup or context, or to simply not ask at all. Although many young adults with social difficulties are unsuccessful in developing and maintaining romantic relationships, most will say that they wish to have romantic partners and may even feel quite lonely.

The purpose of this lesson, as with all of the PEERS® dating etiquette sessions, is not to teach young adults how to casually date multiple people, how to be "players," or how to get lots of people to want to date them. The purpose of the dating lessons is to help motivated young adults develop and maintain close meaningful relationships with romantic partners. The first step in this process is to identify and find appropriate partners and let them know you like them. That was the focus of the previous lesson. The goal of the current lesson is taking these romantic interests a step further by learning how to **ask someone on a date**.

There are several good and bad *Role Play Demonstrations* and *Behavioral Rehearsal Exercises* in this session, focusing on: (1) **asking someone on a date**; (2) **accepting rejection**; and (3) **turning someone down**. Each of the six good and bad *Role Play Demonstrations* will include two parts: the asking and the responding. It is critical that when conducting *Role Play Demonstrations* of **accepting rejection** and **turning someone down**, the asking and responding is either all good or all bad. In other words, if you are going to demonstrate an INAPPROPRIATE example of **accepting rejection**, the behavioral coach should demonstrate **asking the person out** INAPPROPRIATELY and **accepting rejection** INAPPROPRIATELY. Likewise, if you are demonstrating an APPROPRIATE example of **accepting rejection**, the behavioral coach should demonstrate **asking the person out** APPROPRIATELY and **accepting rejection** APPROPRIATELY. To mix appropriate use of skills with inappropriate use of other skills would be confusing to the young adults.

Like the previous lesson, two behavioral coaches are required for this session: one male coach and one female coach. This is not only important to avoid heterosexism in the *Behavioral Rehearsal Exercises*, but to promote comfort through choice in practicing partners for young adults. The group leader is not included in any of the *Role Play Demonstrations* or *Behavioral Rehearsal Exercises* in this session (unless a second same-gendered coach is unavailable). This is because the **Perspective Taking Questions** asked across skills shift focus between the *asker* and the *responder*. Having the group leader ask him or herself the **Perspective Taking Questions** could be potentially awkward, but can be done in the absence of two coaches. As with the previous lesson, all *Behavioral Rehearsal Exercises* are conducted between young adults and behavioral coaches, not between group members, and all occur within the context of the *Didactic Lesson*.

Homework Review

[Go over the following *Homework Assignments* and **troubleshoot** any potential problems. Start with completed homework first. If you have time, you can inquire as to why others were unable to complete the assignment and try to *troubleshoot* how they might get it done for the coming week. When reviewing homework, be sure to relabel descriptions using the *buzzwords* (identified by *bold and italicized* print). Spend the majority of the *Homework Review* on *get-togethers* as this was the most important assignment.]

1. Have a *get-together* with a friend.
   - Say, *"One of the main assignments this week was for you to have a get-together with a friend. Raise your hand if you had a get-together with a friend this week."*
   - Ask the following questions:
     ○ *"Who did you have a get-together with and what did you decide to do?"*
     ○ *"Did you plan the get-together using the five W's?"*
     ○ *"How did the get-together begin?"*
     ○ *"Who picked the activities?"*
     ○ *"Did you trade information and for what percentage of the time?"*
     ○ *"How did the get-together end?"*
     ○ *"Did you and your friend have a good time?"*
     ○ *"Is this someone you might want to hang out with again?"*

Table 11.1 Steps for Beginning and Ending Get-Togethers in Your Home

Beginning the Get-Together	Ending the Get-Together
1. Greet your guest	1. Wait for a pause in activities
2. Invite them in	2. Give a cover story for ending the get-together
3. Introduce them to anyone they don't know	3. Start walking your friend to the door
4. Give them a tour	4. Thank your friend for getting together
5. Offer them refreshments	5. Tell your friend you had a good time
6. Ask them what they want to do	6. Say goodbye and you'll see them later

2. Practice *letting someone know you like them*.
   - Say, *"Another assignment this week was to practice letting someone know you like them. The assignment was NOT to practice unless you are romantically interested in the person. You could also have practiced with social coaches, if you were comfortable. Raise your hand if you did this assignment."*
   - Ask the following questions:
     ○ *"Who did you practice with?"*
     ○ *"What did you do to let them know you liked them?"*
     ○ *"How did the person respond?"*
     ○ *"Does this seem like a good choice and is this someone you might want to go on a date with?"*

3. *Enter and exit group conversations* with social coaches.
   - Say, *"Another assignment this week was to practice entering and exiting group conversations with your social coach and another person. Raise your hand if you did this assignment."*
   - Ask the following questions:
     ○ *"Who did you and your social coach practice with and which steps did you follow?"*
       1. *Listen to the Conversation*
       2. *Watch from a Distance*
       3. *Use a Prop*
       4. *Identify the Topic*
       5. *Find a Common Interest*
       6. *Move Closer*
       7. *Wait for a Pause*
       8. *Mention the Topic*
       9. *Assess Interest*
       10. *Introduce Yourself*
     ○ *"Did it seem like they wanted to talk to you and how could you tell?"*
     ○ *"Did you exit the conversation and which steps did you follow?"*

Table 11.2 Steps for Exiting Conversations

NEVER ACCEPTED	INITIALLY ACCEPTED, THEN EXCLUDED	FULLY ACCEPTED
1. *Keep your cool* 2. *Look away* 3. *Turn away* 4. *Walk away*	1. *Keep your cool* 2. *Look away* 3. *Wait for a BRIEF pause* 4. *Give a BRIEF cover story for leaving* 5. *Walk away*	1. *Wait for a pause* 2. *Give a SPECIFIC cover story for leaving* 3. *Say you'll see them later* 4. *Say goodbye* 5. *Walk away*

4. ***Enter a group conversation*** with peers (could be from the ***source of friends***).
   - Say, *"Another assignment this week was to practice entering group conversations with peers. Raise your hand if you did this assignment."*
   - Ask the following questions:
     - *"Where and with whom did you practice?"*
     - *"Which steps did you follow?"*
     - *"Did it seem like they wanted to talk to you?"*
     - *"How could you tell?"*
       - ***Talking to you?***
       - ***Looking at you?***
       - ***Facing you (they opened the circle)?***
     - *"Did you have to exit the conversation and which steps did you follow?"*

Didactic Lesson: Dating Etiquette: Asking Someone on a Date

- Explain, *"Today, we're going to continue talking about dating etiquette. Last week, we talked about who to date, where to find people to date, and how to let someone know you like them. This week, we're going to talk about how to ask someone on a date."*
- [Present the rules and steps for ***asking someone on a date*** by writing the following bullet points and ***buzzwords*** (identified by ***bold and italicized*** print) on the board. Do not erase the rules and steps until the end of the lesson. Each role play with a ⊙ symbol includes a corresponding role play video from the *PEERS® Role Play Video Library* (www.routledge.com/cw/laugeson).]

Before Asking Someone on a Date

- Explain, *"Before we ever ask someone on a date, we should have done a number of things to let the person know we like them."*
- Present each of the following strategies for ***letting someone know you like them***, and after each example ask, *"Why is it important to . . . (insert the behavior)?"*
  - ***Talk to mutual friends, if you have them.***
  - ***Flirt with your eyes.***
  - ***Give SPECIFIC or GENERAL compliments, depending on how well you know them.***
  - ***Ask them if they're dating anyone.***
  - ***Show interest in them by trading information and finding common interests.***
  - ***Laugh at their jokes when appropriate.***
- Explain, *"There are a few more things we need to do before we ever ask someone on a date."*
- ***Assess their romantic interest in you***
  - Say, *"We also need to assess their romantic interest in us. How can you tell if someone is interested in you romantically?"*
    - Answers: Mutual friends tell you they like you; they flirt back; they appear to enjoy your compliments; they show interest in you by ***trading information***; they ask about your dating status.
  - Ask, *"If they don't seem romantically interested in us, should we ask them out?"*
    - Answer: It's risky to ***ask someone out on a date*** if they don't seem romantically interested in you.

- *Find out if they have a girlfriend or boyfriend*
  - ○ Say, *"We also need to find out if they have a girlfriend or a boyfriend before we ask them on a date. Why is it important to know if they're dating someone?"*
    - Answers: It's disrespectful to ask someone out who is seeing someone else; they are likely to say *"no"* if they are dating someone; it could be awkward and embarrassing.
  - ○ Ask, *"How do we find out if they're dating someone?"*
    - Answers: You could ask a mutual friend; check out their relationship status on their social networking profile page (e.g., Facebook); you could ask them directly.

- *Consider your dating activity options using the five W's*
  - ○ Say, *"Before we ever ask someone on a date, we should also consider our dating activity options. This involves the five W's. What are the five W's?"*
  - ○ **WHO** will be there.
    - Explain, *"Before you ask someone out, you need to decide if this will be a one-on-one date, a double date, or a group date, but be prepared to be flexible."*
    - Ask, *"What is a one-on-one date?"*
      - □ Answer: Just the two of you.
    - Ask, *"What is a double date?"*
      - □ Answer: The two of you with another couple.
    - Ask, *"What is a group date?"*
      - □ Answer: Three couples or more.
    - Ask, *"What is a blind date and who is included?"*
      - □ Answers: **Blind dates** are when the two of you have never met; you may have been set up by friends or family; **blind dates** can be **one-on-one dates**, **double dates**, or **group dates.**
    - Ask, *"What is an online date and who is included?"*
      - □ Answers: **Online dates** are a kind of **blind date**, but with someone you met through an online dating website; **online dates** can be **one-on-one dates**, **double dates**, or **group dates**.
  - ○ **WHAT** you plan to do.
    - Say, *"Before you ask someone out, you need to think about what you're going to do. What should the activity be based on?"*
      - □ Answer: Your **common interests**.
  - ○ **WHEN** it will happen.
    - Say, *"Before you ask someone out, you need to think about when might be a good time for both of you. Do you need to be prepared to be flexible about the day and time?"*
      - □ Answer: Yes.
  - ○ **WHERE** you will meet.
    - Say, *"Before you ask someone out, you need to think about where you might meet. Where are places you might meet?"*
      - □ Answers: Meet them where the date is taking place; meet at their home or your home (only if you know them well); meet in some public place (especially if you don't know them well).
  - ○ **HOW** you will make it happen.
    - Say, *"Before you ask someone out, you also need to figure out how you will make the date happen. What are some things you need to figure out before the date?"*
      - □ Answers: How you will get there (transportation for BOTH of you); how you will get tickets; do you need to make reservations; how will you pay for things.

Asking Someone on a Date

- Explain, *"Once we've let the person know we like them, assessed their romantic interest, found out if they have a girlfriend or boyfriend, and considered our dating activity options, the next step is to ask the person out on a date. There are very specific steps to follow when asking someone on a date."*

Good Role Play: Asking Someone on a Date ⊙

[Two behavioral coaches should do an INAPPROPRIATE role play of *asking someone on a date*. If you do not have two behavioral coaches, the group leader can be a substitute for one of the coaches.]

- Begin by saying, *"We're going to do a role play. Watch this and tell me what (name of behavioral coach 2) is doing WRONG in asking someone on a date."*

Example of an INAPPROPRIATE Role Play

- Behavioral coach 1: (Looking at cell phone)
- Behavioral coach 2: (Walks over quickly, excited) *"Hi, (insert name). Do you want to go out with me?"*
- Behavioral coach 1: (Shocked, stunned, confused) *"Umm . . . I don't think so."*
- Behavioral coach 2: (Persistent) *"Oh come on. Go on a date with me."*
- Behavioral coach 1: (Uncomfortable, confused) *"No, I don't think so."* (Turns away to look at phone)
- Behavioral coach 2: (Persistent) *"No really, we should go out."*
- Behavioral coach 1: (Uncomfortable, annoyed) *"No, I really don't want to."* (Turns away to look at phone)
- Behavioral coach 2: (Persistent) *"But it would be fun!"*
- Behavioral coach 1: (Uncomfortable, awkward)

- End by saying, *"Timeout on that. So what did (name of behavioral coach 2) do WRONG in asking someone on a date?"*
  - Answers: Randomly asked the person out; there was no lead-up to the offer; didn't take no for an answer.
- Ask the following *Perspective Taking Questions*:
  - *"What was that like for (name of coach 1)?"*
    - Answers: Uncomfortable; awkward; annoying.
  - *"What do you think (name of coach 1) thought of (name of coach 2)?"*
    - Answers: Weird; awkward; desperate.
  - *"Is (name of coach 1) going to want to date or talk to (name of coach 2) again?"*
    - Answer: No.
- Ask behavioral coach 1 the same *Perspective Taking Questions*:
  - *"What was that like for you?"*
  - *"What did you think of (name of coach 2)?"*
  - *"Are you going to want to date or talk to (name of coach 2) again?"*

Steps for Asking Someone on a Date

Explain, *"When asking someone on a date, instead of randomly asking them out, there are specific steps we need to follow."*

1. **Wait for an appropriate time to ask**
   - Say, *"The first step for asking someone on a date is to wait for the appropriate time to ask. When are some appropriate times?"*
     - Answers: When no one else is around; when they're not in the middle of doing something; when you're both free to talk; when you're in person; when they're in a good mood.

2. **Trade information**
   - Say, *"The next step for asking someone out is to trade information. Why is it important to trade information before you ask someone out?"*
     - Answer: You don't want to randomly ask them on a date out of the blue.

- Ask, *"Should you have traded information multiple times before?"*
  - Answer: It is less risky to ask someone out that you know and have talked to several times.

3. **Mention your common interest**
   - Say, *"The next step is to mention your common interest. What common interest should you be mentioning?"*
     - Answer: The **common interest** you plan to suggest for your date.

4. **Ask what they're doing at a certain time**
   - Explain, *"After you've traded information for a bit and mentioned the common interest you plan to suggest for your date, the next step is to ask what they're doing at a certain time."*
   - Ask, *"How do you ask what they're doing at a certain time?"*
     - Example: *"What are you doing this weekend?"*
     - Example: *"What are you doing Friday night?"*
   - Explain, *"By asking what they're doing at a certain time, you protect yourself from possible rejection because you haven't actually asked them out yet."*

5. **Assess their interest**
   - Explain, *"After you've asked them what they're doing at a certain time, you need to assess their interest. What are some good signs and bad signs that they're interested in going out with you?"*
     - **GOOD signs**: They say they're available and are smiling; they seem friendly and enthusiastic; they say they're busy, but seem disappointed.
     - **BAD signs**: They say they're busy and seem uncomfortable; they mention a boyfriend or a girlfriend; they say they're available, but seem uncomfortable; they change the subject.
   - Ask, *"If they seem interested, can we proceed with asking them out?"*
     - Answer: Yes.
   - Ask, *"If they DON'T seem interested, should we proceed with asking them out?"*
     - Answers: No; **abort the mission**.

6. **Use your common interest as a cover story for going out**
   - Explain, *"If they seem interested, the next step for asking someone on a date is to use your common interest as a cover story for going out."*
   - Ask, *"What if your common interest is sci-fi movies, what could be a cover story for asking them on a date?"*
     - Answers: Going to the theater to see the latest sci-fi movie; watching sci-fi movies at one of your homes.
   - Ask, *"What if your common interest is sports, what could be a cover story for asking them on a date?"*
     - Answers: Going to a sporting event; watching a game on TV at one of your homes; going to some public place to watch a game together.
   - Ask, *"What if your common interest is Italian food, what could be a cover story for asking them on a date?"*
     - Answers: Going out to eat at an Italian restaurant; making an Italian meal together at one of your homes.

7. **Exchange contact information**
   - Say, *"If they say yes, the next step is to exchange contact information if you don't already have it. How do we exchange contact information?"*
     - Example: *"I should get your number."*
     - Example: *"We should exchange numbers."*
   - Ask, *"If they don't want to give us their number, is that a good sign?"*
     - Answer: No, probably not.
   - Ask, *"What should we do if they don't want to give us their number?"*
     - Answers: Don't try to force them; give them your number and tell them to give you a call or text; be casual; don't expect to hear from them.

8. **Tell them when you'll follow up**
- Explain, *"The last step for asking someone on a date is to tell them when you'll follow up with them."*
- Ask, *"When is it appropriate to call or text after getting someone's number or asking them on a date?"*
  - Answer: Within one or two days of getting their number or planning the date.
- Ask, *"What could be the problem with calling or texting the same day?"*
  - Answers: You could seem overly enthusiastic; they might feel uncomfortable or get **turned off**.
- Ask, *"What could be the problem with waiting three or more days to call or text?"*
  - Answers: You might appear disinterested; they might think you're playing games; they might think you're a player; they might get **turned off**.

Good Role Play: Asking Someone on a Date ⊙

[Two behavioral coaches should do an APPROPRIATE role play of **asking someone on a date**. If you do not have two behavioral coaches, the group leader can be a substitute for one of the coaches.]

- Begin by saying, *"We're going to do a role play. Watch this and tell me what (name of behavioral coach 2) is doing RIGHT in asking someone on a date."*

Example of an APPROPRIATE Role Play

- Behavioral coach 1: (Looking at cell phone)
- Behavioral coach 2: *"Hi, (insert name). How are you?"*
- Behavioral coach 1: *"I'm pretty good. How are you?"*
- Behavioral coach 2: *"I'm fine. So what did you do over the weekend?"*
- Behavioral coach 1: *"I got together with some friends and went to the movies."*
- Behavioral coach 2: *"Oh cool. Did you see that new sci-fi movie we were talking about?"*
- Behavioral coach 1: (Disappointed) *"No, but I want to see that one."*
- Behavioral coach 2: (Casual, friendly) *"Yeah, me too. (pause) Well, what are you doing this weekend?"*
- Behavioral coach 1: (Smiling, flirty) *"I don't have any plans yet."*
- Behavioral coach 2: (Casual, friendly) *"Well, do you want to go see it together?"*
- Behavioral coach 1: (Smiling, flirty) *"Sure. That'd be fun."*
- Behavioral coach 2: (Casual, friendly, flirty) *"Great. So I should probably get your number."* (Takes out phone)
- Behavioral coach 1: (Smiling, friendly) *"Sure. It's 310-555-1212."*
- Behavioral coach 2: (Puts number in phone) *"Okay cool. So why don't I call you tomorrow and we'll make plans."*
- Behavioral coach 1: (Smiling, flirty, friendly) *"That sounds good."*

- End by saying, *"Timeout on that. So what did (name of behavioral coach 2) do RIGHT in asking someone on a date?"*
  - Answers: **Waited for an appropriate time to ask; traded information; mentioned their common interest; asked what they were doing at a certain time; assessed their interest; used their common interest as a cover story for going out; exchanged contact information; told them when they'd follow up.**
- Ask the following *Perspective Taking Questions*:
  - *"What was that like for (name of coach 1)?"*
    - Answers: Nice; flattering; exciting.
  - *"What do you think (name of coach 1) thought of (name of coach 2)?"*
    - Answers: Nice; friendly; cute.
  - *"Is (name of coach 1) going to want to date or talk to (name of coach 2) again?"*
    - Answer: Yes.

- Ask behavioral coach 1 the same *Perspective Taking Questions*:
  - "*What was that like for you?*"
  - "*What did you think of (name of coach 2)?*"
  - "*Are you going to want to date or talk to (name of coach 2) again?*"

Behavioral Rehearsal: Asking Someone on a Date

- Explain, "*Now we're going to have each of you practice asking someone on a date with one of our behavioral coaches.*"
- Go around the room and have each young adult practice *asking someone on a date* with one of the behavioral coaches.
  - Be sure to have at least one male and one female behavioral coach for young adults to practice with.
  - If you only have one behavioral coach, the group leader can substitute for a missing coach of the same gender.
  - Ask, "*Who would you feel more comfortable practicing with, (insert name of female coach) or (insert name of male coach)?*"
- Ask the young adult what they like to do and tell them to imagine the behavioral coach shares that *common interest* and use that as a *cover story* for *asking them out on a date*.
- Encourage young adults to look at the board as they're following the steps.
  - You may need to point to specific steps as they're practicing.
  - Try not to stop the behavioral rehearsal while they're practicing.
- Provide *social coaching* as needed and *troubleshoot* any problems that may arise.
- End by giving a round of applause to each young adult after their practice.

Accepting Rejection

- Explain, "*Even when we follow all the steps for asking someone on a date, we sometimes get rejected. When this happens, it's important to remember that dating is a choice. We don't get to date everyone, and everyone doesn't get to date us. There are some very specific steps we should follow if we get rejected when we ask someone out.*"

Bad Role Play: Accepting Rejection ⊙

[Two behavioral coaches should do an INAPPROPRIATE role play of *accepting rejection*. If you do not have two behavioral coaches, the group leader can be a substitute for one of the coaches.]

- Begin by saying, "*We're going to do a role play. Watch this and tell me what (name of behavioral coach 2) is doing WRONG in accepting rejection.*"

Example of an INAPPROPRIATE Role Play

- Behavioral coach 1: (Looking at cell phone)
- Behavioral coach 2: (Walks over quickly, excited) "*Hi, (insert name). Do you want to go out with me?*"
- Behavioral coach 1: (Shocked, stunned, confused) "*Umm . . . I don't think so.*"
- Behavioral coach 2: (Persistent) "*Oh come on. We should go out sometime!*"
- Behavioral coach 1: (Uncomfortable, confused) "*No, I don't think so.*" (Turns away to look at phone)
- Behavioral coach 2: (Persistent) "*Why not?*"
- Behavioral coach 1: (Uncomfortable, annoyed) "*I just really don't want to.*" (Turns away to look at phone)
- Behavioral coach 2: (Persistent) "*But it would be fun! Just one date?*"
- Behavioral coach 1: (Uncomfortable, awkward) "*No, sorry.*"
- Behavioral coach 2: (Angry) "*You're not sorry. You're just stuck-up!*"
- Behavioral coach 1: (Scared, looking away, trying to find an escape)

- End by saying, *"Timeout on that. So what did (name of behavioral coach 2) do WRONG in accepting rejection?"*
  - ○ Answers: Didn't take no for an answer; asked for a reason; pressured them; got angry.
- Ask the following *Perspective Taking Questions*:
  - ○ *"What was that like for (name of coach 1)?"*
    - ■ Answers: Uncomfortable; awkward; annoying; creepy; scary.
  - ○ *"What do you think (name of coach 1) thought of (name of coach 2)?"*
    - ■ Answers: Weird; desperate; creepy stalker.
  - ○ *"Is (name of coach 1) going to want to date or talk to (name of coach 2) again?"*
    - ■ Answer: No.
- Ask behavioral coach 1 the same *Perspective Taking Questions*:
  - ○ *"What was that like for you?"*
  - ○ *"What did you think of (name of coach 2)?"*
  - ○ *"Are you going to want to date or talk to (name of coach 2) again?"*

Steps for Accepting Rejection

- Explain, *"Instead of pressuring the person or asking for a reason, we should accept the rejection graciously and follow these important steps."*

1. *Keep your cool*
   - Say, *"The first step for accepting rejection when you ask someone on a date is to keep your cool. Why is it important to keep your cool?"*
     - ○ Answers: If you don't *keep your cool*, you will make them uncomfortable; you will look desperate or foolish if you lose your cool; you could get a bad reputation with others; other people might not want to date you.

2. *Make a casual statement of acceptance*
   - Say, *"The next step is to make a casual statement of acceptance. What casual statements could you make to show that you accept the rejection?"*
     - ○ Example: *"Okay. No big deal."*
     - ○ Example: *"That's cool. Just thought I'd ask."*
     - ○ Example: *"That's fine. No worries."*

3. *Shift the subject back to the common interest*
   - Say, *"The next step for accepting rejection is to shift the subject back to the common interest. Why is it a good idea to shift the subject back to what you were talking about before?"*
     - ○ Answers: Because it's awkward to focus on the rejection; it's better to shift away from the offer of a date and talk about your *common interest* again.

4. *Use a cover story before exiting*
   - Say, *"At some point, the conversation will come to an end. It's best to have a cover story for leaving. Why is it important to have a cover story for leaving?"*
     - ○ Answer: So it doesn't seem like you're running away because you're embarrassed or upset.

- Explain, *"While you're following the steps for accepting rejection, you need to do a few more things."*
- *Keep it friendly*
  - ○ Say, *"It's important to keep it friendly when you've been rejected. Why it is important to keep it friendly?"*
    - ■ Answer: Because it's awkward for both of you if it doesn't feel friendly.

- *Don't pressure them to go out with you*
  - ○ Say, *"When someone turns you down for a date, it's important not to pressure them to go out with you. That means don't force the issue and keep asking them out. What could be the problem with pressuring them to go out with you or asking again?"*
    - ■ Answers: It makes them uncomfortable; you seem desperate; they might think you're a creepy stalker; you could get a bad reputation and others may not want to go out with you.

- Ask, *"What if the reason they give could change at some point? For example, what if they say they don't want to date right now. What could you say?"*
  - Example: *"Let me know if you change your mind."*
  - Example: *"If something changes, let me know."*
  - Ask, *"Do you have to say that?"*
    - Answer: No.

- **Don't ask for an explanation**
  - Say, *"Even though we may be curious about why they said 'no,' do we get to ask for an explanation?"*
    - Answer: No.
  - Ask, *"What could be the problem with asking for an explanation when someone turns you down?"*
    - Answers: It makes you look desperate; it could make them uncomfortable; it's awkward.

Good Role Play: Accepting Rejection ⊙

[Two behavioral coaches should do an APPROPRIATE role play demonstrating **accepting rejection**. If you do not have two behavioral coaches, the group leader can be a substitute for one of the coaches.]

- Begin by saying, *"We're going to do a role play. Watch this and tell me what (name of behavioral coach 2) is doing RIGHT in accepting rejection."*

Example of an APPROPRIATE Role Play

- Behavioral coach 1: (Looking at cell phone)
- Behavioral coach 2: *"Hi, (insert name). How are you?"*
- Behavioral coach 1: *"I'm pretty good. How are you?"*
- Behavioral coach 2: *"I'm fine. So what did you do over the weekend?"*
- Behavioral coach 1: *"I got together with some friends and went to the movies."*
- Behavioral coach 2: *"Oh cool. Did you see that new sci-fi movie we were talking about?"*
- Behavioral coach 1: (Disappointed) *"No, but I want to see that one."*
- Behavioral coach 2: (Casual, friendly) *"Yeah, me too. (pause) Well, what are you doing this weekend?"*
- Behavioral coach 1: (Hesitant, slightly nervous) *"I'm not sure."*
- Behavioral coach 2: (Casual, friendly) *"Well, do you want to go see it together?"*
- Behavioral coach 1: (Slightly awkward) *"Actually, I'm kind of interested in someone right now."*
- Behavioral coach 2: (Casual, friendly) *"Okay. No big deal."*
- Behavioral coach 1: (Friendly) *"But thanks for asking."*
- Behavioral coach 2: (Casual, friendly) *"Sure. (pause) Anyway, you really should see that movie. I heard it was pretty good."*
- Behavioral coach 1: (Smiling, friendly) *"Yeah, I heard that, too. I'll totally check it out."*
- Behavioral coach 2: (Pause) *"Well, I better get to class."*
- Behavioral coach 1: (Friendly) *"Yeah, me too."*
- Behavioral coach 2: (Casual, friendly) *"Okay, I'll see you later."*
- Behavioral coach 1: (Friendly) *"Okay, take care."*
- Behavioral coach 2: (Casual, friendly, waves) *"Bye."*
- Behavioral coach 1: (Friendly, waves) *"Bye."*
- Behavioral coaches 1 & 2: (Start walking away)

- End by saying, *"Timeout on that. So what did (name of behavioral coach 2) do RIGHT in accepting rejection?"*
  - Answers: **Kept cool; made a casual statement of acceptance; shifted the subject back to the common interest; used a cover story before exiting; kept it friendly; didn't pressure them; didn't ask for an explanation.**
- Ask the following **Perspective Taking Questions**:
  - *"What was that like for (name of coach 1)?"*

- ■ Answers: Fine; flattering.
  - ○ *"What do you think (name of coach 1) thought of (name of coach 2)?"*
    - ■ Answers: Nice; friendly.
  - ○ *"Is (name of coach 1) going to want to talk to (name of coach 2) again?"*
    - ■ Answer: Yes, probably.
- Ask behavioral coach 1 the same *Perspective Taking Questions*:
  - ○ *"What was that like for you?"*
  - ○ *"What did you think of (name of coach 2)?"*
  - ○ *"Are you going to want to talk to (name of coach 2) again?"*

Behavioral Rehearsal: Accepting Rejection

- Explain, *"Now we're going to have each of you practice asking someone on a date and accepting rejection with one of our behavioral coaches."*
- Go around the room and have each young adult practice **accepting rejection** with one of the behavioral coaches.
  - ○ Be sure to have at least one male and one female behavioral coach for young adults to practice with.
  - ○ If you only have one behavioral coach, the group leader can substitute for a missing coach of the same gender.
  - ○ Ask, *"Who would you feel more comfortable practicing with, (insert name of female coach) or (insert name of male coach)?"*
- Ask the young adult what they like to do and tell them to imagine the behavioral coach shares that **common interest** and use that as a **cover story** for **asking them out on a date**.
- Encourage young adults to look at the board as they're following the steps for **asking them out on a date** and for **accepting rejection**.
  - ○ You may need to point to specific steps as they're practicing.
  - ○ Try not to stop the behavioral rehearsal while they're practicing.
- Provide **social coaching** as needed and **troubleshoot** any problems that may arise.
- End by giving a round of applause to each young adult after their practice.

Turning Someone Down

- Explain, *"Sometimes people we're not interested in may ask us out on dates. When this happens, it's important to remember that dating is a choice. We don't get to date everyone, and everyone doesn't get to date us. That means we don't have to say yes just because someone asks us out. There are some very specific steps we should follow if we need to turn someone down when they ask us out."*

Bad Role Play: Turning Someone Down ⏵

[Two behavioral coaches should do an INAPPROPRIATE role play of **turning someone down**. If you do not have two behavioral coaches, the group leader can be a substitute for one of the coaches.]

- Begin by saying, *"We're going to do a role play. Watch this and tell me what (behavioral coach 1) is doing WRONG in turning someone down."*

Example of an INAPPROPRIATE Role Play

- ○ Behavioral coach 1: (Looking at cell phone)
- ○ Behavioral coach 2: (Walks over quickly, excited) *"Hi, (insert name). Do you want to go out with me?"*
- ○ Behavioral coach 1: (Shocked, outraged) *"Are you kidding? No way!"*
- ○ Behavioral coach 2: (Persistent) *"Oh come on. We should go out sometime."*
- ○ Behavioral coach 1: (Laughs at behavioral coach 2) *"You must be out of your mind!"*

> ○ Behavioral coach 2: (Confused) *"Why not?"*
> ○ Behavioral coach 1: (Rude, making fun of behavioral coach 2) *"Why would you think I'd ever go out with you?"*
> ○ Behavioral coach 2: (Hurt) *"I thought it would be fun."*
> ○ Behavioral coach 1: (Annoyed, dismissive) *"Not in a million years."*

- End by saying, *"Timeout on that. So what did (name of behavioral coach 1) do WRONG in turning someone down?"*
  - ○ Answers: Acted rudely; made fun of them; laughed at them.
- Ask the following *Perspective Taking Questions*:
  - ○ *"What was that like for (name of coach 2)?"*
    - ■ Answers: Embarrassing; hurtful; upsetting.
  - ○ *"What do you think (name of coach 2) thought of (name of coach 1)?"*
    - ■ Answers: Mean; cruel; stuck-up.
  - ○ *"Is (name of coach 2) going to want to talk to (name of coach 1) again?"*
    - ■ Answer: No.
- Ask behavioral coach 2 the same *Perspective Taking Questions*:
  - ○ *"What was that like for you?"*
  - ○ *"What did you think of (name of coach 1)?"*
  - ○ *"Are you going to want to talk to (name of coach 1) again?"*

Steps for Turning Someone Down

Explain, *"Instead of being rude, laughing, or making fun of the other person, we should kindly turn them down following these important steps."*

1. *Keep your cool*
   - Say, *"The first step for turning someone down that asks you on a date is to keep your cool. Why is it important to keep your cool?"*
     - ○ Answers: Because if you lose your cool you might embarrass the other person; you might make them feel bad; you could seem mean or rude; you could get a bad reputation; other people might not want to date you.

2. *Politely turn them down*
   - Say, *"The next step is to politely turn them down. How do we politely turn someone down?"*
     - ○ Example: *"I don't think so."*
     - ○ Example: *"No thank you."*
     - ○ Example: *"I don't think I can."*

3. *Give a cover story for turning them down*
   - Explain, *"People often want to know why they're being turned down, so it's nice to give a cover story or a reason for turning them down. Try not to be too honest if it will hurt their feelings."*
   - Ask, *"What are some cover stories for turning someone down?"*
     - ○ Example: *"I just think of you as a friend."*
     - ○ Example: *"I'm sort of interested in someone else."*
     - ○ Example: *"I'm dating someone right now."* (Don't say this if it's not true.)

4. *Thank them for asking you out*
   - Explain, *"It's generally considered a compliment when someone wants to date you, even if you're not interested in them. That means it's nice to thank them for the offer. How might you thank them for asking you out?"*
     - ○ Example: *"Thanks for asking though."*
     - ○ Example: *"Thanks anyway, I'm flattered."*
     - ○ Example: *"That's nice of you to ask."*

5. *Shift the subject back to the common interest*
   - Say, *"The next step for turning someone down is to shift the subject back to the common interest. Why is it a good idea to shift the subject back to what you were talking about before?"*
     - Answers: Because it's awkward to focus on the rejection; it's better to shift away from the offer and talk about your **common interest** again.

6. *Use a cover story before exiting*
   - Say, *"At some point, the conversation will come to an end. It's best to have a cover story for leaving. Why is it important to have a cover story for leaving?"*
     - Answer: So it doesn't seem like you're running away because you're embarrassed or uncomfortable.

- Explain, *"While you're following the steps for turning someone down, you also need to do a few more things."*

- *Keep it friendly*
  - Say, *"It's important to keep it friendly when you're turning someone down. Why it is important to keep it friendly?"*
    - Answer: Because it's awkward for both of you if it doesn't feel friendly.

- *Don't say yes just because you don't know how to say no*
  - Say, *"Sometimes it can feel awkward to turn someone down. Should you say 'yes' just because you don't know how to say 'no'?"*
    - Answer: No.
  - Ask, *"What could be the problem with saying 'yes' because you don't know how to say 'no'?"*
    - Answers: It's not fair to go out if you don't like them; it will just prolong the inevitable; you shouldn't go out with someone you're not interested in.

- *Don't say yes because you feel sorry for them*
  - Say, *"Sometimes people feel guilty for turning someone down. Should you say 'yes' just because you feel sorry for them?"*
    - Answer: No.
  - Ask, *"What could be the problem with saying 'yes' because you feel sorry for them?"*
    - Answers: It's not fair to them; it will just prolong the inevitable; you shouldn't go out with someone unless you're interested in them.

- *Don't laugh at them or make fun of them*
  - Say, *"Some people laugh and make fun of the people that ask them out. What could be the problem with laughing and making fun of someone who's asked you out on a date?"*
    - Answers: It's mean; it's rude; you seem cruel; you could get a bad reputation; other people may not want to ask you out.

- *Don't tell others they asked you out*
  - Say, *"Although it could be tempting to tell people when someone has asked you out, what could be the problem with telling others that you've turned someone down?"*
    - Answers: People may gossip; it could be embarrassing for the other person; it makes you look bad; you might get a bad reputation; others might be afraid to ask you out in the future.
  - Ask, *"Is it okay to tell your closest friends, social coaches, or your family?"*
    - Answer: Yes, but be kind and don't make fun of the person.

Good Role Play: Turning Someone Down ⊙

[Two behavioral coaches should do an APPROPRIATE role play demonstrating **turning someone down**. If you do not have two behavioral coaches, the group leader can be a substitute for one of the coaches.]

- Begin by saying, *"We're going to do a role play. Watch this and tell me what (name of behavioral coach 1) is doing RIGHT in turning someone down."*

Example of an APPROPRIATE Role Play

o   Behavioral coach 1: (Looking at cell phone)
o   Behavioral coach 2: *"Hi, (insert name). How are you?"*
o   Behavioral coach 1: *"I'm pretty good. How are you?"*
o   Behavioral coach 2: *"I'm fine. So what did you do over the weekend?"*
o   Behavioral coach 1: *"I got together with some friends and went to the movies."*
o   Behavioral coach 2: *"Oh cool. Did you see that new sci-fi movie we were talking about?"*
o   Behavioral coach 1: (Disappointed) *"No, but I want to see that one."*
o   Behavioral coach 2: (Casual, friendly) *"Yeah, me too. (pause) Well, what are you doing this weekend?"*
o   Behavioral coach 1: (Hesitant, slightly nervous) *"I'm not sure."*
o   Behavioral coach 2: (Casual, friendly) *"Well, do you want to go see it together?"*
o   Behavioral coach 1: (Slightly awkward) *"Actually, I don't think that's a good idea. I'm kind of interested in someone right now."*
o   Behavioral coach 2: (Casual, friendly) *"Okay. No big deal."*
o   Behavioral coach 1: (Friendly) *"But thanks for asking. I'm really flattered."*
o   Behavioral coach 2: (Casual, friendly) *"Sure, no worries. Just thought I'd ask."*
o   Behavioral coach 1: *"That's nice. (pause) Anyway, you really should see that movie. I heard it was pretty good."*
o   Behavioral coach 2: (Casual, friendly) *"Yeah, I heard that, too. I'll have to check it out."*
o   Behavioral coach 1: (Pause) *"Well, I guess we better get to class."*
o   Behavioral coach 2: (Casual, friendly) *"Okay, I'll see you later."*
o   Behavioral coach 1: (Friendly) *"Okay, take care."*
o   Behavioral coach 2: (Casual, friendly, waves) *"Bye."*
o   Behavioral coach 1: (Friendly, waves) *"Bye."*
o   Behavioral coaches 1 & 2: (Start walking away)

- End by saying, *"Timeout on that. So what did (name of behavioral coach 1) do RIGHT in turning someone down?"*
  o   Answers: **Kept cool; politely turned him/her down; gave a cover story; thanked him/her; shifted the subject back to the common interest; used a cover story before exiting.**
- Ask the following *Perspective Taking Questions*:
  o   *"What was that like for (name of coach 2)?"*
    ▪   Answers: Fine in the end.
  o   *"What do you think (name of coach 2) thought of (name of coach 1)?"*
    ▪   Answers: Nice; just not interested.
  o   *"Is (name of coach 2) going to want to talk to (name of coach 1) again?"*
    ▪   Answer: Yes, probably.
- Ask behavioral coach 2 the same *Perspective Taking Questions*:
  o   *"What was that like for you?"*
  o   *"What did you think of (name of coach 1)?"*
  o   *"Are you going to want to talk to (name of coach 1) again?"*

Behavioral Rehearsal: Turning Someone Down

- Explain, *"Now we're going to have each of you practice turning someone down with one of our behavioral coaches."*

- Go around the room and have each young adult practice **turning someone down** with one of the behavioral coaches.
  o   Be sure to have at least one male and one female behavioral coach for young adults to practice with.

○   If you only have one behavioral coach, the group leader can substitute for a missing coach of the same gender.

○   Ask, *"Who would you feel more comfortable practicing with, (insert name of female coach) or (insert name of male coach)?"*

●   Ask the young adult what they like to do and tell them the behavioral coach is going to pretend to share that ***common interest*** and use that as a ***cover story*** for ***asking them out on a date***.

●   Tell young adults to follow the steps for ***turning someone down*** when the behavioral coach asks them out.

●   Encourage young adults to look at the board as they're following the steps for ***turning someone down***.

○   You may need to point to specific steps as they're practicing.

○   Try not to stop the behavioral rehearsal while they're practicing.

●   Provide ***social coaching*** as needed and ***troubleshoot*** any problems that may arise.

●   End by giving a round of applause to each young adult after their practice.

DATING ETIQUETTE: ASKING SOMEONE ON A DATE

Young Adult Behavioral Rehearsal

Get-Togethers

Materials Needed

- Indoor games (e.g., video games, card games, board games).
  - If you are going to provide video games as an option, make sure there are enough gaming consoles that each group can play simultaneously together.
  - Do not use small, portable gaming devices as people have to wait to take turns and that can get boring.
  - Several decks of playing cards will be sufficient if you do not have these other resources.
- Optional: iPads or laptops for watching YouTube videos, surfing the Internet, or playing computer games.
  - If you are going to provide iPads or laptops as an option, make sure there are enough that each group can use them simultaneously together.
- [Note: Most PEERS® programs DO NOT have access to gaming consoles, iPads, or laptops. These are luxury items. Just providing a few decks of cards to keep the get-together *activity-based* will be fine.]

Behavioral Rehearsal

- Notify young adults they will be practicing *beginning and ending get-togethers*.
- Break up young adults into small groups (no less than three young adults per group).
- Have EACH young adult practice *beginning a get-together* following the steps.
  - Assign *hosts* and *guests*.
  - One young adult will be the *host*.
  - One young adult will be the *arriving guest*.
  - The other young adult(s) will be the *guest(s) that have already arrived*.
  - Begin by having the *host* verbally go over the steps for *beginning a get-together*.
  - You may need to provide Socratic prompting to young adults for identifying the specific steps for *beginning a get-together* by using some of the following *social coaching questions*:
    - *"What should you do when your guest knocks on the door?"*
    - *"What should you do when they're standing on the doorstep?"*
    - *"What should you do if they've never met your other friends?"*
    - *"What should you do if they've never been to your home?"*
    - *"Do you want to offer them something?"*
    - *"How will you decide what to do?"*
  - The *arriving guest* should step outside and knock on the door.
  - The *guest(s) that have already arrived* should be seated somewhere nearby.
  - Have the *host* follow the steps for *beginning the get-together*.

- ○ You may need to provide Socratic prompting to young adults if they have trouble following the steps by using some of the following *social coaching questions*:
  - ■ *"What should you do when your friend knocks on the door?"*
  - ■ *"Do you think your friend might want to come in?"*
  - ■ *"Have all of your friends met?"*
  - ■ *"Has your friend been to your home?"*
  - ■ *"Do you want to offer your friends something?"*
  - ■ *"How will you and your friends decide what to do?"*
- ○ Once the young adult has practiced, call a *"timeout"* and have the other young adults applaud.
- ○ EACH young adult should practice **beginning a get-together** as a *host*, an *arriving guest*, and a *guest that has already arrived.*
- Have young adults practice following the rules for how to behave **during the get-together** while **trading information**, **finding common interests**, and playing with games and items provided by the treatment team (e.g., video games, card games, board games, iPads, laptops, etc.).
- Have EACH young adult practice **ending a get-together** following the steps.
  - ○ Assign *hosts* and *guests*.
    - ■ One young adult will be the *host*.
    - ■ The other young adults will be the *guests*.
  - ○ Have the *host* verbally go over the steps for **ending a get-together**.
  - ○ You may need to provide Socratic prompting to young adults for identifying the specific steps to **ending a get-together** by using some of the following *social coaching questions*:
    - ■ *"Should you interrupt your friends to end the get-together?"*
    - ■ *"Should you just tell them to leave?"*
    - ■ *"How are they going to find their way out?"*
    - ■ *"Should you thank them for anything?"*
    - ■ *"What should you say if you had a nice time?"*
    - ■ *"What should you say if you're going to see them again?"*
    - ■ *"What's the last thing you should say as they're leaving?"*
  - ○ The *hosts* and *guests* should be seated before they begin the practice so that the *host* has to **stand up and start walking the guests to the door**.
  - ○ Have the *host* follow the steps for **ending the get-together**.
  - ○ You may need to provide Socratic prompting to young adults if they have trouble following the steps by using some of the following *social coaching questions*:
    - ■ *"Do you just tell your friends to leave, or do you need a reason?"*
    - ■ *"How will your friends find their way out?"*
    - ■ *"Do you want to thank them for anything?"*
    - ■ *"What could you say if you had a nice time?"*
    - ■ *"What could you say if you're going to see them again?"*
    - ■ *"What's the last thing you should say as they're leaving?"*
  - ○ *Guests* should actually leave and then come back at the end of the role play.
  - ○ Once the young adult has practiced, call a *"timeout"* and have the other young adults applaud.
  - ○ EACH young adult should practice **ending a get-together** as a *host* and a *guest*.

DATING ETIQUETTE: ASKING SOMEONE ON A DATE

Reunification

- Announce that young adults should join their social coaches.
  - ○ Have young adults stand or sit next to their social coaches.
  - ○ Be sure to have silence and the full attention of the group before starting with *Reunification*.
  - ○ Have young adults generate the content from the lesson while social coaches listen.
- Say, *"Today we talked about dating etiquette and how to ask someone on a date among other things. What are the steps for asking someone on a date?"*
  1. *Wait for an appropriate time to ask*
  2. *Trade information*
  3. *Mention your common interest*
  4. *Ask what they're doing at a certain time*
  5. *Assess their interest*
  6. *Use your common interest as a cover story for going out*
  7. *Exchange contact information*
  8. *Tell them when you'll follow up*
- Say, *"The young adults practiced asking someone on a date. They also practiced handling rejection and politely turning someone down, and the group did a great job. Let's give them a round of applause."*

Homework Assignments

Distribute the *Social Coaching Handout* to young adults and announce the following *Homework Assignments*:

1. Have a *get-together* with a friend.
   - Social coaches should help young adults plan the get-together using the *five W's*:
     - ○ *WHO* they plan to get together with.
     - ○ *WHAT* they plan to do.
     - ○ *WHEN* it will happen.
     - ○ *WHERE* they will meet.
     - ○ *HOW* they will make it happen.
   - Social coaches should go over the rules and steps for *get-togethers* with young adults beforehand.
   - Social coaches should ask young adults the following *social coaching questions* after the *get-together*:
     - ○ *What did you decide to do and who picked the activities?*
     - ○ *Did you trade information and for what percentage of the time?*
     - ○ *What were your common interests and what could you do with that information if you were going to hang out again?*
     - ○ *Did you and your friend have a good time?*
     - ○ *Is this someone you might want to hang out with again?*

2. Practice *letting someone know you like them*.
   - If young adults are interested in someone romantically, use the strategies for *letting someone know you like them*.
     - DO NOT practice unless you are romantically interested in the person.
     - DO NOT ask the person on a date, as we have not covered the rules for having successful dates yet.
   - Young adults should practice *letting someone know you like them* and *asking someone on a date* with social coaches, if comfortable.
   - Social coaches should go over the rules and steps for *letting someone know you like them* and *asking someone on a date* before the practice.
   - Social coaches should ask young adults the following *social coaching questions* after each practice:
     - *Who did you practice with?*
     - *What did you do to let them know you like them?*
     - *How did they respond?*
     - *Does this seem like a good choice and is this someone you might want to go on a date with?*

3. *Enter a group conversation* with peers (could be from the *source of friends*).
   - Social coaches should go over the rules and steps for *entering and exiting group conversations* before the practice.
   - The assignment is NOT to *exit the conversation* unless they naturally need to.
   - Social coaches should ask young adults the following *social coaching questions* after the practice:
     - *Where did you enter a conversation and with whom?*
     - *Which steps did you follow?*
     - *Did it seem like they wanted to talk to you and how could you tell?*
     - *Did you have to exit the conversation and which steps did you follow?*

Individual Check-Out

Individually and privately negotiate with each young adult and social coach:

1. *WHO* they plan to have a *get-together* with in the coming week.
   - *WHAT* they plan to suggest to their friends.
   - *WHEN* and *WHERE* they will suggest to their friends.
   - *HOW* they will make it happen (e.g., tickets, transportation, etc.).

2. How they will practice *letting someone know they like them* and with whom.

3. Where, when, and with whom they plan to *enter a group conversation* with peers.
   - Whether this is an accepting *social group* and how they can tell.

DATING ETIQUETTE: ASKING SOMEONE ON A DATE

Social Coaching Handout

Before Asking Someone on a Date

- *Talk to mutual friends, if you have them.*
- *Flirt with your eyes.*
- *Give SPECIFIC or GENERAL compliments, depending on how well you know them.*
- *Ask them if they're dating anyone.*
- *Show interest in them by trading information and finding common interests.*
- *Laugh at their jokes when appropriate.*
- *Assess their romantic interest in you.*
- *Find out if they have a girlfriend or boyfriend.*
- *Consider your dating activity options using the five W's.*
  - ○ *WHO* will be there.
  - ○ *WHAT* you plan to do.
  - ○ *WHEN* it will happen.
  - ○ *WHERE* you will meet.
  - ○ *HOW* you will make it happen.

Steps for Asking Someone on a Date

1. *Wait for an appropriate time to ask*
2. *Trade information*
3. *Mention your common interest*
4. *Ask what they're doing at a certain time*
5. *Assess their interest*
6. *Use your common interest as a cover story for going out*
7. *Exchange contact information*
8. *Tell them when you'll follow up*

Steps for Accepting Rejection

1. *Keep your cool*
2. *Make a casual statement of acceptance*
3. *Shift the subject back to the common interest*
4. *Use a cover story before exiting*
   - Other rules for accepting rejection:
     - ○ *Keep it friendly*
     - ○ *Don't pressure them to go out with you*
     - ○ *Don't ask for an explanation*

Steps for Turning Someone Down

1. *Keep your cool*
2. *Politely turn them down*
3. *Give a cover story for turning them down*
4. *Thank them for asking you out*
5. *Shift the subject back to the common interest*
6. *Use a cover story before exiting*
   - Other rules for turning someone down:
     - *Keep it friendly*
     - *Don't say yes just because you don't know how to say no*
     - *Don't say yes because you feel sorry for them*
     - *Don't laugh at them or make fun of them*
     - *Don't tell others they asked you out*

Homework Assignments

1. Have a *get-together* with a friend.
   - Social coaches should help young adults plan the get-together using the *five W's*:
     - *WHO* they plan to get together with.
     - *WHAT* they plan to do.
     - *WHEN* it will happen.
     - *WHERE* they will meet.
     - *HOW* they will make it happen.
   - Social coaches should go over the rules and steps for *get-togethers* with young adults before-hand.
   - Social coaches should ask young adults the following *social coaching questions* after the *get-together*:
     - *What did you decide to do and who picked the activities?*
     - *Did you trade information and for what percentage of the time?*
     - *What were your common interests and what could you do with that information if you were going to hang out again?*
     - *Did you and your friend have a good time?*
     - *Is this someone you might want to hang out with again?*

2. Practice *letting someone know you like them*.
   - If young adults are interested in someone romantically, use the strategies for *letting someone know you like them.*
     - DO NOT practice unless you are romantically interested in the person.
     - DO NOT ask the person on a date, as we have not covered the rules for having successful dates yet.
   - Young adults should practice *letting someone know you like them* and *asking someone on a date* with social coaches, if comfortable.
   - Social coaches should go over the rules and steps for *letting someone know you like them* and *asking someone on a date* before the practice.
   - Social coaches should ask young adults the following *social coaching questions* after each practice:
     - *Who did you practice with?*
     - *What did you do to let them know you like them?*
     - *How did they respond?*
     - *Does this seem like a good choice and is this someone you might want to go on a date with?*

3. *Enter a group conversation* with peers (could be from the *source of friends*).
   - Social coaches should go over the rules and steps for *entering and exiting group conversations* before the practice.

- The assignment is NOT to *exit the conversation* unless they naturally need to.
- Social coaches should ask young adults the following *social coaching questions* after the practice:
  - *Where did you enter a conversation and with whom?*
  - *Which steps did you follow?*
  - *Did it seem like they wanted to talk to you and how could you tell?*
  - *Did you have to exit the conversation?*
  - *If you had to exit, which steps did you follow?*

SESSION 11

DATING ETIQUETTE: GOING ON DATES

Social Coaching Therapist Guide

Preparing for the Social Coaching Session

The focus of this lesson is on having successful dates. The rules and steps are similar to those for get-togethers, so there will be some repetition of instruction. Although the majority of young adults in your group are likely to express interest in learning more about dating, it is possible that only a few will actually be actively dating. Consequently, the *Homework Review* on **letting someone know you like them** in this session may be limited. Moreover, not all caregivers will be familiar with the details of their young adult's romantic interests, so there may be even less reporting on these assignments in the social coaching group.

One common question that comes up in the social coaching group in relation to dating etiquette is how to handle issues around physical intimacy. One of the rules presented in this lesson is to **ask permission for any physical contact**. For example, young adults are advised to ask to give a hug or kiss before actually initiating this type of physical contact. The choice to include this rule relates more to the common social errors exhibited by those with Autism Spectrum Disorder (ASD) and other social challenges, and less about what is ecologically valid. In reality, probably only a small minority of people actually ask permission for physical contact. Instead, it is more likely that they read the social cues from their romantic partner in guiding attempts at physical intimacy. However, reading these social cues can be difficult for even the most socially savvy adults. For adults with less developed social cognition, who already struggle with picking up on social cues and reading the signs, knowing when their partner wants to take their relationship to a more physical level will naturally be more difficult. Consequently, it was decided that simply asking permission for physical contact would rectify any major faux pas in this area. Although asking, *"Can I give you a kiss?"* may not sound "smooth" to some social coaches, the truth is that if your partner wants to be kissed, they will be happy to say *"yes,"* and if they don't want to be kissed, be grateful you asked. **Asking permission for physical contact** helps to avoid some of the awkwardness created by misreading the signs. Although young adults rarely object to the idea of asking permission, occasionally you will have a social coach who doesn't feel this behavior is having *"good game."* Take this as an opportunity to explain that the purpose of teaching dating etiquette in PEERS® is not to teach young adults how to have "game" or become "players" when it comes to romance. Instead, the purpose of the dating lessons is to give young adults some basic skills needed to begin to develop meaningful romantic relationships.

Finally, it is important to note that there are many cultural differences when it comes to dating etiquette. Keep this is mind as you present these lessons and modify when necessary. In particular, how couples meet, who they choose to date, what they do on dates and with whom, and even who pays are all highly culturally laden. While this manual was originally developed out of research conducted in North American samples, and the content of the sessions will be most relevant to Western culture, there may still be tremendous differences in how people form romantic attachments even in Western society, so be prepared to be flexible with the material as needed.

Homework Review

[Go over the following *Homework Assignments* and **troubleshoot** any potential problems. Start with completed homework first. If you have time, you can inquire as to why others were unable to complete the assignment and try to **troubleshoot** how they might get it done for the coming week. When reviewing homework, be sure to relabel descriptions using the **buzzwords** (identified by **bold and italicized** print). Spend the majority of the *Homework Review* on **get-togethers** as this was the most important assignment.]

1. Have a **get-together** with a friend.
    *   Say, *"One of the main assignments this week was for young adults to have a get-together with a friend. Who completed this assignment or attempted to complete it?"*
    *   Ask the following questions:
        ○   *"Did you help your young adult plan the get-together using the five W's?"*
        ○   *"What social coaching did you do before the get-together?"*
        ○   *"What did your young adult decide to do and with whom?"*
        ○   *"How did the get-together begin?"*
        ○   *"Who picked the activities?"*
        ○   *"Did they trade information and what percentage of the time?"*
        ○   *"How did the get-together end?"*
        ○   *"What social coaching did you do after the get-together?"*
            ■   Appropriate **social coaching questions**:
                □   **What did you decide to do and who picked the activities?**
                □   **Did you trade information and for what percentage of the time?**
                □   **What were your common interests and what could you do with that information if you were going to hang out again?**
                □   **Did you and your friend have a good time?**
                □   **Is this someone you might want to hang out with again?**
        ○   *"Does this seem like a good choice for a friend and someone your young adult will want to hang out with again?"*

Table 12.1 Steps for Beginning and Ending Get-Togethers in Your Home

Beginning the Get-Together	Ending the Get-Together
1. Greet your guest	1. Wait for a pause in activities
2. Invite them in	2. Give a cover story for ending the get-together
3. Introduce them to anyone they don't know	3. Start walking your friend to the door
4. Give them a tour	4. Thank your friend for getting together
5. Offer them refreshments	5. Tell your friend you had a good time
6. Ask them what they want to do	6. Say goodbye and you'll see them later

2. Practice **letting someone know you like them**.
    *   Say, *"Another assignment this week was for young adults to practice letting someone know they like them. The assignment was NOT to practice unless they are romantically interested in the person. Young adults could also have practiced with social coaches, if they were comfortable. Who completed this assignment or attempted to complete it?"*
    *   Ask the following questions:
        ○   *"What social coaching did you do before the practice?"*
        ○   *"Who did your young adult practice with?"*
        ○   *"What did they do to let them know they liked them?"*
        ○   *"How did the person respond?"*
        ○   *"What social coaching did you do after the practice?"*
            ■   Appropriate **social coaching questions**:
                □   **Who did you practice with?**

    □   *What did you do to let them know you like them?*
    □   *How did they respond?*
    □   *Is this someone you might want to go on a date with?*
  ○   *"Does this seem like a good choice and is this someone they might want to go on a date with?"*

3. *Enter a group conversation* with peers (could be from the *source of friends*).
   - Say, *"Another assignment this week was for young adults to practice entering group conversations with peers. Who completed this assignment or attempted to complete it?"*
   - Ask the following questions:
     - ○ *"Where and with whom did your young adult practice?"*
     - ○ *"What social coaching did you do before the practice?"*
     - ○ *"Which steps did your young adult follow?"*
       1. **Listen to the Conversation**
       2. **Watch from a Distance**
       3. **Use a Prop**
       4. **Identify the Topic**
       5. **Find a Common Interest**
       6. **Move Closer**
       7. **Wait for a Pause**
       8. **Mention the Topic**
       9. **Assess Interest**
       10. **Introduce Yourself**
     - ○ *"What social coaching did you do after the practice?"*
       - ■ Appropriate *social coaching questions*:
         - □ *Where did you enter a conversation and with whom?*
         - □ *Which steps did you follow?*
         - □ *Did it seem like they wanted to talk to you and how could you tell?*
         - □ *Did you have to exit the conversation and which steps did you follow?*

Table 12.2 Steps for Exiting Conversations

NEVER ACCEPTED	INITIALLY ACCEPTED, THEN EXCLUDED	FULLY ACCEPTED
1. Keep your cool 2. Look away 3. Turn away 4. Walk away	1. Keep your cool 2. Look away 3. Wait for a BRIEF pause 4. Give a BRIEF cover story for leaving 5. Walk away	1. Wait for a pause 2. Give a SPECIFIC cover story for leaving 3. Say you'll see them later 4. Say goodbye 5. Walk away

- [Collect the *Social Coaching Homework Assignment Worksheets*. If social coaches forgot to bring the worksheets, have them complete a new form to hold them accountable for the assignments.]

Didactic Lesson: Dating Etiquette: Going on Dates

- Distribute the *Social Coaching Handout*.
  - ○ Sections in **bold print** in the *Social Coaching Therapist Guide* come directly from the *Social Coaching Handout*.
  - ○ Remind social coaches that terms that are in ***bold and italicized*** print are ***buzzwords*** and represent important concepts from the PEERS® curriculum that should be used as much as possible when social coaching.
- Explain, *"Today, we're going to continue talking about dating etiquette. So far, we've talked about how to let someone know you like them and how to ask someone out on a date. In this session, we're going to talk about going on dates. There are several phases for going on dates, including: planning the date, preparing for the date, staying safe on the date, beginning the date, during the date, ending the date, and after the date. We will talk about what young adults need to do during each of these phases."*

Planning the Date

- Explain, *"After you've asked someone on a date and they've accepted, you need to plan the details of the date. Even though you've probably already talked about what you're going to do and when you're going to go out, there are other details you need to finalize."*

- *Follow up using the two-day rule*
  - Explain, *"Part of planning the date involves following up to finalize the details. If you're interested in the person and you don't want to seem like you're playing games, follow up using the two-day rule. That means you should call or text one or two days after getting their number or asking them out."*
  - Ask, *"What could be the problem with calling the same day they give you their number or you ask them out?"*
    - Answers: If you call too soon, they might get scared off; you could seem overly enthusiastic; it might be a turnoff.
  - Ask, *"What could be the problem with calling three or more days after you get their number or ask them out?"*
    - Answers: If you call too late, they might lose interest; they might think you're playing games or trying to be cool; they might think you're a *player* or you seem disinterested; it might be a *turnoff*.

- *Use the five W's to finalize the date*
  - Ask, *"When you follow up, is this a good time to figure out the five W's to finalize your date?"*
    - Answer: Yes (but don't call it the *five W's*).
  - Ask, *"What are the five W's?"*
    - *WHO* will be there.
    - *WHAT* you plan to do.
    - *WHEN* it will happen.
    - *WHERE* you will meet.
    - *HOW* you will make it happen.

- *Confirm the plans right before the date*
  - Say, *"When planning the date, you also need to confirm the plans right before the date. Usually a day or two before the date is appropriate, depending on when you asked them out. Why is it important to confirm your plans?"*
    - Answers: Plans sometimes change; people sometimes forget their plans or get busy; it may not happen if you don't *confirm the plans right before the date*.
  - Explain, *"As social coaches, you can help young adults decide when the right time to confirm the plans for their date is."*

Preparing for the Date

- Explain, *"The next phase of going on dates involves preparing for the date. These are the things we need to do just before the date happens."*

- *Make sure your space is presentable*
  - Say, *"When preparing for your date, you need to make sure your space is presentable. That means if your date is going to where you live or driving in your car, you need to clean up your space. What could be the problem with having a messy home or car on a date?"*
    - Answers: Having a messy home or car is a sign of disrespect for your date; they might think you're a slob; it might be a *turnoff*.

- *Put away anything you don't want your date to share, see, or touch*
  - Say, *"Another important part of preparing for a date involves putting away any personal items you don't want your date to share, see, or touch. Why would it be important to put away these things beforehand?"*

- ■ Answers: Because you don't want to seem rude by telling your date they can't see or touch your things; it's easier to put personal items away in advance so they don't even know they're there.

- **Use good hygiene**
  - ○ Say, *"When preparing for a date, it's also important to use good hygiene. Why is it important to use good hygiene on a date?"*
    - ■ Answers: Good hygiene is a sign of respect for yourself and the person you're dating; poor hygiene is disrespectful to your date; it might be a **turnoff**.
  - ○ Say, *"As social coaches, you may need to provide assistance around good hygiene."*

- **Dress appropriately**
  - ○ Explain, *"When preparing for your date, you also need to think about what you're going to wear. It's important that you dress appropriately for your date."*
  - ○ **Your clothing should match the activity**
    - ■ Say, *"Your clothing should match the activity on your date. What is appropriate clothing for a date?"*
      - □ Example: Casual clothes for a sporting event.
      - □ Example: Nice clothes for dinner and a movie.
      - □ Example: Dressy clothes for a theatrical performance or a fancy restaurant.
    - ■ Explain, *"As social coaches, you may need to provide assistance around appropriate clothing for dates."*
  - ○ **Don't dress too provocatively**
    - ■ Ask, *"Do you think young adults should dress really provocatively for their dates and what could be the problem with that?"*
      - □ Answers: No; their date might get the wrong idea; their date might not take them seriously; their date might think they're just looking for a "hookup."
  - ○ **Try to look your best**
    - ■ Ask, *"Do you think it's important to try to look your best on a date and why is that a good idea?"*
      - □ Answers: Yes; when you try to look your best, it's a sign of respect for your date; it may increase your attractiveness to your date.

Staying Safe on the Date

- Explain, "When preparing for dates, it's also important to think about how to stay safe. For example, a lot of people use online dating websites to meet potential romantic partners. These websites can be very helpful as dating sources, but there are a few precautions we need to take when meeting someone we don't know well."

- **Don't give out your personal contact information at first**
  - ○ Say, *"One way to stay safe when online dating or going out with someone you don't know well is don't give out your personal contact information at first. What is personal contact information?"*
    - ■ Answers: Address; home phone number; last name.
  - ○ Ask, *"What could be the problem with giving out your personal contact information right away?"*
    - ■ Answers: You don't know the person; you don't know if you can trust them yet; you don't know if you want to see or speak to them again.
  - ○ Explain, *"As social coaches, you can help young adults decide when it's the right time to give out personal contact information."*

- **Google your date before you meet**
  - ○ Explain, *"When online dating or going out with someone you don't know well, another way to stay safe is to Google them beforehand. This doesn't mean you should cyber-stalk them, it just means you should check out their online activity and get some background about them before you meet. What are some ways you can do that?"*

- ■ Answers: Carefully review their online dating profile page; friend them on Facebook and check out their postings; if you know their first and last name, you can Google them.

- ● *Let friends and family know where you are and who you're with*
  - ○ Say, *"Another way to stay safe when dating is to let your friends and family know where you are and who you're with when you're on a date. Why would it be a good idea to let people know where you are and who you're with?"*
    - ■ Answers: It's safer when people know where you are and who you're with; if anything happens, people know how and where to find you.

- ● *Drive yourself to and from the date*
  - ○ Say, *"Another way to be safe during your date is to drive yourself to and from the date or find your own alternative form of transportation. Why is it a good idea to drive yourself to and from the date?"*
    - ■ Answers: It's safer; you can leave whenever you want to.
  - ○ Ask, *"What if you don't drive, how can you get to and from the date without accepting a ride from your date?"*
    - ■ Answers: Use public transportation; take a taxi; use Uber; get a ride from a friend, your social coach, or family member; walk or ride a bike there if it's safe and not too far.

- ● *Meet your date in a public place*
  - ○ Say, *"Another way to stay safe when online dating or going out with someone you don't know well is to meet your date in a public place where there are lots of people around. Why would it be a good idea to meet in a public place?"*
    - ■ Answer: It's safer when there are people around.

- ● *Don't go anywhere alone with your date at first*
  - ○ Say, *"Another way to stay safe when you're online dating or going out with someone you don't know well is not to go anywhere alone with your date at first."*
    - ■ *Don't get in the car with your date at first*
    - ■ *Don't take your date home at first*
    - ■ *Don't go to your date's home at first*
  - ○ Ask, *"Why would it be a good idea to avoid going somewhere alone with your date at first?"*
    - ■ Answers: You don't know the person; you don't know if you can trust them yet; you're less safe when you're alone.
  - ○ Explain, *"As social coaches, you can help young adults decide when it's safe to be alone with their date."*

- ● *Check in with friends and family before and after the date*
  - ○ Say, *"Another way to stay safe when online dating or going out with someone you don't know well is to check in with friends and family before and after the date. Why would it be a good idea to check in before and after the date?"*
    - ■ Answers: It's safer when people know what you're doing and when; if anything happens, people know what you're doing and how to find you; others know that you're safe so they won't worry.

Steps for Beginning the Date

- ● Explain, *"Now that we've talked about planning the date, preparing for the date, and being safe on the date, we need to talk about what to do at the beginning of the date. Just like get-togethers with friends, there are specific steps to follow for the beginning of dates."*

1. *Greet your date*
   - ● Say, *"The first step for beginning a date is to greet your date. How should you greet your date?"*
     - ○ Answers: Say hello and ask them how they're doing; some people will hug or give a kiss.
   - ● Say, *"If this is an online date or a blind date, you will also have to introduce yourself. How do people usually introduce themselves?"*
     - ○ Answers: Say, *"Hi, I'm (insert name)"*; some adults also shake hands when meeting for the first time.

2. *Invite them in (if meeting at your home)*
   - Say, *"Assuming this is someone we already know well, the next step is to invite them in if we're meeting in our home. This involves saying something like, 'Come in' and moving out of the doorway so they can come inside. What happens if we forget to invite them in?"*
     - Answers: They end up standing at the door waiting to come in; this can feel awkward for your date.
   - Explain, *"If you're planning to stay at your home for a while, inviting them in may also include taking coats, jackets, or umbrellas."*

3. *Introduce them to anyone they don't know*
   - Say, *"If this is a double date, group date, or you're meeting at your home and they don't know everyone, the next step is to introduce them to anyone they haven't met. Why is it important to introduce them to anyone they don't know?"*
     - Answers: If they don't know everyone, they might feel awkward; they'll feel more comfortable if they know everyone; you could seem inconsiderate if you don't **introduce them to anyone they don't know**.

4. *Show them around (if meeting at your home)*
   - Say, *"If you're meeting in your home and this is the first time your date has been there, you probably want to show them around a little. Why is it important to show your date around?"*
     - Answers: It's polite to **show your date around** if they've never been to your home; it could seem rude to not **show them around**.

5. *Offer them refreshments (if staying at your home)*
   - Say, *"If the date is taking place in your home, or if you plan to stay more than a few minutes, you should offer your date some refreshments. Why would it be a good idea to offer refreshments?"*
     - Answers: It's polite to offer food and/or drinks if you're in your home; your date might be hungry or thirsty; it might seem rude not to offer something.

6. *Ask about your plans*
   - Say, *"The last step is to ask your date about your plans. This helps you to transition to the next part of the date. How do you do that?"*
     - Example: *"So do we still have dinner reservations?"*
     - Example: *"Are we all set for the concert?"*
     - Example: *"Do you still want to watch the game?"*

- [Optional: Show BAD and GOOD *Role Play Video Demonstrations* of **beginning the date** from the *PEERS® Role Play Video Library* (www.routledge.com/cw/laugeson).]

During the Date

- Explain, *"So those are the steps for beginning the date. Now we need to talk about what to do during the date. There are a number of important rules that you need to follow during the date to help things go smoothly."*

- *Show interest in your date*
  - Say, *"When you're on a date, it's important to show interest in your date. How could you show interest in your date?"*
    - Answers: Ask him or her questions; listen to what he or she has to say; make good eye contact.
  - *Smile and make good eye contact*
    - Ask, *"How could smiling and making good eye contact be a way to show interest in your date?"*
      - Answers: When you smile, you show your date that you're enjoying their company; when you make good eye contact, you show that you're interested in your date.
    - Ask, *"Do we still need to flirt with our eyes by making eye contact, giving a slight smile, looking away, and repeating?"*
      - Answer: No.

- Explain, *"Flirting with your eyes is something you do when you don't know the person that well. Once you're on a date with someone, you can smile and maintain eye contact without looking away quickly."*

- *Trade information at least 50% of the time*
  - Say, *"One of the best ways to show interest in your date is by trading information. Why is it important to trade information with your date?"*
    - Answers: This is how you get to know each other; this is how you **find common interests**.
  - Say, *"Just like with get-togethers, we want to be trading information at least 50% of the time. Why is it important to trade information at least half of the time?"*
    - Answer: If we don't **trade information at least 50% of the time**, we may not get to know one another.

- *Laugh at their jokes*
  - Say, *"Another way to show interest in your date is to laugh at their jokes. What should you do if you don't think their joke is funny?"*
    - Answer: **Give a courtesy laugh**.

- *Be polite and respectful*
  - Say, *"During your date, it's also important to be polite and respectful. How can you be polite and respectful to your date?"*
    - Answers: Open and hold doors when appropriate; pull out chairs when appropriate; don't begin eating or drinking until their food or beverages have arrived; use good table manners; don't swear or curse; **don't be argumentative**; **don't police**; **don't tease or make fun of them or others**.

- *Ask your date what they want to do*
  - Ask, *"Why is it important to ask your date what they want to do?"*
    - Answers: **Asking your date what they want to do** is another way to **be polite and respectful** toward your date; it helps ensure that they have a good time.
  - *Don't make all the decisions*
    - Ask, *"What could be the problem with making all the decisions during your date?"*
      - Answers: You might seem controlling or bossy; they might feel like their interests are being ignored.

- *Go with the flow*
  - Say, *"During your date, you also need to be prepared to go with the flow. That means sometimes you need to be flexible and go with whatever is happening that you didn't expect. Why is it important to go with the flow?"*
    - Answers: Plans may change; your date may change his or her mind about what they want to do during the date.
  - Ask, *"What if your date wants to do something that feels unsafe or makes you uncomfortable. Then do you have to go with the flow?"*
    - Answer: No, you don't have to do things that feel unsafe or make you uncomfortable on a date.

- *Give your date compliments*
  - Say, *"It's also nice to give compliments to your date. Remember, this is the equivalent of verbal flirting. What are the rules about giving compliments?"*
    - **Give SPECIFIC compliments when you DON'T know the person well.**
    - **Give SPECIFIC or GENERAL compliments when you know the person well.**
    - **Avoid too many physical compliments.**
    - **Physical compliments should be from the neck up.**

- *Don't flirt with other people*
  - Say, *"When you're on a date with someone, what could be the problem with flirting with someone else during your date?"*

- Answers: It's rude; it's disrespectful; it might seem like you're a player; they might not want to go out with you again.
- *Don't invite people unexpectedly into your date*
  - Ask, *"What could be the problem with inviting people unexpectedly into your date?"*
    - Answers: Your date might think you're rude; he or she might feel neglected.
  - Ask, *"What if your date wants to invite people unexpectedly. What should you do?"*
    - Answers: **Go with the flow in the moment, and remember that dating is a choice; you don't have to go out with them again if it bothers you.**

- *Don't ignore your date*
  - *Don't ignore your date to talk to other people*
    - Say, *"During your date, it's also important not to ignore your date. That means you shouldn't ignore your date to talk to other people. For example, imagine you're on a double date or a group date, what could be the problem with ignoring your date to talk to other people?"*
      - Answers: It's not fun for your date; he or she might feel neglected or ignored; they might not want to go out with you again.
  - *Don't text or make phone calls during your date*
    - Ask, *"Should you be texting or making calls while you're on your date and what could be the problem with that?"*
      - Answers: You shouldn't text or make calls during your date; it's rude to your date; it's ignoring your date.
  - *If you're expecting an important call or text, let your date know in advance and apologize*
    - Ask, *"What if you're expecting an important call or text during your date. What should you do?"*
      - Answer: Let your date know in advance and apologize for the interruption.

- *Suggest a change if you or your date gets bored*
  - Ask, *"Do people sometimes get bored on dates and what should you do?"*
    - Answers: Yes; people may get bored; you should **suggest a change if you or your date gets bored.**
  - Ask, *"How do you suggest a change?"*
    - Answer: You can say, *"How about when we're done with this, we do something else?"*
  - Ask, *"What if your date doesn't want to do what you suggest?"*
    - Answers: **Go with the flow in the moment, and remember that dating is a choice; you don't have to go out with them again if it bothers you.**

- *Avoid risky topics*
  - Say, *"During the date, you probably should avoid talking about risky topics. This is especially true when you're first getting to know one another. What are some risky topics at first?"*
    - Answers: Politics; sex; religion.
  - Ask, *"What could be the problem with talking about politics, sex, or religion when you first start dating?"*
    - Answers: These can be emotionally charged topics; someone could be offended, get upset, or get their feelings hurt.
  - Explain, *"Eventually, you may want to talk about these topics, but it's risky when you're first getting to know someone."*

- *Avoid risky places*
  - Explain, *"During your date, you should also avoid going to risky places. That means avoiding places that might make you or your date uncomfortable. What is risky will depend on you and your date."*
  - Present the following examples by saying, *"What if you or your date . . . ?"* and then follow up by asking, *"What could be some risky places?"*
    - *". . . don't drink alcohol?"*
      - Risky places: Bars; night clubs; dance clubs; raves; fraternity parties; keg parties; certain concerts.
    - *". . . are allergic to or don't like seafood?"*
      - Risky places: Seafood restaurants; sushi restaurants.

- ■ *". . . have sensory issues?"*
  - □ Risky places: Concerts; sporting events; loud restaurants or bars; night clubs; dance clubs; raves.
- ■ *". . . are not interested in getting physically intimate?"*
  - □ Risky places: Hotel rooms; the bedroom in your home; the bedroom in their home; the back seat of a car.

- ● *Be prepared to pay*
  - ○ *The person who asked for the date should pay for the date*
    - ■ Explain, *"The general rule about dating is that the person who asked the other person out is supposed to pay. Should we still be prepared to pay even if we didn't ask the other person out?"*
      - □ Answer: Yes, absolutely.
    - ■ Ask, *"Should the same person have to pay every time?"*
      - □ Answers: Probably not; it's nice to take turns paying when possible; you should at least *offer to pay*.
  - ○ *Always offer to pay and be prepared to pay*
    - ■ Ask, *"We should always offer to pay and be prepared to pay on dates. Does that mean we should always have cash and/or credit cards whenever we go on dates?"*
      - □ Answer: Yes, absolutely.
  - ○ *Be prepared to "go Dutch" or "split the bill"*
    - ■ Ask, *"What if our date offers to 'go Dutch' or 'split the bill.' What does that mean?"*
      - □ Answer: It means you each pay for half or for your portion of the bill.
  - ○ *Use the two-offer rule*
    - ■ Explain, *"Sometimes it can get a little awkward when the bill comes at the end of a date. We should always be prepared to pay and we should always offer to pay. When offering to pay, we should use the two-offer rule."*
    - 1. *Start by offering to pay once.*
      - □ Example: *"Can I get this?"*
      - □ Example: *"Can I help out?"*
      - □ Example: *"Want to split it?"*
    - 2. *If they say no, offer a second time by saying, "Are you sure?"*
    - 3. *If they say no again, thank them.*
    - ■ Explain, *"It's also nice to offer to get the check next time if you plan to go out again. If you do this, you should actually pay the next time."*
    - ■ [Optional: Show *Role Play Video Demonstrations* of the **two-offer rule** from the *PEERS® Role Play Video Library* (www.routledge.com/cw/laugeson).]

Steps for Ending the Date

- ● Explain, *"Just like the beginning of dates involve specific steps that need to be followed, the ending of dates also have very specific steps."*

1. *Wait for a pause in the date*
   - ● Say, *"The first step in ending the date is to wait for a pause in the date. That means don't interrupt what you're doing unless you have to. What could be the problem with interrupting the date to end things?"*
     - ○ Answers: It may seem rude or abrupt; your date may think you don't want to spend time with him or her; it may seem like you're not having a good time.

2. *Have a cover story for ending the date*
   - ● Explain, *"Unless the date naturally ends when the activity is over, you'll need a cover story for ending the date. What are some examples of cover stories, or reasons to end the date?"*
     - ○ Example: *"Well, it's getting late."*
     - ○ Example: *"I guess I better get you home."*
     - ○ Example: *"Well, I have an early class tomorrow."*
     - ○ Example: *"I guess it's getting late and we have work tomorrow."*

3. *Thank them for going out or taking you out*
   - Say, *"The next step for ending a date is to thank them for going out or for taking you out. Why is it important to thank your date?"*
     - Answers: Because it makes them feel nice; it shows that you appreciate them.

4. *Tell them you had a good time if you did*
   - Say, *"The next step is to tell them that you had a good time if you did. Why is it important to tell your date if you had a good time?"*
     - Answers: It shows them that you enjoyed being around them; it makes them feel good; it lets them know you might be interested in going on another date.

5. *Start walking them out*
   - Say, *"Wherever the date may be, you will want to walk out together. That could mean walking out of a restaurant or a movie theater to go to different cars, it could mean walking them to their front door after dropping them off, or it could mean walking them to your door if you're at your home. Why is it important to walk your date out?"*
     - Answers: Because it's rude to make them find their way out; it's rude not to say goodbye at the door or as you're leaving some place.

6. *If you like them, suggest going out again*
   - Say, *"The next step as you're ending a date is to suggest going out again if you like them. How might you say this?"*
     - Example: *"Maybe we could hang out again this weekend."*
     - Example: *"Let's do this again sometime."*
     - Example: *"We should go out again."*
   - Ask, *"What if you don't like them? Should you make plans to go out again?"*
     - Answers: No, you should probably **move on; remember that dating is a choice; you don't have to date everyone and everyone doesn't have to date you.**

7. *Tell them when you'll follow up*
   - Say, *"If you like them and want to see them again, tell them when you'll call or text them next. How do you say that?"*
     - Example: *"I'll call you this weekend."*
     - Example: *"I'll text you in a couple days."*
     - Example: *"I'll give you a call tomorrow."*
   - Explain, *"Then you actually need to follow up when you said you would."*

8. *Say goodbye*
   - Say, *"The last step for ending a date is to say goodbye. This might include a casual 'bye' or 'see you later' or a wave. Some goodbyes even end with a hug or a kiss. But could it be really awkward to go in for a hug or a kiss and the person backs away?"*
     - Answer: Yes.

9. *Ask permission for any physical contact*
   - Say, *"To minimize the risk before we go in for a hug or kiss, we need to ask permission for any physical contact. How do you say that?"*
     - Example: *"Can I give you a hug?"*
     - Example: *"Can I give you a kiss goodnight?"*
   - Explain, *"If they like you, they will be happy to say 'yes.' If they don't like you, be glad you asked!"*

- [Optional: Show BAD and GOOD *Role Play Video Demonstrations* of **ending the date** from the *PEERS® Role Play Video Library* (www.routledge.com/cw/laugeson).]

After the Date

- Explain, *"After we've gone on a date with someone, there are a few things we need to do if we had a nice time and want to see them again."*

- *Make a follow-up call or text the next day*
  - ○ Ask, *"If you like the person and want to go out with them again, should you make a follow-up call or text the next day and why would that be a good idea?"*
    - ■ Answer: When you follow up the next day, it shows that you like them and had a good time.

- *Thank them for going out or taking you out*
  - ○ Say, *"When you follow up, do you want to thank them for going out or taking you out and why would that be a good idea?"*
    - ■ Answers: When you thank them for going out, it shows that you're interested in them; it shows that you appreciate them.

- *Tell them you had a good time if you did*
  - ○ Ask, *"Do you want to tell them you had a good time if you did and why would that be a good idea?"*
    - ■ Answers: It shows them that you enjoyed being with them; it lets them know that you like them.

- *Ask them out again if you like them*
  - ○ Ask, *"Would this be a good time to ask them out again if you like them, or suggest seeing each other again?"*
    - ■ Answer: Yes, definitely.
  - ○ Ask, *"What could be the problem with not suggesting going out again?"*
    - ■ Answers: They may not think you're interested; they may **move on** if you don't seem interested.

- Explain, *"So those are some of the rules and steps to follow when going on dates. Some of your young adults will be practicing this during the week if they have a date."*

Homework Assignments

[Distribute the *Social Coaching Homework Assignment Worksheet* (Appendix I) for social coaches to complete and return at the next session.]

1. Have a *get-together* with a friend.
   - Social coaches should help young adults plan the get-together using the *five W's*:
     - ○ *WHO* they plan to get together with.
     - ○ *WHAT* they plan to do.
     - ○ *WHEN* it will happen.
     - ○ *WHERE* they will meet.
     - ○ *HOW* they will make it happen.
   - Social coaches should go over the rules and steps for *get-togethers* with young adults beforehand.
   - Social coaches should ask young adults the following *social coaching questions* after the *get-together*:
     - ○ *What did you decide to do and who picked the activities?*
     - ○ *Did you trade information and for what percentage of the time?*
     - ○ *What were your common interests and what could you do with that information if you were going to hang out again?*
     - ○ *Did you and your friend have a good time?*
     - ○ *Is this someone you might want to hang out with again?*

2. Practice *letting someone know you like them, ask them on a date,* and/or *go on a date.*
   - If young adults are interested in someone romantically:
     - ○ *Let them know you like them.*
     - ○ *Ask them on a date.*
     - ○ *Go on a date.*
     - ○ DO NOT practice unless you are romantically interested in the person.

- Young adults should practice *letting someone know you like them, asking someone on a date*, and *beginning and ending dates* with social coaches, if comfortable.
- Social coaches should go over the rules and steps for *letting someone know you like them, asking someone on a date*, and *going on dates* before the practice.
- Social coaches should ask young adults the following *social coaching questions* after each practice:
  - *Letting someone know you like them*:
    - *Who did you practice with and what did you do to let them know you like them?*
    - *How did they respond?*
    - *Does this seem like a good choice and is this someone you might want to go on a date with?*
  - *Asking someone on a date*:
    - *Who did you ask on a date and what steps did you follow?*
    - *How did they respond?*
  - *Going on a date*:
    - *What did you decide to do?*
    - *Did you trade information and for what percentage of the time?*
    - *What were your common interests and what could you do with that information if you were going to go on a date again?*
    - *Did you and your date have a good time?*
    - *Does this seem like a good choice and is this someone you might want to go on a date with again?*

3. *Enter a group conversation* with peers (could be from the *source of friends*).
   - Social coaches should go over the rules and steps for *entering and exiting group conversations* before the practice.
   - The assignment is NOT to *exit the conversation* unless they naturally need to.
   - Social coaches should ask young adults the following *social coaching questions* after the practice:
     - *Where did you enter a conversation and with whom?*
     - *Which steps did you follow?*
     - *Did it seem like they wanted to talk to you and how could you tell?*
     - *Did you have to exit the conversation and which steps did you follow?*

Social Coaching Tips

For young adults who are currently (or are considering) online dating, the following *Social Coaching Tips* are suggested:

- Have a discussion about *GOOD choices* and *BAD choices* for online dating websites.
  - Examples of *GOOD choices*: Match, eHarmony, etc.
  - Examples of *BAD choices*: Craigslist, escort services, etc.
- Help your young adult create an account and assist with setting up his or her profile page.
  - Assist with creating appropriate written content and choosing photos.
    - You may need to take photos of your young adult to assist.
- Monitor your young adult's online dating activity, with their approval and collaboration.
  - Review their "matches" and discuss response strategies for communication.
- Start a dialogue about *GOOD choices* and *BAD choices* for potential online dates.
  - Examples of *GOOD choices*: People who share *common interests*, live in the same area, are around the same age, and are seeking a meaningful relationship.
  - Examples of *BAD choices*: People who do not share *common interests*, live far away, are much older or much younger, and are looking for a "hookup."
- Assist young adults with staying safe by using the strategies for *Staying Safe on the Date* outlined in the *Social Coaching Handout* for this lesson.

DATING ETIQUETTE: GOING ON DATES

Young Adult Therapist Guide

Preparing for the Young Adult Session

This lesson is the third of four sessions presented on dating etiquette. While several rules and steps of dating behavior are covered in these sessions, in reality the content merely scratches the surface. Future research using the PEERS® method will delve deeper into exploring additional topics such as forming committed romantic relationships, maintenance of these relationships, sexual intimacy and safety, and managing conflicts and breakups. In the meantime, the current curriculum addresses the basic rules and steps related to dating behavior.

In addition to the rules and steps for planning, preparing, and beginning and ending dates, this session also provides some strategies for how to behave during dates and how to *stay safe on dates*. The latter tools will be most useful for those engaged in (or considering) online dating. Among young adults seen for treatment at the UCLA PEERS® Clinic, the majority of those who were actively dating were connected with online dating websites and found their primary source of dates from these sites. Consequently, staying safe when online dating is a critical component to this lesson. Recommendations such as initially meeting in public places, checking in with family and friends before and after the date, and not going anywhere alone with your date will be highlighted. It's worth noting that these strategies are useful not only when online dating, but also when dating those with whom you don't know well.

Although the previous lesson on dating etiquette focused on how to ask someone on a date, the homework in the previous week did not include the assignment to actually ask someone out. That is because young adults still need the tools provided in this lesson for staying safe and having successful dates. Of the small minority of young adults seen at the UCLA PEERS® Clinic who were dating prior to entering our program, many reported having a handful of *first dates* (usually organized through online dating websites), but very few had *second or third dates*. This session is focused on helping young adults to have more successful *first dates* that lead to future dates. By avoiding many of the common social errors committed by those with social challenges, not to mention socially sophisticated young adults, we will be able to better promote the likelihood of developing more meaningful romantic relationships for those eager to find love.

Homework Review

[Go over the following *Homework Assignments* and **troubleshoot** any potential problems. Start with completed homework first. If you have time, you can inquire as to why others were unable to complete the assignment and try to **troubleshoot** how they might get it done for the coming week. When reviewing homework, be sure to relabel descriptions using the **buzzwords** (identified by **bold and italicized** print). Spend the majority of the *Homework Review* on **get-togethers** as this was the most important assignment.]

1. Have a *get-together* with a friend.
    - Say, *"One of the main assignments this week was for you to have a get-together with a friend. Raise your hand if you had a get-together with a friend this week."*
    - Ask the following questions:
        ○ *"Who did you have a get-together with and what did you decide to do?"*
        ○ *"Did you plan the get-together using the five W's?"*
        ○ *"How did the get-together begin?"*
        ○ *"Who picked the activities?"*
        ○ *"Did you trade information and for what percentage of the time?"*
        ○ *"How did the get-together end?"*
        ○ *"Did you and your friend have a good time?"*
        ○ *"Is this someone you might want to hang out with again?"*

Table 12.1 Steps for Beginning and Ending Get-Togethers in Your Home

Beginning the Get-Together	Ending the Get-Together
1. Greet your guest	1. Wait for a pause in activities
2. Invite them in	2. Give a cover story for ending the get-together
3. Introduce them to anyone they don't know	3. Start walking your friend to the door
4. Give them a tour	4. Thank your friend for getting together
5. Offer them refreshments	5. Tell your friend you had a good time
6. Ask them what they want to do	6. Say goodbye and you'll see them later

2. Practice *letting someone know you like them*.
    - Say, *"Another assignment this week was to practice letting someone know you like them. The assignment was NOT to practice unless you are romantically interested in the person. You could also have practiced with social coaches, if you were comfortable. Raise your hand if you did this assignment."*
    - Ask the following questions:
        ○ *"Who did you practice with?"*
        ○ *"What did you do to let them know you liked them?"*
        ○ *"How did the person respond?"*
        ○ *"Does this seem like a good choice and is this someone you might want to go on a date with?"*

3. *Enter a group conversation* with peers (could be from the *source of friends*).
    - Say, *"Another assignment this week was to practice entering group conversations with peers. Raise your hand if you did this assignment."*
    - Ask the following questions:
        ○ *"Where and with whom did you practice?"*
        ○ *"Which steps did you follow?"*
            1. **Listen to the Conversation**
            2. **Watch from a Distance**
            3. **Use a Prop**
            4. **Identify the Topic**
            5. **Find a Common Interest**
            6. **Move Closer**
            7. **Wait for a Pause**
            8. **Mention the Topic**
            9. **Assess Interest**
            10. **Introduce Yourself**
        ○ *"Did it seem like they wanted to talk to you?"*
        ○ *"How could you tell?"*
            ■ *Talking to you?*

- *Looking at you?*
- *Facing you (they opened the circle)?*
  ○ *"Did you have to exit the conversation and which steps did you follow?"*

Table 12.2 Steps for Exiting Conversations

NEVER ACCEPTED	INITIALLY ACCEPTED, THEN EXCLUDED	FULLY ACCEPTED
1. Keep your cool 2. Look away 3. Turn away 4. Walk away	1. Keep your cool 2. Look away 3. Wait for a BRIEF pause 4. Give a BRIEF cover story for leaving 5. Walk away	1. Wait for a pause 2. Give a SPECIFIC cover story for leaving 3. Say you'll see them later 4. Say goodbye 5. Walk away

Didactic Lesson: Dating Etiquette: Going on Dates

- Explain, *"Today, we're going to continue talking about dating etiquette. So far, we've talked about how to let someone know you like them and how to ask someone out on a date. In this session, we're going to talk about going on dates. There are several phases for going on dates, including: planning the date, preparing for the date, staying safe on the date, beginning the date, during the date, ending the date, and after the date. We will talk about what we need to do during each of these phases."*
- [Present the rules and steps for ***going on dates*** by writing the following bullet points and ***buzzwords*** (identified by ***bold and italicized*** print) on the board. Do not erase the rules and steps until the end of the lesson. Each role play with a ⏵ symbol includes a corresponding role play video from the *PEERS® Role Play Video Library* (www.routledge.com/cw/laugeson).]

Planning the Date

- Explain, *"After you've asked someone on a date and they've accepted, you need to plan the other details of the date. Even though you've probably already talked about what you're going to do and when you're going to go out, there are other details you need to finalize."*

- ***Follow up using the two-day rule***
  ○ Explain, *"Part of planning the date involves following up to finalize your plans. If you're interested in the person and you don't want to seem like you're playing games, follow up using the two-day rule. That means you should call or text one or two days after getting their number or asking them out."*
  ○ Ask, *"What could be the problem with calling the same day they give you their number or you ask them out?"*
    - Answers: If you call too soon, they might get scared; you could seem overly enthusiastic; it might be a ***turnoff***.
  ○ Ask, *"What could be the problem with calling three or more days after you get their number or ask them out?"*
    - Answers: If you call too late, they might lose interest; they might think you're playing games or trying to be cool; they might think you're a ***player*** or you seem disinterested; it might be a ***turnoff***.

- ***Use the five W's to finalize the date***
  ○ Ask, *"When you follow up, is this a good time to figure out the five W's to finalize your date?"*
    - Answer: Yes (but don't call it the ***five W's***).
  ○ Ask, *"What are the five W's?"*
    - ***WHO*** will be there.
    - ***WHAT*** you plan to do.
    - ***WHEN*** it will happen.

- ■ *WHERE* you will meet.
- ■ *HOW* you will make it happen.
  - ○ Explain, *"When you ask them on the date, you should have a general sense of what you're going to do and when, but use the five W's to finalize the plans when you follow up."*

- **Confirm the plans right before the date**
  - ○ Say, *"When planning the date, you also need to confirm the plans right before the date. Usually a day or two before the date is appropriate, depending on when you asked them out. Why is it important to confirm your plans?"*
    - ■ Answers: Plans sometimes change; people sometimes forget their plans or get busy; it may not happen if you don't **confirm the plans right before the date**.
  - ○ Ask, *"What are some examples of things you might say when confirming the plans for a date?"*
    - ■ Example: *"Just checking to see that we're still on for this weekend."*
    - ■ Example: *"Just wanted to make sure we're set for dinner tomorrow."*
    - ■ Example: *"Just calling to say I'll see you tomorrow."*
  - ○ Explain, *"Your social coaches can help you decide when the right time to confirm the plans for your date is."*

Preparing for the Date

- Explain, *"The next phase of going on dates involves preparing for the date. These are the things we need to do just before the date happens."*

- **Make sure your space is presentable**
  - ○ Say, *"When preparing for your date, you need to make sure your space is presentable. That means if your date is going to where you live, you need to make sure your home is presentable. What could be the problem with having a messy home on a date?"*
    - ■ Answers: Having a messy home is a sign of disrespect for your date; they might think you're a slob; it might be a **turnoff**.
  - ○ Say, *"If you're going to be using your car for the date, you also need to make sure it's clean inside and out. What could be the problem with having a messy car on a date?"*
    - ■ Answers: Having a messy car is disrespectful to your date; they might think you're a slob; it might be a **turnoff**.

- **Put away anything you don't want your date to share, see, or touch**
  - ○ Say, *"Another important part of preparing for a date involves putting away any personal items you don't want your date to share, see, or touch. Why would it be important to put away these things beforehand?"*
    - ■ Answers: Because you don't want to seem rude by telling your date they can't see or touch your things; it's easier to put personal items away in advance so they don't even know they're there.

- **Use good hygiene**
  - ○ Say, *"When preparing for a date, it's also important to use good hygiene. What's involved with using good hygiene?"*
    - ■ Answers: Showering using soap and water; washing your hair; brushing your teeth; combing your hair; wearing deodorant.
  - ○ Ask, *"Why is it important to use good hygiene on a date?"*
    - ■ Answer: Good hygiene is a sign of respect for yourself and the person you're dating.
  - ○ Ask, *"What could be the problem with having poor hygiene on a date?"*
    - ■ Answers: Poor hygiene is disrespectful to your date; it might be a **turnoff**.

- **Dress appropriately**
  - ○ Explain, *"When preparing for your date, you also need to think about what you're going to wear. It's important that you dress appropriately for your date."*

- ○ *Your clothing should match the activity*
  - ■ Ask, *"Do you think your clothing should match the activity on your date?"*
    - □ Answer: Yes.
  - ■ Ask, *"What is appropriate clothing for a date?"*
    - □ Example: Casual clothes for a sporting event.
    - □ Example: Nice clothes for dinner and a movie.
    - □ Example: Dressy clothes for a theatrical performance or a fancy restaurant.
  - ■ Explain, *"Your social coaches can help you figure out what's appropriate to wear for the date."*
- ○ *Don't dress too provocatively*
  - ■ Ask, *"Do you think you should dress really provocatively for your date and what could be the problem with that?"*
    - □ Answers: Your date might get the wrong idea; your date might not take you seriously; your date might think you're just looking for a "hookup."
- ○ *Try to look your best*
  - ■ Ask, *"Do you think it's important to try to look your best on your date and why is that a good idea?"*
    - □ Answers: When you try to look your best, it's a sign of respect for your date; it may increase your attractiveness to your date.

Staying Safe on the Date

- Explain, *"When preparing for dates, it's also important to think about how to stay safe. For example, a lot of people use online dating websites to meet potential romantic partners. These websites can be very helpful as dating sources, but there are a few precautions we need to take when meeting someone we don't know well or who we don't have mutual friends in common with."*

- *Don't give out your personal contact information at first*
  - ○ Say, *"One way to stay safe when online dating or going out with someone you don't know well is don't give out your personal contact information at first. What is personal contact information?"*
    - ■ Answers: Address; home phone number; last name.
  - ○ Ask, *"What could be the problem with giving out your personal contact information right away?"*
    - ■ Answers: You don't know the person; you don't know if you can trust them yet; you don't know if you want to see or speak to them again.
  - ○ Explain, *"As you get to know them better, you can begin to share more personal contact information if they're willing to do the same in return. Your social coaches can help you decide when it's the right time."*

- *Google your date before you meet*
  - ○ Explain, *"When online dating or going out with someone you don't know well, another way to stay safe is to Google them beforehand. This doesn't mean you should cyber-stalk them, it just means you should check out their online activity and get some background about them before you meet. What are some ways you can do that?"*
    - ■ Answers: Carefully review their online dating profile page; friend them on Facebook and check out their postings; if you know their first and last name, you can Google them.

- *Let friends and family know where you are and who you're with*
  - ○ Say, *"Another way to stay safe when dating is to let your friends and family know where you are and who you're with when you're on a date. Why would it be a good idea to let people know where you are and who you're with?"*
    - ■ Answers: It's safer when people know where you are and who you're with; if anything happens, people know how and where to find you.

- *Drive yourself to and from the date*
  - ○ Say, *"Another way to be safe during your date is to drive yourself to and from the date or find your own alternative form of transportation. Why is it a good idea to drive yourself to and from the date?"*

- Answers: It's safer; you can leave whenever you want to.
  - ○ Ask, *"What if you don't drive? How can you get to and from the date without accepting a ride from your date?"*
    - Answers: Use public transportation; take a taxi; use Uber; get a ride from a friend, your social coach, or family member; walk or ride a bike there if it's safe and not too far.

- *Meet your date in a public place*
  - ○ Say, *"Another way to stay safe when online dating or going out with someone you don't know well is to meet your date in a public place where there are lots of people around. Why would it be a good idea to meet in a public place?"*
    - Answer: It's safer when there are people around.
  - ○ Ask, *"What could be the problem with meeting away from the public?"*
    - Answer: It's less safe when you are alone.

- *Don't go anywhere alone with your date at first*
  - ○ Say, *"Another way to stay safe when you're online dating or going out with someone you don't know well is not to go anywhere alone with your date at first. Why would it be a good idea to avoid going somewhere alone with your date at first?"*
    - Answers: You don't know the person; you don't know if you can trust them yet; you're less safe when you're alone.
  - ○ *Don't get in the car with your date at first*
    - Ask, *"Should you get in the car with your date at first?"*
      - □ Answer: No.
  - ○ *Don't take your date home at first*
    - Ask, *"Should you take your date home at first?"*
      - □ Answer: No.
  - ○ *Don't go to your date's home at first*
    - Ask, *"Should you go to your date's home at first?"*
      - □ Answer: No.
  - ○ Explain, *"When we don't know our date well, it's safer not to go anywhere alone with them at first. Once you get to know them better, then you can start spending time alone. Your social coach can help you decide when it's the right time."*

- *Check in with friends and family before and after the date*
  - ○ Say, *"Another way to stay safe when online dating or going out with someone you don't know well is to check in with friends and family before and after the date. Why would it be a good idea to check in before and after the date?"*
    - Answers: It's safer when people know what you're doing and when; if anything happens, people know what you're doing and how to find you; others know that you're safe so they won't worry.

Beginning the Date

- Explain, *"Now that we've talked about planning the date, preparing for the date, and being safe on the date, we need to talk about what to do at the beginning of the date. Just like get-togethers with friends, there are specific steps to follow for the beginning of dates."*

Bad Role Play: Beginning the Date ⊙

[Two behavioral coaches should do an INAPPROPRIATE role play of *beginning the date*. If you do not have two behavioral coaches, the group leader can be a substitute for one of the coaches.]

- Begin by saying, *"We're going to do a role play. Watch this and tell me what (name of behavioral coach 2) is doing WRONG in beginning the date."*

Example of an INAPPROPRIATE Role Play

○ (Begin by having behavioral coach 1 step outside)
○ Behavioral coach 1: (Knocks on door)
○ Behavioral coach 2: (Opens door, stands there, doesn't say anything)
○ Behavioral coaches 1 & 2: (Long pause)
○ Behavioral coach 1: (Confused) *"Umm . . . hi, (insert name)."*
○ Behavioral coach 2: (Looking awkward, confused, stunned) *"Hi."*
○ Behavioral coaches 1 & 2: (Long pause)
○ Behavioral coach 1: (Confused, unsure what to do) *"How's it going?"*
○ Behavioral coach 2: (Looking awkward, confused) *"Pretty good."*
○ Behavioral coaches 1 & 2: (Long pause)
○ Behavioral coach 1: (Confused, awkward) *"Did I get the time right? We said 7 o'clock, right?"*
○ Behavioral coach 2: (Surprised) *"Oh . . . yeah."* (Doesn't move out of the doorway)
○ Behavioral coach 1: (Confused, awkward) *"Should I come in or should we just go?"*
○ Behavioral coach 2: (Surprised) *"Oh . . . we can just go."* (Starts to walk out the door)
○ Behavioral coach 1: (Uncomfortable, awkward, confused)

- End by saying, *"Timeout on that. So what did (name of behavioral coach 2) do WRONG in beginning the date?"*
  ○ Answers: Awkwardly stood on the doorstep; never invited the date in.
- Ask the following *Perspective Taking Questions*:
  ○ *"What was that like for (name of coach 1)?"*
    ■ Answers: Uncomfortable, awkward; confusing.
  ○ *"What do you think (name of coach 1) thought of (name of coach 2)?"*
    ■ Answers: Odd; strange; weird; bad date.
  ○ *"Is (name of coach 1) going to want to go on a date with (name of coach 2) again?"*
    ■ Answer: Not sure; not a good start.
- Ask behavioral coach 1 the same *Perspective Taking Questions*:
  ○ *"What was that like for you?"*
  ○ *"What did you think of (name of coach 2)?"*
  ○ *"Would you want to go on a date with (name of coach 2) again?"*

Steps for Beginning the Date

- Explain, *"Instead of having an awkward start, we need to follow the steps for beginning the date, which are similar to the steps for beginning get-togethers."*

1. **Greet your date**
   - Say, *"The first step for beginning a date is to greet your date. How should you greet your date?"*
     ○ Answers: Say hello and ask them how they're doing; some people will hug or give a kiss.
   - Ask, *"If we want to give them a hug or kiss hello, should we ask them first?"*
     ○ Answer: It's less risky to ask before you give a hug or kiss, rather than assuming they are comfortable with that.
   - Say, *"If this is an online date or a blind date, you will also have to introduce yourself. How do people usually introduce themselves?"*
     ○ Answers: Say, *"Hi, I'm (insert name)"*; some adults also shake hands when meeting for the first time.

2. **Invite them in (if meeting at your home)**
   - Say, *"Assuming this is someone we already know well, the next step is to invite them in if we're meeting in our home. This involves saying something like, 'Come in' and moving out of the doorway so they can come inside. What happens if we forget to invite them in?"*
     ○ Answers: They end up standing at the door waiting to come in; this can feel awkward for your date.

- Explain, *"If you're planning to stay at your home for a while, inviting them in may also include taking coats, jackets, or umbrellas."*

3. ***Introduce them to anyone they don't know***
   - Say, *"If this is a double date, group date, or you're meeting at your home and they don't know everyone, the next step is to introduce them to anyone they haven't met. Why is it important to introduce them to anyone they don't know?"*
     - Answers: If they don't know everyone, they might feel awkward; they'll feel more comfortable if they know everyone; you could seem inconsiderate if you don't **introduce them to anyone they don't know**.

4. ***Show them around (if meeting at your home)***
   - Say, *"If you're meeting in your home and this is the first time your date has been there, you probably want to show them around a little. Why is it important to show your date around?"*
     - Answers: It's polite to **show your date around** if they've never been to your home; it could seem rude to not show them around.

5. ***Offer them refreshments (if staying at your home)***
   - Say, *"If the date is taking place in your home, or if you plan to stay more than a few minutes, you should offer your date some refreshments. Why would it be a good idea to offer refreshments?"*
     - Answers: It's polite to offer food and/or drinks if you're in your home; your date might be hungry or thirsty; it might seem rude not to offer something.

6. ***Ask about your plans***
   - Say, *"Even though you should have planned what you're going to do on your date, should you still ask your date about your plans?"*
     - Answer: Yes.
   - Ask, *"How do you ask about your plans?"*
     - Example: *"So do we still have dinner reservations?"*
     - Example: *"Are we all set for the concert?"*
     - Example: *"Do you still want to watch the game?"*
   - Explain, *"Asking about your plans not only helps you to transition to the next part of the date, but gives your date the opportunity to suggest or mention any changes. If there are changes to the plan, be prepared to go with the flow."*

Good Role Play: Beginning the Date ⊙

[The group leader and two behavioral coaches should do an APPROPRIATE role play demonstrating **beginning the date**. If you do not have two behavioral coaches, the group leader can be a substitute for one of the coaches, and a young adult can substitute for the group leader, playing the part of the roommate.]

- Begin by saying, *"We're going to do another role play. Watch this and tell me what (name of behavioral coach 2) is doing RIGHT in beginning the date."*

> Example of an APPROPRIATE Role Play
>
> - (Begin by having behavioral coach 1 step outside)
> - Behavioral coach 1: (Knocks on door)
> - Behavioral coach 2: (Opens door) *"Hi, (insert name)! How are you?"*
> - Behavioral coach 1: *"Hi! I'm fine. How are you?"*
> - Behavioral coach 2: *"Fine, thanks. Come on in."* (Moves aside so behavioral coach 1 can enter)
> - Behavioral coach 1: (Enters) *"Thanks."*
> - Behavioral coach 2: *"I don't think you've met my roommate before. This is (insert name). This is (insert name)."*
> - Behavioral coach 1: *"Nice to meet you."*

○ Group leader: *"You too."*
○ Behavioral coach 2: *"I think I mentioned that (insert name) works at the restaurant we're going to, so we're going to see him/her later."*
○ Behavioral coach 1: *"That's cool."*
○ Behavioral coach 2: (Pause) *"So I know you've never been here before, so let me just show you around real quick."*
○ Behavioral coach 1: *"Thanks."*
○ Behavioral coach 2: (Give a brief imaginary tour)
○ Behavioral coach 2: *"Can I get you something to eat or drink before we go?"*
○ Behavioral coach 1: *"I'm okay. Thanks anyway."*
○ Behavioral coach 2: *"I'm not sure how much time we have before our reservation. Did you want to hang out for a bit or should we get going?"*
○ Behavioral coach 1: *"Maybe we should get going?"*
○ Behavioral coach 2: *"Sure. Sounds good."*

- End by saying, *"Timeout on that. So what did (name of behavioral coach 2) do RIGHT in beginning the date?"*
  ○ Answers: **Greeted the date**; **invited the date in**; **introduced people**; **showed the date around**; **offered refreshments**; **asked about the plans**.
- Ask the following *Perspective Taking Questions*:
  ○ *"What was that like for (name of coach 1)?"*
    ■ Answers: Fine; normal.
  ○ *"What do you think (name of coach 1) thought of (name of coach 2)?"*
    ■ Answers: Friendly; normal; a good date.
  ○ *"Is (name of coach 1) going to want to go on a date with (name of coach 2) again?"*
    ■ Answer: Probably; so far, so good.
- Ask behavioral coach 1 the same *Perspective Taking Questions*:
  ○ *"What was that like for you?"*
  ○ *"What did you think of (name of coach 2)?"*
  ○ *"Would you want to go on a date with (name of coach 2) again?"*

During the Date

- Explain, *"So those are the steps for beginning the date. Now we need to talk about what to do during the date. There are a number of important rules that you need to follow during the date to help things go smoothly."*

- *Show interest in your date*
  ○ Say, *"When you're on a date, it's important to show interest in your date. How could you show interest in your date?"*
    ■ Answers: Ask him or her questions; listen to what he or she has to say; make good eye contact.

- *Smile and make good eye contact*
  ○ Ask, *"How could smiling and making good eye contact be a way to show interest in your date?"*
    ■ Answers: When you smile, you show your date that you're enjoying their company; when you make good eye contact, you show that you're interested in your date.
  ○ Ask, *"Do we still need to flirt with our eyes by making eye contact, giving a slight smile, looking away, and repeating?"*
    ■ Answer: No.
  ○ Explain, *"Flirting with your eyes is something you do when you don't know the person that well. Once you're on a date with someone, you can smile and maintain eye contact without looking away quickly."*

- *Trade information at least 50% of the time*
  - ○ Say, *"One of the best ways to show interest in your date is by trading information. Why is it important to trade information with your date?"*
    - ■ Answers: This is how you get to know each other; this is how you find ***common interests***.
  - ○ Say, *"Just like with get-togethers, we want to be trading information at least 50% of the time. Why is it important to trade information at least half of the time?"*
    - ■ Answer: If we don't ***trade information at least 50% of the time***, we may not get to know one another.
  - ○ Ask, *"What if you decide to go to a movie, should you be trading information throughout half of the movie?"*
    - ■ Answers: No; you should schedule time to talk and hang out before and/or after the movie so you can get to know one another.

- *Laugh at their jokes*
  - ○ Say, *"Another way to show interest in your date is to laugh at their jokes. What should you do if you don't think their joke is funny?"*
    - ■ Answer: ***Give a courtesy laugh***.
  - ○ Ask, *"Why would it be important to give a courtesy laugh if we're trying to show interest in our date?"*
    - ■ Answers: It makes them feel comfortable; you seem friendly; not laughing might make them feel uncomfortable and awkward.

- *Be polite and respectful*
  - ○ Say, *"During your date, it's also important to be polite and respectful. How can you be polite and respectful to your date?"*
    - ■ Answers: Open and hold doors when appropriate; pull out chairs when appropriate; don't begin eating or drinking until their food or beverages have arrived; use good table manners; don't swear or curse; ***don't be argumentative***; ***don't police***; ***don't tease or make fun of them or others***.
  - ○ Ask, *"Why is it important to be polite and respectful during your date?"*
    - ■ Answers: It makes your date feel special; it shows that you have good manners; it shows that you're a nice person.

- *Ask your date what they want to do*
  - ○ Ask, *"Why is it important to ask your date what they want to do?"*
    - ■ Answer: ***Asking your date what they want to do*** is another way to ***be polite and respectful*** toward your date; it helps ensure that they have a good time.
  - ○ *Don't make all the decisions*
    - ■ Say, *"During your date, should you make all the decisions?"*
      - □ Answer: No.
    - ■ Ask, *"What could be the problem with making all the decisions during your date?"*
      - □ Answers: You might seem controlling or bossy; they might feel like their interests are being ignored.

- *Go with the flow*
  - ○ Say, *"During your date, you also need to be prepared to go with the flow. That means sometimes you need to be flexible and go with whatever is happening that you didn't expect. Why is it important to go with the flow?"*
    - ■ Answers: Plans may change; your date may change his or her mind about what they want to do during the date.
  - ○ Ask, *"What if your date is doing things that annoy you or get on your nerves. What should you do?"*
    - ■ Answers: ***Go with the flow in the moment, and remember that dating is a choice; you don't have to go out with them again if something bothers you.***
  - ○ Ask, *"What if your date wants to do something that feels unsafe or makes you uncomfortable. Then do you have to go with the flow?"*
    - ■ Answer: No; you don't have to do things that feel unsafe or make you uncomfortable on a date.

- *Give your date compliments*
  - ○ Say, *"It's also nice to give compliments to your date. Remember, this is the equivalent of verbal flirting. What are the rules about giving compliments?"*
    - ■ **Give SPECIFIC compliments when you DON'T know the person well.**
    - ■ **Give SPECIFIC or GENERAL compliments when you know the person well.**
    - ■ **Avoid too many physical compliments.**
    - ■ **Physical compliments should be from the neck up.**

- *Don't flirt with other people*
  - ○ Say, *"When you're on a date with someone, do you think it's a good idea to flirt with someone else?"*
    - ■ Answer: No, absolutely not.
  - ○ Ask, *"What could be the problem with flirting with someone else during your date?"*
    - ■ Answers: It's rude; it's disrespectful; it might seem like you're a *player*; they might not want to go out with you again.

- *Don't invite people unexpectedly into your date*
  - ○ Ask, *"What do you do if you run into people you know during your date? Should you invite them into your date?"*
    - ■ Answers: No; don't invite them into your date.
  - ○ Ask, *"What could be the problem with inviting people unexpectedly into your date?"*
    - ■ Answers: Your date might think you're rude; he or she might feel neglected.
  - ○ Ask, *"What if your date wants to invite people unexpectedly? What should you do?"*
    - ■ Answers: **Go with the flow in the moment, and remember that dating is a choice**; **you don't have to go out with them again if it bothers you.**

- *Don't ignore your date*
  - ○ *Don't ignore your date to talk to other people*
    - ■ Say, *"During your date, it's also important not to ignore your date. That means you shouldn't ignore your date to talk to other people. For example, imagine you're on a double date or a group date. What could be the problem with ignoring your date to talk to other people?"*
      - □ Answers: It's not fun for your date; he or she might feel neglected or ignored; they might not want to go out with you again.
  - ○ *Don't text or make phone calls during your date*
    - ■ Ask, *"Should you be texting or making calls while you're on your date and what could be the problem with that?"*
      - □ Answers: You shouldn't text or make calls during your date; it's rude to your date; it's ignoring your date.
    - ■ Ask, *"What if your date is texting or making calls during your date. What should you do?"*
      - □ Answers: **Go with the flow in the moment, and remember that dating is a choice; you don't have to go out with them again if it bothers you.**
  - ○ *If you're expecting an important call or text, let your date know in advance and apologize*
    - ■ Ask, *"What if you're expecting an important call or text during your date. What should you do?"*
      - □ Answer: Let your date know in advance and apologize for the interruption.

- *Suggest a change if you or your date gets bored*
  - ○ Ask, *"Do people sometimes get bored on dates and what should you do?"*
    - ■ Answers: Yes, people may get bored; **you should suggest a change if you or your date gets bored**.
  - ○ Ask, *"What could be the problem with saying 'I'm bored' during your date?"*
    - ■ Answers: You would seem rude; it sounds like you're saying your date is boring; they might not want to go out with you again.
  - ○ Say, *"Instead of saying you're bored, you should suggest a change if you or your date gets bored. How do you suggest a change?"*
    - ■ Answer: You can say, *"How about when we're done with this, we do something else?"*

○ Ask, *"What if your date doesn't want to do what you suggest?"*
  ■ Answers: *Go with the flow in the moment, and remember that dating is a choice; you don't have to go out with them again if it bothers you*.

- *Avoid risky topics*
  ○ Say, *"During the date, you probably should avoid talking about risky topics. This is especially true when you're first getting to know one another. What are some risky topics at first?"*
    ■ Answers: Politics; sex; religion.
  ○ Ask, *"What could be the problem with talking about politics, sex, or religion when you first start dating?"*
    ■ Answers: These can be emotionally charged topics; someone could be offended, get upset, or get their feelings hurt.
  ○ Explain, *"Eventually, you may want to talk about these topics, but it's risky when you're first getting to know someone."*

- *Avoid risky places*
  ○ Explain, *"During your date, you should also avoid going to risky places. That means avoiding places that might make you or your date uncomfortable. What is risky will depend on you and your date."*
  ○ Present the following examples by saying, *"What if you or your date . . . ?"* and then follow up by asking, *"What could be some risky places?"*
    ■ *". . . don't drink alcohol?"*
      □ Risky places: Bars; night clubs; dance clubs; raves; fraternity parties; keg parties; certain concerts.
    ■ *". . . are allergic to or don't like seafood?"*
      □ Risky places: Seafood restaurants; sushi restaurants.
    ■ *". . . have sensory issues?"*
      □ Risky places: Concerts; sporting events; loud restaurants or bars; night clubs; dance clubs; raves.
    ■ *". . . are not interested in getting physically intimate?"*
      □ Risky places: Hotel rooms; the bedroom in your home; the bedroom in their home; the back seat of a car.
  ○ Explain, *"During your date, and when planning your date, it's important to avoid going to risky places that might make you or your date uncomfortable."*

- *Be prepared to pay*
  ○ *The person who asked for the date should pay for the date*
    ■ Explain, *"The general rule about dating is that the person who asked the other person out is supposed to pay. Should we still be prepared to pay even if we didn't ask the other person out?"*
      □ Answers: Yes, absolutely.
    ■ Ask, *"Should the same person have to pay every time?"*
      □ Answers: Probably not; it's nice to take turns paying when possible; you should at least *offer to pay*.
  ○ *Always offer to pay and be prepared to pay*
    ■ Ask, *"Should we actually offer to pay even if we didn't ask the other person out?"*
      □ Answer: Yes.
    ■ Ask, *"Does that mean we should always have cash and/or credit cards whenever we go on dates?"*
      □ Answer: Yes, absolutely.
  ○ *Be prepared to "go Dutch" or "split the bill"*
    ■ Ask, *"What if our date offers to 'go Dutch' or 'split the bill?' What does that mean?"*
      □ Answer: It means you each pay for half or for your portion of the bill.
  ○ *Use the two-offer rule*
    ■ Explain, *"Sometimes it can get a little awkward when the bill comes at the end of a date. We should always be prepared to pay and we should always offer to pay. When offering to pay, we should use the two-offer rule."*
      1. *Start by offering to pay once.*
        □ Example: *"Can I get this?"*

        ☐ Example: *"Can I help out?"*

        ☐ Example: *"Want to split it?"*

2. ***If they say no, offer a second time by saying, "Are you sure?"***
3. ***If they say no again, thank them.***

        ☐ Explain, *"It's also nice to offer to get the check next time if you plan to go out again. If you do this, you should actually pay the next time."*

Good Role Play: Two-Offer Rule ⊙

[The group leader and two behavioral coaches should do an APPROPRIATE role play demonstrating ***using the two-offer rule***. If you do not have two behavioral coaches, the group leader can be a substitute for one of the coaches, and a young adult can substitute for the group leader, playing the part of the roommate/waiter.]

- Begin by saying, *"We're going to do a role play. Watch this and tell me what (name of behavioral coach 2) is doing RIGHT in using the two-offer rule."*

> Example of an APPROPRIATE Role Play
>
> ○ Behavioral coaches 1 & 2: (Sitting down)
> ○ Behavioral coach 1: *"That was a great meal."*
> ○ Behavioral coach 2: *"Yeah, it was really good."*
> ○ Group leader: *"Here's your bill. I'll take this when you're ready."* (drops off imaginary bill)
> ○ Behavioral coach 1: (Reaches for the bill)
> ○ Behavioral coach 2: (Reaches for purse or wallet) *"Can I help out?"*
> ○ Behavioral coach 1: *"Oh no, I've got this. But thanks."*
> ○ Behavioral coach 2: (Still holding purse or wallet) *"Are you sure?"*
> ○ Behavioral coach 1: *"Yeah, absolutely. It's on me."*
> ○ Behavioral coach 2: *"Well, thank you. I'll get it next time."*
> ○ Behavioral coach 1: *"That's okay. It's my pleasure. (pause) I'm glad there will be a 'next time'!"*
> ○ Behavioral coaches 1 & 2: (Smiling at each other)

- End by saying, *"Timeout on that. So what did (name of behavioral coach 2) do RIGHT in using the two-offer rule?"*
  - Answers: ***Started by offering to pay***; when the date said "no," ***offered a second time by saying "Are you sure?"*** and when the date said "no" again, ***said "thank you"*** and offered to get the check next time.
- Ask the following ***Perspective Taking Questions***:
  - *"What was that like for (name of coach 1)?"*
    - Answers: Nice; pleasant; normal.
  - *"What do you think (name of coach 1) thought of (name of coach 2)?"*
    - Answers: Friendly; thoughtful; good date.
  - *"Is (name of coach 1) going to want to go on a date with (name of coach 2) again?"*
    - Answer: Yes.
- Ask behavioral coach 1 the same ***Perspective Taking Questions***:
  - *"What was that like for you?"*
  - *"What did you think of (name of coach 2)?"*
  - *"Would you want to go on a date with (name of coach 2) again?"*

Behavioral Rehearsal: Two-Offer Rule

- Explain, *"Now we're going to have each of you practice using the two-offer rule with one of our behavioral coaches using the same example you just saw."*
- Go around the room and have each young adult practice using the ***two-offer rule*** with one of the behavioral coaches while the group watches.

- Be sure to have at least one male and one female behavioral coach for young adults to practice with.
- If you only have one behavioral coach, the group leader can substitute for a missing coach of the same gender.
- Ask, *"Who would you feel more comfortable practicing with, (insert name of female coach) or (insert name of male coach)?"*
- *Have the group leader begin the behavioral rehearsal by saying, "Here's your bill. I'll take this when you're ready."* (Drops off imaginary bill.)
- The behavioral coach should reach for the bill.
- Encourage young adults to look at the board as they're following the steps for using the **two-offer rule**.
  - You may need to point to specific steps as they're practicing.
  - Try not to stop the behavioral rehearsal while they're practicing.
- Provide **social coaching** as needed and **troubleshoot** any problems that may arise.
- End by giving a round of applause to each young adult after their practice.

Ending the Date

- Explain, *"Just like the beginning of dates involve specific steps that need to be followed, the ending of dates also have very specific steps."*
- [The group leader and two behavioral coaches should do an INAPPROPRIATE role play of **ending the date**. If you do not have two behavioral coaches, the group leader can be a substitute for one of the coaches, and a young adult can substitute for the group leader, playing the part of the roommate/waiter.]

Bad Role Play: Ending the Date sc

- Begin by saying, *"We're going to do a role play. Watch this and tell me what (name of behavioral coach 2) is doing WRONG in ending the date."*

> Example of an INAPPROPRIATE Role Play
>
> - Behavioral coaches 1 & 2: (Sitting down)
> - Behavioral coach 1: *"That was a great meal."*
> - Behavioral coach 2: (Distracted, looking around)
> - Group leader: *"Here's your change."* (drops off imaginary bill with change)
> - Behavioral coach 1: *"Thanks!"*
> - Behavioral coach 2: (Distracted, looking around, bored)
> - Behavioral coach 1: (A little pause) *"Well, this was fun."* (Confused, unsure what to do)
> - Behavioral coach 2: (Oblivious, looking around, bored)
> - Behavioral coach 1: (A little pause) *"I'm glad we could get together."* (Confused, unsure what to do)
> - Behavioral coaches 1 & 2: (Long pause)
> - Behavioral coach 2: (Stands up, walks away and leaves)
> - Behavioral coach 1: (Startled, confused)

- End by saying, *"Timeout on that. So what did (name of behavioral coach 2) do WRONG in ending the date?"*
  - Answers: Walked away without saying anything to the date; didn't say thank you; didn't say he/she had a nice time; didn't say goodbye.
- Ask the following **Perspective Taking Questions**:
  - *"What was that like for (name of coach 1)?"*
    - Answers: Confusing; hurtful; shocking.
  - *"What do you think (name of coach 1) thought of (name of coach 2)?"*
    - Answers: Rude; weird; inconsiderate; bad date.

- ○ *"Is (name of coach 1) going to want to go on a date with (name of coach 2) again?"*
  - ■ Answer: No, probably not.
- Ask behavioral coach 1 the same *Perspective Taking Questions*:
  - ○ *"What was that like for you?"*
  - ○ *"What did you think of (name of coach 2)?"*
  - ○ *"Would you want to go on a date with (name of coach 2) again?"*

Steps for Ending the Date

- Explain, *"Instead of having an awkward ending, we need to end dates following the appropriate steps."*

1. *Wait for a pause in the date*
   - Say, *"The first step in ending the date is to wait for a pause in the date. That means don't interrupt what you're doing unless you have to. What could be the problem with interrupting the date to end things?"*
     - ○ Answers: It may seem rude or abrupt; your date may think you don't want to spend time with him or her; it may seem like you're not having a good time.

2. *Have a cover story for ending the date*
   - Explain, *"Unless the date naturally ends when the activity is over, you'll need a cover story for ending the date. What are some examples of cover stories, or reasons to end the date?"*
     - ○ Example: *"Well, it's getting late."*
     - ○ Example: *"I guess I better get you home."*
     - ○ Example: *"Well, I have an early class tomorrow."*
     - ○ Example: *"I guess it's getting late and we have work tomorrow."*
   - Ask, *"What could be the problem with not giving a cover story for leaving or ending a date?"*
     - ○ Answer: Your date may think you don't want to be with him or her anymore.

3. *Thank them for going out or taking you out*
   - Say, *"The next step for ending a date is to thank them for going out or for taking you out. Why is it important to thank your date?"*
     - ○ Answers: Because it makes them feel nice; it shows that you appreciate them.

4. *Tell them you had a good time if you did*
   - Say, *"The next step is to tell them that you had a good time if you did. Why is it important to tell your date you had a good time?"*
     - ○ Answers: It shows them that you enjoyed being around them; it makes them feel good; it lets them know you might be interested in going on another date.
   - Ask, *"What if you didn't have a good time? What should you say then?"*
     - ○ Answers: Don't mention anything about having a good time; just thank them.

5. *Start walking them out*
   - Say, *"Wherever the date may be, you will want to walk out together. That could mean walking out of a restaurant or a movie theater to go to different cars, it could mean walking them to their front door after dropping them off, or it could mean walking them to your door if you're at your home. Why is it important to walk your date out?"*
     - ○ Answers: Because it's rude to make them find their way out; it's rude not to say goodbye at the door or as you're leaving some place.

6. *If you like them, suggest going out again*
   - Say, *"The next step as you're ending a date is to suggest going out again if you like them. How might you say this?"*
     - ○ Example: *"Maybe we could hang out again this weekend."*
     - ○ Example: *"Let's do this again sometime."*
     - ○ Example: *"We should go out again."*

- Say, *"You will need to assess their interest at this point. If they seem interested, do you have to set up an exact date and time for your next date right on the spot?"*
  - Answers: Not unless there is something specific you are proposing to do that takes place at a certain day and time; most of the time, you can follow up later with a call or text to make plans.
- Say, *"If they don't seem interested, should you try to make plans just then?"*
  - Answers: Probably not; you could always follow up later with a call or text to see if they're interested in going out again.
- Ask, *"What if you don't like them. Should you make plans to go out again?"*
  - Answers: No, you should probably move on; remember that dating is a choice; you don't have to date everyone and everyone doesn't have to date you.

7. **Tell them when you'll follow up**
   - Say, *"If you like them and want to see them again, tell them when you'll call or text them next. How do you say that?"*
     - Example: *"I'll call you this weekend."*
     - Example: *"I'll text you in a couple days."*
     - Example: *"I'll give you a call tomorrow."*
   - Explain, *"Then you actually need to follow up when you said you would."*

8. **Say goodbye**
   - Say, *"The last step for ending a date is to say goodbye. This might include a casual 'bye' or 'see you later' or a wave. Some goodbyes even end with a hug or a kiss. Even though a hug or kiss goodnight is pretty common at the end of dates, is it difficult to know if someone wants to be hugged or kissed?"*
     - Answer: Yes.
   - Ask, *"Could it be really awkward to go in for a hug or a kiss and the person backs away?"*
     - Answer: Yes.
   - Ask, *"What can we do to minimize the risk before we go in for a hug or kiss?"*
     - Answer: **Ask permission for any physical contact**.
   - Say, *"Because not everyone is comfortable with physical contact, you should ask before you do anything physical. How do you say that?"*
     - Example: *"Can I give you a hug?"*
     - Example: *"Can I give you a kiss goodnight?"*
   - Explain, *"If they like you, they will be happy to say 'yes.' If they don't like you, be glad you asked!"*

Good Role Play: Ending the Date sc

[The group leader and two behavioral coaches should do an APPROPRIATE role play demonstrating **ending the date**. If you do not have two behavioral coaches, the group leader can be a substitute for one of the coaches, and a young adult can substitute for the group leader, playing the part of the roommate/waiter.]

- Begin by saying, *"We're going to do another role play. Watch this and tell me what (name of behavioral coach 2) is doing RIGHT in ending the date."*

Example of an APPROPRIATE Role Play

- Behavioral coaches 1 & 2: (Sitting down)
- Behavioral coach 1: *"That was a great meal."*
- Behavioral coach 2: *"Yeah, it was really good."*
- Group leader: *"Here's your change."* (drops off imaginary bill with change)
- Behavioral coaches 1 & 2: *"Thanks."*

○ Behavioral coach 2: *"Thanks again for dinner!"*
○ Behavioral coach 1: *"Well thanks for coming out."*
○ Behavioral coach 2: (Pause) *"I guess it's getting kind of late."*
○ Behavioral coach 1: *"Yeah, time flew by."*
○ Behavioral coach 2: *"I had a really nice time."*
○ Behavioral coach 1: *"Me too. It was fun."*
○ Behavioral coaches 1 & 2: (Both stand up and start walking toward the door)
○ Behavioral coach 1: *"Are you sure I can't drive you home?"*
○ Behavioral coach 2: *"Thanks anyway, but my roommate just finished her shift. I'll just catch a ride with him/her."*
○ Behavioral coach 1: *"As long as it's not a problem."*
○ Behavioral coach 2: *"Not at all. (pause) We should do this again sometime."*
○ Behavioral coach 1: *"Definitely, I'd like that. Give me a call if you're free this weekend. Maybe we could get together Saturday night and see that movie you mentioned?"*
○ Behavioral coach 2: *"That would be great! I'll text you tomorrow and we can figure it out."*
○ Behavioral coach 1: *"Sounds good. I'll look forward to it."*
○ Behavioral coaches 1 & 2: (Pause)
○ Behavioral coach 2: *"Can I give you a hug goodnight?"*
○ Behavioral coach 1: *"Of course!"*
○ Behavioral coaches 1 & 2: (Give a nice friendly hug)
○ Behavioral coach 2: *"Okay, thanks. I'll talk to you soon!"*
○ Behavioral coach 1: *"See you soon! Bye!"*

- End by saying, *"Timeout on that. So what did (name of behavioral coach 2) do RIGHT in ending the date?"*
  - Answers: **Waited for a pause in the date; gave a cover story; thanked the date; said he/she had a good time; started walking out; suggested getting together again; said when he/she would follow up; asked to give a hug; said goodbye.**
- Ask the following *Perspective Taking Questions*:
  - *"What was that like for (name of coach 1)?"*
    - Answers: Nice; pleasant; fun; exciting.
  - *"What do you think (name of coach 1) thought of (name of coach 2)?"*
    - Answers: Fun; friendly; cute; good date.
  - *"Is (name of coach 1) going to want to go on a date with (name of coach 2) again?"*
    - Answer: Yes.
- Ask behavioral coach 1 the same *Perspective Taking Questions*:
  - *"What was that like for you?"*
  - *"What did you think of (name of coach 2)?"*
  - *"Would you want to go on a date with (name of coach 2) again?"*

After the Date

- Explain, *"After we've gone on a date with someone, there are a few things we need to do if we had a nice time and want to see them again."*

- *Make a follow-up call or text the next day*
  - Ask, *"If you like the person and want to go out with them again, should you make a follow-up call or text the next day and why would that be a good idea?"*
    - Answer: When you follow up the next day, it shows that you like them and had a good time.

- *Thank them for going out or taking you out*
  - Say, *"When you follow up, do you want to thank them for going out or taking you out and why would that be a good idea?"*

- ■ Answers: When you thank them for going out, it shows that you're interested in them; it shows that you appreciate them.

- *Tell them you had a good time if you did*
  - ○ Ask, *"Do you want to tell them you had a good time if you did and why would that be a good idea?"*
    - ■ Answers: It shows them that you enjoyed being with them; it lets them know that you like them.

- *Ask them out again if you like them*
  - ○ Ask, *"Would this be a good time to ask them out again if you like them, or suggest seeing each other again?"*
    - ■ Answer: Yes, definitely.
  - ○ Ask, *"What could be the problem with not suggesting going out again?"*
    - ■ Answers: They may not think you're interested; they may **move on** if you don't seem interested.

- Explain, *"So those are some of the rules and steps to follow when going on dates. Some of you will be practicing this during the week if you have a date."*

DATING ETIQUETTE: GOING ON DATES

Young Adult Behavioral Rehearsal

Get-Togethers

Materials Needed

- Indoor games (e.g., video games, card games, board games).
  - If you are going to provide video games as an option, make sure there are enough gaming consoles that each group can play simultaneously together.
  - Do not use small, portable gaming devices as people have to wait to take turns and that can get boring.
  - Several decks of playing cards will be sufficient if you do not have these other resources.
- Optional: iPads or laptops for watching YouTube videos, surfing the Internet, or playing computer games.
  - If you are going to provide iPads or laptops as an option, make sure there are enough that each group can use them simultaneously together.
- [Note: Most PEERS® programs DO NOT have access to gaming consoles, iPads, or laptops. These are luxury items. Just providing a few decks of cards to keep the get-together *activity-based* will be fine.]

Behavioral Rehearsal

- Notify young adults they will be practicing *beginning and ending get-togethers*.
- Break up young adults into small groups (no less than three young adults per group).
- Have EACH young adult practice *beginning a get-together* following the steps.
  - Assign *hosts* and *guests*.
    - One young adult will be the *host*.
    - One young adult will be the *arriving guest*.
    - The other young adult(s) will be the *guest(s) that have already arrived*.
  - Begin by having the *host* verbally go over the steps for *beginning a get-together*.
  - You may need to provide Socratic prompting to young adults for identifying the specific steps for *beginning a get-together* by using some of the following *social coaching questions*:
    - *"What should you do when your guest knocks on the door?"*
    - *"What should you do when they're standing on the doorstep?"*
    - *"What should you do if they've never met your other friends?"*
    - *"What should you do if they've never been to your home?"*
    - *"Do you want to offer them something?"*
    - *"How will you decide what to do?"*
  - The *arriving guest* should step outside and knock on the door.
  - The *guest(s) that have already arrived* should be seated somewhere nearby.
  - Have the *host* follow the steps for *beginning the get-together*.

- ○ You may need to provide Socratic prompting to young adults if they have trouble following the steps by using some of the following *social coaching questions*:
    - ■ *"What should you do when your friend knocks on the door?"*
    - ■ *"Do you think your friend might want to come in?"*
    - ■ *"Have all of your friends met?"*
    - ■ *"Has your friend been to your home?"*
    - ■ *"Do you want to offer your friends something?"*
    - ■ *"How will you and your friends decide what to do?"*
  - ○ Once the young adult has practiced, call a "timeout" and have the other young adults applaud.
  - ○ EACH young adult should practice *beginning a get-together* as a *host*, an *arriving guest*, and a *guest that has already arrived*.
- Have young adults practice following the rules for how to behave *during the get-together* while *trading information*, *finding common interests*, and playing with games and items provided by the treatment team (e.g., video games, card games, board games, iPads, laptops, etc.).
- Have EACH young adult practice *ending a get-together* following the steps.
  - ○ Assign *hosts* and *guests*.
    - ■ One young adult will be the *host*.
    - ■ The other young adults will be the *guests*.
  - ○ Have the *host* verbally go over the steps for *ending a get-together*.
  - ○ You may need to provide Socratic prompting to young adults for identifying the specific steps to *ending a get-together* by using some of the following *social coaching questions*:
    - ■ *"Should you interrupt your friends to end the get-together?"*
    - ■ *"Should you just tell them to leave?"*
    - ■ *"How are they going to find their way out?"*
    - ■ *"Should you thank them for anything?"*
    - ■ *"What should you say if you had a nice time?"*
    - ■ *"What should you say if you're going to see them again?"*
  - ○ *"What's the last thing you should say as they're leaving?"*
  - ○ The *hosts* and *guests* should be seated before they begin the practice so that the *host* has to *stand up and start walking the guests to the door*.
  - ○ Have the *host* follow the steps for *ending the get-together*.
  - ○ You may need to provide Socratic prompting to young adults if they have trouble following the steps by using some of the following *social coaching questions*:
    - ■ *"Do you just tell your friends to leave, or do you need a reason?"*
    - ■ *"How will your friends find their way out?"*
    - ■ *"Do you want to thank them for anything?"*
    - ■ *"What could you say if you had a nice time?"*
    - ■ *"What could you say if you're going to see them again?"*
    - ■ *"What's the last thing you should say as they're leaving?"*
  - ○ *Guests* should actually leave and then come back at the end of the role play.
  - ○ Once the young adult has practiced, call a "timeout" and have the other young adults applaud.
  - ○ EACH young adult should practice *ending a get-together* as a *host* and a *guest*.

DATING ETIQUETTE: GOING ON DATES

Reunification

- Announce that young adults should join their social coaches.
  - ○ Have young adults stand or sit next to their social coaches.
  - ○ Be sure to have silence and the full attention of the group before starting with *Reunification*.
  - ○ Have young adults generate the content from the lesson while social coaches listen.
- Say, *"Today, we talked about going on dates. There are several phases for going on dates, including planning, preparing, beginning, ending, and even staying safe. What are some of the rules for DURING the date?"*
  - ○ *Show interest in your date*
  - ○ *Trade information at least 50% of the time*
  - ○ *Laugh at their jokes*
  - ○ *Be polite and respectful*
  - ○ *Ask your date what they want to do*
  - ○ *Go with the flow*
  - ○ *Give your date compliments*
  - ○ *Don't flirt with other people*
  - ○ *Don't invite people unexpectedly into your date*
  - ○ *Don't ignore your date*
  - ○ *Suggest a change if you or your date gets bored*
  - ○ *Avoid risky topics*
  - ○ *Avoid risky places*
  - ○ *Be prepared to pay*
- Explain, *"In addition to talking about going on dates, we also had young adults practice having get-togethers and the group did a great job so we should give them a round of applause."*

Homework Assignments

Distribute the *Social Coaching Handout* to young adults and announce the following *Homework Assignments*:

1. Have a *get-together* with a friend.
   - Social coaches should help young adults plan the get-together using the *five W's*:
     - ○ *WHO* they plan to get together with.
     - ○ *WHAT* they plan to do.
     - ○ *WHEN* it will happen.
     - ○ *WHERE* they will meet.
     - ○ *HOW* they will make it happen.
   - Social coaches should go over the rules and steps for *get-togethers* with young adults beforehand.
   - Social coaches should ask young adults the following *social coaching questions* after the *get-together*:

○ *What did you decide to do and who picked the activities?*
○ *Did you trade information and for what percentage of the time?*
○ *What were your common interests and what could you do with that information if you were going to hang out again?*
○ *Did you and your friend have a good time?*
○ *Is this someone you might want to hang out with again?*

2. Practice *letting someone know you like them, ask them on a date*, and/or *go on a date*.
   - If young adults are interested in someone romantically:
     ○ *Let them know you like them.*
     ○ *Ask them on a date.*
     ○ *Go on a date.*
     ○ DO NOT practice unless you are romantically interested in the person.
   - Young adults should practice *letting someone know you like them, asking someone on a date*, and *beginning and ending dates* with social coaches, if comfortable.
   - Social coaches should go over the rules and steps for *letting someone know you like them, asking someone on a date*, and *going on dates* before the practice.
   - Social coaches should ask young adults the following *social coaching questions* after each practice:
     ○ *Letting someone know you like them*:
       ▪ *Who did you practice with and what did you do to let them know you like them?*
       ▪ *How did they respond?*
       ▪ *Does this seem like a good choice and is this someone you might want to go on a date with?*
     ○ *Asking someone on a date*:
       ▪ *Who did you ask on a date and what steps did you follow?*
       ▪ *How did they respond?*
     ○ *Going on a date*:
       ▪ *What did you decide to do?*
       ▪ *Did you trade information and for what percentage of the time?*
       ▪ *What were your common interests and what could you do with that information if you were going to go on a date again?*
       ▪ *Did you and your date have a good time?*
       ▪ *Does this seem like a good choice and is this someone you might want to go on a date with again?*

3. *Enter a group conversation* with peers (could be from the *source of friends*).
   - Social coaches should go over the rules and steps for *entering and exiting group conversations* before the practice.
   - The assignment is NOT to *exit the conversation* unless they naturally need to.
   - Social coaches should ask young adults the following *social coaching questions* after the practice:
     ○ *Where did you enter a conversation and with whom?*
     ○ *Which steps did you follow?*
     ○ *Did it seem like they wanted to talk to you and how could you tell?*
     ○ *Did you have to exit the conversation and which steps did you follow?*

Individual Check-Out

Individually and privately negotiate with each young adult and social coach:

1. **WHO** they plan to have a *get-together* with in the coming week.
   - **WHAT** they plan to suggest to their friends.
   - **WHEN** and **WHERE** they will suggest to their friends.
   - **HOW** they will make it happen (e.g., tickets, transportation, etc.).

2. How they will practice *letting someone know they like them* and with whom, and whether they plan to *ask them on a date*.
   - *WHO* they plan to have a *date* with in the coming week.
   - *WHAT* they plan to suggest to do.
   - *WHEN* and *WHERE* they will suggest to meet.
   - *HOW* they will make it happen (e.g., tickets, transportation, etc.).

3. Where, when, and with whom they plan to *enter a group conversation* with peers.
   - Whether this is an accepting *social group* and how they can tell.

SESSION 11

DATING ETIQUETTE: GOING ON DATES

Social Coaching Handout

Planning the Date

- *Follow up using the two-day rule*
- *Use the five W's to finalize the date*
- *Confirm the plans right before the date*

Preparing for the Date

- *Make sure your space is presentable*
- *Put away anything you don't want your date to share, see, or touch*
- *Use good hygiene*
- *Dress appropriately*
  - *Your clothing should match the activity*
  - *Don't dress too provocatively*
  - *Try to look your best*

Staying Safe on the Date

- *Don't give out your personal contact information at first*
- *Google your date before you meet*
- *Let friends and family know where you are and who you're with*
- *Drive yourself to and from the date*
- *Meet your date in a public place*
- *Don't go anywhere alone with your date at first*
  - *Don't get in the car with your date at first*
  - *Don't take your date home at first*
  - *Don't go to your date's home at first*
- *Check in with friends and family before and after the date*

Steps for Beginning and Ending the Date

Table 12.3 Steps for Beginning and Ending the Date

Beginning the Date	Ending the Date
1. Greet your date	1. Wait for a pause in the date
2. Invite them in if meeting at your home	2. Have a cover story for ending the date
3. Introduce them to anyone they don't know	3. Thank them for going out or taking you out
4. Show them around if meeting at your home	4. Tell them you had a good time if you did
5. Offer them refreshments if staying at your home	5. Start walking them out
6. Ask about your plans	6. If you like them, suggest going out again
	7. Tell them when you'll follw up
	8. Say goodbye (ask permission for any physical contact)

During the Date

- *Show interest in your date*
  - *Smile and make good eye contact*
- *Trade information at least 50% of the time*
- *Laugh at their jokes*
- *Be polite and respectful*
- *Ask your date what they want to do*
  - *Don't make all the decisions*
- *Go with the flow*
- *Give your date compliments*
  - *Give SPECIFIC compliments when you DON'T know the person well*
  - *Give SPECIFIC or GENERAL compliments when you know the person well*
  - *Avoid too many physical compliments*
  - *Physical compliments should be from the neck up*
- *Don't flirt with other people*
- *Don't invite people unexpectedly into your date*
- *Don't ignore your date*
  - *Don't ignore your date to talk to other people*
  - *Don't text or make phone calls during your date*
  - *If you're expecting an important call or text, let your date know in advance and apologize*
- *Suggest a change if you or your date gets bored*
- *Avoid risky topics*
- *Avoid risky places*
- *Be prepared to pay*
  - *The person who asked for the date should pay for the date*
  - *Always offer to pay and be prepared to pay*
  - *Be prepared to "go Dutch" or "split the bill"*
  - *Use the two-offer rule*
    1. *Start by offering to pay once*
       - *Example: "Can I get this?"*
       - *Example: "Can I help out?"*
       - *Example: "Want to split it?"*
    2. *If they say no, offer a second time by saying, "Are you sure?"*
    3. *If they say no again, thank them.*

After the Date

- *Make a follow-up call or text the next day*
- *Thank them for going out or taking you out*
- *Tell them you had a good time if you did*
- *Ask them out again if you like them*

Homework Assignments

1. Have a *get-together* with a friend.
   - Social coaches should help young adults plan the get-together using the *five W's*:
     - *WHO* they plan to get together with.
     - *WHAT* they plan to do.
     - *WHEN* it will happen.
     - *WHERE* they will meet.
     - *HOW* they will make it happen.
   - Social coaches should go over the rules and steps for *get-togethers* with young adults beforehand.

- Social coaches should ask young adults the following *social coaching questions* after the *get-together*:
  - *What did you decide to do and who picked the activities?*
  - *Did you trade information and for what percentage of the time?*
  - *What were your common interests and what could you do with that information if you were going to hang out again?*
  - *Did you and your friend have a good time?*
  - *Is this someone you might want to hang out with again?*

2. Practice *letting someone know you like them, ask them on a date*, and/or *go on a date*.
   - If young adults are interested in someone romantically:
     - *Let them know you like them.*
     - *Ask them on a date.*
     - *Go on a date.*
     - DO NOT practice unless you are romantically interested in the person.
   - Young adults should practice *letting someone know you like them, asking someone on a date*, and *beginning and ending dates* with social coaches, if comfortable.
   - Social coaches should go over the rules and steps for *letting someone know you like them, asking someone on a date*, and *going on dates* before the practice.
   - Social coaches should ask young adults the following *social coaching questions* after each practice:
     - *Letting someone know you like them*:
       - *Who did you practice with and what did you do to let them know you like them?*
       - *How did they respond?*
       - *Does this seem like a good choice and is this someone you might want to go on a date with?*
     - *Asking someone on a date*:
       - *Who did you ask on a date and what steps did you follow?*
       - *How did they respond?*
     - *Going on a date*:
       - *What did you decide to do?*
       - *Did you trade information and for what percentage of the time?*
       - *What were your common interests and what could you do with that information if you were going to go on a date again?*
       - *Did you and your date have a good time?*
       - *Does this seem like a good choice and is this someone you might want to go on a date with again?*

3. *Enter a group conversation* with peers (could be from the *source of friends*).
   - Social coaches should go over the rules and steps for *entering and exiting group conversations* before the practice.
   - The assignment is NOT to *exit the conversation* unless they naturally need to.
   - Social coaches should ask young adults the following *social coaching questions* after the practice:
     - *Where did you enter a conversation and with whom?*
     - *Which steps did you follow?*
     - *Did it seem like they wanted to talk to you and how could you tell?*
     - *Did you have to exit the conversation?*
     - *If you had to exit, which steps did you follow?*

DATING ETIQUETTE: DATING DO'S AND DON'TS

Social Coaching Therapist Guide

Preparing for the Social Coaching Session

The purpose of this session is to provide an overview of *general dating do's and don'ts* and provide strategies for *handling sexual pressure from romantic partners*. The *dating DO'S* relate to *ecologically valid social skills* used by socially successful adults when dating. The *dating DON'TS* relate to common social errors committed by adults with Autism Spectrum Disorder (ASD) and other social challenges when attempting to date.

The most common question that comes up in the social coaching group in this session relates to handling unwanted sexual advances from strangers. Although an important topic, this lesson does not address this issue. To clarify, the purpose of PEERS® is to help young adults make and keep friends and form romantic relationships when appropriate. Avoiding sexual advances or exploitation from unknown persons, while critically important life skills, do not exactly fall under the umbrella of relationship development. However, useful strategies about how to handle unwanted sexual pressure from romantic partners (or known persons) are provided in this lesson. Social coaches and young adults needing additional guidance related to sexual overtures from strangers should be provided assistance outside of the group in a *side meeting*. Although you may not have time to cover these important issues in the group setting, they should be addressed outside of the group if there is a safety concern.

The majority of social coaches will have very little to report when it comes to dating etiquette during the *Homework Review*. This is probably because very few young adults will actually be actively dating. For social coaches who report that their young adults are interested in dating, use this as an opportunity to troubleshoot ways in which they might help their young adult create opportunities to date. Although not a formal assignment, setting up profiles on legitimate online dating websites is one popular way young adults at the UCLA PEERS® Clinic have been successful at jumpstarting their dating life. Social coaches can be very helpful in navigating this process with young adults. For a review of strategies for helping young adults set up online dating profiles, see the *Social Coaching Tips* from the *Social Coaching Therapist Guide* in *Session 11*.

Homework Review

[Go over the following *Homework Assignments* and **troubleshoot** any potential problems. Start with completed homework first. If you have time, you can inquire as to why others were unable to complete the assignment and try to **troubleshoot** how they might get it done for the coming week. When reviewing homework, be sure to relabel descriptions using the *buzzwords* (identified by *bold and italicized* print). Spend the majority of the *Homework Review* on *get-togethers* as this was the most important assignment.]

1. Have a *get-together* with a friend.
   - Say, *"One of the main assignments this week was for young adults to have a get-together with a friend. Who completed this assignment or attempted to complete it?"*

- Ask the following questions:
  - ○ *"Did you help your young adult plan the get-together using the five W's?"*
  - ○ *"What social coaching did you do before the get-together?"*
  - ○ *"What did your young adult decide to do and with whom?"*
  - ○ *"How did the get-together begin?"*
  - ○ *"Who picked the activities?"*
  - ○ *"Did they trade information and what percentage of the time?"*
  - ○ *"How did the get-together end?"*
  - ○ *"What social coaching did you do after the get-together?"*
    - ■ Appropriate *social coaching questions*:
      - □ **What did you decide to do and who picked the activities?**
      - □ **Did you trade information and for what percentage of the time?**
      - □ **What were your common interests and what could you do with that information if you were going to hang out again?**
      - □ **Did you and your friend have a good time?**
      - □ **Is this someone you might want to hang out with again?**
  - ○ *"Does this seem like a good choice for a friend and someone your young adult will want to hang out with again?"*

Table 13.1 Steps for Beginning and Ending Get-Togethers in Your Home

Beginning the Get-Together	*Ending the Get-Together*
1. Greet your guest	*1. Wait for a pause in activities*
2. Invite them in	*2. Give a cover story for ending the get-together*
3. Introduce them to anyone they don't know	*3. Start walking your friend to the door*
4. Give them a tour	*4. Thank your friend for getting together*
5. Offer them refreshments	*5. Tell your friend you had a good time*
6. Ask them what they want to do	*6. Say goodbye and you'll see them later*

2. Practice *letting someone know you like them, ask them on a date*, and/or *go on a date*.
   - Say, *"Another assignment this week was for young adults to practice letting someone know they like them, ask them on a date, and/or go on a date. The assignment was NOT to practice unless they are romantically interested in the person. Young adults could also have practiced with social coaches, if they were comfortable. Who completed this assignment or attempted to complete it?"*
   - Ask the following questions:
     - ○ *"What social coaching did you do before the practice?"*
     - ○ *"Who did your young adult practice with?"*
     - ○ *"What did they do to let the person know they like them and how did they respond?"*
     - ○ *"Did they ask the person on a date and how did they respond?"*
     - ○ Ask the following questions if they went on a date:
       - ■ *"What did they decide to do?"*
       - ■ *"Did they trade information and for what percentage of the time?"*
       - ■ *"Did they and their date have a good time?"*
     - ○ *"What social coaching did you do after the practice?"*
     - ○ *"Does this seem like a good choice and is this someone they might want to go on a date with (again)?"*

3. *Enter a group conversation* with peers (could be from the *source of friends*).
   - Say, *"Another assignment this week was for young adults to practice entering group conversations with peers. Who completed this assignment or attempted to complete it?"*
   - Ask the following questions:
     - ○ *"Where and with whom did your young adult practice?"*
     - ○ *"What social coaching did you do before the practice?"*
     - ○ *"Which steps did your young adult follow?"*

1. *Listen to the Conversation*
2. *Watch from a Distance*
3. *Use a Prop*
4. *Identify the Topic*
5. *Find a Common Interest*
6. *Move Closer*
7. *Wait for a Pause*
8. *Mention the Topic*
9. *Assess Interest*
10. *Introduce Yourself*

- ○ *"What social coaching did you do after the practice?"*
    - ■ Appropriate *social coaching questions*:
        - □ *Where did you enter a conversation and with whom?*
        - □ *Which steps did you follow?*
        - □ *Did it seem like they wanted to talk to you and how could you tell?*
        - □ *Did you have to exit the conversation and which steps did you follow?*

Table 13.2 Steps for Exiting Conversations

NEVER ACCEPTED	INITIALLY ACCEPTED, THEN EXCLUDED	FULLY ACCEPTED
1. Keep your cool 2. Look away 3. Turn away 4. Walk away	1. Keep your cool 2. Look away 3. Wait for a BRIEF pause 4. Give a BRIEF cover story for leaving 5. Walk away	1. Wait for a pause 2. Give a SPECIFIC cover story for leaving 3. Say you'll see them later 4. Say goodbye 5. Walk away

- [Collect the *Social Coaching Homework Assignment Worksheets*. If social coaches forgot to bring the worksheets, have them complete a new form to hold them accountable for the assignments.]

Didactic Lesson: Dating Etiquette: Dating Do's and Don'ts

- Distribute the *Social Coaching Handout*.
    - ○ Sections in **bold print** in the *Social Coaching Therapist Guide* come directly from the *Social Coaching Handout*.
    - ○ Remind social coaches that terms that are in **bold and italicized** print are **buzzwords** and represent important concepts from the PEERS® curriculum that should be used as much as possible when social coaching.
- Explain, *"Today, we're going to continue talking about dating etiquette. So far, we've talked about how to let someone know you like them, how to ask someone on a date, and how to have a successful date. Today, we're going to talk about general dating do's and don'ts and how to handle sexual pressure from partners."*

Dating DO'S

- Explain, *"There are lots of DO'S and DON'TS when it comes to dating. Let's talk about the DO'S first."*
- **DO remember that dating is a choice**
    - ○ Explain, *"The first cardinal rule of dating is that dating is a choice. We don't get to date everyone and everyone doesn't get to date us."*
    - ○ Ask, *"Just because we like someone, does that mean we get to date them?"*
        - ■ Answer: No.
    - ○ Ask, *"Just because someone likes us, does that mean they get to date us?"*
        - ■ Answer: No.
    - ○ Explain, *"A big part of dating is remembering that dating is a choice and that not every relationship will work out. If it were that easy, everyone would be in a relationship."*

- *DO move on if YOU are not interested*
  - Say, *"Another rule for dating is do move on if YOU are not interested in the person. What could be the problem with continuing to date someone when you're not interested in them romantically?"*
    - Answers: It's not fair to them; it's leading them on; they could get their feelings hurt.

- *DO move on if THEY are not interested*
  - Say, *"Another rule for dating is do move on if THEY are not interested in you. What could be the problem with trying to date someone who's not interested in you romantically?"*
    - Answers: It makes you look desperate; it's not going to work out; you may scare them; you could seem like a stalker; you will probably get hurt.

- *DO be polite and respectful*
  - Explain, *"Another important rule for dating is to be polite and respectful. Why is it important to be polite and respectful to the person you're dating?"*
    - Answers: They may not like you or want to date you if you're not polite and respectful; you might not seem like a nice person if you're rude or disrespectful.
  - Ask, *"How can you be polite and respectful when dating someone?"*
    - Answers: Treat them with kindness; be considerate; use nice words when talking to them; don't call them names; ***don't ignore them***; ***don't police them***; ***don't be argumentative***.

- *DO be honest and truthful*
  - Explain, *"Another important rule when dating is do be honest and truthful. What could be the problem with not being honest or truthful when you're dating someone?"*
    - Answers: They may not trust you; they might think you're a liar; they may not want to date you.
  - Ask, *"What if they ask you how they look, and you don't think they look that great. Should you be honest and truthful and tell them they don't look good?"*
    - Answers: No, that's different; that would be hurtful; that would be impolite.
  - Ask, *"But if they ask you how you feel about them, or if you're dating other people, then do you need to be honest and truthful?"*
    - Answers: Yes, you should be honest about your feelings and your dating status; if you're dating other people, you shouldn't lie about it.
  - Explain, *"When you're honest and truthful about your relationship, you can avoid misunderstandings and hurt feelings. As social coaches, you can help young adults decide what is appropriate to share when being honest and truthful."*

- *DO keep in touch*
  - Say, *"Another important rule for dating is to keep in touch if you like the person. Why is it important to keep in touch if you like someone?"*
    - Answers: It shows that you like them; it keeps their interest; it's polite and respectful.
  - Ask, *"What could be the problem with not keeping in touch if you like them?"*
    - Answers: It seems like you're not interested; they might get their feelings hurt; it could seem like you're playing games; they might lose interest in you; they might not want to date you anymore.
  - Ask, *"What is an appropriate amount of time to keep in touch if you like someone?"*
    - Answers: It depends on the phase of your relationship; when you're casually dating, most people talk at least a few times a week; if you're in a committed relationship, most people talk every day.
  - Explain, *"As social coaches, you can help young adults decide what the appropriate amount of time to keep in touch is."*

- *DO ask permission for any physical contact*
  - Say, *"Another important rule for dating is to ask permission for any physical contact. Can it be difficult to know if someone wants to get physical and could it be really awkward to try to get physical and discover that the other person isn't interested or ready yet?"*
    - Answer: Yes.

- Ask, *"What can we do to minimize the risk of rejection when you want to get physical with someone you're dating?"*
  - Answer: Ask permission for any physical contact.
- Explain, *"Because not everyone is comfortable with physical contact at the same pace, you should ask permission before you do anything physical. The good news is that if they like you, they will be happy to say 'yes.' If they don't like you, be glad you asked first to avoid embarrassment."*

Dating DON'TS

- Explain, *"Just like there are a lot of DO'S when it comes to dating, there are also a lot of DON'TS."*

- *DON'T get too personal at first*
  - Explain, *"When you first start dating someone, it's important not to get too personal at first. That means don't ask too many personal questions or share too much personal information at first."*
  - *Don't ask too many personal questions at first*
    - Ask, *"What could be the problem with asking too many personal questions at first?"*
      - Answers: It could make them uncomfortable; you could seem nosy or intrusive.
  - *Don't share too much personal information at first*
    - Ask, *"What could be the problem with sharing too much personal information at first?"*
      - Answers: It could make them uncomfortable; it could scare them off; you could seem like you're coming on too strong.
  - *Don't disclose any diagnoses at first*
    - Ask, *"Should we be sharing personal information about diagnoses or medical history at first, and what could be the problem with that?"*
      - Answers: No; your date may feel uncomfortable; that might be too much information too soon; you might scare them off; they may not want to go out with you again.

- *DON'T talk about your dating history at first*
  - Explain, *"Another important rule about dating is don't talk about your dating history at first. That means you shouldn't share your lack of dating experience or talk about people you've dated in the past when you first start dating someone."*
  - *Don't share lack of dating experience at first*
    - Ask, *"What could be the problem with sharing your lack of dating experience at first?"*
      - Answers: It could make them uncomfortable; it could scare them off; it could feel like a lot of pressure for them.
  - *Don't share bad dating experiences at first*
    - Ask, *"What could be the problem with sharing bad dating experiences at first?"*
      - Answers: It could seem like you're rude; it might seem like you're not over the other person; it might make your date uncomfortable.
  - *Don't talk about your exes at first*
    - Ask, *"What could be the problem with talking about your exes or your dating history at first?"*
      - Answers: It may make your date uncomfortable; it might make them nervous; they may get jealous; it could be a turn off; they may not want to go out with you again.
    - Ask, *"What if your date asks about your dating history?"*
      - Answers: **Keep it short and sweet**; answer their questions honestly and truthfully, but keep it short and positive, then **change the subject**.
    - Ask, *"After you've dated them for a while, then can you tell them more about your dating history?"*
      - Answer: Yes, once you're in a relationship.

- *DON'T talk about your feelings at first*
  - Say, *"Another rule for dating is don't talk about your feelings at first. What could be the problem with talking about your feelings right away?"*
    - Answers: You might scare them off; you could come on too strong too soon; they might not want to date you again.

- ○ Explain, *"Most people don't start talking about feelings for at least three or four dates. Some people rarely or never talk about feelings. As social coaches, you can help young adults decide when is the right time to start talking about feelings."*

- **DON'T rush the relationship**
  - ○ Say, *"It's also important that when you first start dating someone that you don't rush the relationship. What does it mean to rush the relationship?"*
    - ■ Answers: Moving too quickly; coming on too strong; talking about feelings too soon; assuming you're exclusive before you've talked about your relationship status.
  - ○ Ask, *"What could be the problem with rushing the relationship?"*
    - ■ Answers: If you move too quickly, they might get scared off; you might turn them off if you go too fast.

- **DON'T assume you're a couple**
  - ○ Ask, *"Just because you've gone on a couple of dates with someone, does that mean you're a couple, and what could be the problem with assuming you're a couple?"*
    - ■ Answers: No; you might scare off the other person; it might seem like you're coming on too strong; misunderstandings could happen.
  - ○ Ask, *"How do you know when you're a couple?"*
    - ■ Answer: There is usually a conversation between you and your partner where you make the decision to be exclusive (not see anyone else).
  - ○ Ask, *"When is the right time to have a conversation about being exclusive?"*
    - ■ Answers: It depends on the relationship; most people go on several dates before they decide to be a couple.
  - ○ Explain, *"As social coaches, you can help young adults decide when it's the right time to have a conversation about being exclusive, or not seeing other people."*

- **DON'T kiss and tell**
  - ○ Say, *"Another rule for dating is don't kiss and tell. What does it mean to kiss and tell and what could be the problem with kissing and telling?"*
    - ■ Answers: It means to share the private details of your relationship with other people; it usually involves sharing intimate details about your physical relationship; it's indiscrete and disrespectful to the person you're dating if you kiss and tell.

- **DON'T be a player**
  - ○ Say, *"Another rule for dating is don't be a player. What does it mean to be a player and what could be the problem with being a player?"*
    - ■ Answers: It means to play games with someone when dating; to date multiple people without their knowledge of each other; it's disrespectful and dishonest if they don't know you're dating other people.
  - ○ Ask, *"Does that mean you can't date multiple people at the same time?"*
    - ■ Answer: No, but you should be honest about it.
  - ○ Explain, *"It's fine if you want to keep things casual and date more than one person at a time, as long as you're honest about it. It's when you're not honest that you can seem like a player."*

- **DON'T pressure them**
  - ○ Say, *"Another rule for dating is don't pressure the person you're dating. What could be the problem with pressuring someone to commit to the relationship or get physical before they're ready?"*
    - ■ Answers: It makes the other person uncomfortable; it's not fair to the other person; you seem controlling or needy; they may not want to go out with you.
  - ○ Explain, *"Remember that dating is a choice. Just because you want something from a relationship doesn't mean the other person wants the same thing. It's a choice."*

Handling Sexual Pressure from Partners

- Explain, *"Even though one of the rules for dating is not to pressure the other person, that doesn't mean it won't happen. Sometimes people make sexual offers or even pressure others to do things they don't want to do or are not ready to do. If that happens, there are some very specific steps to follow for handling sexual pressure from romantic partners."*

1. ***Keep your cool***
   - Say, *"The first step for handling sexual pressure from partners is to keep your cool. What does it mean to keep your cool and why would that be important to do?"*
     - Answers: It means stay calm and don't get upset; getting upset may only make matters worse and escalate emotions.

2. ***Tell them what you DON'T want to do***
   - Say, *"The next step for handling sexual pressure is to tell them what you DON'T want to do. This is regardless of whether you want to preserve the relationship or not. Why is it important to be clear about what you DON'T want to do?"*
     - Answers: It's your choice what you do or do not do sexually; if you don't **tell your partner what you DON'T want to do**, they won't know; they can't read your mind.
   - Ask, *"What are some examples of ways to tell them what you DON'T want to do?"*
     - Example: *"I don't want to (state the behavior)."*
     - Example: *"I'm not comfortable with (state the behavior)."*
     - Example: *"I don't (state the behavior)."*
   - Ask, *"What if you're just not ready to do what they're offering right now, but you might be later? How might you say that?"*
     - Example: *"I'm not ready to get physical yet."*
     - Example: *"I'm not comfortable with (state the behavior) right now."*
     - Example: *"I'm not comfortable taking it to the next level yet."*

3. ***Give a cover story***
   - Say, *"If you like the person and you want to preserve the relationship, the next step for handling sexual pressure from a partner is to give a cover story. What are some cover stories or reasons we might not be ready to get more physical with someone we're dating?"*
     - Example: *"I don't know you well enough yet."*
     - Example: *"I don't feel comfortable doing that right now."*
     - Example: *"I like to take things slow."*
   - Ask, *"If you know that you're NEVER going to be comfortable with what they're offering, should you tell them?"*
     - Answer: Yes.
   - Ask, *"If we don't like the person we're dating or we don't care about preserving the relationship, do we have to give a cover story?"*
     - Answer: No.

4. ***Use "I" statements to tell them how you feel***
   - Explain, *"The next step for handling sexual pressure from partners is to use 'I' statements to tell them how you feel. This might include telling them what you need from them or what you want to do moving forward."*
   - Ask, *"What are 'I' statements?"*
     - Answer: Statements that begin with *"I think . . ."* or *"I feel . . ."*
   - Ask, *"What are 'you' statements?"*
     - Answer: Statements that begin with *"You did . . ."* or *"You make me feel . . ."*
   - Ask, *"What could be the problem with using 'you' statements instead of 'I' statements when you're trying to share your feelings or your thoughts?"*
     - Answers: **"You" statements** make people defensive; **"I" statements** are less offensive because they focus on your own feelings and don't place blame.
   - Ask, *"What are some examples of 'I' statements when you're feeling sexually pressured by someone you're dating?"*
     - Example: *"I like you but I need some space."*
     - Example: *"I feel like I need to slow things down."*
     - Example: *"I think I need more time to get to know you."*

- Ask, *"Do you want to sound assertive and confident when using 'I' statements and telling them how you feel, and why would that be important?"*
  - ○ Answers: Yes; they need to know you mean what you're saying.

5. *Change the subject*
   - Say, *"If you like the person and you want to slow things down, but don't want the date to end, the next step is to try changing the subject. What does it mean to change the subject?"*
     - ○ Answers: Talk about something else; do something different; shift the focus of the conversation.

6. *Give a cover story and leave (if still pressured)*
   - Say, *"If you're still feeling sexually pressured, or you simply feel uncomfortable, do you have to stick around?"*
     - ○ Answer: No, absolutely not.
   - Ask, *"What should you do if you're feeling uncomfortable?"*
     - ○ Answer: *Give a cover story* and leave.

7. *Remember dating is a choice*
   - Explain, *"Finally, remember that dating is a choice. If the person you're dating wants to do things you don't want to do, and they continue to pressure you, that may mean they're not a good choice for you."*

- [Optional: Show BAD and GOOD *Role Play Video Demonstrations* of **handling sexual pressure from a partner** from the *PEERS® Role Play Video Library* (www.routledge.com/cw/laugeson).]

Homework Assignments

[Distribute the *Social Coaching Homework Assignment Worksheet* (Appendix I) for social coaches to complete and return at the next session.]

1. Have a *get-together* with a friend.
   - Social coaches should help young adults plan the get-together using the *five W's*:
     - ○ *WHO* they plan to get together with.
     - ○ *WHAT* they plan to do.
     - ○ *WHEN* it will happen.
     - ○ *WHERE* they will meet.
     - ○ *HOW* they will make it happen.
   - Social coaches should go over the rules and steps for *get-togethers* with young adults beforehand.
   - Social coaches should ask young adults the following *social coaching questions* after the *get-together*:
     - ○ *What did you decide to do and who picked the activities?*
     - ○ *Did you trade information and for what percentage of the time?*
     - ○ *What were your common interests and what could you do with that information if you were going to hang out again?*
     - ○ *Did you and your friend have a good time?*
     - ○ *Is this someone you might want to hang out with again?*
2. Practice *letting someone know you like them, ask them on a date,* and/or *go on a date.*
   - If young adults are interested in someone romantically:
     - ○ *Let them know you like them.*
     - ○ *Ask them on a date.*
     - ○ *Go on a date.*
     - ○ DO NOT practice unless you are romantically interested in the person.
   - Young adults should practice *letting someone know you like them, asking someone on a date,* and *beginning and ending dates* with social coaches, if comfortable.

- Social coaches should go over all of the rules and steps for *dating etiquette* before the practice.
- Social coaches should ask young adults the following *social coaching questions* after each practice:
  - *Letting someone know you like them*:
    - *Who did you practice with and what did you do to let them know you like them?*
    - *How did they respond?*
    - *Does this seem like a good choice and is this someone you might want to go on a date with?*
  - *Asking someone on a date*:
    - *Who did you ask on a date and what steps did you follow?*
    - *How did they respond?*
  - *Going on a date*:
    - *What did you decide to do?*
    - *Did you trade information and for what percentage of the time?*
    - *What were your common interests and what could you do with that information if you were going to go on a date again?*
    - *Did you and your date have a good time?*
    - *Does this seem like a good choice and is this someone you might want to go on a date with again?*

3. *Enter a group conversation* with peers (could be from the *source of friends*).
   - Social coaches should go over the rules and steps for *entering and exiting group conversations* before the practice.
   - The assignment is NOT to *exit the conversation* unless they naturally need to.
   - Social coaches should ask young adults the following *social coaching questions* after the practice:
     - *Where did you enter a conversation and with whom?*
     - *Which steps did you follow?*
     - *Did it seem like they wanted to talk to you and how could you tell?*
     - *Did you have to exit the conversation and which steps did you follow?*

Social Coaching Tips

For young adults interested in dating, but having difficulty finding a **dating source**, social coaches may want to consider **matchmaking** options.

- *Matchmaking* involves the process of mutual friends and/or family members introducing prospective romantic partners.
- In some cultures, the process of **matchmaking** between families is the only acceptable form of dating allowed.
  - This form of **matchmaking** may also be related to **arranged marriages**, in which couples are brought together by families for the purpose of marriage.
- In most cultures, **blind dates** (dating someone you have never met in person before) is fairly well known and may be acceptable.
- Some social coaches may choose to assist their young adults with dating by **matchmaking**. This might involve:
  - Setting the young adult up on a **blind date** with a prospective partner known to the social coach.
  - Setting the young adult up on a **blind date** with a prospective partner known to friends and/or family of the social coach.
  - Suggesting that the young adult ask friends and/or family to help with **matchmaking** by setting him or her up on **blind dates** with prospective partners.
- As previously mentioned, there are tremendous cultural differences when it comes to dating etiquette, so be flexible about the methods used to find romantic partners.

DATING ETIQUETTE: DATING DO'S AND DON'TS

Young Adult Therapist Guide

Preparing for the Young Adult Session

In this session, young adults will be given an overview of general *dating do's and don'ts*, as well as strategies for *handling sexual pressure from romantic partners*. There are two *Role Play Demonstrations* provided to outline the steps for handling unwanted sexual pressure in this session. It is recommended that these role plays, as with previous dating etiquette *Role Play Demonstrations*, be conducted by two social coaches when possible, rather than with the group leader. One of the reasons for excluding group leaders in dating etiquette role plays involves professional boundaries. In many cases, group leaders are providing supervision and/or mentorship to behavioral coaches, and therefore demonstrating strategies for *flirting* or *asking someone on a date* may seem uncomfortable or even inappropriate (even though they are not real). Group leaders will need to use their own clinical and professional judgment about what is most appropriate and feasible for these *Role Play Demonstrations*.

The *Role Play Demonstrations* in the current session focus on *handling sexual pressure from a romantic partner*. Given the delicacy of this topic, it is strongly urged that the example given in the manual be used in these role plays and subsequent *Behavioral Rehearsal Exercises*. The example provided in the manual takes place at the conclusion of a date in which one of the behavioral coaches invites the other coach to spend the night. The example is fairly benign when it comes to sexual pressure, which is why it is recommended. More graphic examples of sexual pressure have the capacity to make group members and coaches uncomfortable and could represent a boundary violation. Consequently, it is strongly suggested that the example provided in the manual (or some other fairly benign offer) be given during the role play. Likewise, when conducting the *Behavioral Rehearsal Exercises* with young adults, it is critical that the SAME EXAMPLE be used as that which was demonstrated in the role play. Changing the examples of sexual pressure from one behavioral rehearsal to the next might seem too personal and could result in discomfort and misunderstanding. Instead, use the SAME EXAMPLE of sexual pressure from the *Role Play Demonstrations* with behavioral coaches when conducting the *Behavioral Rehearsal Exercises* with young adults. For example, after the role play involving an invitation to spend the night, the subsequent *Behavioral Rehearsal Exercises* with young adults would include the same type of invitation. Behavioral coaches would begin the behavioral rehearsal by saying, *"I was just wondering . . . it's getting kind of late. Would you like to stay over?"* Then have each young adult follow the steps for *handling sexual pressure from a romantic partner*. Using these methods of demonstration and rehearsal should minimize any discomfort caused by the topic of the lesson.

Homework Review

[Go over the following *Homework Assignments* and *troubleshoot* any potential problems. Start with completed homework first. If you have time, you can inquire as to why others were unable to complete the assignment and try to *troubleshoot* how they might get it done for the coming week. When reviewing homework, be sure to relabel descriptions using the *buzzwords* (identified by *bold and italicized* print). Spend the majority of the *Homework Review* on *get-togethers* as this was the most important assignment.]

1. Have a *get-together* with a friend.
    *   Say, *"One of the main assignments this week was for you to have a get-together with a friend. Raise your hand if you had a get-together with a friend this week."*
    *   Ask the following questions:
        ○   *"Who did you have a get-together with and what did you decide to do?"*
        ○   *"Did you plan the get-together using the five W's?"*
        ○   *"How did the get-together begin?"*
        ○   *"Who picked the activities?"*
        ○   *"Did you trade information and for what percentage of the time?"*
        ○   *"How did the get-together end?"*
        ○   *"Did you and your friend have a good time?"*
        ○   *"Is this someone you might want to hang out with again?"*

Table 13.1 Steps for Beginning and Ending Get-Togethers in Your Home

Beginning the Get-Together	Ending the Get-Together
1. Greet your guest	1. Wait for a pause in activities
2. Invite them in	2. Give a cover story for ending the get-together
3. Introduce them to anyone they don't know	3. Start walking your friend to the door
4. Give them a tour	4. Thank your friend for getting together
5. Offer them refreshments	5. Tell your friend you had a good time
6. Ask them what they want to do	6. Say goodbye and you'll see them later

2. Practice *letting someone know you like them, ask them on a date*, and/or *go on a date*.
    *   Say, *"Another assignment this week was to practice letting someone know you like them, ask them on a date, and/or go on a date. The assignment was NOT to practice unless you're romantically interested in the person. Raise your hand if you did this assignment."*
    *   Ask the following questions:
        ○   *"Who did you practice with?"*
        ○   *"What did you do to let them know you like them and how did they respond?"*
        ○   *"Did you ask them on a date and how did they respond?"*
        ○   Ask the following questions if they went on a date:
            ■   *"What did you decide to do?"*
            ■   *"Did you trade information and for what percentage of the time?"*
            ■   *"What were your common interests and what could you do with that information if you were going to go on a date again?"*
            ■   *"Did you and your date have a good time?"*
        ○   *"Does this seem like a good choice and is this someone you might want to go on a date with (again)?"*

3. *Enter a group conversation* with peers (could be from the *source of friends*).
    *   Say, *"Another assignment this week was to practice entering group conversations with peers. Raise your hand if you did this assignment."*
    *   Ask the following questions:
        ○   *"Where and with whom did you practice?"*
        ○   *"Which steps did you follow?"*
            1. *Listen to the Conversation*
            2. *Watch from a Distance*
            3. *Use a Prop*
            4. *Identify the Topic*

5. *Find a Common Interest*
6. *Move Closer*
7. *Wait for a Pause*
8. *Mention the Topic*
9. *Assess Interest*
10. *Introduce Yourself*
- ○ *"Did it seem like they wanted to talk to you?"*
- ○ *"How could you tell?"*
  - ■ *Talking to you?*
  - ■ *Looking at you?*
  - ■ *Facing you (they opened the circle)?*
- ○ *"Did you have to exit the conversation and which steps did you follow?"*

Table 13.2 Steps for Exiting Conversations

NEVER ACCEPTED	INITIALLY ACCEPTED, THEN EXCLUDED	FULLY ACCEPTED
1. Keep your cool *2. Look away* *3. Turn away* *4. Walk away*	*1. Keep your cool* *2. Look away* *3. Wait for a BRIEF pause* *4. Give a BRIEF cover story for leaving* *5. Walk away*	*1. Wait for a pause* *2. Give a SPECIFIC cover story for leaving* *3. Say you'll see them later* *4. Say goodbye* *5. Walk away*

Didactic Lesson: Dating Etiquette: Dating Do's and Don'ts

- ● Explain, *"Today, we're going to continue talking about dating etiquette. So far, we've talked about how to let someone know you like them, how to ask someone on a date, and how to have a successful date. Today, we're going to talk about general dating do's and don'ts and how to handle sexual pressure from partners."*
- ● [Present the rules and steps for ***dating do's and don'ts*** by writing the following bullet points and ***buzzwords*** (identified by ***bold and italicized*** print) on the board. Do not erase the rules and steps until the end of the lesson. Each role play with a ⊙ symbol includes a corresponding role play video from the *PEERS® Role Play Video Library* (www.routledge.com/cw/laugeson).]

Dating DO'S

- ● Explain, *"There are lots of DO'S and DON'TS when it comes to dating. Let's talk about the DO'S first."*

- ● ***DO remember that dating is a choice***
  - ○ Explain, *"The first cardinal rule of dating is that dating is a choice. We don't get to date everyone and everyone doesn't get to date us."*
  - ○ Ask, *"Just because we like someone, does that mean we get to date them?"*
    - ■ Answer: No.
  - ○ Ask, *"Just because someone likes us, does that mean they get to date us?"*
    - ■ Answer: No.
  - ○ Explain, *"A big part of dating is remembering that dating is a choice and that not every relationship will work out. If it were that easy, everyone would be in a relationship."*

- ● ***DO move on if YOU are not interested***
  - ○ Say, *"Another rule for dating is do move on if YOU are not interested in the person. What could be the problem with continuing to date someone when you're not interested in them romantically?"*
    - ■ Answers: It's not fair to them; it's leading them on; they could get their feelings hurt.
  - ○ Ask, *"Does that mean you can't be friends with them?"*
    - ■ Answers: Not necessarily; you may be able to be friends even if you don't decide to date; remember that ***friendship is also a choice***, so just because you want to be friends doesn't mean they will want to be friends, too.

- • *DO move on if THEY are not interested*
  - ○ Say, *"Another rule for dating is do move on if THEY are not interested in you. What could be the problem with trying to date someone who's not interested in you romantically?"*
    - ■ Answers: It makes you look desperate; it's not going to work out; you may scare them; you could seem like a stalker; you will probably get hurt.
  - ○ Ask, *"Does that mean you can't be friends with them?"*
    - ■ Answers: Not necessarily; you may be able to be friends even if they don't want to date you; remember that *friendship is a choice*, so just because you want to be friends, doesn't mean they will want to be friends, too.

- • *DO be polite and respectful*
  - ○ Explain, *"Another important rule for dating is do be polite and respectful. Why is it important to be polite and respectful to the person you're dating?"*
    - ■ Answers: They may not like you or want to date you if you're not polite and respectful; you might not seem like a nice person if you're rude or disrespectful.
  - ○ Ask, *"How can you be polite and respectful when dating someone?"*
    - ■ Answers: Treat them with kindness; be considerate; use nice words when talking to them; don't call them names; *don't ignore them*; *don't police them*; *don't be argumentative*.

- • *DO be honest and truthful*
  - ○ Explain, *"Another important rule when dating is do be honest and truthful. What could be the problem with not being honest or truthful when you're dating someone?"*
    - ■ Answers: They may not trust you; they might think you're a liar; they may not want to date you.
  - ○ Ask, *"What if they ask you how they look, and you don't think they look that great. Should you be honest and truthful and tell them they don't look good?"*
    - ■ Answers: No, that's different; that would be hurtful; that would be impolite.
  - ○ Ask, *"But if they ask you how you feel about them, or if you're dating other people, then do you need to be honest and truthful?"*
    - ■ Answers: Yes, you should be honest about your feelings and your dating status; if you're dating other people, you shouldn't lie about it.
  - ○ Explain, *"When you're honest and truthful about your relationship, you can avoid misunderstandings and hurt feelings. Your social coaches can help you decide what is appropriate to share when being honest and truthful."*

- • *DO keep in touch*
  - ○ Say, *"Another important rule for dating is to keep in touch if you like the person. Why is it important to keep in touch if you like someone?"*
    - ■ Answers: It shows that you like them; it keeps their interest; it's polite and respectful.
  - ○ Ask, *"What could be the problem with not keeping in touch if you like them?"*
    - ■ Answers: It seems like you're not interested; they might get their feelings hurt; it could seem like you're playing games; they might lose interest in you; they might not want to date you anymore.
  - ○ Ask, *"Does that mean you need to call or text them every 10 minutes?"*
    - ■ Answer: No, that might actually scare them off.
  - ○ Ask, *"What is an appropriate amount of time to keep in touch if you like someone?"*
    - ■ Answers: It depends on the phase of your relationship; when you're casually dating, most people talk at least a few times a week; if you're in a committed relationship, most people talk every day.
  - ○ Explain, *"Your social coaches can help you decide what the appropriate amount of time to keep in touch is."*

- • *DO ask permission for any physical contact*
  - ○ Say, *"Another important rule for dating is to ask permission for any physical contact. Can it be difficult to know if someone wants to get physical?"*
    - ■ Answer: Yes.

- Ask, *"Could it be really awkward to try to get physical and discover that the other person isn't interested or ready yet?"*
  - Answer: Yes.
- Ask, *"What can we do to minimize the risk of rejection when you want to get physical with someone you're dating?"*
  - Answer: ***Ask permission for any physical contact***.
- Explain, *"Because not everyone is comfortable with physical contact at the same pace, you should ask permission before you do anything physical. The good news is that if they like you, they will be happy to say 'yes.' If they don't like you, be glad you asked first to avoid embarrassment."*

Dating DON'TS

- Explain, *"Just like there are a lot of DO'S when it comes to dating, there are also a lot of DON'TS."*

- ***DON'T get too personal at first***
  - Explain, *"When you first start dating someone, it's important not to get too personal at first. That means don't ask too many personal questions or share too much personal information at first."*
  - ***Don't ask too many personal questions at first***
    - Ask, *"What could be the problem with asking too many personal questions at first?"*
      - Answers: Your date may feel uncomfortable; they may not want to go out with you again.
  - ***Don't share too much personal information at first***
    - Ask, *"What could be the problem with sharing too much personal information at first?"*
      - Answers: Your date may feel uncomfortable; it might be too much too soon; they may not want to go out with you again.
  - ***Don't disclose any diagnoses at first***
    - Ask, *"Should we be sharing personal information about diagnoses or medical history at first, and what could be the problem with that?"*
      - Answers: No; your date may feel uncomfortable; that might be too much information too soon; you might scare them off; they may not want to go out with you again.

- ***DON'T talk about your dating history at first***
  - Explain, *"Another important rule about dating is don't talk about your dating history at first. That means you shouldn't share your lack of dating experience or talk about people you've dated in the past when you first start dating someone."*
  - ***Don't share lack of dating experience at first***
    - Ask, *"What could be the problem with sharing your lack of dating experience at first?"*
      - Answers: Your date may feel uncomfortable; they might get scared; it might be too much pressure; they may not want to go out with you again.
    - Ask, *"If it's your first date ever, do you want to tell them that right away, and what could be the problem with doing that?"*
      - Answers: No; you might scare them; it could be too much pressure for them; it might make them feel uncomfortable.
    - Ask, *"After you've dated them for a while, then can you tell them that was your first date?"*
      - Answer: Yes, once you're in a relationship.
  - ***Don't share bad dating experiences at first***
    - Ask, *"What could be the problem with sharing stories of bad dating experiences at first?"*
      - Answers: Your date may feel uncomfortable; it might be too much too soon; it might scare them off; they may not want to go out with you again.
  - ***Don't talk about your exes at first***
    - Ask, *"What could be the problem with talking about your ex-boyfriends or ex-girlfriends at first?"*
      - Answers: It may seem like you're not over your ex; they may get jealous; they may lose interest; they may not want to go out with you again.
    - Ask, *"What if your date asks about your exes or your dating history?"*

- □ Answers: *Keep it short and sweet*; answer their questions honestly and truthfully, but keep it short and positive, then *change the subject.*
  - Ask, *"After you've dated them for a while, then can you tell them more about your exes if they ask?"*
    - □ Answer: Yes, once you're in a relationship.

- **DON'T talk about your feelings at first**
  - Say, *"Another rule for dating is don't talk about your feelings at first. What could be the problem with talking about your feelings right away?"*
    - Answers: You might scare them off; you could come on too strong too soon; they might not want to date you again.
  - Ask, *"What if you really like the person and think about them all the time? Should you tell them that and what could be the problem with doing that?"*
    - Answers: No; you might scare them; they might think you're a stalker; they might not want to go out with you again.
  - Ask, *"After you've dated them for a while, then can you tell them more about your feelings?"*
    - Answer: Yes.
  - Explain, *"Most people don't start talking about feelings for at least three or four dates. Some people rarely or never talk about feelings. Your social coaches can help you decide when it's the right time to start talking about feelings."*

- **DON'T rush the relationship**
  - Say, *"It's also important that when you first start dating someone, you don't rush the relationship. What does it mean to rush the relationship?"*
    - Answers: Moving too quickly; coming on too strong; talking about feelings too soon; assuming you're exclusive before you've talked about your relationship status.
  - Ask, *"What could be the problem with rushing the relationship?"*
    - Answers: If you move too quickly, they might get scared off; you might turn them off if you go too fast.
  - Explain, *"Every relationship moves at a different pace, so you may need to be patient and careful not to move too quickly or rush the relationship."*

- **DON'T assume you're a couple**
  - Ask, *"Just because you've gone on a couple or a few dates with someone, does that mean you're a couple?"*
    - Answer: No.
  - Ask, *"What could be the problem with assuming you're a couple?"*
    - Answers: You might scare off the other person; it might seem like you're coming on too strong; misunderstandings could happen.
  - Ask, *"How do you know when you're a couple?"*
    - Answer: There is usually a conversation between you and your partner where you make the decision to be exclusive (not see anyone else).
  - Ask, *"When is the right time to have a conversation about being exclusive?"*
    - Answers: It depends on the relationship; most people go on several dates before they decide to be a couple.
  - Explain, *"Your social coaches can help you decide when it's the right time to have a conversation about being exclusive, or not seeing other people."*

- **DON'T kiss and tell**
  - Say, *"Another rule for dating is don't kiss and tell. What does it mean to kiss and tell?"*
    - Answers: It means to share the private details of your relationship with other people; it usually involves sharing intimate details about your physical relationship.
  - Ask, *"What could be the problem with kissing and telling?"*
    - Answers: It's indiscrete; it's disrespectful to the person you're dating; that's private information; they may not want to date you again if you *kiss and tell.*
- **DON'T be a player**
  - Say, *"Another rule for dating is don't be a player. What does it mean to be a player?"*

- ■ Answers: It means to play games with someone when dating; to date multiple people without their knowledge of each other.
  - ○ Ask, *"What could be the problem with being a player?"*
    - ■ Answers: It's disrespectful to the people you're dating; it's dishonest if they don't know you're dating other people; it could be hurtful; you could get a bad reputation.
  - ○ Ask, *"Does that mean you can't date multiple people at the same time?"*
    - ■ Answer: No, but you should be honest about it.
  - ○ Explain, *"It's fine if you want to keep things casual and date more than one person at a time, as long as you're honest about it. It's when you're not honest that you can seem like a player."*

- ● **DON'T pressure them**
  - ○ Say, *"Another rule for dating is don't pressure the person you're dating. What does it mean to pressure the other person?"*
    - ■ Answers: Trying to pressure them to do things they don't want to do; trying to get them to commit before they're ready; trying to force them to get physical before they're comfortable.
  - ○ Ask, *"What could be the problem with pressuring someone to commit to the relationship or get physical before they're ready?"*
    - ■ Answers: It makes the other person uncomfortable; it's not fair to the other person; you seem controlling or needy; they may not want to go out with you.
  - ○ Explain, *"Remember that dating is a choice. Just because you want something from a relationship doesn't mean the other person wants the same thing. It's a choice."*

Handling Sexual Pressure from Partners

- ● Explain, *"Even though one of the rules for dating is not to pressure the other person, that doesn't mean it won't happen to us. Sometimes people that we're dating may make sexual offers or even pressure us to do things we don't want to do or that we're not ready to do. For example, they might want us to get physically intimate before we're ready. If that happens, there are some very specific steps we can follow for handling sexual pressure from romantic partners."*

Bad Role Play: Handling Sexual Pressure from Partners ⊙

[Two behavioral coaches should do an INAPPROPRIATE role play of **handling sexual pressure from partners**. If you do not have two behavioral coaches, the group leader can be a substitute for one of the coaches.]

- ● Begin by saying, *"We're going to do a role play. Watch this and tell me what (name of behavioral coach 2) is doing WRONG in handling sexual pressure from a partner."*

Example of an INAPPROPRIATE Role Play

- ○ Behavioral coach 1: *"I had a really nice time with you tonight. Thanks for coming over and letting me make dinner for you."*
- ○ Behavioral coach 2: *"Sure, it was fun."*
- ○ Behavioral coach 1: (Pause) *"I was just wondering . . . it's getting kind of late. (pause) Would you like to stay over?"*
- ○ Behavioral coach 2: (Shocked, overly dramatic) *"Do you mean spend the night with you?! How could you ask me something like that? We've only been dating for two months!"*
- ○ Behavioral coach 1: (Mortified, apologetic) *"I'm so sorry. I didn't mean to offend you. It's just getting late. I thought you might be tired."*
- ○ Behavioral coach 2: (Overreacting, dramatic) *"I can't believe you would ask me something like that! I'm leaving!"* (Storms off and leaves)
- ○ Behavioral coach 1: (Shocked, confused, hurt)

- End by saying, *"Timeout on that. So what did (name of behavioral coach 2) do WRONG in handling sexual pressure from a partner?"*
  - Answers: Got angry and upset; yelled at the date; stormed off.
- Ask the following *Perspective Taking Questions*:
  - *"What was that like for (name of coach 1)?"*
    - Answers: Confusing; hurtful; shocking; offensive.
  - *"What do you think (name of coach 1) thought of (name of coach 2)?"*
    - Answers: Dramatic; overreactive.
  - *"Is (name of coach 1) going to want to go on a date with (name of coach 2) again?"*
    - Answer: No, probably not.
- Ask behavioral coach 1 the same *Perspective Taking Questions*:
  - *"What was that like for you?"*
  - *"What did you think of (name of coach 2)?"*
  - *"Would you want to go on a date with (name of coach 2) again?"*

Steps for Handling Sexual Pressure from Partners

- Explain, *"Instead of getting upset and losing our cool, there are some specific steps we can follow if the person we're dating makes a sexual offer or even pressures us to do things we don't want to do."*

1. **Keep your cool**
   - Say, *"The first step for handling sexual pressure from partners is to keep your cool. What does it mean to keep your cool and why would that be important to do?"*
     - Answers: It means stay calm and don't get upset; getting upset may only make matters worse and escalate emotions.
   - Explain, *"If you like the person and they want to move things to a more physical level before you're ready, a simple conversation may be all you need to solve the problem. They may not be intending to pressure you, so start by keeping your cool."*

2. **Tell them what you DON'T want to do**
   - Say, *"The next step for handling sexual pressure is to tell them what you DON'T want to do. This is regardless of whether you want to preserve the relationship or not. Why is it important to be clear about what you DON'T want to do?"*
     - Answers: It's your choice what you do or do not do sexually; if you don't **tell your partner what you DON'T want to do**, they won't know; they can't read your mind.
   - Ask, *"What are some examples of ways to tell them what you DON'T want to do?"*
     - Example: *"I don't want to (state the behavior)."*
     - Example: *"I'm not comfortable with (state the behavior)."*
     - Example: *"I don't (state the behavior)."*
   - Ask, *"What if you're just not ready to do what they're offering right now, but you might be later? How might you say that?"*
     - Example: *"I'm not ready to get physical yet."*
     - Example: *"I'm not comfortable with (state the behavior) right now."*
     - Example: *"I'm not comfortable taking it to the next level yet."*

3. **Give a cover story**
   - Say, *"If you like the person and you want to preserve the relationship, the next step for handling sexual pressure from a partner is to give a cover story. What are cover stories?"*
     - Answer: *Cover stories* are reasons we do things or don't do things.
   - Ask, *"What are some cover stories or reasons we might not be ready to get more physical with someone we're dating?"*
     - Example: *"I don't know you well enough yet."*
     - Example: *"I don't feel comfortable doing that right now."*
     - Example: *"I like to take things slow."*

- Ask, *"If you know that you're NEVER going to be comfortable with what they're offering, should you tell them?"*
  - ○ Answer: Yes.
- Ask, *"If we don't like the person we're dating or we don't care about preserving the relationship, do we have to give a cover story?"*
  - ○ Answer: No.

4. **Use "I" statements to tell them how you feel**
   - Explain, *"The next step for handling sexual pressure from partners is to use 'I' statements to tell them how you feel. This might include telling them what you need from them or what you want to do moving forward."*
   - Ask, *"What are 'I' statements?"*
     - ○ Answer: Statements that begin with *"I think . . ."* or *"I feel . . ."*
   - Ask, *"What are 'you' statements?"*
     - ○ Answer: Statements that begin with *"You did . . ."* or *"You make me feel . . ."*
   - Ask, *"What could be the problem with using 'you' statements instead of 'I' statements when you're trying to share your feelings?"*
     - ○ Answers: **"You" statements** make people defensive; **"I" statements** are less offensive because they focus on your own feelings and don't place blame.
   - Ask, *"What are some examples of 'I' statements when you're feeling sexually pressured by someone you're dating?"*
     - ○ Example: *"I like you but I need some space."*
     - ○ Example: *"I feel like I need to slow things down."*
     - ○ Example: *"I think I need more time to get to know you."*
   - Ask, *"Do you want to sound assertive and confident when using 'I' statements and telling them how you feel, and why would that be important?"*
     - ○ Answers: Yes; they need to know you mean what you're saying.

5. **Change the subject**
   - Say, *"If you like the person and you want to slow things down, but don't want the date to end, the next step is to try changing the subject. What does it mean to change the subject?"*
     - ○ Answers: Talk about something else; do something different; shift the focus of the conversation.
   - Ask, *"Why is it a good idea to change the subject if you like the person?"*
     - ○ Answer: Because it distracts the conversation away from the awkwardness of the moment.

6. **Give a cover story and leave (if still pressured)**
   - Say, *"If you're still feeling sexually pressured, or you simply feel uncomfortable, do you have to stick around?"*
     - ○ Answer: No, absolutely not.
   - Ask, *"What should you do if you're feeling uncomfortable?"*
     - ○ Answer: **Give a cover story and leave**.
   - Explain, *"If you're in a situation where you feel uncomfortable, or you feel pressured to do something you don't want to do, you can always give a cover story for leaving, and then remove yourself from the situation."*
   - Ask, *"How can you remove yourself?"*
     - ○ Answers: Drive yourself home; call a friend, family member, or social coach to pick you up; call a taxi; take Uber; take public transportation; walk home if not too far.

7. **Remember dating is a choice**
   - Explain, *"Finally, remember that dating is a choice. If the person you're dating wants to do things you don't want to do, and they continue to pressure you, that may mean they're not a good choice for you."*

Good Role Play: Handling Sexual Pressure from Partners ⊙

[Two behavioral coaches should do an APPROPRIATE role play demonstrating *handling sexual pressure from partners*. If you do not have two behavioral coaches, the group leader can be a substitute for one of the coaches.]

- Begin by saying, *"We're going to do another role play. Watch this and tell me what (name of behavioral coach 2) is doing RIGHT in handling sexual pressure from a partner."*

> Example of an APPROPRIATE Role Play
>
> ○ Behavioral coach 1: *"I had a really nice time with you tonight. Thanks for coming over and letting me make dinner for you."*
> ○ Behavioral coach 2: *"Yeah, thanks. It was fun."*
> ○ Behavioral coach 1: (Pause) *"I was just wondering . . . it's getting kind of late. (pause) Would you like to stay over?"*
> ○ Behavioral coach 2: (Calm, assertive, confident) *"Oh thanks, but I'm not really comfortable spending the night yet."*
> ○ Behavioral coach 1: (Casual) *"Okay, that's fine."*
> ○ Behavioral coach 2: (Calm, friendly) *"I just like to take things slow . . . I think I need a little more time to get to know you."*
> ○ Behavioral coach 1: (Reassuring) *"That's cool. I understand."*
> ○ Behavioral coach 2: (Friendly) *"Thanks. (pause) So that was a really great dinner. You're an amazing cook!"*
> ○ Behavioral coach 1: (Smiling) *"Thanks! I'm glad you liked it."*
> ○ Behavioral coach 2: (Friendly) *"I did! Where did you learn to cook like that?"*

- End by saying, *"Timeout on that. So what did (name of behavioral coach 2) do RIGHT in handling sexual pressure from a partner?"*
  - Answers: **Kept cool; told the date what he/she didn't want to do; gave a cover story; used "I" statements; changed the subject.**
- Ask the following *Perspective Taking Questions*:
  - *"What was that like for (name of coach 1)?"*
    - Answer: Fine.
  - *"What do you think (name of coach 1) thought of (name of coach 2)?"*
    - Answers: Assertive; confident; honest.
  - *"Is (name of coach 1) going to want to go on a date with (name of coach 2) again?"*
    - Answer: Yes.
- Ask behavioral coach 1 the same *Perspective Taking Questions*:
  - *"What was that like for you?"*
  - *"What did you think of (name of coach 2)?"*
  - *"Would you want to go on a date with (name of coach 2) again?"*

Behavioral Rehearsal: Handling Sexual Pressure from Partners

- Explain, *"Now we're going to have each of you practice handling sexual pressure from a partner with one of our behavioral coaches using the same example you just saw."*
- Go around the room and have each young adult practice **handling sexual pressure from a partner** using the SAME EXAMPLE from the role play with one of the behavioral coaches while the group watches.
  - Be sure to have at least one male and one female behavioral coach for young adults to practice with.
  - If you only have one behavioral coach, the group leader can substitute for a missing coach of the same gender.

- ○   Ask, *"Who would you feel more comfortable practicing with, (insert name of female coach) or (insert name of male coach)?"*
- Instruct the young adults that the behavioral coach will be offering to have them spend the night in the manner they saw in the role play. They should imagine they are not interested in the offer and should follow the steps for ***handling sexual pressure from partners***.
- Have the behavioral coach begin the role play by saying, *"I was just wondering . . . it's getting kind of late. Would you like to stay over?"*
- Encourage young adults to look at the board as they're following the steps for ***handling sexual pressure from partners***.
  - ○   You may need to point to specific steps as they're practicing.
  - ○   Try not to stop the behavioral rehearsal while they're practicing.
- Provide ***social coaching*** as needed and ***troubleshoot*** any problems that may arise.
- End by giving a round of applause to each young adult after their practice.

DATING ETIQUETTE: DATING DO'S AND DON'TS

Young Adult Behavioral Rehearsal

Get-Togethers

Materials Needed

- Indoor games (e.g., video games, card games, board games).
  - If you are going to provide video games as an option, make sure there are enough gaming consoles that each group can play simultaneously together.
  - Do not use small, portable gaming devices as people have to wait to take turns and that can get boring.
  - Several decks of playing cards will be sufficient if you do not have these other resources.
- Optional: iPads or laptops for watching YouTube videos, surfing the Internet, or playing computer games.
  - If you are going to provide iPads or laptops as an option, make sure there are enough that each group can use them simultaneously together.
- [Note: Most PEERS® programs DO NOT have access to gaming consoles, iPads, or laptops. These are luxury items. Just providing a few decks of cards to keep the get-together *activity-based* will be fine.]

Behavioral Rehearsal

- Notify young adults they will be practicing having *get-togethers*.
  - Note: They will no longer be practicing *beginning and ending get-togethers*.
- Break up young adults into small groups or dyads.
- Have young adults practice following the rules for how to behave *during the get-together* while:
  - ***Trading information.***
  - ***Finding common interests.***
  - Playing with games and items provided by the treatment team (e.g., video games, card games, board games, iPads, laptops, etc.).
- Provide *social coaching* as needed regarding the rules for making and keeping friends.

DATING ETIQUETTE: DATING DO'S AND DON'TS

Reunification

- Announce that young adults should join their social coaches.
  - ○ Have young adults stand or sit next to their social coaches.
  - ○ Be sure to have silence and the full attention of the group before starting with *Reunification*.
  - ○ Have young adults generate the content from the lesson while social coaches listen.
- Say, *"Today, we talked about general dating do's and don'ts and also how to handle sexual pressure from romantic partners. What were the steps for handling sexual pressure from someone you're dating?"*
  1. *Keep your cool*
  2. *Tell them what you DON'T want to do*
  3. *Give a cover story*
  4. *Use "I" statements to tell them how you feel*
  5. *Change the subject*
  6. *Give a cover story and leave (if still pressured)*
  7. *Remember dating is a choice*
- Explain, *"In addition to talking about dating, we also had young adults practice having get-togethers and the group did a great job so we should give them a round of applause."*

Homework Assignments

Distribute the *Social Coaching Handout* to young adults and announce the following *Homework Assignments*:

1. Have a *get-together* with a friend.
   - Social coaches should help young adults plan the get-together using the *five W's*:
     - ○ *WHO* they plan to get together with.
     - ○ *WHAT* they plan to do.
     - ○ *WHEN* it will happen.
     - ○ *WHERE* they will meet.
     - ○ *HOW* they will make it happen.
   - Social coaches should go over the rules and steps for *get-togethers* with young adults beforehand.
   - Social coaches should ask young adults the following *social coaching questions* after the *get-together*:
     - ○ *What did you decide to do and who picked the activities?*
     - ○ *Did you trade information and for what percentage of the time?*
     - ○ *What were your common interests and what could you do with that information if you were going to hang out again?*
     - ○ *Did you and your friend have a good time?*
     - ○ *Is this someone you might want to hang out with again?*
2. Practice *letting someone know you like them, ask them on a date*, and/or *go on a date*.
   - If young adults are interested in someone romantically:

○ *Let them know you like them.*
○ *Ask them on a date.*
○ *Go on a date.*
○ DO NOT practice unless you are romantically interested in the person.
- Young adults should practice *letting someone know you like them, asking someone on a date*, and *beginning and ending dates* with social coaches, if comfortable.
- Social coaches should go over all of the rules and steps for *dating etiquette* before the practice.
- Social coaches should ask young adults the following *social coaching questions* after each practice:
    ○ *Letting someone know you like them:*
        - *Who did you practice with and what did you do to let them know you like them?*
        - *How did they respond?*
        - *Does this seem like a good choice and is this someone you might want to go on a date with?*
    ○ *Asking someone on a date:*
        - *Who did you ask on a date and what steps did you follow?*
        - *How did they respond?*
    ○ *Going on a date:*
        - *What did you decide to do?*
        - *Did you trade information and for what percentage of the time?*
        - *What were your common interests and what could you do with that information if you were going to go on a date again?*
        - *Did you and your date have a good time?*
        - *Does this seem like a good choice and is this someone you might want to go on a date with again?*

3. *Enter a group conversation* with peers (could be from the *source of friends*).
    - Social coaches should go over the rules and steps for *entering and exiting group conversations* before the practice.
    - The assignment is NOT to *exit the conversation* unless they naturally need to.
    - Social coaches should ask young adults the following *social coaching questions* after the practice:
        ○ *Where did you enter a conversation and with whom?*
        ○ *Which steps did you follow?*
        ○ *Did it seem like they wanted to talk to you and how could you tell?*
        ○ *Did you have to exit the conversation and which steps did you follow?*

Individual Check-Out

Individually and privately negotiate with each young adult and social coach:

1. *WHO* they plan to have a *get-together* with in the coming week.
    - *WHAT* they plan to suggest to their friends.
    - *WHEN* and *WHERE* they will suggest to their friends.
    - *HOW* they will make it happen (e.g., tickets, transportation, etc.).

2. How they will practice *letting someone know they like them* and with whom, and whether they plan to *ask them on a date*.
    - *WHO* they plan to have a *date* with in the coming week.
    - *WHAT* they plan to suggest to do.
    - *WHEN* and *WHERE* they will suggest to meet.
    - *HOW* they will make it happen (e.g., tickets, transportation, etc.).

3. Where, when, and with whom they plan to *enter a group conversation* with peers.
    - Whether this is an accepting *social group* and how they can tell.

DATING ETIQUETTE: DATING DO'S AND DON'TS

Social Coaching Handout

Dating DO'S

- *DO remember that dating is a choice*
- *DO move on if YOU are not interested*
- *DO move on if THEY are not interested*
- *DO be polite and respectful*
- *DO be honest and truthful*
- *DO keep in touch*
- *DO ask permission for any physical contact*

Dating DON'TS

- *DON'T get too personal at first*
  - *Don't ask too many personal questions at first*
  - *Don't share too much personal information at first*
  - *Don't disclose any diagnoses at first*
- *DON'T talk about your dating history at first*
  - *Don't share lack of dating experience at first*
  - *Don't share bad dating experiences at first*
  - *Don't talk about your exes at first*
- *DON'T talk about your feelings at first*
- *DON'T rush the relationship*
- *DON'T assume you're a couple*
- *DON'T kiss and tell*
- *DON'T be a player*
- *DON'T pressure them*

Handling Sexual Pressure from Partners

1. *Keep your cool*

2. *Tell them what you DON'T want to do*
   - Example: *"I don't want to (state the behavior)."*
   - Example: *"I'm not comfortable with (state the behavior)."*
   - Example: *"I'm not ready to get physical yet."*
   - Example: *"I'm not comfortable with (state the behavior) right now."*

3. *Give a cover story*
   - Example: *"I don't know you well enough yet."*
   - Example: *"I don't feel comfortable doing that right now."*
   - Example: *"I like to take things slow."*

4. *Use "I" statements to tell them how you feel*
   - Example: *"I like you but I need some space."*
   - Example: *"I feel like I need to slow things down."*
   - Example: *"I think I need more time to get to know you."*

5. *Change the subject*

6. *Give a cover story and leave (if still pressured)*

7. *Remember dating is a choice*

Homework Assignments

1. Have a *get-together* with a friend.
   - Social coaches should help young adults plan the get-together using the *five W's*:
     - ○ *WHO* they plan to get together with.
     - ○ *WHAT* they plan to do.
     - ○ *WHEN* it will happen.
     - ○ *WHERE* they will meet.
     - ○ *HOW* they will make it happen.
   - Social coaches should go over the rules and steps for *get-togethers* with young adults before-hand.
   - Social coaches should ask young adults the following *social coaching questions* after the *get-together*:
     - ○ *What did you decide to do and who picked the activities?*
     - ○ *Did you trade information and for what percentage of the time?*
     - ○ *What were your common interests and what could you do with that information if you were going to hang out again?*
     - ○ *Did you and your friend have a good time?*
     - ○ *Is this someone you might want to hang out with again?*

2. Practice *letting someone know you like them, ask them on a date*, and/or *go on a date*.
   - If young adults are interested in someone romantically:
     - ○ *Let them know you like them.*
     - ○ *Ask them on a date.*
     - ○ *Go on a date.*
     - ○ DO NOT practice unless you are romantically interested in the person.
   - Young adults should practice *letting someone know you like them, asking someone on a date*, and *beginning and ending dates* with social coaches, if comfortable.
   - Social coaches should go over all of the rules and steps for *dating etiquette* before the practice.
   - Social coaches should ask young adults the following *social coaching questions* after each practice:
     - ○ *Letting someone know you like them*:
       - ▪ *Who did you practice with and what did you do to let them know you like them?*
       - ▪ *How did they respond?*
       - ▪ *Does this seem like a good choice and is this someone you might want to go on a date with?*
     - ○ *Asking someone on a date*:
       - ▪ *Who did you ask on a date and what steps did you follow?*
       - ▪ *How did they respond?*
     - ○ *Going on a date*:
       - ▪ *What did you decide to do?*
       - ▪ *Did you trade information and for what percentage of the time?*
       - ▪ *What were your common interests and what could you do with that information if you were going to go on a date again?*

- *Did you and your date have a good time?*
- *Does this seem like a good choice and is this someone you might want to go on a date with again?*

3. *Enter a group conversation* with peers (could be from the *source of friends*).
    - Social coaches should go over the rules and steps for *entering and exiting group conversations* before the practice.
    - The assignment is NOT to *exit the conversation* unless they naturally need to.
    - Social coaches should ask young adults the following *social coaching questions* after the practice:
        - *Where did you enter a conversation and with whom?*
        - *Which steps did you follow?*
        - *Did it seem like they wanted to talk to you and how could you tell?*
        - *Did you have to exit the conversation?*
        - *If you had to exit, which steps did you follow?*

SESSION 13

HANDLING DISAGREEMENTS

Social Coaching Therapist Guide

Preparing for the Social Coaching Session

The focus of this lesson is on helping young adults develop conflict resolution skills to manage arguments and disagreements with friends or romantic partners. This is often a popular session among social coaches who may exclaim, *"I need to share this with my husband"* or *"I could use this with my wife."* It is true that, like many of the skills taught in PEERS®, anyone could benefit from instruction in this area, as disagreements are not uncommon even among healthy friendships and relationships.

Although the lesson is fairly straightforward, one issue that may come up relates to the order of the steps presented for **RESPONDING to disagreements**. The general order for these steps include: (1) **keep your cool**; (2) **listen to the other person**; (3) **repeat what they said**; (4) **explain your side**; (5) **say you're sorry**; and (6) **try to solve the problem**. Although very few social coaches will object to these steps, occasionally there may be criticism of the order. In particular, some social coaches may state that the step for **saying you're sorry** should come earlier in the sequence. In general, the sequence of steps should be maintained, but **saying you're sorry** earlier in the sequence should not be a problem for those who object to the order. However, **explaining your side** should always follow **keeping your cool, listening to the other person**, and **repeating what they said** to ensure that the other person is even willing to hear your explanation. Moreover, most disagreements end with some attempt to **try to solve the problem**, so that step should be somewhere near the end of the sequence. Even more important than maintaining the general sequence of the steps is the importance of following ALL of the steps. Missing only one step could be the difference between conflict resolution and no resolution.

As with most social skills, there are some cultural differences when it comes to strategies for conflict resolution. Even within North America, where the PEERS® intervention was developed, there are some slight cultural differences between the United States and Canada. In having trained thousands of Canadian mental health professionals and educators on the PEERS® method, one common observation is that not only would the step **say you're sorry** come sooner in the sequence for **RESPONDING to disagreements**, it would also come more frequently. The joke among Canadian PEERS® Certified Providers is that the sequence should actually be: **keep your cool, listen to the other person, say you're sorry, repeat what they said, say you're sorry, explain your side, say you're sorry, try to solve the problem**, and **say you're sorry**. Although a humorous anecdote, this frequent observation highlights the cultural differences seen even among close North American neighbors. Consequently, cultural adaptations should be made as needed in this lesson.

Another common question that may come up in this lesson relates to the step in which young adults are told to **repeat what the other person said**. Essentially, this step is intended to involve *active and empathic listening*. The challenge with this step is that many young adults with Autism Spectrum Disorder (ASD) and other social challenges struggle to understand emotions and communicate empathy. They may have difficulty understanding and labeling emotions in themselves and others, which impedes their ability to listen actively and express empathy during disagreements.

Consequently, this lesson presents a simpler alternative to *active and empathic listening* through the rule to **repeat what the other person said**. In this case, young adults are given a sentence stem to help them through the process. Young adults will be instructed that they can demonstrate that they are listening and showing empathy by saying, *"It sounds like . . ."* Examples might include, *"It sounds like you're upset"* or *"It sounds like I made you mad"* or *"It sounds like I hurt your feelings."* Although this sentence stem will help young adults to demonstrate *active and empathic listening*, some social coaches may comment that these statements may sound a bit artificial. If young adults are socially savvy enough to discern the artificiality of these statements, then they may be well equipped enough to provide more empathic responses. In these cases, feel free to have social coaches encourage young adults to use more empathic responses when appropriate. For those who struggle to communicate empathy, sticking to simple sentences that begin with *"It sounds like . . ."* should be sufficient to communicate that they are listening actively.

Homework Review

[Go over the following *Homework Assignments* and **troubleshoot** any potential problems. Start with completed homework first. If you have time, you can inquire as to why others were unable to complete the assignment and try to **troubleshoot** how they might get it done for the coming week. When reviewing homework, be sure to relabel descriptions using the **buzzwords** (identified by **bold and italicized** print). Spend the majority of the *Homework Review* on **get-togethers** as this was the most important assignment.]

1. Have a *get-together* with a friend.
    - Say, *"One of the main assignments this week was for young adults to have a get-together with a friend. Who completed this assignment or attempted to complete it?"*
    - Ask the following questions:
        ○ *"Did you help your young adult plan the get-together using the five W's?"*
        ○ *"What social coaching did you do before the get-together?"*
        ○ *"What did your young adult decide to do and with whom?"*
        ○ *"How did the get-together begin?"*
        ○ *"Who picked the activities?"*
        ○ *"Did they trade information and what percentage of the time?"*
        ○ *"How did the get-together end?"*
        ○ *"What social coaching did you do after the get-together?"*
            ■ Appropriate *social coaching questions*:
                □ **What did you decide to do and who picked the activities?**
                □ **Did you trade information and for what percentage of the time?**
                □ **What were your common interests and what could you do with that information if you were going to hang out again?**
                □ **Did you and your friend have a good time?**
                □ **Is this someone you might want to hang out with again?**
        ○ *"Does this seem like a good choice for a friend and someone your young adult will want to hang out with again?"*

Table 14.1 Steps for Beginning and Ending Get-Togethers in Your Home

Beginning the Get-Together	*Ending the Get-Together*
1. Greet your guest	*1. Wait for a pause in activities*
2. Invite them in	*2. Give a cover story for ending the get-together*
3. Introduce them to anyone they don't know	*3. Start walking your friend to the door*
4. Give them a tour	*4. Thank your friend for getting together*
5. Offer them refreshments	*5. Tell your friend you had a good time*
6. Ask them what they want to do	*6. Say goodbye and you'll see them later*

2. Practice *letting someone know you like them, ask them on a date*, and/or *go on a date*.
   - Say, *"Another assignment this week was for young adults to practice letting someone know they like them, ask them on a date, and/or go on a date. The assignment was NOT to practice unless they are romantically interested in the person. Young adults could also have practiced with social coaches, if they were comfortable. Who completed this assignment or attempted to complete it?"*
   - Ask the following questions:
     - *"What social coaching did you do before the practice?"*
     - *"Who did your young adult practice with?"*
     - *"What did they do to let the person know they like them and how did they respond?"*
     - *"Did they ask the person on a date and how did they respond?"*
     - Ask the following questions if they went on a date:
       - *"What did they decide to do?"*
       - *"Did they trade information and for what percentage of the time?"*
       - *"Did they and their date have a good time?"*
     - *"What social coaching did you do after the practice?"*
     - *"Does this seem like a good choice and is this someone they might want to go on a date with (again)?"*

3. *Enter a group conversation* with peers (could be from the *source of friends*).
   - Say, *"Another assignment this week was for young adults to practice entering group conversations with peers. Who completed this assignment or attempted to complete it?"*
   - Ask the following questions:
     - *"Where and with whom did your young adult practice?"*
     - *"What social coaching did you do before the practice?"*
     - *"Which steps did your young adult follow?"*
       1. *Listen to the Conversation*
       2. *Watch from a Distance*
       3. *Use a Prop*
       4. *Identify the Topic*
       5. *Find a Common Interest*
       6. *Move Closer*
       7. *Wait for a Pause*
       8. *Mention the Topic*
       9. *Assess Interest*
       10. *Introduce Yourself*
     - *"What social coaching did you do after the practice?"*
       - Appropriate *social coaching questions*:
         - *Where did you enter a conversation and with whom?*
         - *Which steps did you follow?*
         - *Did it seem like they wanted to talk to you and how could you tell?*
         - *Did you have to exit the conversation and which steps did you follow?*

Table 14.2 Steps for Exiting Conversations

NEVER ACCEPTED	INITIALLY ACCEPTED, THEN EXCLUDED	FULLY ACCEPTED
1. Keep your cool 2. Look away 3. Turn away 4. Walk away	1. Keep your cool 2. Look away 3. Wait for a BRIEF pause 4. Give a BRIEF cover story for leaving 5. Walk away	1. Wait for a pause 2. Give a SPECIFIC cover story for leaving 3. Say you'll see them later 4. Say goodbye 5. Walk away

- [Collect the *Social Coaching Homework Assignment Worksheets*. If social coaches forgot to bring the worksheets, have them complete a new form to hold them accountable for the assignments.]

Didactic Lesson: Handling Disagreements

- Distribute the *Social Coaching Handout.*
  - Sections in **bold print** in the *Social Coaching Therapist Guide* come directly from the *Social Coaching Handout.*
  - Remind social coaches that terms that are in ***bold and italicized*** print are ***buzzwords*** and represent important concepts from the PEERS® curriculum that should be used as much as possible when social coaching.
- Explain, *"Today, we're going to be talking about handling disagreements. Arguments and disagreements with friends or romantic partners are common, and OCCASIONAL arguments that aren't too explosive shouldn't have to end friendships or relationships. Because we know that OCCASIONAL disagreements are common, it's important to know how to manage them. There are basically two positions young adults may find themselves in when it comes to disagreements. Someone might be upset with them, where they have to RESPOND to a disagreement. Or they might be upset with someone, where they have to BRING UP a disagreement. Let's start by talking about what to do when someone is upset with us and we need to RESPOND to a disagreement."*

Steps for RESPONDING to Disagreements

1. ***Keep your cool***
   - Say, *"The first step for responding to arguments or disagreements with a friend or a partner is to keep your cool. This means you need to stay calm and don't get upset. What are some ways people keep their cool?"*
     - Answers: Take deep breaths; count silently to 10; take some time to cool down before you talk.
   - Ask, *"What could be the problem with losing your cool during a disagreement?"*
     - Answers: If you lose your cool, you may end up saying something you regret or ruining your friendship or relationship; you may make it worse.

2. ***Listen to the other person***
   - Explain, *"The next step for responding to an argument or disagreement with a friend or partner is to listen. That means if someone is upset, you need to listen before you share your side."*
   - Ask, *"Why is it important to listen to the other person's side?"*
     - Answer: Listening is an important part of communication and helps us to understand the other person's perspective.

3. ***Repeat what they said***
   - Explain, *"The next step is to repeat back what they said to let them know you're listening to them."*
   - Ask, *"Why would it be important to repeat back what the other person said?"*
     - Answers: It shows them that you're listening; makes them feel like you care; makes them feel heard; shows that you have empathy.
   - Explain, *"If young adults have trouble with this step, repeating statements might start with the sentence stem, 'It sounds like . . .'"*
     - Example: *"It sounds like you're upset."*
     - Example: *"It sounds like you're angry."*
     - Example: *"It sounds like your feelings are hurt."*
   - Explain, *"Repeating what the other person said is a type of active empathic listening. If you don't repeat what they said, they don't know they've been heard and the argument doesn't tend to be over. Saying, 'It sounds like . . .' is one way to repeat what the person said, but if your young adult can do better than that, then encourage them to try."*

4. ***Explain your side using "I" statements***
   - Explain, *"The next step in responding to a disagreement is to explain your side. Many people will jump to do this step first, but you need to WAIT until you've kept your cool, listened, and repeated what they've said. When you're explaining your side, you should avoid telling the other person that they're wrong. Instead, calmly explain your side of the story."*

- Ask, *"What could be the problem with telling the other person that they're wrong?"*
  - Answers: This will only upset them and escalate the argument or disagreement; they are not likely to agree; they will most likely get more upset with you.
- Explain, *"When you're explaining your side, you also want to use 'I' statements. What are 'I' statements?"*
  - Answer: Statements that begin with *"I think . . ."* or *"I feel . . ."*
- Ask, *"What are 'you' statements?"*
  - Answer: Statements that begin with *"You did . . ."* or *"You make me feel . . ."*
- Ask, *"What could be the problem with using 'you' statements instead of 'I' statements when you're trying to explain your side?"*
  - Answers: **"You" statements** make people defensive; **"I" statements** are less offensive because they focus on your own feelings and don't place blame.
- Ask, *"What are some examples of 'I' statements when you're responding to an argument or disagreement?"*
  - Example: *"I didn't mean to upset you."*
  - Example: *"I think this is a misunderstanding."*
  - Example: *"I feel like this was a miscommunication."*

5. *Say you're sorry*
   - Explain, *"The next step for responding to a disagreement with a friend or partner is to say you're sorry. Even if you don't think you've done anything wrong, it's important to say you're sorry."*
   - Ask, *"Why is it important to say you're sorry when someone is upset?"*
     - Answers: Because the person is feeling bad and wants you to acknowledge that you're sorry they're feeling that way; arguments and disagreements are rarely over until you've said you're sorry in some way.
   - Ask, *"Is it enough to just say, 'sorry' or do you need to say what you're sorry for?"*
     - Answers: You need to say what you're sorry for; if you don't say what you're sorry for, they may ask, *"What are you sorry for?"*
   - Explain, *"Saying that you're sorry doesn't mean that you have to admit guilt or admit you did anything wrong. You can simply say you're sorry they feel that way or you're sorry this happened."*
     - Example: *"I'm sorry you're upset."*
     - Example: *"I'm sorry this happened."*
     - Example: *"I'm sorry your feelings got hurt."*

6. *Try to solve the problem*
   - Explain, *"The last step in responding to an argument or disagreement with a friend or partner is to try to solve the problem. This can be done in several ways."*
     - *Tell them what you'll do differently*
       - Explain, *"One way to try to solve the problem is to tell them what you'll do differently to fix the problem."*
         - Example: *"I'll try not to upset you again."*
         - Example: *"I'll try not to do that again."*
         - Example: *"I'll try to be more careful next time."*
     - *Ask them what they want you to do*
       - Explain, *"Another way to try to solve the problem is to ask them what they want you to do to fix the problem."*
         - Example: *"What can I do to make it up to you?"*
         - Example: *"What would you like me to do?"*
         - Example: *"What can I do to fix this?"*
     - *Suggest what you want them to do*
       - Explain, *"Another way to try to solve the problem is to suggest what you want them to do to fix the problem."*
         - Example: *"I'd like it if you tell me if I hurt your feelings again."*

□ Example: *"I hope you will give me the benefit of the doubt the next time."*

□ Example: *"I'd appreciate it if you let me know the next time this happens."*

○ ***Keep your cool if you can't solve the problem***

■ Ask, *"Can you always solve the problem in an argument or disagreement?"*

□ Answer: Not always.

■ Explain, *"If you can't solve the problem, then you need to keep your cool. Don't expect the other person to admit they're wrong. If you care about your friendship or your relationship, your goal shouldn't be to get them to apologize or admit they're wrong. Your goal should be to try to resolve the conflict."*

○ ***Agree to disagree***

■ Ask, *"Do people sometimes need to agree to disagree and what does that mean?"*

□ Answer: Sometimes we have to agree to have different opinions in arguments and disagreements.

- ***Remember to follow all of the steps***

  ○ Explain, *"If you care about your friend or partner and want to preserve the relationship, you may need to agree to disagree about certain things in order to move forward."*

  ○ Explain, *"It's important to understand that each of the steps doesn't work alone. The steps only work when they're ALL done together. For example, sometimes people have arguments that go on and on and seem like they will never end. This is usually because one or more of the steps haven't been followed."*

  ○ Ask, *"What if the person you're arguing with keeps repeating the same complaints and says things like, 'You just don't get it!' or 'I don't think you understand!' Which step did you forget?"*

    ■ Answer: You didn't **repeat what they said**, so they don't feel heard.

  ○ Ask, *"What if the person you're arguing with keeps asking you questions and says things like, 'I don't understand why you did that!' or 'How could you do that?' Which step did you forget?"*

    ■ Answer: You didn't **explain your side**, so they don't understand.

  ○ Ask, *"What if the person you're arguing with keeps telling you how they feel and says things like, 'You just don't seem to care!' or 'I don't think you even feel bad.' Which step did you forget?"*

    ■ Answer: You didn't **say you're sorry**, so they don't think you care.

  ○ Ask, *"What if the person you're arguing with keeps questioning how you will behave in the future and says things like, 'I just don't know if I can trust you!' or 'How do I know you won't do this again?' Which step did you forget?"*

    ■ Answer: You didn't **try to solve the problem**, so they don't trust you.

  ○ Explain, *"Remember, if you leave out even one step, the argument or disagreement may not be over, so be sure to follow ALL of the steps in this general order."*

- [Optional: Show the Role Play Video Demonstration of **responding to a disagreement** from the *PEERS® Role Play Video Library* (www.routledge.com/cw/laugeson) or **dealing with arguments** from the *FriendMaker* mobile app, then ask the **Perspective Taking Questions** that follow the role play.]

Steps for BRINGING UP Disagreements

- Explain, *"Another part of handling disagreements involves BRINGING UP issues and advocating for yourself. There may be times that your friends or partners do or say things to upset you. Instead of getting mad or saying nothing at all, you need to know how to advocate for yourself and BRING UP these issues. Just like with RESPONDING to disagreements when people are upset with us, there are very specific steps to follow when we're upset and need to BRING UP disagreements."*

1. ***Wait for the right time and place***

   - Say, *"The first step for bringing up disagreements is to wait for the right time and place to talk about the problem. When and where would be the right time and place?"*

     ○ Answers: When you are alone; when you have privacy; when you are both calm; when you have time to talk; when you will not be interrupted.

2. *Keep your cool*
   - Say, *"The next step for bringing up disagreements is to keep your cool. What does it mean to keep your cool?"*
     - ○ Answers: It means stay calm; don't get upset; don't lose your cool.
   - Ask, *"What could be the problem with not keeping your cool?"*
     - ○ Answers: The argument may escalate if you don't keep your cool; you could end up being in the wrong because you didn't handle the situation well; your friendship or relationship could be jeopardized.

3. *Ask to speak privately*
   - Say, *"The next step is to ask to speak to the person privately. Why would it be a good idea to speak privately if you need to bring up something that's upsetting you?"*
     - ○ Answers: You don't want others to know about your private business; it could be embarrassing to both of you if people can hear your conversation; people might gossip about your business; conflict resolution is often done in private.
   - Ask, *"How do you ask to speak privately?"*
     - ○ Example: *"Can I talk to you about something privately?"*
     - ○ Example: *"I need to speak to you about something. Can we go somewhere private?"*
     - ○ Example: *"I think we need to talk. Can I speak to you privately?"*

4. *Explain your side using "I" statements*
   - Explain, *"The next step for bringing up disagreements is to explain your side using 'I' statements. What are 'I' statements?"*
     - ○ Answer: Statements that begin with *"I think . . ."* or *"I feel . . ."*
   - Ask, *"What are some examples of 'I' statements when you're bringing up disagreements?"*
     - ○ Example: *"I felt upset when you canceled our plans."*
     - ○ Example: *"I don't like it when you speak to me that way."*
     - ○ Example: *"I feel hurt when you don't return my texts."*

5. *Listen to the other person*
   - Say, *"The next step for bringing up disagreements is to listen to the other person. Why would it be a good idea to listen to the other person's side if you're upset with them?"*
     - ○ Answers: You won't know why they did or said what they did if you don't listen; they need a chance to explain their side; the argument may not be over if you don't **listen to the other person.**

6. *Repeat what they said*
   - Say, *"The next step for bringing up disagreements is to repeat what they said. Why is it important to repeat what the other person said?"*
     - ○ Answers: They need to know they've been heard; if you don't **repeat what they said,** they may keep explaining their side; the argument may not be over if you don't **repeat what they said.**
   - Ask, *"How do you repeat what they said?"*
     - ○ Answers: Paraphrase or summarize what they said; you can **repeat what they said** using the sentence stem, *"It sounds like . . ."*

7. *Tell them what you need them to do*
   - Explain, *"The next step for bringing up disagreements is to tell them what you need them to do. Most people don't know all the steps for responding to a disagreement, but arguments don't tend to be over if you don't follow ALL of the steps."*
   - Ask, *"If the person you're upset with doesn't follow all of the steps for responding to a disagreement, what can you do?"*
     - ○ Answer: **Tell them what you need them to do.**
   - Ask, *"How do you tell them what you need them to do if they aren't listening to your side?"*
     - ○ Example: *"I need you to give me a chance to explain."*

- ○ Example: *"I need you to listen to what I'm saying."*
- ○ Example: *"Could you give me a chance to explain how I'm feeling?"*
- Ask, *"How do you tell them what you need them to do if they haven't repeated what you said?"*
  - ○ Example: *"Can you see this from my perspective?"*
  - ○ Example: *"Do you understand what I'm saying?"*
  - ○ Example: *"Do you understand why I'm upset?"*
- Ask, *"How do you tell them what you need them to do if they haven't explained their side?"*
  - ○ Example: *"Could you explain how this happened?"*
  - ○ Example: *"Could you help me understand why you did that?"*
  - ○ Example: *"It would help if you could explain where you're coming from."*
- Ask, *"How do you tell them what you need them to do if they haven't said they're sorry?"*
  - ○ Example: *"It would help if I knew you were sorry."*
  - ○ Example: *"I think I would feel better if I knew you were sorry."*
  - ○ Example: *"I think I need to know that you're sorry in order to move on."*

8. ***Try to solve the problem***
   - Explain, *"The last step for bringing up a disagreement with a friend or partner is to try to solve the problem. Just like when responding to arguments and disagreements when someone is upset with us, this can be done in several ways."*
   - ***Tell them what you'll do differently***
     - ○ Explain, *"One way to try to solve the problem is to tell them what you'll do differently."*
       - Example: *"I'll try not to be so sensitive."*
       - Example: *"I'll try not to do that again."*
       - Example: *"I'll try to be more understanding next time."*
   - ***Ask them what they want you to do***
     - ○ Explain, *"Another way to try to solve the problem is to ask them what they want you to do differently."*
       - Example: *"What can I do to avoid this happening again?"*
       - Example: *"What would you like me to do next time?"*
       - Example: *"What can we do to fix this?"*
   - ***Suggest what you want them to do***
     - ○ Explain, *"Another way to try to solve the problem is to suggest what you want them to do differently."*
       - Example: *"I'd like it if you didn't talk to me like that again."*
       - Example: *"I hope you will consider my feelings next time."*
       - Example: *"I'd appreciate it if you talk to me next time this happens."*
   - ***Keep your cool if you can't solve the problem***
     - ○ Ask, *"Can you always solve the problem in an argument or disagreement?"*
       - Answer: Not always.
     - ○ Explain, *"If you can't solve the problem, then you at least need to keep your cool. Don't expect the other person to admit they're wrong. If you care about your friendship or your relationship, your goal shouldn't be to get them to apologize or admit they're wrong. Your goal should be to try to resolve the conflict."*
   - ***Agree to disagree***
     - ○ Ask, *"When we're trying to address a conflict with someone we're upset with, do we sometimes need to agree to disagree?"*
       - Answer: Sometimes we have to ***agree to disagree*** in arguments and disagreements.
     - ○ Explain, *"If you care about your friend or partner, you may need to agree to disagree about certain things in order to preserve the relationship."*

9. ***Remember that friendship and dating is a choice***
   - Say, *"Finally, remember that friendship and dating is a choice. If you get into an argument or disagreement with a friend or partner, and what happens really bothers you, you don't have to be friends with them or date them anymore. Remember that arguments with friends and romantic partners are*

common and OCCASIONAL arguments that aren't too explosive shouldn't have to end your friendship or relationship—but in the end, friendship and dating is a choice."

- Explain, *"Remember, just like with RESPONDING to disagreements, each of the steps for BRINGING UP disagreements doesn't work alone. The steps only work when they're done together. If you leave out a step, the argument may not be over, so be sure to follow ALL of the steps in this general order."*

- [Optional: Show *Role Play Video Demonstrations* of **bringing up a disagreement** from the *PEERS® Role Play Video Library* (www.routledge.com/cw/laugeson).]

Homework Assignments

[Distribute the *Social Coaching Homework Assignment Worksheet* (Appendix I) for social coaches to complete and return at the next session.]

1. Have a *get-together* with a friend.
   - Social coaches should help young adults plan the get-together using the *five W's*:
     ○ *WHO* they plan to get together with.
     ○ *WHAT* they plan to do.
     ○ *WHEN* it will happen.
     ○ *WHERE* they will meet.
     ○ *HOW* they will make it happen.
   - Social coaches should go over the rules and steps for *get-togethers* with young adults beforehand.
   - Social coaches should ask young adults the following *social coaching questions* after the *get-together*:
     ○ *What did you decide to do and who picked the activities?*
     ○ *Did you trade information and for what percentage of the time?*
     ○ *What were your common interests and what could you do with that information if you were going to hang out again?*
     ○ *Did you and your friend have a good time?*
     ○ *Is this someone you might want to hang out with again?*

2. Young adults and social coaches should practice *handling a disagreement*.
   - Go over the rules and steps for *RESPONDING to disagreements* and *BRINGING UP disagreements* before practicing.
   - Social coaches should ask young adults the following *social coaching* and *Perspective Taking Questions* after practicing:
     ○ *Which steps did you follow?*
     ○ *What was that like for me in the end?*
     ○ *What do you think I thought of you in the end?*
     ○ *Do you think I'm going to want to hang out with you again?*

3. Young adults should practice *handling a disagreement* with a friend or romantic partner if relevant.
   - Social coaches should go over the rules and steps for *RESPONDING to disagreements* and *BRINGING UP disagreements* before practicing when possible.
   - Social coaches should ask young adults the following *Perspective Taking Questions* after practicing:
     ○ *Which steps did you follow?*
     ○ *What was that like for you and the other person in the end?*
     ○ *What did you think of each other in the end?*
     ○ *Do you think you'll both want to hang out again?*

4. Practice *letting someone know you like them, ask them on a date, and/or go on a date.*
   - If young adults are interested in someone romantically:

- o *Let them know you like them.*
- o *Ask them on a date.*
- o *Go on a date.*
- o *DO NOT practice unless you are romantically interested in the person.*
- Young adults should practice *letting someone know you like them, asking someone on a date,* and *beginning and ending dates* with social coaches, if comfortable.
- Social coaches should go over all of the rules and steps for *dating etiquette* before the practice.
- Social coaches should ask young adults the following *social coaching questions* after each practice:
  - o *Letting someone know you like them*:
    - *Who did you practice with and what did you do to let them know you like them?*
    - *How did they respond?*
    - *Does this seem like a good choice and is this someone you might want to go on a date with?*
  - o *Asking someone on a date*:
    - *Who did you ask on a date and what steps did you follow?*
    - *How did they respond?*
  - o *Going on a date*:
    - *What did you decide to do?*
    - *Did you trade information and for what percentage of the time?*
    - *What were your common interests and what could you do with that information if you were going to go on a date again?*
    - *Did you and your date have a good time?*
    - *Does this seem like a good choice and is this someone you might want to go on a date with again?*

Social Coaching Tips

When practicing *handling disagreements* with young adults, the following *Social Coaching Tips* are recommended:

- Do not surprise young adults when practicing by "picking a fight" for no reason.
- Plan the practice in advance and go over the rules and steps for *RESPONDING to disagreements* and *BRINGING UP disagreements* beforehand.
- Choose realistic examples of possible disagreements (unless they are too emotionally charged).
- Use *The Science of Making Friends DVD* (Laugeson, 2013) or *FriendMaker* app:
  - o To review steps for *responding to disagreements*.
  - o To view the Role Play Video Demonstration of "dealing with arguments."
  - o To discuss *Perspective Taking Questions* following the video demonstration.
- Use real-life *coachable moments* to practice following the steps for *handling disagreements*.

HANDLING DISAGREEMENTS

Young Adult Therapist Guide

Preparing for the Young Adult Session

The purpose of this lesson is to teach young adults basic skills to resolve arguments and disagreements with peers or romantic partners. Misunderstandings and disagreements are common among young adults, and when infrequent and not too explosive, do not need to result in the termination of friendships or relationships. Yet, some young adults lacking skills for resolving conflict may be unable to see their way out of disagreements and may choose to end relationships. Difficulty with problem resolution is somewhat characteristic of young adults with Autism Spectrum Disorder (ASD), as they have a tendency to think concretely, with little flexibility. For many young adults with ASD, interpreting friendship status may be very black and white. For example, when they are getting along with others, they are friends, but when they are not getting along with others, they are not friends. An important goal of this lesson is to help young adults understand that occasional arguments with friends or partners do not need to result in the dissolution of friendships or relationships. Rather, through appropriate conflict resolution, friendships and relationships should be able to be maintained despite periodic disagreements. For some young adults that find themselves engaged in frequent and/or explosive conflicts with specific friends or partners, they may need to re-examine the appropriateness of their choices.

The greatest challenge in this lesson involves helping young adults understand that they must complete EACH STEP in the series of steps to **RESPOND to disagreements** and **BRING UP disagreements** in order to successfully resolve conflict with others. Many young adults will pick and choose which steps to use, rather than using each of the steps as a whole. Some young adults may disagree with the lesson, making statements such as, *"It never works to just say you're sorry"* or *"It doesn't work to just explain your side."* The reality is that statements such as those are actually true. It rarely does work to ONLY say you are sorry, or ONLY explain your side. It is the combination of ALL of the steps that leads to effective conflict resolution. The *Role Play Demonstrations* will assist you in driving home the point that all of the steps must be followed. In these role plays, two behavioral coaches will demonstrate **handling disagreements** by presenting each step individually and in succession, adding a new step in each phase of the role play, while timing out in between the steps to have young adults identify whether it feels like the argument is over. Conducting the role plays by showing all of the steps together in one unified whole will not convince young adults that they must follow ALL of the steps.

While this lesson may have limited immediate applicability for some young adults, as with all other skills, the maximum effectiveness of the lesson comes with practice between sessions. If there are no peer interactions with conflict, then the young adult may not get to try out the skills being taught in natural social settings. Consequently, it is recommended that you encourage young adults to practice the steps for **handling disagreements** outside of the group with their social coaches during *Homework Assignments*, utilize opportunities for practice during real family conflict, and have young adults and social coaches hold onto the *Social Coaching Handout* for a time when conflict is present in the young adult's friendships or relationships.

Homework Review

[Go over the following *Homework Assignments* and **troubleshoot** any potential problems. Start with completed homework first. If you have time, you can inquire as to why others were unable to complete the assignment and try to **troubleshoot** how they might get it done for the coming week. When reviewing homework, be sure to relabel descriptions using the **buzzwords** (identified by **bold and italicized** print). Spend the majority of the *Homework Review* on **get-togethers** as this was the most important assignment.]

1. Have a **get-together** with a friend.
    - Say, *"One of the main assignments this week was for you to have a get-together with a friend. Raise your hand if you had a get-together with a friend this week."*
    - Ask the following questions:
        ○ *"Who did you have a get-together with and what did you decide to do?"*
        ○ *"Did you plan the get-together using the five W's?"*
        ○ *"How did the get-together begin?"*
        ○ *"Who picked the activities?"*
        ○ *"Did you trade information and for what percentage of the time?"*
        ○ *"How did the get-together end?"*
        ○ *"Did you and your friend have a good time?"*
        ○ *"Is this someone you might want to hang out with again?"*

Table 14.1 Steps for Beginning and Ending Get-Togethers in Your Home

Beginning the Get-Together	*Ending the Get-Together*
1. Greet your guest	*1. Wait for a pause in activities*
2. Invite them in	*2. Give a cover story for ending the get-together*
3. Introduce them to anyone they don't know	*3. Start walking your friend to the door*
4. Give them a tour	*4. Thank your friend for getting together*
5. Offer them refreshments	*5. Tell your friend you had a good time*
6. Ask them what they want to do	*6. Say goodbye and you'll see them later*

2. Practice **letting someone know you like them, ask them on a date**, and/or **go on a date**.
    - Say, *"Another assignment this week was to practice letting someone know you like them, ask them on a date, and/or go on a date. The assignment was NOT to practice unless you're romantically interested in the person. Raise your hand if you did this assignment."*
    - Ask the following questions:
        ○ *"Who did you practice with?"*
        ○ *"What did you do to let them know you like them and how did they respond?"*
        ○ *"Did you ask them on a date and how did they respond?"*
        ○ Ask the following questions if they went on a date:
            ▪ *"What did you decide to do?"*
            ▪ *"Did you trade information and for what percentage of the time?"*
            ▪ *"What were your common interests and what could you do with that information if you were going to go on a date again?"*
            ▪ *"Did you and your date have a good time?"*
        ○ *"Does this seem like a good choice and is this someone you might want to go on a date with (again)?"*

3. **Enter a group conversation** with peers (could be from the **source of friends**).
    - Say, *"Another assignment this week was to practice entering group conversations with peers. Raise your hand if you did this assignment."*
    - Ask the following questions:

- ○ *"Where and with whom did you practice?"*
- ○ *"Which steps did you follow?"*
  1. *Listen to the Conversation*
  2. *Watch from a Distance*
  3. *Use a Prop*
  4. *Identify the Topic*
  5. *Find a Common Interest*
  6. *Move Closer*
  7. *Wait for a Pause*
  8. *Mention the Topic*
  9. *Assess Interest*
  10. *Introduce Yourself*
- ○ *"Did it seem like they wanted to talk to you?"*
- ○ *"How could you tell?"*
  - ■ *Talking to you?*
  - ■ *Looking at you?*
  - ■ *Facing you (they opened the circle)?*
- ○ *"Did you have to exit the conversation and which steps did you follow?"*

Table 14.2 Steps for Exiting Conversations

NEVER ACCEPTED	INITIALLY ACCEPTED, THEN EXCLUDED	FULLY ACCEPTED
1. Keep your cool 2. Look away 3. Turn away 4. Walk away	1. Keep your cool 2. Look away 3. Wait for a BRIEF pause 4. Give a BRIEF cover story for leaving 5. Walk away	1. Wait for a pause 2. Give a SPECIFIC cover story for leaving 3. Say you'll see them later 4. Say goodbye 5. Walk away

Didactic Lesson: Handling Disagreements

- Explain, *"Today, we're going to be talking about handling disagreements. Arguments and disagreements with friends or romantic partners are common, and OCCASIONAL arguments that aren't too explosive shouldn't have to end your friendship or relationship. Because we know that OCCASIONAL disagreements are common, it's important to know how to manage them so they don't hurt our friendships or relationships. There are basically two positions we may find ourselves in when it comes to disagreements. Someone might be upset with us, where we have to RESPOND to a disagreement. Or we might be upset with someone, where we have to BRING UP a disagreement. Let's start by talking about what to do when someone is upset with us and we need to RESPOND to a disagreement."*
- [Present the rules and steps for *handling disagreements* by writing the following bullet points and *buzzwords* (identified by *bold and italicized* print) on the board. Do not erase the rules and steps until the end of the lesson. Each role play with a ▶ symbol includes a corresponding role play video from the *PEERS® Role Play Video Library* (www.routledge.com/cw/laugeson).]

Steps for RESPONDING to Disagreements

1. *Keep your cool*
   - Say, *"The first step for responding to arguments or disagreements with a friend or a partner is to keep your cool. This means you need to stay calm and don't get upset. What are some ways people keep their cool?"*
     - ○ Answers: Take deep breaths; count silently to 10; take some time to cool down before you talk.
   - Ask, *"What could be the problem with losing your cool during a disagreement?"*
     - ○ Answers: If you lose your cool, you may end up saying something you regret or ruining your friendship or relationship; you may make it worse.

2. *Listen to the other person*
   - Explain, *"The next step for responding to an argument or disagreement with a friend or partner is to listen. That means if someone is upset, you need to listen before you share your side."*
   - Ask, *"Why is it important to listen to the other person's side?"*
     - Answer: Listening is an important part of communication and helps us to understand the other person's perspective.

3. *Repeat what they said*
   - Explain, *"The next step is to repeat back what they said to let them know you're listening to them."*
   - Ask, *"Why would it be important to repeat back what the other person said?"*
     - Answers: It shows them that you're listening; makes them feel like you care; makes them feel heard; shows that you have empathy.
   - Explain, *"Repeating statements might start with the sentence stem, 'It sounds like . . .'"*
     - Example: *"It sounds like you're upset."*
     - Example: *"It sounds like you're angry."*
     - Example: *"It sounds like your feelings are hurt."*
   - Have each of the young adults give an example of how to **repeat what the other person said** by presenting the following complaints and then having young adults generate corresponding *repeating statements*.
     - Say, *"I feel bad when you make fun of me."*
       - Example: *"It sounds like what I said made you feel bad."*
     - Say, *"I don't like it when you pull pranks on me."*
       - Example: *"It sounds like I made you upset."*
     - Say, *"I felt embarrassed when you laughed at me in front of everybody."*
       - Example: *"It sounds like I made you feel bad."*
     - Say, *"It hurts my feelings when you don't text me back."*
       - Example: *"It sounds like I hurt your feelings."*
     - Say, *"I felt upset when you said those things."*
       - Example: *"It sounds like I upset you."*
     - Say, *"I don't like it when you tell other people my secrets."*
       - Example: *"It sounds like I hurt your feelings."*
     - Say, *"I don't like it when you talk to me like that."*
       - Example: *"It sounds like you're upset with me."*
     - Say, *"I'm really annoyed that you showed up late."*
       - Example: *"It sounds like you're frustrated with me."*
     - Say, *"I feel hurt when you cancel our plans."*
       - Example: *"It sounds like I hurt your feelings."*
     - Say, *"It makes me mad when you treat me that way."*
       - Example: *"It sounds like you're mad at me."*
   - Explain, *"Repeating what the other person said is a good way to let them know they've been heard. If you don't repeat what they said, they don't know they've been heard and the argument doesn't tend to be over. Saying, 'It sounds like . . .' is one way to repeat what the person said, but if you can do better than that, then go for it."*

4. *Explain your side using "I" statements*
   - Explain, *"The next step in responding to a disagreement is to explain your side. Many people will jump to do this step first, but you need to WAIT until you've kept your cool, listened, and repeated what they've said. When you're explaining your side, you should avoid telling the other person that they're wrong. Instead, calmly explain your side of the story."*
   - Ask, *"What could be the problem with telling the other person that they're wrong?"*
     - Answers: This will only upset them and escalate the argument or disagreement; they are not likely to agree; they will most likely get more upset with you.
   - Explain, *"When you're explaining your side, you also want to use 'I' statements. What are 'I' statements?"*
     - Answer: Statements that begin with *"I think . . ."* or *"I feel . . ."*

- Ask, *"What are 'you' statements?"*
  - Answer: Statements that begin with *"You did . . ."* or *"You make me feel . . ."*
- Ask, *"What could be the problem with using 'you' statements instead of 'I' statements when you're trying to explain your side?"*
  - Answers: ***"You" statements*** make people defensive; ***"I" statements*** are less offensive because they focus on your own feelings and don't place blame.
- Ask, *"What are some examples of 'I' statements when you're responding to an argument or disagreement?"*
  - Example: *"I didn't mean to upset you."*
  - Example: *"I think this is a misunderstanding."*
  - Example: *"I feel like this was a miscommunication."*

5. *Say you're sorry*
- Explain, *"The next step for responding to a disagreement with a friend or partner is to say you're sorry. Even if you don't think you've done anything wrong, it's important to say you're sorry."*
- Ask, *"Why is it important to say you're sorry when someone is upset?"*
  - Answers: Because the person is feeling bad and wants you to acknowledge that you're sorry they're feeling that way; arguments and disagreements are rarely over until you've said you're sorry in some way.
- Ask, *"If you did something wrong, even unintentionally, do you need to say you're sorry?"*
  - Answer: Yes.
- Ask, *"Will the argument be over if you don't say you're sorry?"*
  - Answer: Probably not.
- Ask, *"Is it enough to just say, 'sorry' or do you need to say what you're sorry for?"*
  - Answers: You need to say what you're sorry for; if you don't say what you're sorry for they may ask, *"What are you sorry for?"*
- Ask, *"Does saying you're sorry mean that you're admitting guilt and do you have to admit guilt if you don't think you did anything wrong?"*
  - Answers: Saying sorry is not admitting guilt; you do not have to take the blame if you don't actually believe you did anything wrong.
- Explain, *"Saying that you're sorry doesn't mean that you have to admit guilt or admit you did anything wrong. You can simply say you're sorry they feel that way or you're sorry this happened."*
  - Example: *"I'm sorry you're upset."*
  - Example: *"I'm sorry this happened."*
  - Example: *"I'm sorry your feelings got hurt."*

6. *Try to solve the problem*
- Explain, *"The last step in responding to an argument or disagreement with a friend or partner is to try to solve the problem. This can be done in several ways."*
- *Tell them what you'll do differently*
  - Explain, *"One way to try to solve the problem is to tell them what you'll do differently to fix the problem."*
    - Example: *"I'll try not to upset you again."*
    - Example: *"I'll try not to do that again."*
    - Example: *"I'll try to be more careful next time."*
- *Ask them what they want you to do*
  - Explain, *"Another way to try to solve the problem is to ask them what they want you to do to fix the problem."*
    - Example: *"What can I do to make it up to you?"*
    - Example: *"What would you like me to do?"*
    - Example: *"What can I do to fix this?"*
- *Suggest what you want them to do*
  - Explain, *"Another way to try to solve the problem is to suggest what you want them to do to fix the problem."*
    - Example: *"I'd like it if you tell me if I hurt your feelings again."*

- Example: *"I hope you will give me the benefit of the doubt the next time."*
- Example: *"I'd appreciate it if you let me know the next time this happens."*
- ● *Keep your cool if you can't solve the problem*
  - ○ Ask, *"Can you always solve the problem in an argument or disagreement?"*
    - ■ Answer: Not always.
  - ○ Ask, *"Should you get upset and lose your cool if you can't solve the problem?"*
    - ■ Answers: No; you need to **keep your cool if you can't solve the problem**.
  - ○ Explain, *"If you can't solve the problem, then you need to keep your cool. Don't expect the other person to admit they're wrong. If you care about your friendship or your relationship, your goal shouldn't be to get them to apologize or admit they're wrong. Your goal should be to try to resolve the conflict."*
- ● *Agree to disagree*
  - ○ Ask, *"Do people sometimes need to agree to disagree and what does that mean?"*
    - ■ Answer: Sometimes we have to agree to have different opinions in arguments and disagreements.
  - ○ Explain, *"If you care about your friend or partner and want to preserve the relationship, you may need to agree to disagree about certain things in order to move forward."*

- ● *Remember to follow all of the steps*
  - ○ Explain, *"It's important to understand that each of the steps doesn't work alone. The steps only work when they're ALL done together. For example, sometimes people have arguments that go on and on and seem like they will never end. This is usually because one or more of the steps haven't been followed."*
  - ○ Ask, *"What if the person you're arguing with keeps repeating the same complaints and says things like, 'You just don't get it!' or 'I don't think you understand!' Which step did you forget?"*
    - ■ Answer: You didn't **repeat what they said**, so they don't feel heard.
  - ○ Ask, *"What if the person you're arguing with keeps asking you questions and says things like, 'I don't understand why you did that!' or 'How could you do that?' Which step did you forget?"*
    - ■ Answer: You didn't **explain your side**, so they don't understand.
  - ○ Ask, *"What if the person you're arguing with keeps telling you how they feel and says things like, 'You just don't seem to care!' or 'I don't think you even feel bad.' Which step did you forget?"*
    - ■ Answer: You didn't **say you're sorry**, so they don't think you care.
  - ○ Ask, *"What if the person you're arguing with keeps questioning how you will behave in the future and says things like, 'I just don't know if I can trust you!' or 'How do I know you won't do this again?' Which step did you forget?"*
    - ■ Answer: You didn't **try to solve the problem**, so they don't trust you.

- ● Explain, *"Remember, if you leave out even one step, the argument or disagreement may not be over, so be sure to follow ALL of the steps in this general order."*

Role Play: RESPONDING to a Disagreement ▶

[Two behavioral coaches should do an APPROPRIATE role play demonstrating **RESPONDING to a disagreement** following the steps. Each step should be presented individually and in succession, adding a new step in each phase of the role play. Explain that the behavioral coaches are going to act out a disagreement several times, each time adding a new step. This will illustrate the importance of following EACH STEP.]

- ● Say, "The first two steps for RESPONDING to disagreements are to keep your cool and to listen to the other person. Watch this role play and tell us which steps (name of behavioral coach 2) is following."
  - ○ [Behavioral coach 2 should demonstrate **keeping your cool** and **listening to the other person**.] ▶

Example of an APPROPRIATE but INCOMPLETE Role Play

  - ○ Behavioral coach 1: *"I'm so mad at you, (name of behavioral coach 2)! I heard that you were talking behind my back and you told everyone that I have a crush on (insert a name)."*

○ Behavioral coach 2: (Keeping cool, not getting upset, listening)
○ Behavioral coach 1: *"I can't believe you told everyone that! That was supposed to be a secret. And now everyone knows. That's so uncool."*
○ Behavioral coach 2: (Keeping cool, not getting upset, listening)

- Say, *"Timeout on that. So which of the steps did (name of behavioral coach 2) follow?"*
  ○ Answers: **Kept your cool; listened to the other person.**
- Ask, *"Does it feel like the argument is over?"*
  ○ Answer: No.
- Explain, *"The next step is to repeat what the person said. Watch this and tell us which steps (name of behavioral coach 2) is following."*
- [Behavioral coach 2 should demonstrate **keeping your cool**, **listening to the other person**, and **repeating what the person said** by saying, "It sounds like . . ."] ⊙

Example of an APPROPRIATE but INCOMPLETE Role Play

○ Behavioral coach 1: *"I'm so mad at you, (name of behavioral coach 2)! I heard that you were talking behind my back and you told everyone that I have a crush on (insert a name)."*
○ Behavioral coach 2: (Keeping cool, not getting upset, listening)
○ Behavioral coach 1: *"I can't believe you told everyone that! That was supposed to be a secret. And now everyone knows. That's so uncool."*
○ Behavioral coach 2: *"It sounds like you're really upset with me."*
○ Behavioral coach 1: *"Yeah, I'm upset! I told you that in secret. You weren't supposed to say anything. Now everyone knows my business and is making fun of me."*
○ Behavioral coach 2: (Looks apologetic)

- Say, *"Timeout on that. So which of the steps did (name of behavioral coach 2) follow?"*
  ○ Answers: **Kept your cool; listened to the other person; repeated what they said.**
- Ask, *"Does it feel like the argument is over?"*
  ○ Answer: No.
- Explain, *"The next step is to explain your side using 'I' statements. Watch this and tell us which steps (name of behavioral coach 2) is following."*
- [Behavioral coach 2 should demonstrate **keeping your cool**, **listening to the other person**, **repeating what the person said** by saying, "It sounds like . . . ," and **explaining your side using "I" statements**.] ⊙

Example of an APPROPRIATE but INCOMPLETE Role Play

○ Behavioral coach 1: *"I'm so mad at you, (name of behavioral coach 2)! I heard that you were talking behind my back and you told everyone that I have a crush on (insert a name)."*
○ Behavioral coach 2: (Keeping cool, not getting upset, listening)
○ Behavioral coach 1: *"I can't believe you told everyone that! That was supposed to be a secret. And now everyone knows. That's so uncool."*
○ Behavioral coach 2: *"It sounds like you're really upset with me."*
○ Behavioral coach 1: *"Yeah, I'm upset! I told you that in secret. You weren't supposed to say anything. Now everyone knows my business and is making fun of me."*
○ Behavioral coach 2: (Looks apologetic) *"I didn't realize that was a secret. I didn't think I was talking behind your back because I thought people already knew. I didn't realize people were going to make fun of you."*
○ Behavioral coach 1: *"Well they are and it's your fault! If you hadn't said anything, then none of this would have happened."*
○ Behavioral coach 2: (Looks apologetic)

- Say, *"Timeout on that. So which of the steps did (name of behavioral coach 2) follow?"*

- o Answers: ***Kept your cool; listened to the other person; repeated what they said; explained your side using "I" statements.***
- Ask, *"Does it feel like the argument is over?"*
- o Answer: No.
- Explain, *"The next step is to say you're sorry. Watch this and tell us which steps (name of behavioral coach 2) is following."*
- [Behavioral coach 2 should demonstrate **keeping your cool, listening to the other person, repeating what the person said** by saying, *"It sounds like . . .,"* **explaining your side**, and **saying you're sorry**.] ▶

Example of an APPROPRIATE but INCOMPLETE Role Play

- o Behavioral coach 1: *"I'm so mad at you, (name of behavioral coach 2)! I heard that you were talking behind my back and you told everyone that I have a crush on (insert a name)."*
- o Behavioral coach 2: (Keeping cool, not getting upset, listening)
- o Behavioral coach 1: *"I can't believe you told everyone that! That was supposed to be a secret. And now everyone knows. That's so uncool."*
- o Behavioral coach 2: *"It sounds like you're really upset with me."*
- o Behavioral coach 1: *"Yeah, I'm upset! I told you that in secret. You weren't supposed to say anything. Now everyone knows my business and is making fun of me."*
- o Behavioral coach 2: (Looks apologetic) *"I didn't realize that was a secret. I didn't think I was talking behind your back because I thought people already knew. I didn't realize people were going to make fun of you."*
- o Behavioral coach 1: *"Well they are and it's your fault! If you hadn't said anything, then none of this would have happened."*
- o Behavioral coach 2: (Looks apologetic) *"I'm sorry I upset you. I didn't mean to share your secrets."*
- o Behavioral coach 1: *"Well you did, and it's too late to do anything about it now."*

- Say, *"Timeout on that. So which of the steps did (behavioral coach 2) follow?"*
- o Answers: ***Kept your cool; listened to the other person; repeated what they said; explained your side; said you were sorry.***
- Ask, *"Does it feel like the argument is over?"*
- o Answer: No.
- Explain, *"The next step is to try to solve the problem. Watch this and tell us which steps (name of behavioral coach 2) is following."*
- [Behavioral coach 2 should demonstrate ALL of the steps by **keeping your cool, listening to the other person, repeating what the person said** by saying, *"It sounds like . . .,"* **explaining yourself, saying you're sorry**, and **trying to solve the problem**.] ▶

Example of an APPROPRIATE and COMPLETE Role Play

- o Behavioral coach 1: *"I'm so mad at you, (name of behavioral coach 2)! I heard that you were talking behind my back and you told everyone that I have a crush on (insert name)."*
- o Behavioral coach 2: (Keeping cool, not getting upset, listening)
- o Behavioral coach 1: *"I can't believe you told everyone that! That was supposed to be a secret. And now everyone knows. That's so uncool."*
- o Behavioral coach 2: *"It sounds like you're really upset with me."*
- o Behavioral coach 1: *"Yeah, I'm upset! I told you that in secret. You weren't supposed to say anything. Now everyone knows my business and is making fun of me."*
- o Behavioral coach 2: (Looks apologetic) *"I didn't realize that was a secret. I didn't think I was talking behind your back because I thought people already knew. I didn't realize people were going to make fun of you."*
- o Behavioral coach 1: *"Well they are and it's your fault! If you hadn't said anything, then none of this would have happened."*

> ○ Behavioral coach 2: (Looks apologetic) *"I'm sorry I upset you. I didn't mean to share your secrets."*
> ○ Behavioral coach 1: *"Well you did, and it's too late to do anything about it now."*
> ○ Behavioral coach 2: *"You're right. But I didn't mean for that to happen. From now on, I'll be more careful about telling people your business and I promise not to talk behind your back."*
> ○ Behavioral coach 1: (Long pause) *"Okay, fine."* (Said reluctantly, still a little annoyed)

- Say, *"Timeout on that. So which of the steps did (name of behavioral coach 2) follow?"*
  - ○ Answers: *Kept your cool; listened to the other person; repeated what they said; explained your side; said you were sorry; tried to solve the problem.*
- Ask, *"Does it feel like the argument is over?"*
  - ○ Answers: Yes; as much as it can be for now.
- Ask the following *Perspective Taking Questions*:
  - ○ *"What was that like for (behavioral coach 1) in the end?"*
    - ■ Answers: Controlled; civilized, polite.
  - ○ *"What do you think (behavioral coach 1) thought of (behavioral coach 2) in the end?"*
    - ■ Answers: Good listener; empathic; apologetic.
  - ○ *"Is (behavioral coach 1) going to want to hang out with (behavioral coach 2) again?"*
    - ■ Answer: Yes; the friendship may even be stronger moving forward.
- Ask behavioral coach 1 the same *Perspective Taking Questions*:
  - ○ *"What was that like for you in the end?"*
  - ○ *"What did you think of (behavioral coach 2) in the end?"*
  - ○ *"Would you want to hang out with (behavioral coach 2) again?"*

Behavioral Rehearsal: RESPONDING to a Disagreement

- Explain, *"Now we're going to have each of you practice following the steps for responding to a disagreement. I'm going to pretend to be upset with each of you about something different and you are each going to practice following the steps. We are not going to start and stop like we did with the role play, so feel free to look at the board to make sure you're following the steps."*
- Go around the room and have each young adult practice following each of these steps in a behavioral rehearsal with the group leader while everyone watches.
  - ○ The group leader should accuse each young adult of something different.
  - ○ The young adults should feel free to look at the board in order to follow the steps for **RESPONDING to disagreements**.
  - ○ The group leader may need to point to a certain step on the board if the young adult gets stuck as a reminder of what to do next.
    - ■ Try not to interrupt the behavioral rehearsal to offer verbal prompts.
  - ○ If the young adult does something inappropriate, call a *time-out* and gently point out the error, then have the young adult start again from the beginning until he or she is successful in following all of the steps sequentially.
  - ○ Use different examples of disagreements for each young adult behavioral rehearsal.
    - ■ Examples:
      - □ You're hurt because the young adult made fun of you.
      - □ You're upset because the young adult told your secret.
      - □ You're hurt because the young adult cancelled your weekend plans.
      - □ You're annoyed because the young adult didn't get in touch when they said they would.
      - □ You feel betrayed because the young adult didn't pick you to be on a team project.
      - □ You're mad because the young adult was hanging out with someone you don't like.
      - □ You're hurt because the young adult didn't invite you to his or her get-together.
      - □ You're angry because the young adult laughed when people were teasing you.
      - □ You're upset because the young adult stood you up for lunch.
      - □ You feel betrayed because the young adult didn't come to your defense when someone accused you of something.
- End by giving a round of applause to each young adult after their practice.

Steps for BRINGING UP Disagreements

- Explain, *"Another part of handling disagreements involves BRINGING UP issues and advocating for yourself. There may be times that your friends or partners do or say things to upset you. Instead of getting mad or saying nothing at all, you need to know how to advocate for yourself and BRING UP these issues. Just like with RESPONDING to disagreements when people are upset with us, there are very specific steps to follow when we're upset and need to BRING UP disagreements."*

1. **Wait for the right time and place**
   - Say, *"The first step for bringing up disagreements is to wait for the right time and place to talk about the problem. When and where would be the right time and place?"*
     - Answers: When you are alone; when you have privacy; when you are both calm; when you have time to talk; when you will not be interrupted.

2. **Keep your cool**
   - Say, *"The next step for bringing up disagreements is to keep your cool. What does it mean to keep your cool?"*
     - Answers: It means stay calm; don't get upset; don't lose your cool.
   - Ask, *"What could be the problem with not keeping your cool?"*
     - Answers: The argument may escalate if you don't keep your cool; you could end up being in the wrong because you didn't handle the situation well; your friendship or relationship could be jeopardized.
   - Ask, *"What are some ways people keep their cool?"*
     - Answers: Take deep breaths; silently count to 10; take some time to cool down before you talk.

3. **Ask to speak privately**
   - Say, *"The next step is to ask to speak to the person privately. Why would it be a good idea to speak privately if you need to bring up something that's upsetting you?"*
     - Answers: You don't want others to know about your private business; it could be embarrassing to both of you if people can hear your conversation; people might gossip about your business; conflict resolution is often done in private.
   - Ask, *"How do you ask to speak privately?"*
     - Example: *"Can I talk to you about something privately?"*
     - Example: *"I need to speak to you about something. Can we go somewhere private?"*
     - Example: *"I think we need to talk. Can I speak to you privately?"*

4. **Explain your side using "I" statements**
   - Explain, *"The next step for bringing up disagreements is to explain your side using 'I' statements. What are 'I' statements?"*
     - Answer: Statements that begin with *"I think . . ."* or *"I feel . . ."*
   - Ask, *"What are 'you' statements?"*
     - Answer: Statements that begin with *"You did . . ."* or *"You make me feel . . ."*
   - Ask, *"What could be the problem with using 'you' statements instead of 'I' statements when you're trying to explain your side?"*
     - Answers: **"You" statements** make people defensive; **"I" statements** are less offensive because they focus on your own feelings and don't place blame.
   - Ask, *"What are some examples of 'I' statements when you're bringing up disagreements?"*
     - Example: *"I felt upset when you canceled our plans."*
     - Example: *"I don't like it when you speak to me that way."*
     - Example: *"I feel hurt when you don't return my texts."*

5. **Listen to the other person**
   - Say, *"The next step for bringing up disagreements is to listen to the other person. Why would it be a good idea to listen to other person's side if you're upset with them?"*
     - Answers: You won't know why they did or said what they did if you don't listen; they need a chance to explain their side; the argument may not be over if you don't **listen to the other person**.

6. ***Repeat what they said***
   - Say, *"The next step for bringing up disagreements is to repeat what they said. Why is it important to repeat what the other person said?"*
     - ○ Answers: They need to know they've been heard; if you don't **repeat what they said**, they may keep explaining their side; the argument may not be over if you don't **repeat what they said**.
   - Ask, *"How do you repeat what they said?"*
     - ○ Answers: Paraphrase or summarize what they said; you can **repeat what they said** using the sentence stem, ***"It sounds like . . ."***

7. ***Tell them what you need them to do***
   - Explain, *"The next step for bringing up disagreements is to tell them what you need them to do. Most people don't know all the steps for responding to a disagreement, but arguments don't tend to be over if you don't follow ALL of the steps."*
   - Ask, *"If the person you're upset with doesn't follow all of the steps for responding to a disagreement, what can you do?"*
     - ○ Answer: ***Tell them what you need them to do.***
   - Ask, *"How do you tell them what you need them to do if they aren't listening to your side?"*
     - ○ Example: *"I need you to give me a chance to explain."*
     - ○ Example: *"I need you to listen to what I'm saying."*
     - ○ Example: *"Could you give me a chance to explain how I'm feeling?"*
   - Ask, *"How do you tell them what you need them to do if they haven't repeated what you said?"*
     - ○ Example: *"Can you see this from my perspective?"*
     - ○ Example: *"Do you understand what I'm saying?"*
     - ○ Example: *"Do you understand why I'm upset?"*
   - Ask, *"How do you tell them what you need them to do if they haven't explained their side?"*
     - ○ Example: *"Could you explain how this happened?"*
     - ○ Example: *"Could you help me understand why you did that?"*
     - ○ Example: *"It would help if you could explain where you're coming from."*
   - Ask, *"How do you tell them what you need them to do if they haven't said they're sorry?"*
     - ○ Example: *"It would help if I knew you were sorry."*
     - ○ Example: *"I think I would feel better if I knew you were sorry."*
     - ○ Example: *"I think I need to know that you're sorry in order to move on."*

8. ***Try to solve the problem***
   - Explain, *"The last step in bringing up a disagreement with a friend or partner is to try to solve the problem. Just like when responding to arguments and disagreements when someone is upset with us, this can be done in several ways."*
     - **Tell them what you'll do differently**
     - ○ Explain, *"One way to try to solve the problem is to tell them what you'll do differently."*
       - ▪ Example: *"I'll try not to be so sensitive."*
       - ▪ Example: *"I'll try not to do that again."*
       - ▪ Example: *"I'll try to be more understanding next time."*
     - **Ask them what they want you to do**
     - ○ Explain, *"Another way to try to solve the problem is to ask them what they want you to do differently."*
       - ▪ Example: *"What can I do to avoid this happening again?"*
       - ▪ Example: *"What would you like me to do next time?"*
       - ▪ Example: *"What can we do to fix this?"*
     - **Suggest what you want them to do**
     - ○ Explain, *"Another way to try to solve the problem is to suggest what you want them to do differently."*
       - ▪ Example: *"I'd like it if you didn't talk to me like that again."*
       - ▪ Example: *"I hope you will consider my feelings next time."*
       - ▪ Example: *"I'd appreciate it if you talk to me next time this happens."*

- *Keep your cool if you can't solve the problem*
  - Ask, *"Can you always solve the problem in an argument or disagreement?"*
    - Answer: Not always.
  - Ask, *"Should you get upset and lose your cool if you can't solve the problem?"*
    - Answers: No; you need to *keep your cool if you can't solve the problem*.
  - Explain, *"If you can't solve the problem, then you at least need to keep your cool. Don't expect the other person to admit they're wrong. If you care about your friendship or your relationship, your goal shouldn't be to get them to apologize or admit they're wrong. Your goal should be to try to resolve the conflict."*
- *Agree to disagree*
  - Ask, *"When we're trying to address a conflict with someone we're upset with, do we sometimes need to agree to disagree?"*
    - Answer: Sometimes we have to *agree to disagree* in arguments and disagreements.
  - Explain, *"If you care about your friend or partner, you may need to agree to disagree about certain things in order to preserve the relationship."*

9. *Remember that friendship and dating is a choice*
   - Say, *"Finally, remember that friendship and dating is a choice. Do you have to be friends or date everyone, and does everyone have to be friends or date you?"*
     - Answer: No.
   - Explain, *"If you get into an argument or disagreement with a friend or partner, and what happens really bothers you, you don't have to be friends with them or date them anymore. Remember that arguments with friends and romantic partners are common and OCCASIONAL arguments that aren't too explosive shouldn't have to end your friendship or relationship—but in the end, friendship and dating is a choice."*

Role Play: BRINGING UP a Disagreement ⊙

[Two behavioral coaches should do an APPROPRIATE role play demonstrating **BRINGING UP a disagreement** following the steps. Each step should be presented individually and in succession, adding a new step in each phase of the role play. Explain that the behavioral coaches are going to act out a disagreement several times, each time adding a new step. This will illustrate the importance of following EACH STEP.]

- Say, *"The first three steps for BRINGING UP disagreements are to wait for the right time and place, keep your cool, and ask to speak privately. Watch this role play and tell us which steps (name of behavioral coach 1) is following."*
- [Behavioral coach 1 should demonstrate **waiting for the right time and place**, **keeping your cool**, and **asking to speak privately**.]

> Example of an APPROPRIATE but INCOMPLETE Role Play
>
> - Behavioral coach 1: (Keeping cool, not getting upset) *"Hi, (name of behavioral coach 2). I think we're both on a break, so I was wondering if I could talk to you privately about something."*
> - Behavioral coach 2: (Keeping cool, not getting upset, listening) *"Sure."*

- Say, *"Timeout on that. So which of the steps did (name of behavioral coach 1) follow?"*
  - Answers: **Waited for the right time and place**; **kept cool**; **asked to speak privately**.
- Ask, *"Does it feel like the argument is over?"*
  - Answer: No.
- Explain, *"The next step is to explain your side using 'I' statements. Watch this and tell us which steps (name of behavioral coach 1) is following."*
- [Behavioral coach 1 should demonstrate **waiting for the right time and place**, **keeping your cool**, **asking to speak privately**, and **explaining your side using "I" statements**.] ⊙

Example of an APPROPRIATE but INCOMPLETE Role Play

- ○ Behavioral coach 1: (Keeping cool, not getting upset) *"Hi, (name of behavioral coach 2). I think we're both on a break, so I was wondering if I could talk to you privately about something."*
- ○ Behavioral coach 2: (Keeping cool, not getting upset, listening) *"Sure."*
- ○ Behavioral coach 1: (Keeping cool, not getting upset) *"I'm kind of upset. I just heard that you were talking behind my back and you told everyone that I have a crush on (insert a name)."*
- ○ Behavioral coach 2: (Keeping cool, not getting upset, listening)
- ○ Behavioral coach 1: (Keeping cool, not getting upset) *"I can't believe you told everyone that. That was supposed to be a secret, and now everyone knows."*
- ○ Behavioral coach 2: (Keeping cool, not getting upset, listening)

- • Say, *"Timeout on that. So which of the steps did (name of behavior coach 1) follow?"*
  - ○ Answers: **Waited for the right time and place; kept cool; asked to speak privately; explained your side using "I" statements.**
- • Ask, *"Does it feel like the argument is over?"*
  - ○ Answer: No.
- • Explain, *"The next step is to listen to the other person. Watch this and tell us which steps (name of behavioral coach 1) is following."*
- • [Behavioral coach 1 should demonstrate **waiting for the right time and place, keeping your cool, asking to speak privately, explaining your side using "I" statements**, and **listening to the other person**.] ▶

Example of an APPROPRIATE but INCOMPLETE Role Play

- ○ Behavioral coach 1: (Keeping cool, not getting upset) *"Hi, (name of behavioral coach 2). I think we're both on a break, so I was wondering if I could talk to you privately about something."*
- ○ Behavioral coach 2: (Keeping cool, not getting upset, listening) *"Sure."*
- ○ Behavioral coach 1: (Keeping cool, not getting upset) *"I'm kind of upset. I just heard that you were talking behind my back and you told everyone that I have a crush on (insert a name)."*
- ○ Behavioral coach 2: (Keeping cool, not getting upset, listening)
- ○ Behavioral coach 1: (Keeping cool, not getting upset) *"I can't believe you told everyone that. That was supposed to be a secret, and now everyone knows."*
- ○ Behavioral coach 2: *"It sounds like you're really upset with me."*
- ○ Behavioral coach 1: (Keeping cool, not getting upset) *"Yeah, I am upset. I told you that in secret and I expected you not to say anything. Now everyone knows my business and is making fun of me."*
- ○ Behavioral coach 2: (Looks apologetic) *"I didn't realize that was a secret. I didn't think I was talking behind your back because I thought people already knew. I didn't realize people were going to make fun of you."*

- • Say, *"Timeout on that. So which of the steps did (name of behavior coach 1) follow?"*
  - ○ Answers: **Waited for the right time and place; kept cool; asked to speak privately; explained your side using "I" statements; listened to the other person.**
- • Ask, *"Does it feel like the argument is over?"*
  - ○ Answer: No.
- • Explain, *"The next step is to repeat what they said. Watch this and tell us which steps (name of behavioral coach 1) is following."*
- • [Behavioral coach 1 should demonstrate **waiting for the right time and place, keeping your cool, asking to speak privately, explaining your side using "I" statements, listening to the other person**, and **repeating what they said**.] ▶

Example of an APPROPRIATE but INCOMPLETE Role Play

o   Behavioral coach 1: (Keeping cool, not getting upset) *"Hi, (name of behavioral coach 2). I think we're both on a break, so I was wondering if I could talk to you privately about something."*
o   Behavioral coach 2: (Keeping cool, not getting upset, listening) *"Sure."*
o   Behavioral coach 1: (Keeping cool, not getting upset) *"I'm kind of upset. I just heard that you were talking behind my back and you told everyone that I have a crush on (insert a name)."*
o   Behavioral coach 2: (Keeping cool, not getting upset, listening)
o   Behavioral coach 1: (Keeping cool, not getting upset) *"I can't believe you told everyone that. That was supposed to be a secret, and now everyone knows."*
o   Behavioral coach 2: *"It sounds like you're really upset with me."*
o   Behavioral coach 1: (Keeping cool, not getting upset) *"Yeah, I am upset. I told you that in secret and I expected you not to say anything. Now everyone knows my business and is making fun of me."*
o   Behavioral coach 2: (Looks apologetic) *"I didn't realize that was a secret. I didn't think I was talking behind your back because I thought people already knew. I didn't realize people were going to make fun of you."*
o   Behavioral coach 1: (Keeping cool, not getting upset) *"It sounds like you didn't know it was a secret, but it's still really embarrassing."*
o   Behavioral coach 2: (Apologetic) *"I know. That was my mistake."*

•   Say, *"Timeout on that. So which of the steps did (name of behavioral coach 1) follow?"*
    o   Answers: **Waited for the right time and place; kept cool; asked to speak privately; explained your side using "I" statements; listened to the other person; repeated what they said.**
•   Ask, *"Does it feel like the argument is over?"*
    o   Answer: No.
•   Explain, *"The next step is to tell them what you need them to do. Watch this and tell us which steps (name of behavioral coach 1) is following."*
•   [Behavioral coach 1 should demonstrate **waiting for the right time and place, keeping your cool, asking to speak privately, explaining your side using "I" statements, listening to the other person, repeating what they said,** and **telling them what you need them to do.**] ⊙

Example of an APPROPRIATE but INCOMPLETE Role Play

o   Behavioral coach 1: (Keeping cool, not getting upset) *"Hi, (name of behavioral coach 2). I think we're both on a break, so I was wondering if I could talk to you privately about something."*
o   Behavioral coach 2: (Keeping cool, not getting upset, listening) *"Sure."*
o   Behavioral coach 1: (Keeping cool, not getting upset) *"I'm kind of upset. I just heard that you were talking behind my back and you told everyone that I have a crush on (insert a name)."*
o   Behavioral coach 2: (Keeping cool, not getting upset, listening)
o   Behavioral coach 1: (Keeping cool, not getting upset) *"I can't believe you told everyone that. That was supposed to be a secret, and now everyone knows."*
o   Behavioral coach 2: *"It sounds like you're really upset with me."*
o   Behavioral coach 1: (Keeping cool, not getting upset) *"Yeah, I am upset. I told you that in secret. You weren't supposed to say anything. Now everyone knows my business and is making fun of me."*
o   Behavioral coach 2: (Looks apologetic) *"I didn't realize that was a secret. I didn't think I was talking behind your back because I thought people already knew. I didn't realize people were going to make fun of you."*
o   Behavioral coach 1: (Keeping cool, not getting upset) *"It sounds like you didn't know it was a secret, but it's still really embarrassing."*
o   Behavioral coach 2: (Apologetic) *"I know. That was my mistake."*

- Behavioral coach 1: (Keeping cool, not getting upset) *"It's too late to do anything now, but I need to know you feel badly about this."*
- Behavioral coach 2: (Apologetic) *"Of course I feel badly, I'm sorry. I didn't mean for that to happen."*

- Say, *"Timeout on that. So which of the steps did (name of behavioral coach 1) follow?"*
  Answers: **Waited for the right time and place; kept cool; asked to speak privately; explained your side using "I" statements; listened to the other person; repeated what they said; told them what you needed them to do.**
- Ask, *"Does it feel like the argument is over?"*
  - Answer: Not exactly, but it is close.
- Explain, *"The last step for BRINGING UP disagreements is to try to solve the problem. Watch this and tell us which steps (name of behavioral coach 1) is following."*
- [Behavioral coach 1 should demonstrate **waiting for the right time and place, keeping your cool, asking to speak privately, explaining your side using "I" statements, listening to the other person, repeating what they said, telling them what you need them to do**, and **trying to solve the problem**.] ▶

Example of an APPROPRIATE and COMPLETE Role Play

- Behavioral coach 1: (Keeping cool, not getting upset) *"Hi, (name of behavioral coach 2). I think we're both on a break, so I was wondering if I could talk to you privately about something."*
- Behavioral coach 2: (Keeping cool, not getting upset, listening) *"Sure."*
- Behavioral coach 1: (Keeping cool, not getting upset) *"I'm kind of upset. I just heard that you were talking behind my back and you told everyone that I have a crush on (insert a name)."*
- Behavioral coach 2: (Keeping cool, not getting upset, listening)
- Behavioral coach 1: (Keeping cool, not getting upset) *"I can't believe you told everyone that. That was supposed to be a secret, and now everyone knows."*
- Behavioral coach 2: *"It sounds like you're really upset with me."*
- Behavioral coach 1: (Keeping cool, not getting upset) *"Yeah, I am upset. I told you that in secret and I expected you not to say anything. Now everyone knows my business and is making fun of me."*
- Behavioral coach 2: (Looks apologetic) *"I didn't realize that was a secret. I didn't think I was talking behind your back because I thought people already knew. I didn't realize people were going to make fun of you."*
- Behavioral coach 1: (Keeping cool, not getting upset) *"It sounds like you didn't know it was a secret, but it's still really embarrassing."*
- Behavioral coach 2: (Apologetic) *"I know. I'm really sorry for telling people. That was my mistake."*
- Behavioral coach 1: (Keeping cool, not getting upset) *"It's too late to do anything now, but I need to know you feel badly about this."*
- Behavioral coach 2: (Apologetic) *"Of course I feel badly, I'm sorry. I didn't mean for that to happen."*
- Behavioral coach 1: (Keeping cool, not getting upset) *"Okay, but I'd prefer if you just don't talk about my personal life at all with other people."*
- Behavioral coach 2: (Apologetic) *"Of course. I definitely won't talk about you or your personal business anymore."*

- Say, *"Timeout on that. So which of the steps did (name of behavioral coach 1) follow?"*
  Answers: **Waited for the right time and place; kept cool; asked to speak privately; explained your side using "I" statements; listened to the other person; repeated what they said; told them what you needed them to do and tried to solve the problem.**
- Ask, *"Does it feel like the argument is over?"*
  - Answers: Yes; as much as it can be for now.

- Ask the following *Perspective Taking Questions*:
  - ○ *"What was that like for (behavioral coach 2) in the end?"*
    - ■ Answers: Controlled; civilized, polite.
  - ○ *"What do you think (behavioral coach 2) thought of (behavioral coach 1) in the end?"*
    - ■ Answers: Good communicator; calm; understanding; reasonable.
  - ○ *"Is (behavioral coach 2) going to want to hang out with (behavioral coach 1) again?"*
    - ■ Answer: Yes; the friendship may even be stronger moving forward.
- Ask behavioral coach 2 the same *Perspective Taking Questions*:
  - ○ *"What was that like for you in the end?"*
  - ○ *"What did you think of (behavioral coach 1) in the end?"*
  - ○ *"Would you want to hang out with (behavioral coach 1) again?"*

- Explain, *"So remember, just like with RESPONDING to disagreements, each of the steps for BRINGING UP disagreements doesn't work alone. The steps only work when they're done together. If you leave out a step, the argument may not be over, so be sure to follow ALL of the steps in this general order."*

Behavioral Rehearsal: BRINGING UP a Disagreement

- Explain, *"Now we're going to have each of you practice following the steps for BRINGING UP disagreements. Each of you is going to pretend to be upset with me about something different and you are each going to practice following the steps. We are not going to start and stop like we did with the role play, so feel free to look at the board to make sure you're following the steps."*
- Go around the room and have each young adult practice following each of these steps in a behavioral rehearsal with the group leader while everyone watches.
  - ○ The group leader gives each young adult a different conflict to bring up.
  - ○ The young adults should feel free to look at the board in order to follow the steps for **BRINGING UP Disagreements**.
    - ■ The group leader may need to point to a certain step on the board if the young adult gets stuck as a reminder of what to do next.
      - □ Try not to interrupt the behavioral rehearsal to offer verbal prompts.
    - ■ If the young adult does something inappropriate, call a *timeout* and gently point out the error, then have the young adult start again from the beginning until he or she is successful in following all of the steps sequentially.
  - ○ Use different examples of disagreements for each young adult behavioral rehearsal.
    - ■ Examples:
      - □ The young adult is hurt because you made fun of him or her.
      - □ The young adult is upset because you told his or her secret.
      - □ The young adult is hurt because you cancelled your weekend plans.
      - □ The young adult is annoyed because you didn't get in touch when you said you would.
      - □ The young adult feels betrayed because you didn't pick him or her to be on a team project.
      - □ The young adult is mad because you were hanging out with someone he or she doesn't like.
      - □ The young adult is hurt because you didn't invite him or her to your get-together.
      - □ The young adult is angry because you laughed when people were teasing him or her.
      - □ The young adult is upset because you stood him or her up for lunch.
      - □ The young adult feels betrayed because you didn't come to his or her defense when someone accused them of something.
- End by giving a round of applause to each young adult after their practice.
- Explain, *"So those are the rules and steps for handling disagreements. We know that disagreements with friends or romantic partners are common, and OCCASIONAL arguments that aren't too explosive shouldn't have to end your friendship or relationship, but if you're having frequent and explosive arguments, you may need to consider whether this friend or partner is a good choice."*

HANDLING DISAGREEMENTS

Young Adult Behavioral Rehearsal

Get-Togethers

Materials Needed

- Indoor games (e.g., video games, card games, board games).
  - If you are going to provide video games as an option, make sure there are enough gaming consoles that each group can play simultaneously together.
  - Do not use small, portable gaming devices as people have to wait to take turns and that can get boring.
  - Several decks of playing cards will be sufficient if you do not have these other resources.
- Optional: iPads or laptops for watching YouTube videos, surfing the Internet, or playing computer games.
  - If you are going to provide iPads or laptops as an option, make sure there are enough that each group can use them simultaneously together.
- [Note: Most PEERS® programs DO NOT have access to gaming consoles, iPads, or laptops. These are luxury items. Just providing a few decks of cards to keep the get-together *activity-based* will be fine.]

Behavioral Rehearsal

- Notify young adults they will be practicing having *get-togethers*.
  - Note: They will no longer be practicing *beginning and ending get-togethers*.
- Break up young adults into small groups or dyads.
- Have young adults practice following the rules for how to behave *during the get-together* while:
  - *Trading information*.
  - *Finding common interests*.
  - Playing with games and items provided by the treatment team (e.g., video games, card games, board games, iPads, laptops, etc.).
- Provide *social coaching* as needed regarding the rules for making and keeping friends.

HANDLING DISAGREEMENTS

Reunification

- Announce that young adults should join their social coaches.
  - ○ Have young adults stand or sit next to their social coaches.
  - ○ Be sure to have silence and the full attention of the group before starting with *Reunification*.
  - ○ Have young adults generate the content from the lesson while social coaches listen.
- Say, *"Today, we talked about handling disagreements in terms of responding to and bringing up disagreements. What are the steps for RESPONDING to disagreements?"* (See Table 14.3.)
- Ask, *"What are the steps for BRINGING UP disagreements?"* (See Table 14.3.)

Table 14.3 Steps for Handling Disagreements

RESPONDING TO DISAGREEMENTS	BRINGING UP DISAGREEMENTS
1. Keep your cool *2. Listen to the other person* *3. Repeat what they said* *4. Explain your side using "I" statements* *5. Say you're sorry* *6. Try to solve the problem*	*1. Wait for the right time and place* *2. Keep your cool* *3. Ask to speak privately* *4. Explain your side using "I" statements* *5. Listen to the other person* *6. Repeat what they said* *7. Tell them what you need them to do* *8. Try to solve the problem*

- Explain, *"Young adults practiced handling disagreements and the group did a great job so we should give them a round of applause."*

Homework Assignments

Distribute the *Social Coaching Handout* to young adults and announce the following *Homework Assignments*:

1. Have a *get-together* with a friend.
   - Social coaches should help young adults plan the get-together using the *five W's*:
     - ○ *WHO* they plan to get together with.
     - ○ *WHAT* they plan to do.
     - ○ *WHEN* it will happen.
     - ○ *WHERE* they will meet.
     - ○ *HOW* they will make it happen.
   - Social coaches should go over the rules and steps for *get-togethers* with young adults beforehand.
   - Social coaches should ask young adults the following *social coaching questions* after the *get-together*:
     - ○ *What did you decide to do and who picked the activities?*

      ○   *Did you trade information and for what percentage of the time?*
      ○   *What were your common interests and what could you do with that information if you were going to hang out again?*
      ○   *Did you and your friend have a good time?*
      ○   *Is this someone you might want to hang out with again?*

2. Young adults and social coaches should practice *handling a disagreement*.
- Go over the rules and steps for *RESPONDING to disagreements* and *BRINGING UP disagreements* before practicing.
- Social coaches should ask young adults the following *social coaching* and *Perspective Taking Questions* after practicing:
  - ○ *Which steps did you follow?*
  - ○ *What was that like for me in the end?*
  - ○ *What do you think I thought of you in the end?*
  - ○ *Do you think I'm going to want to hang out with you again?*

3. Young adults should practice *handling a disagreement* with a friend or romantic partner if relevant.
- Social coaches should go over the rules and steps for *RESPONDING to disagreements* and *BRINGING UP disagreements* before practicing when possible.
- Social coaches should ask young adults the following *social coaching* and *Perspective Taking Questions* after practicing:
  - ○ *Which steps did you follow?*
  - ○ *What was that like for you and the other person in the end?*
  - ○ *What did you think of each other in the end?*
  - ○ *Do you think you'll both want to hang out again?*

4. Practice *letting someone know you like them, ask them on a date*, and/or *go on a date*.
- If young adults are interested in someone romantically:
  - ○ *Let them know you like them.*
  - ○ *Ask them on a date.*
  - ○ *Go on a date.*
  - ○ DO NOT practice unless you are romantically interested in the person.
- Young adults should practice *letting someone know you like them, asking someone on a date*, and *beginning and ending dates* with social coaches, if comfortable.
- Social coaches should go over all of the rules and steps for *dating etiquette* before the practice.
- Social coaches should ask young adults the following *social coaching questions* after each practice:
  - ○ *Letting someone know you like them*:
    - ■ *Who did you practice with and what did you do to let them know you like them?*
    - ■ *How did they respond?*
    - ■ *Does this seem like a good choice and is this someone you might want to go on a date with?*
  - ○ *Asking someone on a date*:
    - ■ *Who did you ask on a date and what steps did you follow?*
    - ■ *How did they respond?*
  - ○ *Going on a date*:
    - ■ *What did you decide to do?*
    - ■ *Did you trade information and for what percentage of the time?*
    - ■ *What were your common interests and what could you do with that information if you were going to go on a date again?*
    - ■ *Did you and your date have a good time?*
    - ■ *Does this seem like a good choice and is this someone you might want to go on a date with again?*

Individual Check-Out

Individually and privately negotiate with each young adult and social coach:

1. *WHO* they plan to have a ***get-together*** with in the coming week.
   - *WHAT* they plan to suggest to their friends.
   - *WHEN* and *WHERE* they will suggest to their friends.
   - *HOW* they will make it happen (e.g., tickets, transportation, etc.).

2. When they plan to practice ***handling a disagreement*** with their social coach.

3. How they will practice ***letting someone know they like them*** and with whom, and whether they plan to ***ask them on a date***.
   - *WHO* they plan to have a ***date*** with in the coming week.
   - *WHAT* they plan to suggest to do.
   - *WHEN* and *WHERE* they will suggest to meet.
   - *HOW* they will make it happen (e.g., tickets, transportation, etc.).

HANDLING DISAGREEMENTS

Social Coaching Handout

Steps for RESPONDING to Disagreements*

1. *Keep your cool*

2. *Listen to the other person*

3. *Repeat what they said*
   - Example: *"It sounds like you're upset."*
   - Example: *"It sounds like you're angry."*
   - Example: *"It sounds like your feelings are hurt."*

4. *Explain your side using "I" statements*
   - Example: *"I didn't mean to upset you."*
   - Example: *"I think this is a misunderstanding."*
   - Example: *"I feel like this was a miscommunication."*

5. *Say you're sorry*
   - Example: *"I'm sorry you're upset."*
   - ○ Example: *"I'm sorry this happened."*
   - Example: *"I'm sorry your feelings got hurt."*

6. *Try to solve the problem*
   - *Tell them what you'll do differently*
     - ○ Example: *"I'll try not to upset you again."*
     - ○ Example: *"I'll try not to do that again."*
     - ○ Example: *"I'll try to be more careful next time."*
   - *Ask them what they want you to do*
     - ○ Example: *"What can I do to make it up to you?"*
     - ○ Example: *"What would you like me to do?"*
     - ○ Example: *"What can I do to fix this?"*
   - *Suggest what you want them to do*
     - ○ Example: *"I'd like it if you tell me if I hurt your feelings again."*
     - ○ Example: *"I hope you will give me the benefit of the doubt the next time."*
     - ○ Example: *"I'd appreciate it if you let me know the next time this happens."*
   - *Keep your cool if you can't solve the problem*
   - *Agree to disagree*
   - *Remember to follow all of the steps*

Steps for BRINGING UP Disagreements

1. *Wait for the right time and place*

2. *Keep your cool*

3. *Ask to speak privately*
   - Example: *"Can I talk to you about something privately?"*
   - Example: *"I need to speak to you about something. Can we go somewhere private?"*
   - Example: *"I think we need to talk. Can I speak to you privately?"*

4. *Explain your side using "I" statements*
   - Example: *"I felt upset when you canceled our plans."*
   - Example: *"I don't like it when you speak to me that way."*
   - Example: *"I feel hurt when you don't return my texts."*

5. *Listen to the other person*

6. *Repeat what they said*

7. *Tell them what you need them to do*
   - Example: *"I need you to give me a chance to explain."*
   - Example: *"Can you see this from my perspective?"*
   - Example: *"Could you explain how this happened?"*
   - Example: *"It would help if I knew you were sorry."*

8. *Try to solve the problem*
   - *Tell them what you'll do differently*
     - Example: *"I'll try not to be so sensitive."*
     - Example: *"I'll try not to do that again."*
     - Example: *"I'll try to be more understanding next time."*
   - *Ask them what they want you to do*
     - Example: *"What can I do to avoid this happening again?"*
     - Example: *"What would you like me to do next time?"*
     - Example: *"What can we do to fix this?"*
   - *Suggest what you want them to do*
     - Example: *"I'd like it if you didn't talk to me like that again."*
     - Example: *"I hope you will consider my feelings next time."*
     - Example: *"I'd appreciate it if you talk to me next time this happens."*
   - *Keep your cool if you can't solve the problem*
   - *Agree to disagree*
   - *Remember that friendship and dating is a choice*

Homework Assignments

1. Have a *get-together* with a friend.
   - Social coaches should help young adults plan the get-together using the *five W's*:
     - *WHO* they plan to get together with.
     - *WHAT* they plan to do.
     - *WHEN* it will happen.
     - *WHERE* they will meet.
     - *HOW* they will make it happen.
   - Social coaches should go over the rules and steps for *get-togethers* with young adults beforehand.
   - Social coaches should ask young adults the following *social coaching questions* after the *get-together*:
     - *What did you decide to do and who picked the activities?*
     - *Did you trade information and for what percentage of the time?*
     - *What were your common interests and what could you do with that information if you were going to hang out again?*
     - *Did you and your friend have a good time?*
     - *Is this someone you might want to hang out with again?*

2. Young adults and social coaches should practice *handling a disagreement*.
   - Go over the rules and steps for **RESPONDING to disagreements** and **BRINGING UP disagreements** before practicing.
   - Social coaches should ask young adults the following *social coaching* and *Perspective Taking Questions* after practicing:
     - *Which steps did you follow?*
     - *What was that like for me in the end?*
     - *What do you think I thought of you in the end?*
     - *Do you think I'm going to want to hang out with you again?*

3. Young adults should practice *handling a disagreement* with a friend or romantic partner if relevant.
   - Social coaches should go over the rules and steps for **RESPONDING to disagreements** and **BRINGING UP disagreements** before practicing when possible.
   - Social coaches should ask young adults the following *social coaching* and *Perspective Taking Questions* after practicing:
     - *Which steps did you follow?*
     - *What was that like for you and the other person in the end?*
     - *What did you think of each other in the end?*
     - *Do you think you'll both want to hang out again?*

4. Practice *letting someone know you like them*, *ask them on a date*, and/or *go on a date*.
   - If young adults are interested in someone romantically:
     - *Let them know you like them.*
     - *Ask them on a date.*
     - *Go on a date.*
     - DO NOT practice unless you are romantically interested in the person.
   - Young adults should practice *letting someone know you like them*, *asking someone on a date*, and *beginning and ending dates* with social coaches, if comfortable.
   - Social coaches should go over all of the rules and steps for *dating etiquette* before the practice.
   - Social coaches should ask young adults the following *social coaching questions* after each practice:
     - *Letting someone know you like them*:
       - *Who did you practice with and what did you do to let them know you like them?*
       - *How did they respond?*
       - *Does this seem like a good choice and is this someone you might want to go on a date with?*
     - *Asking someone on a date*:
       - *Who did you ask on a date and what steps did you follow?*
       - *How did they respond?*
     - *Going on a date*:
       - *What did you decide to do?*
       - *Did you trade information and for what percentage of the time?*
       - *What were your common interests and what could you do with that information if you were going to go on a date again?*
       - *Did you and your date have a good time?*
       - *Does this seem like a good choice and is this someone you might want to go on a date with again?*

* See *The Science of Making Friends DVD* (Laugeson, 2013) or *FriendMaker* mobile app for a video Role Play Demonstration of the corresponding rule.

HANDLING DIRECT BULLYING

Social Coaching Therapist Guide

Preparing for the Social Coaching Session

The focus of this lesson is on strategies for handling direct forms of bullying and peer rejection. This includes teasing and physical bullying. Research suggests that one of the strongest predictors of mental health problems among youth is peer rejection. Anxiety and depression, for example, are often strongly predicted by peer rejection during adolescence and even early adulthood. While the focus of PEERS® is on helping young adults make and keep friends and form romantic relationships, the intervention would be incomplete without a discussion about how to handle bullying and other forms of rejection that may prohibit the development of these types of relationships. This will be the focus of the remaining two lessons.

While acts of bullying represent complex sets of distinct behaviors, four general types of bullying behavior have been identified through research. These types include *DIRECT bullying*, which encompasses *verbal bullying* (also known as teasing) and *physical bullying* (which includes aggressive or physical acts). *INDIRECT bullying* includes *electronic bullying* (also known as cyberbullying) and *relational bullying* (which includes rumors, gossip, and social exclusion). The current lesson provides strategies for *handling DIRECT bullying*, while the subsequent lesson in Session 15 will focus on strategies for *handling INDIRECT bullying*.

During the *Didactic Lesson*, you will acknowledge that some of the strategies given to young adults in the past may have been ineffective for *handling teasing*. Many young adults confronted with teasing have been given the advice to ignore the person, walk away, tell someone, or tease them back. Yet, the majority of young adults will say that these strategies usually do not work. While acknowledging this bad advice will help you gain the trust of young adults insofar as they will be more willing to believe what you have to tell them about how to respond appropriately to teasing, some social coaches may express guilt and culpability about having given the wrong advice up until now. You can help ease the collective guilty conscience of the group by normalizing the fact that the vast majority of well-intentioned adults give the same advice, and were probably given similar advice when they were younger. The key here is to dispel the myth that ignoring, walking away, telling someone, or teasing back are useful strategies for *handling teasing*, and instead provide social coaches with the *ecologically valid skills* used by socially accepted young adults.

After you have presented the rules for using *teasing comebacks*, a common issue that may arise involves social coaches' eagerness to create their own *verbal comebacks*. In our experience, most social coaches and young adults are not very skilled at coming up with appropriate replies for teasing, so it is best to stick to the *verbal* and *nonverbal comebacks* listed in this chapter. These comebacks represent *ecologically valid* responses used by socially accepted young adults—so be safe and stick to the list.

The most common issue that comes up in this lesson is that social coaches will want to share stories of bullying that their young adults have experienced. You should limit the time spent by social coaches talking about specific ways in which young adults have been bullied. Instead, gently redirect personal disclosures by saying, *"We know that bullying is very common and can be very painful, but we're not going to spend a lot of time talking about the specific ways our young adults have been bullied. Instead, we're going to focus on what they can do in these situations to make it less likely that they'll be bullied again."* A similar approach is taken in the young adult group, but for a different reason. For young adults, the topic of bullying can be emotionally charged and lead to distress and decompensation if not handled appropriately. Allowing young adults to tell stories of being bullied would prevent some from being able to focus on the lesson and learn the strategies needed to avoid these situations in the future. For social coaches, while these stories may be equally distressing, the major issue for not allowing story-telling is getting off track and not having time to get through the lesson. Consequently, you will need to gently and respectfully redirect both groups if storytelling occurs. If a social coach or young adult appears to be particularly affected by this topic, you may want to speak with them at the end of the group in a *side meeting*.

Homework Review

[Go over the following *Homework Assignments* and **troubleshoot** any potential problems. Start with completed homework first. If you have time, you can inquire as to why others were unable to complete the assignment and try to **troubleshoot** how they might get it done for the coming week. When reviewing homework, be sure to relabel descriptions using the **buzzwords** (identified by **bold and italicized** print). Spend the majority of the *Homework Review* on *get-togethers* as this was the most important assignment.]

1. Have a *get-together* with a friend.
    - Say, *"One of the main assignments this week was for young adults to have a get-together with a friend. Who completed this assignment or attempted to complete it?"*
    - Ask the following questions:
        ○ *"Did you help your young adult plan the get-together using the five W's?"*
        ○ *"What social coaching did you do before the get-together?"*
        ○ *"What did your young adult decide to do and with whom?"*
        ○ *"How did the get-together begin?"*
        ○ *"Who picked the activities?"*
        ○ *"Did they trade information and what percentage of the time?"*
        ○ *"How did the get-together end?"*
        ○ *"What social coaching did you do after the get-together?"*
            ■ Appropriate *social coaching questions*:
                □ **What did you decide to do and who picked the activities?**
                □ **Did you trade information and for what percentage of the time?**
                □ **What were your common interests and what could you do with that information if you were going to hang out again?**
                □ **Did you and your friend have a good time?**
                □ **Is this someone you might want to hang out with again?**
        ○ *"Does this seem like a good choice for a friend and someone your young adult will want to hang out with again?"*

Table 15.1 Steps for Beginning and Ending Get-Togethers in Your Home

Beginning the Get-Together	*Ending the Get-Together*
1. Greet your guest	*1. Wait for a pause in activities*
2. Invite them in	*2. Give a cover story for ending the get-together*
3. Introduce them to anyone they don't know	*3. Start walking your friend to the door*
4. Give them a tour	*4. Thank your friend for getting together*
5. Offer them refreshments	*5. Tell your friend you had a good time*
6. Ask them what they want to do	*6. Say goodbye and you'll see them later*

2. Young adults and social coaches should practice **handling a disagreement**.
    - Say, *"Another assignment this week was for young adults and social coaches to practice handling a disagreement. Who completed this assignment or attempted to complete it?"*

- Ask the following questions:
  - ○ *"What social coaching did you do before the practice?"*
  - ○ *"Which steps did your young adult follow to RESPOND to a disagreement?"*
  - ○ *"Which steps did your young adult follow to BRING UP a disagreement?"*
  - ○ *"What social coaching did you do after the practice?"*
    - ■ Appropriate *social coaching* and *Perspective Taking Questions*:
      - □ *Which steps did you follow?*
      - □ *What was that like for me in the end?*
      - □ *What do you think I thought of you in the end?*
      - □ *Do you think I'm going to want to hang out with you again?*

Table 15.2 Steps for Handling Disagreements

RESPONDING TO DISAGREEMENTS	*BRINGING UP DISAGREEMENTS*
1. Keep your cool *2. Listen to the other person* *3. Repeat what they said* *4. Explain your side using "I" statements* *5. Say you're sorry* *6. Try to solve the problem*	*1. Wait for the right time and place* *2. Keep your cool* *3. Ask to speak privately* *4. Explain your side using "I" statements* *5. Listen to the other person* *6. Repeat what they said* *7. Tell them what you need them to do* *8. Try to solve the problem*

3. Young adults should practice **handling a disagreement** with a friend or romantic partner if relevant.
   - Say, *"Another assignment this week was for young adults to practice handling a disagreement with a friend or romantic partner if relevant. Who completed this assignment or attempted to complete it?"*
   - Ask the following questions:
     - ○ *"Who did your young adult practice with and what was the disagreement?"*
     - ○ *"Which steps did your young adult follow to RESPOND to or BRING UP the disagreement?"*
     - ○ *"What social coaching did you do after the practice?"*
       - ■ Appropriate *social coaching* and *Perspective Taking Questions*:
         - □ *Which steps did you follow?*
         - □ *What was that like for you and the other person in the end?*
         - □ *What did you think of each other in the end?*
         - □ *Do you think you'll both want to hang out again?*

4. Practice **letting someone know you like them, ask them on a date**, and/or **go on a date**.
   - Say, *"Another assignment this week was for young adults to practice letting someone know they like them, ask them on a date, and/or go on a date. The assignment was NOT to practice unless they are romantically interested in the person. Young adults could also have practiced with social coaches, if they were comfortable. Who completed this assignment or attempted to complete it?"*
   - Ask the following questions:
     - ○ *"What social coaching did you do before the practice?"*
     - ○ *"Who did your young adult practice with?"*
     - ○ *"What did they do to let the person know they like them and how did they respond?"*
     - ○ *"Did they ask the person on a date and how did they respond?"*
       - ■ Ask the following questions if they went on a date:
         - □ *"What did they decide to do?"*
         - □ *"Did they trade information and for what percentage of the time?"*
         - □ *"Did they and their date have a good time?"*
     - ○ *"What social coaching did you do after the practice?"*
     - ○ *"Does this seem like a good choice and is this someone they might want to go on a date with (again)?"*
   - [Collect the *Social Coaching Homework Assignment Worksheets*. If social coaches forgot to bring the worksheets, have them complete a new form to hold them accountable for the assignments.]

Didactic Lesson: Handling Direct Bullying

- Distribute the *Social Coaching Handout.*
  - ○ Sections in **bold print** in the *Social Coaching Therapist Guide* come directly from the *Social Coaching Handout.*
  - ○ Remind social coaches that terms that are in ***bold and italicized*** print are ***buzzwords*** and represent important concepts from the PEERS® curriculum that should be used as much as possible when social coaching.
- Explain, *"Today, we're going to be talking about how to handle bullying. We know bullying is very common in adolescence, but unfortunately it also happens with adults. We'll begin our discussion talking about strategies for handling DIRECT bullying, such as teasing and physical bullying. These are DIRECT forms of bullying because they happen directly to the person targeted and not over the Internet or behind their back. In a different lesson, we will talk about handling INDIRECT forms of bullying, such as cyberbullying, rumors, and gossip."*

Handling Teasing

- Explain, *"We're going to begin by talking about teasing, which is essentially bullying with words. One important way to make it less likely that we'll be teased relates to how we react when someone is teasing us. In order for us to know how to react, it's helpful to think about why people tease."*
- Ask, *"Why do people tease?"*
  - ○ Answers: They're trying to get a reaction out of you; they want you to get upset, embarrassed, or tease back because it's fun for them.
- Ask the questions, *"When you get upset . . ."*
  - ○ *". . . are you doing what the teaser wants?"*
    - Answer: Yes.
  - ○ *". . . are you making the teasing fun for the teaser?"*
    - Answer: Yes.
  - ○ *". . . are you MORE likely or LESS likely to get teased again?"*
    - Answer: Definitely MORE likely.
- Say, *"A lot of young adults have been given advice about what to do in response to teasing. What are most young adults told to do in response to teasing?"*
  - ○ Answers: Ignore them; walk away; tell someone; tease them back.
- Explain, *"Unfortunately, most young adults will tell you these strategies usually don't work."*

Strategies for Handling Teasing

- ***Don't ignore the teasing***
  - ○ Ask, *"What happens when you ignore the teasing?"*
    - Answers: They keep teasing; you look weak; you make yourself an easy target.

- ***Don't walk away right away***
  - ○ Ask, *"What happens when you walk away right away?"*
    - Answers: They follow you; they keep teasing; you look weak; you make yourself an easy target.

- ***Don't tell someone right away***
  - ○ Ask, *"What happens when you tell someone right away?"*
    - Answers: You make them mad; they want to retaliate; you may get a reputation as a "snitch," "nark," or "tattletale."

- ***Don't tease them back***
  - ○ Say, *"Some people think that teasing the person back will make it less likely they'll get teased. What could be the problem with teasing them back?"*
    - Answers: You could get into trouble; you might look like the bad guy; you might get a bad reputation; this may be the reaction they're looking for; you'll probably get teased more.

- *Don't banter*
  - ○ Say, *"Some friends like to tease each other, especially men. This kind of teasing is usually done playfully and isn't intended to be hurtful. We call this kind of teasing 'banter.' While banter is very common among young adults, what could be the problem with banter?"*
    - ■ Answers: It could escalate; each person tries to up the ante; eventually, someone could get upset.
  - ○ Explain, *"If our goal is to make and keep friends, we need to understand that banter is very risky. If we want to avoid the risk, we can use the strategies for handling teasing to stop the banter."*

- *Act like what they said didn't bother you*
  - ○ Say, *"Whether it's banter or not, one way you can make the teasing less fun for the teaser is by acting like it didn't bother you. Even if it hurts your feelings, you have to act like it didn't affect you. Why is it important to act like what they said didn't bother you?"*
    - ■ Answers: The teaser doesn't get the reaction they wanted; makes it less fun for the teaser; they will be less likely to tease you in the future.

- *Act like what they said was lame or stupid*
  - ○ Say, *"Another way you can make the teasing less fun for the teaser is by acting like what they said was kind of lame or stupid. Why is it important to act like what they said was lame or stupid?"*
    - ■ Answers: This embarrasses the teaser; makes the teasing less fun; they will be less likely to tease you in the future.

- *Give a short verbal comeback*
  - ○ Say, *"The best way to show someone that their teasing didn't bother you and what they said was kind of lame is to give a SHORT comeback to make fun of what they said. Why is it important to keep your comebacks SHORT?"*
    - ■ Answer: If you say too much, they'll think you care.
  - ○ Say, *"Remember these short verbal comebacks need to give the impression that you don't care and the teasing was lame. A lot of young adults will say things like . . ."*
    - ■ *"Whatever!"*
    - ■ *"Yeah, and?"*
    - ■ *"And?"*
    - ■ *"And your point is?"*
    - ■ *"Am I supposed to care?"*
    - ■ *"And why do I care?"*
    - ■ *"Is that supposed to be funny?"*
    - ■ *"Big deal!"*
    - ■ *"So what!"*
    - ■ *"Who cares?"*
    - ■ *"Tell me when you get to the funny part."*
    - ■ *"Tell me when you get to the punchline."*
    - ■ *"Anyway . . ."* (good comeback to end with and walk away on)
  - ○ *Sound bored*
    - ■ Explain, *"Some people sound bored or indifferent when they use these verbal comebacks. They might say 'Whatever' (said casually with bored indifference)."*
  - ○ *Have an attitude*
    - ■ Explain, *"Other people use these verbal comebacks with lots of attitude. They might say 'WHATEVER!' (said with lots of dramatic flair)."*
    - ■ Say, *"It's up to you to decide which way feels more comfortable for you."*
  - ○ *Always be prepared with at least a few verbal comebacks*
    - ■ Ask, *"Does the teaser usually give up after one teasing comeback?"*
      - □ Answer: No, they usually try a few more times.
    - ■ Explain, *"Because we know they'll probably try teasing a few times, you always need to be prepared with at least a few verbal comebacks."*

- *Verbal comebacks need to make sense*
  - Say, *"It's also important for your verbal comebacks to make sense. What could be the problem if someone said 'You're so stupid!' and I said, 'Am I supposed to care?'"*
    - Answers: You're agreeing with them; that might make the teasing worse.
- **Give a nonverbal comeback**
  - Explain, *"In addition to giving short verbal comebacks, a lot of people will also give a nonverbal comeback that shows they don't care. It's always better to provide a verbal comeback, but if your young adult finds it difficult to use his/her words in these situations, one of the nonverbal comebacks might work. Nonverbal comebacks include . . ."*
    - *Rolling your eyes*
    - *Shrugging your shoulders*
    - *Shaking your head no*
- **Remove yourself after giving teasing comebacks**
  - Say, *"After you've given a few appropriate teasing comebacks, it's a good idea to remove yourself from the situation. You can do this by casually looking away or slowly walking away. What could be the problem with standing there and looking at the person after you've used a few teasing comebacks?"*
    - Answers: It's almost an invitation or a challenge to tease more; you want to give the impression that what they said was lame and that you can't be bothered to listen anymore.
- **Teasing may get worse before it gets better**
  - Explain, *"Sometimes the teaser will be expecting a different reaction from you. Maybe in the past you got upset or teased back. When you stop doing what the teaser expects, they may try a little harder at first. That means the teasing may get worse before it gets better."*
- **Expect the teaser to try again**
  - Explain, *"If you stick with the teasing comebacks, eventually the teaser will get bored and move on, but they may try again in the future. That means even if it seems like the teasing stopped, you should always be ready for them to try again sometime."*
- **Don't use teasing comebacks with physically aggressive people**
  - Explain, *"Teasing comebacks work really well because they kind of embarrass the person teasing us and make it less fun for them. Because they're embarrassing, we don't use teasing comebacks with physically aggressive people."*
  - Ask, *"How do people who get physically aggressive react when they're embarrassed?"*
    - Answer: They usually retaliate with physical aggression.
  - Explain, *"In a few moments, we'll talk about how to handle physical bullying. Those strategies will be more appropriate to use with people who tend to get physically aggressive."*
- **Don't use teasing comebacks with people in authority**
  - Say, *"The last rule for using teasing comebacks is that we should never use them with people in authority. Who are people in authority?"*
    - Answers: Social coaches; parents; professors; university administrators; supervisors; managers; bosses; law enforcement officers.
  - Ask, *"What could be the problem with using teasing comebacks with people in authority?"*
    - Answers: It's disrespectful; you could get in trouble; you could get a bad reputation; you could get kicked out of class; you could get fired.
- [Optional: Show the MALE and FEMALE Role Play Video Demonstrations of *handling verbal teasing* from the *PEERS® Role Play Video Library* (www.routledge.com/cw/laugeson) or *FriendMaker* mobile app, then ask the **Perspective Taking Questions** that follow the role plays.]

Handling Embarrassing Feedback

- Explain, *"Sometimes people say things that are embarrassing and may even be meant to tease us, but they may also be giving us important feedback about how people see us. This is especially true when a lot of people are giving us the same feedback or even when a few people give us the same feedback over and over. Instead of just feeling hurt, we might be able to use this feedback to help us change the way people see us. If we think about what people are trying to tell us when they tease us, we can sometimes do things differently and make it less likely that we'll be teased in the future."*

- Go over the examples of embarrassing feedback listed in Table 15.3 and have social coaches come up with ideas of what young adults could do differently in response to this feedback.
  - Present each example by saying, *"Let's say that a lot of people are giving your young adult negative feedback about . . . (insert example of embarrassing feedback)."*
  - Ask, *"What could they do differently in response to this feedback?"*
  - Have social coaches come up with examples of what young adults could do differently if they wanted to avoid teasing.
  - [Note: Changing things about yourself is a personal choice, so if young adults don't want to change the things they are being teased about, they don't have to.]

Table 15.3 Examples of Embarrassing Feedback and How to Utilize Feedback

Examples of Embarrassing Feedback	Examples of How to Utilize Feedback
Negative feedback about clothing	Consider changing your wardrobe; try to follow the clothing norms of your social group; change and wash clothes regularly; get clothing advice from social coaches, friends, family, sales clerks, personal shoppers, etc.
Negative feedback about body odor	Use deodorant every day; bathe regularly using soap; wash hair with shampoo regularly; wear less cologne/perfume.
Negative feedback about dandruff	Use dandruff shampoo regularly.
Negative feedback about oral hygiene	Brush teeth daily; use mouthwash; floss teeth regularly; use a tongue scraper; chew gum; use breath mints; avoid certain foods; visit the dentist regularly.
Negative feedback about your sense of humor	Pay attention to your humor feedback; consider telling fewer jokes; be a little more serious when first getting to know someone.
Negative feedback about unusual behaviors	Consider changing or discontinuing the behavior if possible.

Handling Physical Bullying

- Explain, *"Now that we've talked about strategies for handling teasing and embarrassing feedback, we need to talk about what to do in cases of physical bullying. Physical bullying might include taking personal items, pranking, or playing practical jokes, or in more extreme cases it could include aggressive acts like pushing, shoving, or throwing things. Even though both types include DIRECT bullying, the strategies for handling physical bullying are very different from the strategies for handling teasing."*
- *Avoid the bully*
  - Say, *"One of the best strategies for handling physical bullying is to avoid the bully. This means we need to stay out of reach of the bully. For example, if the bully has a desk in a certain area of the office, should you walk through that area?"*
    - Answer: Not if you can help it.
  - Ask, *"Why is it important to avoid the bully?"*
    - Answer: If the bully can't FIND you, he or she can't bully you.
- *Plan your route*
  - Say, *"One way to avoid the bully is to plan your route. For example, if you know the bully likes to hang out in a certain area of campus, how could you avoid being in that area?"*
    - Answers: **Plan your route** to avoid that area; go a different way if you can.
- *Lay low when the bully is around*
  - Say, *"Another strategy for handling physical bullying is to lay low when the bully is around. This means you need to fly under the radar, keep a low profile, and don't draw attention to yourself when the bully is near. Why is it important to lay low when the bully is around?"*
    - Answer: **If the bully doesn't notice you, he or she is less likely to bully you.**

- *Don't try to make friends with the bully*
  - ○ Say, *"It's also important not to try to talk to the bully or make friends with the bully. Some people think they can win the bully over, but this almost never works. Instead, it just draws attention to you. What could be the problem with trying to make friends with the bully?"*
    - ▪ Answers: It probably won't work; it will just draw attention to you; they will probably bully you more; they may act like you're friends and then take advantage of you; bullies don't make good friends anyway.

- *Don't provoke the bully*
  - ○ Say, *"Another important rule for handling physical bullying is to avoid provoking the bully. How might you provoke a bully?"*
    - ▪ Answers: Making fun of them; teasing them; laughing at them; pointing out their mistakes; trying to get them in trouble; acting silly around them.
  - ○ Ask, *"What could be the problem with provoking a bully?"*
    - ▪ Answer: They may want to retaliate; the bullying may worsen.

- *Don't tease the bully*
  - ○ Say, *"If we want to avoid provoking the bully, then we need to avoid teasing the bully. What could be the problem with teasing a bully?"*
    - ▪ Answers: They may want to retaliate; the bullying may worsen.

- *Don't police the bully*
  - ○ Ask, *"If we want to avoid provoking the bully, then we also need to avoid policing the bully. What could be the problem with policing the bully for minor offenses, like being late for work or not going to class?"*
    - ▪ Answers: They may want to retaliate; the bullying may worsen; you may look bad.
  - ○ Ask, *"What if the bully is doing something dangerous or illegal that could harm other people. Then should you tell someone?"*
    - ▪ Answer: Yes, definitely.
  - ○ Say, *"If you do have to tell on the bully, should you do this in front of people?"*
    - ▪ Answers: No, you should tell someone privately; don't tell others that you've done this if you can help it.

- *Hang out with other people*
  - ○ Ask, *"Who do bullies like to pick on: people who are by themselves or in a group?"*
    - ▪ Answer: People who are by themselves.
  - ○ Ask, *"Why do bullies like to pick on people who are by themselves?"*
    - ▪ Answer: Because you're an easy target when you're alone and have no one to defend you or stick up for you.
  - ○ Explain, *"One of the most powerful strategies for handling physical bullying is to hang out with other people. This means you should avoid being alone. Bullies like to pick on people when they are alone and unprotected."*

- *Stay near people in authority when the bully is around*
  - ○ Ask, *"If you can't be around friends when the bully is nearby, you can stay near people in authority. Who are some people in authority you could stay near?"*
    - ▪ Answers: Professors; supervisors; managers; bosses.
  - ○ Explain, *"Bullies don't tend to pick on others when people in authority are there, so you can stay near professors, supervisors, managers, or bosses when the bully is around. That doesn't mean you need to hang out with them. It just means you can stay near them when the bully is around."*

- *Make a complaint as a last resort*
  - ○ Say, *"Finally, if all of the strategies for handling physical bullying aren't working, or if you feel threatened or harassed, you should make a complaint. Who could you make a complaint to?"*
    - ▪ Answers: Professor; chair of the department; university administrator; ombudsperson; supervisor; manager; boss; human resources department; personnel department; law enforcement (extreme cases only).

○   Explain, *"Making a complaint is usually a last resort that we only use if the other strategies aren't working or if we feel threatened, harassed, or in danger. As social coaches, be sure to discuss this with your young adults before they make a complaint since this is a serious decision and usually requires some support."*

Homework Assignments

[Distribute the *Social Coaching Homework Assignment Worksheet* (Appendix I) for social coaches to complete and return at the next session.]

1.   Have a *get-together* with a friend.
   - Social coaches should help young adults plan the get-together using the *five W's*:
       ○   *WHO* they plan to get together with.
       ○   *WHAT* they plan to do.
       ○   *WHEN* it will happen.
       ○   *WHERE* they will meet.
       ○   *HOW* they will make it happen.
   - Social coaches should go over the rules and steps for *get-togethers* with young adults beforehand.
   - Social coaches should ask young adults the following *social coaching questions* after the *get-together*:
       ○   *What did you decide to do and who picked the activities?*
       ○   *Did you trade information and for what percentage of the time?*
       ○   *What were your common interests and what could you do with that information if you were going to hang out again?*
       ○   *Did you and your friend have a good time?*
       ○   *Is this someone you might want to hang out with again?*

2.   Young adults and social coaches should practice *handling teasing*.
   - Go over the strategies for *handling teasing* before practicing.
   - Young adults should choose THREE *verbal comebacks* to practice using.
   - Social coaches should use benign teasing comments (i.e., *"Your shoes are ugly"*).
   - Social coaches should ask young adults the following *Perspective Taking Questions* after practicing:
       ○   *What was that like for me?*
       ○   *What do you think I thought of you?*
       ○   *Do you think I'm going to want to tease you again?*

3.   Young adults should practice *handling DIRECT bullying* with a peer if relevant.
   - Social coaches should ask young adults the following *social coaching* and *Perspective Taking Questions* after practicing when relevant:
       ○   *What did you do or say to handle teasing?*
          ▪   *What was that like for the other person?*
          ▪   *What do you think they thought of you?*
          ▪   *Do you think they're going to want to tease you again?*
       ○   *Did they give you any embarrassing feedback and what could you do differently if you didn't want to be teased about that?*
       ○   *What did you do or say to handle physical bullying?*

4.   Young adults and social coaches should practice *handling a disagreement*.
   - Go over the rules and steps for *RESPONDING to disagreements* and *BRINGING UP disagreements* before practicing.
       ○   Social coaches should ask young adults the following *social coaching* and *Perspective Taking Questions* after practicing:
          ▪   *Which steps did you follow?*

- *What was that like for me in the end?*
- *What do you think I thought of you in the end?*
- *Do you think I'm going to want to hang out with you again?*

5. Young adults should practice *handling a disagreement* with a friend or romantic partner if relevant.
   - Social coaches should go over the rules and steps for *RESPONDING to disagreements* and *BRINGING UP disagreements* before practicing when possible.
   - Social coaches should ask young adults the following *social coaching* and *Perspective Taking Questions* after practicing:
     - *Which steps did you follow?*
     - *What was that like for you and the other person in the end?*
     - *What did you think of each other in the end?*
     - *Do you think you'll both want to hang out again?*

6. Practice *letting someone know you like them, ask them on a date,* and/or *go on a date.*
   - If young adults are interested in someone romantically:
     - *Let them know you like them.*
     - *Ask them on a date.*
     - *Go on a date.*
     - DO NOT practice unless you are romantically interested in the person.
   - Young adults should practice *letting someone know you like them, asking someone on a date,* and *beginning and ending dates* with social coaches, if comfortable.
   - Social coaches should go over all of the rules and steps for *dating etiquette* before the practice.
   - Social coaches should ask young adults the following *social coaching questions* after each practice:
     - *Letting someone know you like them*:
       - *Who did you practice with and what did you do to let them know you like them?*
       - *How did they respond?*
       - *Does this seem like a good choice and is this someone you might want to go on a date with?*
     - *Asking someone on a date*:
       - *Who did you ask on a date and what steps did you follow?*
       - *How did they respond?*
     - *Going on a date*:
       - *What did you decide to do?*
       - *Did you trade information and for what percentage of the time?*
       - *What were your common interests and what could you do with that information if you were going to go on a date again?*
       - *Did you and your date have a good time?*
       - *Does this seem like a good choice and is this someone you might want to go on a date with again?*

Social Coaching Tips

For social coaches seeking more detailed information and resources about strategies for *handling DIRECT bullying*, the following recommendations are suggested:

- Social coaches should read *The Science of Making Friends: Helping Socially Challenged Teens and Young Adults* (Laugeson, 2013) with your young adult.
  - Two chapters are included to provide detailed information about *DIRECT bullying*:
    - *Chapter 10: Handling Verbal Teasing.*
    - *Chapter 13: Avoiding Physical Bullying.*

- ○ Chapter summaries for young adults are provided.
  - ○ *Social Coaching Tips* are given for each of the lessons.
- Use *The Science of Making Friends DVD* (Laugeson, 2013) or *FriendMaker* app to:
  - ○ Review the strategies for handling teasing and physical bullying.
  - ○ View the *Role Play Video Demonstrations* of "handling verbal teasing."
  - ○ Male and female examples are provided.
  - ○ Discuss **Perspective Taking Questions** following the video demonstrations.
- Encourage young adults to use the *FriendMaker* mobile app as a "virtual coach" to assist with real-life situations involving:
  - ○ "Handling verbal teasing."
  - ○ "Utilizing embarrassing feedback."
  - ○ "Avoiding physical bullying."

Graduation Announcement

- Distribute the *Graduation Flyer* (see Appendix G for an example).
- Say, *"Graduation is in TWO weeks. That means we will be wrapping things up in two weeks and talking about how to move forward now that our group is coming to an end. In order to celebrate all your hard work, young adults will be having a graduation party and we will all be having a graduation ceremony."*
- You may want to explain the structure of the graduation party and graduation ceremony, which will vary according to resources.
  - ○ Suggestions for the graduation party and ceremony can be found in the *Young Adult Therapist Guide* for Session 16.

HANDLING DIRECT BULLYING

Young Adult Therapist Guide

Preparing for the Young Adult Session

The major goal of this lesson is to give young adults new and more effective strategies for *handling DIRECT bullying*. Although direct forms of bullying such as *verbal bullying* and *physical bullying* are often intertwined, the strategies for handling each of these types of bullying are quite different. Therefore, it is important for you and the young adults to think of these concepts differently in order to choose the more appropriate coping strategy.

As described in the *Preparing for the Social Coaching Session* section of this chapter, four general types of bullying behavior have been identified through research. These types include *DIRECT bullying*, which encompasses *verbal bullying* (i.e., teasing) and *physical bullying* (i.e., aggressive or physical acts), as well as *INDIRECT bullying*, which includes *electronic bullying* (i.e., cyberbullying) and *relational bullying* (i.e., rumors, gossip, and social exclusion). The current lesson provides strategies for handling direct forms of bullying, while Session 15 will focus on strategies for handling indirect forms of bullying.

Many of the young adults in your group will have a long history of being bullied. Consequently, this lesson may be emotionally charged for many of the young adults. You should help to limit the emotional response by not allowing young adults to talk about the specific ways in which they have been bullied. Young adults will be more able to focus on the solutions if they are not distracted by an overwhelming emotional response. By this lesson, the young adults will most likely have developed a cohesive group in which their mutual regard and support for one another will minimize much of the anxiety they may have felt in discussing this topic earlier in the program.

One issue that commonly comes up in this lesson is that young adults may claim that they are *"never teased"* or *"never physically bullied."* Although bullying does decline from adolescence into adulthood, most young adults are still occasionally teased, if not bullied in other ways. Often, these comments represent an attempt to *"save face"* or appear to be above this form of social rejection. It is not important to have young adults confess to being teased or bullied, but it is also important not to make young adults that are being bullied feel embarrassed about their situation. You should normalize this experience for the other young adults by explaining that nearly everyone gets teased or bullied from time to time. Although the experience can be painful, it is not unusual.

Conversely, some young adults will confess to being bullied and will want to go into lengthy stories about these experiences. You should not allow this discussion to go far, as these emotionally charged confessions will make it difficult for young adults to focus on the lesson. Even if one young adult is comfortable talking about his or her experiences of being teased or bullied, another young adult listening to these accounts may become re-traumatized by simply listening to the story. It is helpful for you to gently remind young adults, *"We know that bullying feels really awful and we know that it's fairly common. But we're not going to be talking about the specific ways we've been bullied. Instead, we're going to focus on what we can do in these situations to make it less likely that we'll be bullied in the future."* This clarification will come as a relief to many young adults.

Occasionally, one of the young adults may confess to teasing other young adults or being a bully. You will need to briefly discuss the problems associated with being a bully, but avoid a lengthy discussion on this topic in order to deflect the anxiety that such a disclosure may generate in other young adults. You might say something such as, *"What could be the problem with teasing other people?"* or *"What could be the problem with bullying other people?"* You will open this question up to the group and not call on the person identifying him or herself as a bully. A very brief discussion of why it is bad to be a bully will send the message that this behavior is unacceptable, but avoiding a lengthy discussion will be important to minimize the anxiety this might raise in the others and maintain focus upon strategies for **handling DIRECT bullying**. You will want to end this discussion with a brief moral lesson that teasing or physically bullying other young adults is not a good way to make and keep friends, and you may want to speak privately with the confessor and his or her social coach later if the issue feels unresolved.

When presenting the material about **nonverbal comebacks** to teasing (i.e., rolling eyes, shrugging shoulders, shaking head no), you will conduct a brief behavioral rehearsal to determine whether young adults will be capable of performing the comebacks appropriately. Some young adults with Autism Spectrum Disorder (ASD), or those who have rigid motor movements, may have trouble rolling their eyes or shrugging their shoulders appropriately. Be sure to have each young adult demonstrate how they would do this during the behavioral rehearsal. In the event that they appear awkward (e.g., appear to be having a seizure when rolling their eyes, stiffly lifting their shoulders in an attempt to shrug), let them know that these nonverbal gestures are difficult to do, may not be the best option for them, and that they would be better off using **verbal comebacks** instead. To avoid embarrassment, be sure to let young adults know that not everyone is good at rolling their eyes or shrugging their shoulders, so it's not a big deal. If you feel comfortable, you should make this portion of the lesson fun and playful as you and your behavioral coach act as a judge and jury determining whether the young adults should use these **nonverbal comebacks**. In our experience, this portion of the lesson often includes a good deal of laughter. If you make this portion of the lesson too serious, the young adults may become embarrassed by their inability to use the **nonverbal comebacks**.

When conducting the *Role Play Demonstration* and *Behavioral Rehearsal Exercise* for the teasing portion of this lesson, it will be critical that you use benign teasing remarks. This is because avoiding emotionally charged material will be critical to enabling young adults to learn and practice the strategies. If you were to use more authentic teasing comments such as, *"You're a loser"* or *"You're weird,"* it is likely that some of the young adults would have difficulty concentrating. Do not make this mistake. Instead, stick to the recommended benign teasing remark, *"Your shoes are ugly."* Historically, this teasing remark has not been met with hurt or upset by the young adults, and has allowed them to practice using the **teasing comebacks** with little discomfort. In some settings, choice of footwear is a sensitive issue, so if there is concern that young adults may be offended by teasing comments about their shoes, choose another benign topic to use during practice, but be sure to use the SAME teasing comment for every young adult.

Although it is likely that emotions will initially be elevated during this *Didactic Lesson*, this lesson should ultimately focus on the development of specific strategies for **handling DIRECT bullying** that will lead to a lower probability of being bullied in the future. When the material is presented as described in this chapter, this should actually be an enjoyable and empowering lesson for the young adults.

Homework Review

[Go over the following *Homework Assignments* and **troubleshoot** any potential problems. Start with completed homework first. If you have time, you can inquire as to why others were unable to complete the assignment and try to **troubleshoot** how they might get it done for the coming week. When reviewing homework, be sure to relabel descriptions using the **buzzwords** (identified by **bold and italicized** print). Spend the majority of the *Homework Review* on **get-togethers** as this was the most important assignment.]

1. Have a *get-together* with a friend.
   - Say, *"One of the main assignments this week was for you to have a get-together with a friend. Raise your hand if you had a get-together with a friend this week."*
   - Ask the following questions:
     ○ *"Who did you have a get-together with and what did you decide to do?"*
     ○ *"Did you plan the get-together using the five W's?"*
     ○ *"How did the get-together begin?"*
     ○ *"Who picked the activities?"*
     ○ *"Did you trade information and for what percentage of the time?"*
     ○ *"How did the get-together end?"*
     ○ *"Did you and your friend have a good time?"*
     ○ *"Is this someone you might want to hang out with again?"*

Table 15.1 Steps for Beginning and Ending Get-Togethers in Your Home

Beginning the Get-Together	Ending the Get-Together
1. Greet your guest 2. Invite them in 3. Introduce them to anyone they don't know 4. Give them a tour 5. Offer them refreshments 6. Ask them what they want to do	1. Wait for a pause in activities 2. Give a cover story for ending the get-together 3. Start walking your friend to the door 4. Thank your friend for getting together 5. Tell your friend you had a good time 6. Say goodbye and you'll see them later

2. Young adults and social coaches should practice *handling a disagreement*.
   - Say, *"Another assignment this week was to practice handling a disagreement with your social coach. Raise your hand if you practiced handling a disagreement with your social coach."*
   - Ask the following questions:
     ○ *"Which steps did you follow to RESPOND to a disagreement?"*
     ○ *"Which steps did you follow to BRING UP a disagreement?"*

Table 15.2 Steps for Handling Disagreements

RESPONDING TO DISAGREEMENTS	BRINGING UP DISAGREEMENTS
1. Keep your cool 2. Listen to the other person 3. Repeat what they said 4. Explain your side using "I" statements 5. Say you're sorry 6. Try to solve the problem	1. Wait for the right time and place 2. Keep your cool 3. Ask to speak privately 4. Explain your side using "I" statements 5. Listen to the other person 6. Repeat what they said 7. Tell them what you need them to do 8. Try to solve the problem

3. Young adults should practice *handling a disagreement* with a friend or romantic partner if relevant.
   - Say, *"Another assignment this week was to practice handling a disagreement with a friend or romantic partner if relevant. Raise your hand if you practiced handling a disagreement with a friend or romantic partner."*
   - Ask the following questions:
     ○ *"Who did you practice with and what was the disagreement?"*
     ○ *"Which steps did you follow to RESPOND to or BRING UP the disagreement?"*
     ○ *"What was that like for you and the other person in the end?"*
     ○ *"What did you think of each other in the end?"*
     ○ *"Do you think you'll both want to hang out again?"*

4. Practice *letting someone know you like them*, *ask them on a date*, and/or *go on a date*.
   - Say, *"Another assignment this week was to practice letting someone know you like them, ask them on a date, and/or go on a date. The assignment was NOT to practice unless you're romantically interested in the person. Raise your hand if you did this assignment."*
   - Ask the following questions:
     - *"Who did you practice with?"*
     - *"What did you do to let them know you like them and how did they respond?"*
     - *"Did you ask them on a date and how did they respond?"*
     - Ask the following questions if they went on a date:
       - *"What did you decide to do?"*
       - *"Did you trade information and for what percentage of the time?"*
       - *"What were your common interests and what could you do with that information if you were going to go on a date again?"*
       - *"Did you and your date have a good time?"*
     - *"Does this seem like a good choice and is this someone you might want to go on a date with (again)?"*

Didactic Lesson: Handling Direct Bullying

- Explain, *"Today, we're going to be talking about how to handle bullying. We know bullying is very common in adolescence, but unfortunately it also happens with adults. We'll begin our discussion talking about strategies for handling DIRECT bullying, such as teasing and physical bullying. These are DIRECT forms of bullying because they happen directly to the person targeted and not over the Internet or behind their back. In a different lesson, we will talk about handling INDIRECT forms of bullying, such as cyberbullying, rumors, and gossip. We're not going to be talking about the specific ways we've been bullied, or how it makes us feel. We all know it feels bad to be bullied. Instead, we're going to focus on what we can do in these situations to make it less likely that we'll be bullied again."*
- [Note: If young adults try to talk about specific ways they have been bullied, try to redirect them by saying, *"We're not going to talk about the specific ways we've been bullied. Instead, we're going to talk about what we can do in these situations to make it less likely we'll be bullied again."*]
- [Present the strategies for **handling DIRECT bullying** by writing the following bullet points and **buzzwords** (identified by **bold and italicized** print) on the board. Do not erase the strategies until the end of the lesson. Each role play with a ⊙ symbol includes a corresponding role play video from the *PEERS® Role Play Video Library* (www.routledge.com/cw/laugeson).]

Handling Teasing

- Explain, *"We're going to begin by talking about teasing, which is essentially bullying with words. One important way to make it less likely that we'll be teased relates to how we react when someone is teasing us. In order for us to know how to react, it's helpful to think about why people tease."*
- Ask, *"Why do people tease?"*
  - Answers: They're trying to get a reaction out of you; they want you to get upset, embarrassed, or tease back because it's fun for them.
- Ask the questions, *"When you get upset . . ."*
  - *". . . are you are doing what the teaser wants?"*
    - Answer: Yes.
  - *". . . are you are making the teasing fun for the teaser?"*
    - Answer: Yes.
  - *". . . are you MORE likely or LESS likely to get teased again?"*
    - Answer: Definitely MORE likely.
- Say, *"A lot of us have been given advice about what to do in response to teasing. What are most people told to do in response to teasing?"*
  - Answers: Ignore them; walk away; tell someone; tease them back.

- Ask, *"Do these strategies usually work?"*
  - Answer: Not usually.
- Explain, *"Unlike what you may have heard before, we're not going to suggest that you ignore the teaser, walk away, tell someone, or even tease them back. That's because these strategies usually don't work very well."*

Strategies for Handling Teasing

- ***Don't ignore the teasing***
  - Ask, *"What happens when you ignore the teasing?"*
    - Answers: They keep teasing; you look weak; you make yourself an easy target.
  - Ask, *"Are you MORE likely or LESS likely to get teased?"*
    - Answer: MORE likely.

- ***Don't walk away right away***
  - Ask, *"What happens when you walk away right away?"*
    - Answers: They follow you; they keep teasing; you look weak; you make yourself an easy target.
  - Ask, *"Are you MORE likely or LESS likely to get teased?"*
    - Answer: MORE likely.

- ***Don't tell someone right away***
  - Ask, *"What happens when you tell someone right away?"*
    - Answers: You make them mad; they want to retaliate; you may get a reputation as a "snitch," "nark," or "tattletale."
  - Ask, *"Are you MORE likely or LESS likely to get teased?"*
    - Answer: MORE likely.
  - Ask, *"When would it be appropriate to tell someone?"*
    - Answers: If these strategies don't work and you can't handle the teasing on your own; if you feel physically threatened or harassed.

- ***Don't tease them back***
  - Say, *"Some people think that teasing the person back will make it less likely they'll get teased. What could be the problem with teasing them back?"*
    - Answers: You could get into trouble; you might look like the bad guy; you might get a bad reputation; this may be the reaction they're looking for; you'll probably get teased more.

- ***Don't banter***
  - Say, *"Some friends like to tease each other, especially men. This kind of teasing is usually done playfully and isn't intended to be hurtful. We call this kind of teasing 'banter.' While banter is very common among young adults, what could be the problem with banter?"*
    - Answers: It could escalate; each person tries to up the ante; eventually, someone could get upset.
  - Explain, *"If our goal is to make and keep friends, we need to understand that banter is very risky. If we want to avoid the risk, we can use the strategies for handling teasing to stop the banter."*

- ***Act like what they said didn't bother you***
  - Say, *"Whether it's banter or not, one way you can make the teasing less fun for the teaser is by acting like it didn't bother you. Even if it hurts your feelings, you have to act like it didn't affect you. Why is it important to act like what they said didn't bother you?"*
    - Answers: The teaser doesn't get the reaction they wanted; makes it less fun for the teaser; they will be less likely to tease you in the future.

- ***Act like what they said was lame or stupid***
  - Say, *"Another way you can make the teasing less fun for the teaser is by acting like what they said was kind of lame or stupid. Why is it important to act like what they said was lame or stupid?"*
    - Answers: This embarrasses the teaser; makes the teasing less fun; they will be less likely to tease you in the future.

- *Give a short verbal comeback*
  - ○ Say, *"The best way to show someone that their teasing didn't bother you and what they said was kind of lame is to give a SHORT comeback to make fun of what they said. Why is it important to keep your comebacks SHORT?"*
    - Answer: If you say too much, they'll think you care.
  - ○ Say, *"Remember these short verbal comebacks need to give the impression that you don't care and the teasing was lame. A lot of young adults will say things like . . ."* [Write the following examples on the board. Do not allow young adults to generate their own comebacks, as they are often inappropriate.]:
    - *"Whatever!"*
    - *"Yeah, and?"*
    - *"And?"*
    - *"And your point is?"*
    - *"Am I supposed to care?"*
    - *"And why do I care?"*
    - *"Is that supposed to be funny?"*
    - *"Big deal!"*
    - *"So what!"*
    - *"Who cares?"*
    - *"Tell me when you get to the funny part."*
    - *"Tell me when you get to the punchline."*
    - *"Anyway . . ."* (good comeback to end with and walk away on)
  - ○ *Sound bored*
    - Explain, *"Some people sound bored or indifferent when they use these verbal comebacks. They might say, 'Whatever' (said casually with bored indifference)."*
  - ○ *Have an attitude*
    - Explain, *"Other people use these verbal comebacks with lots of attitude. They might say, 'WHATEVER!' (said with lots of dramatic flair)."*
    - Say, *"It's up to you to decide which way feels more comfortable for you."*
  - ○ *Always be prepared with at least a few verbal comebacks*
    - Ask, *"Does the teaser usually give up after one teasing comeback?"*
      - □ Answer: No, they usually try a few more times.
    - Explain, *"Because we know they'll probably try teasing a few times, you always need to be prepared with at least a few verbal comebacks."*
  - ○ *Verbal comebacks need to make sense*
    - Say, *"It's also important for your verbal comebacks to make sense. What could be the problem if someone said, 'You're so stupid!' and I said, 'Am I supposed to care?'"*
      - □ Answers: You're agreeing with them; that might make the teasing worse.

- *Give a nonverbal comeback*
  - ○ Explain, *"In addition to giving short verbal comebacks, a lot of people will also give a nonverbal comeback that shows they don't care. It's always better to provide a verbal comeback, but if you find it difficult to use your words in these situations, one of the nonverbal comebacks might work for you. Nonverbal comebacks include . . ."*
    - *Rolling your eyes*
    - *Shrugging your shoulders*
    - *Shaking your head no*
  - ○ Explain, *"Not everyone is good at rolling their eyes and shrugging their shoulders. Since we don't want anyone to do something that might look weird, let's go around the room and have everyone demonstrate rolling your eyes and then separately shrugging your shoulders. If you know you can't do it, then you can pass."*
    - Quickly have each young adult demonstrate rolling their eyes.
    - Quickly have each young adult demonstrate shrugging their shoulders.

- ○ You and a coach should decide in the moment and share with the young adult if he or she should use these strategies.
  - Do not let the other young adults weigh in.
  - Keep the interaction fun and playful to avoid embarrassment.
  - Normalize the fact that not everyone can or should do this.
- ○ Say, *"Not everyone should roll their eyes or shrug their shoulders and it's not a big deal. But you should all use your short verbal comebacks no matter what."*

- *Remove yourself after giving teasing comebacks*
  - ○ Say, *"After you've given a few appropriate teasing comebacks, it's a good idea to remove yourself from the situation. You can do this by casually looking away or slowly walking away. What could be the problem with standing there and looking at the person after you've used a few teasing comebacks?"*
    - Answers: It's almost an invitation or a challenge to tease more; you want to give the impression that what they said was lame and that you can't be bothered to listen anymore.

- *Teasing may get worse before it gets better*
  - ○ Explain, *"Sometimes the teaser will be expecting a different reaction from you. Maybe in the past you got upset or teased back. When you stop doing what the teaser expects, they may try a little harder at first. That means the teasing may get worse before it gets better. You still need to stick with your teasing comebacks though."*
  - ○ Ask, *"What could be the problem with not using teasing comebacks and going back to getting upset or teasing back?"*
    - Answers: That's what the teasers want; you'll have proven that if they try hard enough, they can get you to do what they want; this makes it more likely you'll get teased again.

- *Expect the teaser to try again*
  - ○ Explain, *"If you stick with the teasing comebacks, eventually the teaser will get bored and move on, but they may try again in the future. That means even if it seems like the teasing stopped, you should always be ready for them to try again sometime."*
  - ○ Ask, *"Why would they try again?"*
    - Answer: They may try again to see if you'll give them the reaction they're looking for.

- *Don't use teasing comebacks with physically aggressive people*
  - ○ Explain, *"Teasing comebacks work really well because they kind of embarrass the person teasing us and make it less fun for them. Because they're embarrassing, we don't use teasing comebacks with physically aggressive people."*
  - ○ Ask, *"How do people who get physically aggressive react when they're embarrassed?"*
    - Answer: They usually retaliate with physical aggression.
  - ○ Explain, *"In a few moments, we'll talk about how to handle physical bullying. Those strategies will be more appropriate to use with people who tend to get physically aggressive."*

- *Don't use teasing comebacks with people in authority*
  - ○ Say, *"The last rule for using teasing comebacks is that we should never use them with people in authority. Who are people in authority?"*
    - Answers: Social coaches; parents; professors; university administrators; supervisors; managers; bosses; law enforcement officers.
  - ○ Ask, *"What could be the problem with using teasing comebacks with people in authority?"*
    - Answers: It's disrespectful; you could get in trouble; you could get a bad reputation; you could get kicked out of class; you could get fired.

Good Role Play: Handling Teasing ⊙

[The group leader and a behavioral coach should do an APPROPRIATE role play with the group leader **handling teasing** by using **verbal** and **nonverbal comebacks**.]

- Begin by saying, *"We're going to do a role play. Watch this and tell me what I'm doing RIGHT in handling this teasing."*

Example of an APPROPRIATE Role Play

- ○ Behavioral coach: *"Your shoes are ugly!"*
- ○ Group leader: (Rolls eyes) "Whatever." (Said with attitude, then looks away)
- ○ Behavioral coach: *"Seriously, those are some ugly shoes!"*
- ○ Group leader: "Am I supposed to care?" (Said with indifference, then looks away)
- ○ Behavioral coach: *"Well you should care because those are some nasty looking shoes!"*
- ○ Group leader: *"Anyway . . ."* (Shrugs shoulders, shakes head no, and casually walks away)
- ○ Behavioral coach: (Looks defeated)

- Say, *"Timeout on that. So what did I do right in handling that teasing?"*
  - ○ Answers: You used *verbal* and *nonverbal comebacks*; you acted like what was said didn't bother you and was kind of lame; you were *prepared with a few verbal comebacks*; you *removed yourself after giving teasing comebacks*.
- Ask the following *Perspective Taking Questions*:
  - ○ *"What was that like for (name of coach)?"*
    - ■ Answers: Not fun; embarrassing; annoying.
  - ○ *"What do you think (name of coach) thought of me?"*
    - ■ Answers: Not upset; not bothered; indifferent.
  - ○ *"Is (name of coach) going to want to tease me again?"*
    - ■ Answer: Probably not.
- Ask the behavioral coach the same *Perspective Taking Questions*:
  - ○ *"What was that like for you?"*
  - ○ *"What did you think of me?"*
  - ○ *"Would you want to tease me again?"*

Behavioral Rehearsal: Handling Teasing

- Explain, *"Now we're going to have each of you practice using verbal comebacks in response to teasing. Each of you will choose three verbal comebacks from the board to practice. Just like with the role play, we will be teasing you about your shoes."*
- Go around the room and have each young adult individually identify THREE *verbal comebacks* they plan to use when practicing.
  - ○ Discourage young adults' attempts to come up with their own *teasing comebacks*.
  - ○ If the young adult comes up with his or her own response, be sure it fits the parameters of a good response (i.e., short, gives the impression that it didn't bother them and was kind of lame).
- Immediately conduct the behavioral rehearsal using these three *verbal comebacks* once identified, otherwise the young adult may forget what he or she was going to say.
- The group leader should use the benign tease, *"Your shoes are ugly!"*
  - ○ Use the same benign tease for each young adult, otherwise they may take the teasing comments personally.
  - ○ If the young adults would be offended by teasing comments about their shoes, choose another benign teasing remark, but make sure it is the SAME teasing comment for every young adult.
  - ○ Repeat teasing comments THREE times in succession, forcing the young adult to use different *verbal comebacks* each time.
- Young adults should reply with pre-approved *verbal* and *nonverbal* (when appropriate) *comebacks*.
- Give performance feedback and be sure each young adult has mastered the technique before moving on.
  - ○ If the young adult sounds upset, sad, or angry in response to the teasing, gently point this out and have them try again until they give the impression that the teasing didn't bother them.

- DO NOT ALLOW YOUNG ADULTS TO PRACTICE TEASING EACH OTHER.
  - It is never appropriate to have young adults demonstrate or practice inappropriate social behavior.
- End by giving a round of applause to each young adult after their practice.

Handling Embarrassing Feedback

- Explain, *"Sometimes people say things that are embarrassing and may even be meant to tease us, but they may also be giving us important feedback about how people see us. This is especially true when a lot of people are giving us the same feedback or even when a few people give us the same feedback over and over. Instead of just feeling hurt, we might be able to use this feedback to help us change the way people see us. If we think about what people are trying to tell us when they tease us, we can sometimes do things differently and make it less likely that we'll be teased in the future."*
- Go over the examples of embarrassing feedback listed in Table 15.3 and have young adults come up with ideas of what they could do differently in response to this feedback.
  - Present each example by saying, *"Let's say that a lot of people are giving you negative feedback about . . .(insert example of embarrassing feedback)."*
  - Ask, *"What could you do differently in response to this feedback?"*
  - Have young adults come up with examples of what they could do differently if they wanted to avoid teasing.
  - [Note: Changing things about yourself is a personal choice, so if young adults don't want to change the things they are being teased about, they don't have to.]

Table 15.3 Examples of Embarrassing Feedback and How to Utilize Feedback

Examples of Embarrassing Feedback	Examples of How to Utilize Feedback
Negative feedback about clothing	Consider changing your wardrobe; try to follow the clothing norms of your social group; change and wash clothes regularly; get clothing advice from social coaches, friends, family, sales clerks, personal shoppers, etc.
Negative feedback about body odor	Use deodorant every day; bathe regularly using soap; wash hair with shampoo regularly; wear less cologne/perfume.
Negative feedback about dandruff	Use dandruff shampoo regularly.
Negative feedback about oral hygiene	Brush teeth daily; use mouthwash; floss teeth regularly; use a tongue scraper; chew gum; use breath mints; avoid certain foods; visit the dentist regularly.
Negative feedback about your sense of humor	Pay attention to your humor feedback; consider telling fewer jokes; be a little more serious when first getting to know someone.
Negative feedback about unusual behaviors	Consider changing or discontinuing the behavior if possible.

Handling Physical Bullying

- Explain, *"Now that we've talked about strategies for handling teasing and embarrassing feedback, we need to talk about what to do in cases of physical bullying. Physical bullying might include taking personal items, pranking, or playing practical jokes, or in more extreme cases it could include aggressive acts like pushing, shoving, or throwing things. Even though both types include DIRECT bullying, the strategies for handling physical bullying are very different from the strategies for handling teasing."*
- *Avoid the bully*
  - Say, *"One of the best strategies for handling physical bullying is to avoid the bully. This means we need to stay out of reach of the bully. For example, if the bully has a desk in a certain area of the office, should you walk through that area?"*

- ▪ Answer: Not if you can help it.
  - ○ Ask, *"Why is it important to avoid the bully?"*
    - ▪ Answer: *If the bully can't FIND you, he or she can't bully you.*

- ● *Plan your route*
  - ○ Say, *"One way to avoid the bully is to plan your route. For example, if you know the bully likes to hang out in a certain area of campus, how could you avoid being in that area?"*
    - ▪ Answers: *Plan your route* to avoid that area; go a different way if you can.

- ● *Lay low when the bully is around*
  - ○ Explain, *"Another strategy for handling physical bullying is to lay low when the bully is around. This means you need to fly under the radar, keep a low profile, and don't draw attention to yourself when the bully is near."*
  - ○ Ask, *"Why is it important to lay low when the bully is around?"*
    - ▪ Answer: *If the bully doesn't notice you, he or she is less likely to bully you.*

- ● *Don't try to make friends with the bully*
  - ○ Explain, *"It's also important not to try to talk to the bully or make friends with the bully. Some people think they can win the bully over, but this almost never works. Instead, it just draws attention to you."*
  - ○ Ask, *"What could be the problem with trying to make friends with the bully?"*
    - ▪ Answers: It probably won't work; it will just draw attention to you; they will probably bully you more; they may act like you're friends and then take advantage of you; bullies don't make good friends anyway.

- ● *Don't provoke the bully*
  - ○ Say, *"Another important rule for handling physical bullying is to avoid provoking the bully. How might you provoke a bully?"*
    - ▪ Answers: Making fun of them; teasing them; laughing at them; pointing out their mistakes; trying to get them in trouble; acting silly around them.
  - ○ Ask, *"What could be the problem with provoking a bully?"*
    - ▪ Answer: They may want to retaliate; the bullying may worsen.

- ● *Don't tease the bully*
  - ○ Say, *"If we want to avoid provoking the bully, then we need to avoid teasing the bully. What could be the problem with teasing a bully?"*
    - ▪ Answers: They may want to retaliate; the bullying may worsen.

- ● *Don't police the bully*
  - ○ Ask, *"If we want to avoid provoking the bully, then we also need to avoid policing the bully. What could be the problem with policing the bully for minor offenses, like being late for work or not going to class?"*
    - ▪ Answers: They may want to retaliate; the bullying may worsen; you may look bad.
  - ○ Ask, *"What if the bully is doing something dangerous or illegal that could harm other people. Then should you tell someone?"*
    - ▪ Answer: Yes, definitely.
  - ○ Say, *"If you do have to tell on the bully, should you do this in front of people?"*
    - ▪ Answers: No, you should tell someone privately; don't tell others that you've done this if you can help it.
  - ○ Explain, *"If you have to tell on the bully, be sure that you do this privately and away from people. And don't go and tell your friends if you can help it because the bully could find out and might want to get back at you."*

- ● *Hang out with other people*
  - ○ Ask, *"Who do bullies like to pick on: people who are by themselves or in a group?"*
    - ▪ Answer: People who are by themselves.
  - ○ Ask, *"Why do bullies like to pick on people who are by themselves?"*
    - ▪ Answer: Because you're an easy target when you're alone and have no one to defend you or stick up for you.

- Explain, *"One of the most powerful strategies for handling physical bullying is to hang out with other people. This means you should avoid being alone. Bullies like to pick on people when they are alone and unprotected."*

- ***Stay near people in authority when the bully is around***
  - Ask, *"If you can't be around friends when the bully is nearby, you can stay near people in authority. Who are some people in authority you could stay near?"*
    - Answers: Professors; supervisors; managers; bosses.
  - Explain, *"Bullies don't tend to pick on others when people in authority are there, so you can stay near professors, supervisors, managers, or bosses when the bully is around. That doesn't mean you need to hang out with them. It just means you can stay near them when the bully is around."*

- ***Make a complaint as a last resort***
  - Say, *"Finally, if all of the strategies for handling psychical bullying aren't working, or if you feel threatened or harassed, you should make a complaint. Who could you make a complaint to if the bullying is happening at school?"*
    - Answers: Professor; chair of the department; university administrator; ombudsperson.
  - Ask, *"Who could you make a complaint to if the bullying is happening in the work place?"*
    - Answers: Supervisor; manager; boss; human resources department; personnel department.
  - Ask, *"Should we make a complaint the FIRST time someone calls us a name or makes fun of us?"*
    - Answers: No; you should probably try using the other strategies first.
  - Explain, *"Making a complaint is usually a last resort that we only use if the other strategies aren't working or if we feel threatened, harassed, or in danger. Be sure to speak to your social coaches before making a complaint since this is a serious decision and usually requires some support."*

HANDLING DIRECT BULLYING

Young Adult Behavioral Rehearsal

Get-Togethers

Materials Needed

- Indoor games (e.g., video games, card games, board games).
  - If you are going to provide video games as an option, make sure there are enough gaming consoles that each group can play simultaneously together.
  - Do not use small, portable gaming devices as people have to wait to take turns and that can get boring.
  - Several decks of playing cards will be sufficient if you do not have these other resources.
- Optional: iPads or laptops for watching YouTube videos, surfing the Internet, or playing computer games.
  - If you are going to provide iPads or laptops as an option, make sure there are enough that each group can use them simultaneously together.
- [Note: Most PEERS® programs DO NOT have access to gaming consoles, iPads, or laptops. These are luxury items. Just providing a few decks of cards to keep the get-together *activity-based* will be fine.]

Behavioral Rehearsal

- Notify young adults they will be practicing having *get-togethers*.
  - Note: They will no longer be practicing *beginning and ending get-togethers*.
- Break up young adults into small groups or dyads.
- Have young adults practice following the rules for how to behave *during the get-together* while:
  - *Trading information.*
  - *Finding common interests.*
  - Playing with games and items provided by the treatment team (e.g., video games, card games, board games, iPads, laptops, etc.).
- Provide *social coaching* as needed regarding the rules for making and keeping friends.

HANDLING DIRECT BULLYING

Reunification

- Announce that young adults should join their social coaches.
  - ○ Have young adults stand or sit next to their social coaches.
  - ○ Be sure to have silence and the full attention of the group before starting with *Reunification*.
  - ○ Have young adults generate the content from the lesson while social coaches listen.
- Say, *"Today, we talked about strategies for handling DIRECT bullying. This includes teasing and physical bullying. What are some of the verbal comebacks we identified for handling teasing?"*
  - ○ *"Whatever!"*
  - ○ *"Yeah, and?"*
  - ○ *"And?"*
  - ○ *"And your point is?"*
  - ○ *"Am I supposed to care?"*
  - ○ *"And why do I care?"*
  - ○ *"Is that supposed to be funny?"*
  - ○ *"Big deal!"*
  - ○ *"So what!"*
  - ○ *"Who cares?"*
  - ○ *"Tell me when you get to the funny part."*
  - ○ *"Tell me when you get to the punchline."*
  - ○ *"Anyway . . ."*
- Ask, *"What are some of the strategies we identified for handling physical bullying?"*
  - ○ *Avoid the bully*
  - ○ *Plan your route*
  - ○ *Lay low when the bully is around*
  - ○ *Don't try to make friends with the bully*
  - ○ *Don't provoke the bully*
  - ○ *Don't tease the bully*
  - ○ *Don't police the bully*
  - ○ *Hang out with other people*
  - ○ *Stay near people in authority when the bully is around*
  - ○ *Make a complaint as a last resort*
- Explain, *"Young adults practiced handling teasing and the group did a great job so we should give them a round of applause."*

Homework Assignments

Distribute the *Social Coaching Handout* to young adults and announce the following *Homework Assignments*:

1. Have a *get-together* with a friend.
   - Social coaches should help young adults plan the get-together using the *five W's*:

- ○ *WHO* they plan to get together with.
- ○ *WHAT* they plan to do.
- ○ *WHEN* it will happen.
- ○ *WHERE* they will meet.
- ○ *HOW* they will make it happen.
- Social coaches should go over the rules and steps for *get-togethers* with young adults beforehand.
- Social coaches should ask young adults the following *social coaching questions* after the *get-together*:
  - ○ *What did you decide to do and who picked the activities?*
  - ○ *Did you trade information and for what percentage of the time?*
  - ○ *What were your common interests and what could you do with that information if you were going to hang out again?*
  - ○ *Did you and your friend have a good time?*
  - ○ *Is this someone you might want to hang out with again?*

2. Young adults and social coaches should practice *handling teasing*.
   - Go over the strategies for *handling teasing* before practicing.
   - Young adults should choose THREE *verbal comebacks* to practice using.
   - Social coaches should use benign teasing comments (i.e., "Your shoes are ugly").
   - Social coaches should ask young adults the following *Perspective Taking Questions* after practicing:
     - ○ *What was that like for me?*
     - ○ *What do you think I thought of you?*
     - ○ *Do you think I'm going to want to tease you again?*

3. Young adults should practice *handling DIRECT bullying* with a peer if relevant.
   - Social coaches should ask young adults the following *social coaching* and *Perspective Taking Questions* after practicing when relevant:
     - ○ *What did you do or say to handle teasing?*
       - ■ *What was that like for the other person?*
       - ■ *What do you think they thought of you?*
       - ■ *Do you think they're going to want to tease you again?*
     - ○ *Did they give you any embarrassing feedback and what could you do differently if you didn't want to be teased about that?*
     - ○ *What did you do or say to handle physical bullying?*

4. Young adults and social coaches should practice *handling a disagreement*.
   - Go over the rules and steps for *RESPONDING to disagreements* and *BRINGING UP disagreements* before practicing.
   - Social coaches should ask young adults the following *social coaching* and *Perspective Taking Questions* after practicing:
     - ○ *Which steps did you follow?*
     - ○ *What was that like for me in the end?*
     - ○ *What do you think I thought of you in the end?*
     - ○ *Do you think I'm going to want to hang out with you again?*

5. Young adults should practice *handling a disagreement* with a friend or romantic partner if relevant.
   - Social coaches should go over the rules and steps for *RESPONDING to disagreements* and *BRINGING UP disagreements* before practicing when possible.
   - Social coaches should ask young adults the following *social coaching* and *Perspective Taking Questions* after practicing:
     - ○ *Which steps did you follow?*
     - ○ *What was that like for you and the other person in the end?*
     - ○ *What did you think of each other in the end?*
     - ○ *Do you think you'll both want to hang out again?*

6. Practice *letting someone know you like them, ask them on a date*, and/or *go on a date*.
   - If young adults are interested in someone romantically:
     - *Let them know you like them.*
     - *Ask them on a date.*
     - *Go on a date.*
     - DO NOT practice unless you are romantically interested in the person.
   - Young adults should practice *letting someone know you like them, asking someone on a date*, and *beginning and ending dates* with social coaches, if comfortable.
   - Social coaches should go over all of the rules and steps for *dating etiquette* before the practice.
   - Social coaches should ask young adults the following *social coaching questions* after each practice:
     - *Letting someone know you like them*:
       - *Who did you practice with and what did you do to let them know you like them?*
       - *How did they respond?*
       - *Does this seem like a good choice and is this someone you might want to go on a date with?*
     - *Asking someone on a date*:
       - *Who did you ask on a date and what steps did you follow?*
       - *How did they respond?*
     - *Going on a date*:
       - *What did you decide to do?*
       - *Did you trade information and for what percentage of the time?*
       - *What were your common interests and what could you do with that information if you were going to go on a date again?*
       - *Did you and your date have a good time?*
       - *Does this seem like a good choice and is this someone you might want to go on a date with again?*

Graduation Announcement

- Distribute the *Graduation Flyer* (see Appendix G for an example) to young adults.
- Say, *"Graduation is in TWO weeks. That means we will be wrapping things up in two weeks and talking about how to move forward now that our group is coming to an end. In order to celebrate all your hard work, young adults will be having a graduation party and we will all be having a graduation ceremony."*
- You may want to explain the structure of the graduation party and graduation ceremony, which will vary according to resources.
  - Suggestions for the graduation party and ceremony can be found in the *Young Adult Therapist Guide* for Session 16.

Individual Check-Out

Individually and privately negotiate with each young adult and social coach:

1. *WHO* they plan to have a *get-together* with in the coming week.
   - *WHAT* they plan to suggest to their friends.
   - *WHEN* and *WHERE* they will suggest to their friends.
   - *HOW* they will make it happen (e.g., tickets, transportation, etc.).

2. When they plan to practice *handling teasing* with their social coach.

3. When they plan to practice *handling a disagreement* with their social coach.

4. How they will practice *letting someone know they like them* and with whom, and whether they plan to *ask them on a date*.
   - *WHO* they plan to have a *date* with in the coming week.
   - *WHAT* they plan to suggest to do.
   - *WHEN* and *WHERE* they will suggest to meet.
   - *HOW* they will make it happen (e.g., tickets, transportation, etc.).

SESSION 14

HANDLING DIRECT BULLYING

Social Coaching Handout

Handling Teasing*

- *Don't ignore the teasing*
- *Don't walk away right away*
- *Don't tell someone right away*
- *Don't tease them back*
- *Don't banter*
- *Act like what they said didn't bother you*
- *Act like what they said was lame or stupid*
- *Give a short verbal comeback*
  - Examples:
    - *"Whatever!"*
    - *"Yeah, and?"*
    - *"And?"*
    - *"And your point is?"*
    - *"Am I supposed to care?"*
    - *"And why do I care?"*
    - *"Is that supposed to be funny?"*
    - *"Big deal!"*
    - *"So what!"*
    - *"Who cares?"*
    - *"Tell me when you get to the funny part."*
    - *"Tell me when you get to the punchline."*
    - *"Anyway . . ."* (good comeback to end with and walk away on)
  - *Sound bored*
  - *Have an attitude*
  - *Always be prepared with at least a few verbal comebacks*
  - *Verbal comebacks need to make sense*
- *Give a nonverbal comeback*
  - *Rolling your eyes*
  - *Shrugging your shoulders*
  - *Shaking your head no*
- *Remove yourself after giving teasing comebacks*
- *Teasing may get worse before it gets better*
- *Expect the teaser to try again*
- *Don't use teasing comebacks with physically aggressive people*
- *Don't use teasing comebacks with people in authority*

Handling Embarrassing Feedback

Table 15.3 Examples of Embarrassing Feedback and How to Utilize Feedback

Examples of Embarrassing Feedback	Examples of How to Utilize Feedback
Negative feedback about clothing	Consider changing your wardrobe; try to follow the clothing norms of your social group; change and wash clothes regularly; get clothing advice from social coaches, friends, family, sales clerks, personal shoppers, etc.
Negative feedback about body odor	Use deodorant every day; bathe regularly using soap; wash hair with shampoo regularly; wear less cologne/perfume.
Negative feedback about dandruff	Use dandruff shampoo regularly.
Negative feedback about oral hygiene	Brush teeth daily; use mouthwash; floss teeth regularly; use a tongue scraper; chew gum; use breath mints; avoid certain foods; visit the dentist regularly.
Negative feedback about your sense of humor	Pay attention to your humor feedback; consider telling fewer jokes; be a little more serious when first getting to know someone.
Negative feedback about unusual behaviors	Consider changing or discontinuing the behavior if possible.

Handling Physical Bullying

- *Avoid the bully*
    - ○ *If the bully can't FIND you, he or she can't bully you.*
- *Plan your route*
- *Lay low when the bully is around*
    - ○ *If the bully doesn't notice you, he or she is less likely to bully you.*
- *Don't try to make friends with the bully*
- *Don't provoke the bully*
- *Don't tease the bully*
- *Don't police the bully*
- *Hang out with other people*
- *Stay near people in authority when the bully is around*
- *Make a complaint as a last resort*

Homework Assignments

1. Have a *get-together* with a friend.
    - Social coaches should help young adults plan the get-together using the *five W's*:
        - ○ *WHO* they plan to get together with.
        - ○ *WHAT* they plan to do.
        - ○ *WHEN* it will happen.
        - ○ *WHERE* they will meet.
        - ○ *HOW* they will make it happen.
    - Social coaches should go over the rules and steps for *get-togethers* with young adults beforehand.
    - Social coaches should ask young adults the following *social coaching questions* after the *get-together*:
        - ○ *What did you decide to do and who picked the activities?*
        - ○ *Did you trade information and for what percentage of the time?*
        - ○ *What were your common interests and what could you do with that information if you were going to hang out again?*
        - ○ *Did you and your friend have a good time?*
        - ○ *Is this someone you might want to hang out with again?*

2. Young adults and social coaches should practice *handling teasing*.
   - Go over the strategies for *handling teasing* before practicing.
   - Young adults should choose THREE *verbal comebacks* to practice using.
   - Social coaches should use benign teasing comments (i.e., *"Your shoes are ugly"*).
   - Social coaches should ask young adults the following *Perspective Taking Questions* after practicing:
     - *What was that like for me?*
     - *What do you think I thought of you?*
     - *Do you think I'm going to want to tease you again?*

3. Young adults should practice *handling DIRECT bullying* with a peer if relevant.
   - Social coaches should ask young adults the following *social coaching* and *Perspective Taking Questions* after practicing when relevant:
     - *What did you do or say to handle teasing?*
       - *What was that like for the other person?*
       - *What do you think they thought of you?*
       - *Do you think they're going to want to tease you again?*
     - *Did they give you any embarrassing feedback and what could you do differently if you didn't want to be teased about that?*
     - *What did you do or say to handle physical bullying?*

4. Young adults and social coaches should practice *handling a disagreement*.
   - Go over the rules and steps for *RESPONDING to disagreements* and *BRINGING UP disagreements* before practicing.
   - Social coaches should ask young adults the following *social coaching* and *Perspective Taking Questions* after practicing:
     - *Which steps did you follow?*
     - *What was that like for me in the end?*
     - *What did you think of each other in the end?*
     - *Do you think I'm going to want to hang out with you again?*

5. Young adults should practice *handling a disagreement* with a friend or romantic partner if relevant.
   - Social coaches should go over the rules and steps for *RESPONDING to disagreements* and *BRINGING UP disagreements* before practicing when possible.
   - Social coaches should ask young adults the following *social coaching* and *Perspective Taking Questions* after practicing:
     - *Which steps did you follow?*
     - *What was that like for you and the other person in the end?*
     - *What do you think they thought of you in the end?*
     - *Do you think you'll both want to hang out again?*

6. Practice *letting someone know you like them, ask them on a date*, and/or *go on a date*.
   - If young adults are interested in someone romantically:
     - *Let them know you like them.*
     - *Ask them on a date.*
     - *Go on a date.*
     - DO NOT practice unless you are romantically interested in the person.
   - Young adults should practice *letting someone know you like them, asking someone on a date*, and *beginning and ending dates* with social coaches, if comfortable.
   - Social coaches should go over all of the rules and steps for *dating etiquette* before the practice.
   - Social coaches should ask young adults the following *social coaching questions* after each practice:
     - *Letting someone know you like them*:
       - *Who did you practice with and what did you do to let them know you like them?*
       - *How did they respond?*

- Does this seem like a good choice and is this someone you might want to go on a date with?
  ○ *Asking someone on a date*:
    - *Who did you ask on a date and what steps did you follow?*
    - *How did they respond?*
  ○ *Going on a date*:
    - *What did you decide to do?*
    - *Did you trade information and for what percentage of the time?*
    - *What were your common interests and what could you do with that information if you were going to go on a date again?*
    - *Did you and your date have a good time?*
    - *Does this seem like a good choice and is this someone you might want to go on a date with again?*

REMINDER: PEERS® GRADUATION IS IN TWO WEEKS!

* See *The Science of Making Friends* DVD (Laugeson, 2013) or *FriendMaker* mobile app for a video Role Play Demonstration of the corresponding rule.

HANDLING INDIRECT BULLYING

Social Coaching Therapist Guide

Preparing for the Social Coaching Session

The focus of this lesson is on providing strategies for handling indirect forms of bullying. This includes *electronic bullying*, also known as *cyberbullying*, and *relational bullying*, which involves *spreading rumors and gossip*. These are indirect forms of bullying because they generally take place over the Internet or behind the person's back.

The phenomenon of *cyberbullying*, which involves the use of electronic forms of communication to hurt or harass people, has become more common in the past several years, particularly among young adults who frequently use the technologies associated with *cyberbullying*, such as mobile phones and social media. Because *cyberbullying* is a relatively recent phenomenon, some social coaches will be less familiar with the acts associated with *cyberbullying*. Consequently, you should be prepared to provide a brief tutorial on the different types of *cyberbullying*.

To clarify, the act of *cyberbullying* may include sending harassing, threatening, or humiliating messages over cell phones, computers, or social networking sites. Six types of *cyberbullying* have been identified through research:

- **Insulting:** Posting or spreading false information, possibly causing harm to the reputation of the person targeted.
- **Harassment:** Repeatedly sending malicious and harassing messages to a targeted person.
- **Targeting:** Singling out a person and inviting others to attack or make fun of him or her collectively.
- **Identity theft:** Pretending to be someone else to make it appear as though the targeted person said or did things he or she didn't do.
- **Uploading:** Sharing emails or posting images of a person, particularly under embarrassing circumstances.
- **Excluding:** Pressuring others to exclude the targeted person from membership or affiliation with a particular group.

The strategies outlined for *handling cyberbullying* are fairly straightforward and not likely to be met with resistance from social coaches. However, questions about the nature of *cyberbullying* may arise.

Another aspect of **INDIRECT** bullying involves the *spreading of rumors and gossip*. *Spreading rumors and gossip* is one of the more common ways people share information about the personal lives of others. *Rumors and gossip* are very common among young adults. Just consider the popularity of gossip shows and tabloid magazines. Although a distinct type of *relational bullying* often thought of as mean-spirited, heartless, and unkind, *rumors and gossip* may also simply represent a kind of communication that people use to connect and bond when socializing. Research suggests that gossiping may actually enhance social bonding in large groups as a form of shared communication.

Whatever the case may be, it's important to understand that ***rumors and gossip*** are very common and unlikely to be eliminated from the social world in which we live.

The focus of the second half of the *Didactic Lesson* will be on helping social coaches understand the ways in which they can support young adults in ***handling rumors and gossip***. Likening these methods to popular culture is one way to illuminate the practicality of these strategies for social coaches. For example, one of the strategies for ***handling rumors and gossip*** is ***don't try to disprove the rumor***. By trying to disprove or deny the rumor, the target looks defensive and guilty and actually adds fuel to the rumor mill through their denials. To help social coaches understand this common social error, you might have them think of celebrities that have unsuccessfully tried to disprove rumors about themselves, perhaps even suing tabloid magazines and actually fueling the rumor mill, rather than killing the rumor. On the other hand, one of the more proactive strategies for ***handling rumors and gossip*** is to ***spread the rumor about yourself***. This involves discrediting the importance or the believability of the rumor by acknowledging its existence and ***acting amazed that anyone would CARE about or BELIEVE the rumor***. Similarly, to help social coaches understand the utility of this strategy, you might have them think of celebrities who are really good at this, or really bad at this. Although not part of the formal lesson for ***handling rumors and gossip***, this brief exercise is often enjoyable for social coaches and helps to highlight the effectiveness of these strategies.

Homework Review

[Go over the following *Homework Assignments* and **troubleshoot** any potential problems. Start with completed homework first. If you have time, you can inquire as to why others were unable to complete the assignment and try to **troubleshoot** how they might get it done for the coming week. When reviewing homework, be sure to relabel descriptions using the **buzzwords** (identified by **bold and italicized** print). Spend the majority of the *Homework Review* on **get-togethers** as this was the most important assignment.]

1. Have a ***get-together*** with a friend.
   - Say, *"One of the main assignments this week was for young adults to have a get-together with a friend. Who completed this assignment or attempted to complete it?"*
   - Ask the following questions:
     - *"Did you help your young adult plan the get-together using the five W's?"*
     - *"What social coaching did you do before the get-together?"*
     - *"What did your young adult decide to do and with whom?"*
     - *"How did the get-together begin?"*
     - *"Who picked the activities?"*
     - *"Did they trade information and what percentage of the time?"*
     - *"How did the get-together end?"*
     - *"What social coaching did you do after the get-together?"*
       - Appropriate ***social coaching questions***:
         - ***What did you decide to do and who picked the activities?***
         - ***Did you trade information and for what percentage of the time?***
         - ***What were your common interests and what could you do with that information if you were going to hang out again?***
         - ***Did you and your friend have a good time?***
         - ***Is this someone you might want to hang out with again?***
     - *"Does this seem like a good choice for a friend and someone your young adult will want to hang out with again?"*

Table 16.1 Steps for Beginning and Ending Get-Togethers in Your Home

Beginning the Get-Together	Ending the Get-Together
1. Greet your guest 2. Invite them in 3. Introduce them to anyone they don't know 4. Give them a tour 5. Offer them refreshments 6. Ask them what they want to do	1. Wait for a pause in activities 2. Give a cover story for ending the get-together 3. Start walking your friend to the door 4. Thank your friend for getting together 5. Tell your friend you had a good time 6. Say goodbye and you'll see them later

2. Young adults and social coaches should practice *handling teasing*.
   - Say, *"Another assignment this week was for young adults and social coaches to practice handling teasing. Who completed this assignment or attempted to complete it?"*
   - Ask the following questions:
     - *"What social coaching did you do before the practice?"*
     - *"What did your young adult do or say to handle teasing?"*
     - *"What social coaching did you do after the practice?"*
       - Appropriate *Perspective Taking Questions*:
         - **What was that like for me?**
         - **What do you think I thought of you?**
         - **Do you think I'm going to want to tease you again?**

3. Young adults should practice *handling DIRECT bullying* with a peer if relevant.
   - Say, *"Another assignment this week was for young adults to practice handling DIRECT bullying with a peer if relevant. Who completed this assignment or attempted to complete it?"*
   - Ask the following questions:
     - *"Who did your young adult practice with and what was the bullying?"*
     - *"What did your young adult do or say to handle DIRECT bullying?"*
     - *"What social coaching did you do after the practice?"*
       - Appropriate *social coaching* and *Perspective Taking Questions*:
         - **What did you do or say to handle teasing?**
           - **What was that like for the other person?**
           - **What do you think they thought of you?**
           - **Do you think they're going to want to tease you again?**
         - **Did they give you any embarrassing feedback and what could you do differently if you didn't want to be teased about that?**
         - **What did you do or say to handle physical bullying?**

4. Young adults and social coaches should practice *handling a disagreement*.
   - Say, *"Another assignment this week was for young adults and social coaches to practice handling a disagreement. Who completed this assignment or attempted to complete it?"*
   - Ask the following questions:
     - *"What social coaching did you do before the practice?"*
     - *"Which steps did your young adult follow to RESPOND to a disagreement?"*
     - *"Which steps did your young adult follow to BRING UP a disagreement?"*
     - *"What social coaching did you do after the practice?"*
       - Appropriate *social coaching* and *Perspective Taking Questions*:
         - **Which steps did you follow?**
         - **What was that like for me in the end?**
         - **What do you think I thought of you in the end?**
         - **Do you think I'm going to want to hang out with you again?**

Table 16.2 Steps for Handling Disagreements

RESPONDING TO DISAGREEMENTS	BRINGING UP DISAGREEMENTS
1. *Keep your cool*	1. *Wait for the right time and place*
2. *Listen to the other person*	2. *Keep your cool*
3. *Repeat what they said*	3. *Ask to speak privately*
4. *Explain your side using "I" statements*	4. *Explain your side using "I" statements*
5. *Say you're sorry*	5. *Listen to the other person*
6. *Try to solve the problem*	6. *Repeat what they said*
	7. *Tell them what you need them to do*
	8. *Try to solve the problem*

5. Young adults should practice ***handling a disagreement*** with a friend or romantic partner if relevant.
   - Say, *"Another assignment this week was for young adults to practice handling a disagreement with a friend or romantic partner if relevant. Who completed this assignment or attempted to complete it?"*
   - Ask the following questions:
     - *"Who did your young adult practice with and what was the disagreement?"*
     - *"Which steps did your young adult follow to RESPOND to or BRING UP the disagreement?"*
     - *"What social coaching did you do after the practice?"*
       - Appropriate ***social coaching*** and ***Perspective Taking Questions***:
         - **Which steps did you follow?**
         - **What was that like for you and the other person in the end?**
         - **What did you think of each other in the end?**
         - **Do you think you'll both want to hang out again?**

6. Practice ***letting someone know you like them, ask them on a date,*** and/or ***go on a date***.
   - Say, *"Another assignment this week was for young adults to practice letting someone know they like them, ask them on a date, and/or go on a date. The assignment was NOT to practice unless they are romantically interested in the person. Young adults could also have practiced with social coaches, if they were comfortable. Who completed this assignment or attempted to complete it?"*
   - Ask the following questions:
     - *"What social coaching did you do before the practice?"*
     - *"Who did your young adult practice with?"*
     - *"What did they do to let the person know they like them and how did they respond?"*
     - *"Did they ask the person on a date and how did they respond?"*
     - Ask the following questions if they went on a date:
       - *"What did they decide to do?"*
       - *"Did they trade information and for what percentage of the time?"*
       - *"Did they and their date have a good time?"*
     - *"What social coaching did you do after the practice?"*
     - *"Does this seem like a good choice and is this someone they might want to go on a date with (again)?"*
- [Collect the *Social Coaching Homework Assignment Worksheets*. If social coaches forgot to bring the worksheets, have them complete a new form to hold them accountable for the assignments.]

Didactic Lesson: Handling Indirect Bullying

- Distribute the *Social Coaching Handout*.
  - Sections in **bold print** in the *Social Coaching Therapist Guide* come directly from the *Social Coaching Handout*.
  - Remind social coaches that terms that are in ***bold and italicized*** print are ***buzzwords*** and represent important concepts from the PEERS® curriculum that should be used as much as possible when social coaching.
- Explain, *"Today, we're going to be talking about how to handle bullying. In our last session, we talked about strategies for handling DIRECT bullying, such as teasing and physical bullying. These are DIRECT*

forms of bullying because they happen directly to the person. Today, we will talk about handling INDIRECT forms of bullying, such as cyberbullying, rumors, and gossip. These are INDIRECT forms of bullying because they usually happen over the Internet or behind our back. Just like bullying behaviors are completely different, the strategies for handling these different types of bullying are also very different."

Handling Cyberbullying

- Explain, *"One way that people INDIRECTLY bully others is over electronic communication. This is sometimes called cyberbullying. Even though people sometimes tease over electronic communication, the strategies for handling cyberbullying are very different from the ways we handle teasing in person."*
- Ask, *"What are some ways that people cyberbully?"*
  - Answers:
    - Send or forward threatening, harassing, or hurtful email messages, text messages, or instant messages.
    - Spread rumors and gossip on social networking sites.
    - Create social networking pages to target a victim.
    - Post photos or private information on the Internet without consent.
    - Pretend to be someone else in order to humiliate someone or trick someone into revealing personal information.
- Explain, *"There are lots of different ways people bully others over electronic communication. Now we're going to talk about ways to handle these different types of cyberbullying."*

Strategies for Handling Cyberbullying

- ***Don't feed the trolls—don't react***
  - Say, *"Trolling is a term used for people who bully others online by posting harassing and mean comments on social networking sites, message boards, and forums. They do this because it's fun for them and they're trying to get a reaction out of you. What kind of reaction are they trying to get?"*
    - Answer: They're hoping to upset you and get you to put on a show by defending yourself or engaging in a fight.
  - Say, *"Trolls and cyberbullies are not so different from in-person bullies. They're always looking for a reaction. So what happens if you get upset or defend yourself and put up a fight?"*
    - Answer: You make it fun for the cyberbully.
  - Ask, *"When you get upset or put up a fight, does that make it MORE likely or LESS likely that you're going to get cyberbullied again?"*
    - Answer: MORE likely.
  - Explain, *"There's a saying online—'don't feed the trolls.' That means don't react by trying to confront them or beat them at their own game. Even responding by saying, 'whatever' won't work because all of the emotion is lost on the screen. When you react, it's a losing game and you'll only feed their enjoyment and make them want to cyberbully you more. If you don't feed the trolls, they'll probably get bored, move on, and find someone else to bother."*

- ***Have friends stick up for you***
  - Say, *"Just like in-person bullies, cyberbullies like to pick on people who are by themselves. Why do cyberbullies like to pick on people who are by themselves or seem unprotected?"*
    - Answers: Because when you're alone, you have no one to stick up for you or have your back; you are an easier target.
  - Explain, *"One of the strategies for handling cyberbullying is to have a friend stick up for you. We've already talked about how it doesn't do any good for you to defend yourself. That's what the cyberbully or the troll wants. Instead, your young adult can have a friend or a family member around the same age defend him/her to show that they're not alone."*

- ***Lay low online for a while***
  - Explain, *"A lot of cyberbullying happens online, especially on social networking sites. If your young adult is having trouble with people cyberbullying him or her, a good strategy is to lay low online for a while."*

- ○ Ask, *"What does it mean to lay low online and how can that help prevent cyberbullying?"*
  - ■ Answers: Stay off social networking sites for a while; don't post comments on other people's walls or in forums; this creates distance between you and the cyberbullying; it gives you a chance to let the cyberbullying die down; *if the cyberbully can't FIND you, he or she can't bully you.*

- **Block the cyberbully**
  - ○ Explain, *"Since some cyberbullying happens over text messaging, instant messaging, email, and social networking sites where the bully is identifiable, one of the easiest ways to stop cyberbullying is by blocking the cyberbully."*
  - ○ Ask, *"What does it mean to block the cyberbully and how can that help prevent cyberbullying?"*
    - ■ Answers: That means block their messages from ever being delivered to your phone, email, or social networking page; *if the cyberbully can't CONTACT you, he or she can't bully you.*

- **Save the evidence**
  - ○ Say, *"Another good strategy for protecting young adults from cyberbullying is to save the evidence. What does it mean to save the evidence and why is it important to save the evidence?"*
    - ■ Answer: Save any threatening, harassing, or humiliating communications because if the cyberbullying doesn't stop, you may have to report it.
  - ○ Ask, *"What if the cyberbullying happens on a social networking site like Facebook and other people can see it. What should your young adult do?"*
    - ■ Answer: Take a screenshot, save the evidence, and delete the post so other people can't see it.

- **Report cyberbullying as a last resort**
  - ○ Explain, *"In some cases, it may be necessary for young adults to report the cyberbullying to the proper authorities as a last resort. This might include online service providers, webmasters, universities, employers, or in the most extreme cases, even law enforcement. Because knowing when and how to report cyberbullying can be confusing, as social coaches, you will need to work with young adults on deciding if it's appropriate to report the cyberbullying and to whom."*

Handling Rumors and Gossip

- Say, *"Another way that people INDIRECTLY bully others is by spreading rumors and gossip. Rumors and gossip are very common in the workplace and in college settings. Unfortunately, there's very little we can do to prevent people from gossiping. However, it can be very helpful to know why people spread rumors and gossip."*
- Ask, *"Why do people gossip?"*
  - ○ Answers: To be mean; hurt people; get revenge; manipulate others; fulfill a threat; gain attention; increase popularity; as a form of communication.
- Explain the following by saying, *"Rumors and gossip are often used as a . . ."*
  - ○ **Social weapon**
    - ■ Spreading gossip may be mean-spirited and meant to hurt people; to damage the reputation of someone disliked or envied.
  - ○ **Form of social retaliation**
    - ■ Spreading gossip may be used to get revenge on someone for something they've done; to manipulate someone; to fulfill some threat (e.g., *"If you don't do . . . I'll tell everyone . . ."*).
  - ○ **Method to gain attention**
    - ■ Spreading gossip may be a way for some young adults to get attention and feel important (e.g., they know something no one else does).
  - ○ **Method for gaining popularity**
    - ■ Spreading gossip may be a way for some young adults to try to become more popular by capturing the interest and attention of others, and holding power over others.
  - ○ **Form of communication**
    - ■ More often, spreading gossip is just a part of young adults' conversation, and a way to stay current with their social surroundings.

- Explain, *"Because rumors and gossip are often just a form of communication and a way for young adults to stay informed about what's happening around them, there is very little we can do to prevent people from spreading rumors and gossip."*

Avoiding Being the Target of Gossip

- Explain, *"Now that we're clear on WHY people gossip, it will be helpful to know what we can do to make it less likely that people will gossip about us. The first thing we need to think about is how we might avoid being the target of rumors and gossip."*

- ***Avoid being friends with the gossips***
  - ○ Explain, *"The first rule for avoiding being the target of rumors and gossip is to avoid being friends with gossips. 'Gossips' are people who like to start rumors and spread gossip about other people."*
  - ○ Ask, *"What could be the problem with being friends with the gossips?"*
    - ■ Answers: They are likely to spread rumors about you if they get mad at you; it is difficult to trust someone who is a gossip; they may share your secrets; people will believe what they say about you because you're friends; other people may not want to be friends with you because they know you associate with the gossips.

- ***Avoid being enemies with the gossips***
  - ○ Explain, *"The next rule for avoiding being the target of rumors and gossip is to avoid being enemies with the gossips. This means don't get on the bad side of the gossips or their friends by telling their secrets, gossiping about them, making fun of them, or policing them."*
  - ○ Ask, *"What could be the problem with being enemies with the gossips or their friends?"*
    - ■ Answers: This will only provoke them to retaliate against you; you are likely to become the object of their gossip.

- ***Be neutral with the gossips***
  - ○ Say, *"Instead of being friends or enemies with the gossips, you want to be as neutral as possible with the gossips. What does it mean to be neutral?"*
    - ■ Answers: You don't want to be friends and you don't want to be enemies; just stay out of their way and off their radar.

- ***Don't spread rumors about other people***
  - ○ Say, *"Our last rule for avoiding being the target of rumors and gossip is not to spread rumors about other people. What could be the problem with spreading rumors and gossip about other people?"*
    - ■ Answers: Because it's hurtful and people will not want to be friends with you; you may get a bad reputation; the people you gossip about may want to retaliate by gossiping about you.

Handling Being the Target of Gossip

- Explain, *"Even though your young adults may try their best to avoid being the target of gossip, it may still happen, so we need to know what we can do to minimize the impact of gossip when it's focused on them."*

- ***Every instinct we have is WRONG***
  - ○ Explain, *"The interesting thing about being the target of rumors and gossip is that almost every instinct we have in these situations is WRONG!"*
  - ○ Ask, *"What do most people want to do when they are the target of a rumor?"*
    - ■ Answers: Disprove the gossip; defend themselves; get upset; confront the person spreading the gossip.
  - ○ Explain, *"Most people will try to disprove the rumor, deny the rumor, appear upset, or even confront the person spreading the rumor. But in each of these cases, we actually make the rumor stronger by adding fuel to the rumor mill."*

- ***Don't try to disprove the rumor***
  - ○ Say, *"When you're the target of rumors and gossip, a strong instinct is to try to disprove or deny the rumor. What do you look like when you try to deny or disprove the rumor?"*

- ■ Answer: You typically look defensive and guilty.
  - ○ Explain, "*Remember, every instinct we have is WRONG when it comes to rumors and gossip. If you try to disprove the rumor, you'll look defensive and guilty. The new rumor will be how you're freaking out trying to disprove the rumor. That's GOOD GOSSIP and adds fuel to the rumor mill.*"

- ● *Don't appear upset*
  - ○ Say, "*Another common instinct when you're the target of rumors and gossip is to get upset. What could be the problem with appearing upset?*"
    - ■ Answer: You look defensive and guilty.
  - ○ Explain, "*Remember, every instinct we have is WRONG when it comes to rumors and gossip. If you appear upset or stop going to school or work, people may assume you have something to hide. The new rumor will be how upset you are. Again, that's GOOD GOSSIP and adds fuel to the rumor mill.*"

- ● *Act like the rumor doesn't bother you*
  - ○ Explain, "*Even though it's upsetting to be the target of rumors and gossip, you need to act like the rumors don't bother you. Privately, young adults can talk to family and friends, but publically they shouldn't appear upset.*"
  - ○ Ask, "*Why is it important to act like the rumor doesn't bother you?*"
    - ■ Answers: You look less defensive and less guilty if you don't appear upset.

- ● *Don't confront the person spreading the gossip*
  - ○ Explain, "*Sometimes you know who's spreading the rumors about you. In this case, the instinct may be to confront the person spreading the gossip. The problem is this will probably only escalate things and add fuel to the rumor mill.*"
  - ○ Ask, "*What could be the problem with confronting the person spreading the gossip?*"
    - ■ Answers: The person may start spreading even more gossip about you; this may result in an argument or even a fight; the person may feel justified in spreading more gossip about you.
  - ○ Explain, "*Remember, every instinct we have is WRONG when it comes to rumors and gossip. If you confront the person spreading the gossip, you may look defensive and guilty. The new rumor will be how you freaked out and confronted them. Again, that's GOOD GOSSIP and adds fuel to the rumor mill.*"

- ● *Avoid the person spreading the gossip*
  - ○ Say, "*Imagine you know who is spreading the gossip about you. What does everyone expect you to do?*"
    - ■ Answer: They expect you to confront the person spreading the gossip.
  - ○ Say, "*The problem is that even if you don't confront the person spreading the gossip, simply just being in the same place means you can't win no matter what you do. If you don't look at them, what's the new rumor going to be?*"
    - ■ Answer: The new rumor will be how you couldn't even look at them.
  - ○ Ask, "*If you happen to look at them, what's the new rumor going to be?*"
    - ■ Answer: The new rumor will be how you gave them the "evil eye."
  - ○ Explain, "*In this case, you can't win no matter what you do, so it's best if young adults avoid the person spreading the gossip. That doesn't mean stop going to school or work. It just means plan their route and try to avoid them until the rumor dies down.*"

- ● *Act amazed anyone CARES about or BELIEVES the gossip*
  - ○ Explain, "*When you're the target of rumors and gossip, people will ask you about the gossip to see your reaction. Even though your instinct may be to deny or disprove the rumor, that just makes you look guilty. Instead you should act amazed anyone CARES about or BELIEVES the gossip. It doesn't even matter if it's true. If the rumor is true—you can't believe anyone CARES about it. If the rumor isn't true—you can't believe anyone BELIEVES it.*"
  - ○ Provide examples of what to say to **act amazed anyone CARES about the gossip**:
    - ■ "*Can you believe anyone cares about that?*"
    - ■ "*Why would anyone care about that?*"
    - ■ "*People need to get a life.*"
    - ■ "*People need to find a hobby.*"

- ■ *"People seriously need to find something better to talk about."*
- ○ Provide examples of what to say to *act amazed anyone BELIEVES the gossip*:
  - ■ *"Can you believe anyone believes that?"*
  - ■ *"Who would believe that?"*
  - ■ *"People are so gullible."*
  - ■ *"People will believe anything."*
  - ■ *"I can't believe anyone would believe that."*
- ○ Ask, *"Why is it important to act amazed that anyone would CARE about or BELIEVE the gossip?"*
  - ■ Answers: Because it makes the rumor seem silly; people will be less likely to believe the rumor because you've undermined its importance or believability; people will be less likely to continue to spread the rumor because it makes them seem naive or gullible for even caring about or believing it.
- ○ Explain, *"Acting amazed anyone CARES about or BELIEVES the gossip discredits the importance or believability of the gossip."*

- ● *Spread the rumor about yourself*
  - ○ Explain, *"Even though acting amazed anyone would CARE about or BELIEVE the gossip is a good strategy for handling questions about the gossip, young adults should be even more proactive than that. You actually want them to spread the rumor about themselves! That may sound crazy, but it's actually brilliant and works really well! Spreading the rumor about yourself will be a proactive way to discredit the importance or believability of the gossip. There are very specific steps young adults need to follow to spread the rumor about themselves."*

Steps for Spreading the Rumor About Yourself

1. **Find a supportive friend**
   - ● Say, *"The first step for spreading the rumor about yourself is to find a supportive friend. Why would you need to find a supportive friend?"*
     - ○ Answers: This person will have your back and support you; they will agree with what you have to say about the rumor.

2. **Find an audience**
   - ● Say, *"The next step is to find an audience. Why would you want an audience?"*
     - ○ Answer: You want to **spread the rumor about yourself** in front of people who will overhear the conversation so you can discredit the importance or believability of the gossip.

3. **Acknowledge the rumor**
   - ● Say, *"The next step for spreading the rumor about yourself is to acknowledge the rumor. You might do this by saying, 'Have you heard this rumor about me . . . ?' to your supportive friend."*

4. **Act amazed anyone would CARE about or BELIEVE the rumor**
   - ● Explain, *"The next step is to act amazed anyone would CARE about or BELIEVE the rumor using the same statements we talked about before."*
   - ● Ask, *"What are some things you could say to act amazed anyone CARES about or BELIEVES the rumor?"*
     - ○ Examples of answers:
       - ■ *"It's amazing what some people will believe."*
       - ■ *"It's so crazy that people believe that."*
       - ■ *"Can you believe anyone cares about that?"*
       - ■ *"How weird that people even care about that."*
       - ■ *"People need to seriously get a life and find something else to talk about."*
       - ■ *"People need to get a hobby or find something interesting to talk about."*

5. **Repeat with other supportive friends**
   - ● Say, *"The last step for spreading the rumor about yourself is to repeat this with other supportive friends. Why is it important to spread the rumor about yourself with multiple friends?"*

- ○ Answers: Because more people will hear how stupid the old rumor was; it indirectly discredits the rumor in front of multiple people; it takes all the power out of the rumor by making it less important and less believable; few people will want to spread the old rumor because that would make them look silly.
- Ask, *"If you spread the rumor about yourself in front of multiple people and act amazed anyone would care about or believe the rumor, what will the new rumor be?"*
  - ○ Answer: The new rumor will be how stupid the old rumor was.
- Explain, *"Spreading the rumor about yourself will often kill the rumor because the gossip looks stupid. People will be less likely to continue to spread the rumor because they'll look like they don't know what they're talking about. It also takes all of the shock value and power out of the rumor."*

- [Optional: Show the BAD and GOOD *Role Play Video Demonstrations* of **handling rumors and gossip** from the *PEERS®* Role Play Video Library (www.routledge.com/cw/laugeson) or *FriendMaker* mobile app, then ask the *Perspective Taking Questions* that follow the role plays.]

Homework Assignments

[Distribute the *Social Coaching Homework Assignment Worksheet* (Appendix I) for social coaches to complete and return at the next session.]

1. Have a *get-together* with a friend.
   - Social coaches should help young adults plan the get-together using the *five W's*:
     - ○ *WHO* they plan to get together with.
     - ○ *WHAT* they plan to do.
     - ○ *WHEN* it will happen.
     - ○ *WHERE* they will meet.
     - ○ *HOW* they will make it happen.
   - Social coaches should go over the rules and steps for *get-togethers* with young adults beforehand.
   - Social coaches should ask young adults the following *social coaching questions* after the *get-together*:
     - ○ *What did you decide to do and who picked the activities?*
     - ○ *Did you trade information and for what percentage of the time?*
     - ○ *What were your common interests and what could you do with that information if you were going to hang out again?*
     - ○ *Did you and your friend have a good time?*
     - ○ *Is this someone you might want to hang out with again?*

2. Young adults and social coaches should practice *spreading the rumor about yourself*.
   - Go over the strategies for *spreading the rumor about yourself* before practicing.
   - Social coaches should provide an example of a rumor for the young adult to practice *spreading the rumor about yourself*.
   - Social coaches should ask young adults the following *Perspective Taking Questions* after practicing:
     - ○ *What was that like for me?*
     - ○ *What do you think I thought of you?*
     - ○ *Do you think I believed the rumor?*

3. Young adults and social coaches should practice *handling teasing*.
   - Go over the strategies for *handling teasing* before practicing.
   - Young adults should choose THREE *verbal comebacks* to practice using.
   - Social coaches should use benign teasing comments (i.e., *"Your shoes are ugly"*).
   - Social coaches should ask young adults the following *Perspective Taking Questions* after practicing:
     - ○ *What was that like for me?*

   ○   *What do you think I thought of you?*
   ○   *Do you think I'm going to want to tease you again?*

4. Young adults should practice *handling DIRECT or INDIRECT bullying* with a peer if relevant.
    ● Social coaches should ask young adults the following *social coaching* and *Perspective Taking Questions* after practicing when relevant:
        ○   *What did you do or say to handle teasing?*
            ■   *What was that like for the other person?*
            ■   *What do you think they thought of you?*
            ■   *Do you think they're going to want to tease you again?*
        ○   *Did they give you any embarrassing feedback and what could you do differently if you didn't want to be teased about that?*
        ○   *What did you do or say to handle physical bullying?*
        ○   *What did you do to handle cyberbullying?*
        ○   *What did you do or say to handle rumors and gossip?*

5. Young adults should practice *handling a disagreement* with a friend or romantic partner if relevant.
    ● Social coaches should go over the rules and steps for *RESPONDING to disagreements* and *BRINGING UP disagreements* before practicing when possible.
    ● Social coaches should ask young adults the following *social coaching* and *Perspective Taking Questions* after practicing:
        ○   *Which steps did you follow?*
        ○   *What was that like for you and the other person in the end?*
        ○   *What did you think of each other in the end?*
        ○   *Do you think you'll both want to hang out again?*

6. Practice *letting someone know you like them, ask them on a date*, and/or *go on a date*.
    ● If young adults are interested in someone romantically:
        ○   *Let them know you like them.*
        ○   *Ask them on a date.*
        ○   *Go on a date.*
        ○   DO NOT practice unless you are romantically interested in the person.
    ● Young adults should practice *letting someone know you like them, asking someone on a date*, and *beginning and ending dates* with social coaches, if comfortable.
    ● Social coaches should go over all of the rules and steps for *dating etiquette* before the practice.
    ● Social coaches should ask young adults the following *social coaching questions* after each practice:
        ○   *Letting someone know you like them*:
            ■   *Who did you practice with and what did you do to let them know you like them?*
            ■   *How did they respond?*
            ■   *Does this seem like a good choice and is this someone you might want to go on a date with?*
        ○   *Asking someone on a date*:
            ■   *Who did you ask on a date and what steps did you follow?*
            ■   *How did they respond?*
        ○   *Going on a date*:
            ■   *What did you decide to do?*
            ■   *Did you trade information and for what percentage of the time?*
            ■   *What were your common interests and what could you do with that information if you were going to go on a date again?*
            ■   *Did you and your date have a good time?*
            ■   *Does this seem like a good choice and is this someone you might want to go on a date with again?*

Social Coaching Tips

For social coaches seeking more detailed information and resources about strategies for *handling INDIRECT bullying*, the following recommendations are suggested:

- Social coaches should read *The Science of Making Friends: Helping Socially Challenged Teens and Young Adults* (Laugeson, 2013) with your young adult.
  - Two chapters are included to provide detailed information about **INDIRECT bullying**:
    - *Chapter 11: Addressing Cyber Bullying*
    - *Chapter 12: Minimizing Rumors and Gossip*
  - Chapter summaries for young adults are provided.
  - *Social Coaching Tips* are given for each of the lessons.
- Use *The Science of Making Friends DVD* (Laugeson, 2013) or *FriendMaker* app to:
  - Review the strategies for **handling cyberbullying** and **rumors and gossip**.
  - View the *Role Play Video Demonstrations* of "handling rumors and gossip."
    - Good and bad examples are provided.
  - Discuss **Perspective Taking Questions** following the video demonstrations.
- Encourage young adults to use the *FriendMaker* mobile app as a "virtual coach" to assist with real-life situations involving:
  - "Addressing cyberbullying"
  - "Handling rumors and gossip"

Graduation Announcement

- Distribute the *Graduation Flyer* (see Appendix G for an example).
- Say, *"Graduation is next week. That means we will be wrapping things up next week and talking about how to move forward now that our group is coming to an end. In order to celebrate all your hard work, young adults will be having a graduation party and we will all be having a graduation ceremony."*
- You may want to explain the structure of the graduation party and graduation ceremony, which will vary according to resources.
  - Suggestions for the graduation party and ceremony can be found in the *Young Adult Therapist Guide* for Session 16.

HANDLING INDIRECT BULLYING

Young Adult Therapist Guide

Preparing for the Young Adult Session

The focus of the current lesson is on how to appropriately **handle INDIRECT bullying**, which includes **cyberbullying** and **rumors and gossip**. These are more indirect forms of bullying because they often take place over the Internet or behind the person's back. The previous lesson focused on strategies for handling more direct forms of bullying, such as **teasing** and **physical bullying**. As with the previous lesson, the strategies used to handle these specific types of bullying are quite different.

The *Didactic Lesson* on strategies for **handling cyberbullying** will be fairly straightforward. The most common issue that comes up is that young adults may want to tell stories about how they or others have been cyberbullied. It will be important for you to redirect these discussions as they may be rather emotionally charged for group members. Allowing young adults to launch into stories about any form of bullying may cause distress or even decompensation in certain group members, making it difficult to follow the lesson. The simplest way to redirect these discussions is by saying, *"We know that bullying feels really awful and we know that it's fairly common. But we're not going to be talking about the specific ways we've been bullied. Instead, we're going to focus on what we can do in these situations to make it less likely that we'll be bullied in the future."* This same approach should have been taken in the previous session, so you should experience fewer attempts to self-disclose from young adults in the current session. If you are concerned that the disclosure requires further attention, you may choose to have a **side meeting** with the young adult and his or her social coach outside of the group.

The second half of the *Didactic Lesson* focuses on **handling rumors and gossip**, another form of **INDIRECT bullying**. Although often a way of communicating with others, spreading **rumors and gossip** is also a type of **relational bullying**. More common among females, the spreading of **rumors and gossip** may be mean-spirited and intended to hurt others. This type of **social weapon** may be used to retaliate against someone, get revenge on someone for something they've done, or damage the reputation of someone disliked or envied. While people who have a tendency to spread rumors or gossip, commonly referred to as **gossips**, may do this out of malicious intent, it's probably more likely that they're trying to get attention and feel important. Knowing secret details about the personal lives of others is a powerful position and may even increase social standing in the larger peer group. Consequently, many young adults (particularly young women) may spread **rumors and gossip** as a method of increasing their popularity among their peers.

One of the purposes of this lesson is to give young adults the necessary tools for handling situations in which they are the target of **rumors and gossip**. Young adults are taught that it is ineffective to try to **disprove the rumor, appear upset, or confront the person spreading the gossip**. Instead, it is best to **act amazed anyone would CARE about or BELIEVE the gossip**, thereby discrediting the importance or believability of the rumor and making the rumor seem silly. This will make it less "cool" for others to continue to spread the rumor. Young adults are also taught to **spread the rumor about themselves** when they are the target of gossip. This also involves discrediting the importance or believability of the rumor using a more proactive approach. The behavioral rehearsal in which young adults will practice **spreading the rumor about themselves** is often quite lively and entertaining.

Just as with the strategies for *handling teasing* in the previous lesson, this particular skill is often quite empowering for the young adults, and therefore quite enjoyable.

For young adults that are socially isolated or withdrawn, the skills related to *handling rumors and gossip* may be less relevant. However, for young adults that have had a history of peer rejection associated with a *bad reputation*, this skill may be critical in helping to diffuse what are often very challenging social situations.

Homework Review

[Go over the following *Homework Assignments* and *troubleshoot* any potential problems. Start with completed homework first. If you have time, you can inquire as to why others were unable to complete the assignment and try to *troubleshoot* how they might get it done for the coming week. When reviewing homework, be sure to relabel descriptions using the *buzzwords* (identified by *bold and italicized* print). Spend the majority of the *Homework Review* on *get-togethers* as this was the most important assignment.]

1. Have a *get-together* with a friend.
    *   Say, *"One of the main assignments this week was for you to have a get-together with a friend. Raise your hand if you had a get-together with a friend this week."*
    *   Ask the following questions:
        ○ *"Who did you have a get-together with and what did you decide to do?"*
        ○ *"Did you plan the get-together using the five W's?"*
        ○ *"How did the get-together begin?"*
        ○ *"Who picked the activities?"*
        ○ *"Did you trade information and for what percentage of the time?"*
        ○ *"How did the get-together end?"*
        ○ *"Did you and your friend have a good time?"*
        ○ *"Is this someone you might want to hang out with again?"*

Table 16.1 Steps for Beginning and Ending Get-Togethers in Your Home

Beginning the Get-Together	Ending the Get-Together
1. Greet your guest	1. Wait for a pause in activities
2. Invite them in	2. Give a cover story for ending the get-together
3. Introduce them to anyone they don't know	3. Start walking your friend to the door
4. Give them a tour	4. Thank your friend for getting together
5. Offer them refreshments	5. Tell your friend you had a good time
6. Ask them what they want to do	6. Say goodbye and you'll see them later

2. Young adults and social coaches should practice *handling teasing*.
    *   Say, *"Another assignment this week was for you to practice handling teasing with your social coaches. Raise your hand if you practiced handling teasing with your social coach."*
    *   Ask, *"What did you do or say to handle teasing with your social coach?"*
        ○ Have young adults identify *verbal comebacks* and *nonverbal comebacks*.

3. Young adults should practice *handling DIRECT bullying* with a peer if relevant.
    *   Say, *"Another assignment this week was for you to practice handling DIRECT bullying with a peer if relevant. We know teasing and physical bullying are very common, so I expect many of you had the opportunity to practice using these strategies. Raise your hand if you practiced handling DIRECT bullying with a peer."*
    *   Ask the following questions when relevant:
        ○ *"Did you practice handling teasing, physical bullying, or both?"*
        ○ *"What did you do or say to handle teasing? I don't want to know what they said to tease you. I want to know what you said and did to use the teasing comebacks."*

- ○ *"What was that like for the other person?"*
- ○ *"What do you think they thought of you?"*
- ○ *"Do you think they're going to want to tease you again?"*
- ○ *"Did they give you any embarrassing feedback and what could you do differently if you didn't want to be teased about that?"*
- ○ *"What did you do or say to handle physical bullying?"*

4. Young adults and social coaches should practice *handling a disagreement*.
   - Say, *"Another assignment this week was to practice handling a disagreement with your social coach. Raise your hand if you practiced handling a disagreement with your social coach."*
   - Ask the following questions:
     - ○ *"Which steps did you follow to RESPOND to a disagreement?"*
     - ○ *"Which steps did you follow to BRING UP a disagreement?"*

Table 16.2 Steps for Handling Disagreements

RESPONDING TO DISAGREEMENTS	BRINGING UP DISAGREEMENTS
1. Keep your cool 2. Listen to the other person 3. Repeat what they said 4. Explain your side using "I" statements 5. Say you're sorry 6. Try to solve the problem	1. Wait for the right time and place 2. Keep your cool 3. Ask to speak privately 4. Explain your side using "I" statements 5. Listen to the other person 6. Repeat what they said 7. Tell them what you need them to do 8. Try to solve the problem

5. Young adults should practice *handling a disagreement* with a friend or romantic partner if relevant.
   - Say, *"Another assignment this week was to practice handling a disagreement with a friend or romantic partner if relevant. Raise your hand if you practiced handling a disagreement with a friend or romantic partner."*
   - Ask the following questions:
     - ○ *"Who did you practice with and what was the disagreement?"*
     - ○ *"Which steps did you follow to RESPOND to or BRING UP the disagreement?"*
     - ○ *"What was that like for you and the other person in the end?"*
     - ○ *"What did you think of each other in the end?"*
     - ○ *"Do you think you'll both want to hang out again?"*

6. Practice *letting someone know you like them, ask them on a date*, and/or *go on a date*.
   - Say, *"Another assignment this week was to practice letting someone know you like them, ask them on a date, and/or go on a date. The assignment was NOT to practice unless you're romantically interested in the person. Raise your hand if you did this assignment."*
   - Ask the following questions:
     - ○ *"Who did you practice with?"*
     - ○ *"What did you do to let them know you like them and how did they respond?"*
     - ○ *"Did you ask them on a date and how did they respond?"*
     - ○ Ask the following questions if they went on a date:
       - ▪ *"What did you decide to do?"*
       - ▪ *"Did you trade information and for what percentage of the time?"*
       - ▪ *"What were your common interests and what could you do with that information if you were going to go on a date again?"*
       - ▪ *"Did you and your date have a good time?"*
     - ○ *"Does this seem like a good choice and is this someone you might want to go on a date with (again)?"*

Didactic Lesson: Handling Indirect Bullying

- Explain, *"Today, we're going to be talking about how to handle bullying. In our last session, we talked about strategies for handling DIRECT bullying, such as teasing and physical bullying. These are DIRECT forms of bullying because they happen directly to the person. Today, we will talk about handling INDIRECT forms of bullying, such as cyberbullying, rumors, and gossip. These are INDIRECT forms of bullying because they usually happen over the Internet or behind our back. Just like bullying behaviors are completely different, the strategies for handling these different types of bullying are also very different."*

- [Present the strategies for **handling INDIRECT bullying** by writing the following bullet points and **buzzwords** (identified by **bold and italicized** print) on the board. Do not erase the strategies until the end of the lesson. Each role play with a ⊙ symbol includes a corresponding role play video from the *PEERS® Role Play Video Library* (www.routledge.com/cw/laugeson).]

Handling Cyberbullying

- Explain, *"One of the ways that people INDIRECTLY bully others is over electronic communication. This is sometimes called cyberbullying. Even though people sometimes tease over electronic communication, the strategies for handling cyberbullying are very different from the ways we handle teasing in person. We know cyberbullying can be very upsetting, but we're not going to be talking about the specific ways people may have cyberbullied us or how it feels to be bullied. Instead, we're going to focus on what we can do in these situations to make it less likely that we'll be cyberbullied again."*

- [Note: If young adults try to talk about specific ways they have been bullied, try to redirect them by saying, *"We're not going to talk about the specific ways we've been bullied. Instead, we're going to talk about what we can do in these situations to make it less likely we'll be bullied again."*]

- Ask, *"What is cyberbullying?"*
  - Answer: Harassing, threatening, or humiliating people over electronic forms of communication (phones, Internet, social networking sites).

- Ask, *"What do cyberbullies do to other people?"*
  - Answers:
    - Send or forward threatening, harassing, or hurtful email messages, text messages, or instant messages.
    - Spread rumors and gossip on social networking sites.
    - Create social networking pages to target a victim.
    - Post photos or private information on the Internet without consent.
    - Pretend to be someone else in order to humiliate someone or trick someone into revealing personal information.

- Explain, *"There are lots of different ways people bully others over electronic communication. Now we're going to talk about ways to handle these different types of cyberbullying."*

Strategies for Handling Cyberbullying

- ***Don't feed the trolls—don't react***
  - Say, *"Some of you may have heard of 'Internet trolling.' What is a 'troll' and what do trolls do?"*
    - Answers: Trolls are cyberbullies; they enjoy posting negative comments about people online.
  - Explain, *"Trolling is a term used for people who bully others online by posting harassing and mean comments on social networking sites, message boards, and forums. They do this because it's fun for them and they're trying to get a reaction out of you."*
  - Ask, *"What kind of reaction are they trying to get?"*
    - Answer: They're hoping to upset you and get you to put on a show by defending yourself or engaging in a fight.
  - Say, *"Trolls and cyberbullies are not so different from in-person bullies. They're always looking for a reaction. So what happens if you get upset or defend yourself and put up a fight?"*
    - Answer: You make it fun for the cyberbully.

- Ask, *"When you get upset or put up a fight, does that make it MORE likely or LESS likely that you're going to get cyberbullied again?"*
  - Answer: MORE likely.
- Explain, *"There's a saying online—'don't feed the trolls.' That means don't react by trying to confront them or beat them at their own game. Even responding by saying, 'whatever' won't work because all of the emotion is lost on the screen. When you react, it's a losing game and you'll only feed their enjoyment and make them want to cyberbully you more. If you don't feed the trolls, they'll probably get bored, move on, and find someone else to bother."*

- **Have friends stick up for you**
  - Say, *"Just like in-person bullies, cyberbullies like to pick on people who are by themselves. Why do cyberbullies like to pick on people who are by themselves or seem unprotected?"*
    - Answers: Because when you're alone, you have no one to stick up for you or have your back; you are an easier target.
  - Explain, *"One of the strategies for handling cyberbullying is to have a friend stick up for you. We've already talked about how it doesn't do any good for you to defend yourself. That's what the cyberbully or the troll wants. Instead, you can have a friend or a family member around the same age defend you to show that you're not alone."*

- **Lay low online for a while**
  - Explain, *"A lot of cyberbullying happens online, especially on social networking sites. If you're having trouble with people cyberbullying you, a good strategy is to lay low online for a while."*
  - Ask, *"What does it mean to lay low online?"*
    - Answers: Stay off your social networking sites for a while; don't post comments on other people's walls or in forums.
  - Ask, *"What happens when you lay low online for a while and how can that help prevent cyberbullying?"*
    - Answers: It creates distance between you and the cyberbullying; it gives you a chance to let the cyberbullying die down; **if the cyberbully can't FIND you, he or she can't bully you**.
  - Explain, *"Sometimes it can even be helpful to deactivate your Facebook account for a while if that's where the cyberbullying is happening."*

- **Block the cyberbully**
  - Explain, *"Since some cyberbullying happens over text messaging, instant messaging, email, and social networking sites where the bully is identifiable, one of the easiest ways to stop cyberbullying is by blocking the cyberbully."*
  - Ask, *"What does it mean to block the cyberbully and how can that help prevent cyberbullying?"*
    - Answers: That means block their messages from ever being delivered to your phone, email, or social networking page; **if the cyberbully can't CONTACT you, he or she can't bully you**.
  - Explain, *"For example, blocking the cyberbully from Facebook will prevent them from viewing your profile, appearing in your search results or contact lists, and will break any connections you share. Blocking the bully on your phone will prevent them from calling or texting you. Although this strategy doesn't guarantee that the cyberbully won't find you in other areas of the Internet, blocking the cyberbully is a pretty good way to stop contact between you and the bully."*

- **Save the evidence**
  - Say, *"Another good strategy for protecting yourself from cyberbullying is to save the evidence. What does it mean to save the evidence?"*
    - Answer: Save any threatening, harassing, or humiliating communications.
  - Ask, *"Why is it important to save the evidence?"*
    - Answer: Because if the cyberbullying doesn't stop, you may have to report it.
  - Ask, *"What if the cyberbullying happens on a social networking site like Facebook and other people can see it. What should you do?"*
    - Answer: Take a screenshot, save the evidence, and delete the post so other people can't see it.

    ○   Explain, *"If someone sends you threatening or harassing messages or pictures, or posts harmful comments about you on the Internet, you need to save the evidence in case you need to report the cyberbullying."*

- *Report cyberbullying as a last resort*
  - ○ Explain, *"In some cases, it may be necessary for you to report the cyberbullying to the proper authorities. This might include online service providers, webmasters, universities, employers, or in the most extreme cases, even law enforcement."*
  - ○ Ask, *"Would it be important to get help from your social coaches before reporting the cyberbullying and why might that be a good idea?"*
    - ■ Answers: Knowing when and how to report cyberbullying can be confusing; you need to work with your social coaches on this strategy.
  - ○ Explain, *"Reporting cyberbullying is usually a last resort when the other strategies aren't working, or when you feel threatened or harassed. Be sure to get help from your social coaches if you think you need to report the cyberbullying."*

Handling Rumors and Gossip

- Say, *"Another way that people INDIRECTLY bully others is by spreading rumors and gossip. Rumors and gossip are very common in the workplace and in college settings. Unfortunately, there's very little we can do to prevent people from gossiping. However, it can be very helpful to know why people spread rumors and gossip."*
- Ask, *"Why do people gossip?"*
  - ○ Answers: To be mean; hurt people; get revenge; manipulate others; fulfill a threat; gain attention; increase popularity; as a form of communication.
- Explain the following by saying, *"Rumors and gossip are often used as a . . ."*
  - ○ *Social weapon*
    - ■ Spreading gossip may be mean-spirited and meant to hurt people; to damage the reputation of someone disliked or envied.
  - ○ *Form of social retaliation*
    - ■ Spreading gossip may be used to get revenge on someone for something they've done; to manipulate someone; to fulfill some threat (e.g., *"If you don't do . . . I'll tell everyone . . ."*).
  - ○ *Method to gain attention*
    - ■ Spreading gossip may be a way for some young adults to get attention and feel important (e.g., they know something no one else does).
  - ○ *Method for gaining popularity*
    - ■ Spreading gossip may be a way for some young adults to try to become more popular by capturing the interest and attention of others, and holding power over others.
  - ○ *Form of communication*
    - ■ More often, spreading gossip is just a part of young adults' conversation, and a way to stay current with their social surroundings.
- Explain, *"Because rumors and gossip are often just a form of communication and a way for young adults to stay informed about what's happening around them, there is very little we can do to prevent people from spreading rumors and gossip."*

Avoiding Being the Target of Gossip

- Explain, *"Now that we're clear on WHY people gossip, it will be helpful to know what we can do to make it less likely that people will gossip about us. The first thing we need to think about is how we might avoid being the target of rumors and gossip."*

- *Avoid being friends with the gossips*
  - ○ Explain, *"The first rule for avoiding being the target of rumors and gossip is to avoid being friends with gossips. 'Gossips' are people who like to start rumors and spread gossip about other people."*
  - ○ Ask, *"What could be the problem with being friends with the gossips?"*

- Answers: They are likely to spread rumors about you if they get mad at you; it is difficult to trust someone who is a gossip; they may share your secrets; people will believe what they say about you because you're friends; other people may not want to be friends with you because they know you associate with the gossips.

- *Avoid being enemies with the gossips*
  - Explain, *"The next rule for avoiding being the target of rumors and gossip is to avoid being enemies with the gossips. This means don't get on the bad side of the gossips or their friends by telling their secrets, gossiping about them, making fun of them, or policing them."*
  - Ask, *"What could be the problem with being enemies with the gossips or their friends?"*
    - Answers: This will only provoke them to retaliate against you; you are likely to become the object of their gossip.
  - Ask, *"Does that include dating the ex-boyfriend or ex-girlfriend of the gossip?"*
    - Answer: Yes, you may become a target if you date their ex.
  - Ask, *"Does that mean we should never date the ex of a gossip or their friends?"*
    - Answer: No, just be aware of what you're getting into.

- *Be neutral with the gossips*
  - Say, *"Instead of being friends or enemies with the gossips, you want to be as neutral as possible with the gossips. What does it mean to be neutral?"*
    - Answers: You don't want to be friends and you don't want to be enemies; just stay out of their way and off their radar.

- *Don't spread rumors about other people*
  - Say, *"Our last rule for avoiding being the target of rumors and gossip is not to spread rumors about other people. What could be the problem with spreading rumors and gossip about other people?"*
    - Answers: Because it's hurtful and people will not want to be friends with you; you may get a bad reputation; the people you gossip about may want to retaliate by gossiping about you.

Handling Being the Target of Gossip

- Explain, *"Even though we may try our best to avoid being the target of gossip, it may still happen, so we need to know what we can do to minimize the impact of gossip when it's focused on us."*

- *Every instinct we have is WRONG*
  - Explain, *"The interesting thing about being the target of rumors and gossip is that almost every instinct we have in these situations is WRONG!"*
  - Ask, *"What do most people want to do when they are the target of a rumor?"*
    - Answers: Disprove the gossip; defend themselves; get upset; confront the person spreading the gossip.
  - Explain, *"Most people will try to disprove the rumor, deny the rumor, appear upset, or even confront the person spreading the rumor. But in each of these cases, we actually make the rumor stronger by adding fuel to the rumor mill."*
  - Ask, *"What is the rumor mill?"*
    - Answer: The buzz about the latest gossip.

- *Don't try to disprove the rumor*
  - Say, *"When you're the target of rumors and gossip, a strong instinct is to try to disprove or deny the rumor. What do you look like when you try to deny or disprove the rumor?"*
    - Answer: You typically look defensive and guilty.
  - Say, *"One of the problems is that rumors are very difficult to disprove. You can never completely disprove a rumor once it's out there. You could even have evidence that the rumor isn't true, but if you go around trying to convince everyone that it's not true, what will the new rumor be?"*
    - Answer: The new rumor will be how you're freaking out trying to disprove the rumor.
  - Ask, *"So if you try to disprove the rumor, are you making it better or worse for yourself?"*
    - Answer: Worse.

○ Explain, *"Remember, every instinct we have is WRONG when it comes to rumors and gossip. If you try to disprove the rumor, you'll look defensive and guilty. The new rumor will be how you're freaking out trying to disprove the rumor. That's GOOD GOSSIP and adds fuel to the rumor mill."*

- *Don't appear upset*
  ○ Say, *"Another common instinct when you're the target of rumors and gossip is to get upset. What could be the problem with appearing upset?"*
    ■ Answer: You look defensive and guilty.
  ○ Ask, *"What will the new rumor be if you show that you're upset?"*
    ■ Answer: The new rumor will be how upset you are.
  ○ Ask, *"What if you're so upset that you stop going to school or work. What will the new rumor be?"*
    ■ Answer: The new rumor will be how upset you are.
  ○ Ask, *"So if you appear upset or stop going to school or work, are you making it better or worse for yourself?"*
    ■ Answer: Worse.
  ○ Explain, *"Remember, every instinct we have is WRONG when it comes to rumors and gossip. If you appear upset or stop going to school or work, people may assume you have something to hide. The new rumor will be how upset you are. Again, that's GOOD GOSSIP and adds fuel to the rumor mill."*

- *Act like the rumor doesn't bother you*
  ○ Explain, *"Even though it's upsetting to be the target of rumors and gossip, you need to act like the rumors don't bother you. Privately, you can talk to family and friends, but publically don't appear upset."*
  ○ Ask, *"Why is it important to act like the rumor doesn't bother you?"*
    ■ Answer: You look less defensive and less guilty if you don't appear upset.

- *Don't confront the person spreading the gossip*
  ○ Explain, *"Sometimes you know who's spreading the rumors about you. In this case, the instinct may be to confront the person spreading the gossip. The problem is this will probably only escalate things and add fuel to the rumor mill."*
  ○ Ask, *"What could be the problem with confronting the person spreading the gossip?"*
    ■ Answers: The person may start spreading even more gossip about you; this may result in an argument or even a fight; the person may feel justified in spreading more gossip about you.
  ○ Ask, *"What will the new rumor be if you confront the person spreading the gossip?"*
    ■ Answer: The new rumor will be how you freaked out and confronted the person spreading the gossip.
  ○ Ask, *"So if you confront the person spreading the rumor, are you making it better or worse for yourself?"*
    ■ Answer: Worse.
  ○ Explain, *"Remember, every instinct we have is WRONG when it comes to rumors and gossip. If you confront the person spreading the gossip, you may look defensive and guilty. The new rumor will be how you freaked out and confronted them. Again, that's GOOD GOSSIP and adds fuel to the rumor mill."*

- *Avoid the person spreading the gossip*
  ○ Explain, *"One of the difficult things about rumors and gossip is how much people want to talk about them and not let them go. People are always looking for new angles to the story and will be watching you to see how you react."*
  ○ Say, *"Imagine you know who is spreading the gossip about you. What does everyone expect you to do?"*
    ■ Answer: They expect you to confront the person spreading the gossip.
  ○ Explain, *"The problem is that even if you don't confront the person spreading the gossip, simply just being in the same place means you can't win no matter what you do."*
  ○ Ask, *"If you're in the same place and you don't look at the person spreading the gossip, what's the new rumor going to be?"*
    ■ Answer: The new rumor will be how you couldn't even look at them.
  ○ Ask, *"If you're in the same place and you happen to look at the person spreading the gossip, what's the new rumor going to be?"*

- ■ Answer: The new rumor will be how you gave them the "evil eye."
  - ○ Explain, *"In this case, you can't win no matter what you do, so it's best if you avoid the person spreading the gossip about you. That doesn't mean stop going to school or work. It just means plan your route and try to avoid them until the rumor dies down."*

- • *Act amazed anyone CARES about or BELIEVES the gossip*
  - ○ Explain, *"When you're the target of rumors and gossip, people will ask you about the gossip to see your reaction. Even though your instinct may be to deny or disprove the rumor, that just makes you look guilty. Instead you should act amazed anyone CARES about or BELIEVES the gossip. It doesn't even matter if it's true. If the rumor is true—you can't believe anyone CARES about it. If the rumor isn't true—you can't believe anyone BELIEVES it."*
  - ○ Provide examples of what to say to *act amazed anyone CARES about the gossip*:
    - ■ *"Can you believe anyone cares about that?"*
    - ■ *"Why would anyone care about that?"*
    - ■ *"People need to get a life."*
    - ■ *"People need to find a hobby."*
    - ■ *"People seriously need to find something better to talk about."*
  - ○ Provide examples of what to say to *act amazed anyone BELIEVES the gossip*:
    - ■ *"Can you believe anyone believes that?"*
    - ■ *"Who would believe that?"*
    - ■ *"People are so gullible."*
    - ■ *"People will believe anything."*
    - ■ *"I can't believe anyone would believe that."*
  - ○ Ask, *"Why is it important to act amazed that anyone would CARE about or BELIEVE the gossip?"*
    - ■ Answers: Because it makes the rumor seem silly; people will be less likely to believe the rumor because you've undermined its importance or believability; people will be less likely to continue to spread the rumor because it makes them seem naive or gullible for even caring about or believing it.
  - ○ Explain, *"Acting amazed anyone CARES about or BELIEVES the gossip discredits the importance or believability of the gossip."*

- • *Spread the rumor about yourself*
  - ○ Explain, *"Even though acting amazed anyone would CARE about or BELIEVE the gossip is a good strategy for handling questions about the gossip, you want to be even more proactive than that. You actually want to spread the rumor about yourself! That may sound crazy, but it's actually brilliant and works really well!"*

Steps for Spreading the Rumor About Yourself

- • Explain, "Instead of trying to disprove the rumor or sounding upset, you want to spread the rumor about yourself in a way that will discredit the importance or believability of the gossip. There are very specific steps for doing that."

1. *Find a supportive friend*
   - • Say, *"The first step for spreading the rumor about yourself is to find a supportive friend. Why would you need to find a supportive friend?"*
     - ○ Answers: This person will have your back and support you; they will agree with what you have to say about the rumor.

2. *Find an audience*
   - • Say, *"The next step is to find an audience. Why would you want an audience?"*
     - ○ Answer: You want to *spread the rumor about yourself* in front of people who will overhear the conversation so you can discredit the importance or believability of the gossip.
   - • Ask, *"When and where would be good times and places to find an audience?"*
     - ○ Answers: During lunchtime; during breaks at work or school; between classes; when people are hanging out socializing.

3. *Acknowledge the rumor*
   - Say, *"The next step for spreading the rumor about yourself is to acknowledge the rumor. You might do this by saying, 'Have you heard this rumor about me . . . ?' to your supportive friend."*
   - Ask, *"Do you want to get into the juicy details of the rumor?"*
     - Answer: No, just keep it simple; just make only one general statement about the rumor.

4. *Act amazed anyone would CARE about or BELIEVE the rumor*
   - Explain, *"The next step is to act amazed anyone would CARE about or BELIEVE the rumor using the same statements we talked about before."*
   - Ask, *"What are some things you could say to act amazed anyone CARES about or BELIEVES the rumor?"*
     - Examples of answers:
       - *"It's amazing what some people will believe."*
       - *"It's so crazy that people believe that."*
       - *"Can you believe anyone cares about that?"*
       - *"How weird that people even care about that."*
       - *"People need to seriously get a life and find something else to talk about."*
       - *"People need to get a hobby or find something interesting to talk about."*

5. *Repeat with other supportive friends*
   - Say, *"The last step for spreading the rumor about yourself is to repeat this with other supportive friends. Why is it important to spread the rumor about yourself with multiple friends?"*
     - Answers: Because more people will hear how stupid the old rumor was; it indirectly discredits the rumor in front of multiple people; it takes all the power out of the rumor by making it less important and less believable; few people will want to spread the old rumor because that would make them look silly.
   - Ask, *"If you spread the rumor about yourself in front of multiple people and act amazed anyone would care about or believe the rumor, what will the new rumor be?"*
     - Answer: The new rumor will be how stupid the old rumor was.
   - Explain, *"Spreading the rumor about yourself will often kill the rumor because the gossip looks stupid. People will be less likely to continue to spread the rumor because they'll look like they don't know what they're talking about. It also takes all of the shock value and power out of the rumor."*

Bad Role Play: Spreading the Rumor About Yourself ▶

[The group leader and behavioral coach should do an INAPPROPRIATE role play with the group leader unsuccessfully *spreading the rumor about him or herself*.]

- Begin by saying, *"We're going to do a role play. Watch this and tell me what I'm doing WRONG in spreading the rumor about myself. First of all, you should know that (behavioral coach) is my supportive friend and you are the audience, but I am going to be doing TWO things wrong in this role play."*

Example of an INAPPROPRIATE Role Play

- Group leader: (Sounds upset) *"Oh my God, (name of behavioral coach)! You know that rumor that I have a crush on (insert name)?"*
- Behavioral coach: *"Yeah, I heard that."*
- Group leader: (Sounds defensive, panicked) *"That's so not true! You know me. (Insert name) isn't even my type! We don't even have anything in common!"*
- Behavioral coach: (Unsure of the truth) *"I guess. If you say so."*
- Group leader: (Sounds defensive, guilty, hysterical) *"Yeah, I mean that's totally crazy! It's so not true! It's just . . . it's just crazy!"*
- Behavioral coach: (Uncertain) *"Okay."*
- Group leader: (Sounds worried, panicked) *"Seriously, it's totally made up! Don't believe it!"*
- Behavioral coach: (Uncertain, shrugs) *"Okay."*

- End by saying, *"Timeout on that. So what did I do WRONG in trying to spread the rumor about myself?"*
  - Answers: You tried to disprove the rumor; you seemed upset.
- Ask the following *Perspective Taking Questions*:
  - *"What was that like for (name of coach)?"*
    - Answers: Confusing; weird; odd.
  - *"What do you think (name of coach) thought of me?"*
    - Answers: Defensive; guilty; panicked; hysterical.
  - *"Is (name of coach) going to believe me?"*
    - Answers: No; you look too guilty.
- Ask the behavioral coach the same *Perspective Taking Questions*:
  - *"What was that like for you?"*
  - *"What did you think of me?"*
  - *"Did you believe me?"*

Good Role Play: Spreading the Rumor About Yourself ⊙

[The group leader and behavioral coach should do an APPROPRIATE role play with the group leader successfully *spreading the rumor about him or herself*.]

- Begin by saying, *"We're going to do another role play. Watch this and tell me what I'm doing RIGHT in spreading the rumor about myself."*

Example of an APPROPRIATE Role Play

- Group leader & behavioral coach: (Standing around other people who might overhear the conversation)
- Group leader: (Calmly) *"Oh my God, (name of behavioral coach). Did you hear that rumor that I have a crush on (insert name)?"*
- Behavioral coach: *"Yeah, I totally heard that."*
- Group leader: (Casually) *"Who would believe that?"*
- Behavioral coach: *"I don't know who'd believe that."*
- Group leader: (Sounds amazed) *"It's so ridiculous. Why would anyone care anyway?"*
- Behavioral coach: (Agreeing) *"I don't know. Who would care?"*
- Group leader: (Sounds indifferent) *"It's so lame. People need to find something better to talk about."*
- Behavioral coach: *"Absolutely."*
- Group leader: *"I mean get a hobby, right?"*
- Behavioral coach: *"Totally!"*
- Group leader: (Sounds amazed) *"So stupid."*
- Behavioral coach: (Agreeing) *"I know."*

- End by saying, *"Timeout on that. So what did I do RIGHT in spreading the rumor about myself?"*
  - Answers: *Acted amazed anyone would CARE about or BELIEVE the rumor; spread the rumor about yourself* to a person you trusted when there were other people around that might overhear.
- Ask the following *Perspective Taking Questions*:
  - *"What was that like for (name of coach)?"*
    - Answers: Fine; normal.
  - *"What do you think (name of coach) thought of me?"*
    - Answers: Fine; calm; unbothered.
  - *"Is (name of coach) going to believe me?"*
    - Answers: Yes; probably.
- Ask the behavioral coach the same *Perspective Taking Questions*:
  - *"What was that like for you?"*

- ○ *"What did you think of me?"*
- ○ *"Did you believe me?"*

Behavioral Rehearsal: Spreading the Rumor About Yourself

- Explain, *"Now we're going to have each of you practice spreading the rumor about yourself. I will tell you what the rumor is and then you will spread the rumor about yourself to me while everyone else listens."*
- Go around the room and have each young adult practice **spreading the rumor about themselves**.
  - ○ The group leader should provide a different rumor for each young adult.
  - ○ The young adults should feel free to look at the board in order to follow the rules and steps for **spreading the rumor about yourself**.
    - ▪ It is helpful to have some of the **acting amazed** statements on the board (e.g., *"Who would believe that?" "Why would anyone care?"*).
- Use different examples of rumors for each young adult behavioral rehearsal by stating what the rumor is from the list below, and then adding, *"...now spread the rumor about yourself to me."*
  - ○ *"The rumor is you are failing a class ..."*
  - ○ *"The rumor is you got drunk at a party and could not walk ..."*
  - ○ *"The rumor is you have a crush on your coworker ..."*
  - ○ *"The rumor is you were talking behind your friends back ..."*
  - ○ *"The rumor is you don't like your supervisor ..."*
  - ○ *"The rumor is you may not graduate on time ..."*
  - ○ *"The rumor is that you're going to ask out your lab partner ..."*
  - ○ *"The rumor is that you might get fired ..."*
  - ○ *"The rumor is that you got written up at work for being late ..."*
  - ○ *"The rumor is that you got into a huge fight with your boss ..."*
- Give performance feedback and be sure each young adult has mastered the technique of **spreading the rumor about themselves** before moving onto the next young adult.
  - ○ If the young adult sounds upset or tries to disprove the rumor, gently point this out and have them try again until they appropriately **spread the rumor about themselves**.
- End by giving a round of applause to each young adult after their practice.

HANDLING INDIRECT BULLYING

Young Adult Behavioral Rehearsal

Get-Togethers

Materials Needed

- Indoor games (e.g., video games, card games, board games).
  - If you are going to provide video games as an option, make sure there are enough gaming consoles that each group can play simultaneously together.
  - Do not use small, portable gaming devices as people have to wait to take turns and that can get boring.
  - Several decks of playing cards will be sufficient if you do not have these other resources.
- Optional: iPads or laptops for watching YouTube videos, surfing the Internet, or playing computer games.
  - If you are going to provide iPads or laptops as an option, make sure there are enough that each group can use them simultaneously together.
- [Note: Most PEERS® programs DO NOT have access to gaming consoles, iPads, or laptops. These are luxury items. Just providing a few decks of cards to keep the get-together *activity-based* will be fine.]

Behavioral Rehearsal

- Notify young adults they will be practicing having *get-togethers*.
  - Note: They will no longer be practicing *beginning and ending get-togethers*.
- Break up young adults into small groups or dyads.
- Have young adults practice following the rules for how to behave *during the get-together* while:
  - *Trading information.*
  - *Finding common interests.*
  - Playing with games and items provided by the treatment team (e.g., video games, card games, board games, iPads, laptops, etc.).
- Provide *social coaching* as needed regarding the rules for making and keeping friends.

HANDLING INDIRECT BULLYING

Reunification

- Announce that young adults should join their social coaches.
  - ○ Have young adults stand or sit next to their social coaches.
  - ○ Be sure to have silence and the full attention of the group before starting with *Reunification*.
  - ○ Have young adults generate the content from the lesson while social coaches listen.
- Say, *"Today, we talked about strategies for handling INDIRECT bullying. This includes cyberbullying, rumors, and gossip. What are some of the strategies for handling cyberbullying?"*
  - ○ *Don't feed the trolls—don't react*
  - ○ *Have friends stick up for you*
  - ○ *Lay low online for a while*
  - ○ *Block the cyberbully*
  - ○ *Save the evidence*
  - ○ *Report cyberbullying as a last resort*
- Ask, *"What are some of the strategies for handling rumors and gossip when you are the target of gossip?"*
  - ○ *Every instinct we have is WRONG*
  - ○ *Don't try to disprove the rumor*
  - ○ *Don't appear upset*
  - ○ *Act like the rumor doesn't bother you*
  - ○ *Don't confront the person spreading the gossip*
  - ○ *Avoid the person spreading the gossip*
  - ○ *Act amazed anyone CARES about or BELIEVES the gossip*
  - ○ *Spread the rumor about yourself*
- Explain, *"Young adults practiced handling rumors and gossip and the group did a great job so we should give them a round of applause."*

Homework Assignments

Distribute the *Social Coaching Handout* to young adults and announce the following *Homework Assignments*:

1. Have a *get-together* with a friend.
   - Social coaches should help young adults plan the get-together using the *five W's*:
     - ○ *WHO* they plan to get together with.
     - ○ *WHAT* they plan to do.
     - ○ *WHEN* it will happen.
     - ○ *WHERE* they will meet.
     - ○ *HOW* they will make it happen.
   - Social coaches should go over the rules and steps for *get-togethers* with young adults beforehand.
   - Social coaches should ask young adults the following *social coaching questions* after the *get-together*:

- ○ *What did you decide to do and who picked the activities?*
- ○ *Did you trade information and for what percentage of the time?*
- ○ *What were your common interests and what could you do with that information if you were going to hang out again?*
- ○ *Did you and your friend have a good time?*
- ○ *Is this someone you might want to hang out with again?*

2. Young adults and social coaches should practice *spreading the rumor about yourself*.
   - Go over the strategies for *spreading the rumor about yourself* before practicing.
   - Social coaches should provide an example of a rumor for the young adult to practice *spreading the rumor about yourself.*
   - Social coaches should ask young adults the following *Perspective Taking Questions* after practicing:
     - ○ *What was that like for me?*
     - ○ *What do you think I thought of you?*
     - ○ *Do you think I believed the rumor?*

3. Young adults and social coaches should practice *handling teasing*.
   - Go over the strategies for *handling teasing* before practicing.
   - Young adults should choose THREE *verbal comebacks* to practice using.
   - Social coaches should use benign teasing comments (i.e., *"Your shoes are ugly"*).
   - Social coaches should ask young adults the following *Perspective Taking Questions* after practicing:
     - ○ *What was that like for me?*
     - ○ *What do you think I thought of you?*
     - ○ *Do you think I'm going to want to tease you again?*

4. Young adults should practice *handling **DIRECT** or **INDIRECT** bullying* with a peer if relevant.
   - Social coaches should ask young adults the following *social coaching and Perspective Taking Questions* after practicing when relevant:
     - ○ *What did you do or say to handle teasing?*
       - ■ *What was that like for the other person?*
       - ■ *What do you think they thought of you?*
       - ■ *Do you think they're going to want to tease you again?*
     - ○ *Did they give you any embarrassing feedback and what could you do differently if you didn't want to be teased about that?*
     - ○ *What did you do or say to handle physical bullying?*
     - ○ *What did you do to handle cyberbullying?*
     - ○ *What did you do or say to handle rumors and gossip?*

5. Young adults should practice *handling a disagreement* with a friend or romantic partner if relevant.
   - Social coaches should go over the rules and steps for *RESPONDING to disagreements* and *BRINGING UP disagreements* before practicing when possible.
   - Social coaches should ask young adults the following *social coaching* and *Perspective Taking Questions* after practicing:
     - ○ *Which steps did you follow?*
     - ○ *What was that like for you and the other person in the end?*
     - ○ *What did you think of each other in the end?*
     - ○ *Do you think you'll both want to hang out again?*

6. Practice *letting someone know you like them, ask them on a date,* and/or *go on a date*.
   - If young adults are interested in someone romantically:
     - ○ *Let them know you like them.*
     - ○ *Ask them on a date.*
     - ○ *Go on a date.*
     - ○ DO NOT practice unless you are romantically interested in the person.

- Young adults should practice *letting someone know you like them*, *asking someone on a date*, and *beginning and ending dates* with social coaches, if comfortable.
- Social coaches should go over all of the rules and steps for *dating etiquette* before the practice.
- Social coaches should ask young adults the following *social coaching questions* after each practice:
    - *Letting someone know you like them:*
        - *Who did you practice with and what did you do to let them know you like them?*
        - *How did they respond?*
        - *Does this seem like a good choice and is this someone you might want to go on a date with?*
    - *Asking someone on a date:*
        - *Who did you ask on a date and what steps did you follow?*
        - *How did they respond?*
    - *Going on a date:*
        - *What did you decide to do?*
        - *Did you trade information and for what percentage of the time?*
        - *What were your common interests and what could you do with that information if you were going to go on a date again?*
        - *Did you and your date have a good time?*
        - *Does this seem like a good choice and is this someone you might want to go on a date with again?*

Graduation Announcement

- Distribute the *Graduation Flyer* (see Appendix G for an example) to young adults.
- Say, *"Graduation is next week. That means we will be wrapping things up next week and talking about how to move forward now that our group is coming to an end. In order to celebrate all your hard work, young adults will be having a graduation party and we will all be having a graduation ceremony."*
- You may want to explain the structure of the graduation party and graduation ceremony, which will vary according to resources.
    - Suggestions for the graduation party and ceremony can be found in the *Young Adult Therapist Guide* for Session 16.

Individual Check-Out

Individually and privately negotiate with each young adult and social coach:

1. **WHO** they plan to have a *get-together* with in the coming week.
    - **WHAT** they plan to suggest to their friends.
    - **WHEN** and **WHERE** they will suggest to their friends.
    - **HOW** they will make it happen (e.g., tickets, transportation, etc.).

2. When they plan to practice *spreading the rumor about themselves* with their social coach.

3. When they plan to practice *handling teasing* with their social coach.

4. How they will practice *letting someone know they like them* and with whom, and whether they plan to *ask them on a date*.
    - **WHO** they plan to have a *date* with in the coming week.
    - **WHAT** they plan to suggest to do.
    - **WHEN** and **WHERE** they will suggest to meet.
    - **HOW** they will make it happen (e.g., tickets, transportation, etc.).

SESSION 15

HANDLING INDIRECT BULLYING

Social Coaching Handout

Handling Cyberbullying

- *Don't feed the trolls—don't react*
- *Have friends stick up for you*
- *Lay low online for awhile*
  - *If the cyberbully can't FIND you, he or she can't bully you.*
- *Block the cyberbully*
  - *If the cyberbully can't CONTACT you, he or she can't bully you.*
- *Save the evidence*
- *Report cyberbullying as a last resort*

Avoiding Being the Target of Gossip

- *Avoid being friends with the gossips*
- *Avoid being enemies with the gossips*
- *Be neutral with the gossips*
- *Don't spread rumors about other people*

Handling Being the Target of Gossip

- *Every instinct we have is WRONG*
- *Don't try to disprove the rumor*
- *Don't appear upset*
- *Act like the rumor doesn't bother you*
- *Don't confront the person spreading the gossip*
- *Avoid the person spreading the gossip*
- *Act amazed anyone CARES about or BELIEVES the gossip*
  - *Act amazed anyone CARES about the gossip:*
    - *"Can you believe anyone cares about that?"*
    - *"Why would anyone care about that?"*
    - *"People need to get a life."*
    - *"People need to find a hobby."*
    - *"People seriously need to find something better to talk about."*
  - *Act amazed anyone BELIEVES the gossip:*
    - *"Can you believe anyone believes that?"*
    - *"Who would believe that?"*
    - *"People are so gullible."*
    - *"People will believe anything."*
    - *"I can't believe anyone would believe that."*
- *Spread the rumor about yourself**

Steps for Spreading the Rumor About Yourself*

1. *Find a supportive friend*
2. *Find an audience*
3. *Acknowledge the rumor*
4. *Act amazed anyone would CARE about or BELIEVE the rumor*
5. *Repeat with other supportive friends*

Homework Assignments

1. Have a *get-together* with a friend.
   - Social coaches should help young adults plan the get-together using the *five W's*:
     - *WHO* they plan to get together with.
     - *WHAT* they plan to do.
     - *WHEN* it will happen.
     - *WHERE* they will meet.
     - *HOW* they will make it happen.
   - Social coaches should go over the rules and steps for *get-togethers* with young adults beforehand.
   - Social coaches should ask young adults the following *social coaching questions* after the *get-together*:
     - *What did you decide to do and who picked the activities?*
     - *Did you trade information and for what percentage of the time?*
     - *What were your common interests and what could you do with that information if you were going to hang out again?*
     - *Did you and your friend have a good time?*
     - *Is this someone you might want to hang out with again?*

2. Young adults and social coaches should practice *spreading the rumor about yourself*.
   - Go over the strategies for *spreading the rumor about yourself* before practicing.
   - Social coaches should provide an example of a rumor for the young adult to practice *spreading the rumor about yourself*.
   - Social coaches should ask young adults the following *Perspective Taking Questions* after practicing:
     - *What was that like for me?*
     - *What do you think I thought of you?*
     - *Do you think I believed the rumor?*

3. Young adults and social coaches should practice *handling teasing*.
   - Go over the strategies for *handling teasing* before practicing.
   - Young adults should choose THREE *verbal comebacks* to practice using.
   - Social coaches should use benign teasing comments (i.e., *"Your shoes are ugly"*).
   - Social coaches should ask young adults the following *Perspective Taking Questions* after practicing:
     - *What was that like for me?*
     - *What do you think I thought of you?*
     - *Do you think I'm going to want to tease you again?*

4. Young adults should practice *handling DIRECT* or *INDIRECT bullying* with a peer if relevant.
   - Social coaches should ask young adults the following *social coaching and Perspective Taking Questions* after practicing when relevant:
     - *What did you do or say to handle teasing?*
       - *What was that like for the other person?*
       - *What do you think they thought of you?*
       - *Do you think they're going to want to tease you again?*

   ○ *Did they give you any embarrassing feedback and what could you do differently if you didn't want to be teased about that?*

   ○ *What did you do or say to handle physical bullying?*

   ○ *What did you do to handle cyberbullying?*

   ○ *What did you do or say to handle rumors and gossip?*

5. Young adults should practice *handling a disagreement* with a friend or romantic partner if relevant.

  • Social coaches should go over the rules and steps for **RESPONDING** *to disagreements* and **BRINGING UP** *disagreements* before practicing when possible.

  • Social coaches should ask young adults the following *social coaching* and *Perspective Taking Questions* after practicing:

   ○ *Which steps did you follow?*

   ○ *What was that like for you and the other person in the end?*

   ○ *What do you think they thought of you in the end?*

   ○ *Do you think you'll both want to hang out again?*

6. Practice *letting someone know you like them, ask them on a date,* and/or *go on a date.*

  • If young adults are interested in someone romantically:

   ○ *Let them know you like them.*

   ○ *Ask them on a date.*

   ○ *Go on a date.*

   ○ DO NOT practice unless you are romantically interested in the person.

  • Young adults should practice *letting someone know you like them, asking someone on a date,* and *beginning and ending dates* with social coaches, if comfortable.

  • Social coaches should go over all of the rules and steps for *dating etiquette* before the practice.

  • Social coaches should ask young adults the following *social coaching questions* after each practice:

   ○ *Letting someone know you like them*:

    ■ *Who did you practice with and what did you do to let them know you like them?*

    ■ *How did they respond?*

    ■ *Does this seem like a good choice and is this someone you might want to go on a date with?*

   ○ *Asking someone on a date*:

    ■ *Who did you ask on a date and what steps did you follow?*

    ■ *How did they respond?*

   ○ *Going on a date*:

    ■ *What did you decide to do?*

    ■ *Did you trade information and for what percentage of the time?*

    ■ *What were your common interests and what could you do with that information if you were going to go on a date again?*

    ■ *Did you and your date have a good time?*

    ■ *Does this seem like a good choice and is this someone you might want to go on a date with again?*

REMINDER: PEERS® GRADUATION IS NEXT WEEK!

* See *The Science of Making Friends* DVD (Laugeson, 2013) or *FriendMaker* mobile app for a video Role Play Demonstration of the corresponding rule.

MOVING FORWARD AND GRADUATION

Social Coaching Therapist Guide

Preparing for the Social Coaching Session

The major focus of this lesson is on providing suggestions about where to go from here. There is no new material presented in the *Didactic Lesson*, apart from future suggestions. Post-test assessments are recommended for the beginning of the session, particularly if you conducted pre-treatment assessments of social functioning. Suggestions for appropriate outcome measures are provided in Chapter 1 of this manual. In the event that you choose to conduct post-test assessments of treatment outcome, you should plan to lengthen this final session (depending on the number of outcome measures you administer). An additional 30 minutes is recommended if administering more than two measures.

Unlike the young adult group, there is no formal *graduation party* in the social coaching group. However, you may want to suggest that some of the food served at the young adults' *graduation party* be shared with social coaches. Although social coaches are not participating in their own party, they often appreciate the festive atmosphere that food and beverages bring to the group. Even decorating the social coaching room with a banner or two can add to the atmosphere.

The social coaching group will not only include a final wrap-up with suggestions about how to move forward, but should also include a *graduation ceremony* with young adults. The purpose of the *graduation ceremony* is to signify the completion of the group and celebrate the group members' achievements. Providing *Certificates of Completion* (see Appendix H) for young adults is recommended when possible. These certificates serve as a type of diploma that will be a tangible reminder of the work the young adults have accomplished. Although often bittersweet, the *graduation ceremony* should be fun, festive, and focused on a celebration of all the great gains young adults have made in improving their social skills, while acknowledging the hard work that went into these accomplishments. The *graduation ceremony* typically takes about 30 minutes from start to end (allotting time for casual socializing after), so plan your session accordingly.

One of the most common issues that arises at the end of the group is increased anxiety among social coaches and even among the young adults. Social coaches will often worry that the improvements they've witnessed in their young adults will somehow disappear when the group is over. Consequently, they often ask to sign up for the group again in response to this fear. It will be important for you to ease these anxieties by reassuring social coaches that if young adults continue to utilize the skills learned in PEERS®, with support from social coaches, the gains experienced in the group should be maintained. You might even consider citing long-term research findings among youth with Autism Spectrum Disorder (ASD), which found that those who attended PEERS® with a caregiver were not only able to maintain their treatment gains following the conclusion of the group, but in many cases were doing even better socially one to five years after treatment. This is not the normal social trajectory for transitional youth with ASD entering adulthood, and is attributable to the power of including caregivers as social coaches. The notion is that the intervention continues on long after the group is over because social coaches continue to reinforce and coach around the skills.

Despite your reassurances, you may still have social coaches and young adults that insist on returning to the group immediately, for fear of losing newly acquired skills. One effective approach we have used at the UCLA PEERS® Clinic is to say, *"Why don't you wait a few months and see how things go. After a few months, if you still feel like you need to come back, give us a call."* The reality is that very few people call back seeking another round of PEERS®. Instead, you are more likely to receive emails and phone calls with friendly updates sharing all of the exciting developments happening in the young adults' lives.

Given the frequent requests by social coaches and young adults for continued treatment following PEERS®, a common question asked by group leaders relates to the appropriateness of *booster sessions* or *maintenance programs*, which include periodic contact with group members for the purpose of either refining or reinforcing the skills learned in PEERS®. At the time of writing this manual, no research has been conducted to test the efficacy or effectiveness of *booster sessions* or *maintenance programs* using the PEERS® curriculum. However, that is not to say that these types of programs couldn't provide additional treatment gains. At the very least, they are unlikely to cause harm. Future proposed research from the UCLA PEERS® Clinic is anticipated to test the effectiveness of such programs through the implementation of *Club PEERS®*, a maintenance program for alumni of PEERS®. Until greater understanding about the benefits of such programs is known, group leaders are encouraged to meet the post-treatment needs of their families in whatever way works best, but avoid making promises about the utility of *booster sessions* and *maintenance programs*. Another option moving forward will be to encourage social coaches to continue to provide social coaching around the PEERS® skills, and to utilize the additional resources provided in the *Social Coaching Handout.*

Administer Post-Test Assessments (Optional)

[Tracking progress is an essential part of determining whether your program is working. It is how a program maintains quality control. Below is a list of some of the outcome measures we have used in our published research studies with PEERS®. Standardized assessments of social functioning are included. These measures are widely available and have shown significant change following the program.]

- Allow sufficient time to administer post-test assessments if applicable.
  - You may want to lengthen the final session by 30 minutes if you plan to administer more than two post-test assessments (e.g., have participants arrive 30 minutes earlier or plan to stay 30 minutes later).
- Chapter 1 of this manual provides an overview and description of recommended outcome measures.
- Suggested outcome measures to be completed by social coaches might include:
  - *Quality of Socialization Questionnaire* (QSQ; Appendix B).
  - *Social Responsiveness Scale-Second Edition* (SRS-2; Constantino, 2012).
  - *Social Skills Improvement System* (SSIS; Gresham & Elliot, 2008).
  - *Empathy Quotient* (EQ; Baron-Cohen & Wheelwright, 2004).

Homework Review

[Go over the following *Homework Assignments* and **troubleshoot** any potential problems. Focus on completed homework only. When reviewing homework, be sure to relabel descriptions using the **buzzwords** (identified by **bold and italicized** print). Spend the majority of the *Homework Review* on *get-togethers* as this was the most important assignment.]

1. Have a *get-together* with a friend.
   - Say, *"One of the main assignments this week was for young adults to have a get-together with a friend. Who completed this assignment or attempted to complete it?"*
   - Ask the following questions:
     - *"Did you help your young adult plan the get-together using the five W's?"*
     - *"What social coaching did you do before the get-together?"*
     - *"What did your young adult decide to do and with whom?"*
     - *"How did the get-together begin?"*
     - *"Who picked the activities?"*

- ○ *"Did they trade information and what percentage of the time?"*
- ○ *"How did the get-together end?"*
- ○ *"What social coaching did you do after the get-together?"*
  - ■ Appropriate *social coaching questions*:
    - ☐ *What did you decide to do and who picked the activities?*
    - ☐ *Did you trade information and for what percentage of the time?*
    - ☐ *What were your common interests and what could you do with that information if you were going to hang out again?*
    - ☐ *Did you and your friend have a good time?*
    - ☐ *Is this someone you might want to hang out with again?*
- ○ *"Does this seem like a good choice for a friend and someone your young adult will want to hang out with again?"*

Table 17.1 Steps for Beginning and Ending Get-Togethers in Your Home

Beginning the Get-Together	Ending the Get-Together
1. Greet your guest 2. Invite them in 3. Introduce them to anyone they don't know 4. Give them a tour 5. Offer them refreshments 6. Ask them what they want to do	1. Wait for a pause in activities 2. Give a cover story for ending the get-together 3. Start walking your friend to the door 4. Thank your friend for getting together 5. Tell your friend you had a good time 6. Say goodbye and you'll see them later

2. Young adults and social coaches should practice *spreading the rumor about yourself*.
   - Say, *"Another assignment this week was for young adults to practice spreading the rumor about themselves with social coaches. Who completed this assignment or attempted to complete it?"*
   - Ask the following questions:
     - ○ *"What social coaching did you do before the practice?"*
     - ○ *"Which steps did your young adult follow to spread the rumor about him or herself?"*
       1. *Find a supportive friend*
       2. *Find an audience*
       3. *Acknowledge the rumor*
       4. *Act amazed anyone would CARE about or BELIEVE the rumor*
       5. *Repeat with other supportive friends*
     - ○ *"What social coaching did you do after the practice?"*
       - ■ Appropriate *Perspective Taking Questions*:
         - ☐ *What was that like for me?*
         - ☐ *What do you think I thought of you?*
         - ☐ *Do you think I believed the rumor?*

3. Young adults and social coaches should practice *handling teasing*.
   - Say, *"Another assignment this week was for young adults and social coaches to practice handling teasing. Who completed this assignment or attempted to complete it?"*
   - Ask the following questions:
     - ○ *"What social coaching did you do before the practice?"*
     - ○ *"What did your young adult do or say to handle teasing?"*
     - ○ *"What social coaching did you do after the practice?"*
       - ■ Appropriate *Perspective Taking Questions*:
         - ☐ *What was that like for me?*
         - ☐ *What do you think I thought of you?*
         - ☐ *Do you think I'm going to want to tease you again?*

4. Young adults should practice *handling DIRECT* or *INDIRECT bullying* with a peer if relevant.
   - Say, *"Another assignment this week was for young adults to practice handling DIRECT or INDIRECT bullying with a peer if relevant. Who completed this assignment or attempted to complete it?"*
   - Ask the following questions:

- ○ *"Who did your young adult practice with and what was the bullying?"*
- ○ *"What did your young adult do or say to handle the bullying?"*
- ○ *"What social coaching did you do after the practice?"*
    - ■ Appropriate *social coaching* and *Perspective Taking Questions*:
        - □ **What did you do or say to handle teasing?**
        - □ **What was that like for the other person?**
        - □ **What do you think they thought of you?**
        - □ **Do you think they're going to want to tease you again?**
        - □ **Did they give you any embarrassing feedback and what could you do differently if you didn't want to be teased about that?**
        - □ **What did you do or say to handle physical bullying?**
        - □ **What did you do to handle cyberbullying?**
        - □ **What did you do or say to handle rumors and gossip?**

5. Young adults should practice **handling a disagreement** with a friend or romantic partner if relevant.
    - ● Say, *"Another assignment this week was for young adults to practice handling a disagreement with a friend or romantic partner if relevant. Who completed this assignment or attempted to complete it?"*
    - ● Ask the following questions:
        - ○ *"Who did your young adult practice with and what was the disagreement?"*
        - ○ *"Which steps did your young adult follow to RESPOND to or BRING UP the disagreement?"*
        - ○ *"What social coaching did you do after the practice?"*
            - ■ Appropriate *social coaching* and *Perspective Taking Questions*:
                - □ **Which steps did you follow?**
                - □ **What was that like for you and the other person in the end?**
                - □ **What did you think of each other in the end?**
                - □ **Do you think you'll both want to hang out again?**

Table 17.2 Steps for Handling Disagreements

RESPONDING TO DISAGREEMENTS	BRINGING UP DISAGREEMENTS
1. Keep your cool 2. Listen to the other person 3. Repeat what they said 4. Explain your side using "I" statements 5. Say you're sorry 6. Try to solve the problem	1. Wait for the right time and place 2. Keep your cool 3. Ask to speak privately 4. Explain your side using "I" statements 5. Listen to the other person 6. Repeat what they said 7. Tell them what you need them to do 8. Try to solve the problem

6. Practice **letting someone know you like them, ask them on a date**, and/or **go on a date**.
    - ● Say, *"Another assignment this week was for young adults to practice letting someone know they like them, ask them on a date, and/or go on a date. The assignment was NOT to practice unless they are romantically interested in the person. Young adults could also have practiced with social coaches, if they were comfortable. Who completed this assignment or attempted to complete it?"*
    - ● Ask the following questions:
        - ○ *"What social coaching did you do before the practice?"*
        - ○ *"Who did your young adult practice with?"*
        - ○ *"What did they do to let the person know they like them and how did they respond?"*
        - ○ *"Did they ask the person on a date and how did they respond?"*
        - ○ Ask the following questions if they went on a date:
            - ■ *"What did they decide to do?"*
            - ■ *"Did they trade information and for what percentage of the time?"*
            - ■ *"Did they and their date have a good time?"*
        - ○ *"What social coaching did you do after the practice?"*
        - ○ *"Does this seem like a good choice and is this someone they might want to go on a date with (again)?"*

- [Collect the *Social Coaching Homework Assignment Worksheets*. If social coaches forgot to bring the worksheets, have them complete a new form to hold them accountable for the assignments.]

Didactic Lesson: Moving Forward

- Distribute the *Social Coaching Handout.*
  - Sections in **bold print** in the *Social Coaching Therapist Guide* come directly from the *Social Coaching Handout.*
  - Remind social coaches that terms that are in ***bold and italicized*** print are ***buzzwords*** and represent important concepts from the PEERS® curriculum that should be used as much as possible when social coaching.
- Explain, *"Today is our last session of PEERS®, but just because the group is coming to an end doesn't mean that your work has also come to an end. Today, we're going to focus on exactly what you and your young adults will need to do moving forward."*
- **Regularly Attend Social Activities**
  - Say, *"It's essential that your young adults continue to have a source of friends and attend social activities. Why is it important to regularly attend social activities?"*
    - Answer: It gives you a ***source of friends*** with ***common interests***.
  - Explain, *"Young adults need to participate regularly in social activities in order to make friends and even find romantic partners. Social activities should be focused on what your young adult likes to do so that he or she can meet other people with common interests."*
  - Explain, ***"We recommend that young adults attend AT LEAST ONE SOCIAL ACTIVITY A WEEK in order to have access to peers with common interests."***
  - **Criteria for good *social activities*:**
    - **Based on the young adult's interests.**
    - **Meets WEEKLY or at least every other week.**
    - **Includes accepting peers similar in age.**
    - **Includes unstructured time to interact with others.**
  - Explain, *"Remember that social activities should be based on your young adults' interests. The table in your Social Coaching Handout provides some examples of social activities based on interests."*
    - Go over a few examples from Table 17.3 to summarize.

Table 17.3 Possible Social Activities

INTERESTS	RELATED SOCIAL ACTIVITIES
Computers/technology	Take computer classes; attend events through computer/IT department; join a technology related meet-up group; join a technology club; join a computer meet-up group; join a computer club
Video games	Go to adult video arcades with friends; go to gaming conventions; visit gaming stores; join a gaming meet-up group; join a gaming club
Science	Go to science museum events; take science classes; join a science-related meet-up group; join a science club; join a robotics club
Comic books/anime	Attend comic book conventions (i.e., ComicCon); go to comic book/anime stores; take comic book/anime drawing classes; join a comic book/anime meet-up group; join a comic book/anime club
Chess	Visit gaming stores where they play chess; attend chess tournaments; join a chess meet-up group; join a chess club
Cosplay (costume play)	Attend comic book conventions (i.e., ComicCon); take sewing classes to make costumes; join a cosplay meet-up group; join a cosplay club
LARPing (live action role playing)	Attend comic book conventions (i.e., ComicCon); take sewing classes to make costumes; attend LARPing events; join a LARPing meet-up group; join a LARPing club
Movies	Join an audiovisual club; join a movie-related meet-up group; join a movie club

Sports	Try out for a sports team; play sports at community recreation centers or parks; join a sports league; go to sporting events; attend sports camps (e.g., spring training); join a sports-related meet-up group; join a sports club
Cars	Go to car shows; visit car museums; take auto shop courses; join a car-related meet-up group; join a car club
Music	Go to concerts; join the college band; take music classes; join a music-related meet-up group; join a music club

- **Have Regular Get-Togethers**
  - ○ Say, *"Moving forward, it's also essential that young adults have regular get-togethers with friends. Why is it important to have regular get-togethers?"*
    - ■ Answers: Having regular **get-togethers** is how close friendships develop; if you're not having **get-togethers** with your friends, then you're probably not that close.
  - ○ Explain, *"Get-togethers are the way we develop and maintain close friendships. When you're first becoming friends with someone, you should try to have get-togethers to get to know each other better, but even after you've developed a friendship, you need to maintain regular contact by having get-togethers if you want your friendship to be close."*
  - ○ Explain, ***"We recommend that young adults have AT LEAST ONE GET-TOGETHER A WEEK. Having regular get-togethers is how we develop closer and more meaningful relationships with our friends."***
  - ○ **General reminders about *get-togethers*:**
    - ■ *Make plans using the five W's*
    - ■ *Get-togethers should be activity-based and focused on common interests*
    - ■ *Trade information at least 50% of the time*
    - ■ *Keep it short and sweet to start (no more than two hours at first, depending on the activity)*

- **Assess Peer Acceptance Using the Signs of Acceptance**
  - ○ Explain, *"Moving forward, it's also important to continue to assess peer acceptance. It's usually pretty easy for you to know if you want to be friends with someone, but how can you tell if someone wants to be friends with you?"*
    - ■ Answer: See Table 17.4.
  - ○ Ask, *"How can you tell if they don't want to be friends with you?"*
    - ■ Answer: See Table 17.4.

Table 17.4 Signs of Acceptance and Lack of Acceptance

Signs You Are Accepted	Signs You Are Not Accepted
They seek you out to do things individually or in the group	They do not seek you out to do things
They talk to you and respond to your attempts to talk	They ignore you and/or do not respond to your attempts to talk
They give you their contact information	They do not give you their contact information
They ask for your contact information	They do not ask for your contact information
They text message, instant message, email, or call you just to talk	They do not text, instant message, email, or call you
They respond to your text messages, instant messages, emails, or phone calls	They do not accept or return your calls or messages
They invite you to do things	They do not invite you to do things
They accept your invitations to do things	They do not accept your invitations or put off your invitations to do things
They add you to their social networking pages	They ignore your friend requests on social networking sites
They say nice things to you and give you compliments	They laugh at you or make fun of you

- **Remember That Friendship and Dating is a Choice**
  - Explain, *"As you assess peer acceptance, whether it's in friendships or romantic relationships, it's also important to remember that friendship and dating is a choice."*
  - Ask, *"Do we get to be friends with or date everyone?"*
    - Answer: No.
  - Ask, *"Does everyone get to be friends with or date us?"*
    - Answer: No.
  - Explain, *"That's because friendship and dating is a choice. If someone doesn't want to be friends with us or date us, it's not a big deal. We should just move on and find someone who does."*

- **Keep Social Coaching**
  - Say, *"As you move forward, it's also critical that you keep social coaching your young adults. Why do you think it's important to keep social coaching?"*
    - Answers: This is how you promote the use of the skills by young adults; if you don't provide social coaching, they may stop using the skills.
  - Explain, *"One of the reasons PEERS® has been so successful through research trials is because the program includes caregivers and social coaches like you. Involving you in the process ensures that the program continues on long after you have left this group. That means that you need to keep using the buzzwords and the common language we have developed, and follow up with young adults to make sure they're regularly attending social activities and having get-togethers."*

- **Keep Using the PEERS® Skills**
  - Say, *"The last bit of advice we have for you and your young adults as you move forward is to keep using the PEERS skills. Why would it be important to keep using the skills you've learned in PEERS®?"*
    - Answer: The gains young adults have made won't be maintained or improved upon further unless they continue to use the PEERS® skills.
  - Explain, *"Even though this is the last week of our group, that doesn't mean young adults should stop using the PEERS® skills. These are the skills we need for making and keeping friends and forming romantic relationships. Developing and maintaining relationships is a lifelong journey, so plan to use these skills throughout your lives and wherever you go!"*

Additional Resources

- Explain, *"Finally, for those of you looking for a little extra support after the group, we have provided you with some additional resources, which you can find in your Social Coaching Handout."*

- *The Science of Making Friends: Helping Socially Challenged Teens and Young Adults* (Laugeson, 2013)
  - This is a book for teens, young adults, and their social coaches that provides an overview of the skills related to making and keeping friends taught in PEERS®, including:
    - Narrative sections for social coaches with *Social Coaching Tips.*
    - Chapter summaries for teens and young adults.
    - A DVD companion with Role Play Video Demonstrations of corresponding skills, including *Perspective Taking Questions.*
    - Chapter exercises to practice the corresponding skills.

- *FriendMaker* mobile app
  - This mobile application is intended to act as a "virtual social coach" for teens, young adults, and their social coaches.
  - The app provides an overview of the skills related to making and keeping friends taught in PEERS®.
  - Rules and steps of social behavior are broken down into an outline format.
  - Embedded Role Play Video Demonstrations of corresponding skills are included with *Perspective Taking Questions* to follow.

MOVING FORWARD AND GRADUATION

Young Adult Therapist Guide

Preparing for the Young Adult Session

The purpose of this final session of the young adult group is to have a *graduation party* to reward young adults for their hard work throughout the group and to provide closure with fun and celebration. As mentioned in the *Preparing for the Social Coaching Group* section of this chapter, if you plan to conduct post-test assessment, as is recommended, be sure to allot enough time to complete the forms without taking away from the party. In order to provide a feeling of celebration, it is STRONGLY recommended that the treatment team decorate the room for the *graduation party*. Graduation signs and banners are common (and can be recycled), as are balloons, crepe paper, streamers, and festive tablecloths. Young adults will feel more celebratory if the room is decorated, signifying a party atmosphere.

Depending on your resources, you may also want to provide food and beverages for the *graduation party*. You will have to determine what is possible prior to graduation. Most PEERS® graduations include a *potluck party*, where group members bring snacks and desserts to share with everyone. If you plan to serve food, one common issue that may arise is that certain members may have food allergies, dietary restrictions, or unique food preferences. Because it would be difficult to meet the dietary needs and wishes of the entire group, if you do provide food and beverages, it is recommended that you let families know in advance what you will serve and encourage them to bring foods they might enjoy as part of a *potluck*. This should release you of the burden of having to satisfy everyone's culinary needs and tastes. Announcements about graduation, including information about the *potluck party*, should be mentioned during *Reunification* in Sessions 14 and 15 and also stated on the *graduation flyers* distributed in those same sessions.

Throughout the *graduation party* and *ceremony*, the majority of young adults will be cheerful and generally in a festive mood. However, there may be one or two young adults who exhibit visible anxiety and/or sadness in response to the end of the group. While it will be important for you to empathize with this reaction, it is also helpful to redirect any negative moods by focusing on the progress young adults have made and the pride they might feel in their accomplishments. Some of the more anxious young adults may also express an interest in enrolling in the group again. As described in the *Preparing for the Social Coaching Group* section, one helpful approach to such requests might be to say, *"Why don't you wait a few months and see how things go. After a few months, if you still feel like you need to come back, give us a call."* In our experience, once young adults have gotten over the initial anxiety about the group ending, very few express the need to return to the group.

Another common request made by young adults in the final session of PEERS® is to have reunions with their fellow group members. Although the young adults are free to socialize with one another now that the group is coming to an end, and the organization of reunions by the treatment team is unlikely to do any harm, the added effectiveness of these interactions is unknown. Since there is never a one-size-fits-all approach, you will be the best judge for what will be helpful for your young adults with regard to future contact. Whatever you choose with regard to future treatment, be sure to take the opportunity to celebrate all of the wonderful accomplishments made throughout the current group, while acknowledging all of the hard work behind these successes.

Administer Post-Test Assessments (Optional)

[Tracking progress is a useful way to determine whether your program is working. Tracking treatment progress is suggested using comparisons of pre-treatment and post-treatment social functioning. Below is a list of the tests we have used in our published research studies with PEERS®. Several standardized assessments of social functioning are included. These measures are widely available and have shown significant change following the program.]

- Allow sufficient time to administer post-test assessments if applicable. You may want to lengthen the session by 30 minutes in that case.
- Chapter 1 of this manual provides an overview and description of recommended outcome measures.
- Suggested outcome measures to be completed by young adults include:
  ○ Test of Young Adult Social Skills Knowledge (TYASSK; Appendix A).
  ○ Quality of Socialization Questionnaire (QSQ; Appendix B).
  ○ Social and Emotional Loneliness Scale (SELSA; DiTommaso & Spinner, 1993).
  ○ Social Responsiveness Scale-Second Edition (SRS-2; Constantino, 2012).
  ○ Social Skills Improvement System (SSIS; Gresham & Elliot, 2008).
  ○ Empathy Quotient (EQ; Baron-Cohen & Wheelwright, 2004).

Abbreviated Homework Review

[Briefly go over completed homework by asking for a show of hands for those who completed the following assignments. Make a note of the homework completion on the *Homework Compliance Sheet*. Do not spend more than five minutes on the *Homework Review* as the majority of the time should be spent on the *graduation party*.]

1. Have a *get-together* with a friend.
   - Say, *"One of the main assignments this week was for you to have a get-together with a friend. Raise your hand if you had a get-together with a friend this week."*

2. Young adults and social coaches should practice *spreading the rumor about yourself*.
   - Say, *"Another assignment this week was for you to practice spreading the rumor about yourself with your social coaches. Raise your hand if you practiced spreading the rumor about yourself with your social coach."*

3. Young adults and social coaches should practice *handling teasing*.
   - Say, *"Another assignment this week was for you to practice handling teasing with your social coaches. Raise your hand if you practiced handling teasing with your social coach."*

4. Young adults should practice *handling DIRECT or INDIRECT bullying* with a peer if relevant.
   - Say, *"Another assignment this week was for you to practice handling bullying with a peer if relevant. We know bullying is very common, so I expect many of you had the opportunity to practice using these strategies. Raise your hand if you practiced handling bullying with a peer."*

5. Young adults should practice *handling a disagreement* with a friend or romantic partner if relevant.
   - Say, *"Another assignment this week was to practice handling a disagreement with a friend or romantic partner if relevant. Raise your hand if you practiced handling a disagreement with a friend or romantic partner."*

6. Practice *letting someone know you like them, ask them on a date*, and/or *go on a date*.
   - Say, *"Another assignment this week was to practice letting someone know you like them, ask them on a date, and/or go on a date. The assignment was NOT to practice unless you're romantically interested in the person. Raise your hand if you did this assignment."*

Abbreviated Didactic Lesson: Moving Forward

Explain, *"Today is our last session for PEERS® and we're going to celebrate by having a graduation party. Later, we'll have a graduation ceremony with your social coaches. Before we start our party, let's go over a few recommendations we have for moving forward."*

- **Regularly Attend Social Activities**
  - Say, *"It's essential that you continue to have a source of friends and attend social activities. Why is it important to regularly attend social activities?"*
    - Answer: It gives you a source of friends with common interests.
  - Explain, *"We recommend that you attend AT LEAST ONE SOCIAL ACTIVITY A WEEK in order to have access to peers with common interests."*

- **Have Regular Get-Togethers**
  - Say, *"Moving forward, it's also essential that you have regular get-togethers with friends. Why is it important to have regular get-togethers?"*
    - Answers: Having regular **get-togethers** is how close friendships develop; if you're not having **get-togethers** with your friends, then you're probably not that close.
  - Explain, *"We recommend that you have AT LEAST ONE GET-TOGETHER A WEEK. Having regular get-togethers is how we develop closer and more meaningful relationships with our friends."*

- **Assess Peer Acceptance Using the Signs of Acceptance**
  - Explain, *"Moving forward, it's also important to continue to assess peer acceptance. It's usually pretty easy for you to know if you want to be friends with someone, but how can you tell if someone wants to be friends with you?"*
    - Answers: They text you and contact you over electronic communication; invite you to things; accept your invitations; etc.
  - Ask, *"How can you tell if they don't want to be friends with you?"*
    - Answers: They don't text you or contact you over electronic communication; they don't invite you to things; they don't accept your invitations; etc.

- **Remember That Friendship and Dating is a Choice**
  - Explain, *"As you assess peer acceptance, whether it's in friendships or romantic relationships, it's also important to remember that friendship and dating is a choice."*
  - Ask, *"Do we get to be friends with or date everyone?"*
    - Answer: No.
  - Ask, *"Does everyone get to be friends with or date us?"*
    - Answer: No.
  - Explain, *"That's because friendship and dating is a choice. If someone doesn't want to be friends with us or date us, it's not a big deal. We should just move on and find someone who does."*

- **Keep Social Coaching**
  - Say, *"As you move forward, it's also critical that you keep working with your social coaches. Why do you think it's important to keep social coaching?"*
    - Answers: This is how you promote the use of the skills; if you don't allow your social coaches to keep coaching, you may stop using the skills.

- **Keep Using the PEERS® Skills**
  - Say, *"The last bit of advice we have for you as you move forward is to keep using the PEERS® skills. Why would it be important to keep using the skills you've learned in PEERS®?"*
    - Answer: The gains made won't be maintained or improved upon unless you continue to use the PEERS® skills.
  - Explain, *"Even though this is the last week of our group, that doesn't mean you should stop using the PEERS® skills. These are the skills we need for making and keeping friends and forming romantic relationships. We'll provide you with some additional resources in the Social Coaching Handout, but just remember that developing and maintaining relationships is a lifelong journey, so plan to use these skills throughout your lives and wherever you go!"*

Suggestions for the Graduation Party

- It is STRONGLY RECOMMENDED that the young adult group room be decorated prior to the *graduation party* to add to the festive atmosphere.
  - See the *Preparing for Young Adult Session* for the current session for suggestions.
- It is recommended that some basic food and beverages be provided at the *graduation party* by the treatment team.
  - In North America, delivery pizza is a popular food item for PEERS® *graduation parties*.
  - If serving food and beverages, be sure to have plates, napkins, cups, and silverware available.
- Consider organizing a *potluck party* in which group members bring snacks and desserts for the party.
  - If you are planning a *potluck party*, young adults and social coaches should have been notified prior to the party for planning purposes.
  - Notices about *potluck parties* are usually stated in the *graduation flyer* and mentioned during the *graduation announcements* in Sessions 14 and 15.
- Young adults should be encouraged to talk and socialize during the *graduation party*, much like they would during a group *get-together*.
- The group leader and behavioral coaches should give the young adults space to enjoy their *graduation party* with each other.
- Young adults often enjoy watching a movie in the background, playing games, and/or listening to music while talking.
  - It is recommended that a selection of movies be provided by the treatment team.
    - Be sure the content of whatever movies are available will not be offensive to certain group members (e.g., certain PG-13 and R-rated movies include violence, nudity, and profanity that may be offensive to some).
    - If a movie is watched, be sure young adults are actually interacting with one another and talking during the movie.
    - The movie should be more of a background activity than the focus of attention.
  - It is recommended that a selection of games be provided by the treatment team.
    - These could be games used during the *Behavioral Rehearsal Exercises* focused on having mock *get-togethers*.
    - Allow young adults to work out the choice in games among themselves.
  - Young adults may also choose to play music during the party (usually through their mobile phones).
    - If young adults decide to listen to music, allow them to work out the choices in music among themselves.
- The *graduation party* should be unstructured time for the young adults to socialize.
  - Many young adults will exchange contact information at this point (or after the *graduation ceremony*). This is perfectly appropriate now that the group is coming to an end.
- Be sure to encourage a fun, festive, and socially engaging atmosphere throughout the *graduation party*.

MOVING FORWARD AND GRADUATION

Graduation Ceremony

Suggestions for the Graduation Ceremony

[The *graduation ceremony* typically takes about 30 minutes from start to end (allotting for casual socializing after), so plan your session accordingly.]

- Announce that young adults should join their social coaches.
  - Have young adults stand or sit next to their social coaches.
- Distribute the *Social Coaching Handout* to young adults.
- The group leaders and behavioral coaches should be at the front of the room with the young adults and social coaches seated facing them.
- Announce the start of the *Graduation Ceremony*.
  - Be sure to have silence and the full attention of the group before starting the *Graduation Ceremony*.
- The group leaders conduct the *Graduation Ceremony*.
- The group leaders begin by complimenting the young adults and social coaches on the hard work they have done.
  - Comment on the progress the group has made as a whole.
  - Avoid mentioning specific details about young adults since comments will never be equal and feelings might get hurt.
- The behavioral coaches may also want to make a few comments about the progress shown by the young adults and the hard work and dedication shown by social coaches.
- The group leaders should then announce the presentation of the *Certificates of Completion* and explain how the ceremony will work:
  - When young adults hear their names called, they will come to the front of the room to receive a *Certificate of Completion* (see Appendix H for an example).
  - Everyone will clap and cheer for them.
  - The group leaders will shake the hand of the young adult and then hand him or her the *Certificate of Completion* with the other hand.
  - The young adult should also shake the hand of any behavioral coaches (or give *high fives*).
  - Everyone will continue to clap and cheer until the young adult has returned to his or her seat.
- Group leaders present the *Certificates of Completion*.
  - While the group does a drum roll for dramatic effect, say, *"The first/next PEERS® Certificate of Completion goes to (insert name)!"*
  - Call each young adult up to the front of the room and present him or her with a *Certificate of Completion*.
  - Have the group clap and cheer after each name is called.
  - Be sure the young adult shakes the hand of the group leaders and behavioral coaches (or gives *high fives*).

- ○ Encourage the group to clap and cheer again as each young adult returns to his or her seat.
  - Say, *"Another round of applause for (insert name)!"*
  - Say, *"Give it up for (insert name)!"*
- After the final *Certificate of Completion* is awarded, make a few final comments about the wonderful progress the group has made.
- Remind the young adults and social coaches that just because the group is over, does not mean that they should stop using the PEERS® skills
- Encourage them to keep practicing what they have learned so that they can continue to make and keep friends and develop romantic relationships.
- Wish them well and end with a final round of applause.
- [Optional: Distribute fresh copies of all 16 *Social Coaching Handouts* as a "graduation gift" to young adults and social coaches. Providing a fresh set of the *Social Coaching Handouts* will help ensure that group members have access to all of the information provided in PEERS® moving forward.]

SESSION 16

MOVING FORWARD AND GRADUATION

Social Coaching Handout

Suggestions Moving Forward

- **Regularly Attend Social Activities**
  - ○ We recommend that young adults attend *AT LEAST ONE SOCIAL ACTIVITY A WEEK* in order to have access to peers with ***common interests***.
  - ○ Criteria for a good ***social activities***:
    - ▪ Based on the young adult's interests.
    - ▪ Meets WEEKLY or at least every other week.
    - ▪ Includes accepting peers similar in age.
    - ▪ Includes unstructured time to interact with others.

Table 17.3 Possible Social Activities

INTERESTS	RELATED SOCIAL ACTIVITIES
Computers/technology	Take computer classes; attend events through computer/IT department; join a technology related meet-up group; join a technology club; join a computer meet-up group; join a computer club
Video games	Go to adult video arcades with friends; go to gaming conventions; visit gaming stores; join a gaming meet-up group; join a gaming club
Science	Go to science museum events; take science classes; join a science-related meet-up group; join a science club; join a robotics club
Comic books/anime	Attend comic book conventions (i.e., ComicCon); go to comic book/anime stores; take comic book/anime drawing classes; join a comic book/anime meet-up group; join a comic book/anime club
Chess	Visit gaming stores where they play chess; attend chess tournaments; join a chess meet-up group; join a chess club
Cosplay (costume play)	Attend comic book conventions (i.e., ComicCon); take sewing classes to make costumes; join a cosplay meet-up group; join a cosplay club
LARPing (live action role playing)	Attend comic book conventions (i.e., ComicCon); take sewing classes to make costumes; attend LARPing events; join a LARPing meet-up group; join a LARPing club
Movies	Join an audiovisual club; join a movie-related meet-up group; join a movie club
Sports	Try out for a sports team; play sports at community recreation centers or parks; join a sports league; go to sporting events; attend sports camps (e.g., spring training); join a sports-related meet-up group; join a sports club
Cars	Go to car shows; visit car museums; take auto shop courses; join a car-related meet-up group; join a car club
Music	Go to concerts; join the college band; take music classes; join a music-related meet-up group; join a music club

- **Have Regular Get-Togethers**
  - We recommend that young adults have *AT LEAST ONE GET-TOGETHER A WEEK.*
  - Having regular get-togethers is how we develop closer and more meaningful relationships with our friends.
  - General reminders about *get-togethers*:
    - *Make plans using the five W's*
    - *Get-togethers should be activity-based and focused on common interests*
    - *Trade information at least 50% of the time*
    - *Keep it short and sweet to start (no more than two hours at first, depending on the activity)*

- **Assess Peer Acceptance Using the Signs of Acceptance**

Table 17.4 Signs of Acceptance and Lack of Acceptance

Signs You Are Accepted	Signs You Are Not Accepted
They seek you out to do things individually or in the group	They do not seek you out to do things
They talk to you and respond to your attempts to talk	They ignore you and/or do not respond to your attempts to talk
They give you their contact information	They do not give you their contact information
They ask for your contact information	They do not ask for your contact information
They text message, instant message, email, or call you just to talk	They do not text message, instant message, email or call
They respond to your text messages, instant messages, emails, or phone calls	They do not accept or return your calls or messages
They invite you to do things	They do not invite you to do things
They accept your invitations to do things	They do not accept your invitations or put off your invitations to do things
They add you to their social networking pages	They ignore your friend requests on social networking sites
They say nice things to you and give you compliments	They laugh at you or make fun of you

- **Remember That Friendship and Dating is a Choice**
- **Keep Social Coaching**
- **Keep Using the PEERS® Skills**

Additional Resources

- *The Science of Making Friends: Helping Socially Challenged Teens and Young Adults* (Laugeson, 2013)
  - This is a book for teens, young adults, and their social coaches that provides an overview of the skills related to making and keeping friends taught in PEERS®, including:
    - Narrative sections for social coaches with *Social Coaching Tips*.
    - Chapter summaries for teens and young adults.
    - A DVD companion with Role Play Video Demonstrations of corresponding skills, including *Perspective Taking Questions*.
    - Chapter exercises to practice the corresponding skills.

- *FriendMaker* mobile app
  - This mobile application is intended to act as a "virtual social coach" for teens, young adults, and their social coaches.

- ○ The app provides an overview of the skills related to making and keeping friends taught in PEERS®.
- ○ Rules and steps of social behavior are broken down into an outline format.
- ○ Embedded *Role Play Video Demonstrations* of corresponding skills are included with ***Perspective Taking Questions*** to follow.

THANK YOU FOR BEING A PART OF PEERS®!
WE WISH YOU THE BEST OF LUCK MOVING FORWARD!

TEST OF YOUNG ADULT SOCIAL SKILLS KNOWLEDGE (TYASSK)

Instructions:

The following items are about making and keeping friends and romantic relationships. After you read each item, there will be a couple of choices to choose from. Decide which choice is the best by bubbling in the best answer. Only choose one answer per item.

---

1. The most important part of having a conversation is to:
   - ○ Trade information
   - ○ Make sure the other person is laughing and smiling

2. When starting a conversation:
   - ○ Wait for the person to notice you
   - ○ Find a common interest

3. If your friend mispronounces a word, you should:
   - ○ Not police them
   - ○ Politely point out their mistake to be helpful

4. If you discover that you and a friend like the same thing:
   - ○ Be repetitive
   - ○ Don't be repetitive

5. It's ALWAYS a good idea to try to make friends with someone who:
   - ○ Has lots of friends and is popular
   - ○ Likes the same things as you

6. Friendship is a:
   - ○ Choice
   - ○ Gift

7. When you want to exchange contact information with someone:
   - ○ Go up and nicely ask them for their number
   - ○ Use a cover story

8. How many messages can you leave in row without hearing back from a person?
   - ○ 1–2
   - ○ 3–4

9. After you make a joke, it's a good idea to pay attention to:
   - ○ Whether the other person is laughing
   - ○ Your humor feedback

10. It is ALWAYS a good sign if someone laughs at your jokes:
    - ○ True
    - ○ False

11. When you're trying to meet a new group of people, it's a good idea to go up and say hello and introduce yourself:
    - ○ True
    - ○ False

12. When you're trying to enter a group conversation, the FIRST thing you should do is:
    - ○ Watch and listen to the conversation
    - ○ Make a comment about what they're saying

13. If you try to enter a group conversation and the people exclude you:
    - ○ Start to look away
    - ○ Make sure they can hear you

14. If you try to join ten different conversations, on average how many times out of ten are you likely to be rejected:
    - ○ 7 out of 10
    - ○ 5 out of 10

15. When having a friend over for a get-together at your home:
    - ○ Tell your friend what you're going to do
    - ○ Have your friend choose the activity

16. If you're having a friend over for a get-together and someone else unexpectedly texts that you really like:
    - ○ Ask your friend if you can invite them over
    - ○ Text them later

17. When you're interested in someone romantically, it's a good idea to:
    - ○ Talk to mutual friends
    - ○ Not tell people until you're sure they like you

18. When you're flirting with someone, you should make eye contact, smile, and keep looking at them:
    - ○ True
    - ○ False

19. When you're asking someone on a date, you should:
    - ○ Tell them you like them and ask if they'll go out with you
    - ○ Ask what they're doing on a certain day and time

20. If you ask someone on a date and they turn you down, it's okay to politely ask them for a reason:
    - O True
    - O False

21. At the end of a date, if you want to kiss goodnight, you should:
    - O Ask your date if you can kiss him or her
    - O Wait for a sign they want to be kissed

22. When you're on a first date it's a good idea to give general compliments:
    - O True
    - O False

23. When you FIRST start dating someone, you should:
    - O Tell them about your dating history
    - O Avoid talking about your dating history

24. If a date you like is pressuring you to get physical and you're not ready, you should:
    - O Date someone else
    - O Change the subject

25. The FIRST thing you should do when you get into an argument is:
    - O Listen and keep your cool
    - O Explain your side

26. When a friend accuses you of doing something you didn't do:
    - O Say you're sorry that this happened
    - O Explain your side until they believe you

27. If someone is teasing you and calling you names:
    - O Ignore them or walk away
    - O Give a teasing comeback

28. A good strategy for handling chronic bullying is:
    - O Try to make friends with the person so they won't bully you
    - O Don't try to make friends with the person

29. If someone spreads a rumor about you that isn't true, you should:
    - O Spread the rumor about yourself
    - O Confront the person that started the rumor

30. If someone is gossiping behind your back, you should:
    - O Let them know that the gossip hurts your feelings
    - O Act amazed that anyone would believe the gossip

Test of Young Adult Social Skills Knowledge
(TYASSK)

Scoring Key

SCORING:

Items highlighted gray reflect correct answers. One point should be given per correct answer. Scores range from 0–30. Higher scores reflect better knowledge of young adult social skills.

---

1. The most important part of having a conversation is to:
   - O Trade information
   - O Make sure the other person is laughing and smiling

2. When starting a conversation:
   - O Wait for the person to notice you
   - O Find a common interest

3. If your friend mispronounces a word, you should:
   - O Not police them
   - O Politely point out their mistake to be helpful

4. If you discover that you and a friend like the same thing:
   - O Be repetitive
   - O Don't be repetitive

5. It's ALWAYS a good idea to try to make friends with someone who:
   - O Has lots of friends and is popular
   - O Likes the same things as you

6. Friendship is a:
   - O Choice
   - O Gift

7. When you want to exchange contact information with someone:
   - O Go up and nicely ask them for their number
   - O Use a cover story

8. How many messages can you leave in row without hearing back from a person?
   - O 1–2
   - O 3–4

9. After you make a joke, it's a good idea to pay attention to:
    - ○ Whether the other person is laughing
    - ○ Your humor feedback

10. It is ALWAYS a good sign if someone laughs at your jokes:
    - ○ True
    - ○ False

11. When you're trying to meet a new group of people, it's a good idea to go up and say hello and introduce yourself:
    - ○ True
    - ○ False

12. When you're trying to enter a group conversation, the FIRST thing you should do is:
    - ○ Watch and listen to the conversation
    - ○ Make a comment about what they're saying

13. If you try to enter a group conversation and the people exclude you:
    - ○ Start to look away
    - ○ Make sure they can hear you

14. If you try to join ten different conversations, on average how many times out of ten are you likely to be rejected:
    - ○ 7 out of 10
    - ○ 5 out of 10

15. When having a friend over for a get-together at your home:
    - ○ Tell your friend what you're going to do
    - ○ Have your friend choose the activity

16. If you're having a friend over for a get-together and someone else unexpectedly texts that you really like:
    - ○ Ask your friend if you can invite them over
    - ○ Text them later

17. When you're interested in someone romantically, it's a good idea to:
    - ○ Talk to mutual friends
    - ○ Not tell people until you're sure they like you

18. When you're flirting with someone, you should make eye contact, smile, and keep looking at them:
    - ○ True
    - ○ False

19. When you're asking someone on a date, you should:
    - ○ Tell them you like them and ask if they'll go out with you
    - ○ Ask what they're doing on a certain day and time

20. If you ask someone on a date and they turn you down, it's okay to politely ask them for a reason:
    - ○ True
    - ○ False

21. At the end of a date, if you want to kiss goodnight, you should:
    - ○ Ask your date if you can kiss him or her
    - ○ Wait for a sign they want to be kissed

22. When you're on a first date it's a good idea to give general compliments:
    - ○ True
    - ○ False

23. When you FIRST start dating someone, you should:
    - ○ Tell them about your dating history
    - ○ Avoid talking about your dating history

24. If a date you like is pressuring you to get physical and you're not ready, you should:
    - ○ Date someone else
    - ○ Change the subject

25. The FIRST thing you should do when you get into an argument is:
    - ○ Listen and keep your cool
    - ○ Explain your side

26. When a friend accuses you of doing something you didn't do:
    - ○ Say you're sorry that this happened
    - ○ Explain your side until they believe you

27. If someone is teasing you and calling you names:
    - ○ Ignore them or walk away
    - ○ Give a teasing comeback

28. A good strategy for handling chronic bullying is:
    - ○ Try to make friends with the person so they won't bully you
    - ○ Don't try to make friends with the person

29. If someone spreads a rumor about you that isn't true, you should:
    - ○ Spread the rumor about yourself
    - ○ Confront the person that started the rumor

30. If someone is gossiping behind your back, you should:
    - ○ Let them know that the gossip hurts your feelings
    - ○ Act amazed that anyone would believe the gossip

Test of Young Adult Social Skills Knowledge
(TYASSK)

Administration

- The TYASSK is intended to provide an assessment of the social skills knowledge of young adults.
- The TYASSK can be completed by young adults individually or during a group administration.
- For young adults with significant language delay and/or reading impairment, it is recommended that the TYASSK be administered orally.
- The TYASSK may be used as a pre-test, post-test, and/or follow-up assessment of treatment outcome.

Item Content

- The TYASSK is a criterion-based measure.
- The 30-items that make up the TYASSK are derived from young adult session content.
- Two items are taken from each of the 15 didactic lessons.
- These items are considered to be central to the social skills lessons.

Skills	Items
Conversational skills	1–4
Sources of friends	5–6
Electronic communication	7–8
Humor	9–10
Peer entry	11–12
Peer exiting	13–14
Get-togethers	15–16
Dating etiquette	17–24
Conflict resolution	25–26
Peer rejection	27–30

QUALITY OF SOCIALIZATION QUESTIONNAIRE - YOUNG ADULT (QSQ-YA)

We are interested in the number of get-togethers you have had in the last month. A get-together is any time that young adults follow through with a commitment to spend time together.

- It may be a planned activity like going to the movies, playing videogames, or hanging out.
- It may be organized well in advance or spontaneously that same day.
- It may be with one other young adult or a group of young adults.

1. How many *get-togethers* did you organize in the last month? _____
2. How many *romantic dates* did you organize in the last month? _____

3. Please list the **first names** of all of the friends who came to your get-togethers **in the last month**. If you did not organize a get-together or a date with other young adults in the last month, leave the section below blank.

Friend's first name _____   Friend's first name _____
Friend's first name _____   Friend's first name _____
Friend's first name _____   Friend's first name _____

4. How did you and your friends get along at your LAST get-together?
Circle the number below that describes how true each sentence is.

	Not at all true	Just a little true	Pretty much true	Very much true
We didn't share games or personal items	0	1	2	3
We got along well	3	2	1	0
We got upset with each other	0	1	2	3
We had fun	3	2	1	0
We argued with each other	0	1	2	3
We enjoyed each other	3	2	1	0
We criticized or teased each other	0	1	2	3
We shared the conversation	3	2	1	0
We were bossy with each other	0	1	2	3
We needed someone else to solve problems	0	1	2	3
We didn't hang out with each other	0	1	2	3
We annoyed each other	0	1	2	3

5. How many *get-togethers* were you invited to in the last month? _____
6. How many *romantic dates* were you invited to in the last month? _____

7. Fill in the **first names** of your friends who invited you for a get-together **in the last month**. If you were not invited to a get-together or a date in the last month, leave the section below blank.

Friend's first name _____   Friend's first name _____
Friend's first name _____   Friend's first name _____
Friend's first name _____   Friend's first name _____

Quality of Socialization Questionnaire – Caregiver (QSQ-C)

We are interested in the number of get-togethers your young adult has had in the last month. A get-together is any time that young adults follow through with a commitment to spend time together.
- It may be a planned activity like going to the movies, playing videogames, or hanging out.
- It may be organized well in advance or spontaneously that same day.
- It may be with one other young adult or a group of young adults.

1. **How many *get-togethers* did your young adult organize in the last month?** _____
2. **How many *romantic dates* did your young adult organize in the last month?** _____

3. Please list the **first names** of all of the friends who came to your young adult's get-togethers **in the last month**. If he/she did not organize a get-together or a date with other young adults in the last month, leave the section below blank.

Friend's first name _____   Friend's first name _____
Friend's first name _____   Friend's first name _____
Friend's first name _____   Friend's first name _____

4. How did your young adult and his/her friends get along at their LAST get-together?
Circle the number below that describes how true each sentence is.

	Not at all true	Just a little true	Pretty much true	Very much true
They didn't share games or personal items	0	1	2	3
They got along well	3	2	1	0
They got upset with each other	0	1	2	3
They had fun	3	2	1	0
They argued with each other	0	1	2	3
They enjoyed each other	3	2	1	0
They criticized or teased each other	0	1	2	3
They shared the conversation	3	2	1	0
They were bossy with each other	0	1	2	3
They needed someone else to help solve problems	0	1	2	3
They didn't hang out with each other	0	1	2	3
They annoyed each other	0	1	2	3

5. **How many *get-togethers* was your young adult invited to in the last month?** _____
6. **How many *romantic dates* was your young adult invited to in the last month?** _____

7. Fill in the **first names** of the friends who invited your young adult for a get-together **in the last month**. If he/she was not invited to a get-together or a date in the last month, leave the section below blank.

Friend's first name _____   Friend's first name _____
Friend's first name _____   Friend's first name _____
Friend's first name _____   Friend's first name _____

Quality of Socialization Questionnaire (QSQ)
Administration and Scoring Key

QSQ-YA Administration:

- The QSQ-YA takes approximately 5 minutes to complete.
- Most young adults can complete this measure independently.
- It should be orally administered to young adults with reading or comprehension difficulties.
- The QSQ-YA should be administered at pre-test, post-test, and follow-up (optional).

QSQ-C Administration:

- The QSQ-C takes approximately 5 minutes to complete.
- It should be completed independently by the caregiver.
- The QSQ-C should be administered at pre-test, post-test, and follow-up (optional).

QSQ-YA and QSQ-C Scoring Key:

Social Initiation Scale:

1. The number of HOSTED get-togethers in the last month.
2. The number of HOSTED romantic dates in the last month.
3. The number of different friends that the young adult HOSTED during get-togethers and/or dates in the last month.

Conflict Scale:

4. Measures degree of conflict during the last get-together.
   - Calculate the total Conflict Scale Score by summing the scores from the items in the box.
   - Scores greater than 3.5 indicate significant conflict.

Social Reciprocity Scale:

5. The number of INVITED get-togethers in the last month.
6. The number of INVITED romantic dates in the last month.
7. The number of different friends who INVITED the young adult over for get-togethers and/or dates in the last month.

PLANNED ABSENCE SHEET

It is very important for social coaches and young adults to attend **EVERY SESSION** of *PEERS*®. However, if you know that you have to be absent for a session, please mark those dates that you know you will not be able to attend below.

Young Adult's Name: _____

Social Coach's Name: _____

SESSION	DATE	PLANNED ABSENCE
1	[insert date]	
2	[insert date]	
3	[insert date]	
4	[insert date]	
5	[insert date]	
6	[insert date]	
7	[insert date]	
8	[insert date]	
9	[insert date]	
10	[insert date]	
11	[insert date]	
12	[insert date]	
13	[insert date]	
14	[insert date]	
15	[insert date]	
16	[insert date]	Graduation

Advanced information about planned absences will be used to determine if a particular session needs to be rescheduled based on the anticipated number of absences.

Please return this sheet at the FIRST or SECOND group meeting of *PEERS*® if you have any planned absences.

PHONE ROSTER

This phone roster is to be used to complete the IN-GROUP CALLS OR VIDEO CHATS. Please use this table to keep track of the person you are assigned to call each week and note the day and time of the scheduled call.

Name	Phone Number	Week 1 Day/time	Week 2 Day/time	Week 3 Day/time	Week 4 Day/time	Week 5 Day/time	Week 6 Day/time

IN-GROUP CALL OR VIDEO CHAT ASSIGNMENT LOG

WEEK 1

Caller _____   Receiver _____
Caller _____   Receiver _____
Caller _____   Receiver _____
Caller _____   Receiver _____
Caller _____   Receiver _____
Caller _____   Receiver _____

WEEK 2

Caller _____   Receiver _____
Caller _____   Receiver _____
Caller _____   Receiver _____
Caller _____   Receiver _____
Caller _____   Receiver _____
Caller _____   Receiver _____

WEEK 3

Caller _____   Receiver _____
Caller _____   Receiver _____
Caller _____   Receiver _____
Caller _____   Receiver _____
Caller _____   Receiver _____
Caller _____   Receiver _____

WEEK 4

Caller _____   Receiver _____
Caller _____   Receiver _____
Caller _____   Receiver _____
Caller _____   Receiver _____
Caller _____   Receiver _____
Caller _____   Receiver _____

WEEK 5

Caller _____   Receiver _____
Caller _____   Receiver _____
Caller _____   Receiver _____
Caller _____   Receiver _____
Caller _____   Receiver _____
Caller _____   Receiver _____

WEEK 6

Caller _____   Receiver _____
Caller _____   Receiver _____
Caller _____   Receiver _____
Caller _____   Receiver _____
Caller _____   Receiver _____
Caller _____   Receiver _____

HOMEWORK COMPLIANCE SHEET

PEERS® Homework Compliance Sheet

Week	1	2	3	4	5	6	7	8	9	10	11	12	13	14	15	16
Date																

C = Completed   P = Partially Completed   I = Incomplete

Name	Personal Item	Practice w/ Coach	In-Group Call	Sources of Friends	Start & Maintain Convo	Humor Feedback	Enter & Exit Convo	Get-Togethers	Dating	Disagree ment	Bullying	Comments / Notes

SAMPLE GRADUATION FLYER

[Insert day of week and date]

Testing: [insert time of post-testing]
Graduation party: [insert time]

Please Note the Time Change

[Insert date] is the last meeting of PEERS. We will begin the evening by doing post-testing with social coaches and young adults. **Please plan to arrive 30 minutes earlier.**

We will wrap-up our 16th meeting with the social coaches, while the young adults attend their graduation party. At the end of the meeting, we will all assemble for a brief Graduation Ceremony.

We would appreciate it if everyone would kindly consider bringing a treat to the party as a potluck.

Patient confidentiality prohibits photography.

SAMPLE CERTIFICATE OF COMPLETION

PEERS®

Program for the Education and Enrichment of Relational Skills

Certificate of Completion

Presented to

Johnny Example

For the successful completion of PEERS®

Date including year

Group Leader Name and Signature

Group Leader Name and Signature

SOCIAL COACHING HOMEWORK ASSIGNMENT WORKSHEETS (WEEKS 1–15)

SOCIAL COACHING HOMEWORK ASSIGNMENT WORKSHEET: WEEK 1

Please fill out this worksheet *before* the next session and bring it with you to the group. Answer each question and write any additional comments in the space provided.

Young Adult's Name:

	Did you review the rules with your young adult before practicing the skill?	*Did your young adult complete the assignment?*	*Did you social coach and praise your young adult when they practiced the skill?*
In-group call or video chat: • *Before the call* o *Did your young adult set up a day and time to make the call?* • *During the call* o *Did your young adult trade information and find a common interest?* • *After the call* o *Did you ask your young adult what the common interest was?* o *Did you ask, "What could you do with that information if you were going to hang out?"*			
Starting a conversation & trading information with the social coach: • *Did you and your young adult find a common interest?* • *Did you ask, "What could we do with that information if we were going to hang out?"*			

SOCIAL COACHING HOMEWORK ASSIGNMENT WORKSHEET: WEEK 2

Please fill out this worksheet *before* the next session and bring it with you to the group. Answer each question and write any additional comments in the space provided.

Young Adult's Name:

	Did you review the rules with your young adult before practicing the skill?	*Did your young adult complete the assignment?*	*Did you social coach and praise your young adult when they practiced the skill?*

In-group call or video chat:
• *Before the call*
  o *Did your young adult set up a day and time to make the call?*
• *During the call*
  o *Did your young adult trade information and find a common interest?*
• *After the call*
  o *Did you ask your young adult what the common interest was?*
  o *Did you ask, "What could you do with that information if you were going to hang out?"*			

Starting and maintaining a conversation with the social coach: • *Did you and your young adult find a common interest?* • *Did you ask, "What could we do with that information if we were going to hang out?"*			

SOCIAL COACHING HOMEWORK ASSIGNMENT WORKSHEET: WEEK 3

Please fill out this worksheet *before* the next session and bring it with you to the group. Answer each question and write any additional comments in the space provided.

Young Adult's Name:

	Did you review the rules with your young adult before practicing the skill?	*Did your young adult complete the assignment?*	*Did you social coach and praise your young adult when they practiced the skill?*
Finding a source of friends: • *Did you and your young adult discuss and decide on social activities to enroll in?*			

In-group call or video chat:
 • *Before the call*
    o *Did your young adult set up a day and time to make the call?*
 • *During the call*
    o *Did your young adult trade information and find a common interest?*
 • *After the call*
    o *Did you ask your young adult what the common interest was?*
    o *Did you ask, "What could you do with that information if you were going to hang out?"*			

Starting and maintaining a conversation with the social coach: • *Did you and your young adult find a common interest?* • *Did you ask, "What could we do with that information if we were going to hang out?"*			
Did your young adult bring a personal item to trade information?			

SOCIAL COACHING HOMEWORK ASSIGNMENT WORKSHEET: WEEK 4

Please fill out this worksheet *before* the next session and bring it with you to the group. Answer each question and write any additional comments in the space provided.

Young Adult's Name:

	Did you review the rules with your young adult before practicing the skill?	*Did your young adult complete the assignment?*	*Did you social coach and praise your young adult when they practiced the skill?*
Finding a source of friends: • *Did you and your young adult discuss and decide on social activities to enroll in?*			
Starting a conversation & trading information with a peer: • *Did you ask the appropriate social coaching questions after your young adult had the conversation?*			

In-group call or video chat:
 • *Before the call*
     o *Did your young adult set up a day and time to make the call?*
 • *During the call*
     o *Did your young adult trade information and find a common interest?*
 • *After the call*
     o *Did you ask your young adult what the common interest was?*
     o *Did you ask, "What could you do with that information if you were going to hang out?"*			

Starting and ending phone calls & trading information with the social coach: • *Did you and your young adult find a common interest?* • *Did you ask, "What could we do with that information if we were going to hang out?"*			
Did your young adult bring a personal item to trade information?			

SOCIAL COACHING HOMEWORK ASSIGNMENT WORKSHEET: WEEK 5

Please fill out this worksheet *before* the next session and bring it with you to the group. Answer each question and write any additional comments in the space provided.

Young Adult's Name:

	Did you review the rules with your young adult before practicing the skill?	*Did your young adult complete the assignment?*	*Did you social coach and praise your young adult when they practiced the skill?*
Finding a source of friends: • *Did you and your young adult discuss and decide on social activities to enroll in?*			
Starting a conversation & trading information with a peer: • *Did you ask the appropriate social coaching questions after your young adult had the conversation?*			
Paying attention to humor feedback: • *Did you PRIVATELY ask the appropriate social coaching questions if your young adult happened to tell jokes?*			

In-group call or video chat:
• *Before the call*
  o *Did your young adult set up a day and time to make the call?*
• *During the call*
  o *Did your young adult trade information and find a common interest?*
• *After the call*
  o *Did you ask your young adult what the common interest was?*
  o *Did you ask, "What could you do with that information if you were going to hang out?"*			

Did your young adult bring a personal item to trade information?			

SOCIAL COACHING HOMEWORK ASSIGNMENT WORKSHEET: WEEK 6

Please fill out this worksheet *before* the next session and bring it with you to the group. Answer each question and write any additional comments in the space provided.

Young Adult's Name:

	Did you review the rules with your young adult before practicing the skill?	*Did your young adult complete the assignment?*	*Did you social coach and praise your young adult when they practiced the skill?*
Finding a source of friends: • *Did you and your young adult discuss and decide on social activities to enroll in?*			
Entering a group conversation with social coaches: • *Did your young adult practice entering a group conversation with you and another person?* • *Did you ask the appropriate social coaching questions after the practice?*			
Entering a group conversation with peers: • *Did your young adult enter a group conversation with peers?* • *Did you ask the appropriate social coaching questions afterwards?*			
Paying attention to humor feedback: • *Did you PRIVATELY ask the appropriate social coaching questions if your young adult happened to tell jokes?*			
Finding a source of friends: • *Did you and your young adult discuss and decide on social activities to enroll in?*			

(continued on p. 494)

	Did you review the rules with your young adult before practicing the skill?	Did your young adult complete the assignment?	Did you social coach and praise your young adult when they practiced the skill?

In-group call or video chat:
• *Before the call*
  o *Did your young adult set up a day and time to make the call?*
• *During the call*
  o *Did your young adult trade information and find a common interest?*
• *After the call*
  o *Did you ask your young adult what the common interest was?*
  o *Did you ask, "What could you do with that information if you were going to hang out?"*			

Did your young adult bring a personal item to trade information?			

SOCIAL COACHING HOMEWORK ASSIGNMENT WORKSHEET: WEEK 7

Please fill out this worksheet *before* the next session and bring it with you to the group. Answer each question and write any additional comments in the space provided.

Young Adult's Name:

	Did you review the rules with your young adult before practicing the skill?	*Did your young adult complete the assignment?*	*Did you social coach and praise your young adult when they practiced the skill?*

Entering and exiting a group conversation with social coaches:
 • *Did your young adult practice entering and exiting a group conversation with you and another person?*
 • *Did your young adult practice exiting when:*
     o *Never accepted*
     o *Initially accepted and then excluded*
     o *Fully accepted*
 • *Did you ask the appropriate social coaching questions after the practice?*			

Entering a group conversation with peers: • *Did your young adult enter a group conversation with peers?* • *Did you ask the appropriate social coaching questions afterwards?*			
Paying attention to humor feedback: • *Did you PRIVATELY ask the appropriate social coaching questions if your young adult happened to tell jokes?*			

SOCIAL COACHING HOMEWORK ASSIGNMENT WORKSHEET: WEEK 8

Please fill out this worksheet *before* the next session and bring it with you to the group. Answer each question and write any additional comments in the space provided.

Young Adult's Name:

	Did you review the rules with your young adult before practicing the skill?	*Did your young adult complete the assignment?*	*Did you social coach and praise your young adult when they practiced the skill?*
Having a get-together: • *Did you help your young adult plan the get-together using the five W's?* • *Did you ask the appropriate social coaching questions after the get-together?*			

Entering and exiting a group conversation with social coaches:
• *Did your young adult practice entering and exiting a group conversation with you and another person?*
• *Did your young adult practice exiting when:*
  o *Never accepted*
  o *Initially accepted and then excluded*
  o *Fully accepted*
• *Did you ask the appropriate social coaching questions after the practice?*			

Entering a group conversation with peers: • *Did your young adult enter a group conversation with peers?* • *Did you ask the appropriate social coaching questions afterwards?*			
Paying attention to humor feedback: • *Did you PRIVATELY ask the appropriate social coaching questions if your young adult happened to tell jokes?*			

SOCIAL COACHING HOMEWORK ASSIGNMENT WORKSHEET: WEEK 9

Please fill out this worksheet *before* the next session and bring it with you to the group. Answer each question and write any additional comments in the space provided.

Young Adult's Name:

	Did you review the rules with your young adult before practicing the skill?	*Did your young adult complete the assignment?*	*Did you social coach and praise your young adult when they practiced the skill?*
Having a get-together: • *Did you help your young adult plan the get-together using the five W's?* • *Did you ask the appropriate social coaching questions after the get-together?*			
Letting someone know you like them: • *Did your young adult identify someone they were interested in romantically?* • *Did you practice some of the strategies for letting someone know you like them?* • *Did your young adult let someone know they like them?* • *Did you ask the appropriate social coaching questions after each practice?*			

Entering and exiting a group conversation with social coaches:
• *Did your young adult practice entering and exiting a group conversation with you and another person?*
• *Did your young adult practice exiting when:*
   o *Never accepted*
   o *Initially accepted and then excluded*
   o *Fully accepted*
• *Did you ask the appropriate social coaching questions after the practice?*			

SOCIAL COACHING HOMEWORK ASSIGNMENT WORKSHEET: WEEK 10

Please fill out this worksheet *before* the next session and bring it with you to the group. Answer each question and write any additional comments in the space provided.

Young Adult's Name:

	Did you review the rules with your young adult before practicing the skill?	*Did your young adult complete the assignment?*	*Did you social coach and praise your young adult when they practiced the skill?*
Having a get-together: • *Did you help your young adult plan the get-together using the five W's?* • *Did you ask the appropriate social coaching questions after the get-together?*			
Letting someone know you like them: • *Did your young adult identify someone they were interested in romantically?* • *Did you practice some of the strategies for letting someone know you like them?* • *Did your young adult let someone know they like them?* • *Did you ask the appropriate social coaching questions after each practice?*			
Entering a group conversation with peers: • *Did your young adult enter a group conversation with peers?* • *Did you ask the appropriate social coaching questions afterwards?*			

SOCIAL COACHING HOMEWORK ASSIGNMENT WORKSHEET: WEEK 11

Please fill out this worksheet *before* the next session and bring it with you to the group. Answer each question and write any additional comments in the space provided.

Young Adult's Name:

	Did you review the rules with your young adult before practicing the skill?	*Did your young adult complete the assignment?*	*Did you social coach and praise your young adult when they practiced the skill?*
Having a get-together: • *Did you help your young adult plan the get-together using the five W's?* • *Did you ask the appropriate social coaching questions after the get-together?*			
Letting someone know you like them and asking them on a date: • *Did your young adult identify someone they were interested in romantically?* • *Did you practice some of the strategies for letting someone know you like them and asking them on a date?* • *Did your young adult let someone know they like them and did they ask them on a date?* • *Did you ask the appropriate social coaching questions after each practice?*			
Entering a group conversation with peers: • *Did your young adult enter a group conversation with peers?* • *Did you ask the appropriate social coaching questions afterwards?*			

SOCIAL COACHING HOMEWORK ASSIGNMENT WORKSHEET: WEEK 12

Please fill out this worksheet *before* the next session and bring it with you to the group. Answer each question and write any additional comments in the space provided.

Young Adult's Name:

	Did you review the rules with your young adult before practicing the skill?	*Did your young adult complete the assignment?*	*Did you social coach and praise your young adult when they practiced the skill?*
Having a get-together: • *Did you help your young adult plan the get-together using the five W's?* • *Did you ask the appropriate social coaching questions after the get-together?*			
Letting someone know you like them and asking them on a date: • *Did your young adult identify someone they were interested in romantically?* • *Did you practice some of the strategies for letting someone know you like them and asking them on a date?* • *Did your young adult let someone know they like them and did they ask them on a date?* • *Did you ask the appropriate social coaching questions after each practice?*			
Entering a group conversation with peers: • *Did your young adult enter a group conversation with peers?* • *Did you ask the appropriate social coaching questions afterwards?*			

SOCIAL COACHING HOMEWORK ASSIGNMENT WORKSHEET: WEEK 13

Please fill out this worksheet *before* the next session and bring it with you to the group.
Answer each question and write any additional comments in the space provided.

Young Adult's Name:

	Did you review the rules with your young adult before practicing the skill?	*Did your young adult complete the assignment?*	*Did you social coach and praise your young adult when they practiced the skill?*
Having a get-together: • *Did you help your young adult plan the get-together using the five W's?* • *Did you ask the appropriate social coaching questions after the get-together?*			
Handling a disagreement with the social coach: • *Did you practice the steps for responding to disagreements with your young adult?* • *Did you practice the steps for bringing up disagreements with your young adult?* • *Did you ask the appropriate social coaching questions after each practice?*			
Handing a disagreement with a friend or romantic partner: • *Did your young adult practice handling a disagreement with a friend or romantic partner?* • *If so, did you review the steps and ask the appropriate social coaching questions afterwards?*			
Letting someone know you like them and asking them on a date: • *Did your young adult identify someone they were interested in romantically?* • *Did you practice some of the strategies for letting someone know you like them and asking them on a date?* • *Did your young adult let someone know they like them and did they ask them on a date?* • *Did you ask the appropriate social coaching questions after each practice?*			

SOCIAL COACHING HOMEWORK ASSIGNMENT WORKSHEET: WEEK 14

Please fill out this worksheet *before* the next session and bring it with you to the group. Answer each question and write any additional comments in the space provided.

Young Adult's Name:

	Did you review the rules with your young adult before practicing the skill?	*Did your young adult complete the assignment?*	*Did you social coach and praise your young adult when they practiced the skill?*
Having a get-together: • *Did you help your young adult plan the get-together using the five W's?* • *Did you ask the appropriate social coaching questions after the get-together?*			
Handling teasing with the social coach: • *Did you practice the strategies for handing teasing with your young adult?* • *Did your young adult choose three verbal comebacks BEFORE practicing?* • *Did you use benign teasing comments?* • *Did you ask the appropriate social coaching questions after practicing?*			
Handling direct bullying with peers: • *Did your young adult practice handling direct bullying with a peer?* • *If so, did you ask the appropriate social coaching questions after practicing?*			
Handling a disagreement with the social coach: • *Did you practice the steps for responding to disagreements with your young adult?* • *Did you practice the steps for bringing up disagreements with your young adult?* • *Did you ask the appropriate social coaching questions after each practice?*			

SOCIAL COACHING HOMEWORK ASSIGNMENT WORKSHEET: WEEK 14 (Cont.)

	Did you review the rules with your young adult before practicing the skill?	*Did your young adult complete the assignment?*	*Did you social coach and praise your young adult when they practiced the skill?*
Handing a disagreement with a friend or romantic partner: • *Did your young adult practice handling a disagreement with a friend or romantic partner?* • *If so, did you review the steps and ask the appropriate social coaching questions afterwards?*			
Letting someone know you like them and asking them on a date: • *Did your young adult identify someone they were interested in romantically?* • *Did you practice some of the strategies for letting someone know you like them and asking them on a date?* • *Did your young adult let someone know they like them and did they ask them on a date?* • *Did you ask the appropriate social coaching questions after each practice?*			

SOCIAL COACHING HOMEWORK ASSIGNMENT WORKSHEET: WEEK 15

Please fill out this worksheet *before* the next session and bring it with you to the group. Answer each question and write any additional comments in the space provided.

Young Adult's Name:

	Did you review the rules with your young adult before practicing the skill?	Did your young adult complete the assignment?	Did you social coach and praise your young adult when they practiced the skill?
Having a get-together: • Did you help your young adult plan the get-together using the five W's? • Did you ask the appropriate social coaching questions after the get-together?			
Spreading the rumor about yourself with the social coach: • Did you practice the strategies for spreading the rumor about yourself with your young adult? • Did you provide an example of a rumor for the young adult to practice with? • Did you ask the appropriate social coaching questions after practicing?			
Handling teasing with the social coach: • Did you practice the strategies for handing teasing with your young adult? • Did your young adult choose three verbal comebacks BEFORE practicing? • Did you use benign teasing comments? • Did you ask the appropriate social coaching questions after practicing?			
Handling direct or indirect bullying with peers: • Did your young adult practice handling direct or indirect bullying with a peer? • If so, did you ask the appropriate social coaching questions after practicing?			

SOCIAL COACHING HOMEWORK ASSIGNMENT WORKSHEET: WEEK 15 (Cont.)

	Did you review the rules with your young adult before practicing the skill?	*Did your young adult complete the assignment?*	*Did you social coach and praise your young adult when they practiced the skill?*
Handing a disagreement with a friend or romantic partner: • *Did your young adult practice handling a disagreement with a friend or romantic partner?* • *If so, did you review the steps and ask the appropriate social coaching questions afterwards?*			
Letting someone know you like them and asking them on a date: • *Did your young adult identify someone they were interested in romantically?* • *Did you practice some of the strategies for letting someone know you like them and asking them on a date?* • *Did your young adult let someone know they like them and did they ask them on a date?* • *Did you ask the appropriate social coaching questions after each practice?*			

REFERENCES

Adolphs, R., Sears, L., & Piven, J. (2001). Abnormal processing of social information from faces in autism. *Journal of Cognitive Neuroscience, 13*(2), 232–240.

Allen, K. D., Wallace, D. P., Renes, D., Bowen, S. L., & Burke, R. V. (2010). Use of video modeling to teach vocational skills to adolescents and young adults with autism spectrum disorders. *Education and Treatment of Children, 33*(3), 339–349.

Altman, I., & Taylor, D. (1973). *Social penetration: The development of interpersonal relationships.* New York: Holt, Rinehart & Winston.

Anckarsäter, H., Stahlberg, O., Larson, T., Hakansson, C., Jutblad, S. B., Niklasson, L., & Rastam, M. (2006). The impact of ADHD and autism spectrum disorders on temperament, character, and personality development. *American Journal of Psychiatry, 163,* 1239–1244.

Attwood, T. (2000). Strategies for improving the social integration of children with Asperger syndrome. *Autism, 4,* 85–100.

Attwood, T. (2003). Frameworks for behavioral interventions. *Child and Adolescent Psychiatric Clinics of North America, 12,* 65–86.

Azmitia, M. (2002). Self, self-esteem, conflicts, and best friendships in early adolescence. In T. M. Brinthaupt (Ed.), *Understanding early adolescent self and identity: Applications and interventions* (pp. 167–192). Albany, NY: State University of New York Press.

Barnhill, G. P. (2007). Outcomes in adults with Asperger syndrome. *Focus on Autism and Other Developmental Disabilities, 22,* 116–126.

Barnhill, G. P., Cook, K. T., Tebbenkanmp, K., & Myles, B. S. (2002). The effectiveness of social skills intervention targeting nonverbal communication for adolescents with Asperger syndrome and related pervasive developmental delays. *Focus on Autism and Other Developmental Disabilities, 17,* 112–118.

Baron-Cohen, S. (1988). Social and pragmatic deficits in autism: Cognitive or affective? *Journal of Autism and Developmental Disorders, 18*(3), 379–402.

Baron-Cohen, S. (1995). *Mindblindness: An Essay on Autism and Theory of Mind.* Cambridge, MA: MIT Press.

Baron-Cohen, S., Leslie, A., & Frith, U. (1985). Does the autistic child have a "theory of mind"? *Cognition, 21,* 37–46.

Baron-Cohen, S., & Wheelwright, S. (2004). The empathy quotient: An investigation of adults with Asperger syndrome or high functioning autism, and normal sex differences. *Journal of Autism and Developmental Disorders, 34*(2), 163–175.

Barry, T. D., Klinger, L. G., Lee, J. M., Palardy, N., Gilmore, T., & Bodin, S. D. (2003). Examining the effectiveness of an outpatient clinic-based social skills group for high-functioning children with autism. *Journal of Autism and Developmental Disorders, 33,* 685–701.

Baumeister, R. F., Zhang, L., & Vohs, K. D. (2004). Gossip as cultural learning. *Review of General Psychology, 8,* 111–121.

Bauminger, N., & Kasari, C. (2000). Loneliness and friendship in high-functioning children with autism. *Child Development, 71,* 447–456.

Bauminger, N., Shulman, C., & Agam, G. (2003). Peer interaction and loneliness in high-functioning children with autism. *Journal of Autism and Developmental Disorders, 33,* 489–507.

Bauminger, N., Solomon, M., Aciezer, A., Heung, K., Gazit, L., Brown, J., & Rogers, S. J. (2008). Children with autism and their friends: A multidimensional study in high functioning autism spectrum disorders. *Journal of Abnormal Child Psychology, 36,* 135–150.

Baxter, A. (1997). The power of friendship. *Journal on Developmental Disabilities, 5*(2), 112–117.

Beauchamp, M. H., & Anderson, V. (2010). SOCIAL: An integrative framework for the development of social skills. *Psychological Bulletin, 136*(1), 39.

Beaumont, R., & Sofronoff, K. (2008). A multi-component social skills intervention for children with Asperger syndrome: The Junior Detective Training Program. *Journal of Child Psychology and Psychiatry, 49,* 743–753.

Bellini, S. (2004). Social skill deficits and anxiety in high-functioning adolescents with autism spectrum disorders. *Focus on Autism and Other Developmental Disabilities, 19*(2), 78–86.

Bellini, S., & Akullian, J. (2007). A meta-analysis of video modeling and video self-modeling interventions for children and adolescents with autism spectrum disorders. *Exceptional Children, 73*(3), 264–287.

Bellini, S., Peters, J. K., Benner, L., & Hopf, A. (2007). A meta-analysis of school-based social skills interventions for children with autism spectrum disorders. *Remedial and Special Education, 28*(3), 153–162.

Berndt, T. J., Hawkins, J. A., & Jiao, Z. (1999). Influences of friends and friendships on adjustment to junior high school. *Merrill-Palmer Quarterly, 45*, 13–41.

Bock, M. A. (2007). The impact of social-behavioral learning strategy training on the social interaction skills of four students with Asperger syndrome. *Focus on Autism and Other Developmental Disabilities, 22*, 88–95.

Bordia, P., DiFonzo, N., Haines, R., & Chaseling, E. (2005). Rumors denials as persuasive messages: Effects of personal relevance, source, and message characteristics. *Journal of Applied Social Psychology, 35*, 1301–1331.

Boulton, M. J., & Underwood, K. (1992). Bully/victim problems among middle school children. *British Journal of Educational Psychology, 62*, 73–87.

Bowler, D. M., Gaigg, S. B., & Gardiner, J. M. (2008). Subjective organization in the free recall learning of adults with Asperger's syndrome. *Journal of Autism and Developmental Disorders, 38*, 104–113.

Brown, B. B., & Lohr, M. J. (1987). Peer-group affiliation and adolescent self-esteem: An integration of ego-identity and symbolic-interaction theories. *Journal of Personality and Social Psychology, 52*, 47–55.

Buhrmester, D. (1990). Intimacy of friendship, interpersonal competence, and adjustment during preadolescence and adolescence. *Child Development, 61*, 1101–1111.

Buhrmester, D., & Furman, W. (1987). The development of companionship and intimacy. *Child Development, 58*, 1101–1113.

Bukowski, W. M., Hoza, B., & Boivin, M. (1993). Popularity, friendship, and emotional adjustment during early adolescence. In B. Laursen (Ed.), *Close friendships in adolescence* (pp. 23–37). San Francisco, CA: Jossey-Bass.

Bukowski, W. M., Hoza B., & Boivin, M. (1994). Measuring friendship quality during pre- and early adolescence: The development and psychometric properties of the Friendship Qualities Scale. *Journal of Social and Personal Relationships, 11*(3), 471–484.

Burack, J. A., Root, R., & Zigler, E. (1997). Inclusive education for students with autism: Reviewing ideological, empirical, and community considerations. In D. J. Cohen & F. Volkmar (Eds.), *Handbook of autism and pervasive developmental disorders* (pp. 796–807) New York: Wiley.

Capps, L., Sigman, M., & Yirmija, N. (1996). Self-competence and emotional understanding in high-functioning children with autism. *Annual Progress in Child Psychiatry and Child Development*, 260–279.

Carter, A. S., Davis, N. O., Klin, A., & Volkmar, F. R. (2005). Social development in autism. In F. R. Volkmar, R. Paul, A. Klin, & D. Cohen (Eds.), *Handbook of autism and pervasive developmental disorders* (pp. 312–334). Hoboken, NJ: John Wiley & Sons.

Castorina, L. L., & Negri, L. M. (2011). The inclusion of siblings in social skills training groups for boys with Asperger syndrome. *Journal of Autism and Developmental Disorders, 41*, 73–81.

Cederlund, M., Hagberg, B., & Gillberg, C. (2010). Asperger syndrome in adolescent and young adult males. Interview, self- and parent assessment of social, emotional, and cognitive problems. *Research in Developmental Disabilities, 31*, 287–298.

Chang, Y. C., Laugeson, E. A., Gantman, A., Dillon, A. R., Ellingsen, R., & Frankel, F. (2013). Predicting treatment success in social skills training for adolescents with Autism Spectrum Disorders: The UCLA Program for the Education and Enrichment of Relational Skills. *Autism: The International Journal of Research and Practice.* DOI: 1362361313478995.

Charlop-Christy, M. H., & Daneshvar, S. (2003). Using video modeling to teach perspective taking to children with autism. *Journal of Positive Behavior Interventions, 5*(1), 12–21.

Charlop-Christy, M. H., Le, L., & Freeman, K. A. (2000). A comparison of video modeling with in vivo modeling for teaching children with autism. *Journal of Autism and Developmental Disorders, 30*(6), 537–552.

Chevallier, C., Kohls, G., Troiani, V., Brodkin, E. S., & Schultz, R. T. (2012). The social motivation theory of autism. *Trends in Cognitive Sciences, 16*(4), 231–239.

Chung, K. M., Reavis, S., Mosconi, M., Drewry, J., Matthews, T., & Tassé, M. J. (2007). Peer-mediated social skills training program for young children with high-functioning autism. *Research in Developmental Disabilities, 28*(4), 423–436.

Church, C., Alisanski, S., & Amanullah, S. (2000). The social, behavioral, and academic experiences of children with Asperger syndrome. *Focus on Autism and Other Developmental Disabilities, 15*, 12–20.

Coie, J. D., Dodge, K. A., & Kupersmidt, J. B. (1990). Peer group behavior and social status. In S. R. Asher & J. D. Coie (Eds.), *Peer rejection in childhood* (pp. 17–59). New York: Cambridge University Press.

Coie, J. D., & Kupersmidt, J. B. (1983). A behavioral analysis of emerging social status. *Child Development, 54*, 1400–1416.

Coie, J., Terry, R., Lenox, K., Lochman, J., & Hyman, C. (1995). Childhood peer rejection and aggression as predictors of stable patterns of adolescent disorder. *Development and Psychopathology, 7*, 697–713.

Collins, W. A., & Madsen, S. D. (2006). Personal relationships in adolescence and early adulthood. In A. L. Vangelisti & D. Perlman (Eds.), *The Cambridge handbook of personal relationships* (pp. 191–209). New York: Cambridge University Press.

Constantino, J. N. (2012). *Social Responsiveness Scale.* Los Angeles, CA: Western Psychological Services.

Constantino, J. N., & Todd, R. D. (2005). Intergenerational transmission of subthreshold autistic traits in the general population. *Biological Psychiatry, 57*, 655–660.

Crick, N. R., & Grotpeter, J. K. (1996). Children's treatment by peers: Victims of relational and overt aggression. *Development and Psychopathology, 8*, 367–380.

Crick, N. R., & Ladd, G. W. (1990). Children's perceptions of the outcomes of social strategies: Do the ends justify being mean? *Developmental Psychology, 26*, 612–620.

Croen, L. A., Grether, J. K., Hoogstrate, J., & Selvin, S. (2002). The changing prevalence of autism in California. *Journal of Autism and Developmental Disorders, 32*, 207–215.

DeRosier, M. E., & Marcus, S. R. (2005). Building friendships and combating bullying: Effectiveness of S.S.GRIN at one-year follow-up. *Journal of Clinical Child and Adolescent Psychology, 24*, 140–150.

DiSalvo, C. A., & Oswald, D. P. (2002). Peer-mediated interventions to increase the social interaction of children with autism consideration of peer expectancies. *Focus on Autism and Other Developmental Disabilities, 17*(4), 198–207.

DiTommaso, E., & Spinner, B. (1993). The development and initial validation of the Social and Emotional Loneliness Scale for Adults (SELSA). *Personality and Individual Differences, 14*(1), 127–134.

Dodge, K. A., Schlundt, D. C., Schocken, I., & Delugach, J. D. (1983). Social competence and children's sociometric status: The role of peer group entry strategies. *Merrill-Palmer Quarterly, 29*, 309–336.

Eaves, L. C., & Ho, H. H. (2008). Young adult outcome of autism spectrum disorders. *Journal of Autism and Developmental Disorders, 38*(4), 739–747.

Elder, L. M., Caterino, L. C., Chao, J., Shacknai, D., & De Simone, G. (2006). The efficacy of social skills treatment for children with Asperger syndrome. *Education & Treatment of Children, 29*, 635–663.

Emerich, D. M., Creaghead, N. A., Grether, S. M., Murray, D., & Grasha, C. (2003). The comprehension of humorous materials by adolescents with high-functioning autism and Asperger's Syndrome. *Journal of Autism and Developmental Disorders, 33*, 253–257.

Fraley, R., & Davis, K. E. (1997). Attachment formation and transfer in young adults' close friendships and romantic relationships. *Personal Relationships, 4*, 131–144.

Frankel, F. (1996). *Good Friends are Hard to Find: Help Your Child Find, Make, and Keep Friends.* Los Angeles, CA: Perspective Publishing.

Frankel, F., & Myatt, R. (2003). *Children's Friendship Training.* New York: Brunner-Routledge.

Frankel, F., Myatt, R., Whitham, C., Gorospe, C., & Laugeson, E. A. (2010). A controlled study of parent-assisted Children's Friendship Training with children having Autism Spectrum Disorders. *Journal of Autism and Developmental Disorders, 40*, 827–842.

Frith, U. (2004). Emanuel Miller lecture: Confusions and controversies about Asperger syndrome. *Journal of Child Psychology and Psychiatry, 45*, 672–686.

Gantman, A., Kapp, S. K., Orenski, K, & Laugeson, E. A. (2012). Social skills training for young adults with high-functioning autism spectrum disorders: A randomized controlled pilot study. *Journal of Autism and Developmental Disorders, 42*(6), 1094–1103.

Gauze, C., Bukowski, W. M., Aquan-Assee, J., & Sippola, L. K. (1996). Interactions between family environment and friendship and associations with self-perceived well-being during early adolescence. *Child Development, 67*, 2201–2216.

George, T. P., & Hartmann, D. P. (1996). Friendship networks of unpopular, average, and popular children. *Child Development, 67*, 2301–2316.

Gerhardt, P. F., & Lainer, I. (2011). Addressing the needs of adolescents and adults with autism: A crisis on the horizon. *Journal of Contemporary Psychotherapy, 41*, 37–45.

Gillott, A., & Standen, P. J. (2007). Levels of anxiety and sources of stress in adults with autism. *Journal of Intellectual Disabilities, 11*(4), 359–370.

Golan, O., & Baron-Cohen, S. (2006). Systemizing empathy: Teaching adults with Asperger syndrome or high-functioning autism to recognize complex emotions using interactive multimedia. *Development and Psychopathology, 18*(2), 591–617.

Goldstein, A. P., & McGinnis, E. (2000). *Skill Streaming the Adolescent: New Strategies and Perspectives for Teaching Prosocial Skills.* Champaign, IL: Research Press.

Gonzalez-Lopez, A., & Kamps, D. M. (1997). Social skills training to increase social interactions between children with autism and their typical peers. *Focus on Autism and Other Developmental Disabilities, 12*(1), 2–14.

Gougeon, N. A. (2010). Sexuality and autism: A critical review of selected literature using a social-relational model of disability. *American Journal of Sexuality Education, 5*(4), 328–361.

Gralinski, J. H., & Kopp, C. (1993). Everyday rules for behavior: Mother's requests to young children. *Developmental Psychology, 29*, 573–584.

Gresham, F., & Elliott, S. N. (2008). *Social Skills Improvement System (SSIS) Rating Scales.* San Antonio, TX: Pearson Education.

Gresham, F. M., Sugai, G., & Horner, R. H. (2001). Interpreting outcomes of social skills training for students with high-incidence disabilities. *Exceptional Children, 67*, 331–345.

Griffin, H. C., Griffin, L. W., Fitch, C. W., Albera, V., & Gingras, H. G. (2006). Educational interventions for individuals with Asperger Syndrome. *Intervention in School and Clinic, 41*, 150–155.

Harper, C. B., Symon, J. B., & Frea, W. D. (2008). Recess is time-in: Using peers to improve social skills of children with autism. *Journal of Autism and Developmental Disorders, 38*(5), 815–826.

Hartup, W. W. (1993). Adolescents and their friends. In B. Laursen (Ed.), *Close friendships in adolescence.* San Francisco, CA: Jossey-Bass. (pp. 3–22).

Hauck, M., Fein, D., Waterhouse, L., & Feinstein, C. (1995). Social initiations by autistic children to adults and other children. *Journal of Autism and Developmental Disorders, 25*(6), 579–595.

Head, A. M., McGillivray, J. A., & Stokes, M. A. (2014). Gender differences in emotionality and sociability in children with autism spectrum disorders. *Molecular Autism, 5*(1), 1.

Hendricks, D. (2010). Employment and adults with autism spectrum disorders: Challenges and strategies for success. *Journal of Vocational Rehabilitation, 32*(2), 125–134.

Hendricks, D. R., & Wehman, P. (2009). Transition from school to adulthood for youth with autism spectrum disorders: Review and recommendations. *Focus on Autism and Other Developmental Disabilities.*

Hill, E. L. (2004). Executive dysfunction in autism. *Trends in Cognitive Sciences, 8*, 26–32.

Hillier, A., Fish, T., Coppert, P., & Beversdorf, D. Q. (2007). Outcomes of a social and vocational skills support group for adolescents and young adults on the autism spectrum. *Focus on Autism and Other Developmental Disabilities, 22*, 107–115.

Hillier, A. J., Fish, T., Siegel, J. H., & Beversdorf, D. Q. (2011). Social and vocational skills training reduces self-reported anxiety and depression among young adults on the autism spectrum. *Journal of Developmental and Physical Disabilities, 23*(3), 267–276.

Hodgdon, L. Q. (1995). Solving social-behavioral problems through the use of visually supported communication. In K. A. Quill (Ed.), *Teaching children with autism: Strategies to enhance communication and socialization* (pp. 265–286). New York: Delmar.

Hodges, E., Boivin, M., Vitaro, F., & Bukowski, W. M. (1999). The power of friendship: Protection against an escalating cycle of peer victimization. *Developmental Psychology, 35*, 94–101.

Hodges, E., Malone, M. J., & Perry, D. G. (1997). Individual risk and social risk as interacting determinants of victimization in the peer group. *Developmental Psychology, 33*, 1032–1039.

Hodges, E. V. E., & Perry, D. G. (1999). Personal and interpersonal antecedents and consequences of victimization by peers. *Journal of Personality & Social Psychology, 76*, 677–685.

Hollingshead, A. B. (1975). *Four factor index of social status.* (Available from P.O. Box 1965, Yale Station, New Haven, CT 06520, USA.)

Howlin, P. (2000). Outcome in adult life for more able individuals with autism or Asperger syndrome. *Autism, 4*(1), 63–83.

Howlin, P., Alcock, J., & Burkin, C. (2005). An 8 year follow-up of a specialist supported employment service for high-ability adults with autism or Asperger syndrome. *Autism, 9*(5), 533–549.

Howlin, P., & Goode, S. (1998). Outcome in adult life for people with autism, Asperger syndrome. In F. R. Volkmar (Ed.), *Autism and pervasive developmental disorders* (pp. 209–241). New York: Cambridge University Press.

Howlin, P., Mawhood, L., & Rutter, M. (2000). Autism and developmental receptive language disorder: A follow-up comparison in early adult life. II: Social, behavioural, and psychiatric outcomes. *Journal of Child Psychology and Psychiatry, 41*(5), 561–578.

Howlin, P., & Yates, P. (1999). The potential effectiveness of social skills groups for adults with autism. *Autism, 3*(3), 299–307.

Hume, K., Loftin, R., & Lantz, J. (2009). Increasing independence in autism spectrum disorders: A review of three focused interventions. *Journal of Autism and Developmental Disorders, 39*, 1329–1338.

Humphrey, N., & Symes, W. (2010). Perceptions of social support and experience of bullying among pupils with autistic spectrum disorders in mainstream secondary schools. *European Journal of Special Needs Education, 25*, 77–91.

Hurlbutt, K., & Chalmers, L. (2002). Adults with autism speak out perceptions of their life experiences. *Focus on Autism and Other Developmental Disabilities, 17*(2), 103–111.

Jobe, L. E., & White, S. W. (2007). Loneliness, social relationships, and a broader autism phenotype in college students. *Personality and Individual Differences, 42*(8), 1479–1489.

Johnson, S. A., Blaha, L. M., Houpt, J. W., & Townsend, J. T. (2010). Systems factorial technology provides new insights on global-local information processing in autism spectrum disorders. *Journal of Mathematical Psychology, 54,* 53–72.

Kandalaft, M. R., Didehbani, N., Krawczyk, D. C., Allen, T. T., & Chapman, S. B. (2013). Virtual reality social cognition training for young adults with high-functioning autism. *Journal of Autism and Developmental Disorders, 43*(1), 34–44.

Kapp, S. K., Gantman, A., & Laugeson, E. A. (2011). Transition to adulthood for high-functioning individuals with autism spectrum disorders. In M. R. Mohammadi (Series Ed.), *A comprehensive book on autism spectrum disorders.*

Kasari, C., & Locke, J. (2011). Social skills interventions for children with autism spectrum disorders. In D. G. Amaral, G. Dawson and D. H. Geschwind (Eds.), *Autism Spectrum Disorders* (pp. 1156–1166). New York: Oxford University Press.

Kasari, C., Rotheram-Fuller, E., Locke, J., & Gulsrud, A. (2012). Making the connection: Randomized controlled trial of social skills at school for children with autism spectrum disorders. *Journal of Child Psychology and Psychiatry, 53*(4), 431–439.

Kerbel, D., & Grunwell, P. (1998). A study of idiom comprehension in children with semantic-pragmatic difficulties. Part I: Task effects on the assessment of idiom comprehension in children. *International Journal of Language and Communication Disorders, 33,* 1–22.

Klin, A. (2011). From Asperger to modern day. In D. G. Amaral, G. Dawson and D. H. Geschwind (Eds.), *Autism Spectrum Disorders* (pp. 44–59). New York: Oxford University Press.

Klin, A., Jones, W., Schultz, R., & Volkmar, F. (2003). The enactive mind, or from actions to cognition: Lessons from autism. *Philosophical Transactions of the Royal Society of London B: Biological Sciences, 358*(1430), 345–360.

Klin, A., & Volkmar, F. R. (2003). Asperger syndrome: Diagnosis and external validity. *Child and Adolescent Psychiatric Clinics of North America, 12,* 1–13.

Klin, A., Volkmar, F. R., & Sparrow, S. S. (2000). *Asperger Syndrome.* New York: Guilford.

Kobayashi, R., & Murata, T. (1998). Behavioral characteristics of 187 young adults with autism. *Psychiatry and clinical neurosciences, 52*(4), 383–390.

Koegel, L. K., Koegel, R. L., Hurley, C., & Frea, W. D. (1992). Improving social skills and disruptive behavior in children with autism through self-management. *Journal of Applied Behavior Analysis, 25,* 341–353.

Koning, C., & Magill-Evans, J. (2001). Social and language skills in adolescent boys with Asperger syndrome. *Autism, 5,* 23–36.

Krasny L., Williams B. J., Provencal S., & Ozonoff, S. (2003). Social skills interventions for the autism spectrum: Essential ingredients and a model curriculum. *Child and Adolescent Psychiatric Clinics of North America, 12*(1), 107–122.

Landa, R., Klin, A., Volkmar, F., & Sparrow, S. (2000). Social language use in Asperger syndrome and high-functioning autism. *Asperger Syndrome,* 125–155.

Larson, R., & Richards, M. H. (1991). Daily companionship in late childhood and early adolescence: Changing developmental contexts. *Child Development, 62,* 284–300.

Lasgaard, M., Nielsen, A., Eriksen, M. E., & Goossens, L. (2009). Loneliness and social support in adolescent boys with autism spectrum disorders. *Journal of Autism and Developmental Disorders, 40,* 218–226.

Laugeson, E. A., Ellingsen, R., Sanderson, J., Tucci, L., & Bates, S. (2014). The ABC's of teaching social skills to adolescents with autism spectrum disorders in the classroom: The UCLA PEERS program. *Journal of Autism and Developmental Disorders.* DOI: 10.1007/s10803–014–2108–8.

Laugeson, E. A., & Frankel, F. (2010). *Social Skills for Teenagers with Developmental and Autism Spectrum Disorders: The PEERS Treatment Manual.* New York: Routledge.

Laugeson, E. A., Frankel, F., Gantman, A., Dillon, A. R., & Mogil, C. (2012). Evidence-based social skills training for adolescents with autism spectrum disorders: The UCLA PEERS program. *Journal of Autism and Developmental Disorders, 42*(6), 1025–1036.

Laugeson, E. A., Frankel, F., Mogil, C., & Dillon, A. R. (2009). Parent-assisted social skills training to improve friendships in teens with autism spectrum disorders. *Journal of Autism and Developmental Disorders, 39,* 596–606.

Laugeson, E. A., Gantman, A., Kapp, S. K., Orenski, K., & Ellingsen, R. (2015). A randomized controlled trial to improve social skills in young adults with autism spectrum disorder: The UCLA PEERS® program. *Journal of Autism and Developmental Disorders,* 1–12. DOI: 10.1007/s10803–015–2504–8.

Laugeson, E. A., Paley, B., Frankel, F., & O'Connor, M. (2011). *Project Good Buddies trainer workbook.* Atlanta, GA: U.S. Department of Health and Human Services, Centers for Disease Control and Prevention.

Laugeson, E. A., Paley, B., Schonfeld, A., Frankel, F., Carpenter, E. M., & O'Connor, M. (2007). Adaptation of the Children's Friendship Training program for children with fetal alcohol spectrum disorders. *Child and Family Behavior Therapy, 29*(3), 57–69.

Laugeson, E. A., & Park, M. N. (2014). Using a CBT approach to teach social skills to adolescents with autism spectrum disorder and other social challenges: The PEERS® method. *Journal of Rational-Emotive and Cognitive Behavioral Therapy*. DOI: 10.1007/s10942-014-0181-8.

Laursen, B., & Koplas, A. L. (1995). What's important about important conflicts? Adolescents' perceptions of daily disagreements. *Merrill-Palmer Quarterly, 41*, 536–553.

Little, L. (2001). Peer victimization of children with Asperger spectrum disorders. *Journal of the American Academy of Child and Adolescent Psychiatry, 40*, 995.

McGuire, K. D., & Weisz, J. R. (1982). Social cognition and behavior correlates of preadolescent chumship. *Child Development, 53*, 1478–1484.

Macintosh, K., & Dissanayake, C. (2006). Social skills and problem behaviours in school aged children with high-functioning autism and Asperger's disorder. *Journal of Autism and Developmental Disorders, 36*(8), 1065–1076.

McKenzie, R., Evans, J. S. B. T., & Handley, S. J. (2010). Conditional reasoning in autism: Activation and integration of knowledge and belief. *Developmental Psychology, 46*, 391–403.

Mandelberg, J., Frankel, F., Cunningham, T., Gorospe, C., & Laugeson, E. A. (2013). Long-term outcomes of parent-assisted social skills intervention for high-functioning children with autism spectrum disorders. *Autism: The International Journal of Research and Practice*. DOI: 10.1177/1362361312472403.

Mandelberg, J., Laugeson, E. A., Cunningham, T. D., Ellingsen, R., Bates, S., & Frankel, F. (2014). Long-term treatment outcomes for parent-assisted social skills training for adolescents with autism spectrum disorders: The UCLA PEERS program. *Journal of Mental Health Research in Intellectual Disabilities, 7*(1), 45–73. DOI: 10.1080/19315864.2012.730600.

Marriage, K. J., Gordon, V., & Brand, L. (1995). A social skills group for boys with Asperger's syndrome. *Australian & New Zealand Journal of Psychiatry, 29*, 58–62.

Mathur, S. R., Kavale, K. A., Quinn, M. M., Forness, S. R., & Rutherford Jr, R. B. (1998). Social skills interventions with students with emotional and behavioral problems: A quantitative synthesis of single-subject research. *Behavioral Disorders*, 193–201.

Matson, J. L. (2007). Determining treatment outcome in early intervention programs for autism spectrum disorders: A critical analysis of measurement issues in learning based interventions. *Research in Developmental Disabilities, 28*, 207–218.

Matson, J. L., Dempsey, T., & Fodstad, J. C. (2009). The effect of autism spectrum disorders on adaptive independent living skills in adults with severe intellectual disability. *Research in Developmental Disabilities, 30*(6), 1203–1211.

Matson, J. L., Dempsey, T., & LoVullo, S. V. (2009). Characteristics of social skills for adults with intellectual disability, autism and PDD-NOS. *Research in Autism Spectrum Disorders, 3*(1), 207–213.

Matson, J. L., Fodstad, J. C., & Rivet, T. T. (2009). The relationship of social skills and problem behaviors in adults with intellectual disability and autism or PDD-NOS. *Research in Autism Spectrum Disorders, 3*(1), 258–268.

Matson, J. L., Matson, M. L., & Rivet, T. T. (2007). Social-skills treatments for children with autism spectrum disorders: An overview. *Behavior Modification, 31*, 682–707.

Matson, J. L., & Wilkins, J. (2007). A critical review of assessment targets and methods for social skills excesses and deficits for children with autism spectrum disorders. *Research in Autism Spectrum Disorders, 1*(1), 28–37.

Mehzabin, P., & Stokes, M. A. (2011). Self-assessed sexuality in young adults with high-functioning autism. *Research in Autism Spectrum Disorders, 5*(1), 614–621.

Mesibov, G. B. (1984). Social skills training with verbal autistic adolescents and adults: A program model. *Journal of Autism and Developmental Disorders, 14*, 395–404.

Mesibov, G. B. (1992). Treatment issues with high-functioning adolescents and adults with autism. In E. Schopler & G. B. Mesibov (Eds.), *High-functioning individuals with autism* (pp. 143–155). New York: Springer US.

Mesibov, G. B., & Stephens, J. (1990). Perceptions of popularity among a group of high-functioning adults with autism. *Journal of Autism and Developmental Disorders, 20*, 33–43.

Miller, P. M., & Ingham, J. G. (1976). Friends, confidants and symptoms. *Social Psychiatry, 11*, 51–58.

Morgan, S. H., & Morgan, H. (1996). *Adults with Autism: A Guide to Theory and Practice*. Cambridge: Cambridge University Press.

Morrison, L., Kamps, D., Garcia, J., & Parker, D. (2001). Peer mediation and monitoring strategies to improve initiations and social skills for students with autism. *Journal of Positive Behavior Interventions, 3*, 237–250.

Müller, E., Schuler, A., & Yates, G. B. (2008). Social challenges and supports from the perspective of individuals with Asperger syndrome and other autism spectrum disabilities. *Autism, 12*, 173–190.

Murray, D. S., Ruble, L. A., Willis, H., & Molloy, C. A. (2009). Parent and teacher report of social skills in children with autism spectrum disorders. *Language, Speech and Hearing Services in Schools, 40*, 109–115.

Nelson, J., & Aboud, F. E. (1985). The resolution of social conflict between friends. *Child Development, 56*, 1009–1017.

Newcomb, A. F., & Bagwell, C. L. (1995). Children's friendship relations: A meta-analytic review. *Psychological Bulletin, 117*, 306–347.

Newcomb, A. F., Bukowski, W. M., & Pattee, L. (1993). Children's peer relations: A meta-analytic review of popular, rejected, neglected, controversial, and average sociometric status. *Psychological Bulletin, 113*, 99–128.

Newman, B., Reinecke, D. R., & Meinberg, D. L. (2000). Self-management of varied responding in three students with autism. *Behavioral Interventions, 15*, 145–151.

Nikopoulos, C. K., & Keenan, M. (2003). Promoting social initiation in children with autism using video modeling. *Behavioral Interventions, 18*(2), 87–108.

Njardvik, U., Matson, J. L., & Cherry, K. E. (1999). A comparison of social skills in adults with autistic disorder, pervasive developmental disorder not otherwise specified, and mental retardation. *Journal of Autism and Developmental Disorders, 29*(4), 287–295.

O'Connor, A. B., & Healy, O. (2010). Long-term post-intensive behavioral intervention outcomes for five children with autism spectrum disorder. *Research in Autism Spectrum Disorders, 4*, 594–604.

O'Connor, M. J., Frankel, F., Paley, B., Schonfeld, A. M., Carpenter, E., Laugeson, E., & Marquardt, R. (2006). A controlled social skills training for children with fetal alcohol spectrum disorders. *Journal of Consulting and Clinical Psychology, 74*(4), 639–648.

O'Connor, M., Laugeson, E. A., Mogil, C., Lowe, E., Welch-Torres, K., Keil, V., & Paley, B. (2012). Translation of an evidence-based social skills intervention for children with prenatal alcohol exposure in a community mental health setting. *Alcoholism: Clinical and Experimental Research, 36*(1), 141–152.

Olweus, D. (1993). Bullies on the playground: The role of victimization. In C. H. Hart (Ed.), *Children on playgrounds* (pp. 45–128). Albany, NY: State University of New York Press.

Orsmond, G. L., Krauss, M. W., & Selzter, M. M. (2004). Peer relationships and social and recreational activities among adolescents and adults with autism. *Journal of Autism and Developmental Disorders, 34*, 245–256.

Ousley, O. Y., & Mesibov, G. B. (1991). Sexual attitudes and knowledge of high-functioning adolescents and adults with autism. *Journal of Autism and Developmental Disorders, 21*(4), 471–481.

Ozonoff, S., & Miller, J. N. (1995). Teaching theory of mind: A new approach to social skills training for individuals with autism. *Journal of Autism and Developmental Disorders, 25*, 415–433.

Parker, J. G., & Asher, S. R. (1993). Friendship and friendship quality in middle childhood: Links with peer group acceptance and feelings of loneliness and social dissatisfaction. *Developmental Psychology, 29*, 611–621.

Parker, J., Rubin, K., Price, J., & de Rosier, M. (1995). Peer relationships, child development, and adjustment. In D. Cicchetti, & D. Cohen (Eds.), *Developmental psychopathology, vol 2: Risk, disorder, and adaptation* (pp. 96–161). New York: Wiley.

Parsons, S., & Mitchell, P. (2002). The potential of virtual reality in social skills training for people with autistic spectrum disorders. *Journal of Intellectual Disability Research, 46*(5), 430–443.

Perry, D. G., Kusel, S. J., & Perry, L. C. (1988). Victims of aggression. *Developmental Psychology, 24*, 807–814.

Perry, D. G., Williard, J. C., & Perry, L. C. (1990). Peer perceptions of the consequences that victimized children provide aggressors. *Child Development, 61*, 1310–1325.

Phillips, C. A., Rolls, S., Rouse, A., & Griffiths, M. D. (1995). Home video game playing in schoolchildren: A study of incidence and patterns of play. *Journal of Adolescence, 18*, 687–691.

Putallaz, M., & Gottman, J. M. (1981). An interactional model of children's entry into peer groups. *Child Development, 52*, 986–994.

Rao, P. A., Beidel, D. C., & Murray, M. J. (2008). Social skills interventions for children with Asperger's syndrome or high-functioning autism: A review and recommendations. *Journal of Autism and Developmental Disorders, 38*, 353–361.

Rapin, I. (1999). Appropriate investigations for clinical care versus research in children with autism. *Brain and Development, 21*, 152–156.

Reichow, B., & Volkmar, F. R. (2010). Social skills interventions for individuals with autism: Evaluation for evidence-based practices within a best evidence synthesis framework. *Journal of Autism and Developmental Disorders, 40*, 149–166.

Remington, A., Swettenham, J., Campbell, R., & Coleman, M. (2009). Selective attention and perceptual load in autism spectrum disorder. *Psychological Science, 20*, 1388–1393.

Renty, J. O., & Roeyers, H. (2006). Quality of life in high-functioning adults with autism spectrum disorder: The predictive value of disability and support characteristics. *Autism, 10*(5), 511–524.

Riggio, R. (1989). Assessment of basic social skills. *Journal of Personality and Social Psychology, 51*, 649–660.

Rogers, S. J. (2000). Interventions that facilitate socialization in children with autism. *Journal of Autism and Developmental Disorders, 30*(5), 399–409.

Rubin, Z., & Sloman, J. (1984). How parents influence their children's friendships. In M. Lewis (Ed.), *Beyond the dyad* (pp. 223–250). New York: Plenum.

Sansosti, F. J., & Powell-Smith, K. A. (2006). Using social stories to improve the social behavior of children with Asperger syndrome. *Journal of Positive Behavior Interventions, 8*, 43–57.

Schopler, E., & Mesibov, G. B. (Eds.). (1983). *Autism in Adolescents and Adults.* New York: Springer Science & Business Media.

Schopler, E., & Mesibov, G. B. (Eds.). (2013). *High-functioning Individuals with Autism*. New York: Springer Science & Business Media.

Schopler, E., Mesibov, G. B., Kunce, L. J. (1998). *Asperger's Syndrome or High Functioning Autism?* New York: Plenum Press.

Shantz, D. W. (1986). Conflict, aggression and peer status: An observational study. *Child Development, 57*, 1322–1332.

Shattuck, P., Seltzer, M., Greenberg, M. M., Orsmond, G. I., Bolt, D., Kring, S., et al. (2007). Change in autism symptoms and maladaptive behaviors in adolescents and adults with an autism spectrum disorder. *Journal of Autism and Developmental Disorders, 37*, 1735–1747.

Shore, S. (2002). Dating, marriage and autism. *Advocate, 4*(3), 24–27.

Shtayermann, O. (2007). Peer victimization in adolescents and young adults diagnosed with Asperger's syndrome: A link to depressive symptomatology, anxiety symptomatology and suicidal ideation. *Issues in Comprehensive Pediatric Nursing, 30*, 87–107.

Shukla-Mehta, S., Miller, T., & Callahan, K. J. (2009). Evaluating the effectiveness of video instruction on social and communication skills training for children with autism spectrum disorders: A review of the literature. *Focus on Autism and Other Developmental Disabilities*.

Sigman, M., & Ruskin, E. (1999). Continuity and change in the social competence of children with autism, Down syndrome, and developmental delays. *Monographs of the Society for Research in Child Development, 64*, 114.

Simpson, A., Langone, J., & Ayres, K. M. (2004). Embedded video and computer based instruction to improve social skills for students with autism. *Education and Training in Developmental Disabilities*, 240–252.

Smith, K. R., & Matson, J. L. (2010). Social skills: Differences among adults with intellectual disabilities, co-morbid autism spectrum disorders and epilepsy. *Research in Developmental Disabilities, 31*(6), 1366–1372.

Smith T., Scahill, L., Dawson, G., Guthrie, D., Lord, C., & Odom, S., et al. (2007). Designing research studies on psychosocial interventions in autism. *Journal of Autism and Developmental Disorders, 37*, 354–366.

Solomon, M., Goodlin-Jones, B., & Anders, T. F. (2004). A social adjustment enhancement intervention for high-functioning autism, Asperger's syndrome, and pervasive developmental disorder NOS. *Journal of Autism & Developmental Disabilities, 34*(6), 649–668.

Sperry, L. A., & Mesibov, G. B. (2005). Perceptions of social challenges of adults with autism spectrum disorder. *Autism, 9*(4), 362–376.

Starr, E., Szatmari, P., Bryson, S., & Zwaigenbaum, L. (2003). Stability and change among high-functioning children with pervasive developmental disorders: A 2-year outcome study. *Journal of Autism and Developmental Disorders, 33*, 15–22.

Stokes, M. A., & Kaur, A. (2005). High-functioning autism and sexuality a parental perspective. *Autism, 9*(3), 266–289.

Stokes, M., Newton, N., & Kaur, A. (2007). Stalking, and social and romantic functioning among adolescents and adults with autism spectrum disorder. *Journal of Autism and Developmental Disorders, 37*(10), 1969–1986.

Sullivan, A., & Caterino, L. C. (2008). Addressing the sexuality and sex education of individuals with autism spectrum disorders. *Education and Treatment of Children, 31*(3), 381–394.

Sutton, J., Smith, P. K., & Swettenham, J. (1999). Bullying and 'theory of mind': A critique of the 'social skills deficit' view of anti-social behaviour. *Social Development, 8*(1), 117–127.

Swain, D., Scarpa, A., White, S., & Laugeson, E. (2015). Emotion Dysregulation and Anxiety in Adults with ASD: Does Social Motivation Play a Role? *Journal of Autism and Developmental Disorders*, 1–7. DOI: 10.1007/s10803–015–2567–6.

Tantam, D. (2003). The challenge of adolescents and adults with Asperger syndrome. *Child and Adolescent Psychiatric Clinics of North America, 12*, 143–163.

Taylor, J. L., & Seltzner, M. M. (2010). Changes in autism behavioral phenotype during the transition to adulthood. *Journal of Autism and Developmental Disorders, 40*, 1431–1446.

Tetreault, A. S., & Lerman, D. C. (2010). Teaching social skills to children with autism using point-of-view video modeling. *Education and Treatment of Children, 33*(3), 395–419.

Thurlow, C., & McKay, S. (2003). Profiling "new" communication technologies in adolescence. *Journal of Language and Social Psychology, 22*, 94–103.

Tissot, C. (2009). Establishing a sexual identity case studies of learners with autism and learning difficulties. *Autism, 13*(6), 551–566.

Travis, L. L., & Sigman, M. (1998). Social deficits and interpersonal relationships in autism. *Mental Retardation and Developmental Disabilities Research Reviews, 4*, 65–72.

Tse, J., Strulovitch, J., Tagalakis, V., Meng, L., & Fombonne, E. (2007). Social skills training for adolescents with Asperger syndrome and high functioning autism. *Journal of Autism and Developmental Disorders, 37*, 1960–1968.

Turner-Brown, L. M., Perry, T. D., Dichter, G. S., Bodfish, J. W., & Penn, D. L. (2008). Brief report: Feasibility of social cognition and interaction training for adults with high functioning autism. *Journal of Autism and Developmental Disorders, 38*(9), 1777–1784.

VanBergeijk, E., Klin, A., & Volkmar, F. (2008). Supporting more able students on the autism spectrum: College and beyond. *Journal of Autism and Developmental Disorders, 38*(7), 1359–1370.

Van Bourgondien, M. E., & Mesibov, G. B. (1987). Humor in high-functioning autistic adults. *Journal of Autism and Developmental Disorders, 17*, 417–424.

Van Bourgondien, M. E., Reichle, N. C., & Palmer, A. (1997). Sexual behavior in adults with autism. *Journal of Autism and Developmental Disorders, 27*(2), 113–125.

Van Bourgondien, M. E., Reichle, N. C., & Schopler, E. (2003). Effects of a model treatment approach on adults with autism. *Journal of Autism and Developmental Disorders, 33*(2), 131–140.

Venter, A., Lord, C., & Schopler, E. (1992). A follow-up study of high-functioning autistic children. *Journal of Child Psychology and Psychiatry, 33*(3), 489–597.

Volkmar, F. R., & Klin, A. (1998). Asperger syndrome and nonverbal learning disabilities. In E. Schopler, G. B. Mesibov, & L. J. Kunce (Eds.), *Asperger syndrome or high functioning autism?* (pp. 107–121). New York: Plenum Press.

Wang, P., & Spillane, A. (2009). Evidence-based social skills interventions for children with autism: A meta-analysis. *Education and Training in Developmental Disabilities*, 318–342.

Warm, T. R. (1997). The role of teasing in development and vice versa. *Journal of Developmental & Behavioral Pediatrics, 18*, 97–101.

Webb, B. J., Miller, S. P., Pierce, T. B., Strawser, S., & Jones, P. (2004). Effects of social skills instruction for high-functioning adolescents with autism spectrum disorders. *Focus on Autism and Other Developmental Disabilities, 19*, 53–62.

Weiss, M. J., & Harris, S. L. (2001). Teaching social skills to people with autism. *Behavior Modification, 25*(5), 785–802.

Wentzel, K. R., Barry, C. M., & Caldwell, K. A. (2004). Friendships in middle school: Influences on motivation and school adjustment. *Journal of Educational Psychology, 96*, 195–203.

White, S. W. (2011). *Social Skills Training for Children with Asperger Syndrome and High-functioning Autism.* New York: Guilford Press.

White, S. W., Koenig, K., & Scahill, L. (2007). Social skills development in children with autism spectrum disorders: A review of the intervention research. *Journal of Autism and Developmental Disorders, 37*, 1858–1868.

White, S. W., Koenig, K., & Scahill, L. (2010). Group social skills instruction for adolescents with high-functioning autism spectrum disorders. *Focus on Autism and Other Developmental Disabilities, 25*, 209–219.

White, S. W., & Robertson-Nay, R. (2009). Anxiety, social deficits, and loneliness in youth with autism spectrum disorders. *Journal of Autism and Developmental Disorders, 39*, 1006–1013.

Whitehouse, A. J., Durkin, K., Jaquet, E., & Ziatas, K. (2009). Friendship, loneliness and depression in adolescents with Asperger's syndrome. *Journal of Adolescence, 32*, 309–322.

Williams, T. I. (1989). A social skills group for autistic children. *Journal of Autism and Developmental Disorders, 19*(1), 143–155.

Wing, L. (1983). Social and interpersonal needs. In E. Schopler & G. Mesibov (Eds.), *Autism in adolescents and adults* (pp. 337–354). New York: Plenum Press.

Wing, L. (1988). The continuum of autistic characteristics. In E. Schopler & G. B. Mesibov (Eds.), *Diagnosis and assessment in autism* (pp. 91–110). New York: Springer US.

Wing, L. (1992). Manifestations of social problems in high-functioning autistic people. In E. Schopler & G. B. Mesibov (Eds.), *High-functioning individuals with autism* (pp. 129–142). New York: Springer US.

Winter, M. (2003). *Asperger Syndrome: What Teachers Need to Know.* London, UK: Jessica Kingsley Publishers.

Wong, C., Odom, S. L., Hume, K. A., Cox, A. W., Fettig, A., Kucharczyk, S., & Schultz, T. R. (2015). Evidence-based practices for children, youth, and young adults with autism spectrum disorder: A comprehensive review. *Journal of Autism and Developmental Disorders, 45*(7), 1951–1966.

Wood, J. J., Drahota, A., Sze, K., Har, K., Chiu, A., & Langer, D. A. (2009). Cognitive behavioral therapy for anxiety in children with autism spectrum disorders: A randomized, controlled trial. *Journal of Child Psychology and Psychiatry, 50*, 224–234.

Wood, J. J., Drahota, A., Sze, K., Van Dyke, M., Decker, K., Fujii, C., Bahng, C., Renno, P., Hwang, W., & Spiker, M. (2009). Effects of cognitive behavioral therapy on parent-reported autism symptoms in school-aged children with high-functioning autism. *Journal of Autism and Developmental Disabilities, 39*, 1608–1612.

Woodward, L. J., & Fergusson, D. M. (2000). Childhood peer relationship problems and later risks of educational under-achievement and unemployment. *Journal of Child Psychology and Psychiatry, 41*, 191–201.

Yoo, H. J., Bahn, G., Cho, I. H., Kim, E. K., Kim, J. H., Min, J. W., Lee, W. H., Seo, J. S., Jun, S. S., Bong, G., Cho, S., Shin, M.S., Kim, B. N., Kim, J. W., Park, S., & Laugeson. E. A. (2014). A randomized controlled trial of the Korean version of the PEERS® parent-assisted social skills training program for teens with ASD. *Autism Research.*

INDEX